Sybex's Quick Tour of Windows 95

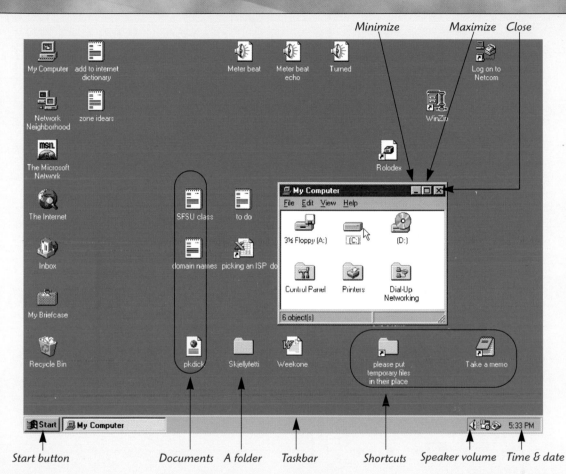

Minimize   Maximize   Close

Start button   Documents   A folder   Taskbar   Shortcuts   Speaker volume   Time & date

The Desktop *is where your programs, files, and shortcuts reside.*

My Computer *allows you to browse the contents of your computer, open folders, open documents, and run programs.*

Network Neighborhood *gives you direct access to other computers (and shared resources, such as printers).*

The Microsoft Network *dials up your connection to Microsoft's online service.*

The Internet *starts up the Internet Explorer, a World Wide Web browser (available only with Plus!).*

Inbox *starts Microsoft Exchange and opens your inbox, so you can see if you have any new mail.*

My Briefcase *is a new feature for keeping documents consistent as you move them between computers.*

Recycle Bin *makes it easy to delete and undelete files.*

The Start button *pops up the Start menu, from which you can run just about every program.*

The Taskbar *displays a button for every running program.*

Create **shortcuts** *on your Desktop for frequently used programs and documents.*

Every window has a **Minimize, Maximize** *(alternating with Restore), and* **Close** *button. The Close button is new; the others just look different.*

FORMATTING A FLOPPY DISK

To format a floppy disk, first double-click the My Computer icon. Put the floppy in the disk drive. Then right-click the 3½ Floppy icon in the My Computer window and choose Format. The Format dialog box appears.

If you want some density other than the standard 1.44MB, click the Capacity drop-down list box and choose another option. To give the disk a label, click in the Label box and type one. Then click Start.

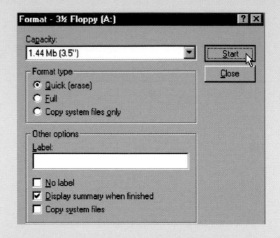

USEFUL KEYBOARD SHORTCUTS

TASK	KEYSTROKE
Get help	F1
Quit a program	Alt+F4
Pop up shortcut menu for selected item	Shift+F10
Pop up the Start menu	Ctrl+Esc
Cut a selection	Ctrl+X
Copy a selection	Ctrl+C
Paste a selection	Ctrl+V
Delete a selection	Delete
Undo the last action	Ctrl+Z
Select all items in window	Ctrl+A
Refresh a window	F5
Open folder one level up from current one	Backspace
Close a folder and all its parents	Shift and click Close button
Rename a selection	F2
Find a file starting with current folder	F3
Delete a selection without putting it in Recycle Bin (be careful!)	Shift+Delete
View a selection's properties	Alt+Enter or Alt+double-click
Copy an icon	Ctrl+click and drag
Create a shortcut from an icon	Ctrl+Shift+click and drag

Sybex Inc.
2021 Challenger Drive
Alameda, CA 94501
Tel: 510-523-8233 · 800-227-2346
Fax: 510-523-2373

You have all kinds of control over the appearance of Windows. You can get to the Display Properties dialog box to change the look via the Control Panel, but the easiest shortcut is to right-click in any empty area of the Desktop and select Properties. The Display Properties dialog box comes up with the Background tab selected.

- *Choose a desktop pattern or wallpaper design.*

- *Choose **Screen Saver** to select a screen saver or stop using one.*

- *Choose **Appearance** to change the look of the windows and dialog boxes.*

- *Choose **Settings** to change the color palette or screen resolution.*

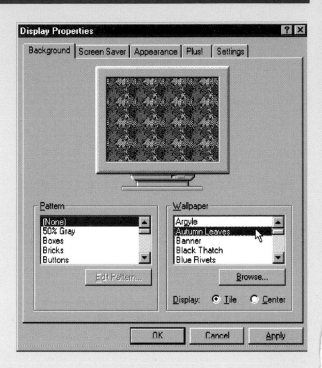

No one likes having to set up a printer, but Windows has made it fairly unthreatening. Choose Start ➤ Settings ➤ Printer (or open My Computer and double-click Printers). Your Printers window will open.

- *To modify an existing Printer, right-click it and choose Properties.*

- *To create a new Printer, double-click the Add Printer icon and follow the instructions in the Add Printer Wizard.*

- *To change the default printer, right-click a printer and choose Set as Default.*

Just press the Start button to do almost anything.

Running a Program

To start a program, click Start ➤ Programs, choose a program folder (if necessary), and then point to a program.

- *Choose a program or program group from a submenu.*
- *Reopen one of the last 15 documents you've worked on.*
- *Change the way Windows is set up or add a printer.*
- *Search for a missing document, folder, or program.*
- *Get online help.*
- *Run a program directly, the old-fashioned (DOS) way.*
- *Turn off or restart your computer.*

Putting a Program, Folder, or Document on the Start Menu

First, open the folder that contains the program you want to put on the Start menu. Then click the program icon and drag it onto the Start button. (If you want to get a look at the hierarchy of the programs on the Start submenus—so that you can move things around—right-click on the Start button and choose Open.)

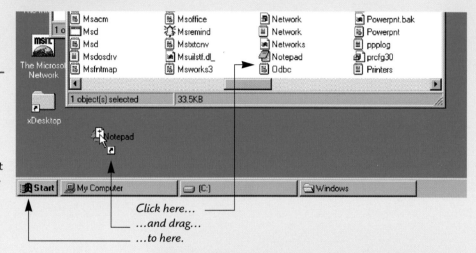

Click here...
...and drag...
...to here.

Finding Files and Folders Quickly

Unlike Windows 3.1's cumbersome Search command in the File Manager, Windows 95 has a simple-to-use Find command. To try it, select Start ➤ Find ➤ Files or Folders.

Type the name of the file you're looking for (or just part of it), then click Find Now.

A window will open, showing the files as Windows finds them.

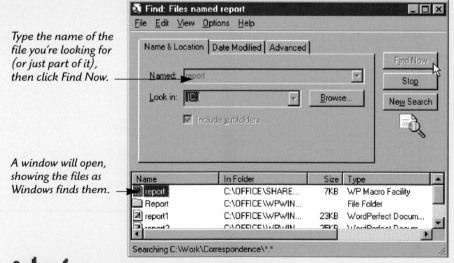

Sybex's Quick Tour of Windows 95

Sure, Windows 3.1 enabled you to use the mouse to scroll, click menus, and interact with dialog boxes, but now just about every feature of Windows can be clicked on (with either button), double-clicked, and/or dragged.

Selecting Things

Click most things to select them. Shift-click to add all intervening items to a selection. Ctrl-click to add an individual item to a selection. Click and drag to lasso and select several items (click in an empty space before starting to drag—otherwise, you'll drag the item itself).

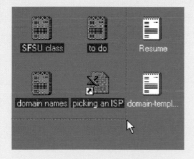

Right-Click Dragging

If you click with the left button and drag, Windows 95 will either copy the icon (for example, when dragging from or to a floppy) or move the icon (for example, when dragging from one folder to another).

For more control, right-click on an icon and drag it. When you release the mouse button, a menu pops up.

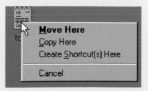

Things You Can Right-Click On

Right-click on an item to pop up a shortcut menu. Every icon's shortcut menu has Properties as its last choice —each object on your computer has a set of properties associated with it, which you can view or change.

■ My Computer

Explore displays a File Manager-like view of folders and files.

■ Any folder, document, or program icon

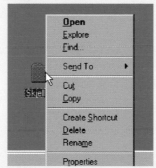

Send To sends documents directly to a floppy, printer, or fax machine.

■ The Start button

Open lets you make changes to the Start menu.

■ The Recycle Bin

■ The Desktop

Arrange Icons sorts them by name, type, size, or date.

New creates a new folder, document, or shortcut on the Desktop.

■ The Taskbar

■ A Taskbar button

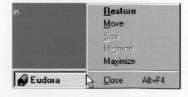

■ Undo
After you move, copy, create a shortcut from, or delete an icon, the next time you right-click anywhere you can undo your last action. The menu will have a choice like Undo Move or Undo Delete.

Every running program, open folder, and drive gets a button on the Taskbar. Dialog boxes do not.

You can switch to any task by clicking its button. When you get a lot of things going at once, the Taskbar can get crowded, as you can see in example 1 below.

Making the Taskbar Bigger

To make more room on the Taskbar, click it along its top edge and drag it up. You'll get something more like example 2.

Moving the Taskbar

If you'd prefer to have the Taskbar at the top of the screen, so the Start menu will pull down like a menu on the menu bar, just click the Taskbar (not one of the buttons on it) and drag it to the top of the screen. It will look similar to example 3.

You can also put the Taskbar at the left or right edge of the screen to get something that looks like the taskbars shown to the right. In either position, the Taskbar can be stretched up to half the width of the screen.

Changing the Way the Taskbar Works

You can customize the Taskbar by right-clicking on an empty portion of it and choosing Properties. This brings up the Properties dialog box.

Check or uncheck the options (the preview area shows you the effects of your choices). Uncheck **Always on top** if you want the Taskbar to be covered by other windows. Check **Auto hide** if you want the Taskbar to stay hidden until you move your mouse toward it.

Task-Switching with Alt+Tab

Another easy way to switch from task to task is to hold down the Alt key and press Tab repeatedly. This worked in Windows 3.1 too. But now when you do this, a plaque will appear showing all the running programs as

icons, with the currently selected one labeled in a box at the bottom of the plaque. Press Tab until the program you want is highlighted and then release both the Tab and the Alt keys.

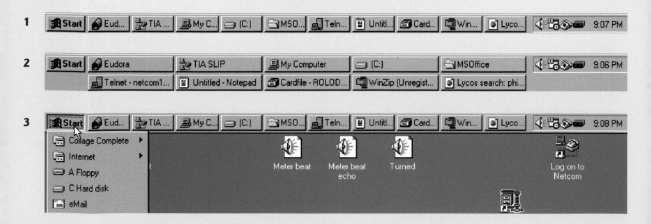

The basic routine for poking around your computer is to double-click on folder icons and select programs or documents from folder windows.

Starting with My Computer

Usually, you'll start by double-clicking My Computer, which gives you a view of all the drives and devices attached to your computer. Double-click the C: icon to look at the contents of your hard disk.

Then double-click one of the folders in the C: window to open another window, and so on, and so on.

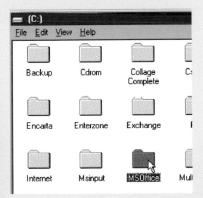

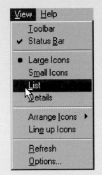

Besides the Large Icons view, you can also choose List view (shown below). Or you can choose Details view to see more information about a folder or file, such as size, type of file it is, and date it was last changed.

If you'd prefer that each new folder opens up in the same window, instead of creating a new window (which can get very irritating when you end up with numerous open windows on your screen), select View ➢ Options ➢ Browse folders by using a single window.

Renaming, Copying, or Moving an Icon

In Windows 95, an icon can represent a document, folder, program, or shortcut. The rules for manipulating an icon are the same no matter what the icon corresponds to.

To rename an icon, select it and click in the label below it (wait a few seconds for the text in the label to become highlighted). Then type a new name (up to 255 characters, including spaces if you like) and press Enter.

To copy an icon, the easiest way is to right-click on it and select Copy. Then move to the destination, right-click again, and select Paste. To move an icon, right-click on it and select Cut. Then move to the destination, right-click, and select Paste.

This is a big change from Windows 3.1! Before, the convenience of cutting, copying, and pasting was limited to the text and other contents of application windows. Now just about every item on the screen can be dragged, dropped, cut, copied, and pasted.

Or, you can just hold down Ctrl and drag a copy of an icon to a new location. (A safer way to copy an icon is to right-click on it, drag to a new location, and then choose Copy from the menu that pops up.)

One of the best new features of Windows 95 is shortcuts. Each shortcut you create takes up only a small amount of disk space, but can save you time and energy by opening a program or document that you'd otherwise have to hunt around for. You can recognize a shortcut by the little doubling-back arrow in the bottom-left corner of its icon.

Putting a Shortcut on the Desktop

There are many ways to do this. If you have a document or program already visible on the screen and want to create a shortcut to it on the desktop, right-click on the icon, drag it onto the Desktop, and then choose Create Shortcut(s) Here. You can also start from the Desktop when the "target" of your shortcut-to-be is not readily available.

Right-click on the Desktop, select New, and then Shortcut.

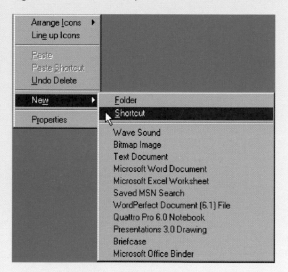

This brings up the Create Shortcut wizard. If you don't know the command line for the program you want, click the Browse button. This brings up an Open-style dialog box; work your way through various folders until you find the program you want to make a shortcut to. Then click the Open button, click Next (or type a different name for the shortcut and click Next), and click Finish when you're done. Voila! Your shortcut appears on the Desktop.

Making a Keyboard Shortcut

Once you've created a shortcut icon, you can also set up a keyboard shortcut to launch the program (or open the document) automatically.

Right-click the shortcut icon and choose Properties. Click the Shortcut tab in the Properties dialog box, click inside the Shortcut Key box, and then press the keyboard shortcut you want. It will appear in the box as you press it.

Shows the default folder for the program

Controls how the program's window appears when you first run it (other choices are Minimized and Maximized)

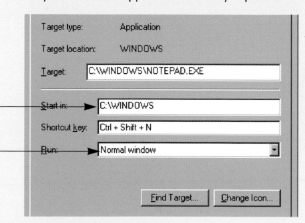

▼▼▼▼▼

MASTERING
AUTOCAD® 13
FOR WINDOWS®

Second Edition

George Omura

▼▼▼▼▼

MASTERING
AUTOCAD® 13
FOR WINDOWS®

Second Edition

George Omura

San Francisco

Paris

Düsseldorf

Soest

Acquisitions Manager: Kristine Plachy
Developmental Editor: Richard Mills
Editors: Neil Edde, Carol Henry, Doug Robert, Laura Arendal
Technical Editor: Robin Hansen
Series Designer: Ingrid Owen
Desktop Specialists: Deborah Maizels, Alissa Feinberg, Deborah A. Bevilacqua
Production Coordinators: Taris Duffié, Nathan Johanson
Indexer: Ted Laux
Cover Art: John Corrigan
Cover Designer: Design Site
Cover Photography: Mark Johann
Cover Photo Art Direction: Ingalls & Associates
Screen reproductions produced with Collage Complete

Library of Congress Card Number: 95-72706
ISBN: 0-7821-1858-5

Manufactured in the United States of America
10 9 8 7 6 5 4 3

you discover a defect in the media during this warranty period, you may obtain a replacement of identical format at no charge by sending the defective media, postage prepaid, with proof of purchase to:

SYBEX Inc.
Customer Service Department
1151 Marina Village Parkway
Alameda, CA 94501
(510) 523-8233
Fax: (510) 523-2373
e-mail: info@sybex.com

After the 90-day period, you can obtain replacement media of identical format by sending us the defective disk, proof of purchase, and a check or money order for $10, payable to SYBEX.

Disclaimer

SYBEX makes no warranty or representation, either expressed or implied, with respect to this media or its contents, its quality, performance, merchantability, or fitness for a particular purpose. In no event will SYBEX, its distributors, or dealers be liable to you or any other party for direct, indirect, special, incidental, consequential, or other damages arising out of the use of or inability to use the media or its contents even if advised of the possibility of such damage.

The exclusion of implied warranties is not permitted by some states. Therefore, the above exclusion may not apply to you. This warranty provides you with specific legal rights; there may be other rights that you may have that vary from state to state. The pricing of the book with the Software by SYBEX reflects the allocation of risk and limitations on liability contained in this agreement of Terms and Conditions.

Shareware Distribution

This Software media may contain various programs that are distributed as shareware. Copyright laws apply to both shareware and ordinary commercial software, and the copyright Owner(s) retains all rights. If you try a shareware program and continue using it, you are expected to register it. Individual programs differ on details of trial periods, registration, and payment. Please observe the requirements stated in appropriate files.

Copy Protection

None of the files on the disk is copy-protected. However, in all cases, reselling or redistributing these files without authorization is expressly forbidden except as specifically provided for by the Owner(s) therein.

ACKNOWLEDGMENTS
▼ ▼ ▼ ▼ ▼

Thanks and much gratitude go to everyone who helped create this book. I'd like to thank Neil Edde, coordinating editor, for keeping his cool and expertly managing this project; Doug Robert, for helping with the editing; and Robin Hansen, technical reviewer, for her comments, tips, and advice. Thanks also go to Richard Mills, developmental editor, who started things off and gave encouragement along the way.

A special thanks to Carol Henry of C^2 Editorial Services who contributed much to the quality and tone of this book. Thanks for everything, Carol.

Many thanks go to the SYBEX production staff for its efforts to get this book out on the usual impossible schedule: production assistant Taris Duffié, desktop publisher Deborah Maizels, and everyone else who lent a hand during the process.

At Autodesk, Art Cooney, technical support, gave invaluable advice, Lisa Senauke provided the greatly needed prerelease software, and Jim Quanci and Kathy Keopke helped with general questions.

And finally, a thanks to my family, Cynthia, Arthur, and Charles for their encouragement and understanding of an "orbiting" parent.

CONTENTS AT A GLANCE
▼▼▼▼▼

Part Four

Modeling and Imaging in 3D

Part Five

Customization: Taking AutoCAD to the Limit

Appendices

TABLE OF CONTENTS
▼ ▼ ▼ ▼ ▼

Part Two

Building on the Basics

Part Three

Becoming an Expert

14   Getting and Exchanging Data from Drawings

Part Four

Modeling and Imaging in 3D

Part Five

Customization—Taking AutoCAD to the Limit

Appendices

Introduction
▼ ▼ ▼ ▼ ▼

Welcome to *Mastering AutoCAD 13 for Windows*. As many readers have already discovered, *Mastering AutoCAD* offers a unique blend of tutorial and source book that offers everything you need to get started and stay ahead with AutoCAD.

HOW TO USE THIS BOOK

Rather than just showing you how each command works, *Mastering AutoCAD 13 for Windows* shows you AutoCAD in the context of a meaningful activity: you will learn how to use commands together to reach a goal. It also provides a foundation on which you can build your own methods for using AutoCAD and become an AutoCAD expert yourself. For this reason, I haven't covered every single command or every permutation of a command response. The AutoCAD help system (described in *Chapter 2*) and the AutoCAD Reference Manual are quite adequate for this purpose. You should think of this book as a way to get a detailed look at AutoCAD as it is used on a real project. As you follow the exercises, I encourage you to also explore AutoCAD on your own, applying the techniques you learn to your own work.

If you are not an experienced user, you may want to read *Mastering AutoCAD 13 for Windows* as a tutorial from front to back, since later chapters rely on the skills and information you learned in earlier ones. To help you navigate, the exercises are shown in numbered steps. *Mastering AutoCAD 13 for Windows* can also be used as a ready reference for your day-to-day problems and questions about commands. Optional exercises at the end of each chapter will help you review what you have learned.

GETTING INFORMATION FAST

If you are already familiar with AutoCAD, you will appreciate the Fast Tracks at the beginning of each chapter. Fast Tracks are highly encapsulated instructions on the use of commands and functions found in the chapter. They include the page number in the chapter where you can find a more detailed description of the function or command. If you only need to refresh your memory on how to do something, check the Fast Tracks first.

I've also included marginal comments labeled as *Notes*, *Tips*, and *Warnings*. Notes supplement the main text; Tips are designed to make practice easier; and Warnings steer you away from pitfalls. Also, in each chapter you will find more extensive tips and discussions in the form of specially screened *sidebars*. Together they provide a wealth of information gathered over years of using AutoCAD on a variety of projects in different office environments. You may want to browse through the book, just reading the margin notes and side bars, to get an idea of how they might be useful to you.

In *Appendices D* and *E*, I provide tables of all the system variables and commands with comments on their use and options. And in *Appendix F* you'll find labeled illustrations of the many toolbars available with AutoCAD for Windows.

WHAT TO EXPECT

Mastering AutoCAD 13 for Windows is divided into five parts, each representing a milestone in your progress toward becoming an expert AutoCAD user. Here is a description of those parts and what they will show you.

Part One: The Basics

As with any major endeavor, you must begin by tackling small, manageable tasks. In this first part, you will get familiar with the way AutoCAD looks and feels. *Chapter 1*, *This Is AutoCAD*, shows you how to get around in AutoCAD. In *Chapter 2*, *Creating Your First Drawing*, you will learn how to start and exit the program and how to respond to Auto-CAD commands. *Chapter 3*, *Learning the Tools of the Trade*, tells you how to set up a work area, edit objects, and lay out a drawing. In *Chapter 4*, *Organizing Your Work*, you will explore some tools unique to CAD: symbols, blocks, and layers. As you are introduced to AutoCAD, you will also get a chance to make some drawings that you can use later in the book and perhaps even in future projects of your own.

Part Two: Building on the Basics

Once you have the basics down, you will begin to explore some of Auto-CAD's more subtle qualities. *Chapter 5, Editing for Productivity*, tells you how to reuse drawing setup information and parts of an existing drawing. In *Chapter 6, Managing a Large Drawing*, you will learn how to assemble and edit a large drawing file. *Chapter 7, Printing and Plotting*, shows you how to get your drawing onto hard copy. *Chapter 8, Adding Text to Drawings*, tells you how to annotate your drawing and edit your notes. *Chapter 9, Using Dimensions*, gives you practice in using automatic dimensioning, another unique CAD capability. Along the way, I will be giving you tips on editing and problems you may encounter as you begin to use AutoCAD for more complex tasks.

Part Three: Becoming an Expert

At this point, you will be on the verge of becoming a real expert. *Part Three* is designed to help you polish your existing skills and give you a few new ones. *Chapter 10, Storing and Linking Data with Graphics*, tells you how to attach information to drawing objects and how to link your drawing to database files. In *Chapter 11, Entering Pre-existing Drawings*, you will learn three techniques for transferring paper drawings to Auto-CAD. In *Chapter 12, Power Editing*, you will complete the apartment building tutorial, and in the process, will learn how to integrate what you've learned so far and gain some tips on working in groups. *Chapter 13, Drawing Curves and Solid Fills*, gives you an in-depth look at some special drawing objects such as spline and fitted curves. In *Chapter 14, Getting and Exchanging Data from Drawings*, you will practice getting information about a drawing, and will learn how AutoCAD can interact with other applications, such as spreadsheets and desktop-publishing programs. You'll also learn how to copy and paste data.

Part Four: Modeling and Imaging in 3D

While 2D drafting is AutoCAD's workhorse application, AutoCAD's 3D capabilities give you a chance to expand your ideas and look at them in a new light. *Chapter 15, Introducing 3D*, covers AutoCAD's basic features for creating three-dimensional drawings. *Chapter 16, Using Advanced 3D Features*, introduces you to some of the program's more powerful 3D capabilities. *Chapter 17, Rendering and Animating 3D Drawings* shows how you can use the AutoCAD Renderer for this purpose. *Chapter 18, Mastering 3D Solids*, is a guided tour of AutoCAD Release 13's new solid modeling feature.

Part Five: Customization— Taking AutoCAD to the Limit

In the last part of the book, you will learn how you can take full control of AutoCAD. *Chapter 19, Introduction to Customization*, gives you a gentle introduction to the world of AutoCAD customization. You'll learn how to load and use existing utilities that come with AutoCAD. *Chapter 20, Exploring AutoLISP*, shows you how you can tap the power of this programming language to add new functions to AutoCAD. *Chapter 21, Integrating AutoCAD into Your Projects and Organization*, shows you how you can adapt AutoCAD to your own work style. Customizing menus, line types, and screens are only three of the many topics.

The Appendices

Finally, this book has five appendices. *Appendix A, Hardware and Software Tips*, should give you a start on selecting hardware appropriate for AutoCAD. It also provides tips on improving AutoCAD's performance and troubleshooting. *Appendix B, Installing and Setting Up AutoCAD*, contains an installation and configuration tutorial that you should follow before starting *Chapter 1* if AutoCAD is not already installed on your system. You should read *Appendix C, What's on the Companion CD-ROM*, around the time you read *Chapter 19*. This appendix describes the utilities available on the Companion CD. *Appendix D, System and Dimension Variables*, will illuminate the references to the system variables scattered throughout the book. *Appendix D* also discusses the many dimension settings and system features AutoCAD has to offer. *Appendix E, Standard AutoCAD Commands*, provides a listing of all the AutoCAD commands, with a brief description of their functions and options. Finally, *Appendix F* shows the major toolbars in AutoCAD and what all the buttons do.

THE MINIMUM SYSTEM REQUIREMENTS

This book assumes you have an IBM-compatible 80486 computer that will run AutoCAD and support a mouse. Your computer should have at least one disk drive capable of reading a $3\frac{1}{2}''$ 1.44 MB disk, and a hard disk with 100 MB or more free space (about 70 MB for the AutoCAD program and another 30 MB available for drawing files and work space for AutoCAD). A CD-ROM is a preferred option as it makes installation easier, and it allows you to take advantage of AutoCAD's online documentation. In addition to these requirements, you should also have a Windows permanent swap file of at least 40 MB. Consult your Windows manual or *Appendix A* of this book for more on swap files.

AutoCAD Release 13 runs best on systems with at least 16 MB or more of RAM, though you can get by with 12 MB. However, AutoCAD also needs about 450K of standard DOS memory free, which is memory below the 640K DOS limit.

Your computer should also have a high-resolution monitor and a color display card. The current standard is the Video Graphics Array or VGA display, though most computers sold offer an enhanced version of the VGA called Super VGA. This is quite adequate for most AutoCAD work. The computer should also have at least one serial port. If you have only one, you should consider having another one installed, or at least getting a switch box. I also assume you are using a mouse and have the use of a dot-matrix printer or a plotter. AutoCAD Release 13 does not run on older 80286-based computers or on 80386-based computers without a math coprocessor.

If you want a more detailed explanation of hardware options with AutoCAD, look at *Appendix A*. You will find a general description of the available hardware options and their significance to AutoCAD.

DOING THINGS IN STYLE

Much care has been taken to see that the stylistic conventions in this book—the use of upper- or lowercase letters, italic or boldface type, and so on—will be the ones most likely to help you learn AutoCAD. On the whole, their effect should be subliminal. You may find it useful, however, to be conscious of the following rules that we have followed:

1. Pull-down selections are shown by a series of menu options separated by the ➤ symbol.
2. Keyboard entries are shown in boldface (e.g., enter **Rotate** ↵).
3. Command line entries are also shown in boldface, but in a different font (e.g., type **Array** ↵).

For most functions, I'll describe how to select options from toolbar buttons and tool palettes. In addition, where applicable, I'll include related command names in parentheses. By providing command names, continuity will be maintained for those readers already familiar with the DOS version of AutoCAD.

▼ TIP

If you have a Web browser and an Internet service provider, check out my Web page http://wyp.net/users/omura/ aec.htm. You'll find links to the latest news and software updates to AutoCAD and other Autodesk products. Check out the AutoCAD-related newsgroups to find the answers to those nagging questions about AutoCAD, or tour the AutoCAD-related on-line magazines. You'll also find a link to Sybex, so you can stay in touch with the publishers of this book.

ALL THIS, AND SOFTWARE TOO

Finally, I have included a CD containing a wealth of utilities, symbols libraries, and sample programs that can greatly enhance your use of AutoCAD. *Appendix C* gives you detailed information about the CD. Here's a brief rundown of what's available. Check it out!

SOFTWARE YOU CAN USE RIGHT AWAY

An AEC add-on to AutoCAD offers the typical symbols and wall and door utilities needed to construct architectural drawings. A PostScript add-on turns AutoCAD into a PostScript drawing tool for desktop publishing. Both these add-ons are full working versions. Other software includes printing and plotting shareware utilities that let you output high resolution plots from standard dot-matrix printers.

If you are using the World Wide Web to publish your AutoCAD drawings, you'll be interested in the Autodesk WHIP! Utilities on the CD. These enable you to publish your AutoCAD drawings on a Web page so that your clients and consultants can easily review them. Included is a plug-in to Netscape 2.0 or greater that lets you view, zoom, and pan over your published drawings.

FINDING WHAT YOU WANT IN THE THIRD-PARTY WORLD

When you're ready to expand into third-party products, we've included the latest Autodesk Resource Guide. This is a comprehensive online database of nearly every third-party hardware and software product available for AutoCAD. Many of the programs in the Resource Guide include demos and screen shots, so you can get a better idea of what is offered.

DRAWING FILES FOR THE EXERCISES

We've even included drawing files from the exercise in this book. These are provided so that you can pick up an exercise anywhere in the book, without having to work through the book from front to back.

NEW FEATURES OF AUTOCAD RELEASE 13 FOR WINDOWS 95

Windows 95 is an excellent operating system for AutoCAD R13. It offers the full 32-bit environment that AutoCAD requires to perform to its fullest potential while maintaining compatibility with Windows 3.1 and DOS software. For AutoCAD users, Windows 95 offers a great alternative to Windows NT in stand-alone and small network environments.

To take full advantage of Windows 95, you must have AutoCAD R13 version C4 or greater. With version C4 you will be able to:

OPEN MULTIPLE INSTANCES OF AUTOCAD

This feature enables you to have several AutoCAD sessions running at the same time, each with a different file open. This can be useful if you are editing files that contain cross-references.

USE LONG FILE NAMES

Windows 95 allows you to use file names longer than the old DOS limit of eight characters plus the file-name extension. Now file names can be as long as 256 characters. AutoCAD R13 version C4 enables you to take advantage of this feature by allowing you to add more descriptive names to your CAD files.

WORK FASTER

Overall performance of AutoCAD under Windows 95 is now on par with the DOS version and, in some cases, even surpasses the DOS version, especially where large files are concerned.

TAKE ADVANTAGE OF OLE 2.0

The latest features of OLE are supported in AutoCAD, including:

In-place editing of pasted objects

Drag-and-drop support for placing objects

Advanced scripting for control over multiple applications

NEW FEATURES OF RELEASE 13

In addition to the above-mentioned capabilities, you can take advantage of the many other enhancements that R13 provides. The following is a summary of R13's new features, including the chapter number and section name where each particular feature is discussed:

- A more Windows-like interface (Chapter 1, "Taking a Guided Tour").
- File Preview when opening files (Chapter 1, "Opening an Existing File").
- Zoom In/Out single-click options on toolbar and View menu (Chapter 1, "Getting a Closer Look").
- Explode blocks inserted with nonuniform X, Y, and Z scaling (Chapter 4, "Unblocking and Modifying a Block").
- Objects can be combined into named groups (Chapter 4, "Grouping Objects").
- Basic layer settings can be controlled from a drop-down list in the Properties toolbar (Chapter 4, "Working on Layers").

- Line-type scales can be assigned to objects individually (Chapter 4, "Assigning Line Types to Layers").
- Browse and search capabilities that include thumbnail views of drawing files (Chapter 4, "Finding Files on Your Hard Disk").
- Osnap option called *From* allows you to select a point relative to another point (Chapter 5, "Using and Editing Lines").
- Ray and Xline layout objects simplify editing and layout functions (Chapter 5, "Using Construction Lines as Tools").
- Lengthen tool allows you to accurately change the length of lines and arcs (Chapter 5, "Changing the Length of Objects").
- Multiline object draws complex multiple lines that can include complex line types (Chapter 5, "Drawing Parallel Lines," and Chapter 21, "Creating Complex Line Types").
- Multilines can be joined and edited using new Mledit tools (Chapter 5, "Joining and Editing Multilines").
- Purge can now be executed at any time during a drawing session (Chapter 5, "Selectively Removing Unused Elements").
- Features added to Boundary Hatch, including associative hatching and island detection (Chapter 6, "Adding Hatch Patterns to Your Drawings").
- Dialog box for editing and creating text styles (Chapter 8, "Choosing Fonts and Special Characters").
- Mtext text objects allow you to enter blocks of text (Chapter 8, "Entering Large Blocks of Text").
- Spelling checker with customizing capability (Chapter 8, "Checking Spelling").
- Easier font substitution (Chapter 8, "Substituting Fonts").
- Streamlined dimensioning commands (Chapter 9, "Drawing Linear Dimensions").
- Curved leader tool (Chapter 9, "Adding a Note with an Arrow").
- Tolerance Notation tools for mechanical drafting (Chapter 9, "Adding Tolerance Notation").
- Streamlined external database access (Chapter 10, "Accessing External Databases").

- Easier selection of overlapping objects through Selection Cycling (Chapter 12, "Selection Cycling").
- True Spline curves including ellipses (Chapter 13, "Using True Spline Curves").
- OLE Client support allows you to paste spreadsheets, database, text, bitmap graphics, video clips, and sound into AutoCAD files (Chapter 14, "Adding Sound, Motion, and Photos to Your Drawings").
- Built-in 3D solid modeler (Chapter 18, "Mastering 3D Solids").
- Customizable toolbars and toolbar icons (Chapter 21, "Customizing Tool Palettes").
- Individual pull-down menu groups can be added on the fly without replacing the entire menu file (Chapter 21, "Adding Your Own Pull-Down Menu").
- Line types can now include text or complex shapes (Chapter 21, "Creating Complex Line Types").
- ARX APIs for serious customization through Microsoft Visual C++.

THE AUTOCAD PACKAGE

This book assumes you are using AutoCAD Release 13 for Windows. If you are using an earlier version of AutoCAD, you will want to refer to *Mastering AutoCAD Release 12*, which is available for both DOS and Windows. If you are using the DOS version of AutoCAD Release 13, you will want to refer to *Mastering AutoCAD Release 13 for DOS*.

▼ NOTE

You may find the AutoCAD manuals pretty intimidating, especially if you feel uncomfortable with user manuals in the first place. But it's worth taking some time to browse through them and get to know their content, just in case you run into problems later.

THE MANUALS

You receive seven manuals with AutoCAD. They are:

- The AutoCAD Command Reference
- The AutoCAD User's Guide
- The Customization Guide
- Learning AutoCAD for DOS and UNIX

- The Documentation Guide
- The Installation Guide for DOS
- The Installation Guide for Windows

You'll probably want to read the installation guide for Windows first, then browse through the Command Reference and User's Guide to get a feel for the kind of information available there. You may want to save the Customization Guide for later, when you've become more familiar with AutoCAD.

THE DISKS

AutoCAD comes on a single disk and CD combination. Optionally, you can get AutoCAD on a set of diskettes. Before you do anything else, make copies of your disks and put the originals in a safe place.

THE DIGITIZER TEMPLATE

▼ NOTE

I won't specifically discuss the use of the digitizer for selecting commands, since the process is straightforward. If you are using a digitizer, you can use its puck like a mouse for the all of exercises in this book.

If you intend to use a digitizer tablet in place of a mouse, Autodesk also provides you with a digitizer template. Commands can be selected directly from the template by pointing at the command on the template and pressing the pick button. Each command is shown clearly by name and a simple icon. Commands are grouped on the template by the type of operation the command performs. Before you can use the digitizer template, you must configure the digitizer. See *Appendix A, Hardware and Software Tips*, for a more detailed description of digitizing tablets and *Appendix B* for instructions on configuring the digitizer.

PART ONE

THE

■

BASICS

As with any major endeavor, you must begin by tackling small, manageable tasks. In this first part, you will get familiar with the way AutoCAD looks and feels. *Chapter 1, This Is AutoCAD*, shows you how to get around the Auto-CAD screen. In *Chapter 2, Creating Your First Drawing*, you will learn how to start and exit the program and how to respond to AutoCAD commands. *Chapter 3, Learning the Tools of the Trade*, tells you how to set up a work area, edit objects, and lay out a drawing. In *Chapter 4, Organizing Your Work*, you will explore some tools unique to AutoCAD: symbols, blocks, and layers. As you are introduced to AutoCAD, you will also get a chance to make some drawings that you can use later in the book and perhaps even in your own future projects.

1

▼ ▼ ▼ ▼ ▼

THIS IS AUTOCAD

FAST TRACK

9 ▶ The AutoCAD drawing editor has six main components

These are the pull-down menu bar, the toolbars, the drawing area, the two floating tool palettes, the prompt area and command prompt lines, and the status line. A seventh component, the Aerial View window, can be displayed optionally.

9 ▶ To tell AutoCAD what you want to do

Select commands from either the pull-down menu, a toolbar, or a floating tool palette, or enter instructions at the command prompt with the keyboard.

13 ▶ To select locations in the drawing area

Position the crosshair cursor at the location you want, and press the mouse/pick button.

14 ▶ To select a menu option

Highlight option name and press mouse/pick button; this is called *clicking on* a menu option. Or click twice on the option; this is called double-clicking.

15 ▶ To get a brief description of the pull-down menu items

Click on a menu bar item and drag the highlight bar down into the pull-down menu. As each option is highlighted, a description appears in the status line.

18 ▶ To quickly find out the role of a button on a toolbar or tool palette

Place the arrow cursor on the button for a moment. The name of the button (a tool tip) appears nearby, and a brief description of the button's function appears in the status line.

22 ▶ **To hide a tool palette**

Click on the button in the upper-right corner of the palette window.

22 ▶ **To display a tool palette**

Select Tools ➤ Toolbars and click on the desired tool palette name.

25 ▶ **To open a file from the file dialog box**

Place the arrow cursor on the file name, and press the mouse/pick button twice in rapid succession. This is called *double-clicking*.

28 ▶ **To quickly enlarge an area of your drawing**

Choose View ➤ Zoom ➤ In.

31 ▶ **To erase an object**

Click on the Erase button in the Modify tool palette, select the object you wish to erase, and press ↵.

33 ▶ **To exit a file**

Choose File ➤ Exit. You will be prompted to save your changes, if any.

34 ▶ **To close one file and open another**

Choose File ➤ Open.

▼ NOTE

OLE stands for *Object Linking and Embedding*—a Windows feature that lets different applications share documents. See *Chapter 14* for a more detailed discussion of OLE.

▼ NOTE

Windows NT and Windows 95 users will notice an impressive improvement in performance over Windows 3.1.

AutoCAD has undergone a major facelift. Even if you are a seasoned AutoCAD user, the Windows version of Release 13 will pleasantly surprise you. If you have been using AutoCAD for DOS, you won't regret moving to Windows—it contains many features you won't find in the DOS version. For example, you can use Windows OLE to paste documents directly into AutoCAD from Excel, Windows Paint, or any other programs that support OLE as a server. And, as in Release 12, you can export AutoCAD drawings directly to other OLE clients. This means no more messy conversions and reworking to get spreadsheet, database, text or other data into AutoCAD. It also means that if you want to include a photograph in your AutoCAD drawing, all you have to do is cut and paste.

With Windows, you have the freedom to arrange AutoCAD's screen by clicking and dragging its components. The Windows version of AutoCAD 13 offers many time-saving tools not found in the DOS version, such as a drop-down list for layer settings and line types, tool palettes for easy access to all of AutoCAD's commands, and flyout menus that remember the last item you selected. You even have an expanded help system, with online tutorials and full documentation.

If you are new to AutoCAD, this is the version you may have been waiting for before purchasing the software. Even with its many new features, the programmers at Autodesk have managed to make AutoCAD easier to use. Release 13 is fully compliant with the Windows interface guidelines, and is designed to conform with the Microsoft Office standard interface. So if you are familiar with the Microsoft Office suite of programs, you will feel right at home with AutoCAD Release 13.

In this first chapter, you will look at many of AutoCAD's basic operations, such as opening and closing files, getting a close-up look at part of a drawing, and making changes to a drawing.

TAKING A GUIDED TOUR

First, you will get a chance to familiarize yourself with the AutoCAD screen and how you communicate with AutoCAD. Along the way, you

The Basics

will also get a feel for how to work with this book. Don't worry about understanding or remembering everything that you see in this chapter. You will get plenty of opportunities to probe the finer details of the program as you work through the later tutorials. If you are already familiar with earlier versions of AutoCAD, you may want to read through this chapter anyway, to get acquainted with new features and the graphical interface. To help you remember the material, you will find a brief exercise at the end of each chapter. For now, just enjoy your first excursion into AutoCAD.

▼ NOTE

If you are using Windows 3.1, start Windows, open the AutoCAD program group, then double-click on the AutoCAD program icon.

1. Start your computer and, if you are using Windows 95 on a network, enter your login password.

2. Once in Windows 95, choose Programs ➤ AutoCAD R13 ➤ AutoCAD R13 from the Start menu in the lower-left corner of the screen.

You will see a message telling you that AutoCAD is loading. Then AutoCAD's drawing editor window appears, with an opening greeting telling you which version of AutoCAD you are using, who the program is registered to, and the AutoCAD dealer's name and phone number should you need help.

MESSAGE TO VETERAN AUTOCAD USERS

Autodesk is committed to the Windows operating environment. The result is a graphical user interface that is easier on the AutoCAD neophyte, but perhaps a bit foreign to a veteran AutoCAD user.

If you've been using AutoCAD for a while, and you prefer the older interface, you can still enter AutoCAD commands from the keyboard (though this may become a thing of the past in subsequent releases), and you can still mold AutoCAD's interface into one that is more familiar to you.

First, you may want to restore the side menu that appears in the DOS version of AutoCAD. Here's how it's done:

1. Select Options ➤ Preferences.

2. At the Preferences dialog box, check the Screen Menu check box to enable this option.

3. Click on the Save to ACAD.INI radio button to turn on this option.

4. Finally, click on OK. The side menu will appear.

Also, if you're more comfortable with the AutoCAD Release 12–style pull-down menus, use the Menu command and load the Acadfull.MNU file; you'll find it in the \Acadr13\WIN\Support subdirectory. This menu contains many of the Draw and Modify options found in the DOS version of AutoCAD Releases 12 and 13.

Finally, a word of caution: If you are accustomed to pressing Ctrl-C to cancel an operation, you must now retrain yourself to press the Esc (Escape) key. Ctrl-C now conforms to the Windows standard, making this key-combination a shortcut for saving marked items to the Clipboard. Similarly, instead of using F1 to view the full text window, you must use F2. F1 is most commonly reserved for the Help function in Windows applications.

THE AUTOCAD WINDOW

The AutoCAD program window is divided into six parts:

▼ NOTE

A seventh hidden component, the Aerial View window, displays your entire drawing and lets you select close-up views of parts of your drawing. After you're more familiar with AutoCAD, consult *Chapter 6* for more on this feature.

- Pull-down menu bar

- Toolbars

- Floating tool palettes

- Drawing area

- Command prompt and prompt area

- Status line

Figure 1.1 shows a typical layout of the AutoCAD program window. Along the top is the *menu bar*, and at the bottom are the *command prompt* and the *status line*. Just below the menu bar are the *toolbars*. The rest of the screen is occupied by the *drawing area*. Within the drawing area are two *floating tool palettes*. The toolbars and floating tool palettes are really just two versions of the same thing, as you will soon see.

Many of the elements within the AutoCAD window can be easily moved and reshaped. Figure 1.2 demonstrates how different AutoCAD can look after some simple rearranging of window components.

▼ NOTE

A *layer* is like an overlay that allows you to separate different types of information. AutoCAD allows an unlimited number of layers. On new drawings the default layer is 0. You'll get a detailed look at layers and the meaning of the icons in *Chapter 4*.

The menu bar at the top of the drawing area (illustrated in Figure 1.3) offers pull-down menus from which you select commands in a typical Windows fashion. The toolbars offer a variety of commands through icon buttons and drop-down lists. For example, the *layer* name or number you are presently working on is displayed in a drop-down list in the toolbar. The layer name is preceded by icons that inform you of the status of the layer. The tools, icons, and lists on the toolbar are plentiful, and you'll learn more about all of them later in this chapter and as you work through this book.

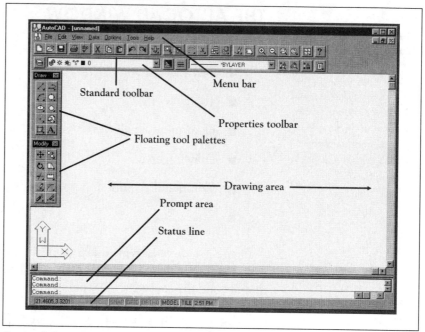

Figure 1.1:   A typical arrangement of the elements of the AutoCAD window

The floating tool palettes (Figure 1.4) offer commands that create new objects and edit existing ones. These are just two of many palettes available to you.

The drawing area—your workspace—occupies most of the screen. Everything you draw appears in this area. As you move your mouse around, you will see crosshairs move within the drawing area. This is your drawing cursor. It lets you point to locations in the drawing area.

At the bottom of the drawing area, the status line (see Figure 1.5) gives you information at a glance about the drawing. For example, the coordinate readout toward the far left of the status line tells you the location of your cursor. Let's practice using the coordinate readout and drawing cursor.

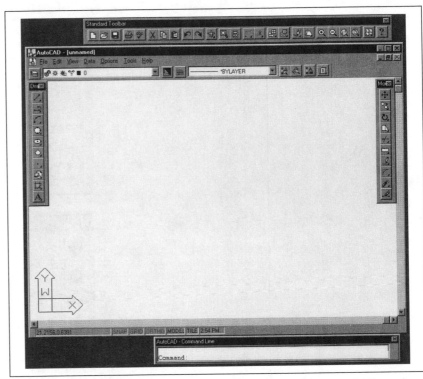

Figure 1.2:   An alternative arrangement of the elements of the AutoCAD window

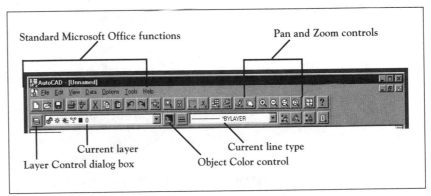

Figure 1.3:   The components of the menu bar and toolbar

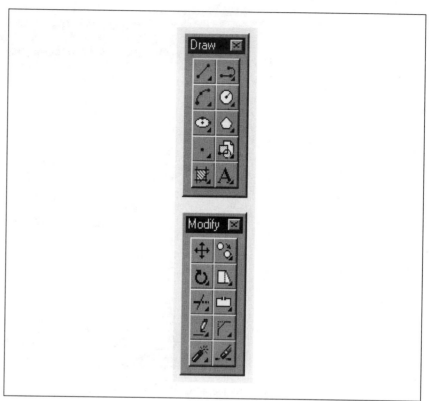

Figure 1.4: The floating tool palettes

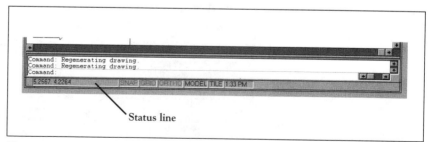

Figure 1.5: The status line and command prompt window

Picking Points

1. Move the cursor around in the drawing area, and note how the coordinate readout changes as you move to tell you the cursor's location. It shows the coordinates in an X,Y format.

2. Now place the cursor in the middle of the drawing area, and press the mouse/pick button and immediately let it go. Move the cursor, and a rectangle follows. This is a *selection window*; you'll learn more about this window in *Chapter 2*.

3. Move the cursor a bit in any direction; then press and let go of the mouse/pick button again. Notice that the rectangle disappears. You have just picked a point.

4. Try picking several more points in the drawing area.

You will notice that tiny crosses appear where you picked points. These are called *blips*—markers that show where you've selected points. They do not become a permanent part of your drawing, nor do they print onto hardcopy output.

UCS Icon

In the lower-left corner of the drawing area, you see a thick, L-shaped arrow outline. This is the *user coordinate system* (UCS) icon, which tells you your orientation in the drawing. This icon becomes helpful as you start to work with complex 2D drawings and 3D models. The X and Y inside the icon indicate the x- and y-axes of your drawing. The W tells you that you are in what is called the *world coordinate system*. We will discuss this icon in detail in *Chapter 16*. For now, you can use it as a reference to tell you the direction of the axes.

The Prompt Area

At the bottom of the screen, just above the status line, is a small horizontal window, which is the *prompt area*. Here you'll see displayed AutoCAD's responses to your input. Right now, it shows the word

"Command:". This tells you that AutoCAD is waiting for your instructions. As you click on a point in the drawing area, you'll see the message "Other corner." At the same time, the cursor starts to draw a selection window which disappears when you click on another point.

It is important to pay special attention to messages displayed in the prompt area, because this is how AutoCAD communicates with you. Besides giving you messages, the prompt area records your activity in AutoCAD. You can use the scroll bar to the right of the prompt area to review previous messages. You can also enlarge the prompt area for a better view. (We'll discuss this in more detail in *Chapter 2*.)

Now let's look at the window components in detail.

THE PULL-DOWN MENUS

As with many Windows programs, the pull-down menus available on the menu bar offer a quicker way to access the general controls and settings for AutoCAD. Within these menus you'll find the commands and functions that are the heart of AutoCAD. By clicking menu items, you can cut and paste items to and from AutoCAD, change the settings that make AutoCAD work the way you want it to, set up the general organization of windows within the AutoCAD window, access the help system, and much more.

The pull-down menu options perform three basic functions:

▼ TIP

To close a pull-down menu without selecting anything, press the Esc (Escape) key. Or you can click on any other part of the AutoCAD window or on another pull-down menu.

- Display additional menu choices

- Display a dialog box that contains settings you can change

- Issue a command that requires keyboard or drawing input. As you select commands and options, AutoCAD provides additional help for you, in the form of brief descriptions of each menu option, which appear in the status line.

Here's an exercise that lets you practice with the pull-down menus and get acquainted with AutoCAD's interface:

1. Place your arrow cursor on Options in the pull-down menu bar. Press the mouse/pick button and hold it down. The list

of items that appear are the commands and settings that let you set up your AutoCAD environment. Don't worry if you don't understand them; you'll get to know them in later chapters.

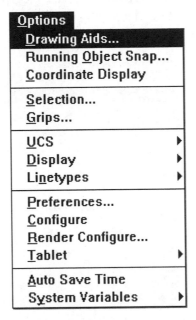

2. While still holding down the mouse/pick button, move the highlight cursor slowly down the list of menu items. As you highlight each item, notice that a description of it appears in the status line at the bottom of the AutoCAD window. These descriptions help you choose the menu option you need.

3. Some of the menu items have triangular pointers to their right. This means the command has additional choices. Highlight the Display item, and you'll see another set of options appear to the right of the menu.

This second set of options is called a *cascading menu*. Whenever you see a pull-down menu item with the triangular pointer, you know that this item opens a cascading menu offering a more detailed set of options.

You might have noticed that other pull-down menu options are followed by three periods, or an ellipsis (…). This indicates that the option brings up a dialog box, as the following exercise demonstrates:

4. In the menu bar, click on Options again, but this time, don't hold down the mouse/pick button.

5. Click on the Preferences… item. The Preferences dialog box appears:

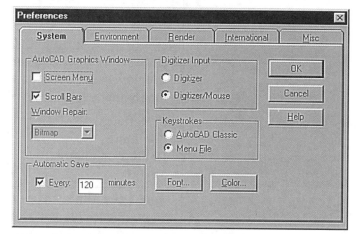

This dialog box contains several "pages," indicated by the tabs across the top, that contain settings for controlling what AutoCAD shows you on its screens, where you want it to look for special files, and other "housekeeping" settings. *Appendix B* describes this dialog box in more detail.

6. Click the Cancel button on the right side of the dialog box.

The third type of item you'll find on pull-down menus is a command that directly executes an AutoCAD operation.

7. Click on Options again in the menu bar.

The Basics

8. In the Options menu, click on Auto Save Time. The Options menu closes, and a message appears in the command line:

New value for SAVETIME <120>:

This message is asking you to enter a new value for the Savetime setting, which controls how frequently AutoCAD performs an automatic save. The item between the < > brackets is the current setting: 120 minutes. You will often be asked for further information through the command line.

9. Type **20** ↵. When you type your response, it, too, will appear in the command line. Then the word Command: returns to the command line. You have just changed AutoCAD's automatic save feature to automatically save files every 20 minutes instead of every two hours. (Let this be a reminder to give your eyes a rest!)

At this point you've seen how most of AutoCAD's commands work.

▼ TIP

Savetime is an AutoCAD setting called a *system variable*. You'll learn more about these variables as you work through the tutorial. For a full list and description of all the variables, consult *Appendix C*.

▼ COMMUNICATING WITH AUTOCAD

AutoCAD is the perfect servant: It does everything you tell it to, and no more. You communicate with AutoCAD using the pull-down menus, and the buttons on toolbars and tool palettes. These devices invoke AutoCAD *commands*. A command is a single-word instruction you give to AutoCAD telling it to do something, such as draw a line (the Line button in the Draw tool palette) or erase an object (the Erase button in the Modify tool palette). Whenever you invoke a command, by either typing it in or selecting a menu or tool palette item, AutoCAD responds by presenting messages to you in the command prompt area, or by displaying a *dialog box*.

The messages in the command prompt area often tell you what to do next, or they offer a list of options. A command will often present several messages, which you answer to complete the command.

A dialog box is like a form you fill out on the computer screen. It lets you adjust settings or make selections from a set of options pertaining to a command. You'll get a chance to work with commands and dialog boxes later in this chapter.

THE TOOL PALETTES AND TOOLBARS

Just as the pull-down menus give you control over the general operation of AutoCAD, the commands in the toolbars and tool palettes do the nitty-gritty work of creating new objects and editing existing ones. These commands are grouped by action type. For example, the Modify palette contains functions that modify existing objects in a drawing. The Draw palette contains tools needed to create new objects. And so on.

The icon buttons in the toolbars and palettes perform three types of actions, just like the pull-down menu commands: They display further options, open dialog boxes, and issue commands that require keyboard or cursor input.

The Tool Palettes

▼ NOTE

Tool tips are available for the tool palettes' icons as well as the toolbars'.

AutoCAD's tool palettes contain icons that represent commands. To help you understand each icon, a *tool tip* appears just below the arrow cursor when you rest the cursor on an icon. Each tool tip helps you identify the icon with its function.

1. Move the cursor onto one of the toolbar icons and leave it there for a second or two. Notice that the command's name appears nearby—this is the tool tip. In the status line, a brief description of the button's purpose appears. See Figure 1.6.

2. Move the cursor across the toolbar. As you do, notice that the tool tips and status-line descriptions change to describe each button.

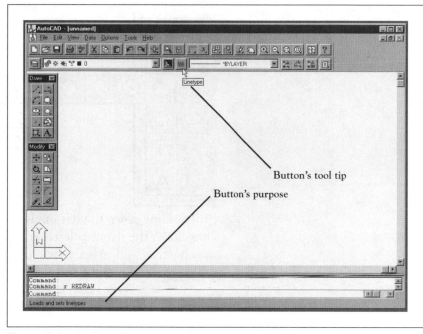

Figure 1.6:   Each toolbar button tells you what it does.

Flyouts   Most toolbar icons start a command as soon as you click on them, but other icons will display a set of additional icons (similar to the cascading menus) that are related to the tool you have selected. This set of additional icons is called a *flyout palette*. If you've used other Windows graphics programs, chances are you've seen flyouts. Look closely at the toolbars on your screen or in Figure 1.6, and you'll be able to identify which toolbar icons have flyouts; they'll have a small right-pointing arrow in the lower-right corner of the palette button.

Let's see how a flyout works:

1. Move the cursor to the Circle tool button in the Draw palette. Click and hold the left mouse button to display the flyout palette. Don't release the mouse button.

▼ **TIP**
Remember: When an instruction says "click on," you should lightly press the mouse/pick button until you hear a click, and then immediately let it go. Don't hold it down.

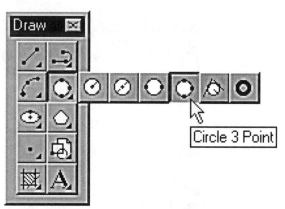

2. Still holding down the left mouse button down, move the cursor over the flyout palette, and notice that the tool tips appear here, as well. Also, notice the description at the bottom of the AutoCAD window.

As you can see, you get a lot of feedback from AutoCAD!

The Toolbars

One unique characteristic of AutoCAD's toolbars is their mobility. In fact, a toolbar in its standard location is really a floating tool palette in its *docked* position. This means it is placed against the top and side borders of the AutoCAD window, so that the toolbar occupies a minimal amount of space. If you want to, you can move the toolbar to any location on your desktop, thus turning it into a floating tool palette.

Later in this section you'll find descriptions of all AutoCAD's toolbars, but first try the following exercise to move the Object Properties toolbar away from its current position in the AutoCAD window:

1. Move the arrow cursor so that it points to the border of the Object Properties toolbar, as shown here:

▼ NOTE

Terminology to Remember:
The action you perform in steps 2 and 3 of this exercise—holding down the mouse/pick button while simultaneously moving the mouse—is called *click and drag*. (If you have used other Windows applications, you already know this.) From now on, we will use "click and drag" to describe this type of action.

2. Press and hold down the left mouse button. Notice that a gray rectangle appears by the cursor.

3. Still holding down the mouse button, move the mouse downward. The gray box follows the cursor.

4. When the gray box is over the drawing area, release the mouse button, and the Object Properties toolbar—now a floating tool palette—moves to its new location.

You can now move the Object Properties tool palette to any location on the screen that suits you. You can also change the shape of the palette; try this:

5. Place the cursor on the bottom-edge border of the Object Properties tool palette. The cursor becomes a double-headed arrow, as shown here:

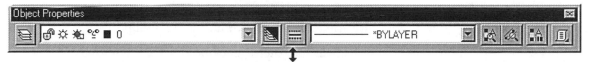

6. Click and drag the border downward. The gray rectangle jumps to a new, taller rectangle as you move the cursor.

7. When the gray rectangle changes to the shape you want, release the mouse button to reform the tool palette.

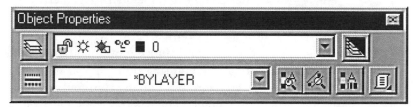

8. To move the tool palette back into its docked position as a toolbar, place the arrow cursor on ("point to") the palette's title bar, and slowly click and drag the palette so the cursor is in position in the upper-left corner of the AutoCAD window. Notice how the gray outline of the palette changes as it approaches its docked position.

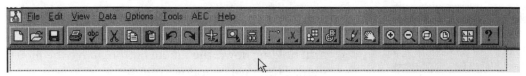

9. When the outline of the object properties palette is near its docked position, release the mouse button. The palette, once again a toolbar, moves back into its previous position in the AutoCAD window.

Thus you can move and reshape any of AutoCAD's tool palettes to place them out of the way yet still have them at the ready to give you quick access to commands. You can also put them away altogether when you don't need them and bring them back at will, as shown in these next steps:

10. Click on the Close button in the upper-left corner of the Draw floating tool palette. This is the small square button with the rectangle in it. The palette disappears.

11. To recover the palette, click on the Tools pull-down menu and then on Toolbars (Tools ➤ Toolbars).

12. In the Toolbars cascading menu, click on Draw. The toolbar reappears in the drawing window.

AutoCAD will remember your palette arrangement between sessions. When you exit and then reopen AutoCAD later, the AutoCAD window will appear just as you left it.

You may have noticed several other tool palettes listed in the Toolbars cascading menu that don't appear in the AutoCAD window. To keep the screen from becoming cluttered, many of the palettes are not placed on the screen. The palettes you'll be using most are displayed first; others that are less frequently used are kept out of sight until they are needed. Here are brief descriptions of all the palettes available from the Tools ➤ Toolbars menu:

> **Draw:** Commands for creating common objects, including lines, arcs, circles, curves, ellipses, and text. This palette appears in the AutoCAD window by default.

▼ NOTE

You can also use the Tool Window button on the Standard toolbar to recover a closed tool palette. Click on the Tool Windows button, and in the Tool Windows flyout, click on the button for the tool palette you want.

▼ NOTE

Terminology to Remember: To show a menu/command combination, we will use the notation *Menu* ➤ *Command*—for example, Tools ➤ Toolbars. For commands/options from cascading menus, we will use *Menu* ➤ *Command* ➤ *Option* ➤ *Option…*—for example, Tools ➤ Toolbars ➤ Draw.

Modify: Commands for editing existing objects. You can Move, Copy, Rotate, Erase, Trim, Extend, and so on.

Dimensioning: Commands that help you dimension your drawings. See *Chapter 9*.

Solids: Commands for creating 3D solids. See *Chapter 18*.

Surfaces: Commands for creating 3D surfaces. See *Chapters 15* and *16*.

External References: Commands that control cross-referencing of drawings. See *Chapters 6* and *12*.

Attribute: Commands for creating and editing object attributes. See *Chapter 10*.

Render: Commands to operate AutoCAD's rendering feature. See *Chapter 17*.

External Database: Commands for linking objects to external databases. See *Chapter 10*.

Miscellaneous: A mixed bag of commands that are used infrequently, yet are helpful in special situations.

Select Objects: Tools for modifying the method used to select objects on the screen. See *Chapter 2*.

Object Snap: Tools to help you select specific points on objects, such as endpoints and midpoints. See *Chapter 3*.

Point Filters: Tools for fine-tuning the selection of coordinates. See *Chapter 15*.

UCS: Tools for setting up a plane on which to work. This is most useful for 3D modeling, but it can be helpful in 2D drafting, as well. See *Chapter 16*.

View: Tools for saving views of a drawing, and quickly obtaining standard orthogonal views of 3D objects. See *Chapter 6* for saving views and *Chapter 18* for orthogonal views of 3D objects.

The Basics

Object Properties: Commands for manipulating the properties of objects. This palette is normally docked below the pull-down menu bar.

Standard Toolbar: The most frequently used commands for view control, file management, and editing. This palette is normally docked below the pull-down menu bar.

You'll get to work with all of the palettes as you work through this book. Or, if you plan to use the book as a reference rather than working through it as a chapter-by-chapter tutorial, any exercise you try will tell you which palette to use for performing a specific operation.

▼ MENUS VS. THE KEYBOARD

Throughout this book, you will be told to select commands and command options from the pull-down menus, toolbars, and tool palettes. For new and experienced users alike, menus and tool buttons offer an easy-to-remember method for accessing commands. You can also enter commands and command options through the keyboard, at the command prompt at the bottom of the AutoCAD window. In fact, if you are familiar with the DOS version of AutoCAD, you may prefer using the keyboard over the menus.

Keyboard entry of commands can speed up drawing input, since this method of communicating with AutoCAD eliminates paging through the many layers of menus and cryptic icons—the time savings will be even better if you use the command abbreviations or aliases. Also, knowing these basic AutoCAD commands in addition to the pull-down menus will allow you to work on any AutoCAD system, no matter what kind of custom menus and programs are used by that system. As you work through the tutorial, we'll show you the keyboard equivalents of pull-down menu options and palette icon buttons, in parentheses.

In addition to the traditional AutoCAD keyboard commands, you can use *accelerator keys*—special keystrokes that open and activate pull-down menu options. You might have noticed that the commands in the menu bar and the items in the pull-down menus each have an underlined character. By pressing the Alt key followed by the key corresponding to the underlined character, you activate that command or option, without having to engage the mouse. For example, to issue File ➤ Open, press Alt, then F, then finally O (**Alt-F O**).

Finally, if you are feeling adventurous, you can create your own single-key shortcuts for executing commands, by adding them to the AutoCAD menu file. We'll discuss customization of the menus, icon palettes, and keyboard shortcuts in *Chapter 21*.

WORKING WITH AUTOCAD

Now that you've been introduced to the drawing editor, let's try using a few of AutoCAD's commands. First, you'll open a sample file and make a few simple modifications to it. In the process, you'll get familiar with some common methods of operation in AutoCAD.

OPENING AN EXISTING FILE

In this exercise, you will get a chance to see and use a typical file dialog box. To start with, you will open an existing file.

1. From the menu bar, choose File ➤ Open. A file dialog box appears. This is a typical Windows file dialog box, with an added twist; notice the large Preview box on the right. It allows you to preview a drawing before you open it, thereby saving time while searching for files.

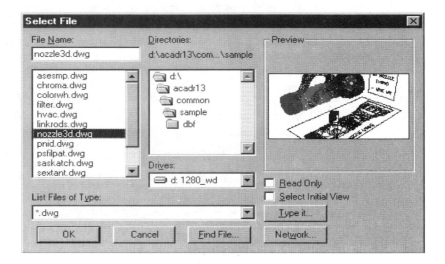

2. In the Directories list in the center, locate the directory named Sample (you may need to scroll down the list to find it). Point to it, and then double-click—press the mouse/pick button twice in rapid succession. (If you're having trouble opening files with a double-click, here's another way to do it until you are more proficient with the mouse: Click on the file once to highlight it, and then double-click on it or click the OK button.) The file list on the left changes to show the contents of the Sample directory.

3. Move the arrow to the file named Nozzle3d, and click on it. Notice that the name now appears in the File Name input box above the file list. Also, the Preview box now shows a thumbnail image of the file.

4. Click on the OK button at the bottom of the dialog box. AutoCAD proceeds to open the Nozzle3d file, as shown in Figure 1.7.

The Nozzle3d file opens to display the entire drawing, in the same state as when you last saved it. Also, the AutoCAD window's title bar displays the name of the drawing. This offers easy identification of the file.

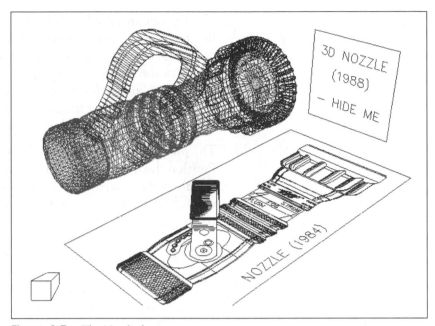

Figure 1.7:   The Nozzle drawing

GETTING A CLOSER LOOK

Usually, you will want to get a closer look at a part of your drawing. To do that in the Nozzle3D drawing, use the Zoom command (View ➤ Zoom). To tell AutoCAD what area you wish to enlarge, you will use what is called a *window*.

1. Choose View ➤ 3D Viewpoint Presets ➤ Plan View ➤ World. Your view changes to display a two-dimensional view looking down on the drawing.

2. Choose View ➤ Zoom ➤ Window.

3. The prompt area displays First corner:. Look at the dotted-line rectangle shown in panel 1 of Figure 1.8. Move the crosshair cursor on your screen to about where the lower-left corner of the square is in the figure; then press the mouse/pick button. Move the cursor, and you see the rectangle appear, one corner fixed on the point you just picked, while the other corner follows the cursor.

4. The prompt area now displays First corner: Other corner:. Position the other corner of the window so it encloses the handle of the nozzle, as shown in the figure, and press the mouse/pick button. The handle enlarges to fill the screen (panel 2 of Figure 1.8).

In this exercise, you used the Window option of the Zoom command to define an area to enlarge for your close-up view. You saw how Auto-CAD prompts you to indicate first one corner of the window, then the other. These messages are helpful for first-time users of AutoCAD. You will be using the Window options frequently—not just to define views, but also to select objects for editing.

Getting a close-up view of your drawing is crucial to working accurately with a drawing, but you'll often want to return to a previous view to get the overall picture. To do so, choose View ➤ Zoom ➤ Previous. Do this now, and the previous view—one showing the entire nozzle—returns to the screen.

You can also quickly enlarge or reduce your view using Zoom In and Zoom Out, as follows:

1. Choose View ➤ Zoom ➤ In. Your view enlarges to show more detail.

2. Choose View ➤ Zoom ➤ Out. The view changes back to include more of the drawing.

▼ NOTE

You can also zoom in and out using the Zoom In and Zoom Out buttons in the Standard toolbar. These icons look like magnifying glasses, with a plus sign for Zoom In and a minus sign for Zoom Out.

▼ NOTE

If you are using the C4 upgrade and have configured AutoCAD to use the WHIP display driver, you have two more display commands at your disposal. Type **RTPAN** at the command prompt and the cursor changes into a hand. You can then drag your view across the display in real time. Type **RTZOOM** and the cursor changes into a magnifying glass. You can then zoom in or out in real time. RTPAN and RTZOOM can also be used transparently (see the sidebar "Zooming and Panning during Other Commands" in Chapter 6).

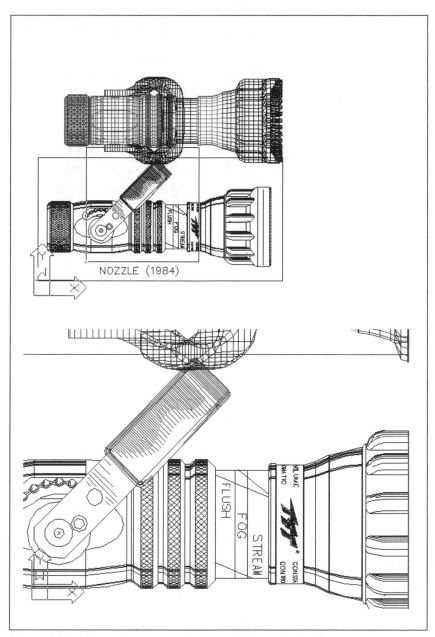

Figure 1.8: Placing the Zoom window around the nozzle handle

THE AERIAL VIEW WINDOW

The Aerial View window is an optional AutoCAD display tool. It gives you an overall view of your drawing, no matter how much magnification you may be using for the drawing editor. Aerial View also makes it easier to get around in a large-scale drawing. You'll find that this feature is best suited to more complex drawings that cover great areas, such as site plans, topographical maps, or city planning documents.

We won't discuss this view much here in the first chapter, as it can be a bit confusing for the first-time AutoCAD user. As you become more comfortable with AutoCAD, however, you may want to try it out. You'll find a detailed description in *Chapter 6*.

SAVING A FILE AS YOU WORK

It is a good idea to periodically save your file as you work on it. You can save it under its original name (with File ➤ Save), or under a different name (with File ➤ Save As), thereby creating a new file.

By default, AutoCAD automatically saves your work at 120-minute intervals under the name AUTO.SV$; this is known as the *autosave* feature. Using system variables, you can change the name of the autosaved file and control the time between autosaves. See the sidebar, "Using AutoCAD's Automatic Save Feature," in *Chapter 3* for details.

First try the Save command. This quickly saves the drawing in its current state without exiting the program.

Choose File ➤ Save. You will notice some disk activity while Auto-CAD saves the file to the hard disk. As an alternative to picking File ➤ Save from the menus, you can type **Alt-F S**. This is the accelerator key, also called hotkey, for the File ➤ Save command.

Now try the Save As command. This command brings up a dialog box that allows you to save the current file under a new name.

▼ TIP

You can also issue the File ➤ Save command by entering **Qsave** ↵ into the command prompt line.

1. Choose File ➤ Save As or type **Saveas** ↵ at the command prompt. The Select File dialog box appears. Note that the current file name, Nozzle3d, is highlighted in the File Name input box at the bottom of the dialog box.

2. Type **Myfirst**. As you type, the name Nozzle3d disappears from the input box and is replaced by Myfirst. You don't need to enter the .DWG file name extension. AutoCAD adds it to the file name automatically when it saves the file.

3. Click on the OK button. The dialog box disappears, and you will notice some disk activity.

You now have a copy of the nozzle file under the name Myfirst.DWG, and the name of the file displayed in the AutoCAD window's title bar has changed to Myfirst. From now on, when you use the File ➤ Save option, your drawing will be saved under its new name. Saving files under a different name can be useful when you are creating alternatives or when you just want to save one of several ideas you are trying out.

MAKING CHANGES

You will be making frequent changes to your drawings. In fact, one of the AutoCAD's chief advantages is the ease with which you can make changes. The following exercise shows you a typical sequence of operations involved in making a change to a drawing.

▼ TIP

You can also issue the Erase command by typing **Erase** ↵ at the command prompt.

1. From the Modify tool palette, click on the Erase icon (the one with a pencil eraser touching paper). This activates the Erase command.

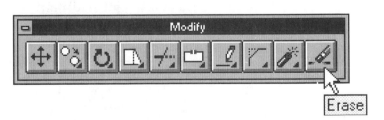

Notice that the cursor has turned into a small square; this square is called the *pickbox*. You also see Select object: in the command prompt area.

2. Place the pickbox on the diagonal pattern of the nozzle handle (see Figure 1.9) and click on it. The 2D image of the nozzle becomes highlighted. The pickbox and the Select object: prompt remain, telling you that you can continue to select objects.

3. Now press ⏎. The nozzle and the rectangle disappear. You have just erased a part of the drawing.

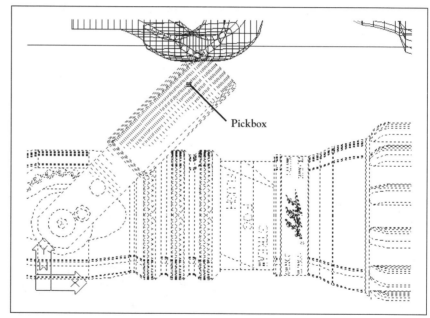

Pickbox

Figure 1.9:   Erasing a portion of the Nozzle handle

In this exercise, you first issued the Erase command, and then selected an object by clicking on it using a pickbox. The pickbox tells you that you must select items on the screen. Once you've done that, you press ⏎ to move on to the next step. This sequence of steps is common to many of the commands you will work with in AutoCAD.

The Basics | I

CLOSING AUTOCAD

When you are done with your work on one drawing, you can open another drawing, or temporarily leave AutoCAD, or close AutoCAD entirely. To close a file and exit AutoCAD, you use the Exit option on the File menu.

▼ NOTE

You can also issue the Exit command by typing **Quit** ⏎ at the command prompt, or you can double-click on the Control menu box in the upper-left corner of the AutoCAD window.

1. Choose File ➤ Exit, the last item in the menu. A dialog box appears, asking you "Save changes to Myfirst?" and offering three buttons, labeled Yes, No, and Cancel.

2. Click the No button. AutoCAD exits the nozzle drawing and closes without saving your changes.

Whenever you attempt to exit a drawing that has been changed, you will get this same inquiry box. This request for confirmation is a safety feature that lets you change your mind and save your changes before you exit AutoCAD. In the previous exercise, you discarded the changes you made, so the nozzle drawing reverts back to its state before you erased the handle.

If you only want to exit AutoCAD temporarily, you can minimize it so it appears as an icon in the lower-left corner of the Windows desktop. You do this by clicking on the down-arrow button in the upper-right corner of the AutoCAD window. Alternatively, you can use the Alt-Tab key-combination to switch to another program.

IF YOU WANT TO EXPERIMENT...

Try opening and closing some of the sample drawing files.

1. Start AutoCAD by double-clicking on the AutoCAD program icon in the AutoCAD program group.

2. Click on File ➤ Open.

3. Use the dialog box to open the Myfirst file again. Notice that the drawing appears on the screen with the handle enlarged. This is the view you had on screen when you used the Save command in the earlier exercise.

4. Erase the handle, as you did in the earlier exercise.

5. Click on File ➤ Open again. This time, open the Dhouse file. Notice that you get the Save Changes inquiry box you saw when you used the Exit option earlier. File ➤ Open acts just like Exit, but instead of exiting AutoCAD altogether, it closes the current file and then opens a different one.

6. Click on the No button. The 3D Dhouse drawing opens.

7. Click on File ➤ Exit. Notice that you exit AutoCAD without getting the Save Changes dialog box. This is because you didn't make any changes to the Dhouse file.

2

CREATING YOUR FIRST DRAWING

Understanding the AutoCAD Interface

Drawing Lines

Giving Distance and Direction

Drawing Arcs

Selecting Objects for Editing

Specifying Point Locations for
Moves and Copies

Using Grips

Selecting Specific Geometric Elements

Getting Help

FAST TRACK

43 ▶ To draw a series of line segments

Choose Line from the Draw tool palette's Line flyout, and click on the drawing area where you want to place lines.

47 ▶ To cancel a command or to exit a dialog box without changing anything

Press the Esc key.

48 ▶ To specify exact distances from a picked point in polar coordinates

Type **@**, the distance, **<**, and the angle. Use no spaces between characters. For example, to specify a distance of 4 at an angle of 30 degrees, type **@4<30** ↵.

50 ▶ To specify exact distances from a picked point in horizontal and vertical distances

Type **@**, the horizontal distance, a comma, and the vertical distance. For example, to specify a location that is 4 units to the right and 6 units up, type **@4,6** ↵.

52 ▶ To get rid of blips that clutter the screen

Choose View ➤ Redraw View.

53 ▶ To select a command option using the keyboard

Note the option's capitalized letters in the prompt, type those letters in, and press ↵.

In this chapter we'll examine some of AutoCAD's basic functions and practice with the drawing editor by building a simple drawing to use in later exercises. We'll discuss giving input to AutoCAD, interpreting prompts, and getting help when you need it. We'll also cover the use of coordinate systems to give AutoCAD exact measurements for objects. You'll see how to select objects you've drawn, and how to specify base points for moving and copying.

If you're not a beginning AutoCAD user, you might want to move on to the more complex material in *Chapter 3*. You can use the files supplied on the companion disk of this book to continue the tutorials at that point.

GETTING TO KNOW THE DRAW TOOL PALETTE

Your first task in learning how to draw in AutoCAD is to try and draw a line. But before you begin drawing, take a moment to familiarize yourself with the tool palette you'll be using more than any other to create objects with AutoCAD: the Draw tool palette.

1. Start AutoCAD just as you did in the first chapter, by opening the AutoCAD program group and double-clicking on the AutoCAD icon.

2. Move the arrow cursor to the upper-left icon in the Draw palette, and rest it there so that the tool tip appears.

3. Slowly move the arrow cursor over the other buttons in the Draw tool palette, and read each tool tip.

▼ NOTE

Moving the arrow cursor onto an element on the screen is also referred to as "pointing to" that element.

In most cases, you'll be able to guess what each button does by looking at its icon. The icon with an arc, for instance, indicates that the button draws arcs; the one with the ellipse shows that the button draws ellipses; and so on. The tool tip gives you more information on the use of the button. For example, if you point to the Arc icon just below the Line icon, the tool tip reads "3 Point." This tells you the button draws an arc using 3 points that you supply by picking points in the drawing area.

Figure and Table 2.1 will aid you in navigating the two main tool palettes (Draw and Modify), and you'll get experience with many of AutoCAD's tool buttons as you work through this book.

As you saw in *Chapter 1*, clicking on a button issues a command. Clicking *and dragging* a button, however, opens a flyout, which offers further options for that tool.

1. Click and drag the Arc button. The Arc flyout appears. As you can see, there are a number of additional ways you can draw an arc.

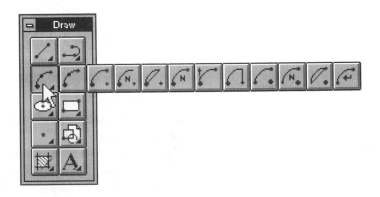

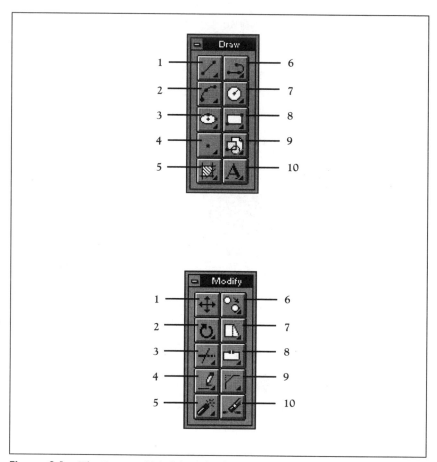

Figure 2.1: The Draw and Modify tool palettes. The options available from each tool button are listed by number in Table 2.1.

2. Move the cursor across the flyout to about the middle, until the tool tip reads "Arc Start End Direction," and then let go of the mouse button. Notice that the icon representing the Arc tool now changes and becomes the icon from the flyout that represents Arc Start End Direction. By releasing the mouse you've also issued the Arc command with the Start End Direction option.

Table 2.1: The Options That Appear on the Draw and Modify Tool
Palettes and Flyouts

Draw Tool Palette	
1	Line Construction Line Ray
2 (Arc)	3 Point Start Center End Start Center Angle Start Center Length Start End Angle Start End Direction Start End Radius Center Start End Center Start Angle Center Start Length Continue
3 (Ellipse)	Center Axis End Arc
4	Point Divide Measure
5	Hatch PostScript Fill
6	Polyline 3D Polyline Multiline Spline
7	Center Radius Center Diameter 2 Point 3 Point Tantan Radius Donut
8	Rectangle Polygon 2D Solid Region Boundary
9	Insert Block Block
10	Text Dtext Single Line Text

Modify Tool Palette	
1	Move
2	Rotate 3D Rotate Align
3	Trim Extend
4	Edit Polyline Edit Multiline Edit Spline Edit Text Edit Hatch
5	Explode Union Subtract Intersection
6	Copy Offset Mirror 3D Mirror Rectangular Array Polar Array 3D Rectangular Array 3D Polar Array
7	Stretch Scale Lengthen (Change) Point
8 (Break)	1 Point 1 Point Select 2 Point 2 Point Select
9	Chamfer Fillet
10	Erase

3. Press Esc twice to exit the Arc command.

▼ **TIP**

If you find you are working a lot with one particular flyout, you can easily turn a flyout into a floating tool palette, so all the flyout options are readily available with a single click. See *Chapter 21* for details on how to do this.

By making the most recently selected option on a flyout the default option for the tool palette button, AutoCAD gives you quick access to frequently used commands. A word of caution, however: This feature can confuse the first-time AutoCAD user. Also, the grouping of options on the flyout menus are not always self-explanatory—even to a veteran AutoCAD user. Refer to Table 2.1 when you need help.

Don't be too concerned if you don't understand all the options you see in the table. You will get to know them as you work with AutoCAD and the tutorials in this book. Now let's get down to the business of drawing.

▼ WORKING WITH TOOL PALETTES

As you work through the exercises, this book will show you graphics of the icons to choose, along with the palette or flyout that contains the icon. Don't be alarmed, however, if the palettes you see in the examples don't look exactly like those on your screen. To save page space, the palettes and flyouts have been placed horizontally for the illustrations; the ones on your screen may be oriented vertically, or in the case of the Draw and Modify palettes, in a two column-setup. Though the shape of your palettes and flyouts may differ from the ones you see in this book, the contents are the same. So when you see a graphic showing an icon, focus on the icon itself with its tool tip name, along with the name of the palette in which it is shown.

STARTING YOUR FIRST DRAWING

In *Chapter 1*, you looked at a pre-existing sample drawing. This time you will begin to draw on your own, by creating a door that will be used in later exercises. First, though, you must learn how to tell AutoCAD what you want and, even more importantly, to understand what Auto-CAD wants from you.

1. Choose File ➤ New.

2. When the Create New Drawing dialog box appears, type **Door**. As you type, the name appears in the New Drawing Name input box.

▼ NOTE

When the No Prototype check box in the Create New Drawing dialog box is checked, AutoCAD creates a new file using the standard AutoCAD default settings. This is an important feature in all your AutoCAD work. (For more on prototype files, see *Chapter 5*.) This book assumes you are using the standard default settings.

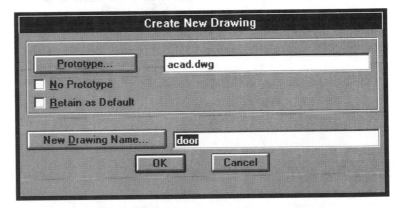

3. Be sure the No Prototype check box is checked. Then click on the OK button or press Enter. The AutoCAD opening message appears briefly and a new file is opened.

The new file shows a drawing area roughly 12 inches wide by 9 inches high. To check this for yourself, move the crosshair cursor to the upper-right corner of the screen, and observe the value shown in the coordinate readout. This is the standard AutoCAD default drawing area for new drawings.

4. Point to the Line icon on the Draw palette. (Remember, "point to" means "move the arrow cursor to.")

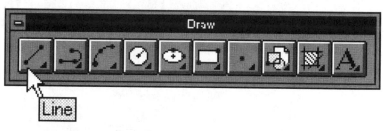

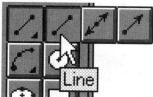

Click and drag with the left mouse button, but don't release the button. A flyout appears:

5. While still holding down the mouse button, move the arrow cursor across the flyout to a different icon button. Hold it there for a second until the tool tip appears. Continue to move the cursor, and watch the tool tips appear for each option.

6. Point to the line icon and release the mouse button. You've just issued the LINE command. AutoCAD responds in two ways. First, you see the message

From point:

in the command prompt, asking you to select a point to begin your line. Also, the cursor has changed its appearance; it no longer has a square in the crosshairs. This is a clue telling you to pick a point to start a line.

7. Using the mouse/pick button, select a point on the screen near the center. As you select the point, AutoCAD adds

To point:

to the prompt.

Now as you move the mouse around, you will notice a line with one end fixed on the point you just selected, and the other end following the cursor, as you move the mouse (see panel 1 of Figure 2.2). This action is called *rubber-banding*.

You will also see a tiny cross marking the first endpoint of the line. This cross is called a *blip*, and it appears every time you select a point during a command. Though they show up on the screen, *blips* are not part of the drawing; they are a visual aid to you as you draw. AutoCAD provides a setting that lets you turn off blips. We will discuss this command in *Chapter 13*.

Now continue with the LINE command.

8. Move the cursor to a point to the right of the first point you selected, and press the mouse/pick button again. The first rubber-banding line is now fixed between the two points you selected, and a second rubber-banding line appears (see panel 2 of Figure 2.2).

9. If the line you drew isn't the exact length you want, you can back up during the LINE command and change it. To do this, click on Undo in the Standard toolbar, or type **U** from the keyboard and press ↵.

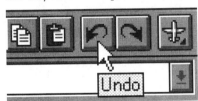

Now the line you drew previously will rubber-band as if you hadn't selected the second point to fix its length.

From now on, this crosshair cursor without the small box will be referred to as the *point selection mode* of the cursor. If you look ahead to Figure 2.8, you'll see all the different modes of the drawing cursor.

You've just drawn, and then undrawn, a line at an arbitrary length. The LINE command is still active. There are two things that tell you that you are in the middle of a command, as mentioned in step 6 above. If you don't see the word Command in the command prompt, you know a command is still active. Also, the cursor will be the plain crosshair without the little box at its intersection.

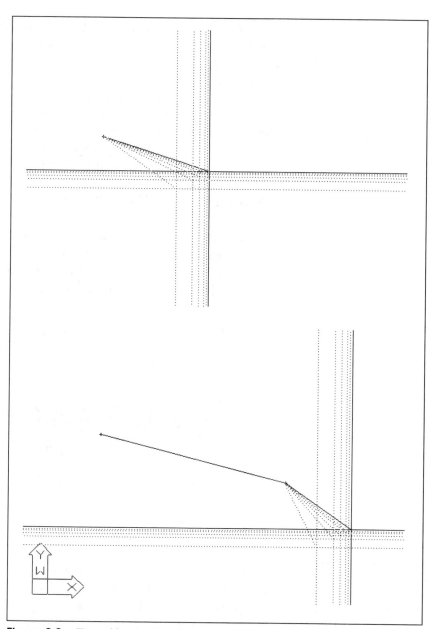

Figure 2.2: Two rubber-banding lines

The Basics   I

GETTING OUT OF TROUBLE

Beginners and experts alike are bound to make a few mistakes. Before you get too far into the tutorial, here are some powerful yet easy-to-use tools to help you recover from accidents.

Backspace [←] If you make a typing error, you can use the Backspace key to back up to your error, and then retype your command or response. Backspace is located in the upper-right corner of the main keyboard area.

Escape [Esc] This is perhaps the single most important key on your keyboard. When you need to quickly exit a command or dialog box without making changes, just press the Escape key in the upper-left corner of your keyboard. Press it twice if you want to make absolutely sure you've canceled a command.

Tip: Use the Escape key before editing with grips or issuing commands through the keyboard. You can also use it to clear grip selections.

U ↵ If you accidentally change something in the drawing and want to reverse that change, click on the Undo button in the Standard toolbar (the left-pointing curved arrow). Or type **U ↵** at the command prompt. Each time you do this, AutoCAD will undo one operation at a time, in reverse order—so the last command performed will be undone first, then the next to last, and so on. The prompt will display the name of the command being undone, and the drawing will revert to its state prior to that command. You can undo everything back to the beginning of an editing session, if you need to.

Redo If you accidentally Undo one too many commands, you can redo the last undone command, by clicking on the Redo button (the right-pointing curved arrow) in the Standard toolbar. Or type **Redo** ↵. Unfortunately, Redo only restores one command.

SPECIFYING DISTANCES WITH COORDINATES

Next, you will continue with the Line command to draw a *plan view* (an overhead view) of a door, to no particular scale. Later you will resize the drawing to use in future exercises. The door will be 3.0 units long and 0.15 units thick. To specify these exact distances in AutoCAD, you can use either *relative polar coordinates* or *Cartesian coordinates*.

SPECIFYING POLAR COORDINATES

To enter the exact distance of 3 units to the right of the last point you selected, do the following:

1. Type **@3<0.** As you type, the letters appear in the command prompt.

2. Press ↵. A line appears, starting from the first point you picked and ending 3 units to the right of it (see Figure 2.3). You have just entered a relative polar coordinate.

The at sign (**@**) you entered tells AutoCAD that the distance you are specifying is from the last point you selected. The 3 is the distance, and the less-than symbol (**<**) tells AutoCAD that you are designating the angle at which the line is to be drawn. The last part is the value for the angle, which in this case is 0. This is how to use *polar coordinates* to communicate distances and direction to AutoCAD.

Angles are given based on the system shown in Figure 2.4, where 0° is a horizontal direction from left to right, 90° is straight up, 180° is horizontal from right to left, and so on. You can specify degrees, minutes, and seconds of arc if you want to be that exact. We'll discuss angle formats in more detail in *Chapter 3*.

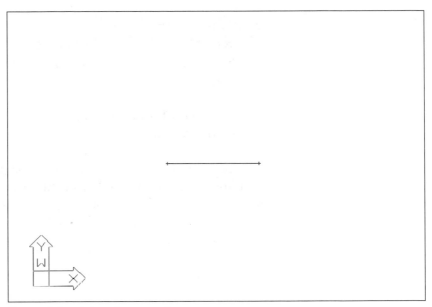

Figure 2.3: A line three units long

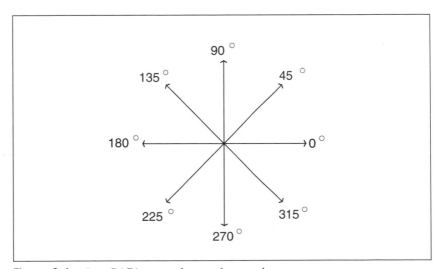

Figure 2.4: AutoCAD's system for specifying angles

SPECIFYING RELATIVE CARTESIAN COORDINATES

For the next line segment, let's try another method of specifying exact distances.

1. Enter **@0,.15** ↲. A short line appears above the endpoint of the last line.

Once again, the @ tells AutoCAD that the distance you specify is from the last point picked. But in this example, you give the distance in x and y values. The x distance, 0, is given first, followed by a comma, and then the y distance, 0.15. This is how to specify distances in relative Cartesian coordinates.

2. Enter **@-3,0** ↲. The result is a drawing that looks like Figure 2.5.

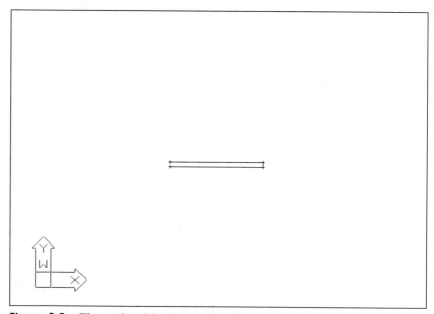

Figure 2.5: Three sides of the door in the plan

▼ NOTE

If you are using the C4 upgrade, you can also use the Direct Distance method for drawing objects. For example, to use this method with the LINE command, point the rubber-banding line in the direction you want to draw the line, then type the distance and press ↵. If you are drawing orthogonal lines, you can improve data entry speed by turning on Ortho mode.

The distance you entered in step 2 was also in x,y values, but here you used a negative value to specify the x distance. Positive values in the Cartesian coordinate system are from left to right and from bottom to top (see Figure 2.6). If you want to draw a line from right to left, you must designate a negative value.

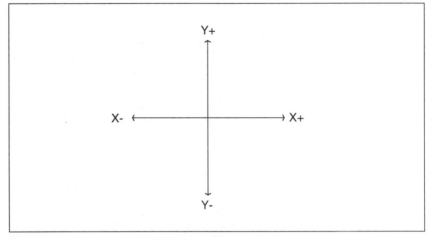

Figure 2.6:   Positive and negative Cartesian coordinate directions

▼ TIP

To finish drawing a series of lines without closing them, you can press Esc, or ↵, or the Spacebar.

3. Now type **C** ↵. A line connecting the first and last points of a sequence of lines is drawn (see Figure 2.7), and the Line command terminates.

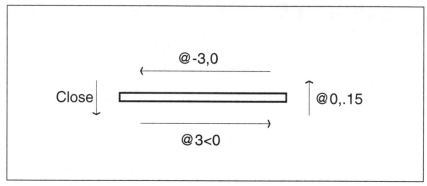

Figure 2.7: Distance and direction input for the door

CLEANING UP THE SCREEN

By now, with all the blips, the screen looks a bit messy. To clean up a screen image, use the Redraw command. Choose View ➤ Redraw View, or click on the Redraw button in the toolbar. The screen quickly redraws the objects, clearing them of the blips.

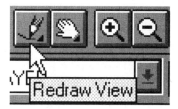

Another command, Regen, does the same thing as Redraw, but also updates the drawing database—which means it takes a lot longer to restore the drawing. In general, you will want to avoid Regen, though at times using it is unavoidable. You will examine regens in *Chapter 7*.

INTERPRETING THE CURSOR MODES AND UNDERSTANDING PROMPTS

The key to working with AutoCAD successfully is understanding the way it interacts with you. In this section you will become familiar with some of the ways AutoCAD prompts you for input. Understanding the format of the messages in the prompt area and recognizing other events on the screen will help you learn the program more easily.

As the command prompt aids you with messages, the cursor also gives you clues about what to do. Figure 2.8 illustrates the various modes of the cursor and gives a brief description of the role of each mode. Take a moment to study this figure.

CHOOSING COMMAND OPTIONS

Many commands in AutoCAD offer several options, which are often presented to you in the prompt. Here, we'll use the Arc command, issued from the keyboard, to illustrate the format of AutoCAD's prompts. Usually, in a floor-plan drawing, an arc is drawn to indicate the direction of a door swing. Figure 2.9 shows some of the other standard symbols used in architectural style drawings. Next, you'll draw the arc for the door you started in the previous exercise.

> ▼ NOTE
>
> The *default* is the option Auto-CAD assumes you intend to use unless you don't tell it otherwise.

1. Start the command by typing **Arc** ↵. The prompt Center/<Start point>: appears, and the cursor changes to point selection mode.

Let's examine this Center/<Start point>: prompt. It contains two options. The *default* option always appears between angle brackets (< >), and all other options are separated by slashes (/). If you choose to take the default, Start point, you can input a point by clicking on a location on the screen or by entering a coordinate.

> ▼ NOTE
>
> When you see a set of options in the prompt, note their capitalization. If you choose to respond to prompts using the keyboard, these capitalized letters are all you need to enter to select that option. In some cases, the first two letters are capitalized to differentiate two options that begin with the same letter, such as LAyer and LType.

2. Type **C** ↵ to select the Center option. The prompt Center: appears. Notice that you only had to type in the C and not the whole word Center.

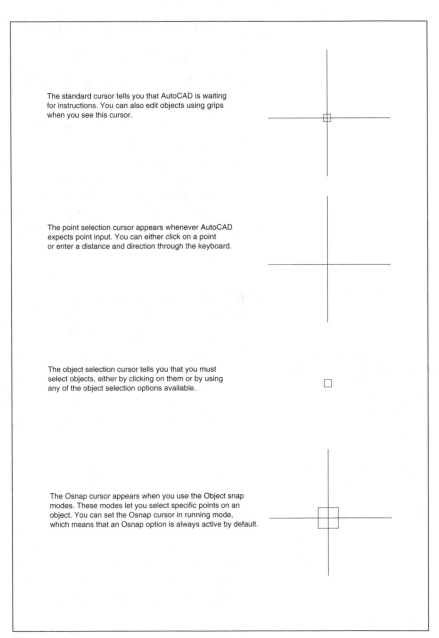

The standard cursor tells you that AutoCAD is waiting for instructions. You can also edit objects using grips when you see this cursor.

The point selection cursor appears whenever AutoCAD expects point input. You can either click on a point or enter a distance and direction through the keyboard.

The object selection cursor tells you that you must select objects, either by clicking on them or by using any of the object selection options available.

The Osnap cursor appears when you use the Object snap modes. These modes let you select specific points on an object. You can set the Osnap cursor in running mode, which means that an Osnap option is always active by default.

Figure 2.8:   The drawing cursor's modes

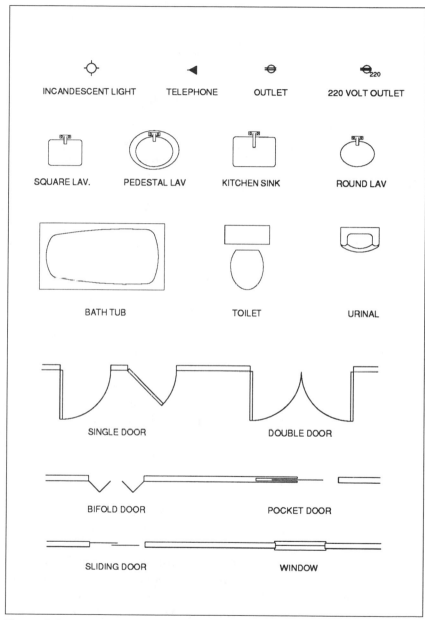

Figure 2.9: Samples of standard symbols used in architectural drawings

3. Now pick a point representing the center of the arc near the upper-left corner of the door (see panel 1 of Figure 2.10). The prompt Start point: appears.

4. Type **@3<0**. The prompt Angle/Length of chord/<End point>: appears.

5. Move the mouse, and you will see a temporary arc originating from a point 3 units to the right of the center point you selected and rotating about that center, as in panel 2 of Figure 2.10.

As the prompt indicates, you now have three options. You can enter an angle, length of chord, or the endpoint of the arc. The default, indicated by **<End point>** in the prompt, is to pick the arc's endpoint. Again, the cursor is in a point selection mode, telling you it is waiting for point input. To select this default option, you need only pick a point on the screen indicating where you want the endpoint.

6. Pick a point directly vertical from the center of the arc. The arc is now fixed in place, as in panel 3 of Figure 2.10.

You could have selected the Center Start End icon from the Arc flyout of the Draw palette and obtained the same results as in the foregoing exercise. However, this exercise has given you some practice working with AutoCAD's prompts and entering keyboard commands—a skill you will need when you start to use some of the more advanced AutoCAD functions.

As you can see, AutoCAD has a distinct structure in its prompt messages. You first issue a command, which in turn offers options in the form of a prompt. Depending on the option you select, you will get another set of options or you will be prompted to take some action, such as picking a point, selecting objects, or entering a value.

As shown in Figure 2.11, the sequence is something like a tree. As you work through the exercises, you will become intimately familiar with this routine. Once you understand the workings of the tool palettes, command prompts, and dialog boxes, you can almost teach yourself the rest of the program!

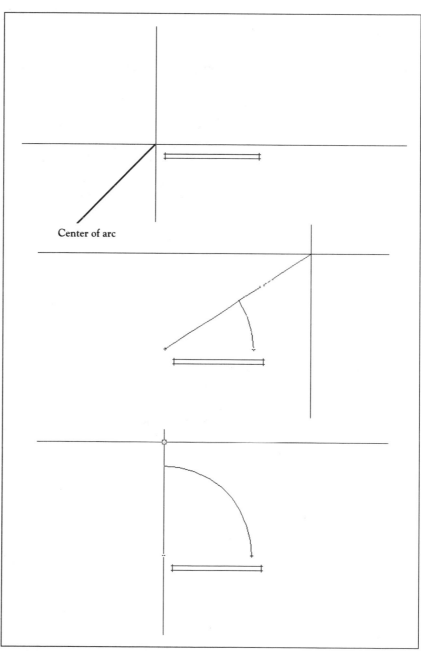

Center of arc

Figure 2.10:   Using the Arc command

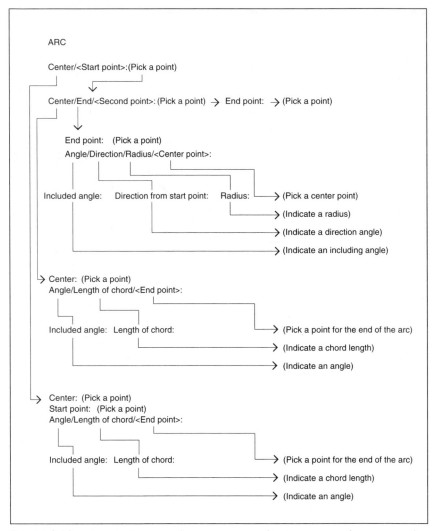

Figure 2.11:   A typical command structure, using the Arc command as an example

SELECTING OBJECTS

AutoCAD provides many options for selecting objects. This section has two parts: The first part deals with object selection methods unique to AutoCAD. The second part deals with the more common selection method used in most popular graphic programs, the *Noun/Verb* method. It's a good idea to familiarize yourself with these two methods early on, since they play a major role in working with AutoCAD.

SELECTING OBJECTS IN AUTOCAD

Many AutoCAD commands prompt you to Select objects:. Along with this prompt, the cursor will change from crosshairs to a small square (see Figure 2.8). Whenever you see this object-selection prompt and the square cursor, you have several options while making your selection. Often, as you select objects on the screen, you will change your mind about a selection or accidentally pick an object you do not want. Let's take a look at most of the selection options available in AutoCAD, and learn what to do when you make the wrong selection.

1. Choose Move from the Modify palette.

2. At the Select objects prompt, click on the two horizontal lines that compose the door. As you saw in the last chapter, whenever AutoCAD wants you to select objects, the cursor turns into the small square pickbox. This tells you that you are in *object-selection mode*. As you pick an object, it is *highlighted*, as shown in Figure 2.12.

▼ TIP

If you need to select objects by their characteristics rather than by their location, *Chapter 12* describes the Object Selection Filters tool. This feature lets you easily select a set of objects based on their properties, including object type, color, layer assignment, and more.

▼ NOTE

Highlighting means an object changes from a solid image to one composed of dots. When you see an object highlighted on the screen, you know that you have chosen that object to be acted upon by whatever command you are currently using.

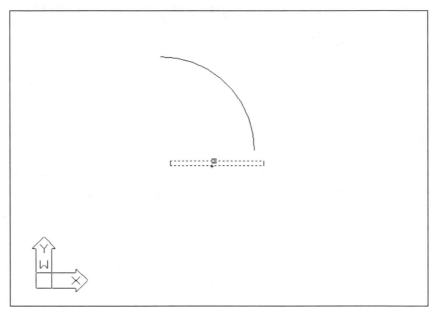

Figure 2.12: Selecting the lines of the door and seeing them highlighted

3. After making your selections, you may decide to deselect
   some items. Click on Undo in the Standard toolbar, or enter
   U ↵ from the keyboard.

Notice that one line is no longer highlighted. The Undo
option deselects objects, one at a time, in reverse order of
selection.

4. There is another way to deselect objects: Hold down the
   Shift key and click on the remaining highlighted line. It reverts to a solid line, showing you that it is no longer selected
   for editing.

I

The Basics

By now you have deselected both lines. Let's try using another method for selecting groups of objects.

5. Another option for selecting objects is to *window* them. Click and drag on the Select Objects button (on the Standard toolbar). Here is the flyout that appears (shown horizontally to conserve space):

6. Point to the Select Window icon, and release the mouse button. The cursor changes to a point-selection cursor, and the prompt changes to

   First corner:

7. Click on a point below and to the left of the rectangle representing the door. As you move your cursor across the screen, the window appears, and stretches across the drawing area.

8. Once the window completely encloses the door but not the arc, press the mouse/pick button and all of the door will be highlighted. This window selects only objects that are completely enclosed by the window, as shown in Figure 2.13.

9. Now that you have selected the entire door but not the arc, press ⏎. *It is important to remember to press ⏎ as soon as you have finished selecting the objects you want to edit.* You must tell AutoCAD when you have finished selecting object. A new prompt, Base point or displacement:, appears. The cursor changes to its point selection mode.

Now you have seen how the selection process works in AutoCAD—but we've left you in the middle of the Move command. In the next section, we'll discuss the prompt that's now on your screen, and see how to input base points and displacement distances.

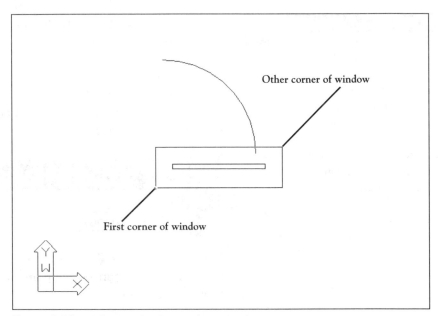

Figure 2.13: Selecting the door within a window

Providing Base Points

When you move or copy objects, AutoCAD prompts you for a *base point,* which is a difficult concept to grasp. AutoCAD must be told specifically *from* where and *to* where the move occurs. The base point is the exact location from which you determine the distance and direction of the move. Once the base point is determined, you can tell AutoCAD where to move the object in relation to that point.

1. To select a base point, hold down the Shift key and press the right mouse button. A menu pops up on the screen. This is the Object Snap (Osnap) menu.

From
Endpoint
Midpoint
Intersection
Apparent Intersection
Center
Quadrant
Perpendicular
Tangent
Node
Insertion
Nearest
Quick,
None
.X
.Y
.Z
.XZ
.YZ
.XY

2. Pick Intersection from the Osnap menu. The Osnap menu disappears, and a square appears on the cursor (see Figure 2.8).

3. Pick the lower-right corner of the door. Whenever you see the square in the cursor, you don't have to point exactly at the intersection. Just get the intersection within the square, and AutoCAD will find the exact point where the two lines meet (see Figure 2.14).

4. At the Second point of displacement: prompt, hold down the Shift key and press the right mouse button again. In the Osnap menu, pick Endpoint.

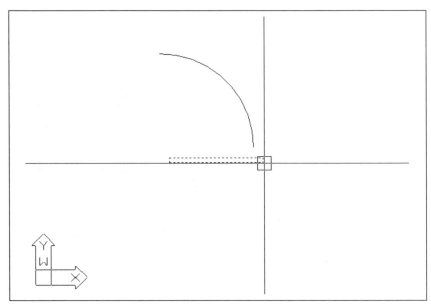

Figure 2.14: Using the Osnap cursor

5. Now pick the lower-right end of the arc you drew earlier. (Remember, you need to place only the end of the arc within the square.) The door moves so that the intersection of the door connects exactly with the endpoint of the arc (see Figure 2.15).

As you can see, the Osnap overrides allow you to select specific points on an object. You used Endpoint and Intersect in this exercise, but other options are available. We will look at some of those later.

If you want to specify an exact distance and direction by typing in a value, you can select any point on the screen as a base point. Or you can just type @ followed by ↵ at the base point prompt; then enter the second point's location in relative coordinates. Remember that @ means the last point selected. In this next exercise, you'll try moving the entire door an exact distance of 1 unit in a 45° angle.

1. Pick Move from the Modify palette again.

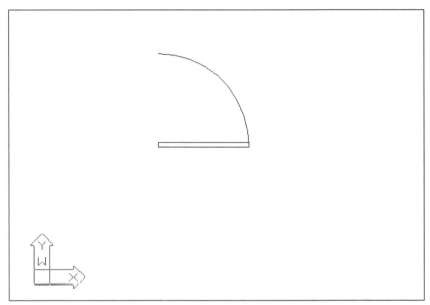

Figure 2.15:   The finished door

2. Click and drag to open the Select Objects flyout from the Standard toolbar, and click the Select Previous icon. The set of objects you selected in the previous command is highlighted.

3. You're still in the object selection mode, so click on the arc to include it in the set of selected objects. Now the entire door, including the arc, is highlighted (see Figure 2.16).

4. Now press ↵ to tell AutoCAD you have finished your selection. The cursor changes to point selection mode.

5. At the Base point or displacement prompt, pick a point on the screen between the door and the left side of the screen (see Figure 2.16).

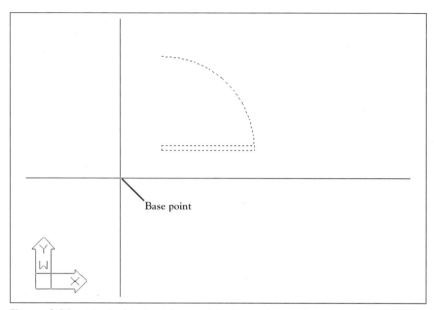

Figure 2.16:   The highlighted door and the base point just left of the door

6. Move the cursor around slowly and notice that the door moves as if the base point you selected were attached to the door. The door moves with the cursor, at a fixed distance from it. This demonstrates how the base point relates to the objects you select.

7. Now type **@1<45** ↵. The door will move to a new location on the screen at a distance of 1 unit from its previous location and at an angle of 45°.

This exercise illustrates that the base point does not have to be on the object you are manipulating—provided you enter specific distances with the keyboard. The base point can be virtually anywhere on your drawing. You also saw how you can reselect a group of objects that were selected previously, without having to duplicate the selection process.

OTHER SELECTION OPTIONS

There are several other selection options you haven't tried yet. The following describes these other options. You'll see how these options work in exercises later in this book. Or if you are adventurous, try them out now on your own. To use these options, type their keyboard abbreviations (shown in brackets in the following list) at any Select objects: prompt, or click on them in the Standard toolbar's Select Objects flyout.

Select All [All ↵] selects all the objects in a drawing except those in frozen or locked layers (see *Chapter 4* for more on layers).

Auto [Au ↵] forces the standard automatic window or crossing window when a point is picked and no object is found. A standard window is produced when the two window corners are picked from left to right. A crossing window is produced when the two corners are picked from right to left. Once this option is selected, it remains active for the duration of the current command. Auto is intended for use on systems where the Automatic selection feature has been turned off. This has no menu equivalent.

Select Crossing [C ↵] is similar to the Select Window option but will select anything that *crosses through* the window you define.

Select Crossing Polygon [Cp ↵] acts exactly like WPolygon (see below) but, like the Select Crossing option, will select anything that crosses through a polygon boundary.

Select Fence [F ↵] selects objects that are crossed over by a temporary line called a *fence*. The operation is like crossing out the objects you want to select with a line. When you invoke this option, you can then pick points, as when you are drawing a series of line segments. When you are done drawing the fence, press ↵.

Select Last [L ↵] selects the last object you input.

Multiple [M ↵] lets you select several objects first, before AutoCAD highlights them. In a very large file, picking objects individually can cause AutoCAD to pause after each pick, while it locates and highlights each object. The Multiple option can speed things up by letting you first pick all the objects quickly, and then high-light them all by pressing ↵. This has no menu equivalent.

Select Previous [P ↵] selects the last object or set of objects that was edited or changed.

Single [Si ↵] forces the current command to select only a single ob-ject. If you use this option, you can pick a single object; then the current command will act on that object as if you had pressed ↵ im-mediately after selecting the object. This has no menu equivalent.

Select Window [W ↵] forces a standard selection window. This op-tion is useful when your drawing area is too crowded to place a win-dow around a set of objects. It prevents you from accidentally selecting an object with a single pick when you are placing your window.

Select Window Polygon [Wp ↵] lets you select objects by enclos-ing them in an irregularly shaped polygon boundary. When you use this option, you see the prompt First polygon point. You then pick points to define the polygon boundary. As you pick points, the prompt Undo/<Endpoint of line> appears. Select as many points as you need to define the boundary. You can Undo boundary line segments as you go, by clicking on the Undo button on the Stand-ard toolbar or by pressing the U key. With the boundary defined, press ↵. The bounded objects are highlighted and the Select ob-ject prompt returns, allowing you to use more selection options.

▼ TIP

This chapter presents the standard AutoCAD method for object selection. Auto-CAD also offers selection methods with which you may be more familiar. Refer to the section on the Object Selec-tion Settings dialog box in *Ap-pendix B* to learn how you can control object selection meth-ods. This appendix also de-scribes how you can change the size of the pickbox cursor.

SELECTING OBJECTS BEFORE THE COMMAND: NOUN/VERB

Nearly all graphics programs today have tacitly acknowledged the *noun/verb* method for selecting objects. This method requires you to se-lect objects *before* you issue a command to edit them. The next set of exercises shows you how to use the noun/verb method in AutoCAD.

You have seen that when AutoCAD is waiting for a command, it dis-plays the crosshair cursor with the small square. This square is actually a pickbox superimposed on the cursor. It tells you that you can select objects, even while the command prompt appears at the bottom of the screen and no command is currently active. The square momentarily disappears when you are in a command that asks you to select points. From now on, we'll refer to this crosshair cursor with the small box as the *standard cursor*.

Now try moving objects by first selecting them and then using the Move command.

1. First, press Esc to make sure AutoCAD isn't in the middle of a command you may have accidentally issued. Then click on the arc. The arc is highlighted, and you may also see squares appear at its endpoints and midpoint. These squares are called *grips*. You'll get a chance to work with them a bit later.

2. Choose Move from the Modify palette.

3. At the Base point: prompt, pick any point on the screen. The prompt To point: appears, and the cursor changes to point selection mode.

4. Type @1<0 ↵. The arc moves to a new location 1 unit to the right.

In this exercise, you picked the arc *before* issuing the MOVE command. Then, when you clicked the Move button, you didn't see the object-selection prompt. Instead, AutoCAD assumed you wanted to move the arc you had selected and went directly to the base point prompt.

Using Autoselect

Next you will move the rest of the door in the same direction by using the Autoselect feature.

1. Pick a point just above and to the left of the rectangle representing the door. Be sure not to pick the door itself. Now a window appears that you can drag across the screen as you move the cursor. If you move the cursor to the left of the last

▼ **TIP**

In previous exercises, you were able to deselect objects using the Undo selection options. With Noun/Verb selection turned on, you can only deselect objects by holding down the Shift key and simultaneously picking an object or using a window.

point selected, the window appears dotted (see panel 1 of Figure 2.17). If you move the cursor to the right of that point, it appears solid (see panel 2 of Figure 2.17).

2. Now pick a point below and to the right of the door, so that the door is completely enclosed by the window, as shown in panel 2 of Figure 2.17. The door is highlighted (and again, you may see small squares appear at the line's endpoints and midpoints).

3. Start the MOVE command again. Just as in the last exercise, the base point prompt appears.

4. Pick any point on the screen; then enter **@1<0** ↵. The door joins with the arc.

The two different windows you have just seen—the solid one and the dotted one—represent a *standard window* and a *crossing window*. If you use a standard window, anything that is completely contained within the window will be selected. If you use a crossing window, anything that crosses through the window will be selected. These two types of windows start automatically when you click on any blank portion of the drawing area with a standard cursor or point selection cursor; hence the name Autoselect.

Next, you will select objects with an automatic crossing window.

1. Pick a point below and to the right of the door. As you move the cursor to the left, the crossing (dotted) window appears.

2. Select the next point so that the window encloses the door and part of the arc (see Figure 2.18). The entire door, including the arc, highlights.

3. Start the MOVE command.

4. Pick any point on the screen; then enter **@1<180**. The door moves back to its original location.

You'll find that the Autoselect standard and crossing windows are all you need when selecting objects. They will really save you time, so you'll want to get familiar with these features.

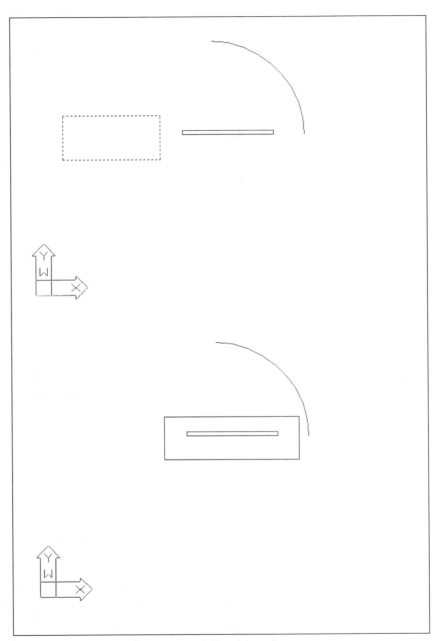

Figure 2.17:   The dotted window and the solid window

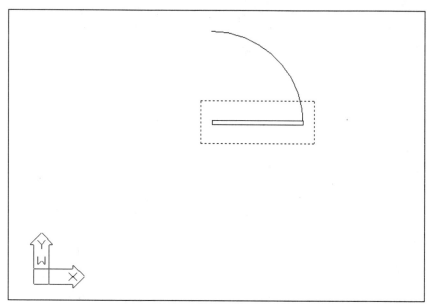

Figure 2.18: The door enclosed by a crossing window

Before we continue, you need to use File ➤ Save to save the Door file. You won't want to save the changes you make in the next section, so saving now will store the current condition of the file on your hard disk for safekeeping.

RESTRICTIONS ON NOUN/VERB OBJECT SELECTION

If you prefer to work *with* the Noun/Verb selection feature, you should know that its use is limited to the following subset of AutoCAD commands, listed here in no particular order.

Array	Mirror	Wblock	Block
Dview	Move	Explode	Change
Erase	Rotate	Chprop	Hatch
Scale	Copy	List	Stretch

The Basics

For all other modifying or construction-oriented commands, the Noun/Verb selection method is inappropriate, because for those commands you must select more than one set of objects.

If you want to take a break, now is a good time to do it. If you wish, you can exit AutoCAD and return to this point in the tutorial later. When you return, start AutoCAD and open the Door file.

EDITING WITH GRIPS

▼ WARNING

If you did not see small squares appear on the door in the previous exercise, your version of AutoCAD may have the Grips feature turned off. Before continuing with this section, refer to the information on grips in *Appendix B*.

Earlier, when you selected the door, little squares appeared at the endpoints and midpoints of the lines and arcs. These squares are called *grips*. Grips can be used to make direct changes to the shape of objects, or to quickly move and copy them.

So far, you have seen how operations in AutoCAD have a discrete beginning and ending. For example, to draw an arc, you first issue the Arc command and then go through a series of operations, including answering prompts and picking points. When you are done, you have an arc and AutoCAD is ready for the next command.

The Grips feature, on the other hand, plays by a different set of rules. Grips offer a small yet powerful set of editing functions that don't conform to the lockstep command/prompt/input routine you have seen so far. As you work through the following exercises, it will be helpful to think of the Grips feature as a "subset" to the standard method of operation within AutoCAD.

To practice using the grips feature, you'll make some temporary modifications to the door drawing.

STRETCHING LINES USING GRIPS

In this exercise, you'll stretch one corner of the door by grabbing the grip points of two lines.

1. Press Esc to make sure AutoCAD has your attention and you're not in the middle of a command. Click on a point below and to the left of the door to start a selection window.

2. Click above and to the right of the rectangular part of the door to select it.

3. Place the cursor on the lower-left corner grip of the rectangle, *but don't press the pick button yet.* Notice that cursor jumps to the grip point.

4. Move the cursor to another grip point. Notice again how the cursor jumps to it. When placed on a grip, the cursor moves to the exact center of the grip point. This means, for example, that if the cursor is placed on an endpoint grip, it is on the exact endpoint of the object.

5. Move the cursor to the upper-left corner grip of the rectangle and click on it. The grip becomes a solid color, and is now a *hot grip.* The prompt displays the following message:

```
**STRETCH**
<Stretch to point>/Base point/Copy/Undo/eXit:
```

This prompt tells you that the Stretch mode is active. Notice the options shown in the prompt. As you move the cursor, the corner follows and the lines of the rectangle stretch (see Figure 2.19).

6. Move the cursor upward toward the top end of the arc and pick that point. The rectangle deforms, with the corner placed at your pick point (see Figure 2.19).

Here you saw that a command called **STRETCH** is issued simply by clicking on a grip point. As you will see, a handful of other hot-grip commands are also available.

1. Click on the grip point that you moved before.

2. Enter **B** ↵. The prompt changes to Base point:.

3. Click on a point to the right of the hot grip. Now as you move the cursor, the hot grip moves relative to the cursor.

▼ **NOTE**

When you select a grip by clicking on it, it turns a solid color and is known as a *hot grip.* You can control the size and color of grips using the Grips dialog box (see *Appendix B*).

▼ **NOTE**

When you click on the corner grip point, AutoCAD selects the overlapping grips of two lines. When you stretch the corner away from its original location, the endpoints of both lines follow.

The Basics

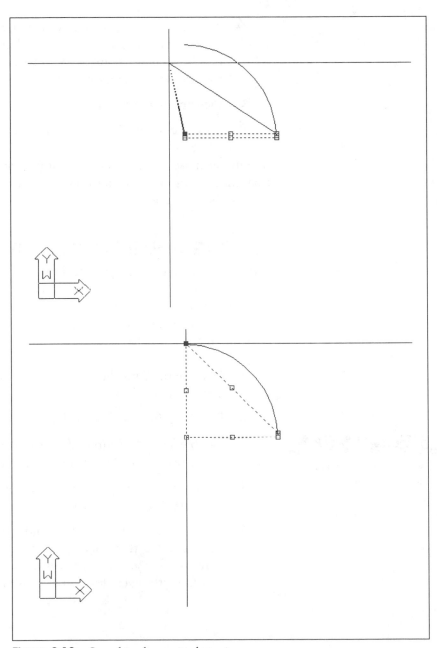

Figure 2.19: Stretching lines using hot grips

4. Type **C** ↵ to select the Copy option, and enter **@1<-90**. Instead of moving the hot grip and changing the lines, copies of the two lines are made, with their endpoints 1 unit below the first set of endpoints.

5. Pick another point just below the last. More copies are made.

6. Press ↵ or enter **X** ↵ to exit the Stretch mode.

In this exercise, you were shown that you can select a base point other than the hot grip. You also saw how you can specify relative coordinates to move or copy a hot grip.

MOVING AND ROTATING WITH GRIPS

As you've just seen, the Grips feature offers an alternative method of editing your drawings. You've already seen how you can stretch endpoints, but there is much more you can do with grips. The next exercise demonstrates some other options. You will start by undoing the modifications you made in the last exercise.

1. Click on the Undo button in the Standard toolbar, or type **U** ↵. The copies of the stretched lines disappear.

2. Press ↵ again. The deformed door snaps back to its original form.

3. Choose View ➤ Redraw View to clean up the display. Now you're ready to make a rotated copy of the door.

4. Select the entire door by first clicking on a blank area below and to the right of the door.

5. Move the cursor to a location above and to the left of the rectangular portion of the door, and click. Since you went from right to left, you created a crossing window. Recall that this selects anything enclosed and crossing through the window.

▼ **TIP**

Pressing ↵ at the command prompt causes AutoCAD to repeat the last command entered—in this case, **U**.

6. Click on the lower-left grip of the rectangle to turn it into a hot grip. Now as you move your cursor, the corner stretches.

7. Press ↵ or the Spacebar. The prompt changes to

   MOVE
   <Move to point>/Base point/Copy/Undo/eXit:

   Now as you move the cursor, the entire door moves with it.

8. Position the door near the center of the screen and click there. The door moves to the center of the screen. Notice that the command prompt returns, yet the door remains highlighted, telling you that it is still selected for the next operation.

9. Click on the lower-left grip again, and press ↵ or the Spacebar twice. This time, the command prompt changes to

   ROTATE <Rotation angle>/Base point/copy/Undo/Reference/eXit:

   As you move the cursor, the door rotates about the grip point.

10. Position the cursor so that the door rotates 180° (see Figure 2.20). Then, while holding down the Shift key, press the mouse/pick button. A copy of the door appears in the new rotated position, leaving the original door in place.

11. Press ↵ to exit the Rotate mode.

▼ NOTE

You've seen how the MOVE command is duplicated in a modified way as a hot-grip command. Other hot-grip commands (**STRETCH**, **ROTATE**, **SCALE**, and **MIRROR**) also have similar counterparts in the standard set of AutoCAD commands. You'll see how those work later in this book.

After you've completed any operation using grips, the objects are still highlighted with their grips still active. To clear the grip selection, press Esc twice.

In this exercise, you saw how new hot-grip commands appear as you press ↵. Two more commands, **SCALE** and **MIRROR**, are also available by continuing to press ↵ while a hot grip is selected. The commands then repeat if you continue to press ↵. The Shift key acts as a shortcut to the Copy option.

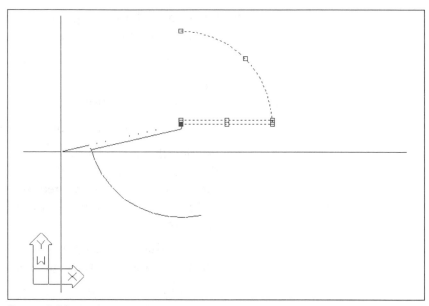

Figure 2.20: Rotating and copying the door using a hot grip

▼
■
■
■
■

A QUICK
SUMMARY OF THE GRIP FEATURE

The exercises in this chapter using hot grips include only a few of
the Grips options. You'll get a chance to use other hot-grip commands
in later chapters. Meanwhile, here is a summary of Grips.

- Clicking on endpoint grips causes those endpoints to
  stretch.

- Clicking on midpoint grips of lines causes the entire line
  to move.

- If two objects meet end to end and you click on their overlapping grips, both grips are selected simultaneously.

- You can select multiple grips by holding down the Shift key and clicking on the desired grips.

- When a hot grip is selected, the Stretch, Move, Rotate, Scale, and Mirror commands are available to you.

- You can cycle through the Stretch, Move, Rotate, Scale, and Mirror commands by pressing ↵ while a hot grip is selected.

- All the hot-grip commands allow you to make copies of the selected objects.

- All the hot-grip commands allow you to select a base point other than the originally selected hot grip.

GETTING HELP

Eventually, you will find yourself somewhere without documentation and you will have a question about an AutoCAD feature. AutoCAD provides an online help facility that will give you information on nearly any topic related to AutoCAD.

▼ NOTE

You can also press F1 to open the AutoCAD Help window. If you are in the middle of a command, you can type **'help** ↵ at the command prompt to get information about your current activity.

1. Click on Help in the menu bar and choose Contents. A Help window appears. This window shows the contents of the Help system at a glance. Notice that several items appear in color and are underlined. When you click on these items, you will get further information.

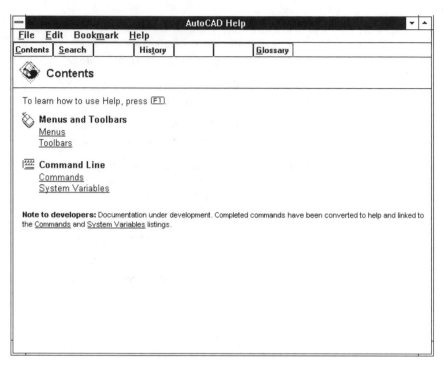

2. Scan down the screen until you see the topic named Commands, and click on it. A list of AutoCAD commands appears.

3. At the top of the list is an abbreviated alphabet. Below, you see a list of commands that begin with the characters A through C. You can click on the characters at the top to show more commands. For now, click on the word Copy. A detailed description of the Copy command appears.

4. Click on the Search button at the top of the window. The Search dialog box appears, with a list of topics in alphabetical order. You can enter a word to search for, or you can choose a topic in the list box.

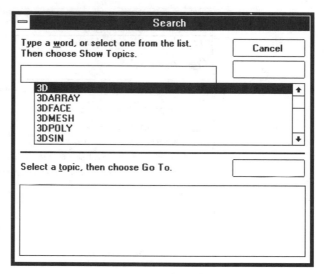

5. Type the word **Change.** The list box immediately goes to the word Change in the list.

6. Press ↵. At the bottom of the dialog box, the words "CHANGE Command" appear in the Go To list box.

7. Click on the Go To button, and you get a description of the CHANGE command.

You can go directly to the Search dialog box by clicking on Help ➤ Search for Help On. If you need more detailed information on using the help system, click on Help ➤ How to Use Help.

AutoCAD also provides *context-sensitive help* to give you information related to the command you are currently using. To see how this works, try the following:

1. Click on the Move button in the Modify tool palette to start the MOVE command.

2. Type **'Help** ↵. The Help window appears, with a description of the MOVE command.

3. Click on the OK button or press Esc.

4. Press Esc to exit the MOVE command.

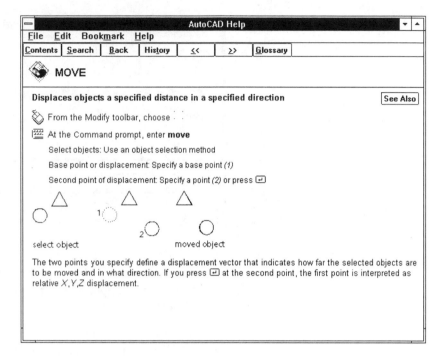

DISPLAYING MORE OF THE PROMPT TEXT

Some commands produce more information than will fit in the prompt area. This frequently happens when you are trying to get information about your drawing. The following exercise shows how you can get an enlarged view of messages that have scrolled past the prompt area.

1. Click on the List button in the Standard toolbar (it's the icon that's a piece of paper with writing on it). At the bottom of the desktop, the AutoCAD Text Window appears. This window keeps a record of the most recent activity in AutoCAD. You can open the window at any time to view its contents.

2. At the Select objects: prompt, click on one of the arcs and press ↵. Information about the arc is displayed in the prompt area, but the information is too long to fit on the three lines.

3. Press F2 to open the AutoCAD Text Window. Toward the bottom is the list of the arc's properties (you'll get a detailed look at this information later in this book).

4. To go back to the drawing editor, click on the Minimize key in the upper-right corner of the Text Window, or press F2 again.

5. Repeat steps 3 and 4 a few times and see what happens.

6. Now you are done with the door drawing, so choose File ➤ Exit.

7. At the Save Changes? dialog box, click on the No button. (You've already saved this file in the condition you want it in, so you need not save it again at this time.)

IF YOU WANT TO EXPERIMENT...

Try drawing the latch shown in Figure 2.21.

1. Start AutoCAD, open a new file, and name it **Latch**.

2. When you get to the drawing editor, use the Line command to draw the straight portions of the latch. Start a line as indicated in the figure; then enter relative coordinates from the keyboard. For example, for the first line segment, enter **@4<180** to draw a line segment 4 units long from right to left.

3. Draw an arc for the curved part. To do this, click and drag the 3 Point button from the Draw palette, and then click on Arc Start End Direction on the flyout.

4. Use the Endpoint Osnap override, and pick the endpoint indicated in the figure to start your arc.

5. Using the Endpoint Osnap override again, click on the endpoint above where you started your line. A rubber-banding line and a temporary arc appear.

6. Position your cursor so the ghosted arc looks like the one in the figure, and press the mouse/pick button to draw in the arc.

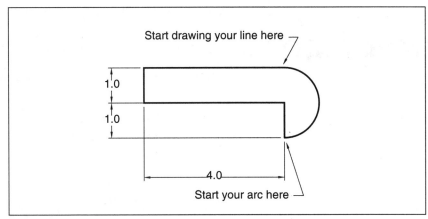

Figure 2.21:   Try drawing this latch. Dimensions are provided for your reference.

3

LEARNING THE TOOLS OF THE TRADE

Setting Up a Work Area

Designating the Measurement System

Understanding Scale in AutoCAD

Using Snaps, Grids, and the Coordinate Readout

Enlarging and Reducing Your View of the Drawing

Trimming and Making Parallel Copies of Objects

Laying Out a Drawing with Lines

FAST TRACK

89 ▶ To enable the use of feet and inch measurement

Click on Data ➤ Units. In the Units Control dialog box, click on the Architectural button

93 ▶ To define a work area

Determine the area you need, based on the scale of your drawing and final sheet size. Then use the Limits command (Data ➤ Drawing Limits) to define the area in AutoCAD. See Table 3.2

98 ▶ To set the grid spacing

Click on Options ➤ Drawing Aids, and enter the grid spacing in the X Spacing input box under the Grid group. Turn the grid on and off by pressing F7 or Ctrl-G.

99 ▶ To force the cursor to snap to regularly spaced intervals

Click on Options ➤ Drawing Aids, and enter the snap spacing in the X Spacing input box under the Snap group. Turn snap on and off by pressing F9 or Ctrl-B.

101 ▶ To cycle among the dynamic/relative/absolute coordinate readout

Press F6.

106 ▶ To copy an object

In the Modify tool palette, click and drag Copy and choose Offset from the flyout. Select the object(s) you want to copy. Pick a base point for the copy, then either pick another point or enter a relative coordinate.

107 ▶ To trim an object

Click on Trim in the Modify tool palette. First select the objects *to which* you want to trim, and then select the objects you want to trim.

114 ▶ To make a parallel copy of an object

In the Modify tool palette, click and drag Copy and choose Offset from the flyout. Enter the distance away from the original you want the copy to be. Then select the object of which to make the parallel copy, and indicate the direction of the copy.

124 ▶ To join two objects with an arc

In the Modify palette, click and drag Chamfer and choose Fillet from the flyout. Enter **R** ↵ and then enter the radius of the joining arc. Start Fillet again, and pick the two objects you want to join.

So far we have covered the most basic information you need to understand the workings of AutoCAD. Now you will put your knowledge to work. In this architectural tutorial, which begins here and continues through Chapter 12, you will draw a studio apartment building. The tutorial illustrates how to use AutoCAD commands and will give you a solid understanding of the basic AutoCAD package. With these fundamentals, you can use AutoCAD to its fullest potential, regardless of the kinds of drawings you intend to create or the enhancement products you may use in the future.

In this chapter you will start drawing an apartment's bathroom fixtures. In the process, you will learn how to use AutoCAD's basic tools.

SETTING UP A WORK AREA

Before beginning most drawings, you will want to set up your work area. To do this you must determine the *measurement system*, the *drawing sheet size*, and the *scale* you want to use. The default work area is roughly 9″×12″ at full scale, given a decimal measurement system where 1 unit equals 1 inch. If these are appropriate settings for your drawing, then you don't have to do any setting up. It is more likely, however, you will be doing drawings of various sizes and scales. For example, you may want to create a drawing in a measurement system where you can specify feet, inches, and fractions of inches, at 1″=1′ scale, and print the drawing on an $8\frac{1}{2} \times 11''$ sheet of paper. In this section, you will learn how to set up a drawing the way you want.

SPECIFYING UNITS

Start by creating a new file called Bath.

1. Start up AutoCAD; then pick File ➤ New.

2. In the Create New Drawing dialog box, enter the name **Bath**.

3. Make sure the No Prototype check box is checked, and click on OK to open the new file.

▼ NOTE

Although you could start drawing in the drawing editor immediately after starting up AutoCAD and then save the file later under the name Bath, use File ➤ New for this exercise—in case you are using a system that has an altered default setup for new files. We'll discuss default setups in *Chapter 5*.

The first thing you will want to tell AutoCAD is the *unit style* you intend to use. So far, you've been using the default, which is decimal inches. In this style, whole units represent inches, and decimal units are decimal inches. If you want to be able to enter distances in feet, then you must change the unit style to one that accepts feet as input. This is done through the Units Control dialog box.

1. Choose Data ➤ Units…. The Units Control dialog box appears. Let's look at a few of the options available.

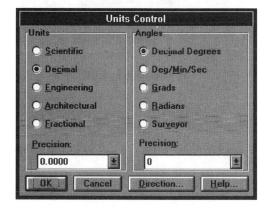

2. Notice the unit styles listed in the Units group. Click on the Architectural button.

3. Click on the down-pointing arrow in the Precision drop-down list at the bottom of the Units group. Notice the options available. You can set the smallest unit AutoCAD will display in this drawing. For now, leave this setting at its default value of 1/16″.

4. Click on the Direction… button at the bottom of the dialog box. The Direction Control dialog box appears. This dialog box lets you set the direction for the 0° angle and the direction for positive degrees. For now, don't change these settings—you'll read more about them in a moment. Click on the Cancel button.

▼ TIP

The Units Control settings can also be controlled using several system variables. To set the unit style, you can type **'lunits** ↵ at the command prompt. (The apostrophe lets you enter this command while in the middle of other commands.) At the New value for Lunits <2> prompt, enter **4** for Architectural. See *Appendix D* for other settings.

▼ NOTE

This dialog box has two button groups: Units and Angles. Both groups contain Precision settings in drop-down lists near the bottom of the dialog. These lists let you control the degree of precision AutoCAD uses for distances and angles. The Units group lets you select the type of measurement unit you want to use; in the Angles group you select the angle type.

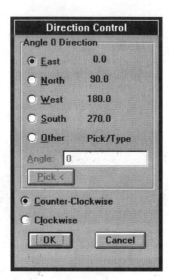

5. Click on OK in the main Units Control dialog box to return to the drawing.

You picked Architectural measurement units for this tutorial, but your own work may require a different unit style. You saw the unit styles available in the Units Control dialog box. Table 3.1 shows examples of how the distance 15.5 is entered in each of these styles.

Table 3.1: Measurement Systems Available in AutoCAD

Measurement System	AutoCAD's Display of Measurement
Scientific	1.55E+01 (inches)
Decimal	15.5000 (inches)
Engineering	1'-3.5" (input as 1'3.5")
Architectural	1'-3 1/2" (input as 1'3-1/2")
Metric	15.5000 (converted to metric at plot)
Fractional	15 1/2" (input as 15-1/2")

In the previous exercise, you needed to change only one setting. Let's take a look at the other Units Control settings in more detail. As you read, you may want to refer to the illustration of the Units Control dialog box.

FINE-TUNING THE MEASUREMENT SYSTEM

Most of the time, you will be concerned only with the Units and Angles setting groups of the Units Control dialog box. But as you saw from the exercise, you can control many other settings related to the input and display of units.

The Precision drop-down list in the Units group lets you specify the smallest unit value that you want AutoCAD to display in the status line and in the prompts. If you choose a measurement system that uses fractions, the Precision list will include fractional units. This setting can also be controlled with Buprec system variables.

The Angles group lets you set the style for displaying angles. You have a choice of five angle styles: decimal degrees, degrees/minutes/seconds, grads, radians, and surveyor's units. In the Angles group's Precision drop-down list, you can determine the degree of accuracy you want AutoCAD to display for angles. These settings can also be controlled with the Aunits and Auprec system variables.

The Direction Control dialog box lets you set the direction of the base angle, 0°. The default base angle (and the one used throughout this book) is a direction from left to right. However, there may be times when you will want to designate another direction as the 0° base angle. You can also tell AutoCAD which direction is positive, either clockwise or counterclockwise. In this book we use the default, counterclockwise. These settings can also be controlled with the Angbase and Angdir system variables.

▼ TIP

To find the distance between two points, choose Distance from the List flyout on the Standard toolbar, or type **Dist** ↵ and then click on the two points. But if you find that this command doesn't give you an accurate distance measurement, examine the Units/Precision option in the Units Control dialog box. If it is set too high, the value returned by Dist may be rounded to a value greater than your tolerances allow, even though the distance is drawn accurately.

▼ NOTE

You can find out more about system variables in *Appendix D*.

THINGS TO WATCH OUT FOR WHEN ENTERING DISTANCES

When you are using Architectural units, there are two points you should be aware of:

- Hyphens are used only to distinguish fractions from whole inches.

- You cannot use spaces while giving a dimension. For example, you can specify eight feet, four and one-half inches as **8'4– 1/2"** or **8'4.5,** but *not* as **8'–4 1/2".**

These idiosyncrasies are a source of confusion to many architects and engineers new to AutoCAD, since the program often *displays* architectural dimensions in the standard architectural format but does not allow you to *enter* dimensions that way.

When inputting distances and angles in unusual situations, here are some tips:

- When entering distances in inches and feet, you can omit the inch (") sign.

- You can enter fractional distances and angles in any format you like, regardless of the current unit system. For example, you can enter a distance as **@1/2<1.5708r** even if your current unit system is set for decimal units and decimal degrees (**1.5708r** is the radian equivalent of 90°).

- If you have your angle units set to degrees, grads, or radians, you do not need to specify *g*, *r*, or *d* after the angle. You *do* have to specify *g*, *r*, or *d*, however, if you want to use these units when they are not the current default angle system.

- If your current angle system is set to something other than degrees, but you want to input angles in degrees, you can use a double less-than symbol (<<) in place of the single less-than symbol (<) to override the current angle system of measure. The << also assumes the base angle of 0° to be a direction from left to right and the positive direction to be counterclockwise.

▼
■
■
■
■

- If your current angle system uses a different base angle and direction (other than left to right for 0° and a counter-clockwise direction for positive angles), and you want to specify an angle in the standard base direction, you can use a triple less-than symbol (<<<) to indicate angle.

- You can specify a denominator of any size when specifying fractions. However, you should be aware that the value you have set for the maximum number of digits to the right of decimal points (under the Units setting) will restrict the actual fractional value AutoCAD will use. For example, if your units are set for a maximum of 2 digits of decimals and you give a fractional value of $\frac{5}{32}$, AutoCAD will round it out to $\frac{3}{16}$ or 0.16.

- You are allowed to enter decimal feet for distances in the architectural unit style.

SETTING UP THE DRAWING LIMITS

One of the big advantages in using AutoCAD is that you can draw at full scale; you aren't limited to the edges of a piece of paper the way you are in manual drawing. But you still have to consider what will happen when you want a printout of your drawing. If you're not careful, you may create a drawing that won't fit on the paper size you want at the scale you want. You must limit your drawing area to one that can be scaled down to fit on a standard sheet size.

In order to set up the drawing work area, you need to understand how standard sheet sizes translate into full-scale drawing sizes. Tables 3.2 and 3.3 list widths and heights of drawing areas in inches and millimeters, respectively, according to scales and final printout sizes. The scales are listed in the far left column; the output sheet sizes are listed across the top.

Let's take an example: To find the area needed in AutoCAD for your Bath drawing, for instance, look across from the scale 1″=1′ to the column that reads $8\frac{1}{2}″\times11″$ at the top. You'll find the value 102×132. This means the drawing area needs to fit within an area 102″ by 132″ (8.5 feet by 11 feet) in AutoCAD in order to fit a printout of a 1″=1′-0″ scale drawing on an $8\frac{1}{2}\times11″$ sheet of paper. You will want the drawing area

Table 3.2: Work Area in Drawing Units (Inches) by Scale and Plotted Sheet Size

Scale	8½"×11"	11"×17"	17"×22"	18"×24"	22"×34"	24"×36"	30"×42"	36"×48"
3"=1'	34×44	44×68	68×88	72×96	88×136	96×144	120×168	144×192
1½"=1'	68×88	88×136	136×176	144×192	176×272	192×288	240×336	288×384
1"=1'	102×132	132×204	204×264	216×288	264×408	288×432	360×504	432×576
3/4"=1'	136×176	176×272	272×352	288×384	352×544	384×576	480×672	576×768
1/2"=1'	204×264	264×408	408×528	432×576	528×816	576×864	720×1008	864×1152
1/4"=1'	408×528	528×816	816×1056	864×1152	1056×1632	1152×1728	1440×2016	1728×2304
1/8"=1'	816×1056	1056×1632	1632×2112	1728×2304	2112×3264	2304×3456	2880×4032	3456×4608
1/16"=1'	1632×2112	2112×3264	3264×4224	3456×4608	4224×6528	4608×6912	5760×8064	6912×9216
1/32"=1'	3264×4224	4224×6528	6528×8448	6912×9216	8448×13056	9216×13824	11520×16128	13824×18432
1"=10'	1020×1320	1320×2040	2040×2640	2160×2880	2640×4080	2880×4320	3600×5040	4320×5760
1"=20'	2040×2640	2640×4080	4080×5280	4320×5760	5280×8160	5760×8640	7200×10080	8640×11520
1"=30'	3060×3960	3960×6120	6120×7920	6480×8640	7920×12240	8640×12960	10800×15120	12960×17280
1"=40'	4080×5280	5280×8160	8160×10560	8640×11520	10560×16320	11520×17280	14400×20160	17280×23040
1"=50'	5100×6600	6600×10200	10200×13200	10800×14400	13200×20400	14400×21600	18000×25200	21600×28800
1"=60'	6120×7920	7920×12240	12240×15840	12960×17280	15840×24480	17280×25920	21600×30240	25920×34560

The Basics

Table 3.3: Work Area in Metric Units (Millimeters) by Scale and Plotted Sheet Size

Scale	A0 841mm×1189mm (33.11″×46.81″)	A1 594mm×841mm (23.39″×33.11″)	A2 420mm×594mm (16.54″×23.39″)	A3 297mm×420mm (11.70″×16.54″)	A4 210mm×297mm (8.27″×11.70″)
1:2	1682mm×2378mm	1188mm×1682mm	840mm×1188mm	594mm×840mm	420mm×594mm
1:5	4205mm×5945mm	2970mm×4205mm	2100mm×2970mm	1485mm×2100mm	1050mm×1485mm
1:10	8410mm×11890mm	5940mm×8410mm	4200mm×5940mm	2970mm×4200mm	2100mm×2970mm

to be oriented horizontally, so that the 11 feet will be in the x-axis and the 8.5 feet will be in the y-axis.

Now that you know the area you need, you can use the Limits command to set up the area.

1. Choose Data ➤ Drawing Limits or type **Limits** ↵ at the command prompt.

2. At the ON/OFF/<Lower left corner> <0′–0″,0′–0″>: prompt, specify the lower-left corner of your work area. Press ↵ to accept the default.

3. At the Upper right corner <1′0″,0′9″>: prompt, specify the upper-right corner of your work area. (The default is shown in brackets.) Enter **132,102**. Or if you prefer, you can enter **11′,8′6.**

4. Next, choose View ➤ Zoom ➤ All. Though it appears that nothing has changed, your drawing area is now set to a size that will allow you to draw your bathroom at full scale.

5. Move the cursor to the upper-right corner of the drawing area and watch the coordinate readout. You will see that now the upper-right corner has a Y coordinate of 8′6. The X coordinate will vary depending on the proportion of your AutoCAD window. The coordinate readout also displays distances in feet and inches.

In step 5 above, the coordinate readout shows you that your drawing area is larger than before, but there are no visual clues to tell you where you are or what distances you are dealing with. To help you get your bearings, you can use the Grid mode, which you will learn about shortly. But first, let's take a closer look at scale factors and how they work.

UNDERSTANDING SCALE FACTORS

All the drawing sizes in Table 3.2 were derived by using scale factors. Table 3.3 shows scale factors as they relate to standard drawing scales.

▼ TIP

If you get the message ****Outside limits**, it means you have selected a point outside the area defined by the limits of your drawing *and* the Limits command's limits-checking feature is on. (Some third-party programs may use the limits-checking feature.) If you must select a point outside the limits, issue the Limits command and then enter **off** at the ON/OFF <Lower left corner>... prompt to turn off the limits-checking feature.

▼ TIP

The scale factor for fractional inch scales is derived by multiplying the denominator of the scale by 12, then dividing by the numerator. For example, the scale factor for $\frac{1}{4}''=1'-0''$ is $(4\times12)/1$, or 48/1. For whole-foot scales like $1''=10'$, multiply the feet side of the equation by 12. Metric scales require simple decimal conversions.

These scale factors are the values by which you multiply the desired final printout size to get the equivalent full-scale size. For example, if you have a sheet size of 11×17″, and you want to know the equivalent full-scale size for a $\frac{1}{4}''$-scale drawing, you multiply the sheet measurements by 48. In this way, 11″ becomes 528″ (48×11) and 17″ becomes 816″ (48×17). Your work area must be 528″ by 816″ if you intend to have a final output of 11″ by 17″ at $\frac{1}{4}''=1'$. You can divide these inch measurements by 12″ to get 44′×68′.

If you are using the metric system, the drawing scale can be used directly as the scale factor. For example, a drawing scale of 1:10 would have a scale factor of 10; a drawing scale of 1:50 would have a scale factor of 50, and so on.

You will be using scale factors to specify text height and dimension settings, so getting to understand them now will pay off later.

Table 3.4: Scale Conversion Factors

Scale Factors for Engineering Drawing Scales								
1″= n	10′	20′	30′	40′	50′	60′	100′	200′
Scale factor	120	240	360	480	600	720	1200	2400

Scale Factors for Architectural Drawing Scales								
n=1′-0″	$\frac{1}{16}''$	$\frac{1}{8}''$	$\frac{1}{4}''$	$\frac{1}{2}''$	$\frac{3}{4}''$	1″	$1\frac{1}{2}''$	3″
Scale factor	192	96	48	24	16	12	8	4

USING THE AUTOCAD MODES AS DRAFTING TOOLS

After you have set up your work area, you can begin the plan of a typical bathroom in your studio. We will use this example to show you some of AutoCAD's drawing aids. These tools might be compared to a background grid (the *grid mode*), scale (the *coordinate readout*), and a T square and triangle (the *ortho mode*). The drawing modes can be indispensable tools when used properly. The Drawing Aids dialog box helps you visualize the modes in an organized manner and simplifies their management.

USING THE GRID MODE AS A BACKGROUND GRID

Using the *grid mode* is like having a grid under your drawing to help you with layout. In AutoCAD, the grid mode also lets you see the limits of your drawing and helps you visually determine the distances you are working with in any given view. In this section, you will learn how to control the grid's appearance. The F7 key toggles the grid mode on and off; you can also double-click on the Grid button in the status bar.

▼ **TIP**

You can use the Gridunit system variable to set the grid spacing. Enter **'Gridunit** ⏎, and at the **New value for** GRIDUNIT <0'0",0'0">: prompt, enter **10,10**. Note that the Gridunit value must be entered as an x,y coordinate.

1. Press F7, or hold down the Ctrl key and press **G**. An array of dots appears. These dots are the *grid points*. They will not print or plot with your drawing. If the grid seems too dense, you can alter the grid spacing by using the Grid command.

2. Choose Options ➤ Drawing Aids... to display the Drawing Aids dialog box, showing all the mode settings. You see four button groups: Modes, Snap, Grid, and Isometric Snap/Grid. Let's start with the Grid group.

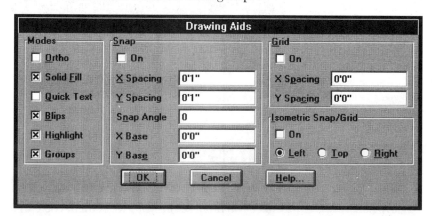

3. Notice that the X Spacing input box contains a value of 0'0".
   Above that, the On check box contains an X, telling you
   that the grids are turned on.

4. Double-click on the X Spacing input box. The 0'0" highlights. You can now type in a new value for this setting.

5. Enter **10** ↵ for 10". Notice that the Y Spacing input box
   automatically changes to 0'10". AutoCAD assumes you want
   the X and Y grid spacing to be the same, unless you specifically ask for a different Y setting.

6. Click on OK. The grid now appears with a 10" spacing in
   your drawing area.

With the grid at a 10-unit spacing, the grid doesn't clutter the screen.
Since the grid will appear only within the drawing limits, you are better
able to see your work area. Next, you'll see how the snap mode works.

USING THE SNAP MODE

The *snap mode* has no equivalent in hand drafting. This mode forces the
cursor to step a specific distance. It is useful if you want to maintain accuracy while entering distances with the cursor. The F9 key toggles the
snap mode on and off. Or, just like the grid mode, there is a Snap button
in the status line that you can double-click.

1. Press F9 or hold down the Ctrl key and press **B**; then move
   the cursor slowly around the drawing area. Notice how the
   cursor seems to move in "steps" rather than in a smooth motion. Also note that the left end of the status line reads Layer
   0 Snap, which tells you that the snap mode is on.

2. Choose Options ➤ Drawing Aids. The Drawing Aids dialog
   box appears again.

3. In the Snap group of the dialog box, double-click on the X
   Spacing input box, and enter **4** ↵. As with the Grid setting,
   AutoCAD assumes you want the X and Y snap spacing to be
   the same, unless you specifically ask for a different Y setting.

▼ **TIP**

If you want to change an entry
in an input box, you can double-
click on it to highlight the
whole entry, and then replace
the entry by simply typing in a
new one. If you just want to
change a part of the entry,
click on the input box and
then use the cursor keys to
move the vertical bar cursor to
the exact character you want
to change. You can use the
Backspace key to delete
characters.

▼ **TIP**

You can use the Snapunit system variable to set the snap
spacing. Enter **'Snapunit** ↵,
then at the **New value for**
SNAPUNIT <0'0",0'0">:
prompt, enter **4,4**. Note that
the Snapunit value must be entered as an x,y coordinate.

4. Click on OK, and start moving the cursor around. Notice how it steps at a greater distance than before—4" to be exact.

The other options in the Snap group of the Drawing Aids dialog box allow you to set the snap origin point (X Base and Y Base), rotate the cursor to an angle other than its current 0–90° (Snap angle), and set the horizontal snap spacing to a value different from the vertical spacing (X Spacing and Y Spacing). You can also adjust other settings, such as the grid/snap orientation that allow isometric-style drawings (Isometric Snap/Grid). We will look at these features in *Chapters* 6 and 15.

USING GRID AND SNAP TOGETHER

You can set the grid spacing to be the same as the snap setting, allowing you to see every snap point. Let's take a look at how grid and snap work together.

1. Open the Drawing Aids dialog box.

2. Double-click on the X Spacing input box in the Grid group, and enter 0 ↲.

3. Click on OK. Now the grid spacing has changed to reflect the 4" snap spacing. Move the cursor, and watch it snap to the grid points.

4. Open the Drawing Aids dialog box again.

5. Double-click on the X Spacing input box in the Snap group, and enter 1 ↲.

6. Click on OK. The grid automatically changes to conform to the new snap setting. When the grid spacing is set to 0, the grid then aligns with the snap points. At this density, the grid is overwhelming.

7. Open the Drawing Aids dialog box again.

8. Double-click on the X Spacing input box in the Grid group, and enter **10** ↲.

9. Click on OK. The grid spacing is now at 10 again, a more reasonable spacing for the current drawing scale.

USING THE COORDINATE READOUT AS YOUR SCALE

Now you will draw the first item in the bathroom: the toilet. It is composed of a rectangle representing the tank, and a truncated ellipse representing the seat.

As you move the cursor over the drawing area, the coordinate readout dynamically displays its position in absolute Cartesian coordinates. This allows you to find a position on your drawing by locating it in reference to the drawing origin—0,0—which is in the lower-left corner of the sheet. You can also set the coordinate readout to display relative coordinates. Throughout these exercises, coordinates will be provided to enable you to select points using the dynamic coordinate readout. (If you want to review the discussion of AutoCAD's coordinates display, see *Chapter 1*.)

▼ NOTE

The ortho mode (also available under Modes in the Drawing Aids dialog box) is analogous to the T square and triangle. Note that the word Ortho appears on the status line to tell you that the ortho mode is on.

1. Click on the Line icon on the Draw palette.

2. Using your coordinate readout for guidance, start your line at the coordinate 5′–7″, 6′–3″.

3. Choose Option ➤ Coordinate Display or press F6 until you see the relative polar coordinates appear in the coordinate readout at the bottom of the AutoCAD window. Polar coordinates allow you to see your current location in reference to the last point selected. This is helpful when you are using a command that requires distance and direction input.

4. Move the cursor until the coordinate readout lists 1′–10″< 0, and pick this point. As you move the cursor around, the rubber-banding line follows it at any angle.

5. You can also force the line to be orthogonal. Press F8, or hold down the Ctrl key and press **O** to toggle on the ortho mode, and move the cursor around. Now the rubber-banding line will only move vertically or horizontally.

6. Move the cursor down until the coordinate readout lists
    0'– 9"< 270.

7. Continue drawing the other two sides of the rectangle by us-
    ing the coordinate readout. You should have a drawing that
    looks like Figure 3.1.

By using the snap mode in conjunction with the coordinate readout,
you can measure distances as you draw lines. This is similar to how you
would draw using a scale. Be aware that the smallest distance the coordinate readout will register depends on the area you have displayed in
your drawing area. For example, if you are displaying an area the size of
a football field, the smallest distance you can indicate with your cursor may
be 6". On the other hand, if your view shows an area of only one square
inch, you can indicate distances as small as $\frac{1}{1000}$" using your cursor.

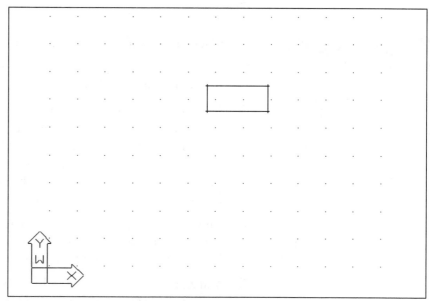

Figure 3.1:   A plan view of the toilet tank

EXPLORING THE DRAWING PROCESS

In this section, you will look at some of the more common commands and use them to complete this simple drawing. As you draw, watch the prompts and notice how your responses affect them. Also note how you use existing drawing elements as reference points.

While drawing with AutoCAD, you create gross geometric forms to determine the basic shapes of objects, and then modify the shapes to fill in detail. This is where the differences between drawing with Auto-CAD and manual drafting become more apparent.

AutoCAD offers 14 basic types of drawing objects, four of which are new in Release 13. The object types from earlier versions of AutoCAD are lines, arcs, circles, text, traces, polylines, points, solids, and 3D faces. The four new types are true ellipses, elliptical arcs, spline curves, solids, and Multiline text. All drawings are built on these objects. In addition, there are five different 3D meshes, which are three-dimensional surfaces composed of 3D faces. You are familiar with lines and arcs; these, along with circles, are the most commonly used objects. As you progress through the book, we will introduce you to the other objects and how they are used.

LOCATING AN OBJECT IN REFERENCE TO OTHERS

As great a program as AutoCAD is, it has been sorely lacking an accurate representation of ellipses and spline curves—until now. Release 13 fills this gap with true ellipses and curves, or NURBS. NURBS stands for Non-Uniform Rational B-Splines—a fancy term meaning that curved objects are based on accurate mathematical models. When you trim the ellipse in a later exercise, it becomes a NURBS curve, not a segmented polyline as in earlier versions of AutoCAD. You'll learn more about curves in *Chapter 13*.

To define the toilet seat, you will use an ellipse.

1. Click and drag the Ellipse icon in the Draw palette. You can also type **ellipse** ↵ to start the Ellipse command.

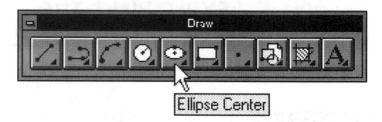

and then select Ellipse Axis Endpoint from the flyout.

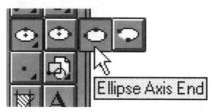

2. At the Arc/Center/<Axis endpoint 1>: prompt, pick the midpoint of the bottom horizontal line of the rectangle. Do this by bringing up the Osnap overrides and selecting Midpoint; then pick the bottom line. (Remember, to bring up the Osnap menu, Shift-click the right mouse button.)

3. At the Axis endpoint 2: prompt, move the cursor down until the coordinate readout lists 1'–10"< 270.

4. Pick this as the second axis endpoint.

5. At the <Other axis distance>/Rotation: prompt, move the cursor horizontally from the center of the ellipse until the coordinate readout lists 0'–8"< 180.

6. Pick this as the axis distance defining the width of the ellipse. Your drawing should look like Figure 3.2.

GETTING A CLOSER LOOK

During the drawing process, you will want to enlarge areas of a drawing to more easily edit its objects. In *Chapter 1*, you already saw how the Zoom command is used for this purpose.

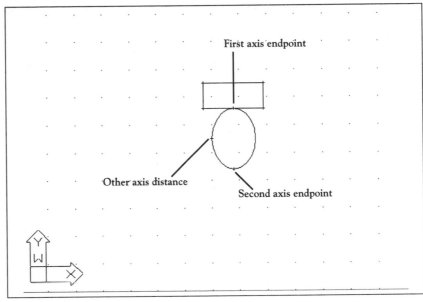

Figure 3.2: The ellipse added to the tank

1. Choose View ➤ Zoom ➤ Window. You can also enter **Zoom** ↵ or pick Zoom ➤ Zoom Window from the Standard toolbar.

2. At the First corner: prompt, pick a point below and to the left of your drawing at coordinate 5'–0", 3'–6".

3. At the Other corner: prompt, pick a point above and to the right of the drawing at coordinate 8'–3", 6'–8", so that the toilet is completely enclosed by the view window. The toilet enlarges to fill more of the screen (see Figure 3.3).

MODIFYING AN OBJECT

Now let's see how editing commands are used to construct an object. To define the back edge of the seat, let's put a copy of the line defining the front of the toilet tank, about 3" toward the center of the ellipse.

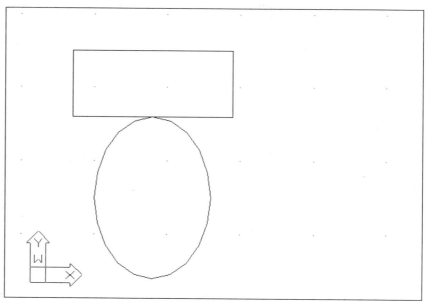

Figure 3.3: A close-up of the toilet drawing

1. Click on Copy Object in the Modify palette. You can also type **Copy** ↵, or use grips to copy the line (see *Chapter 2*).

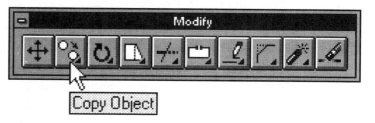

2. At the Select object: prompt, pick the horizontal line that touches the top of the ellipse. The line is highlighted. Press ↵ to confirm your selection.

3. At the <Base point or displacement>/Multiple: prompt, pick a base point near the line. Then move the cursor down until the coordinate readout lists 0'–3"< 270.

4. Pick this point. Your drawing should look like Figure 3.4.

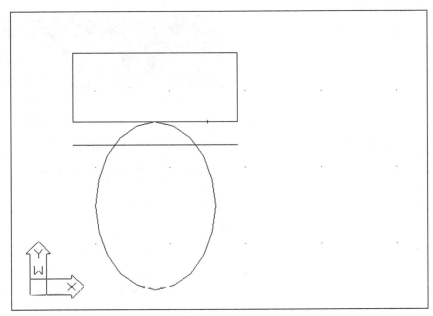

Figure 3.4:   The line copied down

You will have noticed that the COPY command acts exactly like the Move command you used in *Chapter 2*, except that Copy does not alter the position of the objects you select.

Trimming an Object

Now you must delete the part of the ellipse that is not needed. You will use the TRIM command to trim off parts of the ellipse.

1. First, turn the snap mode off by pressing F9. Snap may be a hindrance at this point in your editing session, because it may keep you from picking the points you want. Snap mode forces the cursor to move to points at a given interval, so you will have difficulty selecting a point that doesn't fall exactly at one of those intervals.

2. Click on Trim in the Modify palette. You can also type **Trim** ↵ to start the Trim command.

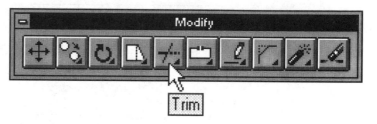

You will see this prompt:

Select cutting edges: (Projmode=UCS, Edgemode=No extend)
Select objects:

3. Click on the line you just created—the one that crosses through the ellipse—and press ↵ to finish your selection.

4. At the <Select object to trim>/Project/Edge/Undo: prompt, pick the topmost portion of the ellipse above the line. This trims the ellipse back to the line.

SELECTING CLOSE OR OVERLAPPING OBJECTS

At times, you will want to select an object that is in close proximity to or beneath another object, and AutoCAD won't obey your mouse click. It's frustrating when you click on the desired object but AutoCAD selects the one next to it instead. To help you make your selections in these situations, AutoCAD provides *Object Selection Cycling*, which is new with Release 13. To use it, hold down the Ctrl key while simultaneously clicking on the object you want to select. If the wrong object is highlighted, press the mouse/pick button again (you needn't hold down the Ctrl key for the second pick), and the next object in close proximity will be highlighted. If several objects are overlapping or close together, continue to press the mouse/pick button until the correct object is highlighted.

In step 2 of the foregoing exercise, the TRIM command produces two messages in the prompt. The first message, Select cutting edges..., tells you that you must first select objects to define *the edge to which you wish to trim*. In step 4, you are again prompted to select objects, this time to select the *objects to trim*. TRIM is one of a handful of AutoCAD commands that asks you to select two sets of objects: The first set defines a boundary, and the second is the set of objects you want to edit. The two sets of objects are not mutually exclusive. You can, for example, select the cutting edge objects as objects to trim. The next exercise shows how this works.

First you will undo the Trim you just did. Then you will use the Trim command again in a slightly different way to finish off the toilet.

1. Click on the Undo button in the Standard toolbar, or enter **U** ↵ at the command prompt. The top of the ellipse reappears.

2. Start the TRIM command again by clicking on it in the Modify palette.

3. At the Select cutting edges... Select objects prompt, click on the ellipse and the line crossing the ellipse (see panel 1 of Figure 3.5).

4. Press ↵ to finish your selection and move to the next step.

5. At the <Select object to trim>/Project/Edge/Undo: prompt, click on the top portion of the ellipse, as you did in the previous exercise. The ellipse trims back.

6. Click on a point near the left end of the trim line, past the ellipse. The line trims back to the ellipse.

7. Click on the other end of the line. The right side of the line trims back to meet the ellipse. Your drawing should look like panel 2 of Figure 3.5.

8. Press ↵ to exit the Trim command.

9. Erase any remnants of the ellipse.

▼ NOTE

These new Trim options—Project, Edge, and Undo—are described just below.

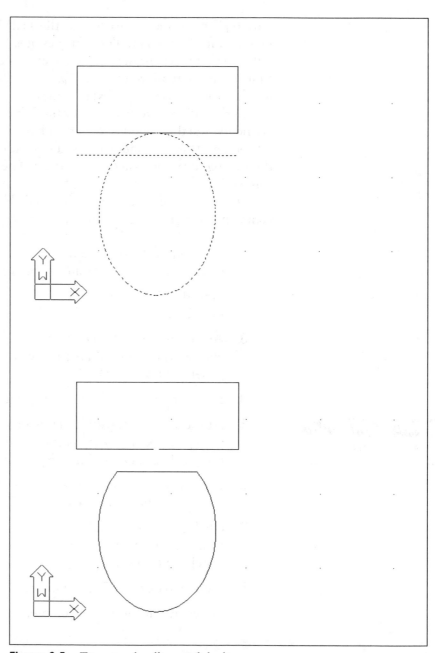

Figure 3.5: Trimming the ellipse and the line

Here you saw how the ellipse and the line are both used as trim objects, as well as the objects to be trimmed.

The Trim Options

Release 13 offers three options for the Trim command: Edge, Project, and Undo. As described in the following paragraphs, these options give you a higher degree of control over how objects are trimmed.

Edge [E] allows you to trim an object to an apparent intersection, even if the cutting-edge object does not intersect the object to be trimmed (see the top of Figure 3.6). Edge offers two options, Extend and No Extend. These can also be set using the Edgemode system variable.

Project [P] is useful when working on 3D drawings. It controls how AutoCAD trims objects that are not coplanar. Project offers three options: None, UCS, and View. None causes Trim to ignore objects that are on different planes, so that only coplanar objects will be trimmed. If you choose UCS, the Trim command trims objects based on a plan view of the current UCS and then disregards whether the objects are coplanar or not (see the middle of Figure 3.6). View is similar to UCS but uses the current view's "line of sight" to determine how non-coplanar objects are trimmed (see the bottom of Figure 3.6).

Undo [U] causes the last trimmed object to revert to its original length.

You've just seen one way to construct the toilet. However, there are many ways to construct objects. For example, you could have just trimmed the top of the ellipse, as you did in the first Trim exercise, then used the Grips feature to move the endpoints of the line to meet the endpoints of the ellipse. As you become familiar with AutoCAD, you will start to develop your own ways of working, using the tools best suited to your style.

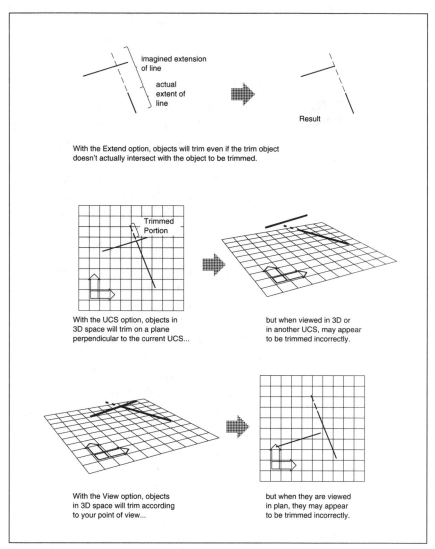

Figure 3.6: The TRIM command's options

PLANNING AND LAYING OUT A DRAWING

For the next object, the bathtub, you will use some new commands to lay out parts of the drawing. This will help you get a feel for the kind of planning you must do to use AutoCAD effectively. You'll also get a chance to use some of the keyboard shortcuts built into AutoCAD. First, though, go back to the previous view of your drawing, and arrange some more room to work.

1. Choose View ➤ Zoom ➤ Previous. Your view will return to the one you had before the last Zoom command (Figure 3.7).

You'll begin the bathtub by using the Line command to draw a rectangle 2'–8"×5'–0" on the left side of the drawing area. This time, you'll use the Line command's keyboard shortcut.

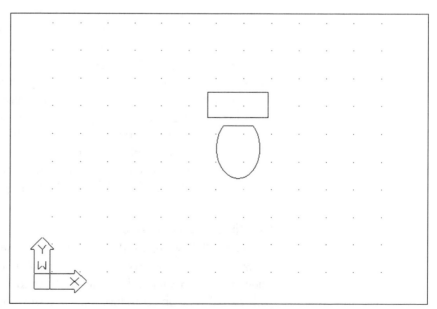

Figure 3.7:   The finished toilet

2. Turn snap mode on by pressing F9.

3. Type **L** ↵, and at the From point prompt, pick the coordinate location 0′–9″, 0′–10″.

4. Type **@2′8″<0** ↵ for the first side of the tub.

5. Type **@5′<90** ↵ for the next side.

6. Type **@2′8″<180** ↵ for the next side.

7. Type **C** ↵ to close the rectangle.

Now you have the outline of the tub. Notice that when you enter feet and inches through the keyboard, you must avoid hyphens or spaces. Thus *2 feet 8 inches* is typed as *2′8″*.

MAKING A PRELIMINARY SKETCH

The following exercise will show you how planning ahead will make your use of AutoCAD more efficient. When drawing a complex object, you will often have to do some layout before you do the actual drawing. This is similar to drawing an accurate pencil sketch using construction lines that you later trace over to produce a finished drawing. The advantage of doing this in AutoCAD is that your drawing doesn't lose any accuracy between the sketch and the final product. Also, AutoCAD allows you to use the geometry of your sketch to aid you in drawing. While planning your drawing, think about what it is you want to draw, and then decide what drawing elements will help you create that object.

You will use the OFFSET command to establish reference lines to help you draw the inside of the tub. This is where the Osnap overrides are quite useful. See the sidebar, "The Osnap Options."

Setting Up a Layout

The OFFSET option on the Copy flyout of the Modify palette allows you to make parallel copies of a set of objects, such as the lines forming the outside of your tub. OFFSET is different from the COPY command; OFFSET allows only one object to be copied at a time, but it can remember the distance you specify. The OFFSET option does not work with all types of objects. Only lines, arcs, circles, and 2D polylines can be offset.

The Basics | **I**

THE OSNAP OPTIONS

Here is a summary of all the available Osnap options. You've already used many of these options in this and the previous chapter. Pay special attention here to those options you haven't yet used in the exercises but may find useful to your style of work. The full name of each option is followed by its keyboard shortcut name in brackets. To use these options, you can enter either the full name or abbreviation at any point prompt. You can also pick these options from the pop-up menu obtained by Shift-clicking on the right mouse button.

Tip: Sometimes you'll want to have one or more of these Osnap options available as the default selection. You can set Osnaps to be on at all times (called a running Osnap). Use the Running Osnap option on the Object Snap flyout, or click on Options ➤ Running Object Snaps from the pull-down menu.

Apparent Intersection [apint] selects the apparent intersection of two objects. This is useful when you want to select the intersection of two objects that do not actually intersect. You will be prompted to select the two objects.

Center [cen] selects the center of an arc or circle. You must click on the arc or circle itself, not its apparent center.

Endpoint [endp] selects all the endpoints of lines, polylines, arcs, curves, and 3dface vertices.

From [fro] selects a point relative to a picked point. For example, you can select a point that is 2 units to the left and 4 units to the right of a circle's center.

Insert [ins] selects the insertion point of text, blocks, xrefs, and overlays.

Intersection [int] selects the intersection of objects.

Midpoint [mid] selects the midpoint of a line or arc. In the case of a polyline, it select the midpoint of the polyline segment.

Nearest [nea] selects a point on an object nearest the pick point.

Node [nod] selects a point object.

None [non] temporarily turns off running Osnaps.

Perpendicular [per] selects a position on an object that is perpendicular to the last point selected. Normally, this option is not valid for the first point selected in a string of points.

Quadpoint [qua] selects the nearest cardinal (north, south, east, or west) point on an arc or circle.

Quick [qui], by sacrificing accuracy, improves the speed at which AutoCAD selects geometry. You use Quick in conjunction with one of the other Osnap options. For example, to speed up the selection of an intersection, you would enter **QUICK,INT** ↵ at a point prompt, and then select the intersection of two objects.

Tangent [tan] selects a point on an arc or circle that represents the tangent from the last point selected. Like the Perpendicular option, Tangent is not valid for the first point in a string of points.

In this exercise, you will use standard lines to layout your drawing. Lines are best suited for the layout of the bathtub in this situation. In Chapter 5 you will learn about two other objects, Xlines and Rays, which are specifically designed to help you layout a drawing.

1. In the Modify palette, click and drag the Copy button to display the flyout, and select Offset.

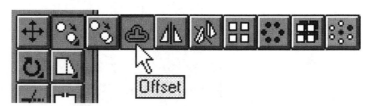

2. At the Offset distance or Through <Through>: prompt, enter **3** ↵. This enters the distance of 3″ as the offset distance.

3. At the Select object to offset: prompt, click on the bottom line of the rectangle you just drew.

4. At the Side to offset? prompt, pick a point inside the rectangle. A copy of the line appears. You don't have to be exact about where you pick the side to offset; AutoCAD only wants to know on which side of the line you want to make the offset copy.

5. The prompt Select an object to offset: appears again. Click on another side to offset; then click again on a point inside the rectangle.

6. Continue to offset the other two sides. Then offset these four new lines inside the rectangle toward the center. You will have a drawing that looks like Figure 3.8.

7. When you are done, exit the OFFSET command by pressing ⏎.

▼ NOTE

Notice that Offset is now the default button on the Modify palette, where Copy Object was when you first opened AutoCAD.

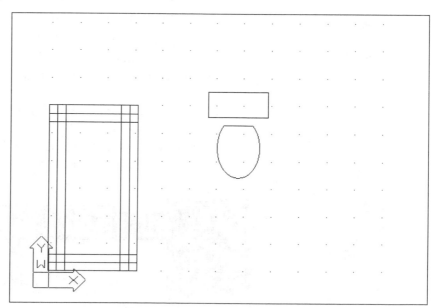

Figure 3.8: The completed layout

USING THE LAYOUT

Now you will begin to draw the inside of the tub, starting with the narrow end. You will use your offset lines as references to construct the arcs that make up the tub.

▼ TIP

Remember that you bring up the Osnap menu by Shift-clicking the right mouse button.

1. In the Draw palette, click and drag the Arc button to open the flyout, and select 3 Points. (See Figure 3.9 for an explanation of 3 Points and the other Arc options.)

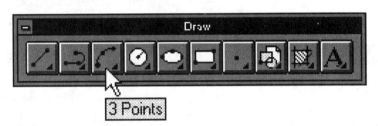

2. Using the Intersection Osnap override, click on the intersection of the two lines located at coordinate 2′–11″, 5′–4″.

3. Using the Midpoint Osnap override, pick the midpoint of the second horizontal line near the top.

4. Finally, pick the intersection of the two lines at coordinate 1′–3″, 5′–4″. An arc appears. Panel 1 of Figure 3.10 shows the sequence we've just described.

Next you will draw an arc for the left side of the tub.

5. In the Draw palette, click and drag the Arc button and select Start End Direction from the flyout:

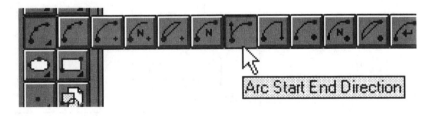

The Basics

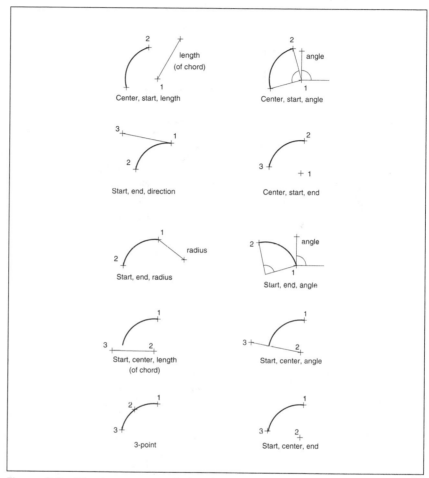

Figure 3.9: The Arc options and what they mean

and then type **@** ↵. This selects the last point you picked as the start of the next arc.

6. At the End point prompt, use the Intersection Osnap override to pick the intersection of the two lines at coordinate 1'–0", 1'–4" in the lower-left corner of the tub. See panel 2 of Figure 3.10 for the location of this point.

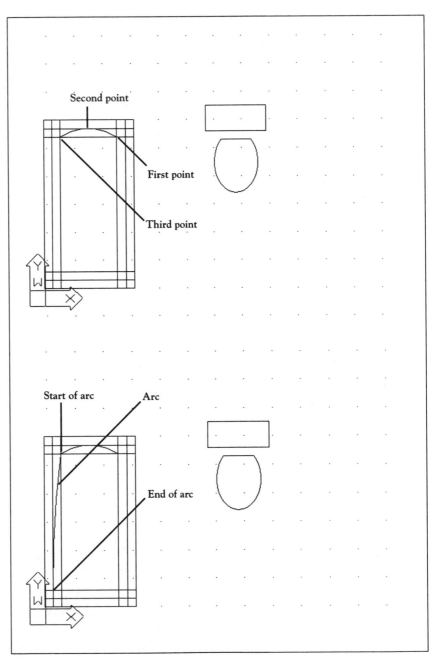

Figure 3.10: The top, left side, and bottom of the tub

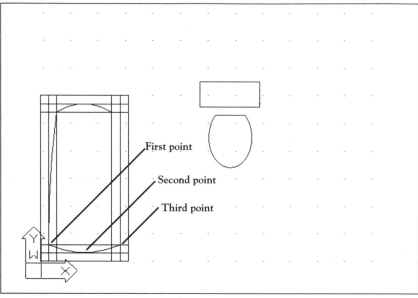

Figure 3.10: The top, left side, and bottom of the tub (continued)

▼ TIP

In step 7, the rubber-banding line indicates the direction of the arc. Be sure ortho mode is off, because ortho will force the rubber-banding line and the arc in a direction you don't want. Check the status line; if "Ortho" appears as solid black, not gray, press F8 to turn ortho off.

7. You will see the arc drag as you move the cursor, along with a rubber-banding line from the starting point of the arc. Move the cursor to the left of the dragging arc until it touches the middle line on the left side of the tub. Then pick that point (see panel 2 of Figure 3.10).

Now you will draw the bottom of the tub.

8. Click and drag the Arc button in the Draw palette, and select 3 Points from the flyout.

9. Using the Osnap overrides, pick the endpoint of the bottom of the arc just drawn.

10. Using the Osnap overrides, pick the midpoint of the middle horizontal line at the bottom of the tub.

11. Finally, pick the intersection of the two lines at coordinate 3′–2″, 2′–1″ (see panel 3 of Figure 3.10).

Now create the right side of the tub by mirroring the left side.

12. Click and drag Offset from the Modify palette, and select Mirror from the flyout.

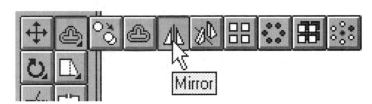

13. At the object-selection prompt, pick the long arc on the left side of the tub. The arc highlights. Press ↵ to indicate that you've finished your selection.

14. At the First point of mirror line: prompt, pick the midpoint of the top horizontal line.

15. At the Second point: prompt, turn on the ortho mode and pick a point directly below the last point selected.

16. At the Delete old objects?<N> prompt, press ↵ to accept the default, No. A mirror image of the arc you picked appears on the right side of the tub. Your drawing should look like Figure 3.11.

Erasing the Layout Lines

▼ TIP

If the following exercise doesn't work as described, be sure you have the Noun/Verb selection setting turned on. See *Appendix B* for details.

For the next step, you will erase the layout lines you created with Offset command. But this time, try selecting the lines *before* issuing the ERASE command.

1. Click on each internal layout line individually.

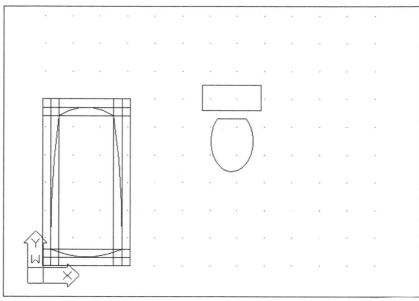

Figure 3.11: The inside of the tub completed

new

If you have problems selecting just the lines, try using a window to select single lines. (Remember, a window selects only objects that are completely within the window.) You might also try the Object Selection Cycling option, as explained in the sidebar, "Selecting Close or Overlapping Objects."

2. Once all the layout lines are highlighted, enter **E** ↵. This is a keyboard shortcut to entering the ERASE command.

You will notice that parts of the arcs you drew are missing. Don't be alarmed; they are still there. When an object that overlaps another object is changed or moved in any way, the overlapped object seems to disappear. This frequently occurs while you are using Modify ➤ Change, Fillet, Move, Mirror, and Erase.

To correct this, enter **R** ↵. The screen redraws, and your drawing should look like Figure 3.12.

▼ TIP

When preparing to erase an object that is close to other objects, you may want to select the object first, using the Noun/Verb method. This way you can carefully select objects you want to erase before you actually invoke the Erase command. You can also use Object Selection Cycling, as described in the sidebar, "Selecting Close or Overlapping Objects."

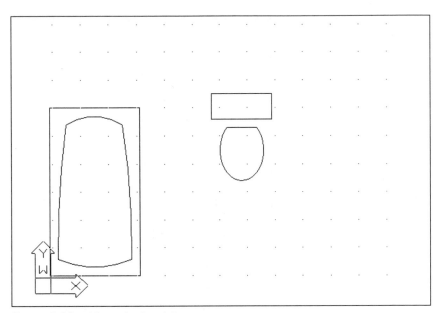

Figure 3.12:   The redisplayed drawing

PUTTING ON THE FINISHING TOUCHES

The inside of the tub still has some sharp corners. To round out these corners, you can use the versatile FILLET command (on the Modify tool palette). FILLET allows you to join lines and arcs end to end, and it can add a radius where they join, so there is a smooth transition from arc to arc or line to line. FILLET can join two lines that do not intersect, and it can trim two crossing lines back to their point of intersection.

1. Click and drag Chamfer from the Modify palette, and select Fillet from the flyout. You can also type **Fillet** ↵ at the command prompt to start the FILLET command.

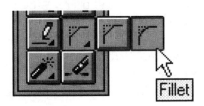

2. At the Polyline/Radius/Trim/<Select first object>: prompt, enter **R** ↵.

3. At the Enter fillet radius <0'0">: prompt, enter **4** ↵. This tells AutoCAD that you want a 4" radius for your fillet.

4. Press ↵ to invoke the FILLET command again; this time, pick two adjacent arcs. The fillet arc joins the two larger arcs.

5. Press ↵ again and fillet another corner. Repeat until all four corners are filleted. Your drawing should look like Figure 3.13.

6. Save the Bath file and exit AutoCAD.

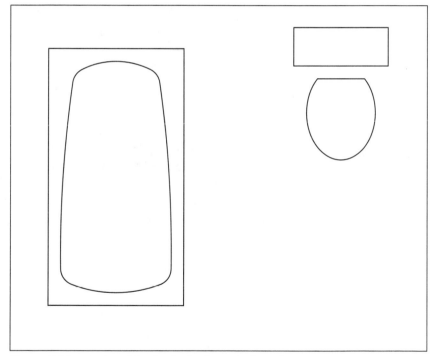

Figure 3.13:   A plot of the finished toilet and tub

USING AUTOCAD'S AUTOMATIC SAVE FEATURE

As you work with AutoCAD, you may notice that AutoCAD periodically saves your work for you. Your file is saved not as its current file name, but as a file called Auto.SV$. The default time interval between automatic saves is 120 minutes. You can change this interval by doing the following:

1. Enter **Savetime** ↵ at the command prompt.

2. At the New value for SAVETIME < 120 >: prompt, enter the desired interval, in minutes. Or, to disable the automatic save feature entirely, enter **0** at the prompt.

IF YOU WANT TO EXPERIMENT...

As you draw, you will notice that you are alternately creating objects, then copying and editing them. This is where the difference between hand-drafting and CAD really begins to show.

Try drawing the part shown in Figure 3.14. The figure shows you what to do, step by step. Take particular note of how you are applying the concepts of layout and editing to this drawing.

The Basics

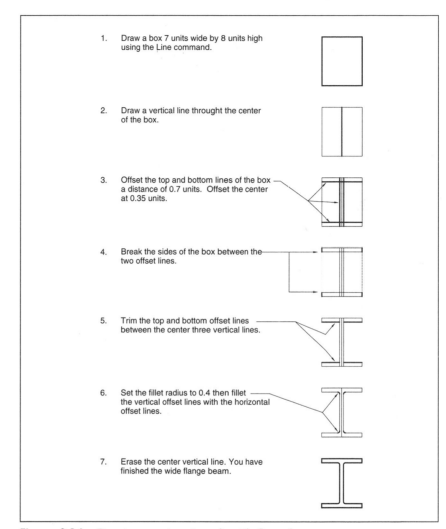

1. Draw a box 7 units wide by 8 units high using the Line command.

2. Draw a vertical line throught the center of the box.

3. Offset the top and bottom lines of the box a distance of 0.7 units. Offset the center at 0.35 units.

4. Break the sides of the box between the two offset lines.

5. Trim the top and bottom offset lines between the center three vertical lines.

6. Set the fillet radius to 0.4 then fillet the vertical offset lines with the horizontal offset lines.

7. Erase the center vertical line. You have finished the wide flange beam.

Figure 3.14: Drawing a section view of a wide flange beam

4

ORGANIZING YOUR WORK

Creating Symbols Using Blocks

Placing a Block

Restoring Erased Objects

Breaking Down a Block into Its
Component Objects

Creating Layers and Assigning Objects
to Them

Controlling Color

Controlling Layers

Using Line Types Such As Dotted and
Dashed Lines

FAST TRACK

158 ▶ To change the color of a layer

In the Layer Control dialog box, highlight the name of the layer you want to change, and click on the Set Color button. Double-click on the desired color in the Select Color dialog box.

159 ▶ To change the layer assignment of an object

Click on the Properties button in the Object Properties toolbar. Select the objects whose layer assignment you want to change and press ↵. At the Change Properties dialog box, click on the Layer button. Double-click on the layer name you want for the selected objects.

163 ▶ To make a layer the current default layer

Click on Data ➤ Layers. In the list of layers, select the layer you want to make the current default. Then click on the Current button near the bottom of the list.

170 ▶ To turn a layer off

Click on Data ➤ Layers. In the list of layers, select the layer or layers you want to turn off. Then click on the Off button.

173 ▶ To change the line-type assignment of a layer

Click on Data ➤ Layers. Select the name of the layer you want to change, and click on the Set Ltype button. In the Select Linetype dialog box, double-click on the desired line type. If the desired line type is not shown, you need to load it from the external file, as described just below.

174 ▶ To load a line type

Enter **Ddltype** ↵ at the command prompt, and click on the Load button. In the list, select the line type you want to load.

Drawing the tub and toilet in *Chapter 3* may have taken what seemed to you an inordinate amount of time. As you continue to use Auto-CAD, however, you will learn to draw objects more quickly. You will also need to draw fewer of them, because you can save drawings as symbols to be used like rubber stamps, duplicating drawings instantaneously wherever they are needed. This will save you a lot of time when you're composing drawings.

To make effective use of AutoCAD, you should begin a *symbols library* of drawings you use frequently. A mechanical designer might have a library of symbols for fasteners, cams, valves, or any type of parts for his or her application. An electrical engineer might have a symbols library of capacitors, resistors, switches, and the like. And a circuit designer will have yet another unique set of frequently used symbols. On this book's companion disk, you'll find a variety of ready-to-use symbols libraries. Check them out—you're likely to find some you can use.

In Chapter 3 you drew two objects, a bathtub and a toilet, that architects often use. In this chapter, you will see how to create symbols from those drawings. You will also learn about layers and how you can use them to organize information.

CREATING A SYMBOL

To save a drawing as a symbol, you use the Block command. If you use a word processor, you are probably familiar with the idea of a block. In word processing, a block is used to group words or sentences together so they can be copied elsewhere within the same file, to other files, or to a separate disk for future use. AutoCAD uses blocks in a similar fashion. Within a file, you can turn parts of your drawing into blocks that can be saved and recalled at any time. You can also use entire existing files as blocks.

1. Start AutoCAD and open the existing Bath file. Use the one you created in *Chapter 3*, or open 04-BATH.DWG on the companion CD. The drawing appears just as you left it in the last session.

---

2. In the Draw tool palette, click and drag Insert Block, and choose Block from the flyout. (Or type **Block** ↵ at the command prompt to start the BLOCK command.)

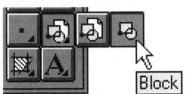

3. The prompt BLOCK Block name (or ?): appears, asking you to supply a name for the block you are about to define. Type **Toilet** ↵.

4. The prompt Insertion base point: asks you to select a base point for the block. (The insertion base point of a block is similar to the base point you used as a handle on an object in *Chapter 2.*) Using the Osnap overrides, pick the midpoint of the back of the toilet.

5. You now see the familiar object-selection prompt. Click on a point below and to the left of the toilet. Then window the entire toilet; it will be highlighted.

6. Press ↵ to confirm your selection, and the toilet disappears. It is now a block with the name Toilet.

7. Repeat the blocking process for the tub, but this time use the upper-left corner of the tub as the insertion base point and give the block the name **Tub**.

▼ NOTE

The insertion base point of a block is similar to the base point you used as a handle on an object in Chapter 2.

▼ NOTE

You can press ↵ to start Block again.

RECALLING BLOCKED OR ERASED OBJECTS

When you turn an object into a block, it is stored within the drawing file, ready to be recalled at any time. The block remains part of the drawing file even when you end the editing session. When you open the file again, the block will be available for your use. A block acts like a single object, even though it is really made up of several objects. It can only be modified by unblocking it using the EXPLODE command. You can then edit it and turn it back into a block. We will look at the block-editing process later in this chapter.

If for some reason you want to restore the object you just turned into a block, you can use the OOPS command. The OOPS command can also be used in any situation where you want to restore an object you erased by accident.

▼ NOTE

Oops is also on the Miscellaneous tool palette (Tools ➤ Toolbars ➤ Miscellaneous).

1. Type **Oops** ↵. The tub reappears in its former condition, not as a block.

2. You won't need this restored tub, so click on the Undo button on the Standard toolbar or type **U** ↵ to undo the OOPS command. Be careful not to press ↵ more than once!

OOPS is also useful when you want to create several blocks that are only slightly different. For example, suppose you want several versions of the tub. You can save the tub as a block, then use OOPS to restore it, then modify it to a different shape, and then save this new tub as a different block.

INSERTING A SYMBOL

Although the tub and toilet blocks disappeared, they can be recalled at any time, as many times as you want. In the following exercise you'll first draw the interior walls of the bathroom and then insert the tub and toilet.

▼ TIP

If you're in a hurry, enter **Insert** ↵ at the command prompt, then enter **Tub** ↵, and then go to step 6.

1. Draw a rectangle 5′×7$\frac{1}{2}$′. Orient the rectangle so the long sides go from left to right and the lower-left corner is at coordinate 1′–10″, 1′–10″. Your drawing will look like Figure 4.1.

2. In the Draw tool palette, click and drag Block and choose Insert Block from the flyout.

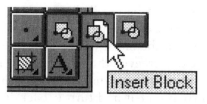

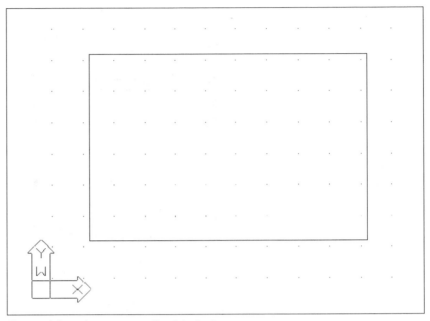

Figure 4.1: The interior walls of the bathroom

The Insert dialog box appears:

Insert

Block

[Block...] [   ]

[File...] [   ]

Options

☒ Specify Parameters on Screen

Insertion Point   Scale   Rotation

X: [0"]   X: [1"]   Angle: [0]

Y: [0"]   Y: [1"]

Z: [0"]   Z: [1"]

☐ Explode

[OK]   [Cancel]   [Help...]

3. Click on the Block button at the top of the dialog box. The Defined Blocks dialog box appears, with a list of the available blocks in the current drawing.

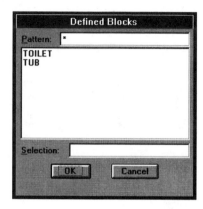

4. Double-click on the block name TUB. The Insert dialog box returns with TUB in the input box next to the Block button.

5. Click on OK. AutoCAD prompts you for more information.

6. At the Insertion point: prompt, move the cursor across the screen slowly. Notice that a preview image of the tub appears and follows the cursor. The upper-left corner you picked for the tub's base point is now on the cursor intersection.

7. Pick the upper-left intersection of the room as your insertion point. Notice that as you move your cursor, the preview image of the tub appears distorted.

8. At the X scale factor <1> / Corner / XYZ: prompt, press ↵ to accept the default, 1.

9. At the Y scale factor (default=X): prompt, press ↵ to accept (default=X). This means you are accepting that the X scale equals the Y scale, which in turn equals 1.

10. At the Rotation angle <0>: prompt, press ↵ to accept the default of 0. You should have a drawing that looks like panel 1 of Figure 4.2.

▼ NOTE

The X scale factor and Y scale factor prompts let you stretch the block in one direction or another. You can even specify a negative value to mirror the block. The defaults on these prompts is always 1, which inserts the block or file at the same size as it were created.

11. Repeat steps 2 through 10, but this time, in steps 3 and 4 click on the Block input box and enter **toilet**. Place the toilet along the top of the rectangle representing the room, just to the right of the tub at coordinate 5'–8", 6'–10", as shown in panel 2 of Figure 4.2.

You might have noticed that as you moved the cursor in step 7, the tub became distorted. This demonstrates how the X and Y scale factors can affect the item being inserted. Also, in step 10, you can see the tub rotate as you move the cursor. You can pick a point to fix the block in place, or you can enter a rotation value. The default 0° angle inserts the block or file with the orientation at which it was created.

USING AN EXISTING DRAWING AS A SYMBOL

Now you need a door into the bathroom. Since you have already drawn a door and saved it as a file, you can bring the door into this drawing file and use it as a block.

1. In the Draw palette, click and drag Block and choose Insert Block from the flyout.

2. In the Insert dialog box, click on the File button just below the Block button. The Select Drawing File dialog box appears.

3. Double-click on the Door file name in the file list.

4. As you move the cursor around, you will notice the door appear above and to the right of the cursor intersection, as in Figure 4.3.

5. At this point, the door looks too small for this bathroom. This is because you drew it 3 units long, which translates to 3". Pick a point near coordinate 7'–2",2'–4", so that the door is placed in the lower-right corner of the room.

▼ TIP

You can also browse your hard disk by looking at thumbnail views of the drawing files in a directory. See "Locating Files on Your Hard Disk" later in this chapter.

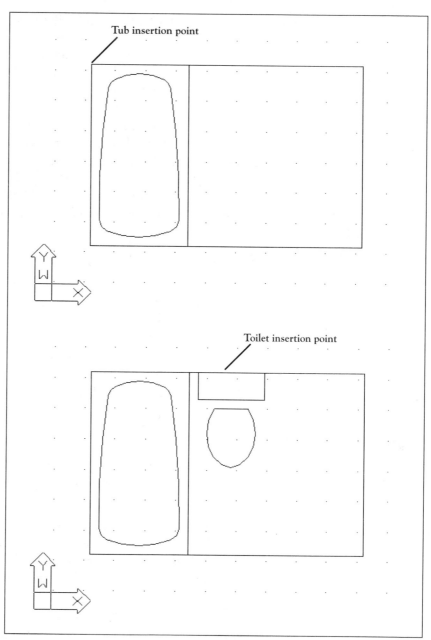

Figure 4.2: The bathroom, first with the tub and then with the toilet inserted

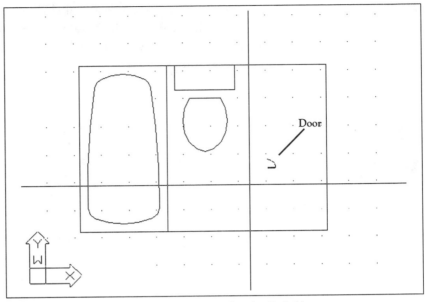

Figure 4.3: The door drawing being inserted in the Bath file

6. If you take the default setting for the X scale of the inserted block, the door will remain 3″ long. However, as mentioned earlier, you can specify a smaller or larger size for an inserted object. In this case, you want a 3′ door. To get that from a 3″ door, you need an X scale factor of 12. (You may want to look again at Table 3.3 in *Chapter 3* to see how this is determined.) Enter **12** ↵ now, at the X scale factor prompt.

7. Press ↵ twice to accept the default y = x and the rotation angle of 0°.

Now the command prompt appears, but nothing seems to happen to the drawing. This is because, when you enlarged the door, you also enlarged the distance between the base point and the object. This brings up another issue to be aware of when you're considering drawings as symbols. All drawings have base points. The default base point is the absolute coordinate 0,0, otherwise known as the *origin*, located in the lower-left corner of any new drawing. When you drew the door in *Chapter 2*, you didn't specify the base point. So, when you try to bring the door into this drawing, AutoCAD uses the origin of the door drawing as its base point (see Figure 4.4).

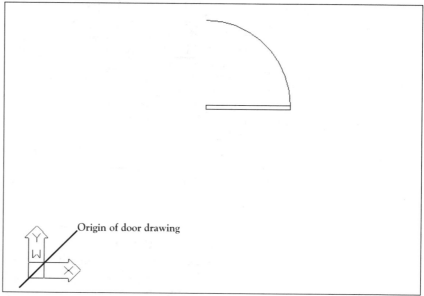

Origin of door drawing

Figure 4.4:   The origin of the door drawing

Since the door appears outside the bathroom, you must first use the Zoom ➤ All option to show more of the drawing, and then the Move command on the Modify palette to move the door to the right side wall of the bathroom. Let's do this now.

1. Click on View ➤ Zoom ➤ All from the pull-down menu. The view of the room shrinks away and the door is revealed. Notice that it is now the proper size for your drawing (see Figure 4.5).

The Basics

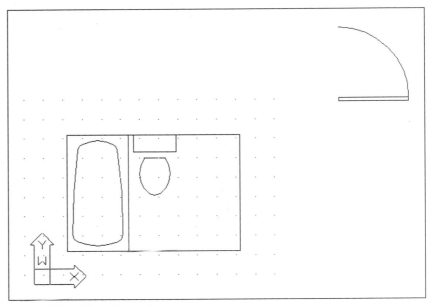

Figure 4.5:   The enlarged door

2. Choose Move from the Modify palette.

3. To pick the door you just inserted, at the Select objects: prompt, click on a point anywhere on the door and press ↵. Notice that now the entire door highlights. This is because a block is treated like a single object, even though it may be made up of several lines, arcs, etc.

4. At the Base point: prompt, pick the lower-left corner of the door.

5. At the Second point: prompt, use the Nearest Osnap override, and position the door so your drawing looks like Figure 4.6.

Because the door is an object you will use often, it should be a common size, so you don't have to specify an odd value every time you insert it. It would also be helpful if the door's insertion base point were in a

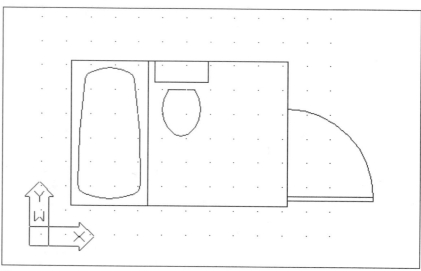

Figure 4.6:   The door on the right side wall of the bathroom

more convenient location. Next, you will modify the Door block to better suit your needs.

▼ TIP

If the REGENAUTO setting is turned off, you will have to issue a REGEN command to see changes made to redefined blocks. See *Chapter 6* for more on REGENAUTO.

UNBLOCKING AND MODIFYING A BLOCK

To modify a block, you break it down into its components, edit them, and then turn them back into a block. This is called *redefining* a block. If you redefine a block that has been inserted in a drawing, each occurrence of that block will change to reflect the new definition. You can use this block redefinition feature to make rapid changes to a design.

To separate a block into its components, you use the Explode command. As of Release 13 of AutoCAD, you can explode blocks that are inserted with differing X, Y, and Z Scale values. You can also explode mirrored blocks.

1. Choose Explode from the Modify palette. You can also type **Explode** ↵ to start the EXPLODE command.

2. Click on the door and press ↵ to confirm your selection.

Now you can edit the individual objects that make up the door, if you so desire. In this case, you only want to change the door's insertion point, because you have already made it a more convenient size. So now you'll turn the door back into a block, this time using the door's lower-left corner for its insertion base point.

▼ TIP

You can simultaneously insert and explode a block by clicking on the Explode check box in the lower-left corner of the Insert dialog box.

3. In the Modify palette, click and drag Insert Block and select Block from the flyout.

4. At the Block name prompt, enter **Door** for the name of the block. The following prompt appears:

    Block DOOR already exists.
    Redefine it? <N>

    AutoCAD provides this prompt so you won't inadvertently change a block you want to leave alone.

5. Enter **Y** ↵ for Yes.

6. At the Insertion base point: prompt, pick the lower-left corner of the door; then proceed with the rest of the command.

▼ TIP

To mirror an object using Grips, first be sure Grips is on. Select the objects to mirror, click on a grip, and then press the right mouse button until you see the ** MIRROR ** message in the prompt.

7. Now insert the door again, using the Block button in the Insert dialog box. This time, however, use the Nearest Osnap override and pick a point on the right side wall of the bathroom, near coordinate 9′–4″, 2′–1″.

8. After you complete this, use the Grips feature to mirror the door, using the wall as the mirror axis so that the door is inside the room. Your drawing will look like Figure 4.7.

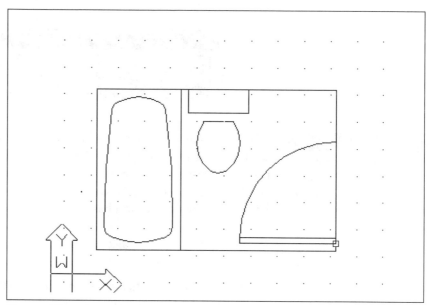

Figure 4.7:   The bathroom floor plan thus far

SAVING A BLOCK AS A DRAWING FILE

You've seen that, with very little effort, you can create a symbol that can be placed anywhere in a file. Suppose you want to use this symbol in other files. When you create a block using the Block command, the block exists within the current file only until you save it as a drawing file on disk. For an existing drawing that has been brought in and modified, such as the door, the drawing file on disk associated with that door is not automatically updated. To reflect the changes you made to the door block, you must update the door file. You do this using the Export option on the File menu. Let's see how this works.

In the next exercise, you'll get a chance to see how this works, and to try some new options in the File dialog box. Start by turning the tub and toilet blocks into individual files on disk.

The Basics

I

▼ TIP

If you prefer, you can skip step 2, and then in step 3 enter the full file name including the .DWG extension, as in **Tub.DWG.**

▼ NOTE

AutoCAD gives you the option to save a block's file under the same name as the original block or with a different name. Usually you will want to use the same name, which you can do by entering an equals sign (=) after the prompt.

1. Click on File ➤ Export. The Export Data dialog box opens. This dialog box is a simple file dialog box.

2. Open the List Files of Type drop-down list and select Drawing (*.DWG).

3. Double-click on the File Name input box and enter **Tub**. The dialog box closes.

4. At the Block name prompt, enter the name of the block you wish to save on disk as the tub file—in this case, also Tub. The tub block is now saved as a file.

5. Repeat steps 1 through 3 for the toilet block. Give the file the same name as the block.

REPLACING EXISTING FILES WITH BLOCKS

The WBLOCK command does the same thing as File ➤ Export, but output is limited to AutoCAD .DWG files. (Veteran AutoCAD users will want to note that WBLOCK is now incorporated into the File ➤ Export command.) Let's try using the WBLOCK command this time, to save the door block you modified.

1. Issue the WBLOCK command by typing **Wblock** ↵.

2. At the Create Drawing File dialog box, enter the file name **Door**. A warning message appears:

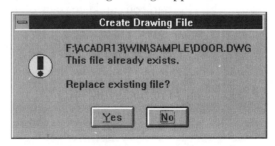

3. In this case, you want to update the door you drew in *Chapter 2*, so click on Yes. The new door will replace the old one.

4. Save the current drawing.

In this exercise, you typed the WBLOCK command at the command prompt instead of using File ➤ Export. The results are the same, regardless of which method you use.

OTHER USES FOR BLOCKS

So far, you have used Block to create symbols, and the EXPORT and WBLOCK commands to save those symbols to disk. As you can see, symbols can be created and saved at any time while you are drawing. You have made the tub and toilet symbols into drawing files that you can see when you check the contents of your current directory.

However, creating symbols is not the only use for Insert Block, Block, Export, and WBLOCK. You can use them in any situation that requires grouping objects (though you may prefer to use the more flexible Object Group command discussed in the next section). Export and WBLOCK also allow you to save a part of a drawing to disk. You will see instances of these other uses of Block, Export, and WBLOCK throughout *Chapters 5–8* and in *Chapter 12*.

Block, Export, and WBLOCK are extremely versatile and, if used judiciously, can boost your productivity and simplify your work. If you are not careful, however, you can also get carried away and create more blocks than you can keep track of. Planning your drawings helps you determine which elements will work best as blocks, and to recognize situations where other methods of organization will be more suitable.

The Basics   **I**

AN ALTERNATIVE TO BLOCKS

Another way to create symbols is by creating *shapes*. Shapes are special objects made up of lines, arcs, and circles. They can regenerate faster than blocks, and they take up less file space. Unfortunately, shapes are considerably more difficult to create and less flexible to use than blocks.

You create shapes by using a coding system developed by Autodesk. The codes define the sizes and orientations of lines, arcs, and circles. You first sketch your shape, then convert it into the code, and then copy that code into a DOS text file. We won't get into detail on this subject, so if you want to know more about shapes, look in Chapter 3 of your *AutoCAD Customization Manual*.

One way to get around the difficulty of creating shapes is to purchase one of the third-party software products available for this purpose. These are add-on programs capable of converting AutoCAD drawings into shape libraries. They usually require that you draw your shape within a predefined area in a special drawing file supplied with the software. If you intend to do drawings that will be composed mostly of very simple symbols, you may want to look into this alternative. Since AutoCAD fonts are created in the same way shapes are, these programs also make it possible to create your own fonts.

Another way of using symbols is to use AutoCAD's *cross-reference* capabilities. Cross-referenced files are those inserted into a drawing in a way similar to blocks—the difference is that cross-referenced files do not actually become part of the drawing's database. Instead, they are loaded along with the current file at start-up time. It is as if AutoCAD opens several drawings at once: the main file you specify when you start AutoCAD, and any cross-referenced files associated with the main file.

▼ NOTE

Third-party developers of software for making shapes often advertise in *Cadalyst* magazine. You can contact the magazine at *Cadalyst*, Aster Publishing, P.O. Box 10460, Eugene, OR 97440-2460. Telephone: (503) 343-1200.

By keeping cross-referenced files independent from the current file, you make sure that any changes made to the cross-referenced file will automatically appear in the current file. You don't have to update the cross-referenced file as you must for blocks. For example, if you used the Attach option on the External Reference palette (to be discussed in *Chapter 12*) to insert the Tub drawing, and you later made changes to the tub, the next time you opened the Bath file, you would see the new version of the tub.

Cross-referenced files are especially useful in workgroup environments, where several people are working on the same project. One person might be updating several files that have been inserted into a variety of other files. Before cross-referencing was available, everyone in the workgroup would have had to be notified of the changes and update all the affected blocks in all the drawings that contained them. With cross-references, the updating is automatic. There are many other features unique to these files, discussed in more detail in *Chapters* 6 and *12*.

GROUPING OBJECTS

Blocks are an extremely useful tool, but for some situations, they are too restricting. At times, you will want to group objects together so they are connected, yet can still be edited individually. For example, consider a space planner who has to place workstations in a floor plan. Though each workstation is basically the same, there may be some slight variations in each station that would make the use of blocks unwieldy. A better way is to draw a prototype workstation, and then turn it into a group. The group can be copied into position, then edited for each individual situation, without the group's losing its identity as a group. The following exercises demonstrate how this works.

1. Open the office1.DWG drawing from the companion CD.

2. Use the Zoom command to enlarge just the view of the workstation, as shown in panel 1 of Figure 4.8.

3. In the Standard toolbar, choose Object Group.

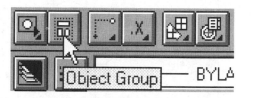

The Object Grouping dialog box appears.

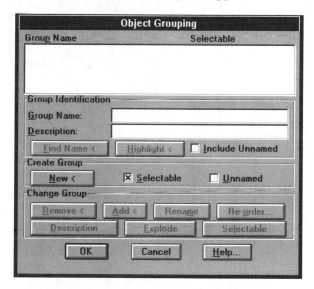

4. Type **Station1**. As you type, your entry appears in the Group Name input box.

5. Click on New in the Create Group button group, about midway in the dialog box. The dialog box temporarily disappears to allow you to select objects for your new group.

6. At the Select objects: prompt, window the entire workstation and press ↵. The Object Grouping dialog box returns.

7. Click OK. You have just created a group.

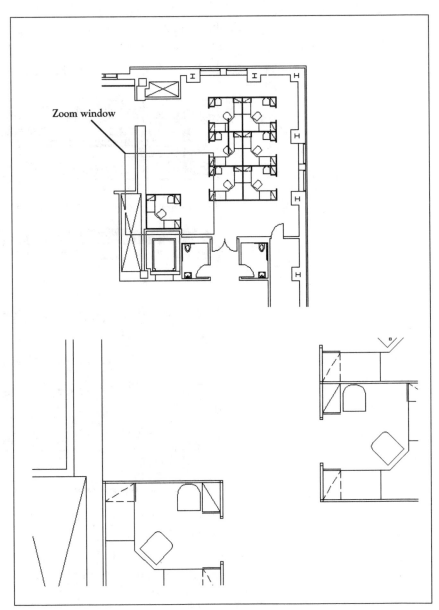

Figure 4.8: A workstation in an office plan

Now, whenever you want to select the workstation, you can click on any part of it and the entire group will be selected. At the same time, you will still be able to modify individual parts of the group—the desk, partition, and so on—without losing the grouping of objects.

Modifying Members of a Group

Next, you will make copies of the original group and modify the copies. Figure 4.9 is a sketch of the proposed layout that uses the new workstations. Look carefully, and you'll see that some of the workstations are missing a few of the standard components that exist in the Station1 group. One pair of stations has a partition removed; another station has no desk. The next exercise shows you how to complete your drawing to reflect the design requirements of the sketch.

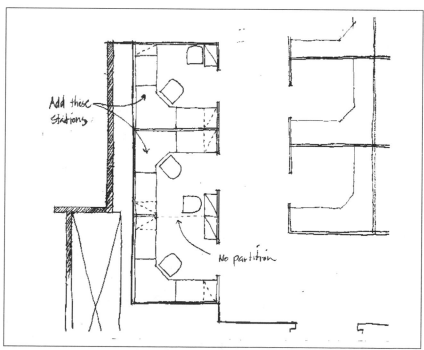

Figure 4.9: A sketch of the new office layout

1. Click on Copy in the Modify palette, and click on the Station1 group you just created. Notice that you can click on any part of the station to select the entire station.

2. At the Base point prompt, enter **@** ↵. Then enter **@8′2″<90** to copy the workstation 8 feet, 2 inches vertically.

3. Issue the COPY command again, but this time click on the copy of the workstation you just created. Notice that it, too, is a group.

4. Copy this workstation 8′2″ vertically, just as you did the original workstation.

5. Next, you'll use Grips to mirror the first workstation copy. Click on the middle workstation to highlight it, and notice that grips appear for all the entities in the group.

6. Click on the grip in the middle-left side, as shown in Figure 4.10.

7. Press ↵ four times until you see the ****MIRROR**** prompt. Notice that a temporary mirror image of the workstation follows the movement of your cursor.

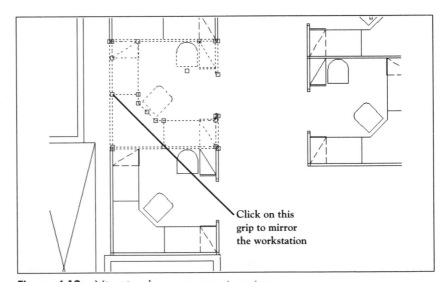

Figure 4.10: Mirroring the new group using grips

8. Turn on the ortho mode, and pick a point directly to the right of the hot grip you picked in step 6. The workstation is mirrored to a new orientation.

Now that you've got the workstations laid out, you need to remove some of the partitions between the new workstations. If you had used blocks for the workstations, you would have to first explode the workstations whose partitions you wish to edit. Groups, however, let you make changes without undoing their grouping.

▼ TIP

You can also use the Pickstyle system variable to control groupings. See *Appendix C* for more on Pickstyle.

1. Press Ctrl-A. This temporarily turns off groupings.

2. Using a window, erase the short partition that divides the two copies of the workstations, as shown in Figure 4.11.

3. Press Ctrl-A again to turn groupings back on.

4. To check your workstations, click on one of them to see if all of its components are highlighted together.

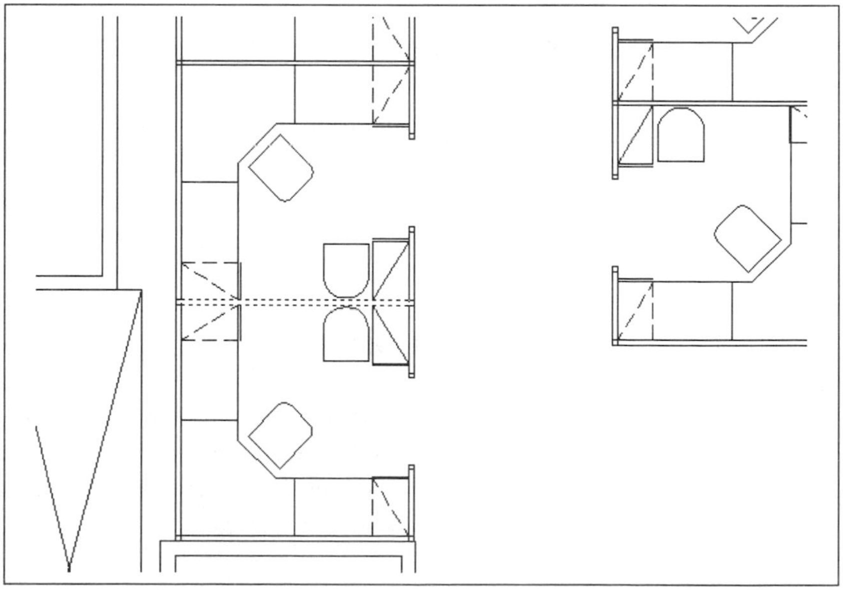

Figure 4.11:   Removing the partitions between two workstations in a group

Working with the Object Grouping Dialog Box

Each group has a unique name, and you can also attach a brief description. When you copy a group, AutoCAD assigns an arbitrary name to the newly created group. Copies of groups are unnamed, but still can be listed in the Object Grouping dialog box by clicking the Unnamed check box. You can use the Rename button in the Object Grouping dialog box to rename new groups appropriately.

Objects within a group are not bound solely to that group. One object can be a member of several groups, and you can have nested groups.

Here are descriptions of the options available in the Object Grouping dialog box.

Group Identification   Use this button group to identify your groups, using unique elements that let you remember what each group is for.

Group Name input box lets you create a new group by naming it first.

Description input box lets you include a brief description of the group.

Find Name button lets you find the name of a group by temporarily closing the dialog box so you can click on a group.

Highlight button highlights a group selected from the group list. This helps you locate a group in a crowded drawing.

Include Unnamed check box determines whether unnamed groups are included in the Group Name list. Check this box to include copies of groups for processing by this dialog box.

Create Group   Here's where you control how a group is created.

New lets you create a new group. It temporarily closes the dialog box so you can select objects for grouping. To use this button, you must have either entered a group name or checked the Unnamed check box.

Selectable check box lets you control whether the group you will create is selectable or not. See the description of the Selectable button in the Change Group just below.

Unnamed check box lets you create a new group without naming it.

Change Group   These buttons are available only when a group name is highlighted in the Group Name list at the top of the dialog box.

Remove lets you remove objects from a group

Add lets you add objects to a group. While using this option, grouping is temporarily turned off to allow you to select objects from other groups.

Rename lets you rename a group.

Reorder lets you change the order of objects in a group.

Description lets you modify the description of a group.

Explode separates a group into its individual components.

Selectable turns individual groupings on and off. When a group is selectable, it is selectable as a group. When a group is not selectable, the individual objects in a group can be selected, but not the group.

ORGANIZING INFORMATION WITH LAYERS

Another AutoCAD tool for organization is the *layer*. Layers are like overlays on which you keep various types of information (see Figure 4.12). In a floor plan of a building, for example, you want to keep the walls, ceiling, plumbing fixtures, wiring, and furniture separate, so you can display or plot them individually or combine them in different ways. It's also a good idea to keep notes and reference symbols about each element of

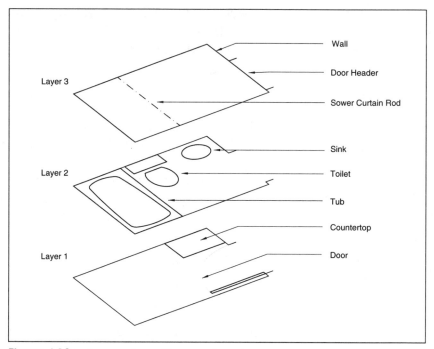

Figure 4.12: A comparison of layers and overlays

the drawing, as well as the drawing's dimensions, on their own layers. As your drawing becomes more complex, the various layers can be turned on and off to allow easier display and modification.

For example, one of your consultants may need a plot of just the dimensions and walls, without all the other information; another consultant may need only a furniture layout. Using manual drafting, you would have to redraw your plan for each consultant. With AutoCAD, you can turn off the layers you don't need and plot a drawing containing only the required information. A carefully planned layering scheme helps you produce a document that combines the different types of information needed in each case.

Using layers also enables you to modify your drawings more easily. For example, suppose you have an architectural drawing with separate layers for the walls, the ceiling plan, and the floor plan. If any change occurs in the wall locations, you can turn on the ceiling plan layer to see where the new wall locations will affect the ceiling, and then make the proper adjustments.

AutoCAD allows an unlimited number of layers, and you can name each layer anything you want.

CREATING AND ASSIGNING LAYERS

To continue with your bathroom, you will create some new layers.

1. Open the Bath file. To display the Layer Control dialog box, click on Data ➤ Layers, or click on the Layers button in the Object Properties toolbar.

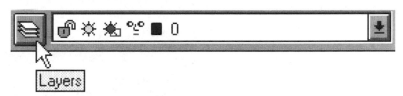

▼ **NOTE**

The Layer Control dialog box shows you at a glance the status of your layers. Right now, you only have two layers, but as your work expands, so will the number of layers. You will then find this dialog box indispensable.

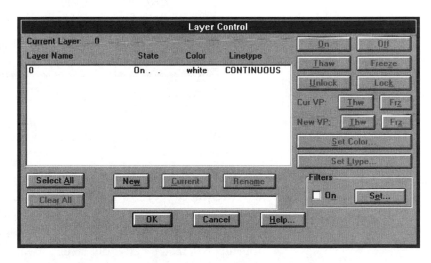

2. Type **Wall**. As you type, your entry appears in the input box at the bottom of the dialog box (just above the OK button).

3. When you are done typing, click on the New button just above the input box. The new layer appears in the large list box in the center of the dialog box.

4. Click on the Wall layer now shown in the list. The item is highlighted, and some of the buttons to the right become available (no longer grayed out).

5. Click on the Set Color button to display the Select Color dialog box, showing you the selection of colors available.

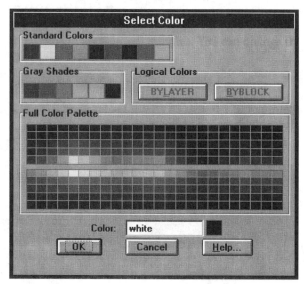

6. In the top row of Standard Colors, click on the green square and then on OK.

7. When the Layer Control dialog box returns, click on OK to close it.

Controlling Layers through the Layer Command

You have seen how the Layer Control dialog box makes it easy to view and edit layer information, and how layer colors can be easily selected from an on-screen palette. But layers can also be controlled through the command prompt.

1. First press Esc to make sure any current command is canceled.

2. At the command prompt, enter **Layer** ↵. The following prompt appears:

   ?/Make/Set/New/ON/OFF/Color/Ltype/Freeze/Thaw/Lock/Unlock:

   You'll learn about many of the options in this prompt as you work through this chapter.

3. Enter **N** ↵ to select the New option.

4. At the New layer name(s) prompt, enter **Wall2** ↵. The ?/Make/Set/New... prompt appears again.

5. Enter **C** ↵.

6. At the Color prompt, enter **Yellow** ↵. Or you can enter **2** ↵, the numeric equivalent to the color yellow in AutoCAD.

7. At the Layer Names for color 2 (yellow) <0>: prompt, enter **Wall2** ↵. The ?/Make/Set/New... prompt appears again.

8. Press ↵ to exit the LAYER command.

Each method of controlling layers has its own advantages: The Layer Control dialog box offers more information about your layers at a glance. On the other hand, the LAYER command offers a quick way to control and create layers if you're in a hurry. Also, if you intend to write custom macros, you will want to know how to use the Layer command as opposed to the dialog box, because dialog boxes cannot be controlled through scripts.

Assigning Layers to Objects

When you create an object, that object is assigned to the current layer. Until now, only one layer has existed, layer 0—which contains all the objects you've drawn so far. Now that you've created some new layers, you can reassign objects to them using the Properties button on the Object Properties toolbar.

1. Choose Properties from the Object Properties toolbar.

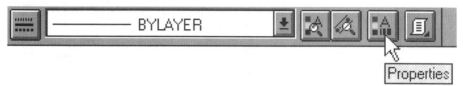

2. At the Select objects prompt, click on the four lines rep-
    resenting the bathroom walls. If you have problems sin-
    gling out the wall to the left, use a window to select the
    wall line.

3. Press ↵ to confirm your selection. The Change Properties dia-
    log box appears.

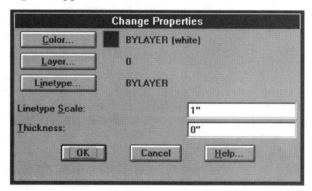

    This dialog box allows you to change the layer assign-
    ment, color, line type, and thickness of an object. You'll
    learn about line types and object thickness in later
    chapters.

4. Click on the Layer button. Next you see the Select Layer dia-
    log box, listing all the existing layers, including the ones you
    just created.

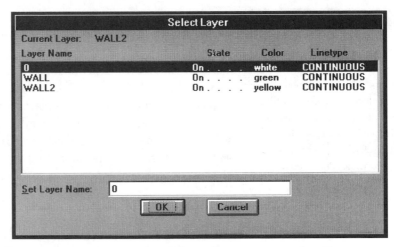

5. Double-click on the Wall layer. You return to the Change Properties dialog box.

6. Click on OK to close the dialog box.

The bathroom walls are now on the new layer, Wall, and the walls are changed to green. Layers are more easily distinguished from one another when colors are used to set them apart.

Next, you will practice the commands you learned in this section by creating some new layers and changing the layer assignments of the rest of the objects in your bathroom.

1. Bring up the Layer Control dialog box (use Data ➤ Layers, or click on the Layers button in the Object Properties toolbar). Create a new layer called **Fixture** and give it the color blue.

2. Use the Change Properties dialog box (click the Properties button on the Object Properties toolbar) to change the tub and toilet to the Fixture layer.

3. Now create a new layer for the door, name the layer **Door,** and make it red.

4. Change the door to the Door layer.

▼ **NOTE**

Within a block, you can change the color assignment and line type of only the objects that are on layer 0. See the sidebar, "Controlling Colors and Line Types of Blocked Objects."

5. Create three more layers for the ceiling, door jambs, and floor. Assign magenta to Ceiling, green to Jamb, and cyan to Floor.

In step 4 above, you used a dialog box that offered several options for modifying the block. When you click the Properties button on the Object Properties toolbar, the dialog box displayed will depend on whether you have selected one object or several. With only one object selected, AutoCAD presents options that apply specifically to that object. With several objects selected, you'll see a more limited set of options, because AutoCAD can change only the properties that are common to all the objects selected.

CONTROLLING COLORS AND LINE TYPES OF BLOCKED OBJECTS

Layer 0 has special importance to blocks. When objects assigned to layer 0 are used as parts of a block, those objects take on the characteristics of the layer on which the block is inserted. On the other hand, if those objects are on a layer other than 0, they will maintain their original layer characteristics even if you insert or change that block to another layer. For example, suppose the tub is drawn on the Door layer, instead of on layer 0. If you turn the tub into a block and insert it on the Fixture layer, the objects the tub is composed of will maintain their assignment to the Door layer, although the Tub block is assigned to the Fixture layer.

It might help to think of the block function as a clear plastic bag that holds together the objects that make up the tub. The objects inside the bag maintain their assignment to the Door layer even while the bag itself is assigned to the Fixture layer.

AutoCAD also allows you to have more than one color or line type on a layer. You can use the Color and Linetype buttons in the Change Properties dialog box (the Object Properties button on the Standard toolbar) to alter the color or line type of an object on layer 0, for example. That object then maintains its assigned color and line type—no matter what its layer assignment. Likewise, objects specifically assigned a color or line type will not be affected by their inclusion into blocks.

I

The Basics

WORKING ON LAYERS

So far you have created layers and then assigned objects to those layers. However, the current layer is still 0, and every new object you draw will be on layer 0. Here's how to change the current layer.

▼ NOTE

You can also use the LAYER command to reset the current layer. To do this here, enter **Layer** at the command prompt, and at the ?/Make… prompt, enter **S** for set. At the New current layer prompt, enter **Jamb** and then press ↵ twice to exit the LAYER command.

1. Click on the arrow button next to the layer name on the Object Properties toolbar. A drop-down list opens, showing you all the layers available in the drawing.

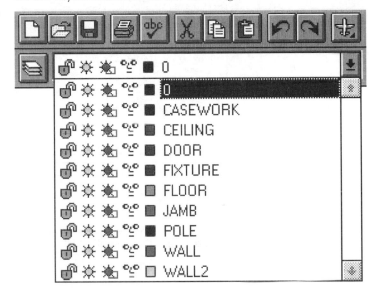

Notice the icons that appear next to the layer names; these control the status of the layer. You'll learn how to work with these icons later in this chapter. Also notice the box directly to the left of each layer name. This shows you the color of the layer.

2. Click on the Jamb layer name. The drop-down list closes, and the name Jamb appears in the toolbar's layer name box. Jamb is now the current layer.

3. Zoom in to the door, and draw a 5″ line; start at the lower-right corner of the door and draw toward the right.

4. Draw a similar line from the top-right end of the arc. Your drawing should look like Figure 4.13.

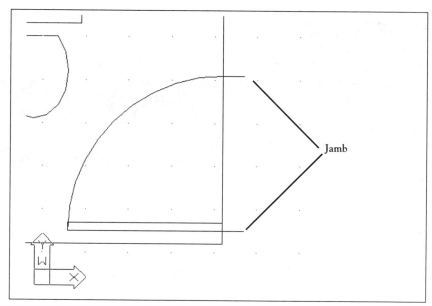

Figure 4.13:   Door at wall with door jamb added

Because you assigned the color green to the Jamb layer, the two lines you just drew to represent the door jambs are green. This gives you immediate feedback about what layer you are on as you draw.

Now you will use the part of the wall between the jambs as a line representing the door header (the part of the wall above the door). To do this, you will have to cut the line into three line segments, and then change the layer assignment of the segment between the jambs.

1. In the Modify palette, click and drag 1 Point and choose 1 Point Select from the flyout.

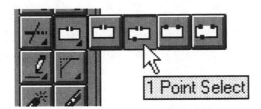

2. At the Select objects prompt, click on the wall between the two jambs.

3. At the Enter first point prompt, use the Endpoint Osnap override to pick the endpoint of the door's arc that is touching the wall.

4. Click on 1 Point Select from the Modify palette, and then repeat steps 2 and 3, this time using the jamb near the door hinge location to locate the break point.

5. Now change the line between the two jambs to the Ceiling layer. When you complete this change, the line turns to magenta, telling you it is now on the Ceiling layer.

6. Click on View ➤ Zoom ➤ Previous to return to the previous view.

The set of buttons under the 1 Point Select option issues the Break command. When you choose any of these options, you'll see Break appear at the command prompt, followed by another prompt. This command allows you to cut an object at a single point. You can also use Break to create a gap in an object.

Now you'll finish the bathroom by adding a sink to a layer named Casework.

1. Using the Layer Control dialog box, create a layer called **Casework**.

2. When the Casework layer name appears in the layer list, highlight it and click on the Current check box.

3. Click on the Set Color button. Using the Set Color dialog box, choose blue and click OK. When you exit the Layer Control dialog box, the status line indicates that the current layer is Casework.

Now you'll add the sink. Notice that as you draw, the objects will appear in blue, the color of the Casework layer.

4. Click on View ➤ Zoom ➤ All.

5. Click on Rectangle in the Draw tool palette, and draw a rectangle 28″×18″ representing a sink countertop. Orient the countertop so that it fits into the upper-right corner of the room, as shown in Figure 4.14. Use coordinate 7′–0″, 5′–4″ for the lower-left corner of the countertop.

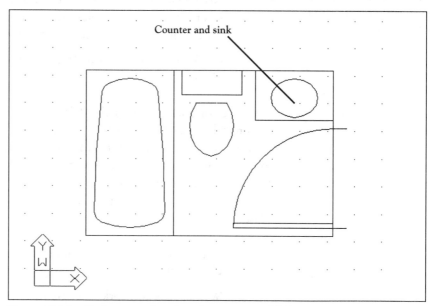

Figure 4.14: Bathroom with sink and countertop added

The Basics

6. Use the Ellipse tool from the Draw palette and draw an ellipse 17″×14″ in the center of the countertop.

7. Use the Change Properties dialog box to change the ellipse to the Fixture layer. Your drawing will look like Figure 4.14.

CONTROLLING LAYER VISIBILITY

We mentioned earlier that at times you'll want to be selective about what layers you are working with on a drawing. In this bathroom, there is a door header that would normally appear only in a reflected ceiling plan. To turn off a layer so that it becomes invisible, use the Off button in the Layer Control dialog box.

1. Open the Layer Control dialog box.

2. Click on the Ceiling layer in the layer list.

3. Click on the Off button to the right of the list.

4. Click on the OK button to exit the dialog box. When you return to the drawing, the header disappears because you have made it invisible by turning off its layer (see Figure 4.15).

You can also control layer visibility using the layer drop-down list on the Object Properties toolbar.

1. On the Object Properties toolbar, click on the arrow button to open the layer name drop-down list.

2. Find the Ceiling layer, and notice the icon that looks like a face with its eyes closed. This tells you that the layer is off and not visible.

3. Click on the face icon; the eyes open.

4. Now click on the drawing area to close the layers list, and the door header reappears.

Figure 4.16 explains the role of the other icons in the layers drop-down list.

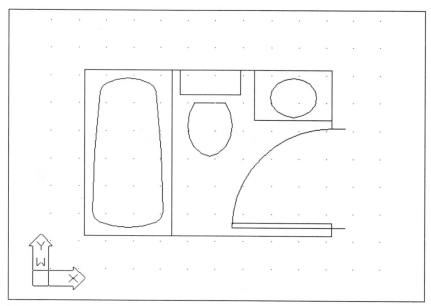

Figure 4.15: Bathroom with Ceiling layer turned off

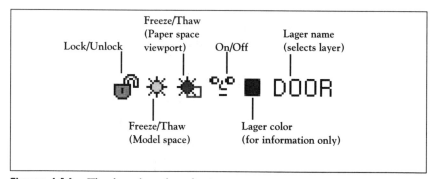

Figure 4.16: The drop-down layer list icons

I

The Basics

FINDING THE LAYERS YOU WANT

With only a handful of layers, its fairly easy to find the layer you want to turn off. This becomes much more difficult, however, when the number of layers exceeds 20 or 30. The Layer Control dialog box offers the Filters option to help you search through your layer names to find specific ones.

To use filters, you click on the Set button of the Filters group at the lower-right of the Layer Control dialog box. In the Set Layer Filters dialog box, you can specify the layers you want to show in the layer list by indicating the layers' characteristics.

Set Layer Filters	
On/Off:	Both
Freeze/Thaw:	Both
Lock/Unlock:	Both
Current Vport:	Both
New Vports:	Both
Layer Names:	*
Colors:	*
Ltypes:	*
Reset	
OK	Cancel	Help...

▼ **TIP**

The asterisk in **C-*** is called a *wildcard character*. Wildcards can be used to help locate names in DOS and AutoCAD.

Now suppose you have several layers whose names begin with C-, such as C-lights, C-header, and C-pattern, and you want to display only those layers in the Layer Control dialog box. To do this, you enter **C-*** in the Layer Names input box and then click on OK. Now only the layers whose names begin with C- will appear in the list of layers. You can then easily turn all these layers off, and change their color assignment or other settings quickly, without involving other layers you don't want to touch.

The other two input boxes, Colors and Ltypes, let you control what layers appear in the list by virtue of their color or line-type assignments.

In the five drop-down lists at the top of the dialog box, you can designate the layers to include in the layer list by virtue of the status: On/Off, Freeze/Thawed, Locked/Unlocked, and so forth. See the sidebar, "Other Layer Options."

As the number of layers in a drawing grows, you will find layer filters to be an indispensable tool. Also, keep in mind the wildcard feature as you name layers: You can use it to group layers and later quickly select those groups to turn on and off.

Now try changing the layer settings again, turning off all the layers except Wall and Ceiling and leaving just a simple rectangle. In the exercise, you'll get a chance to experiment with the On/Off options of the Layer Control dialog box.

▼ NOTE

To delete all the objects on a layer, set the current layer to the one you want to edit, and then freeze or lock all the others. Click on Erase in the Modify palette. Then click and drag Select Window in the Standard toolbar and choose Select All from the flyout.

1. Click on the Layers button in the Object Properties toolbar, or on Data ➤ Layers in the pull-down menus.

2. Click on the Select All button in the bottom-left corner of the dialog box, to highlight the entire list of layers.

3. Click on the Wall and Ceiling layers, to deselect them and thus exempt them from your next action.

4. Click on the Off button in the upper-right corner of the dialog box. The list changes to show that the selected layers have been turned off.

5. Click on the OK button. A message appears, warning you that the current layer will be turned off. Click OK. The drawing now appears with only the Wall and Ceiling layers displayed (see Figure 4.17).

6. Open the Layer Control dialog box again, click on the Select All button, and then click on the On button to turn on all the layers at once.

7. Click on OK to return to the drawing.

The Basics

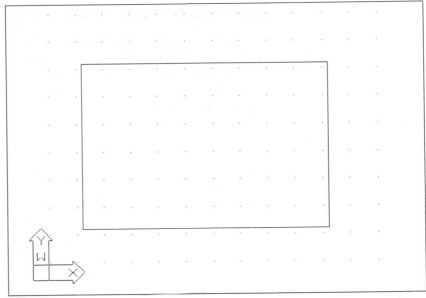

Figure 4.17: Bathroom with all layers except Wall and Ceiling turned off

▼ OTHER LAYER OPTIONS

You may have noticed the Freeze and Thaw buttons in the Layer Control dialog box. These options are similar to the On and Off buttons—however, Freeze not only makes layers invisible, it also tells AutoCAD to ignore the contents of those layers when you use the **All** response to the Select object: prompt. Freezing layers can also save time when you issue a command that regenerates a complex drawing. This is because AutoCAD ignores objects on frozen layers during a regen. You will get firsthand experience with Freeze and Thaw in *Chapter 6*.

Another pair of Layer Control options, Lock and Unlock, offer a function similar to Freeze and Thaw. If you lock a layer, you will be able to view and snap to objects on that layer, but you won't be able to edit those objects. This feature is useful when you are working on a crowded drawing and you don't want to accidentally edit portions of it. You can lock all the layers except those you intend to edit, and then proceed to work without fear of making accidental changes.

ASSIGNING LINE TYPES TO LAYERS

You will often want to use different line types to show hidden lines, center lines, fence lines or other noncontinuous lines. You can set a layer to have not only a color assignment but also a line-type assignment. AutoCAD comes with several line types, as shown in Figure 4.18. You can also create your own line types (see *Chapter 21*).

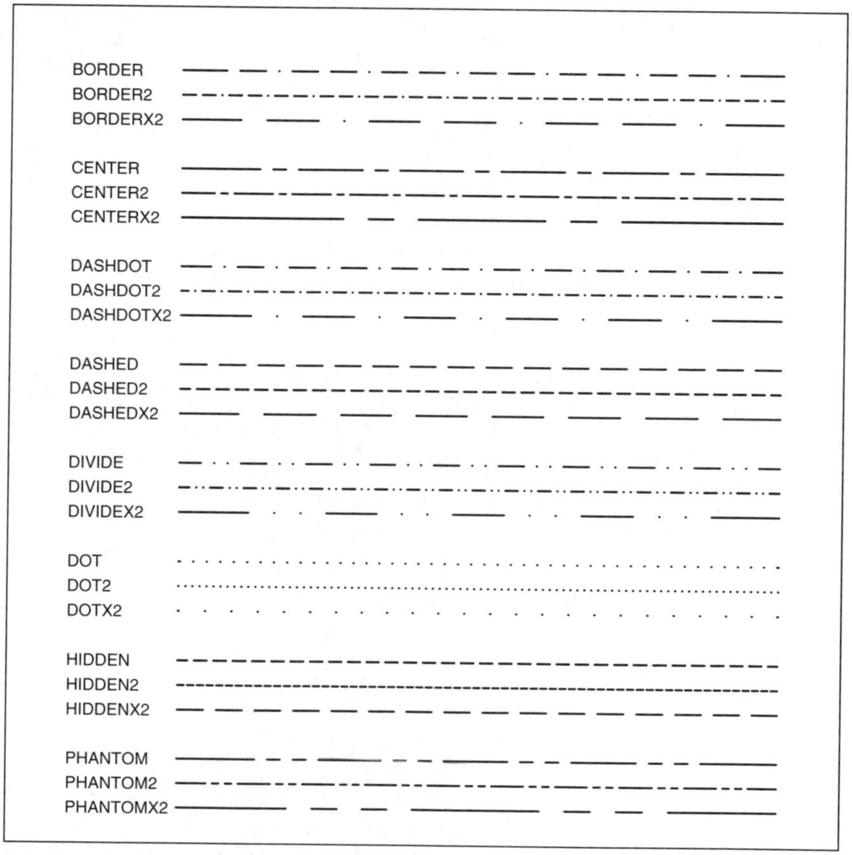

Figure 4.18: Standard AutoCAD line types

AutoCAD stores line-type descriptions in an external file named ACAD.LIN. You can edit this file in a word processor to create new line types or to modify existing ones. You will see how this is done in *Chapter 21*.

To see how line types work, add a dash-dot line in the bathroom plan to indicate a shower-curtain rod.

▼ TIP

If you are in a hurry, you can simultaneously load a line type and assign it to a layer by using the LAYER command. In this exercise, you would enter **Layer** ↵ at the command prompt, then enter **L** ↵, **dashdot** ↵, **pole** ↵, and then ↵ to exit the LAYER command.

1. Click on Data ➤ Layers.

2. Enter **Pole** in the input box and click on New. Click on the Pole layer to highlight it in the layer list.

3. Click on the Set Ltype button to display the Select Linetype dialog box, showing the line types that have already been loaded into the drawing.

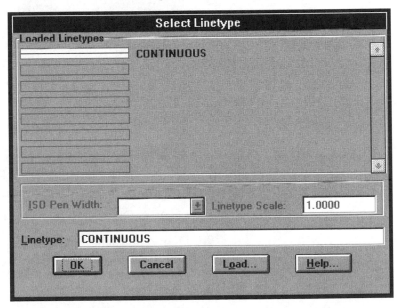

4. Click on the Load button at the bottom of the dialog box. The Load or Reload Linetype dialog box appears.

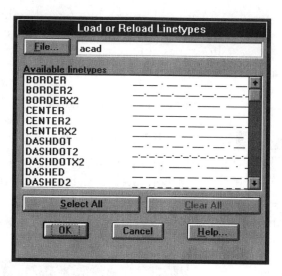

5. In the Available Linetypes list, click to highlight the sample view of the DASHDOT line type, and then click OK.

6. Notice that the DASHDOT line type is now added to the line types available in the Select Linetype dialog box. Click to highlight this line type, and then click on OK to exit the Select Linetype dialog box.

7. In the Layer Control dialog box, make sure the Pole layer is the current default layer by clicking on the Current button. DASHDOT is now listed as the line type for the Pole layer.

8. Click on OK to exit the dialog box.

9. Draw a line across the opening of the tub area, from coordinate 4′–4″, 1′–10″ to coordinate 4′–4″, 6′–10″.

Although you have designated that this line is to be a DASHDOT line, it appears to be solid. Zoom in to a small part of the line, and you'll see that the line is indeed as you specified.

Since you are working at a scale of 1″=1′, you must adjust the scale of your line types accordingly. This, too, is accomplished in the Layer Control dialog box.

▼ **TIP**

You can also use the Ltscale system variable to set the line-type scale. Type **Ltscale** ↵, and at the LTSCALE New scale factor <1.0000> prompt, enter **12** ↵.

1. Click on the Linetype button in the Object Properties tool-bar, or on Data ➤ Linetype in the pull-down menus. The Select Linetype dialog box appears.

2. Double-click on the Linetype Scale input box, and type **12** ↵. This is the scale conversion factor for a 1"=1' scale (see Table 3.3).

3. Click on OK, then again on OK at the Layer Control dialog box. The drawing regenerates, and the shower-curtain rod is displayed in the line type and at the scale you designated. Your drawing will look like Figure 4.19.

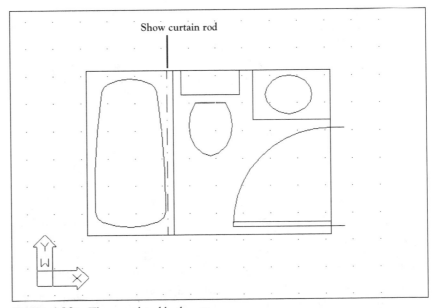

Figure 4.19:   The completed bathroom

▼ **TIP**

If you change the line type of a layer or object but the object remains a continuous line, check the Ltscale system variable. It should be set to your drawing scale factor. If this doesn't work, set the Viewres system variable to a higher value (see *Chapter* 6).

new

▼ **TIP**

The Linetype Scale setting in the Object Creation dialog box can also be set using the Celtscale system variable.

Remember that if you assign a line type to a layer, everything you draw on that layer will be of that line type. This includes arcs, polylines, circles, and traces. As explained in the "Setting Individual Colors, Line Types, and Line-Type Scales" sidebar, you can also assign different colors and line types to individual objects, rather than relying on their layer assignment to define color and line type. However, you may want to avoid assigning colors and line types directly to objects until you have some experience with AutoCAD and a good grasp of your drawing's organization.

The ability to assign line-type scales to individual objects is new in Release 13. You change the line-type scale of an object, using the Properties button on the Object Properties toolbar. Or you can set a default line-type scale for all new objects, with the Data ➤ Object Creation command or the Object Creation button on the Object Properties toolbar. At the Object Creation dialog box, you change the value in the Linetype Scale input box as desired.

When individual objects are assigned a line-type scale, they are still affected by the global line-type scale set by the Ltscale system variable. For example, say you assign a line-type scale of 2 to the curtain rod in the previous example. This scale would then be multiplied by the global line-type scale of 12, for a final line-type scale of 48.

If the objects you draw appear in a different line type from that of the layer they are on, check the default line type, using the Object Creations Modes dialog box. Click on Data ➤ Object Creation or use the Object Creation button on the Object Properties toolbar. This dialog box is similar to the Change Properties dialog box you saw earlier, and is described in detail in *Chapter 15*. The Linetype... button opens the same Select Linetype dialog box you saw earlier. In the Linetype input box, choose Bylayer. Also, check the line-type scale of the object itself, using the Properties button. A different line-type scale can make a line appear to have an assigned line type that may not be what you expect. See the sidebar, "Setting Individual Colors, Line Types, and Line-Type Scales."

If you are working through the tutorial, your last task here is to set up an insertion point for the current drawing, to facilitate its insertion into other drawings in the future.

1. Type **Base** ↵.

2. At the Base point <0'–0",0'–0">: prompt, pick the upper-left corner of the bathroom. The bathroom drawing is now complete.

SETTING INDIVIDUAL COLORS, LINE TYPES, AND LINE-TYPE SCALES

If you prefer, you can set up AutoCAD to assign specific colors and line types to objects, instead of having objects take on the color and line-type settings of the layer on which they reside. Normally, objects are given a default color and line type called Bylayer, which means each object takes on the color or line type of its assigned layer. (You've probably noticed the word Bylayer in the Object Properties toolbar.)

Use the Properties button on the Object Properties toolbar to change the color or line type of existing objects. This button opens a dialog box that lets you set the properties of individual objects. For new objects, use the Color button on the Object Properties toolbar to set the current default color to red (for example), instead of Bylayer. The Color button opens the Select Color dialog box, where you select your color from a palette. Then everything you draw will be red, regardless of the current layer color.

For line types, you can use the Line Type drop-down list in the Object Properties toolbar to select a default line type for all new objects. The list only shows line types that have already been loaded into the drawing, so you must have first loaded a line type before you can select it.

▼

■

■

■

■

Another possible color and line-type assignment is Byblock, which is also set with the Properties button. Byblock makes everything you draw white, until you turn your drawing into a block and then insert the block on a layer with an assigned color. The objects then take on the color of that layer. This behavior is similar to that of objects drawn on layer 0. The Byblock line type works similarly to the Byblock color.

Finally, if you want to set the line-type scale for each individual object, instead of relying on the global line-type scale (the Ltscale system variable), you can use the Properties button to modify the line-type scale of individual objects. Or you can use the Object Creation Modes dialog box (via the Object Creation button in the Object Properties toolbar) to set the line-type scale to be applied to new objects. In place of using the Properties button, you can set the Celtscale system variable to the line-type scale you want for new objects.

▼ TIP

If you just want to quickly check what layer an object is on, click on the Properties button in the Standard toolbar, and then click on the object in question. You will get a dialog box showing you the basic properties of the object, including its layer setting.

▼ NOTE

The Space property you see listed for the Tub block designates whether the object resides in Model Space or Paper Space. You'll learn more about these spaces in *Chapters* 6 and 12.

KEEPING TRACK OF BLOCKS AND LAYERS

The Insert and the Layer Control dialog boxes let you view the blocks and layers available in your drawing, by listing them in a window. The Layer Control dialog box also includes information on the status of layers. However, you may forget what layer an object resides on. The List button on the Object Properties toolbar enables you to get information about individual objects, as well as blocks.

1. Choose List from the Object Properties toolbar.

2. At the object-selection prompt, click on the tub and then press ↵. The AutoCAD Text Window appears.

3. In the Text Window, you will see not only the layer that the tub is on, but its space, insertion point, name, color, line type, rotation angle, and scale.

USING THE LOG FILE FEATURE

Eventually, you will want a permanent record of block and layer listings. This is especially true if you work on drawing files that are being used by others. Here's a way to get a permanent record of the layers and blocks within a drawing, using the Log File option under the Environment Preferences:

1. Minimize the Text Window (click on the down arrow in the upper-right corner).

2. Click on Options ➤ Preferences. The Preferences dialog box appears. Notice the file folder-style tabs along the top of the dialog box. Each tab opens a different page of options.

3. Click on the Environment tab at the top of the dialog box.

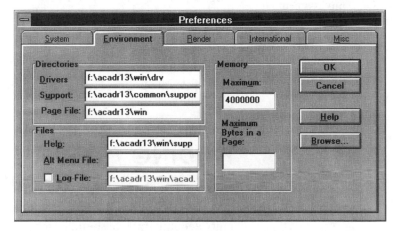

4. Click on the Log File Open check box in the lower-left corner of the Environment page. An X appears in the check box, and the location of the log file appears next to it.

5. Click on OK; then type **Layer** ↵ at the command prompt, then **?** ↵ ↵. The AutoCAD Text Window appears, and a listing of all the layers scrolls into view.

6. Press F2 to return to the AutoCAD drawing screen. Then click on Options ➤ Preferences to reopen the Preferences dialog box.

7. Click on the Environment tab again, uncheck the Log File Open check box, and click on OK.

8. Use the Windows Notepad to open the AutoCAD log file, ACAD.LOG, located in the \ACADR13\WIN directory. You will see that the layer listing is recorded there.

With the Log File feature, you can record virtually anything that appears in the command prompt. You can even record an entire AutoCAD session. The log file can also be helpful in constructing script files to automate tasks. To have hard copy of the log file, print it from an application such as Windows Notepad or your favorite word processor.

If you wish, you can arrange to keep the ACAD.LOG file in a directory other than the default AutoCAD Support subdirectory. This setting, too, is on the Environment page of the Preferences dialog box. There you can set the path and file name for the log file.

And here's a tip: Once you've settled on a location on disk for the log file, use the File Manager to associate the log file with the Windows Notepad or Write application. Then click and drag the file to the AutoCAD program group. This gives you quick access to your log file by simply double-clicking on its icon in the AutoCAD program group.

▼ NOTE

See *Appendix B* for more on AutoCAD Environment settings.

FINDING FILES ON YOUR HARD DISK

As your library of symbols and files grows, you may begin to have difficulty keeping track of them. Fortunately, AutoCAD offers a utility that lets you quickly locate a file anywhere in your computer. The Find File utility searches your hard disk for specific files. You can have it search one drive or several, or you can limit the search to one directory. You can limit the search to specific file names or use DOS wildcards to search for files with similar names.

The following exercise steps you through a sample Find File task:

▼ TIP

Find File can also be accessed using the Find File button in any AutoCAD file dialog box.

1. Click on File ➤ Open. In the Select File dialog box, click on Find File to display the Browse/Search dialog box.

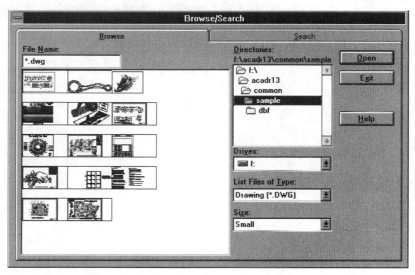

The Basics

The Browse/Search dialog box has two tabs, Browse and Search. In the Browse page are all the drawings in the current directory, displayed as thumbnail views so you can easily identify them. You can open a file by double-clicking on its thumbnail view, or by entering its name in the File Name input box at the top.

The Size drop-down list in the Browse page of the Browse/Search dialog box lets you choose the size of the thumbnail views shown in the list box—small, medium and large. You can scroll through the views using the scroll bars at the top and side of the list box.

2. Click on the Search tab to open the page of Search functions. Use the Search Pattern input box to enter the name of the file for which you wish to search. The default is *.DWG, which will cause Find File to search for all AutoCAD drawing files. Several other input boxes help you set a variety of other search criteria, such as the date stamp of the drawing, the type of drawing, and the drive and path to be searched. For now, leave these settings as is.

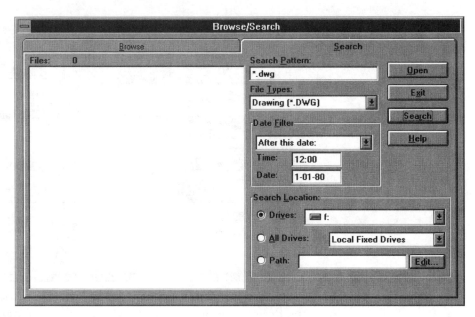

3. Click on the Search button. In a few seconds, a listing of files that meet the criteria specified in the input boxes appears in the Files list on the left, along with thumbnail views of each file. You can click on a file name in the list, and then click on the Open button to open the file in the drawing editor.

4. When ready, click on Exit to exit the Browse/Search dialog box, and then click on Cancel to exit the Open File dialog box.

In this exercise you performed a search using the default settings. These settings caused AutoCAD to search for files with the .DWG file name extension, created after midnight on January 1, 1980, in the \ACADWIN directory.

Here are descriptions of the items in the Browse/Search dialog box:

Search Pattern lets you give specific file-name search criteria using DOS wildcard characters.

File Types lets you select from a set of standard file types.

Time and Date let you specify a cutoff time and date. Files created before the specified time and date are ignored.

Drives lets you specify the drives to search.

All Drives lets you search all the drives on your computer.

Path lets you specify a path to search.

The **Search** button begins the search process.

The **Open** button opens the file highlighted in the file list, after a search is performed.

The **Help** button provides information on the use of Browse/Search.

The **Edit** button next to the Path box opens another dialog box, displaying a directory tree from which you can select a search path.

INSERTING SYMBOLS WITH DRAG AND DROP

If you prefer to manage your symbols library using the Windows File Manager, or to use another third-party file manager for locating and managing your symbols, you'll appreciate AutoCAD's support for Drag and Drop. With this feature, you can click and drag a file from the File Manager into the AutoCAD window. AutoCAD will automatically start the Insert command to insert the file. Drag and Drop also works with a variety of other AutoCAD support files. Table 4.1 shows a list of files with which you can use Drag and Drop, and the functions associated with them.

Table 4.1: AutoCAD Support for Drag and Drop

File Type	Command Issued	Function Performed When File Is Dropped
.DXF	Dxfin	Imports .DXF files
.DWG	Insert, Plot	Imports or plots drawing files
.TXT	Dtext	Imports texts via Dtext
.LIN	Linetype	Loads line types
.MNU, .MNX	Menu	Loads menus

Table 4.1: AutoCAD Support for Drag and Drop (continued)

File Type	Command Issued	Function Performed When File Is Dropped
.PS	Psin	Imports PostScript files
.PSB, .SHP, .SHX	Style	Loads fonts or shapes
.SCR	Script	Runs script
.LSP	(Load..)	Loads AutoLISP routine
.EXE, .EXP	(Xload..)	Loads ADS application

IF YOU WANT TO EXPERIMENT...

▼ TIP

Use the Osnap modes you learned about in *Chapter 2* to select the insertion points.

If your application is not architecture, you may want to experiment with creating some other types of symbols. You might also start thinking about a layering system that suits your particular needs.

Open a new file called Mytemp. In it, create layers named 1 through 8 and assign each layer the color that corresponds to its number. For example, give layer 1 the color 1 (red), layer 2 the color 2 (yellow) and so on. Draw each part shown in Figure 4.20, and turn each part into a file on disk using the WBLOCK command. When WBLOCK prompts you for a file name, use the name indicated for each part in the figure. For the insertion point, also use the points indicated in the figure. Use the Osnap modes (*Chapter 2*) to select the insertion points.

When you are done creating the parts, exit the file using File ➤ Exit, and then open a new file. Set up the drawing as an engineering drawing with a scale of $\frac{1}{4}''=1''$ on an $11''\times17''$ sheet. Create the drawing in Figure 4.21 using the Insert Block command to place your newly created parts.

The Basics

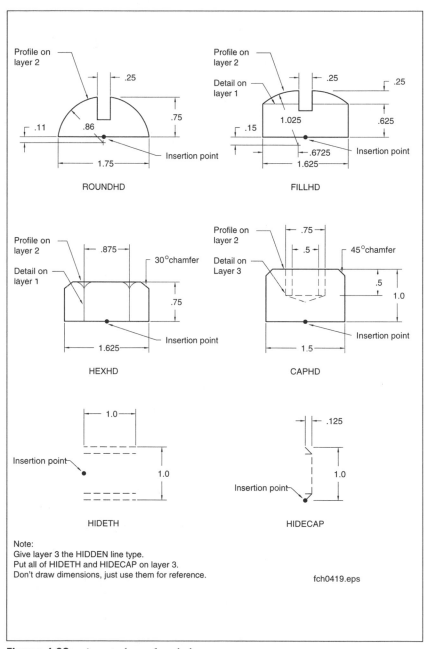

Figure 4.20: A typical set of symbols

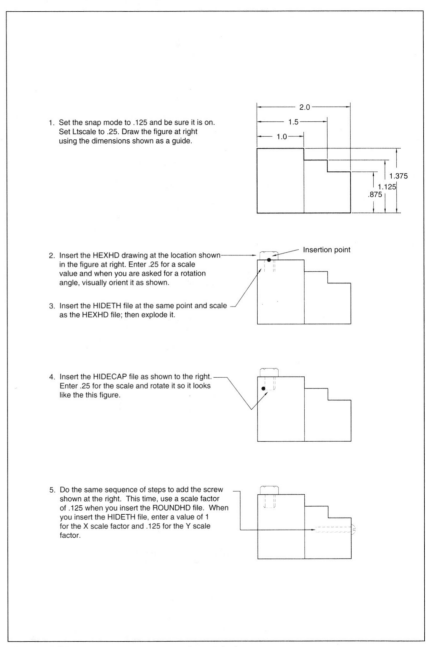

1. Set the snap mode to .125 and be sure it is on. Set Ltscale to .25. Draw the figure at right using the dimensions shown as a guide.

2. Insert the HEXHD drawing at the location shown in the figure at right. Enter .25 for a scale value and when you are asked for a rotation angle, visually orient it as shown.

3. Insert the HIDETH file at the same point and scale as the HEXHD file; then explode it.

4. Insert the HIDECAP file as shown to the right. Enter .25 for the scale and rotate it so it looks like the this figure.

5. Do the same sequence of steps to add the screw shown at the right. This time, use a scale factor of .125 when you insert the ROUNDHD file. When you insert the HIDETH file, enter a value of 1 for the X scale factor and .125 for the Y scale factor.

Figure 4.21: Draw this part using the symbols you create

PART TWO

BUILDING
■
ON THE
■
BASICS

Once you have the basics down, you will begin to explore AutoCAD in more detail. *Chapter 5, Editing for Productivity*, tells you how to reuse drawing setup information and parts of an existing drawing. In *Chapter 6, Enhancing Your Drawing Skills*, you will learn how to assemble and edit a large drawing file. *Chapter 7, Printing and Plotting*, shows you how to get your drawing onto hard copy. *Chapter 8, Adding Text to Drawings*, tells you how to annotate your drawing and edit your notes. *Chapter 9, Using Dimensions*, gives you practice in using automatic dimensioning, another unique CAD capability. Along the way, I will be giving you tips on editing and problems you may encounter as you begin to use AutoCAD for more complex tasks.

5

EDITING FOR PRODUCTIVITY

Using Existing Drawings as Prototypes for New Drawings

Making Circular or Column and Row Copies

Using Construction Lines

Marking Regular Intervals along a Line or Arc

Drawing Parallel Lines

Removing Unused Elements Such As Blocks and Layers

Understanding Methods for Constructing New Drawings

FAST TRACK

193 ▶ To use an existing file as a prototype for a new file

Click on File ➤ New. In the Create New Drawing dialog box, make sure the No Prototype check box is unchecked. Then enter the file name of the existing prototype file in the input box at the top.

195 ▶ To open a file and protect it from accidental editing

Click on File ➤ Open, select the file you want, and click on the Read Only mode check box.

196 ▶ To create a circular pattern of copies

Click and drag on Copy Object from the Modify palette then select Polar Array. Select the objects you want to copy. Enter the total number of items you want, enter the degrees to fill, and specify whether or not you want the copies rotated as they are copied.

197 ▶ To create row and column copies

Click and drag Copy Object from the Modify palette then select Rectangular Array. Select the objects you want to copy. Specify the number of vertical rows and horizontal columns you want, and enter the row and column spacing.

205 ▶ To create randomly spaced copie

Click on Copy Object from the Modify palette and select the objects. Enter **M** ↵ and then click on the locations where you want the copies. You can also use the move mode of the Grips feature to make multiple random copies.

207 ▶ To reuse layers from another drawing

Insert the drawing containing the layers and other settings you want. If the inserted drawing contains objects you don't want, use Data ➤ Purge to remove them.

211 ▶ To construct walls from existing single lines

Click and drag Copy Object from the Modify palette then select Offset. Place parallel copies of lines at wall thickness, and then use Fillet from the Chamfer flyout of the Modify palette to join lines end to end for corners.

219 ▶ To extend lines to points in space

Draw a Ray or Construction Line pointing in a direction that intersects another line at the desired point in space. Then use the FILLET command to join the construction line with the line you want to extend.

222 ▶ To draw an opening in a wall

Use the Offset option of the Construction Line (Xline) command to create a new construction line perpendicular to the wall where you want the opening. Offset the new Xline to the width of the opening, and then use Modify ▶ Break to break the wall lines between the two Xlines. Then use Trim from the Modify palette to trim the construction lines to the wall.

228 ▶ To locate an exact distance along an arc

Click and drag Point from the Draw palette then select Measure. Then click on the arc near the endpoint you wish to measure from. Enter the distance you want to measure. You'll see Xs appear along the arc at the distance specified.

231 ▶ To export part of a drawing as a drawing file for use in other drawings

Click on File ▶ Export... and enter a name for the new file, including the .DWG extension. At the Block name prompt, press ↵ and select a base point; then select the objects you want to export. Type **Oops** ↵ at the command prompt to restore the exported objects.

There are at least five commands devoted to duplicating objects, ten if you include the Grips options. Why so many? If you're an experienced drafter, you know that technical drawing is often tedious. So AutoCAD offers a variety of ways to reuse existing geometry, thereby automating much of the repetitive work usually associated with manual drafting.

In this chapter, as you finish drawing the studio apartment unit, you will explore some of the ways to exploit existing files and objects while constructing your drawing. For example, you will use existing files as prototypes for new files, eliminating the need to set up layers, scales, and sheet sizes for similar drawings. With AutoCAD you can also duplicate objects in multiple arrays. You have already seen how to use the Osnap overrides on objects to locate points for drawing complex forms. We will look at other ways of using lines to aid your drawing.

And, because you will begin to use Zoom more in the exercises of this chapter, we will review this command as we go along. We'll also introduce you to the PAN command—another tool to help you get around in your drawing.

You're already familiar with many of the commands you will use to draw the apartment unit. So, rather than going through every step of the drawing process, we will sometimes ask you to copy the drawing from a figure, using notes and dimensions as guides and putting objects on the indicated layers. If you have trouble remembering a command you've already learned, just go back and review the appropriate section of the book.

USING AN EXISTING DRAWING AS A PROTOTYPE

AutoCAD allows you to use an existing drawing as the starting point, or *prototype*, for a new drawing. A prototype is a file that contains the necessary settings or objects for making a drawing. In fact, AutoCAD uses a prototype drawing called Acad.DWG for all new files.

You can also use your own files as prototypes. For example, you may want to create a second drawing with the same scale and sheet size as an existing drawing. You may even want to use some of the objects, layers, and blocks in it. By using the existing file to begin your new one, you can save a lot of time.

CHANGING THE STANDARD AUTOCAD PROTOTYPE DRAWING

In earlier exercises where you created new files, you have typically worked with the No Prototype option turned on in the Create New File dialog box. This ensured that you were working with the standard AutoCAD settings. With the No Prototype option turned on, Auto-CAD ignores the Acad.DWG prototype file and constructs a new drawing based on its own built-in default settings. With No Prototype left turned off, AutoCAD uses the Acad.DWG file as the prototype for the new drawing. The Acad.DWG file itself is left untouched.

If you are working on a system with a nonstandard Acad.DWG prototype file (also known as a template file), and you want to create a file based on the standard AutoCAD file, you can still do so by ensuring the No Prototype option is checked. But you may have several sets of default settings you would like to maintain. In this case, you can create several empty drawing files, each with its own default settings. One may have layers already set up; another may have predefined blocks ready to use. When you want to use one of these files as a prototype, you proceed as if you were opening a new file, and at the Create New File dialog box, you uncheck No Prototype. Then enter the name of the prototype in the input box just above the No Prototype check box.

The following exercise guides you through creating and using a prototype drawing for your studio's kitchenette. Because the kitchenette will use the same layers, settings, scale, and sheet size as the bathroom drawing, you can use the Bath file as a prototype.

▼ TIP

If you find most of the default AutoCAD settings unsatisfactory for your application, you can open Acad.DWG and reset the defaults as you please. Then, leave the No Prototype check box unchecked whenever you create a new file.

1. Start AutoCAD in the usual way.

2. Click on File ➤ New. The Create New Drawing dialog box appears.

Building on the Basics

II

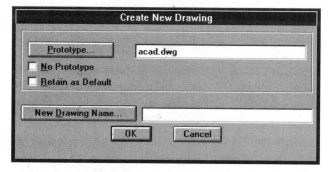

3. If the No Prototype check box is checked, click on it to turn it off. This tells AutoCAD you want to use a prototype file.

4. Click on the input box beside the Prototype button at the top of the dialog box, and type **Bath** as the name of the file you want to use as a prototype. You can also click on the Prototype... button to open the Prototype Drawing File dialog box, from which you can locate a particular file.

5. Click on the file name input box at the bottom of the dialog box, and type **kitchen** as the name of your new drawing.

6. Click OK, and the bathroom drawing appears on the screen.

▼ TIP

This dialog box also gives you the option of completely replacing an existing file, by clicking on the New Drawing Name... button. This opens a typical File dialog box in which you select the name of the file to be replaced. But you'll want to use this option carefully, because you run the risk of overwriting important existing files.

Although the bathroom drawing now in the drawing editor looks like the Bath drawing, this does not mean that you have opened the Bath file. Because the Kitchen file is using the Bath file as a prototype, the Kitchen drawing contains everything that's in the Bath drawing, including its objects. You don't need these objects, however, so erase them. Your new kitchenette file still contains the layers and settings used in the Bath file, and is already set up for a 1″=1′ drawing on an $8^1/_2 \times 11″$ drawing area.

▼

■

■

■

■

OPENING A FILE AS READ-ONLY

When you open an existing file, you might have noticed the Read Only Mode check box in the Open Drawing dialog box. If you open a file with this option checked, AutoCAD will not let you save the file under its original name. You can still edit the drawing any way you please, but if you attempt to use File ➤ Save, you will get the message "Drawing file is write-protected." You can, however, save your changed file under another name.

The read-only mode provides a way to protect important files from accidental corruption. It also offers another method for reusing settings and objects from existing files by letting you open a file as a prototype, then saving the file under another name.

COPYING AN OBJECT MULTIPLE TIMES

Now let's explore the tools that let you quickly duplicate objects. First you will draw the gas range top. In the process you will learn how to use the ARRAY command to create *arrays* (or multiple copies) of an object, and to control the number and orientation of the copies.

MAKING CIRCULAR COPIES

To start the range top, you have to first set the layer on which you want to draw, and then draw a circle representing the edge of one burner.

1. Set the current layer to Fixture, and toggle the snap mode on.

2. Click on Circle Center Radius from the Draw palette.

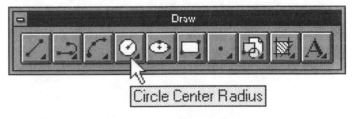

▼ NOTE

An array can be in either a circular pattern called a *polar array*, or a matrix of columns and rows called a *rectangular array*.

▼ TIP

You can also enter **C** ↵ at the command prompt to start the CIRCLE command. The Center, Radius options are the defaults for CIRCLE.

II

Building on the Basics

3. At the 3P/2P/TTR/<Center point>: prompt, pick a point at coordinate 4',4'.

4. At the Diameter/<Radius>: Drag prompt, enter **3** ↵. The circle appears.

Now you're ready to use the ARRAY command to draw the burner grill. You will first draw one line representing part of the grill, and then use Array to create the copies.

1. Draw a line 4" long starting from the coordinate 4'–1", 4'–0" and ending to the right of that point.

2. Zoom into the circle and line to get a better view. Your drawing should look like Figure 5.1.

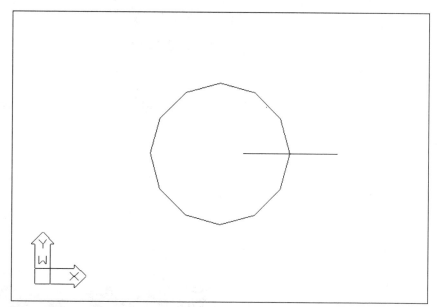

Figure 5.1: A close-up of the circle and line

▼ **TIP**

You can also type **Array** ↵ to start the ARRAY command. Then, after confirming your selection of objects in step 5, type **P** ↵.

3. Click and drag Copy Object from the Modify palette, then select Polar Array.

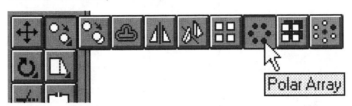

4. At the Select object: prompt, enter **L** ↵. This highlights the line you just drew.

5. Press ↵ to confirm your selection.

6. At the Center point of array prompt, pick the center of the circle using the Center Osnap override. Be sure you click on the circle's circumference.

7. At the Number of items prompt, enter **8** ↵. This tells Auto-CAD you want seven copies plus the original.

8. At the Angle to fill (+=ccw,-=cw) <360>: prompt, press ↵ to accept the default. The default value of 360 tells Auto-CAD to copy the objects so that they are spaced evenly over a 360° arc. (If you had instead entered 180°, the lines would be evenly spaced over a 180° arc, filling only half the circle.)

9. At the Rotate objects as they are copied? <Y>: prompt, press ↵ again to accept the default. The line copies around the center of the circle, rotating as it copies. Your drawing will look like Figure 5.2.

▼ **NOTE**

If you want to copy in a clockwise (CW) direction, you must enter a minus sign (−) before the number of degrees.

▼ **NOTE**

In step 9, you could have the line maintain its horizontal orientation as it is copied around, by entering **N** ↵. But since you want it to rotate about the array center, accept the default, **Y**.

MAKING ROW AND COLUMN COPIES

Now you will draw the other three burners of the gas range by creating a rectangular array from the burner you just drew. You will first zoom back a bit to get a view of a larger area. Then you will proceed with the ARRAY command.

II

Building on the Basics

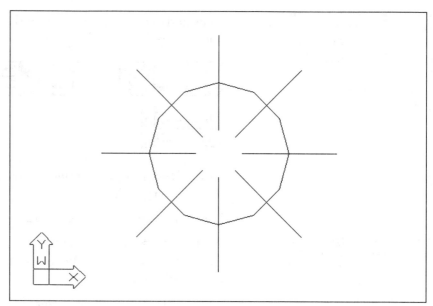

Figure 5.2: The completed gas burner

1. Choose View ➤ Zoom ➤ Scale.

2. Enter **.5x** ↵. Your drawing will look like Figure 5.3.

▼ TIP

If you're not too fussy about the amount you want to zoom out, you can choose View ➤ Zoom ➤ Out to quickly re-duce your view.

Entering **.5x** for the Zoom Scale value tells AutoCAD you want a view that reduces the width of the current view to fill half the display area, allowing you to see more of the work area. If you specify a Scale value greater than 1 (5, for example), you will magnify your current view. If you leave off the x, your new view will be in relation to the draw-ing limits rather than the current view.

Now you will finish the range top. Here you will get a chance to use the Rectangular Array option to create three additional burners.

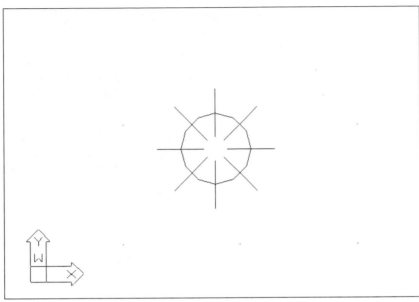

Figure 5.3:   A 0.5x magnification of the preceding view

▼ TIP

You can also type **Array** ↵ to start the ARRAY command. Then, after confirming your selection of objects in step 4, type **R** ↵.

3. Click and drag Polar Array from the Modify palette then select Rectangular Array.

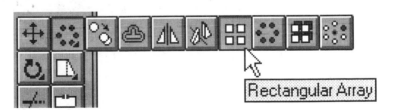

4. At the Select objects: prompt, use the Window selection option to window the entire burner. Then press ↵ to confirm your selection.

5. As mentioned earlier, a rectangular array is a matrix of columns and rows. At the Number of rows (----) <1> prompt, enter **2** ↵. This tells AutoCAD the number of copies you want vertically.

6. At the Number of columns (¦ ¦ ¦ ¦) <1> prompt, enter 2 ↵ again. This tells AutoCAD the number of copies you want horizontally.

7. At the Unit cell or distance between rows (----) prompt, enter 14 ↵. This tells AutoCAD that the vertical distance between the rows of burners is 14″.

8. At the Distance between columns (¦ ¦ ¦ ¦) prompt, enter 16 ↵ to tell AutoCAD you want the horizontal distance between the columns of burners to be 16″. Your screen will look like Figure 5.4.

AutoCAD usually draws a rectangular array from bottom to top, and from left to right. You can reverse the direction of the array by giving negative values for the distance between columns and rows.

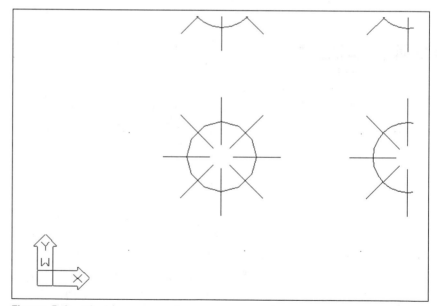

Figure 5.4: The burners arrayed

▼ TIP

At times you may want to do a rectangular array at an angle. To accomplish this you must first set the Snap angle setting in the Drawing Aids dialog box (Options ➤ Drawing Aids) to the desired angle. Then proceed with the AR-RAY command.

You can also use the cursor to graphically indicate an *array cell* (see Figure 5.5). An array cell is a rectangle defining the distance between rows and columns. You may want to use this option when an object is available to use as a reference from which to determine column and row distances. For example, you may have drawn a crosshatch pattern, as on a calendar, within which you want to array an object. You would use the intersections of the hatch lines as references to define the array cell, which would be one square in the hatch pattern.

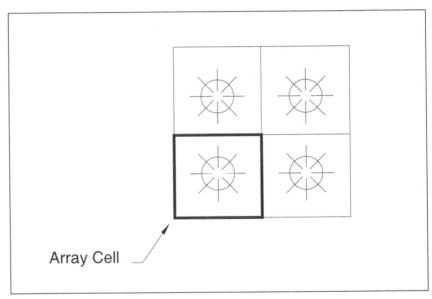

Figure 5.5: An array cell

▼ NOTE

Pan is especially helpful when you have magnified an area to do some editing, and you need to get to part of the drawing that is near your current view.

Using Pan

Notice that most of the burners do not appear on the display shown in Figure 5.4. To move the view over so you can see all the burners, you can use the PAN command. Pan is similar to Zoom in that it changes your view of the drawing; however, Pan does not alter the magnification of the view the way Zoom does. Rather, Pan maintains the current

II

Building on the Basics

magnification while moving your view across the drawing, just as you would pan a camera across a landscape.

1. Click on View ➤ Pan ➤ Point, or type P ↵ at the command prompt.

2. At the 'PAN Displacement: prompt, pick a point near coordinate 3′–7″, 3′–7″.

3. At the Second point: prompt, turn the ortho mode off if it is still on, and then move the cursor to the lower-left corner of the screen, as shown in Figure 5.6. The rubber-banding line you see indicates the pan displacement. Pick this point. Your drawing will be panned to the view shown in Figure 5.7.

You may have noticed the other options in the View ➤ Pan cascading menu. These options provide an easy way to pan your view in the direction they indicate. Use these options if you want to quickly pan across

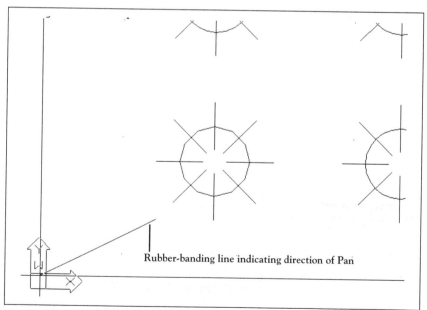

Rubber-banding line indicating direction of Pan

Figure 5.6: A rubber-banding line indicating pan displacement

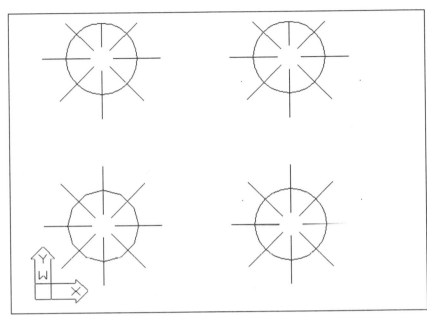

Figure 5.7: The panned view of the gas range

your view and you don't need to be exact about the distance or direction. The Pan options are also duplicated in the Pan button flyout of the standard toolbar.

The burners are still not entirely visible in your panned view, because the current zoom magnification is too great for you to see the entire range.

1. Type Z ↵.

2. At the All/Center/Dynamic... prompt, enter 1 ↵. This has the effect of zooming back out to include an area equivalent to the limits of your drawing.

3. Now complete the kitchenette as indicated in Figure 5.8.

▼ **NOTE**

Although you can also use View ➤ Zoom ➤ All to see the range, the method shown in the foregoing exercise lets you get to an overall view without causing a screen regeneration (regen). In a dense drawing, regens can slow you down. You'll learn more about regens in *Chapter 6*.

Building on the Basics

II

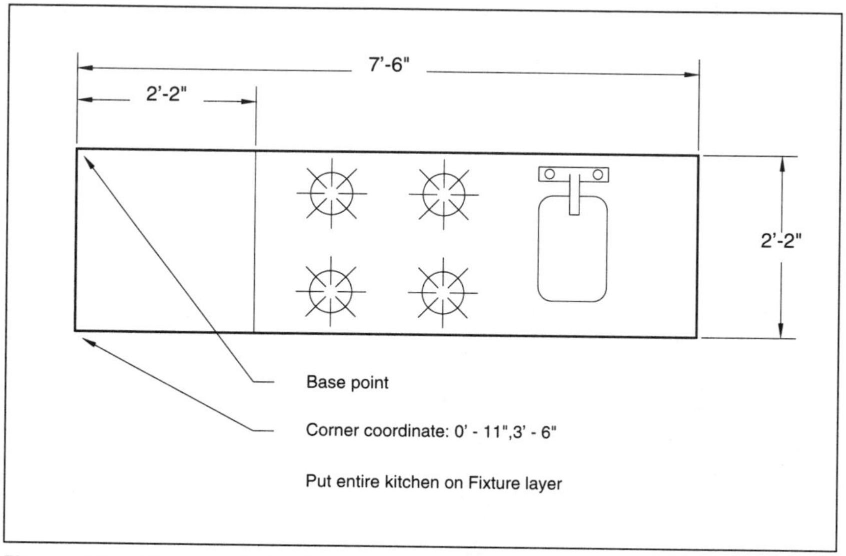

Figure 5.8: Drawing the kitchenette

You will be using this drawing as a symbol, inserting it into the overall plan of the studio unit. To facilitate accurate placement of the kitchenette, you will want to change the location of the base point of this drawing to the upper-left corner of the kitchenette. This will then be the "handle" of the drawing.

1. At the command prompt, type BASE ↵.

2. At the Base point <1'–10",6'–10",0'–0"> prompt, pick the upper-left corner of the kitchenette as indicated in Figure 5.8. The kitchenette drawing is complete.

3. Click on File ➤ Save.

MAKING RANDOM MULTIPLE COPIES

The Construct ➤ Array command is useful when you want to make multiple copies in a regular pattern. But what if you need to make copies in a random pattern? You have two alternatives for accomplishing this: the COPY command's Multiple option, and the Grips feature's Move mode.

To use the COPY command to make random multiple copies:

1. Click on Copy Object from the Modify palette.

2. At the Select object prompt, select the objects you want to copy and press ↵ to confirm your selections.

3. At the <Base point or displacement>/Multiple: prompt, enter **M** ↵ to select the Multiple option.

4. At the Base point prompt, select a base point as usual.

5. At the Second point prompt, select a point for the copy. You will be prompted again for a second point, allowing you to make yet another copy of your object.

6. Continue to select points for more copies as desired.

7. Press ↵ to exit the COPY command when you are done.

When you use the Grips feature to make multiple random copies, you get an added level of functionality, since you can also rotate, mirror, and stretch copies by pressing the right mouse button. Of course, you must have the Grips feature turned on; it is usually on by default but you may find yourself on a system that has it turned off for some reason.

1. Press the Escape key twice to make sure you are not in the middle of a command, then select the objects you want to copy.

2. Click on a grip point as your base point. The ** STRETCH ** prompt appears, telling you that you are in the stretch mode.

3. Press the right mouse button once to change to the move mode. You'll see ** MOVE ** in the prompt area.

4. Move the cursor to the location for your copy and, while holding down the Shift key, click on the new location. Or you can enter **C** ↵ to issue the Copy option before you click on the new location.

5. If desired, click on other locations for more copies, without holding down the Shift key.

DEVELOPING YOUR DRAWING

As mentioned briefly in *Chapter 3*, when using AutoCAD, you first create the most basic forms of your drawing; then you refine them. In this section you will create two drawings—the studio apartment unit and the lobby—that demonstrate this process in more detail.

First you will construct a typical studio apartment unit using the drawings you have created thus far. In the process, you will explore the use of lines as reference objects.

You will also further examine how to use existing files as blocks. In *Chapter 4*, you inserted a file into another file. There is no limit to the size or number of files you can insert. As you may already have guessed, you can also *nest* files and blocks, that is, insert blocks or files within other blocks or files. Nesting can help reduce your drawing time by allowing you to build one block out of smaller blocks. For example, you can insert your door drawing into the bathroom plan. The bathroom plan can in turn be inserted into the studio unit plan, which also contains doors. Finally, the unit plan can be inserted into the overall floor plan for the studio apartment building.

IMPORTING SETTINGS

In this exercise, you will use the Bath file as a prototype for the studio unit plan. However, you must make a few changes to it first. Once the changes are made, you will import the bathroom and thereby import the layers and blocks contained in the bathroom file.

As you go through this exercise, observe how the drawings begin to evolve from simple forms to complex, assembled forms.

1. First, open the Bath file.

2. Use the BASE command and select the upper-left corner of the bathroom as the new base point for this drawing, so you can position the Bath file more accurately.

3. Save the Bath file.

4. Open a new file called **Unit**. This time, make sure the No Prototype check box is checked.

5. Use Data ➤ Units… to set the unit style to Architectural.

6. Use Data ➤ Drawing Limits to set up a $\frac{1}{4}''=1'-0''$ scale, drawing on an $8\frac{1}{2}\times11''$ sheet. This means your limits should include an area 528″ wide by 408″ high.

7. Turn the snap mode on and set the grid aspect to 12″.

8. Begin the unit by drawing two rectangles, one 14′ wide by 24′ long, and the other 14′ wide by 4′ long. Place them as shown in Figure 5.9.

9. Use Insert Block on the Draw palette to insert the bathroom drawing using the upper-left corner of the unit's interior as the insertion point (see Figure 5.10). You can use the Endpoint Osnap override to accurately place the bathroom. Use a scale factor of 1.0 and a rotation angle of 0°.

10. Use the Properties button on the Object Properties toolbar to change all the lines you drew to the Wall layer.

By inserting the bathroom, you imported the layers and blocks contained in the Bath file. You were then able to move previously drawn objects to the imported layers. As a quick way of setting up layers, you could set up several drawings containing different layering schemes and then insert them into new drawings. This method is similar to using an existing drawing as a prototype, but it allows you to start work on a drawing before deciding which template to use.

▼ NOTE

If you need help setting up a drawing, turn to the instructions at the start of *Chapter 3*.

▼ WARNING

If two drawings contain the same layers and blocks, and one of these drawings is imported into the other, the layer settings and block definitions of the *current* file will take priority over those of the *imported* file. This is a point to remember in cases where the layer settings and block definitions are different in the two files.

Building on the Basics

II

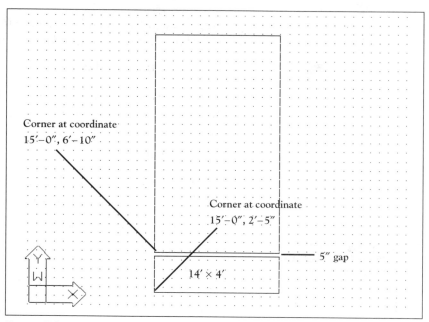

Figure 5.9: The apartment unit interior and balcony

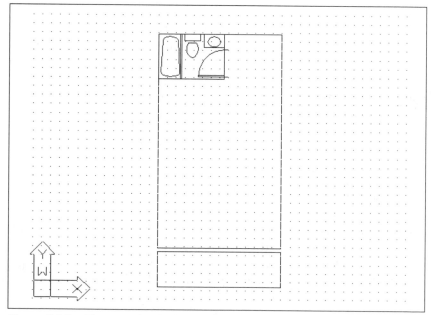

Figure 5.10: The unit after the bathroom is inserted

▼ IMPORTING SETTINGS FROM CROSS-REFERENCED FILES

As explained in the *Chapter 4* sidebar, "An Alternative to Blocks," you can use the External Reference (Xref) Attach option to use another file as a background or cross-referenced file. Cross-referenced files are similar to blocks except that they do not actually become part of the current drawing's database; nor do the settings from the cross-referenced file automatically become part of the referencing drawing.

If you want to import layers, line types, text styles, and so forth from a cross-referenced file, you must use the XBIND command, which you will learn more about as you work through this book. XBIND allows you to attach dimension style settings (discussed in *Chapter 9* and in *Appendix C*), layers, line types, or text styles (discussed in *Chapter 8*) from a cross-referenced file to the current file.

You can also use XBIND to turn a cross-referenced file into an ordinary block, thereby importing all the new settings contained in that file.

See *Chapter 12* for a more detailed description of how to use the External References (XREF) and XBIND commands.

II

Building on the Basics

USING AND EDITING LINES

You will draw lines in the majority of your work, so it is important to know how to manipulate lines to your best advantage. In this section, you will look at some of the more common ways to use and edit these fundamental drawing objects. The following exercises show you the process of drawing lines, rather than just how individual commands work.

Roughing In the Line Work

The bathroom you inserted in the last section has only one side of its interior walls drawn (walls are usually shown by double lines). In this next exercise, you will draw the other side. Rather than trying to draw the wall in perfectly the first time, you will "sketch" in the line work and then work through a clean-up process, in a way similar to manual drafting.

1. Zoom into the bathroom so that the entire bathroom and part of the area around it are displayed on the screen, as in Figure 5.11.

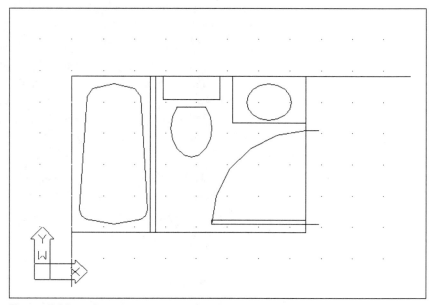

Figure 5.11: The enlarged view of the bathroom

2. Use Data ➤ Layers to make Wall the current layer.

3. Start the LINE command. Click on From from the Osnap menu. This option lets you select a point relative to another point.

4. At the From prompt, click on the lower-right corner of the bathroom. Nothing appears in the drawing area yet.

5. Type **@5<–90** ⏎. Now a line starts 5″ below the lower-right corner of the bathroom.

6. Continue the line horizontally to the left, to slightly cross the left wall of the apartment unit, as illustrated in panel 1 of Figure 5.12.

In the foregoing exercise, the From Osnap override allows you to specify a point in space relative to the corner of the bathroom. In step 5, you used a polar coordinate to indicate the distance from the corner at which you wanted the line to start. You can also use relative or absolute Cartesian coordinates. Now let's continue with the line work.

1. Draw another line upward from the endpoint of the top door jamb at coordinate 22′–11″, 29′–2″ to meet the top wall of the unit. Use the ortho mode and the Perpendicular Osnap override to pick the top wall of the unit. This causes the line to end precisely on the wall line in perpendicular position, as in panel 2 of Figure 5.12.

2. Draw a line connecting the two door jambs. Then change that line to the Ceiling layer.

3. Draw a line 6″ downward from the endpoint of the jamb nearest the corner at coordinate 22′–11″, 26′–0″, as shown in panel 1 of Figure 5.13.

Cleaning Up the Line Work

You've drawn some of the wall lines, approximating their endpoint locations. Next you will use the FILLET command to join lines exactly end to end.

1. Click and drag Chamfer from the Modify palette then select Fillet.

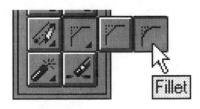

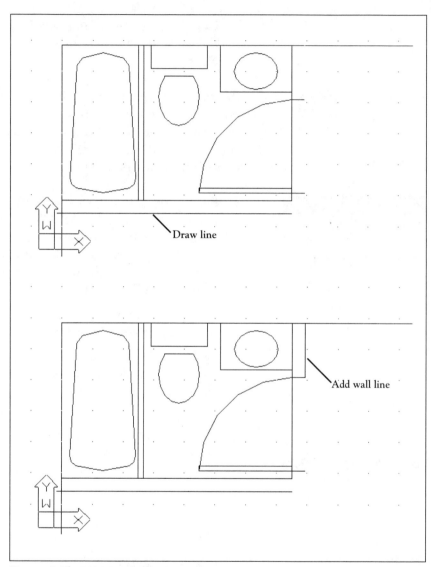

Figure 5.12: The first wall line and the wall line by the door

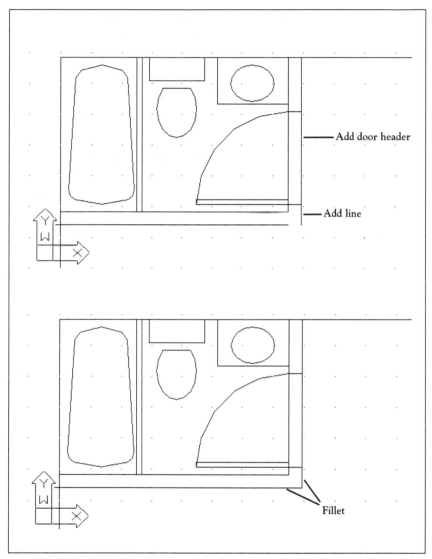

Building on the Basics

Figure 5.13: The corner of the bathroom wall, and the filleted wall around the bathroom

2. Type **R** ↵ **0** ↵ to set the fillet radius to 0, then press ↵ to repeat the FILLET command.

3. Fillet the two lines by picking the vertical line at coordinate 22′–11″, 25′–7″ and the horizontal line at coordinate 22′–0″, 25′–5″. Notice that these points lie on the portion of the line you want to keep. Your drawing will look like panel 2 of Figure 5.13.

4. Fillet the bottom wall of the bathroom with the left wall of the unit. Make sure the points you pick on the wall lines are on the side of the line you want to keep, not the side you want trimmed.

5. Fillet the top wall of the unit with the right side wall of the bathroom.

6. Use View ➤ Redraw View to refresh the drawing. Your drawing should now look like Figure 5.14.

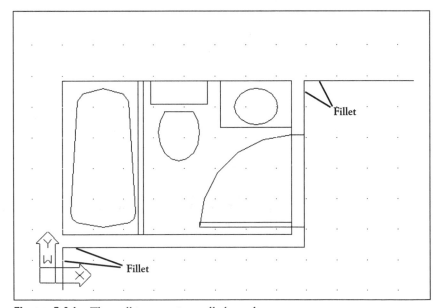

Figure 5.14: The wall intersections, all cleaned up

Fillet joins two nonparallel lines exactly end to end. Remember: Where you select the lines will affect how the lines are joined. As you select objects for Fillet, the side of the line you click on is the side that remains when the lines are joined. Figure 5.15 illustrates how Fillet works and shows what the fillet options do.

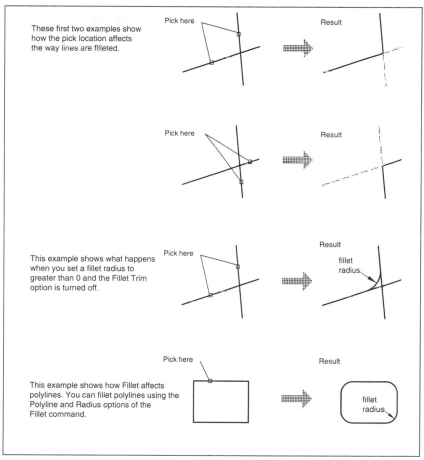

Figure 5.15:   The place where you click on the object to select it determines what part of an object gets filleted.

▼ **TIP**

If you didn't complete the
kitchen earlier in this chapter,
you can insert the Kitchen file
from the companion disk.

▼ **NOTE**

If you need some help with
the BREAK command, see
"Modifying an Object" in
Chapter 3, and the sidebar,
"The Break Options," here in
Chapter 5.

Now let's finish this end of the Unit plan.

1. Use Insert Block from the Draw palette to place the kitchen drawing at the wall intersection at coordinate 15′–0″, 25′–5″. (You
   can also insert the kitchen at approximately the place where you
   want it, and then move it into a more exact position.)

2. Press ↵ three times to accept the default X and Y Scale factors of 1.0, and a Rotation Angle of 0°.

3. Pan your view so that the upper-right corner of the bathroom
   is in the center of the drawing area, as illustrated in panel 1
   of Figure 5.16.

4. Insert a door on the unit wall at coordinate 23′–4″, 30′– 10″.
   Then press ↵ twice to accept the default Scale factors.

5. At the Rotation angle prompt, enter **270** ↵. Or use the cursor (make sure the ortho mode is on) to orient the door so
   that it is swinging *into* the unit.

6. Make sure the door is on the Door layer.

7. Add 5″ door jambs, click and drag 1 Point from the Modify
   palette, and select 2 Point Select to break the header over
   the door (see panel 2 of Figure 5.16). Be sure the door jambs
   are on the Jamb layer.

8. Draw the door header on the Ceiling layer.

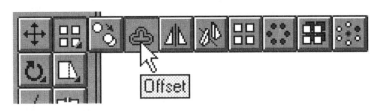

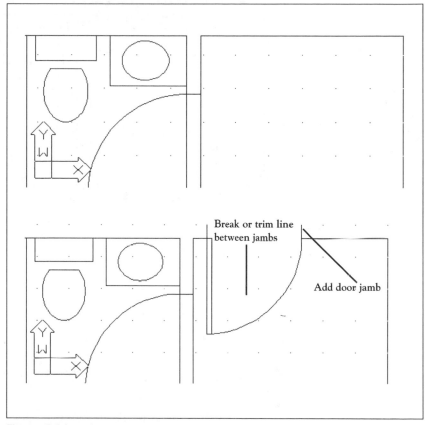

Figure 5.16:   The view after using Pan, with the door inserted and the jamb and header added

9. Click and drag Rectangular Array from the Modify palette and select Offset. Offset the top wall lines of the unit and the door header up 5″, so they connect with the top end of the door jamb, as shown in Figure 5.17. Don't forget to include the short wall line from the door to the bathroom wall.

10. Save your file.

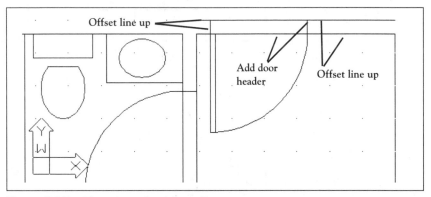

Figure 5.17:   The other side of the wall

▼

THE BREAK OPTIONS

In the exercise for finishing the Unit plan, you used a new option—
2 Point Select—in the Break flyout button menu of the Modify palette. Here are descriptions of all the options available for the Break
flyout.

1 Point Select   breaks an object at a single point, so the object
becomes two contiguous objects. You are prompted to first select
an object and then the point where the break is to occur.

1 Point   performs the same function as 1 Point Select, but you
are only prompted to select an object. The break is placed at the
point of selection.

2 Point Select   breaks an object so that there is a gap in the object. You are prompted to first select the object and then to pick
two points defining the location of the gap.

2 Point   also produces a gap in an object, but instead of prompt-
ing you to select the object and two points, 2 Point uses the
point of selection as the first point in the gap. You are then
prompted for the other end of the break or gap.

Using Construction Lines as Tools

new

Now you need to extend the upper wall line 5″ beyond the right-side interior wall of the unit. To accomplish this, you will draw some line objects specifically designed to help with layout. Start by drawing a Ray line.

1. Click and drag Line from the Draw menu then select Ray.

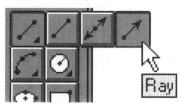

2. At the Start point prompt, start the Ray line from the upper-right corner of the unit at coordinate 29′–0″, 30′–10″ (see panel 1 of Figure 5.18).

3. Type @ **1<45**. The Ray line appears. Press ↵ to exit the RAY command.

4. Fillet this Ray with the wall line you wish to extend, and then erase the Ray when you are done. Your drawing should look like panel 2 of Figure 5.18.

5. Click on View ➤ Zoom ➤ Previous to view the left side of the unit.

6. Draw another Ray at 135°. Then use Fillet to join this line with the wall line (see Figure 5.19).

7. Erase the last Ray you drew.

8. Click on View ➤ Zoom ➤ All to view the entire drawing. It will look like Figure 5.20.

In this exercise, you used Rays to help accurately position two other lines used for the exterior walls of the studio unit. This shows that you can freely use objects to help construct your drawing.

▼ **NOTE**

A Ray is a line of infinite length that starts from a point you select. For this reason, it didn't matter what length value you entered in step 3. As you continue this exercise, you will use the ray to help you locate one side of a wall.

Building on the Basics

II

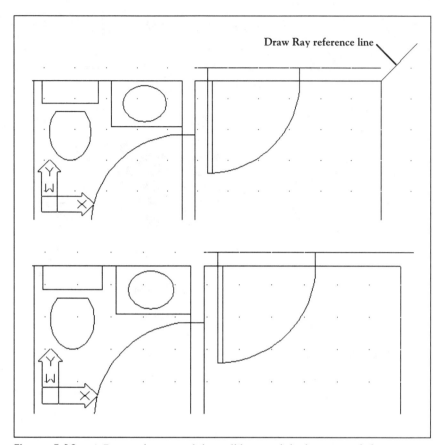

Figure 5.18: A Ray used to extend the wall line; and the line, extended

Now you will finish the balcony by adding a sliding glass door and a rail. Again, you will use lines for construction as well as for parts of the drawing. First, you'll add the door jamb by drawing an Xline. An Xline is a line that has an infinite length, but unlike the Ray, it extends in both directions. After drawing the Xline, you'll use it to quickly position the door jambs.

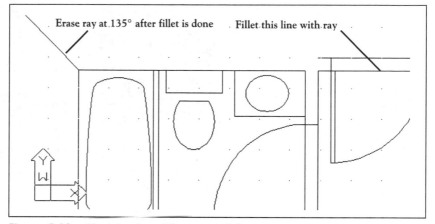

Figure 5.19: The left-side wall line, extended

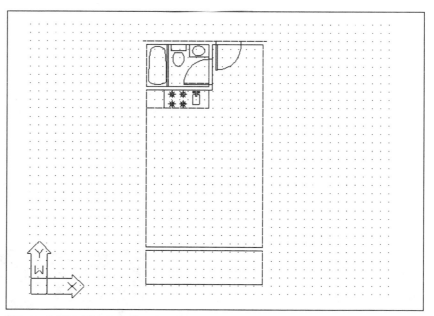

Figure 5.20: The unit plan thus far

1. Zoom into the balcony area.

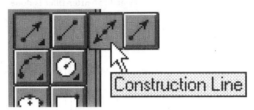

2. Click and drag Ray from the Draw palette, then select Construction Line. This starts the XLINE command, and you'll see this prompt:

   Hor/Ver/Ang/Bisect/Offset/<From point>:

3. Type **O** ↵ to select the Offset option of the XLINE command.

4. At the Offset distance prompt, type **4'** ↵.

5. At the Select object prompt, click on the wall line at the right of the unit.

6. At the Side to offset prompt, click on a point to the left of the wall. The Xline appears (see panel 1 of Figure 5.21).

7. At the Select object prompt, click on the left wall line, and then click to the right of the wall to create another Xline.

Next, you'll adjust the Xlines to form the jambs.

8. Click on Trim from the Modify palette.

9. Select the Xlines and the two horizontal lines representing the wall between the unit and the balcony, and press ↵.

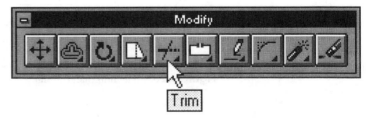

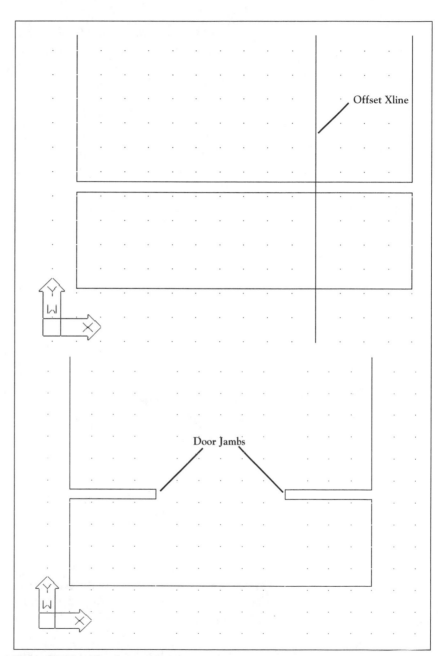

Figure 5.21: The door opening

10. Click on the horizontal lines at any point between the Xlines. Then click on the Xlines above and below the horizontal lines to trim them. Your drawing will look like panel 2 of Figure 5.21.

11. Add lines on the Ceiling layer to represent the door header.

12. Now draw lines between the two jambs (on the Door layer) to indicate a sliding glass door (see Figure 5.22).

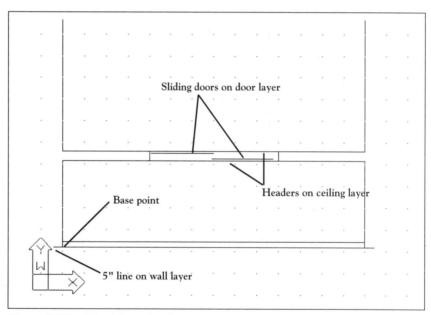

Figure 5.22:   The sliding glass door

The XLINE Options   There is more to the XLINE command than you have seen in the exercises of this chapter. Here is a list of the XLINE options and their use:

Hor   draws horizontal Xlines as you click on points

Ver   draws vertical Xlines as you click on points

Angle   draws Xlines at a specified angle as you pick points

Bisect   draws Xlines bisecting an angle or a location between two points

The wall facing the balcony is now complete. To finish off the unit, you need to show a hand rail and the corners of the balcony wall.

1. Offset the bottom line of the balcony 3″ toward the top of the drawing.

2. Create a new layer called **F-rail,** and assign this line to it.

3. Add a 5″ horizontal line to the lower corners of the balcony, as shown in Figure 5.22.

4. Now type **Base** ↵ to set the base point at the lower-left corner of the balcony, at the coordinates 15′, 2′–5″.

5. Change the lines indicating walls to the Wall layer, and put the sliding glass door on the Door layer (see Figure 5.22).

6. Zoom back to the previous view. Your drawing should now look like Figure 5.23.

7. Click on File ➤ Save to save the drawing.

Your studio apartment unit plan is now complete. The exercises you've just completed show you a typical set of operations you'll perform while building your drawings. In fact, nearly 80 percent of what you will do in AutoCAD is represented here.

Now, to review the drawing process, and to create a drawing you'll use later, draw the apartment house's lobby. As you follow the steps, refer to Figure 5.24.

1. Create a new file called **Lobby,** using the Unit file as a prototype.

2. Erase the entire unit.

3. Begin by drawing the three main rectangles representing the outlines of the stair shaft, the elevator shaft, and the lobby.

II

Building on the Basics

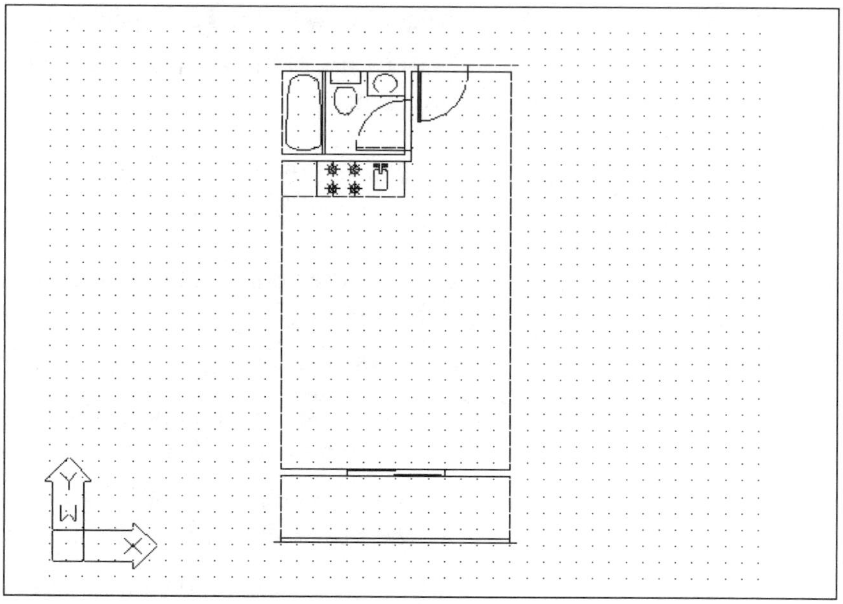

Figure 5.23: The completed studio apartment unit

4. To draw the stairs, offset the stair shaft's left wall to the right a distance of 4′. This creates the first line representing the steps.

5. Array this line in one row of ten columns, using an 11″ column spacing.

6. Draw the center line dividing the two flights of stairs.

7. Draw the elevator and insert the door. Practice using Xlines here.

8. Draw in the door jambs, and edit the door openings to add the door headers. Your plan should resemble the one in Figure 5.24, panel 4.

9. Once you are finished, save the Lobby file.

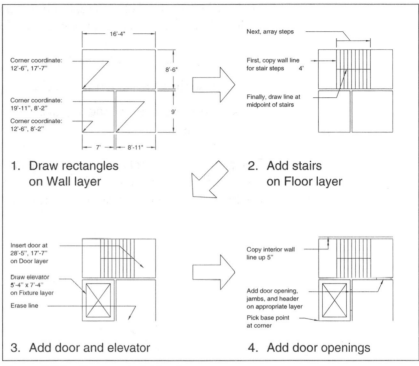

Figure 5.24: Drawing the lobby plan

> **▼ NOTE**
>
> As is usual in floor plans, the elevator is indicated by the box with the large X through it, and the stair shaft is indicated by the box with the row of vertical lines through it.

FINDING DISTANCES ALONG ARCS

You've seen how you can use lines to help locate objects and geometry in your drawing. But if you need to find distances along a curved object such as an arc, lines don't always help. Following are two ways of finding exact distances on arcs. Try these exercises when you're not working through the main tutorial.

Finding a Point a Particular Distance from Another Point

At times you'll need to find the location of a point on an arc that lies at a known distance from another point on the arc. The distance could be described as a cord of the arc, but how do you find the exact cord location? To find a cord along an arc, do the following:

1. Click on Circle Center Radius from the Draw palette.
2. Use the Osnap overrides to click on the endpoint of the arc.
3. At the End of diameter/<radius> prompt, enter the length of the cord.

The point where the circle intersects the arc is the endpoint of the cord distance from the endpoint of the arc (see Figure 5.25). You can then use the Intersect Osnap override to select the circle and arc intersection.

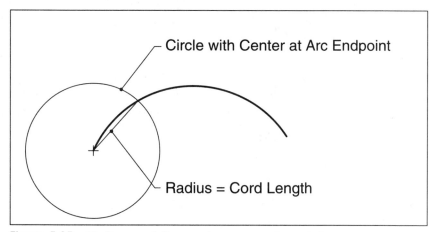

Figure 5.25: Finding a cord distance along an arc using a circle

Finding an Exact Distance Along an Arc

To find an exact distance along an arc (nonlinear), do the following:

▼ **TIP**

You can also set the point style by setting the Pdmode system variable to 3. See *Appendix C* for more on Pdmode.

1. Type **Ddptype** ↵ to open the Point Style dialog box.
2. At the Point Style dialog box, click on the icon that looks like an X, in the top row. Also be sure the Set Size Relative to Screen radio button is selected. Then click on OK.

3. Click and drag Point from the Draw palette then select Measure.

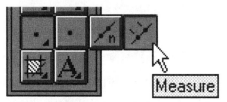

4. At the Select object to measure prompt, click on the arc near the end from which you wish to find the distance.

5. At the <Segment length>/Block prompt, enter the distance you are interested in. A series of Xs appears on the arc, marking off the specified distance along the arc. You can select the exact location of the Xs using the Node Osnap override (Figure 5.26).

The MEASURE command also works on Bezier curves. You'll get a more detailed look at the MEASURE command in *Chapter 13*.

As you work with AutoCAD, you'll find that constructing temporary geometry such as the circle and points in the two foregoing examples will help you solve problems in new ways. Don't hesitate to experiment!

II

Building on the Basics

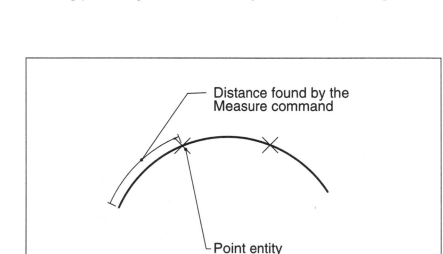

Figure 5.26: Finding an exact distance along an arc using points and the MEASURE command

Remember, you've always got the Save and U commands to help you recover from mistakes.

CHANGING THE LENGTH OF OBJECTS

Suppose, after finding the length of an arc, you realize you need to lengthen the arc by a specific amount. The Modify ➤ Lengthen command lets you lengthen or shorten arcs, lines, splines, and elliptical arcs. Here's how to lengthen an arc:

1. Click and drag Stretch from the Modify palette then select Lengthen.

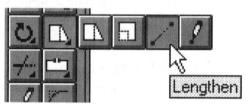

2. At the DElta/Percent/Total/DYnamic/,Select object>: prompt, type **T** ↵.

3. At the Angle/<Enter total length (1.0000)>: prompt, enter the length you want for the arc.

4. At the <Select object to change>/Undo: prompt, click on the arc you wish to change. Be sure to click at a point nearest the end you want to lengthen. The arc increases in length to the size you specified.

Modify ➤ Lengthen will also shorten an object if it is currently longer than the value you enter.

In this short example, we have demonstrated how to change an object to a specific length. You can use other criteria to change an object's length, using these options available in the LENGTHEN command:

DElta lets you lengthen or shorten an object by a specific length. To specify an angle rather than a length, use the Angle suboption.

Percent is for increasing or decreasing the length of an object by a percentage of its current length.

Total lets you specify the total length or angle of an object.

DYnamic lets you graphically change the length of an object using your cursor.

CREATING A NEW DRAWING USING PARTS FROM ANOTHER DRAWING

In this section you will use the WBLOCK command (which you learned in *Chapter 4*), to create a separate stair drawing using the stair you've already drawn for the lobby. Later, in *Chapter 6*, you will use this new stair drawing for a fire escape. Although you haven't turned the existing stair into a block, you can still use WBLOCK to turn parts of a drawing into a file.

1. Click on File ➤ Export….

2. When the Export Data File dialog box appears, enter **stair.dwg** in the file name input box and click OK. By including the .DWG file name extension, AutoCAD knows that you want to export to a drawing file and not some other format such as a .DXF or .WMF format file.

3. At the Block name prompt, press ↵. This tells AutoCAD that you want to create a file from part of the drawing, rather than a block.

4. At the Insertion base point: prompt, pick the lower-right corner of the stair shaft, at coordinate 28'–10", 17'–7". This tells AutoCAD the base point for the new drawing.

5. At the Select objects prompt, use a window to select the stair shaft, as shown in Figure 5.27.

6. When the stair shaft, including the door, is highlighted, press ↵ to confirm your selection. The stair disappears.

7. Since you want the stair to remain in the lobby drawing, use the OOPS command to bring it back.

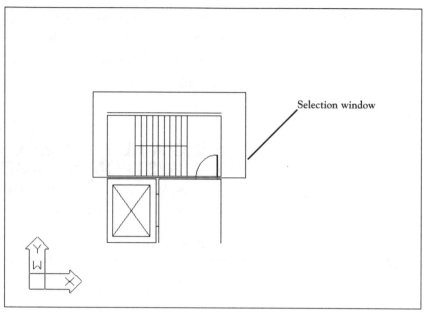

Figure 5.27: A selection window enclosing the stair shaft

DRAWING PARALLEL LINES

Frequently, when working on an architectural project, you will first do your schematic layout using simple lines for walls. Then, later, as the design requirements begin to take shape, you can start to add more detailed information about the walls—for example, indicating wall materials or locations for insulation. AutoCAD provides *Multilines* (the MLINE command)—double lines that can be used to represent walls. Mline can also be customized to display solid fills, center lines, and additional line types shown in Figure 5.28. You can save your custom Multilines as Mline styles, which are in turn saved in special files for easy access from other drawings.

The following exercise shows you how you might continue to build information into your drawings by using Multilines to indicate wall types.

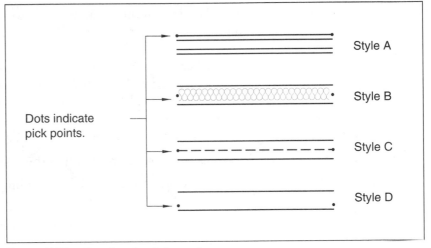

Figure 5.28: Samples of multiline styles

▼ NOTE

The first line in the prompt area gives you the current settings for Mline. You'll learn more about those settings in an upcoming section.

1. Click and drag Polyline from the Draw palette then select Multiline. You'll see two lines in the prompt area:

    Justification = Top, Scale = 1.00, Style = Standard
    Justification/Scale/STyle/<From point>:

    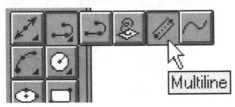

2. At the Justification/Scale/Style/<From Point>: prompt, type **S** ↵ (for Scale).

3. At the Set Mline Scale <0.00>: prompt, type **5** ↵.

4. Pick a point to start the double line.

5. Continue to select points to draw more double line segments, or type **C** ↵ to close the series of lines.

II

Building on the Basics

Let's take a look at the meaning of the Mline settings included in the prompt you saw in steps 1 and 2 above.

Justification   controls how far off center the double lines are drawn. The default sets the double lines equidistant from the points you pick. By changing the justification value to be greater than or less than 0, you can have AutoCAD draw double lines off center from the pick points.

Scale   lets you set the width of the double line.

Close   closes a sequence of double lines, much as the LINE command's Close option does.

Style   lets you select a style for Multilines. You can control the number of lines in the Multiline, as well as the line types used for each line in the Multiline style, by using the MLEDIT command (discussed in the next section).

CUSTOMIZING MULTILINES

In *Chapter 4* you learned how to make a line appear dashed or dotted, using line types. In a similar way, you can control the appearance of Multilines using the MLSTYLE command. With MLSTYLE you can

- Set the number of lines that appear in the Multiline

- Control the color of each line

- Control the line type of each line

- Apply a fill between the outermost lines of a Multiline

- Control if and how ends of Multilines are closed

To activate Mlstyle, you can either select Data ➤ Multiline Style…
from the pull-down menu, or type **Mlstyle** ↵ at the command prompt.
Here is the Multiline Styles dialog box:

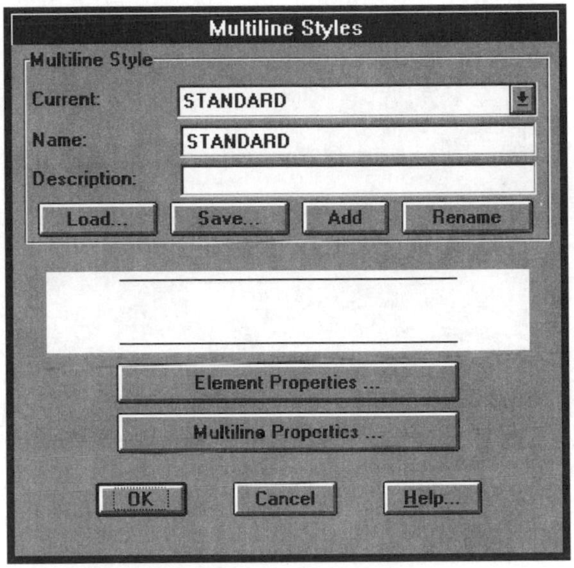

At the top of the dialog, a group of buttons and input boxes allows you
to select the Multiline Style you want to works with. The Current pop-
up list offers you a selection of existing styles. In the Name input box
you can name a new style you are creating, or rename an existing style.
Description lets you attach a description to an Mline style for easy identification. You use the Add and Save buttons to create and save Multiline styles as files so they can be accessed by any AutoCAD drawing, and
with the Load button you retrieve a saved style for use in the current
drawing. Rename lets you change the name of an Mline style (the default style in a new drawing is called Standard).

In the lower half of the Multiline Styles dialog box are two buttons—
Element Properties and Multiline Properties—that allow you to make
adjustments to the Mline style currently indicated at the top of the dialog box. This Mline is also previewed in the middle of the dialog box.

Element Properties

In the Element Properties dialog box, you control the properties of the individual elements of the style, including the number of lines that appear in the Mline, their color, and the distance they appear from your pick points.

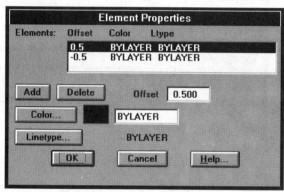

▼ **TIP**

You can easily indicate an insulated wall in an architectural drawing by adding a third center line (offset of 0.0), and giving that center line a Batting line type from the Ltypeshp.LIN file. This line type draws an S-shaped pattern typically used to represent fiberglass batt insulation in a floor plan. Also, see the sections on line-type customization in *Chapter 21*, to see how other wall patterns can be created.

For example, click on the Add button, and another line is added to your Multiline. The offset distance of the new line appears in the list box. The default value for new lines is 0.0, which places the line at the center of the standard Multiline. To delete a line, highlight its offset value in the list box and click the Delete button. To change the amount of offset, highlight it and enter a new value in the Offset input box.

To change the color and line type of individual lines, use the Color... and Linetype... buttons, which open the Color and Select Linetype dialog boxes you have worked with. In Figure 5.29 you see some examples of Multilines and their corresponding Element Properties settings.

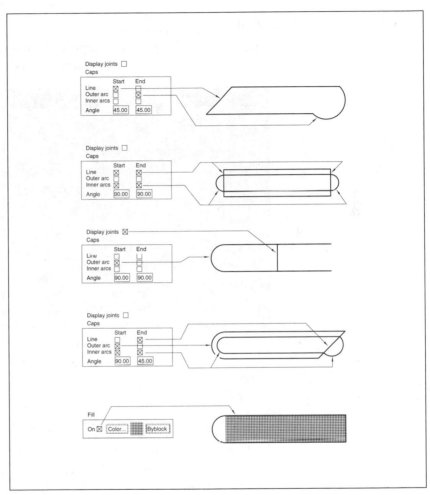

Figure 5.29: Samples of Mline styles you can create

Multiline Properties

The Multiline Properties... button lets you control how the Mline is capped at its ends, as well as whether joints are displayed.

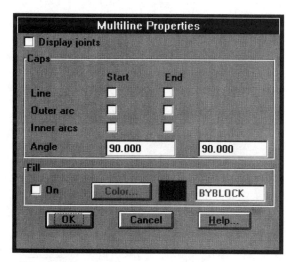

A solid-filled Multiline can be used where you need to fill in a wall with a solid shade (or *poche,* to use the drafting term). You can quickly add a poche by setting one Multiline offset to be 0.0 and the other to be the width of the wall. Then trace either the inside or outside of the wall to be poched, using the Multiline style with the Fill option turned on.

To turn a cap on, you click on the check box next to the type of cap you want. If you prefer, you can give your Multiline style a solid fill, using the Fill check box.

JOINING AND EDITING MULTILINES

Multilines are unique in their ability to combine several line types and colors into one entity. For this reason, you need special tools to edit them. On the Modify menu, the Edit Multiline option (and the MLE-DIT command) have the sole purpose of allowing you to join Multilines in a variety of ways, as demonstrated in Figure 5.30.

Here's how the MLEDIT command is used:

1. Click and Drag Edit Polyline from the Modify palette then select Multiline. The Multiline Edit Tools dialog box appears

CLOSED CROSS Trims one of two intersecting Multlines so that they apper overlapping.	
OPEN CROSS Trims the outer lines of two intersecting Multilines.	
MERGED CROSS Joins two multilines into one Multiline.	
CLOSED TEE Trims the leg of a tee intersection to the first line.	
OPEN TEE Joins the outer lines of a Multiline tee intersection.	
MERGED TEE Joins all the lines in a Multiline tee intersection.	
CORNER JOINT Joins two Multilines into a corner joint.	
ADD VERTEX Adds a vertex to a Multiline. The vertex can later be moved.	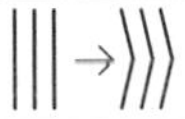
DELETE VERTEX Deletes a vertex to straighten a Multiline.	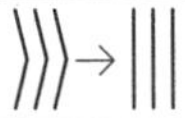
CUT SINGLE Creates an opening in a single line of a Multiline.	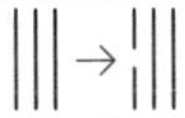
CUT ALL Creates a break across all lines in a Multiline.	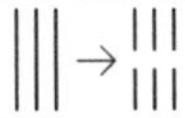
WELD ALL Closes a break in a Multiline.	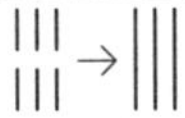

Figure 5.30: The MLEDIT options and their meaning

(see Figure 5.31), offering a variety of ways to edit your Multilines.

2. Click on the graphic that best matches the edit you want to perform.

3. Select the Multilines you want to join or edit.

Building on the Basics

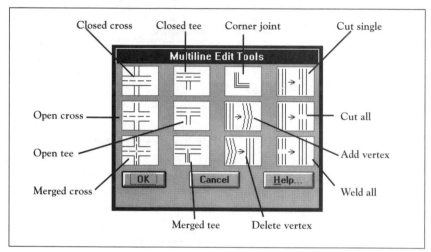

Figure 5.31:   Multiline Edit Tools

ELIMINATING BLOCKS, LAYERS, LINE TYPES, SHAPES, AND STYLES

A prototype may contain blocks and layers you don't need in your new file. For example, the lobby you just completed contains the bathroom block because you used the Unit file as a prototype. Even though you erased this block, it remains in the drawing file's database. It is considered "unused" because it doesn't appear as part of the drawing. Such extra blocks can slow you down by increasing the amount of time needed to open the file. They will also increase the size of your file unnecessarily. There are two commands for eliminating unused elements from a drawing: PURGE and WBLOCK.

SELECTIVELY REMOVING UNUSED ELEMENTS

The PURGE command (Data ➤ Purge) is used to remove unused individual blocks, layers, line types, shapes, and text styles from a drawing file. You will want to purge your drawing of unused elements, to help keep the file size down and to make layer maintenance easier.

As you will see in the Data ➤ Purge cascading menu and the PURGE command prompt, you can purge other unused drawing elements, such as line types and layers, as well. Bear in mind, however, that PURGE will not delete certain primary drawing elements—namely, layer 0, the Continuous line type, and the standard text style. Unlike previous versions of AutoCAD, you can now Purge at any time during your edit session.

1. Click on File ➤ Open and open the Lobby file. (Remember, you saved this file to disk, so now you are simultaneously closing the file and reopening the saved version.)

2. Click on Data ➤ Purge ➤ Blocks.

3. At the Purge block BATH? <N> prompt, enter **Y** ↵. The Purge block prompt will repeat for each unused block in the file. Continue to enter **Y** ↵ to all the prompts until the PURGE command is completed.

4. Use File ➤ Save to save the file to disk.

The Lobby file is now purged of most, but not all, of the unused blocks. Now let's take a look at how to delete all the unused elements at once.

REMOVING ALL UNUSED ELEMENTS

PURGE does not remove nested blocks on its first pass. For example, although you purged the Bath block from the Lobby file, it still contains the Tub and Toilet blocks that were nested in the Bath block. To remove them using PURGE, you must start the command again and remove the nested blocks. For this reason, PURGE can be a time-consuming way to delete large numbers of elements.

In contrast, the WBLOCK command (File ➤ Export...) enables you to remove *all* unused elements, including blocks, nested blocks, layers, line types, shapes, and styles, all at once. You cannot select specific elements or types of elements to remove.

II

Building on the Basics

Be careful: In a given file, there may be a block that is unused but that you want to keep, so you may want to keep a copy of the unpurged file.

1. If you've exited the Lobby file, open it again.

2. Click on File ➤ Export....

3. At the Export Data File dialog box, enter **Lobby1.DWG**. This tells AutoCAD to create a new file called Lobby1, which will be the Lobby file with the unused elements removed.

4. At the Block name prompt, enter * ↵. This tells AutoCAD that you want to create a new file containing all the drawing elements of the current file, including settings. AutoCAD saves the current file to disk, omitting all the unused blocks, layers, and so forth.

5. Now open the Lobby1 file and click on Insert Block from the Draw palette.

6. Click on the Block button to get a view of blocks contained in this file. Note that the list shows only the Door block. All the unused blocks have been purged.

Remember: Though WBLOCK offers a quick way of clearing out the deadwood in a file, the command indiscriminately strips a file of all unused elements. So exercise care when you use this method of purging files.

IF YOU WANT TO EXPERIMENT...

Try using the techniques you learned in this chapter to create new files. Use the files you created in *Chapter 4* as prototypes to create the symbols shown in Figure 5.32.

▼ NOTE

If you specify an existing file, you will get a warning message telling you that a file with that name already exists and a request to confirm if you want to replace it. Click on **Yes** to replace the file or **No** to enter a new name.

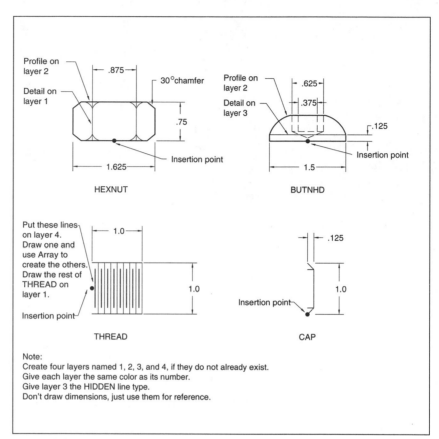

Profile on layer 2

Detail on layer 1

.875

30°chamfer

.75

1.625

Insertion point

HEXNUT

Profile on layer 2

Detail on layer 3

.625

.375

.125

Insertion point

1.5

BUTNHD

Put these lines on layer 4.
Draw one and use Array to create the others.
Draw the rest of THREAD on layer 1.

Insertion point

1.0

1.0

THREAD

.125

1.0

Insertion point

CAP

Note:
Create four layers named 1, 2, 3, and 4, if they do not already exist.
Give each layer the same color as its number.
Give layer 3 the HIDDEN line type.
Don't draw dimensions, just use them for reference.

Figure 5.32: Mechanical symbols

Building on the Basics

II

ENHANCING YOUR DRAWING SKILLS

Reducing Wait Times by Controlling Regen

Improving Performance through Smart Use of the Virtual Display

Improving Performance Using Layers

Saving Views of Your Drawing

Adding Hatch Patterns to Your Drawing

Placing Hatch Patterns Exactly Where You Want Them

Organizing Your Drawings with Cross-Referencing

FAST TRACK

253 ▶ To get a quick overall view of your drawing

Click Aerial View from the Standard Toolbar. You'll get an overall view of your drawing from which you can select a view.

256 ▶ To prevent annoying accidental regens

At the command prompt, type **Regenauto ↵ Off ↵**.

256 ▶ To quickly save a view that you will want to refer to later

Set up the view you want to save. At the command prompt, type **VIEW ↵ S ↵**. Then enter a name for the view, using no spaces.

258 ▶ To recall a view

Click on View ➤ Named Views. Double-click on the name of the view you want to restore.

260 ▶ To open a file to a specific view

When you open the file, choose the Select Initial View option in the Open dialog box. Just before the file begins to display, you will see a list of the views available in the drawing. Double-click on the view you want to open.

262 ▶ To get to part of a drawing not currently visible while in the middle of another command

Use the Aerial View window, or View ➤ Pan, or View ➤ Named Views....

262 ▶ To set up a drawing to allow the hiding of object sets

Group objects into blocks; then assign the blocks to their own unique layers. Freeze and thaw the block layers to hide or redisplay their contents.

266 ▶ To add a hatch pattern to an area

Click on Hatch ➤ from the Draw palette. To select a pattern, click on the Pattern Type sample graphic until the pattern you want appears, or choose the pattern name from the Pattern pop-up list. Click on Pick Points, then on any point inside the area to be hatched. Click on Preview Hatch to check the pattern in place, or Apply to add the pattern to the drawing.

271 ▶ To generate a polyline outline of the hatch boundary

Once you've defined a boundary, click the Advanced... button in the Boundary Hatch dialog box. In the Advanced Options dialog box, turn on Retain Boundaries, and proceed to hatch the selected area.

272 ▶ To specifically position a hatch pattern

Use the Snapbase system variable to set the origin of the hatch pattern.

282 ▶ To globally replace one block with another block

Type **Insert** ↵. At the Block name prompt, enter the block name followed by an equals sign, then the name of the new block or file name. Do not insert spaces between the names and the equals sign.

284 ▶ To add a cross-reference (Xref) file

Choose Attach from the External Reference palette. At the dialog box, double-click on the name of the file you wish to add as a cross-reference, and answer the rest of the prompts.

285 ▶ To tell AutoCAD to save changes made to layers in a cross-referenced file

Type **Visretain** ↵ at the command prompt. At the New value for VIS-RETAIN <0> prompt, enter **1**.

Now that you have created drawings of a typical apartment unit, and the apartment house's lobby and stairs, you can assemble them to complete the first floor of the apartment house. In this chapter, you will take full advantage of AutoCAD's features to enhance your drawing skills, as well as to reduce the time it takes for you to create accurate drawings.

As your drawing becomes larger, you will find that you need to use the ZOOM and PAN commands more often. And as the drawing becomes more dense, screen regenerations will take longer, so we'll look at ways to take control of regens through the careful use of display options. Larger drawings also require some special editing techniques. You will learn how to assemble drawings in ways that will save you time and effort as your design progresses. Along the way, you'll see how you can enhance the appearance of your drawings by adding hatch patterns.

ASSEMBLING THE PARTS

Start by creating a new file for the first floor, and inserting and copying the unit file.

1. Open a new file, called **Plan**, to contain the drawing of the apartment house's first floor. This is the file that you will use to assemble the unit plans into an apartment building.

2. Set up the drawing for a $\frac{1}{8}''=1'-0''$ scale on an 18″×24″ drawing area.

3. Create a layer called **Plan1** and make it the current layer.

4. Turn the snap mode on, and set the grid to 5′.

5. Insert the Unit.DWG drawing at coordinate 31′–5″, 43′–8″. Accept the default values at all the prompts, since you want to insert this drawing just as you drew it.

6. Zoom in to the apartment unit plan.

7. Draw a line from the upper-right corner of the unit's interior, at coordinate 45′–5″, 72′–1″, to the right 2.5″.

8. Use the endpoint of the new 2.5″ line to mirror the unit plan to the right. You will thus get a 5″ wall thickness between studio units. Keep the original unit plan in place. Your drawing should look like Figure 6.1.

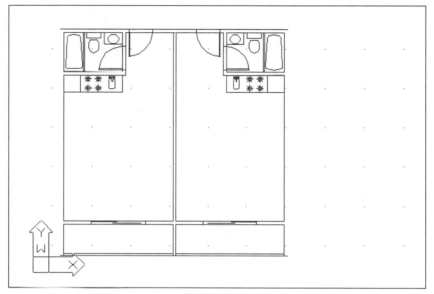

Figure 6.1:   The unit plan mirrored

9. Now erase the short line you used as a mirror reference, and draw another line vertically from the same corner a distance of 24″.

10. Use the endpoint of the 24″ line to mirror the two unit plans on a horizontal axis.

11. Click on View ➤ Zoom ➤ Extents to get a view of the four plans. Your drawing will look like Figure 6.2.

▼ NOTE

The Extents option forces the entire drawing to fill the screen at the leftmost side of the display area.

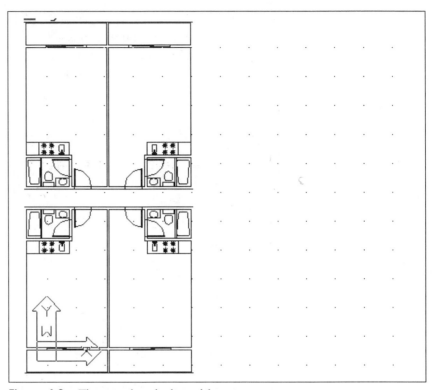

Figure 6.2: The unit plan, duplicated four times

12. Erase the reference line, and copy the four units horizontally a distance of 28′–11″, the width of two units.

13. Insert the lobby at coordinate 89′–1″, 76′–1″.

14. Copy all the unit plans to the right 74′–5″, the width of four units plus the width of the lobby.

▼ **NOTE**

From this point on, we will use the nickname "Zoom All" to refer to the View ➤ Zoom ➤ All command.

15. Click on View ➤ Zoom ➤ All ("Zoom All") to view the entire drawing, which will look like Figure 6.3.

16. Now use the File ➤ Save option to save this file to disk.

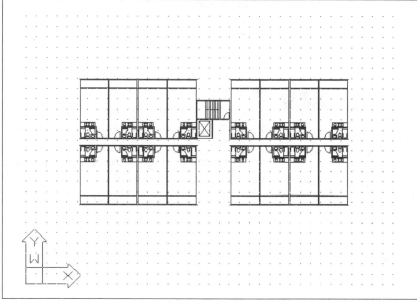

Figure 6.3:   The Plan drawing

CONTROLLING REGENERATION

To understand how to control the amount of time AutoCAD takes to show you your drawings as you work on them, you need to understand the difference between *regenerating* and *redrawing*.

AutoCAD uses two types of numbers for storing and displaying drawings: integers and floating-point numbers. The drawing database is stored in a floating-point format; the display is modeled using integers. When AutoCAD does a *regeneration* ("regen"), it converts the floating-point drawing database into an integer format that is in turn used to generate the display you see on the screen. This integer display format, called the *virtual display,* is a computer model of the actual display you see on the screen. AutoCAD can recalculate these integers much faster than the floating-point coordinates in the drawing database. As long as you select view windows within the virtual display area, your zooming speed will be as fast as a redraw.

Redrawing is used to *refresh* the screen drawing area by clearing blips and restoring any lines that appear to get lost during editing. This redraw takes as little as one-tenth the time of a regeneration. And regeneration of a typical architectural drawing can take half a minute or more if you are using a 486 PC or similar computer. At that rate, you may find yourself spending more time waiting for a drawing to regenerate than you spend on actual editing. With this in mind, you can appreciate the speed of redrawing while moving around in your drawing.

You may have noticed that your drawing takes considerably longer now to regen during the Zoom All command than it did before. This is because AutoCAD must recalculate more information during commands that regenerate the drawing. Zoom All and a handful of other AutoCAD commands cause the program to regenerate the drawing.

In this section, you will discover how to minimize the number of regenerations during an editing session, thus making it easier to create a large and complex drawing. You can control regeneration in three ways:

- By using the virtual screen to speed up zooming and panning

- By saving views to return to without zooming

- By freezing layers that do not need to be viewed or edited

We will explore these methods in the upcoming sections.

USING THE VIRTUAL SCREEN

The virtual display can be turned on or off using the VIEWRES command. The Viewres setting is on by default. Although you can turn it off or on by typing **Viewres ↵ No ↵** at the command prompt, I wouldn't recommend this. The VIEWRES command also controls the smoothness of line types, arcs, and circles when they appear in an enlarged view. With the virtual screen active, line types sometimes appear as continuous even when they are supposed to be dotted or dashed. You may have noticed in previous chapters how on the screen, arcs appear to be segmented lines, though they are always plotted as smooth curves. You can adjust the VIEWRES value to control the number of segments an arc appears to have: the lower the value, the fewer the segments and

---

▼ TIP

If you want to get an overall view of your drawing and the virtual display *without* triggering a regen, click on View ➤ Zoom ➤ Vmax or by typing **Zoom ↵ V ↵**. This gives you a view of the extents of your drawing plus some additional space, but it may zoom out too far for some purposes.

▼ TIP

A good value for the VIEWRES setting is 1000. At this setting, line types display properly, and arcs and circles have a reasonably smooth appearance. At the same time, redraw speed is not noticeably degraded.

the faster the redraw and regeneration. However, a low VIEWRES value will cause noncontinuous line types to appear as continuous.

Another way to accelerate screen redraw is to keep your drawing limits to a minimum area. If the limits are set unnecessarily large, Auto-CAD may slow down noticeably. Also, make sure the drawing origin falls within the drawing limits.

Using the Aerial View

▼ **TIP**

The View ➤ Zoom ➤ Dynamic option performs a similar function to the Aerial View Window, but instead of opening a separate window, Dynamic temporarily displays the overall view in the drawing area.

Lets take a tour of a tool that lets you navigate the Virtual Screen. It's called the Aerial View.

1. Click on Aerial View from the Standard Toolbar. The Aerial View window appears, as shown in Figure 6.4.

2. Move your cursor over to Aerial View window. Notice that you have a dotted cross hair cursor in the window. This is the Aerial View zoom cursor.

3. Click on a point below and to the left of the apartment plan. A view window appears.

4. Click on a point above and to the right of the first unit in the lower left corner so the view window encloses the unit. Your view in the Drawing area enlarges to display the area you just selected. You also see a bold rectangle in the Aerial View window showing the location of your drawing area view.

The Aerial View doesn't zoom in. It continues to display the overall view of your drawing. The bold rectangle shows you exactly where you are in the overall drawing at any given time. This feature is especially useful when you need to zoom in close to a part of a drawing.

II

Building on the Basics

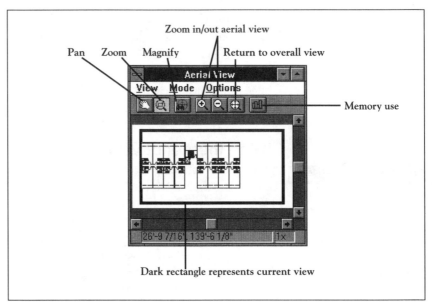

Figure 6.4: The Aerial View window and its components

Now let's look at the pan feature on the Aerial View toolbar. The pan feature can be helpful if you are moving or copying objects from one part of a drawing to another.

1. Choose Mode ➤ Pan from the Aerial View menu bar or click on the Pan button on the Aerial View toolbar. Now as you move your cursor over the Aerial View window, you see a dotted rectangle. This lets you pan to any location in the view.

2. Move the dotted rectangle so it encloses the set of units above the ones currently being displayed in the drawing area. Your view immediately pans to that area.

Again, the view in the Aerial View window doesn't change during the pan, allowing you to visualize where you are in the overall drawing.

Now lets look at the Magnified View feature. This feature lets you search for detail in your drawing, much as you would using a magnifying lens on a map.

Building on the Basics

II

▼ NOTE

When the Magnified View feature is activated, the view in the Aerial View window shows an enlarged view of the area in that rectangle. As you move the rectangle in the drawing area, the Aerial View window changes dynamically, like a magnifying glass passing over the drawing area.

1. Click and drag the button that looks like a pair of binoculars, then drag your mouse into the drawing area. Notice that you now have a gray rectangle that follows the motion of your mouse.

2. Place the rectangle over a bathroom in one of the units, then let go of the mouse button. Your drawing zooms into the bathroom area.

The Aerial View window is a great tool when you are working on a drawing that requires a lot of magnification in your zoomed-in views. You may not find it very helpful on drawings that don't require lots of magnification, like the bathroom drawing you worked on in *Chapters 3* and *4*.

You were able to use the major features of the Aerial view in this exercise. Here are a few more features you can try on your own:

View ➤ Zoom In   zooms in on the view in the Aerial View window.

View ➤ Zoom Out   zooms out on the view in the Aerial View window.

View ➤ Global   displays an overall view of your drawing in the Aerial View window. Global is like a View ➤ Zoom ➤ Extents option for the Aerial View.

Options ➤ Auto Viewport   controls whether a selected viewport is automatically displayed in the Aerial View window. When checked, this option will cause the Aerial View window to automatically display the contents of a viewport when it becomes active. (see *Chapters 12* and *16* for more on viewports.)

Options ➤ Dynamic Update   controls how often changes in your drawing are updated in the Aerial View. When this option is checked, the Aerial View window is updated as you work. You may want to turn this feature off in very complex drawing as it can slow down redraw times.

Options ➤ Locator Magnification…   brings up a dialog box that lets you control the magnification of the Spyglass feature. A higher number increases magnification.

Options ➤ Display Statistics…   displays the memory use of the display list. The display list is the coordinate data Auto-CAD uses to store and update the virtual display.

▼ PREVENTING ACCIDENTAL REGENS

Another way to control regeneration is by setting the Regenmode system variable to 0 (zero). You can also use the REGENAUTO command to accomplish the same thing, by typing **Regenauto ↵ Off ↵**.

If you then zoom or pan to a region outside of the virtual display, AutoCAD tells you it is about to regenerate the drawing and asks if you are sure you want to proceed. Also, commands that normally regenerate a drawing will give the message Regen queued. For example, when you globally edit attributes, redefine blocks, thaw frozen layers, change the LTSCALE setting, or, in some cases, change a text's style, you will get the Regen queued message.

You must then use the REGEN command to display the effects of these commands. If you don't care whether you see the changes, then you won't have to regenerate the drawing. The drawing database will still be updated when you save or end the file.

▼ NOTE

If you have configured Auto-CAD to use the WHIP display driver, regens are generally less of a problem until you start to work with very large, multimegabyte files.

SAVING VIEWS

Now let's look at another way of controlling screen regeneration: saving views. A few walls in the Plan drawing are not complete. You'll need to zoom in to the areas that need work to add the lines, but these areas are spread out over the drawing. You could use the Aerial View window to view each area. There is, however, another way to edit widely separated areas: First, save views of the areas you want to work on, and then jump from saved view to saved view. This technique is especially helpful when you know you will often want to return to a specific area of your drawing.

1. First close the Aerial View window by double-clicking on the button in the upper-left corner of the window.

2. Click on View ➤ Zoom ➤ All to get an overall view of the plan.

3. Click on View ➤ Named Views…. The View Control dialog box appears.

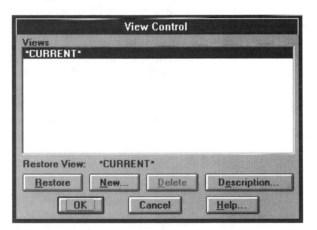

4. Click on the New… button. The Define New View dialog box appears.

5. Click on the Define Window button. Notice that the grayed options become available.

6. Click on Window <. The dialog boxes momentarily disappear.

7. At the First corner prompt, click on the coordinate 26′–3″, 40′–1″.

8. At the Other corner prompt, click on the coordinate 91′–2″, 82′–8″. The dialog boxes reappear.

9. Type **First** for the name of the view you just defined. As you type, the name appears in the New Name input box.

10. Click on the Save View button. The Define New View dialog box closes, and you see FIRST listed in the View Control list.

11. Repeat steps 3 through 9 to define five more views, named SECOND, THIRD, etc. Use Figure 6.5 as a guide for where to define the windows. Click OK when you are done.

Now let's see how you recall these views that you've saved.

1. With the View Control dialog box open, click on FIRST in the list of views.

2. Click the Restore button and then click OK. Your screen displays the first view you selected.

3. Set the current layer to Wall, and proceed to add the stairs and exterior walls of the building, as shown in Figure 6.6.

4. Use the View Control dialog box again to restore the view named SECOND. Then add the wall indicated in Figure 6.7.

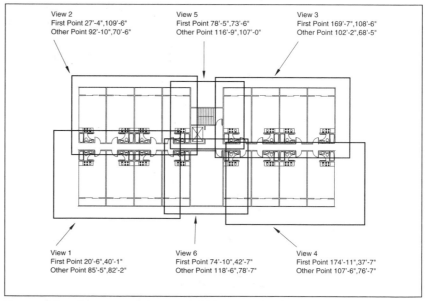

Figure 6.5: Save view windows in these locations for the Plan drawing.

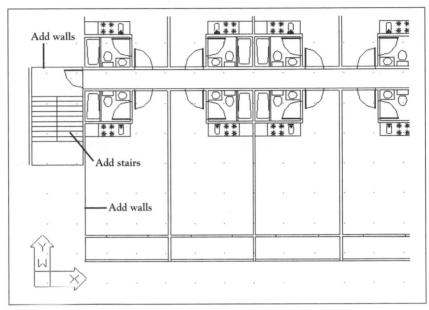

Figure 6.6: The stairs added to the restored Wall view

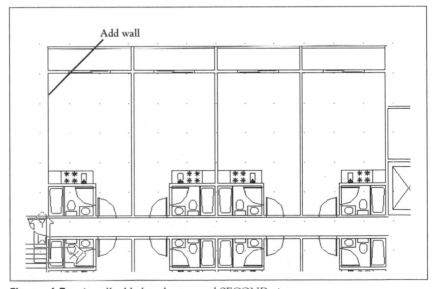

Figure 6.7: A wall added to the restored SECOND view

5. Continue to the other views and add the rest of the exterior walls, as you have done with FIRST and SECOND. Use the three panels of Figure 6.8 as a guide to completing the views.

If you prefer, you can use the keyboard to invoke the VIEW command and thus avoid all the dialog boxes.

1. Click on View ➤ Zoom ➤ All.

2. Enter **View** ↵ at the command prompt.

3. At the View name to save prompt, enter **Overall** ↵.

4. Now save the Plan file to disk.

As you can see, this is a quick way to save a view. With the name OVERALL assigned to this view, you can easily recall the overall view at any time. (The View ➤ Zoom ➤ Vmax option gives you an overall view, too, but it may zoom out too far for some purposes.)

▼
■
■
■
■

OPENING A FILE TO A PARTICULAR VIEW

The Open Drawing dialog box contains a Select Initial View check box. If you open an existing drawing with this option checked, you are greeted with a Select Initial View dialog box just before the opened file appears on the screen. This dialog box lists any views saved in the file. You can then go directly to a view by double-clicking on the view name. If you have saved views and you know the name of the view you want, using Select Initial View saves time when you're opening very large files.

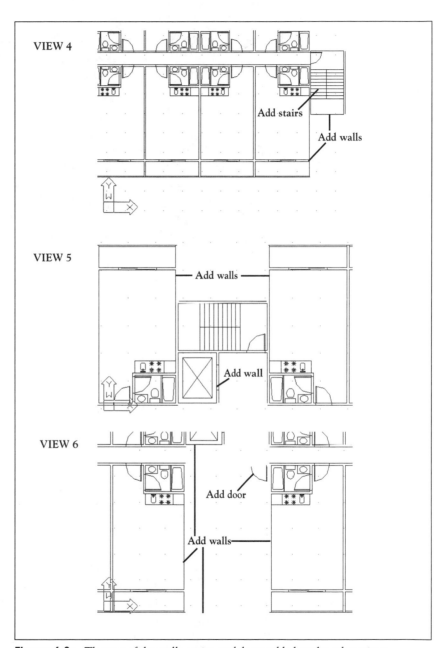

Figure 6.8: The rest of the walls, stairs, and doors added to the other views

ZOOMING AND PANNING DURING OTHER COMMANDS

At times you may want to perform a task that requires you to pan beyond the current view while you're in the middle of another command. For example, suppose you have the view named FIRST on screen and you want to draw a line from the lower-left corner of the building to the upper-right corner. To draw a line, pick the starting point of the line, and then click on View ➤ Pan ➤ Point, and pan your view so that the upper-right corner of the building appears on the screen. Once the view appears, the Line command automatically continues and you can pick the other corner. Likewise, you can use the Aerial View window to zoom or pan over your drawing while in the middle of another command.

Note: This only works within the virtual screen area, and you cannot use Zoom's All or Extents options. But you *can* use the Vmax option or the View command to get an overall view of the virtual screen area while in another command.

Commands that can be used in the middle of other commands are called *transparent commands*. A handful of standard AutoCAD commands, as well as all the system variables, are accessible as transparent commands.

FREEZING LAYERS TO CONTROL REGENERATION TIME

As mentioned earlier, you may wish to turn certain layers off altogether to plot a drawing containing only selected layers. But even when a layers are turned off, AutoCAD still takes the time to redraw and regenerate them. The Data ➤ Layers… command's Freeze option acts like the Off option, except that Freeze causes AutoCAD to ignore frozen layers when redrawing and regenerating a drawing. This is the third method of controlling regeneration in AutoCAD. By freezing layers that are not needed for reference or editing, you can speed up drawing regenerations. But Freeze also affects blocks in a way that Off does not. Try this:

▼ TIP

You can freeze and thaw individual layers by clicking on the Sun icon in the layer pop-up list in the Properties toolbar.

1. Set the current layer to 0.

2. Turn on all the layers in the drawing, and then turn off the Plan1 layer. Nothing happens, because none of the objects were drawn on that layer.

3. Choose Data ➤ Layers. Then choose the Plan1 layer from the list and click on Freeze. (Note that you cannot freeze the current layer.)

4. Click on OK. Every block you inserted disappears.

Even though none of the objects within the inserted blocks were drawn on layer Plan1, when Plan1 is frozen, so are the blocks assigned to that layer. To help you understand what Freeze does to blocks, let's return to the clear plastic bag analogy we used in *Chapter 4*. If a block function is like a plastic bag that holds objects together, you can further think of the bag as an object that is not affected by the Layers command's Off option.

In the last exercise, the items inside the bag were assigned to layers independent of the bag's (block's) layer assignment. When you turned off the layer assigned to the bag, nothing happened because the bag is unaffected by the Layers ➤ Off option, and none of the objects within the bag are on the layer you turned off. However, you can freeze the layer assigned to the bag, causing the bag and its contents to disappear. Figure 6.9 helps you visualize this concept.

▼ NOTE

For more on cross-referencing vs. inserting, see "Cross-Referencing Drawings" later in this chapter.

With respect to the Freeze option, cross-referenced files inserted using the XREF command also act like blocks. For example, you can Xref several drawings on different layers. Then, when you want to view a particular Xref drawing, you can freeze all the layers except the one containing that drawing.

Another technique uses individual layers to store parts of a drawing that you may want to plot separately. For example, three floors in your apartment house plan may contain the same information, with some specific variation on each floor. In this case, you can have one layer

II

Building on the Basics

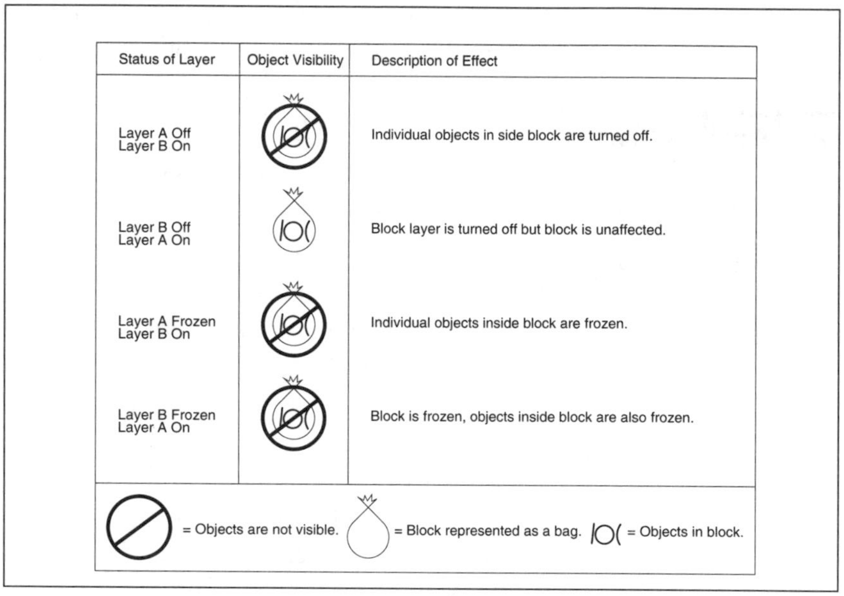

Status of Layer	Object Visibility	Description of Effect
Layer A Off Layer B On		Individual objects in side block are turned off.
Layer B Off Layer A On		Block layer is turned off but block is unaffected.
Layer A Frozen Layer B On		Individual objects inside block are frozen.
Layer B Frozen Layer A On		Block is frozen, objects inside block are also frozen.

⊘ = Objects are not visible.   = Block represented as a bag. |O(= Objects in block.

Figure 6.9: A graphic showing the relationship of the Layers ➤ Freeze option to block

contain blocks of the objects common to all floors. Another layer contains the blocks and objects specific to the first floor, and additional layers contain information specific to the second and third floors. When you want to view or plot one floor, you can freeze the layers associated with the others. You will practice this technique in *Chapter 12*.

Using layers and blocks in these ways requires careful planning and record keeping. It also makes your files quite large, slowing down overall regeneration time and complicating any transfer of files from your hard disk to floppy disks. If used successfully, however, layer-freezing techniques can save substantial time when you're working with drawings that use repetitive objects or that require similar information that can be overlaid.

Now "thaw" layer Plan1 that you froze earlier, turn off the Ceiling layer, and use File ➤ Exit to exit the Plan file.

UNDERSTANDING MODEL SPACE AND PAPER SPACE

▼ NOTE

The VPORTS command (View ➤ Tiled Viewports) only works in Model Space. In Model Space, you can use VPORTS to split your screen into several viewports, which can neither be plotted nor shaped and controlled individually the way Paper Space viewports can. See *Chapter 16* for details.

So far, you've looked at ways to help you get around in your drawing while using a single view. You also have the capability to set up multiple views of your drawing, called *viewports*. Viewports are accessed by using two modes of display: *Paper Space* and *Model Space*.

To get a clear understanding of these two modes, imagine that your drawing is actually a full-size replica or model of the object you are drawing. Your computer screen is your window into a "room" where this model is being constructed, and the keyboard and mouse are your means of access to this room. You can control your window's position in relation to the object through the use of the View ➤ Pan and ➤ Zoom commands. You can also construct or modify the model by using drawing and editing commands. This room is your *Model Space*.

So far, you have been working on your drawings by looking through a single "window." Now suppose you have the ability to step back and add windows with different views looking into your Model Space. The effect is as if you have several video cameras in your Model Space "room," each connected to a different monitor: You can view all your windows at once on your computer screen, or enlarge a single window to fill the entire screen. Further, you can control the shape of your windows and easily switch from one window to another. This is what *Paper Space* is like.

Paper Space lets you set up several views into your drawing Model Space. Each view acts like an individual virtual screen. One window can have an overall view of your drawing, while another can be a close-up. Layer visibility can also be controlled individually for each window, allowing you to display different versions of the same area of your drawing. You can move, copy, and stretch viewports, and even overlap them, just as you do objects.

If you draw something in Paper Space, it doesn't become part of Model Space, but it can be plotted. This is significant because, as you will see in *Chapter 12*, Paper Space lets you plot several views of the same drawing on one sheet of paper. You can even include drawing borders and notes that appear only in Paper Space. In this function, you might think of Paper Space as a kind of page-layout area where you can "paste up" different views of your drawing. Figure 6.10 shows the Plan drawing set up in Paper Space mode to display several views.

II

Building on the Basics

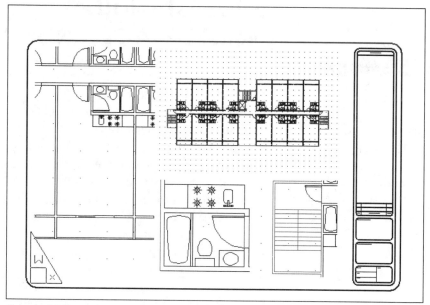

Figure 6.10: Different views of the same drawing in Paper Space

We will discuss using Paper Space in more detail in *Chapter 12*. For now, let's continue with our look at working with large drawings.

ADDING HATCH PATTERNS TO YOUR DRAWINGS

To help communicate your ideas to others, you will want to add graphic elements that represent types of materials, special regions, or textures. AutoCAD provides *hatch patterns* for quickly placing a texture over an area of your drawing. In this section, you will add a hatch pattern to the floor of the studio apartment unit, thereby instantly enhancing the appearance of one drawing. Then later in the chapter you'll learn how you can quickly update all the units in the overall floor plan to reflect the changes in the unit.

SETTING UP FOR THE HATCH

The first step is to provide a layer for the hatch pattern.

1. Open the Unit file and zoom into the bathroom and kitchen-ette area.

2. Create a new layer called **Flr-pat**.

3. Make Flr-pat the current layer.

DEFINING THE HATCH

new

1. Click on the Hatch button on the Draw Palette or type **Bhatch** ↵.

The Boundary Hatch dialog box appears.

Building on the Basics   **II**

▼ NOTE

The Boundary Hatch dialog box lets you set the hatch pattern (Pattern Type and Pattern Properties), pick a point that is bounded by the area to be hatched (Pick Points), select objects to define the hatch area (Select Objects), and use advanced boundary selection options for complex hatch patterns (Advanced...). Other options let you preview the hatch pattern in place (Preview Hatch), or view the hatch boundaries (View Selections).

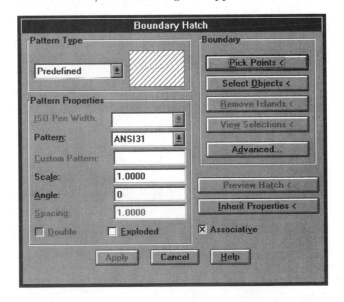

▼ **TIP**

Say you want to add a hatch pattern you have previously inserted. You may think that you have to guess at its scale and rotation angle. But with the Inherit Properties option in the Boundary Hatch dialog box, you can select a previously inserted hatch pattern as a prototype for the current hatch pattern. This feature does not work with Exploded hatch patterns however.

2. Under Pattern Type, open the pop-up list and select User-Defined. The User-Defined option lets you define a simple crosshatch pattern by specifying the line spacing of the hatch and whether it is a single- or double-hatch pattern. The Angle and Spacing input boxes become available in the Pattern Properties group, so you can enter values.

3. Double-click on the Spacing input box and enter **6**. This tells AutoCAD you want the hatch's line spacing to be 6″. Leave the Angle value at 0, since we want the pattern to be aligned with the bathroom.

4. Click on the Double check box (at the bottom of the Pattern Properties group). This tells AutoCAD you want the hatch pattern to run both vertically and horizontally.

5. Click on the Pick Points button. The dialog box momentarily disappears, allowing you to pick a point inside the area you want hatched.

6. Click on a point anywhere inside the bathroom floor area, away from the toilet. Notice that a highlighted outline appears in the bathroom. This is the boundary AutoCAD has selected to enclose the hatch pattern. It outlines everything including the door swing arc; however, it misses the toilet.

7. Press ↵ to return to the dialog box, and click on the Select Objects button.

8. Click on the toilet to highlight it, and press ↵ to return to the Boundary Hatch dialog box.

9. Click on the Preview Hatch button. The hatch pattern appears everywhere on the floor except where the door swing occurs.

10. Click on Pick Points again, pick a point inside the door swing, and press ↵.

11. Click on Preview Hatch again. The hatch pattern now covers the entire floor area.

12. Click on the Apply button to place the hatch pattern in the drawing.

Draw ➤ Hatch lets you first define the boundary within which you want to place a hatch pattern. You do this by simply clicking on a location inside the boundary area, as in step 6. AutoCAD finds the actual boundary for you.

USING THE ADVANCED HATCH OPTIONS

You might have noticed that, in the case of the toilet, you only had to select it to include it into the boundary region for the hatch pattern. Think of the toilet as a "nested" boundary area to be excluded from hatching. You can control how AutoCAD treats these nested boundaries by selecting options available with the Advanced... button in the Boundary Hatch dialog box. This button displays the Advanced Options dialog:

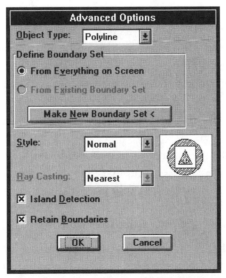

In addition to controlling the nesting of hatch patterns, the Advanced Options let you fine-tune other aspects of hatch pattern creation.

Building on the Basics

II

Style   The Style pop-up list in the middle of the dialog box controls how nested boundaries affect the hatch pattern. When you select a Style option, the graphic to the right of the pop-up list shows an example of the effect of the selected option. The Style options include the following:

Normal   causes the hatch pattern to alternate between nested boundaries. The outer boundary is hatched; then, if there is a closed object within the boundary, it is not hatched. If there is another closed object *inside* the first closed object, *that* object is hatched. This is the default setting.

Outer   applies the hatch pattern to an area defined by the outermost boundary and any boundaries nested within the outermost boundary. Any boundaries nested within the nested boundaries are ignored.

Ignore   applies the hatch pattern to the entire area within the outermost boundary, ignoring any nested boundaries.

> **▼ NOTE**
>
> Hatch patterns are like blocks, in that they act like single objects. You can explode a hatch pattern to edit its individual lines. You can also automatically explode the hatch after it is placed in the drawing, by selecting the Exploded check box in the Pattern Properties group of the Boundary Hatch dialog box.

Object Type   This pull-down list lets you select the type of object used to define the boundary. The default is Polyline, which creates a simple outline using a polyline. The other option is Region, which creates an object that is like a flat plane in the shape of the hatch area.

Define Boundary Set   Within this group, you'll find the following:

From Everything on Screen   is on by default, unless you have already used Boundary Hatch to generate a hatch boundary. If it isn't already on, clicking this button creates a new boundary set based on everything visible on the screen. This operation can take some time if the current view is dense with objects.

From Existing Working Set   is on by default if you have already used Boundary Hatch to generate a hatch boundary. This setting simply indicates that a boundary set already exists and

will be used unless the From Everything on Screen option button is selected or you click the Make New Boundary Set button.

Make New Boundary Set lets you select the objects from
which you want AutoCAD to determine the hatch boundary.
The screen clears and lets you select objects. This option dis-
cards previous boundary sets.

Ray Casting

Ray Casting This is a pull-down list that lets you control how
AutoCAD searches for a boundary when Island Detection (described
next) is not used. The options are Nearest (the default), −X, +X, −Y,
and +Y. With Nearest selected, AutoCAD searches for a boundary by
starting with the object nearest to the point you pick when you use the
Pick Points button in the Boundary Hatch dialog box. The −X and −Y
options cause AutoCAD to search in negative X or negative Y direction for the first object in the boundary. The +X and +Y options cause
AutoCAD to search in a positive X or positive Y direction.

Island Detection

Island Detection This check box controls the Island Detection
feature, a new method of finding boundaries used by AutoCAD Release 13. It is capable of finding nested areas and islands more easily
than the older Ray Casting method.

Retain Boundaries

Retain Boundaries The Boundary Hatch command works by
creating temporary 2D regions which are like 2D planes or polyline
outlines of the hatch area. These polyline boundaries are automatically
removed after the hatch pattern is inserted. If you want to retain the
polyline boundaries in the drawing, make sure the Retain Boundaries
check box is turned on. Retaining the boundary can be useful in situations where you know you will be hatching the area more than once,
or if you are hatching a fairly complex area. It is also useful if you want
to know the hatched area's dimensions in square inches or feet. This
option is only available if a boundary is already defined.

Building on the Basics

II

THINGS TO WATCH OUT FOR WHILE USING BOUNDARY HATCH

Here are a few tips on using the Boundary Hatch feature:

- Watch out for boundary areas that are part of a very large block. AutoCAD will examine the entire block when defining boundaries. This can take time if the block is quite large.

- The Boundary Hatch feature is view dependent; that is, it locates boundaries based on what is visible in the current view. To ensure that AutoCAD finds every detail, zoom in to the area to be hatched.

- If the area to be hatched will cover a very large area yet will require fine detail, first outline the hatch area using a polyline (see *Chapter 13* for more on Polylines). Then use the Select Object option in the Boundary Hatch dialog box to select the polyline boundary manually, instead of depending on Boundary Hatch to find the boundary for you.

- Consider turning off layers that might interfere with Auto-CAD's ability to find a boundary. For example, in the previous exercise, you could have turned off the Door layer, and then used Pick Points to locate the boundary of the hatch pattern.

- Boundary Hatch works on nested blocks as long as the nested block entities are parallel to the current UCS and are uniformly scaled in the x- and y-axes.

POSITIONING HATCH PATTERNS ACCURATELY

In the last exercise, the hatch pattern was placed in the bathroom without regard for the location of the lines that make up the pattern. In most cases, however, you will want to control where the lines of the pattern are placed.

Hatch patterns use the same origin as the snap origin. By default, this origin is the same as the drawing origin, 0,0. You can change the snap origin (and thus the hatch pattern origin) by using the Snapbase system variable.

The following exercise guides you through the process of placing a hatch pattern accurately, using the example of adding floor tile to the kitchenette.

▼ TIP

You can also click on Graphic in the Pattern Type list to "page" through each of the predefined hatch patterns.

1. Pan your view so that you can see the area below the kitchenette, and draw the 3′–0″×8′–0″ outline of the floor tile area, as shown in Figure 6.11.

2. At the command prompt, type **Snapbase** ⏎.

3. At the New value for SNAPBASE <0′–0″,0′–0″>: prompt, use the Endpoint Osnap override and click on the lower-left corner of the area you just defined (see Figure 6.11).

4. Click on Draw ➤ Hatch.

5. At the Boundary Hatch dialog box, make sure Predefined is selected in the Pattern Type pull-down list.

II

Building on the Basics

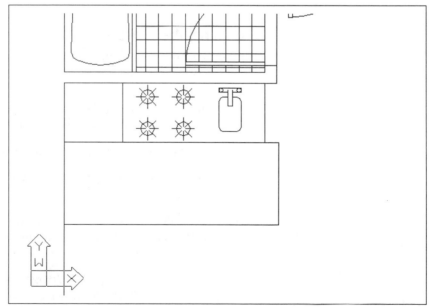

Figure 6.11:   The area below the kitchenette showing the outline of the floor tile area

6. In the Pattern Properties group, open the Pattern pull-down list and select AR-PARQ1. The graphic to the right of the Pattern Type list box changes to show what AR-PARQ1 looks like.

7. Click on the Pick Points button.

8. Click on the interior of the area to be tiled, and press ↵.

9. Click on Apply. A parquet-style tile pattern appears in the defined area.

Notice that each tile is shown whole; none of the tiles is cut off as in the bathroom example. This is because you first used the Snapbase system variable to set the origin for the hatch pattern. You can now move the Snapbase setting back to the 0,0 setting and not affect the hatch pattern.

In the foregoing exercise, you got a chance to use a predefined hatch pattern. Figure 6.12 shows you all the patterns available. You can also create your own custom patterns, as described in *Chapter 21*.

Changing the Hatch Area

Suppose you want to enlarge the tiled area of the kitchenette by one tile. Here's how it's done.

1. Click on the outline border of the hatch pattern you just created. Notice that grips appear around the hatch pattern area.

2. Shift-click on the grip in the lower-left corner of the hatch area.

3. With the lower-left grip highlighted, Shift-click on the lower-right grip.

4. Now click on the lower-left grip again, but don't Shift-click this time. Move the mouse and notice how the hatch boundary moves with it.

5. At the <Stretch to point>/Basepoint/Copy/Undo/eXit prompt, enter **@12<–90** to widen the hatch pattern by 1 foot. The hatch pattern adjusts to the new size of the boundary.

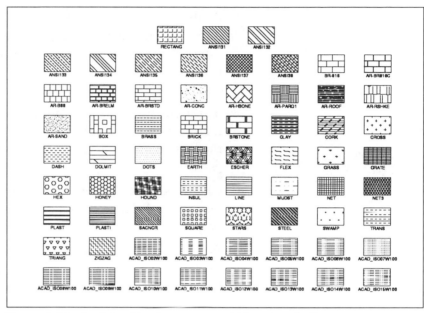

Figure 6.12: Predefined hatch patterns available in AutoCAD

MODIFYING A HATCH PATTERN

Like everything else, you or someone involved in your project will eventually want to change a hatch pattern in some way. In previous versions of AutoCAD, changing hatch patterns was a tedious process. Release 13 makes it a lot easier, as demonstrated in the following exercise.

1. Click and drag Edit Polyline from the Modify palette then select Edit Hatch, or type **Hatchedit** ↵ at the command prompt.

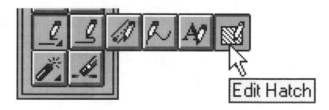

II

Building on the Basics

2. At the Select hatch object: prompt, click on the hatch pattern area. The Boundary Hatch dialog box appears again. You can now select any option that is available (not grayed out) to modify the hatch pattern.

3. Choose Predefined from the Pattern Type list box; then click on the graphic beside the Pattern Type list box. Notice how it changes and how, as it changes, the name of the pattern in the Pattern Properties group changes with it, to identify the pattern.

4. Choose AR-BRSTD from the Pattern pop-up list in the Pattern Properties group. Click the Apply button to change the hatch pattern area to the new pattern.

5. We want to keep the old pattern in our drawing, so click on the Undo button on the standard toolbar twice or type **U** ↵ twice to return to the previous hatch pattern.

As you saw in the last exercise, not all the Boundary Hatch options are available to you. Still, you can change the pattern to a predefined or custom pattern, or to one that exists in the drawing. You can also change the angle and scale of a pattern, as well as the origin. Remember, in order to change the hatch origin, you must set the snap origin before you use the HATCHEDIT command.

A Review of Other Boundary Hatch Options

Before exiting this section, you might want to look over the descriptions of options in the Boundary Hatch dialog box that weren't discussed in the exercises.

ISO Pen Width lets you select a pen width to associate with the hatch patterns. These pen widths are meaningful only when used with the ISO standard hatch patterns. When you set the ISO pen width, the scale of the pattern is adjusted accordingly. However, you must manually set the width of the actual plotter pen at plot time.

Exploded   draws the hatch pattern as individual objects, instead of an associative hatch pattern.

Associative   draws a hatch pattern that will automatically update whenever the boundary of the hatch pattern changes.

Remove Islands   allows you to remove nested or island boundaries that have been included when you pick a point to define a boundary. This is useful when you want to force a hatch pattern to fall inside an island that occurs in a boundary.

View Selections   lets you review the boundaries that have been selected at any given time during the Boundary Hatch process.

Inherit Properties   lets you designate a hatch pattern, scale, and angle by selecting an existing hatch pattern in your drawing. When you choose this option, the dialog box momentarily disappears so you can select a pattern from your drawing. The properties of the selected pattern become the settings for the current boundary hatch session.

Default Properties   sets the Boundary Hatch options to their current default settings.

SPACE PLANNING AND HATCH PATTERNS

Suppose you are working on a plan within which you are constantly repositioning equipment and furniture, or in the process of designing the floor covering. You may be a little hesitant to place a hatch pattern on the floor because you don't want to have to rehatch the area every time you move a piece of equipment or change the flooring. You have two options in this situation: You can use polyline outlines, or you can put AutoCAD's 3D features to work.

Outlining the Area and the Blocks

The first option is to outline the floor area with a polyline; then you outline your equipment with polylines also. Make sure the outlining polylines are on their own layer. Turn off all layers except the layer for the floor pattern and the outlining polylines. Finally, choose Hatch

II

Building on the Basics

from the Draw palette to hatch the floor, making sure the polylines out-lining your equipment are included in the boundary set. This way, whenever you move equipment or furniture in your plan, you can simply erase the old hatch pattern and repeat the HATCH command.

Using 3D Features to Trick AutoCAD

The second option requires the use of some 3D features of AutoCAD. First, draw the equipment at an elevation above the floor level by setting up AutoCAD to draw objects with a Z coordinate other than 0. Use the 3DFACE command to generate a 3D surface that matches the outline of the equipment. Or, if your equipment outline is a fairly complex shape, use a region (regions are discussed in *Chapter 18*). Make sure the 3Dfaces are drawn at an elevation that places them between the floor and the equipment. Turn each individual piece of equipment, complete with 3Dface, into blocks or groups so that you can easily move around. Once this is done, hatch the entire floor, making sure the hatch pattern is at an elevation below the 3Dface elevation (see Figure 6.13).

As you work with the drawing, the floor pattern will show through the equipment. (Don't worry—when it is time to plot your drawing, you can use the PLOT command's Hide option, discussed in *Chapter 15*, or the View ➤ Floating Viewports ➤ Hideplot option, discussed in *Chapter 18*.) This causes anything behind the 3Dface to be hidden in the plotter output, which means any hatch pattern underneath your equipment will not appear. You can also use the HIDE command from time to time to see what your design will look like, without having to wait for hard copy—like using paper cutouts over a plan.

Using AutoCAD 3D features this way can save you time and give you more flexibility in your work. And although the HIDE command takes a minute or two to do its work, it is still faster than rehatching an area each time you make a change to its configuration. For more on the 3D functions mentioned here, see *Part IV* of this book.

▼ **NOTE**

See *Chapter 15* for more on drawing objects in 3D.

▼ **WARNING**

One drawback to this 3D method is that the HIDE command turns solids and wide polylines into outlines.

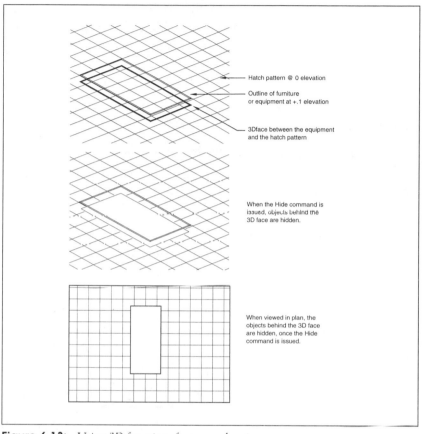

Figure 6.13: Using 3D functions for space planning

Hatch pattern @ 0 elevation

Outline of furniture
or equipment at +.1 elevation

3Dface between the equipment
and the hatch pattern

When the Hide command is
issued, objects behind the
3D face are hidden.

When viewed in plan, the
objects behind the 3D face
are hidden, once the Hide
command is issued.

Building on the Basics

UPDATING BLOCKS

This method does not update
exploded blocks. If you plan to
use this method to update parts
of a drawing, do not explode the
blocks you plan to update. See
"Updating and Modifying a
Block" in *Chapter 4*.

As you progress through a design project, you make countless revisions.
With traditional drafting methods, revising a drawing like our studio
apartment floor plan takes a good deal of time. If the bathroom layout
is changed, for example, you have to erase every occurrence of the bathroom and redraw it 16 times. With AutoCAD, on the other hand, revising this drawing can be a very quick operation. The studio unit you
just modified can be updated throughout the overall plan drawing by

replacing the current Unit block with the updated Unit file. AutoCAD automatically updates all occurrences of the Unit block. The following exercise shows you how this is accomplished.

1. Start by opening the Plan file.

2. When the drawing begins to appear, press the Escape key to cancel the initial regeneration.

3. Click on Insert Block from the Draw Palette.

4. Click on the File button, and from the Select Drawing File dialog box, double-click on the Unit file name.

5. Click on OK. A warning message tells you that a block already exists with the same name as the file. You have the option to cancel the operation or redefine the block in the current drawing.

6. Click on Redefine. Your prompt displays a series of messages telling you that AutoCAD is ignoring duplicate blocks. Then, the drawing will regenerate (unless you have REGENAUTO turned off; see the sidebar, "Preventing Accidental Regens").

7. At the Insertion point prompt, press Esc. You do this because you really don't want to insert a Unit plan into your drawing, but rather are just using the Insert feature to update an existing block.

8. If REGENAUTO is turned off, type **Regen** ↵ to turn it on.

9. Now zoom in to one of the units. You will see that the floor tile appears in the unit as you drew it in the Unit file (see Figure 6.14).

Nested blocks must be updated independent of the parent block. For example, if you had modified the Toilet block while editing the Unit file, and then updated the Unit drawing in the Plan file, the old Toilet block would not have been updated. Even though the toilet is part of

▼ NOTE

You need not wait for a drawing to regenerate in order to edit it, so canceling this regeneration can save some time when you update blocks.

▼ NOTE

If REGENAUTO is turned off, you must use the REGEN command to force a regeneration of the drawing before the updated Unit block will appear on the display, even though the drawing database has been updated.

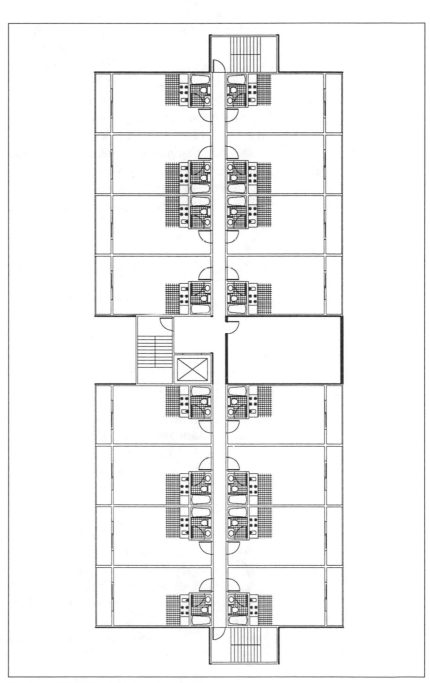

Figure 6.14: The Plan drawing thus far

the Unit file, it is still a unique, independent block in the Plan file, and AutoCAD will not modify it unless specifically instructed to do so. In this situation, you must edit the original Toilet file, and then update it in both the Plan and Unit files.

Also, block references and layer settings of the current file take priority over those of the imported file. For example, if a file to be imported has layers of the same name as the current file, but those layers have color and line-type assignments that are different from the current file's, the current file's layer color and line-type assignments will determine those of the imported file. This does not mean, however, that the actual imported file on disk is changed; only the inserted drawing is affected.

▼
■
■
■
■

SUBSTITUTING BLOCKS

In the example under the section "Updating Blocks," you update a block in your Plan file using the File option in the Insert dialog box. In that exercise, the block name and the file name were the same. You can also *replace* a block with another block or file of a different name. Here's how to do this:

1. Type **Insert** ↵ at the command prompt.

2. At the Block name (or ?) <>: prompt, enter **unit=alternate** ↵ where **alternate** is the name of the replacing block or file name. You will get the message Block unit redefined, and if REGENAUTO is turned off, your drawing will regenerate.

3. At the Insertion point: prompt, press Esc.

You can use this method of replacing blocks if you would like to see how changing one element of your project can change your design. You might, for example, draw three different apartment unit plans, each with a unique name. You could then generate and plot three apartment house designs in a fraction of the time it would take you to do it by hand.

Block substitution can also reduce a drawing's complexity and accelerate regenerations. To do this, you temporarily replace large, complex blocks with schematic versions of those blocks. For example, you might replace the Unit block in the Plan drawing with another drawing that contains just a single-line representation of the walls and bathroom fixtures. You would still have the wall lines for reference when inserting other symbols or adding mechanical or electrical information, but the drawing would regenerate much faster. When doing the final plot, you would reinsert the original Unit block showing every detail.

CROSS-REFERENCING DRAWINGS

In this chapter's discussion about freezing layers, we mentioned that you can use cross-referenced drawing files in a way similar to using blocks. To accomplish this, you use the External Reference (XREF) command. The difference between these cross-referenced (Xref) files and files inserted with the Insert Block option from the Draw palette is that Xref files do not actually become part of the drawing's database. Instead, they are "loaded" along with the current file at start-up time. It is as if Auto-CAD were opening several drawings at once: the currently active file you specify when you start AutoCAD, and any file inserted with XREF.

If you keep Xref files independent from the current file, any changes you make to the cross-reference will automatically appear in the current file. You don't have to manually update the Xref file as you do blocks. For example, if you used XREF to insert the Unit file into the Plan file, and you later made changes to the Unit file, the next time you opened the Plan file you would see the new version of the Unit file in place of the old.

Another advantage to cross-referenced files is that since they do not actually become part of a drawing's database, drawing size is kept to a minimum. This translates to more efficient use of your hard disk space.

▼ NOTE

Cross-referenced (Xref) files, like blocks, cannot be edited. You can, however, use Osnap overrides to snap to location in an Xref file, or freeze the Xref file's layer to make it invisible.

Building on the Basics

II

OPENING THE EXTERNAL REFERENCE PALETTE

The next exercise shows how you can use an External Reference in place of an inserted block to construct the studio apartment building. You'll start by creating a new unit file by copying the old one. Then you bring a new palette, the External Reference Palette, to the screen.

1. Use the Windows File Manager to make a copy of the Unit file and name the copy **Unitxref.DWG**.

2. Open a new file called **Planxref,** and set up the drawing for a $\frac{1}{8}$"=1'–0" scale on an 11"×17" drawing area.

3. Click on Tools ➤ Toolbars ➤ External Reference to open the External Reference toolbar. You can also click and drag the Aerial View button on the standard toolbar, then select External Reference. The new toolbar appears in the drawing area.

With the External Reference palette on the screen, you can access any of the External Reference functions with a single click.

ATTACHING A DRAWING AS A CROSS REFERENCE

Now you're ready to do the actual attaching of a drawing.

▼ NOTE

Another way to attach a drawing is to enter **Xref** ↵ at the command prompt. The prompt response that you see contains the same options as those found on the External Reference toolbar. Since attach is the default option, press ↵ to attach a file.

1. Click on Attach from the External Reference toolbar.

2. At the Select File to Attach dialog box, click on the file named unitxref. You see the message Unitxref loaded in the prompt area.

3. At the Insertion point: prompt, insert the drawing at coordinate 31'–5",43'–8". The rest of the XREF command acts just like the INSERT command. Press ↵ at all the prompts to accept the defaults.

4. Once the Unitxref file appears, make several copies of it in the same way you made copies of the Unit plan in the first part of this chapter.

5. Save the Planxref file. Then open Unitxref.

6. Erase the hatch pattern for the floors, and save the file.

7. Open Planxref again, and notice what happens to the Unitxref file you inserted using the External Reference command.

Here you saw how a cross-referenced file doesn't have to be updated the way blocks do. Also, you avoid the task of having to update nested blocks, since AutoCAD updates nested cross-references, as well as un-nested cross-references.

OTHER DIFFERENCES BETWEEN CROSS-REFERENCING AND INSERTING

Here are a few other differences between cross-referenced files (Xref) and inserted files that you will want to keep in mind:

- Any new layers, text styles, or line types brought in with cross-referenced files do not become part of the current file. You must use the options on the All flyout on the External Reference palette to import these items.

- If you make changes to the layers of a cross-referenced file, those changes will not be retained when the file is saved, unless you set the Visretain system variable to 1. Visretain will then instruct AutoCAD to remember any layer color or visibility settings from one editing session to the next.

II

Building on the Basics

■ To segregate layers on a cross referenced file from the ones in the current drawing, the cross-referenced file's layers are prefixed with their file's name. A vertical bar separates the file-name prefix and the layer name, as in Unitxref | wall.

■ Cross-referenced files cannot be exploded. You can, however, convert a cross-reference file into a block, then explode it. To do this, you must use the All option on the External Reference palette. This option turns all cross-referenced files into blocks.

■ If a cross-referenced file is renamed or moved to another location on your hard disk, AutoCAD won't be able to find that file when it opens other files to which the cross-reference is attached. If this happens, you must use the Path option on the External Reference palette to tell AutoCAD where to find the cross-reference file.

Cross-referenced files are especially useful in workgroup environments where several people are working on the same project. For example, one person might be updating several files that are inserted into a variety of other files. Using blocks, everyone in the workgroup would have to be notified of the changes and then update all the affected blocks in all the drawings that contained them. With cross-referenced files, however, the updating is automatic, so you avoid confusion about which files need to have their blocks updated.

THE EXTERNAL REFERENCE PALETTE OPTIONS

There are many other features unique to cross-referenced files. Let's briefly look at some of the options under the External Reference palette we haven't yet discussed.

Overlay attaches a file as a cross-reference without including any files that might be attached to the cross-reference. This avoids multiple attachments of other files and eliminates the possibility of circular references (referencing the current file into itself through another file).

▼ TIP

You can convert a single cross-referenced file into a block by typing **Xref** ⏎ **B** ⏎, then enter the name of the cross-reference file to be converted.

Reload lets you update an Xref file that has been modified since you opened your current file. This is useful when you are working in a network environment and you know that someone is concurrently editing a cross-referenced file that you need.

Clip simultaneously attaches and creates a paper space viewport of an external file.

List displays a list of all files attached to the current open file.

To aid in housekeeping, AutoCAD maintains a log file that keeps a record of all your cross-reference file activity. The name of the file is the same as the drawing file it is associated with, except that the .XLG extension is used. This file stores a record of cross-referenced files and their associated blocks. AutoCAD creates this file automatically if it does not already exist. If it does exist, AutoCAD will append further records of cross-reference activity.

IF YOU WANT TO EXPERIMENT...

If you'd like to see firsthand how block substitution works, try doing the exercise in Figure 6.15. It shows how quickly you can change the configuration of a drawing by careful use of block substitution. As you work through the exercise, keep in mind that some planning is required to use blocks in this way. If you know that you will have to try various configurations in a drawing, you can plan to set up files to accommodate them.

You might also want to try the exercise using the External Reference palette's Attach option in place of inserting files as blocks. Once you've attached the cross-reference, try detaching it by using the External Reference palette's Detach option. When you get the prompt Xref(s) to Detach, enter the name of the cross-referenced file.

By now, you may be anxious to see how your drawings look on paper. In the next chapter you will explore the use of AutoCAD's printing and plotting commands.

II

Building on the Basics

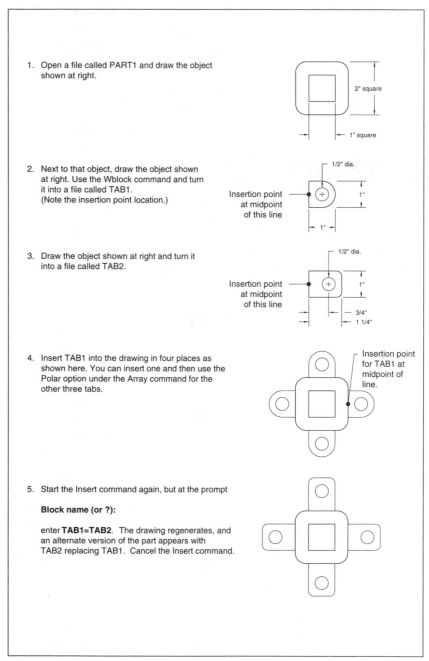

1. Open a file called PART1 and draw the object shown at right.

   2" square

   1" square

2. Next to that object, draw the object shown at right. Use the Wblock command and turn it into a file called TAB1.
   (Note the insertion point location.)

   1/2" dia.

   Insertion point at midpoint of this line

   1"

   1"

3. Draw the object shown at right and turn it into a file called TAB2.

   1/2" dia.

   Insertion point at midpoint of this line

   1"

   3/4"

   1 1/4"

4. Insert TAB1 into the drawing in four places as shown here. You can insert one and then use the Polar option under the Array command for the other three tabs.

   Insertion point for TAB1 at midpoint of line.

5. Start the Insert command again, but at the prompt

   Block name (or ?):

   enter **TAB1=TAB2**. The drawing regenerates, and an alternate version of the part appears with TAB2 replacing TAB1. Cancel the Insert command.

Figure 6.15: An exercise in block substitution

7

▼ ▼ ▼ ▼ ▼

PRINTING AND PLOTTING

Setting Plotter Origin

Selecting Paper Sizes

Controlling Dashed and Filled
Wide Lines

Controlling What Gets Printed

Setting Scale and Drawing Location

Setting Line Weights

Setting Plotter Speed

Previewing a Plot before Plotting

Using Scripts to Automate Plotting

FAST TRACK

292 ▶ **To start printing or plotting**

Click on File ➤ Print.

294 ▶ **To select a plotter or printer**

Click on the Device and Default Selection button in the Plot Configuration dialog box. Then click on the desired output device in the list.

297 ▶ **To select a paper size**

In the Plot Configuration dialog box, click the Size button. Click on a sheet size in the Paper Size dialog box, or use the Width and Height input boxes to enter a custom size.

299 ▶ **To plot a 3D drawing and remove hidden lines**

In the Plot Configuration dialog box, turn on the Hide Lines option in the Additional Parameters group. This is not necessary, however, if you are plotting paper space viewports that have the Hideplot option turned on (View ➤ Floating Viewports ➤ Hideplot). See *Chapter 12* for more on paper space and *Chapter 18* for more on Hideplot.

299 ▶ **To save a plot to a file for later plotting**

Before you plot, click the File Name button in the Additional Parameters group, and then enter the name you want for the plot file.

309 ▶ **To adjust the location of a plot on the paper**

In the Plot Configuration dialog box, click on the Rotation and Origin button. At the next dialog box, enter offset values in the X Origin and Y Origin input boxes. Use negative values for offsets to the left or down.

310 ▶ To control the orientation of the image on the paper

Click the Rotation and Origin button under Scale, Rotation, and Origin, and then rotate the image by selecting an option from the Plot Rotation and Origin dialog box.

310 ▶ To control line weights

In the Plot Configuration dialog box, click the Pen Assignments button. Assign pens of different weights to the various drawing colors, by highlighting a color item in the list box and entering the appropriate pen assignment settings in the Modify Values input boxes.

313 ▶ To make sure pen widths don't enlarge the area of solid fills

In the Plot Configuration dialog box, turn on the Adjust Area Fill option in the Additional Parameters group. Make sure the Pen Width setting in the Pen Assignment dialog box corresponds to the actual pen width setting of your plotter.

315 ▶ To view a plot before you commit it to paper

In the Plot Configuration dialog box, turn on the Full option in the Plot Preview group. Then click the Preview button.

316 ▶ To save plotter settings for easy retrieval

In the Plot Configuration dialog box, click the Device and Default Selection button. Then click Save Defaults To File. At the Save To File dialog box, enter the name you want for the settings file.

▼ NOTE

For more information on choosing between printers and plotters, see *Appendix A*.

Getting hard copy output from AutoCAD is something of an art. You'll need to be intimately familiar with both your output device and the settings available in AutoCAD. You will probably spend a good deal of time experimenting with AutoCAD's plotter settings and your printer or plotter to get your equipment set up just the way you want.

With the huge array of output options available, this chapter can only provide a general discussion of plotting. It is up to you to work out the details and fine-tune the way you and AutoCAD together work with your plotter. Here we'll take a look at the features available in Auto-CAD and discuss some general rules and guidelines to follow when setting up your plots. We'll also discuss alternatives to using a plotter, such as plotter service bureaus and common dot-matrix printers. There won't be much in the way of a tutorial, so consider this chapter more of a reference.

PLOTTING THE PLAN

To see firsthand how the PLOT command works, try plotting the Plan file.

1. First, be sure your printer or plotter is connected to your computer and is turned on.

2. Start AutoCAD and open the Plan file.

3. Click on View ➤ Zoom ➤ All to display the entire drawing.

4. Click on File ➤ Print or type Plot ↵ at the command prompt. The Plot Configuration dialog box appears.

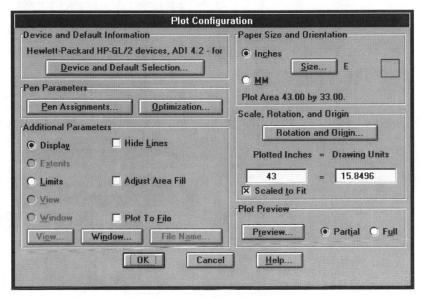

5. Click on OK. The dialog box closes and you see the following message:

   Command: PLOT Effective plotting area: 10.50 wide by 7.59 high

   The width and height values shown in this message will depend your system setup.

6. Your plotter or printer will print out the plan to no particular scale. You may see various messages while AutoCAD is plotting. When the plot is done, you see the message

   Regeneration done 100% Plot complete.

You've just done your first printout. Now let's take a look at the wealth of settings available when you plot, starting with the selection of an output device.

SELECTING AN OUTPUT DEVICE

Many of you have more than one output device. You may have a laser printer for your word-processed documents, in addition to a plotter. You may also require PostScript file output for presentations. AutoCAD offers you the flexibility to use several types of devices, quickly and easily.

When you configure AutoCAD, you have the option to specify more than one output device. Once you've configured several printers and plotters, you can select the desired device using the Device and Default Selection button. The current default device is shown just above this button. When you click this button, you will see the Device and Default Selection dialog box.

```
┌────────────────────────────────────────────────────────┐
│               Device and Default Selection               │
│ ┌─Select Device──────────────────────────────────────┐  │
│ │ Manufacturer:   Hewlett-Packard HP-GL/2 devices, ADI 4.2 - for Autodesk by │
│ │ Port:   LPT1                                         │  │
│ │ ┌─────────────────────────────────────────────────┐ │  │
│ │ │ Hewlett-Packard HP-GL/2 devices, ADI 4.2 - for Autodesk by HP │ │
│ │ │ System Printer ADI 4.2 - by Autodesk, Inc        │ │  │
│ │ │ Raster file export ADI 4.2 - by Autodesk, Inc    │ │  │
│ │ │                                                   │ │  │
│ │ └─────────────────────────────────────────────────┘ │  │
│ └────────────────────────────────────────────────────┘  │
│ ┌─File Defaults──────────────────────────────────────┐  │
│ │  [ Save Defaults To File... ]  [ Get Defaults From File... ] │
│ └────────────────────────────────────────────────────┘  │
│ ┌─Device Specific Configuration──────────────────────┐  │
│ │ [ Show Device Requirements... ] [ Change Device Requirements... ] │
│ └────────────────────────────────────────────────────┘  │
│              [   OK   ]    [ Cancel ]                     │
└────────────────────────────────────────────────────────┘
```

USING THE WINDOWS SYSTEM PRINTER

Under Windows, you have even more output options since Windows itself offers you the option to output to a wide range of plotters and printers. If you configure AutoCAD to use the System Printer, AutoCAD will then use the Windows output device. You set the Windows output device through the Printers option of the Windows Control Panel application. Consult your Windows manual for more on the use of output devices and Windows.

To select a device, highlight the device name from the list and click on OK. The rest of the Plot Configuration options will then reflect the requirements of the chosen device. For this reason, be sure you select the output device you want, *before* you adjust the other plotter settings.

UNDERSTANDING YOUR PLOTTER'S LIMITS

If you're familiar with a word processor or desktop publishing program, you know that you can set the margins of a page, thereby telling the program exactly how far from each edge of the paper you want the text to appear. With AutoCAD, you don't have that luxury. To accurately place a plot on your paper, you must know the plotter's *hard clip limits*. The hard clip limits are like built-in margins, beyond which the plotter will not plot. These limits vary from plotter to plotter (see Figure 7.1).

It is crucial that you know your printer/plotter's hard clip limits, in order to accurately place your drawings on the sheet. Take some time to study your plotter manual and find out exactly what these limits are. Then make a record of them and store it somewhere, in case you or someone else needs to format a sheet in a special way.

Hard clip limits for printers are often dependent on the software that drives them. You may need to consult your printer manual, or use the trial-and-error method of plotting samples to see how they come out.

Once you've established the limits of your plotter or printer, you can begin to lay out your drawings to fit within those limits (see "Setting the Output's Origin and Rotation" later in this chapter). You can then establish some standard drawing limits based on your plotter's limits.

KNOWING YOUR PLOTTER'S ORIGINS

▼ NOTE

These origin placements also apply to plotter-emulation software that allows you to plot to a raster printer using the HPGL or Houston Instrument Graphic Language formats.

Another important consideration is the location of your plotter's origin. For example, the Hewlett-Packard 7470 and 7475 use the lower-left corner of the plot area as the origin. Larger-format Hewlett-Packard plotters use the center of the plot area as the origin. When you plot a drawing that is too large to fit the sheet on a 7475 plotter, the image is pushed toward the top and to the right of the sheet (see Figure 7.2).

II

Building on the Basics

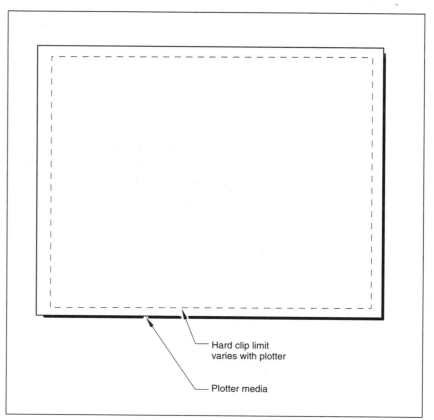

Figure 7.1: The hard clip limits of a plotter

When you plot a drawing that is too large to fit on an HP 7580 plotter, the image is pushed outward in all directions from the center of the sheet.

In each situation, the origin determines a point of reference from which you can relate your drawing in the computer to the physical output. Once you understand this, you are better equipped to accurately place your electronic drawing on the physical media.

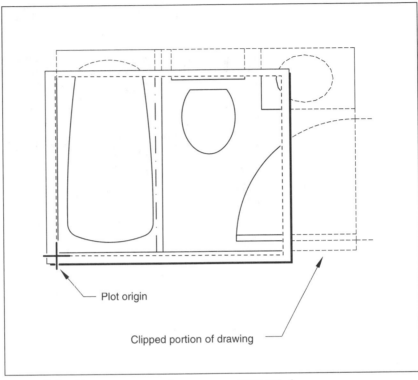

Figure 7.2:   Plotting an oversized image on an HP 7475 plotter

SELECTING A
PAPER SIZE AND ORIENTATION

Next let's look at the Paper Size and Orientation button group in the Plot Configuration dialog box. This is where you determine the size of your media and the standard unit of measure you will use. The Inches and MM radio buttons let you determine the unit of measure you want to work with in this dialog box. This is the unit of measure you will use when specifying sheet sizes and view locations on the sheet. If you choose MM, sheet sizes are shown in millimeters, and you must specify distances and scales in millimeters for other options.

▼ TIP

If you need to convert from inches to millimeters, the scale factor is 1″ = 25.4 mm.

Once you've chosen a unit of measure, you can click on the Size... button to select a sheet size. This brings up the Paper Size dialog box.

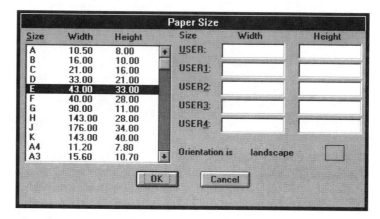

The range of sheet sizes will vary, depending on what plotter you have selected in the Device and Default selection option (described later). To select a sheet size, you simply highlight it in the list box on the left and click OK. Optionally, you can enter a nonstandard sheet size in the input boxes to the right. As you can see, you can store up to five custom sheet sizes.

CONTROLLING THE APPEARANCE OF OUTPUT

On the left side of the Plot Configuration dialog box is the Additional Parameters button group. These options give you the most control over the appearance of your plot. From here, you can control what gets plotted and how.

DESIGNATING HIDDEN LINES, FILLS, AND OUTPUT DESTINATION

Let's start by looking at the three check boxes down the right side of this group. Using these check boxes, you can tell AutoCAD to store the plot in a file on disk, instead of sending the plot data to a plotter or printer for immediate output. You can specify whether to plot a 3D drawing with hidden lines removed, or whether your plotter is to compensate for pen widths when drawing solid fills.

Hide Lines

The Hide Lines check box is generally only used for 3D images. When this option is on, AutoCAD will remove hidden lines from a 3D drawing as it is plotted. This operation will add a minute or two to your plotting time.

Hide Lines is not required for Paperspace viewports that have been set to hide lines using the Hideplot option of the MVIEW command (View ➤ Floating Viewports ➤ Hideplot).

Adjust Area Fill

Generally, compensation for pen width is critical only when you are producing drawings as a basis for photo etchings or similar artwork, where close tolerances must be adhered to.

Turning on Adjust Area Fill tells AutoCAD to compensate for pen width around the edges of a solid filled area in order to maintain dimensional accuracy of the plot. To understand this feature, you need to understand how most plotters draw solid areas.

Plotters draw solid fills by first outlining the fill area and then cross-hatching the area with a series of lines, much as you would do by hand. For example, if a solid filled area is drawn at a width of 0.090″, the plotter will outline the area using the edge of the outline as the centerline for the pen, and then proceed to fill the area with a cross-hatch motion. Unfortunately, by using the outline as the centerline for the pen, the solid fill's actual width is 0.090″ *plus* the width of the pen.

When you check the Adjust Area Fill box, AutoCAD pulls in the outline of the solid area by half the pen width. To determine the amount of offset to use, AutoCAD uses the pen width setting you enter under the Pen Assignments dialog box (described later in this chapter). Figure 7.3 illustrates the operation of Adjust Area Fill.

Plot To File

You may need a special Windows utility to download your plot file to a plotter. There is a shareware utility called Dspooler on the companion disk in this book. Dspooler lets you download a Hewlett-Packard plot file to an HP or compatible plotter through the serial port.

Turn this option on when you want to divert your printout to a file on disk and print it later. This can be useful if you are in an office in which a plotter is shared among several CAD stations. When the plotter is busy, plot to a file. Later you can download the plot file when your plotter is available.

II

Building on the Basics

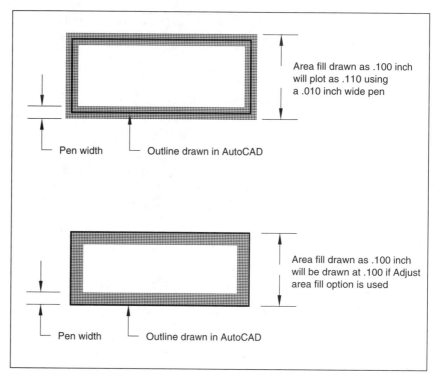

Figure 7.3: A solid area without pen-width compensation and with pen-width compensation

To use this option, do the following:

1. Click the Plot To File check box.

2. Click on the File Name button (just below the check box). You'll see the Create Plot File dialog box, which is the same as the one used for most other file creation operations.

3. Enter the name for your plot file, or just accept the default file name, which is usually the same as the current file. The .PLT file name extension is the default.

4. Click on OK to accept the file name.

DETERMINING WHAT TO PRINT

The radio buttons on the left side of the Additional Parameters button group let you specify which part of your drawing you wish to plot. You might notice some similarities between these settings and the ZOOM command options.

Display

This is the default option; it tells AutoCAD to plot what is currently displayed on the screen (see panel 1 of Figure 7.4). If you let AutoCAD fit the drawing onto the sheet (that is, you check the Scaled to Fit check box), the plot will be exactly the same as what you see on your screen (panel 2 of Figure 7.4).

Extents

The Extents option draws the entire drawing, eliminating any space that may border the drawing (see Figure 7.5). If you let AutoCAD fit the drawing onto the sheet (that is, you check the Scaled to Fit check box), the plot will display exactly the same thing that you would see on the screen had you clicked on View ➤ Zoom ➤ Extents.

At times, when using the Extents plot option, you may find that you don't get exactly the same plot as your drawing extents. When a drawing changes in size, AutoCAD will often have to recalculate its size twice, by performing two drawing regenerations to display the drawing extents. When plotting, AutoCAD doesn't do the second regeneration, so you end up with the wrong display. To avoid this problem, you may want to use the VIEW command (View ➤ Named Views...) to set up a view of the area you want to plot, and then click the View... button (described later in "Controlling Scale and Location"). This will ensure that you will always get the plot you want, regardless of drawing extents.

▼ WARNING

Using the Extents option can yield unexpected results. If you want reliable plotter output, avoid using Extents if possible. Instead, use the View ➤ Named Views to save views for plotting.

II

Building on the Basics

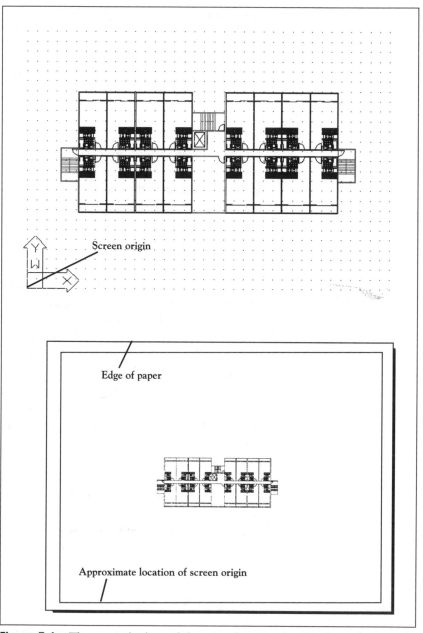

Figure 7.4: The screen display and the printed output when Display is chosen and no Scale is used (the drawing is scaled to fit the sheet)

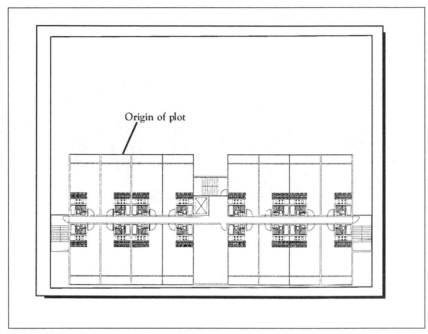

Origin of plot

Figure 7.5: The printed output when Extents is chosen

Limits

The Limits printing option uses the limits of the drawing to determine what to print (see Figure 7.6). If you let AutoCAD fit the drawing onto the sheet (by selecting Scaled to Fit), the plot will display exactly the same thing that you would see on the screen had you clicked on View ➤ Zoom ➤ All.

View

The View printing option uses a previously saved view to determine what to print (see Figure 7.7). To use this option, you must first create a view. Then click on the View... button in the Plot Configuration dialog box, and double-click on the desired view name from the dialog box list that appears.

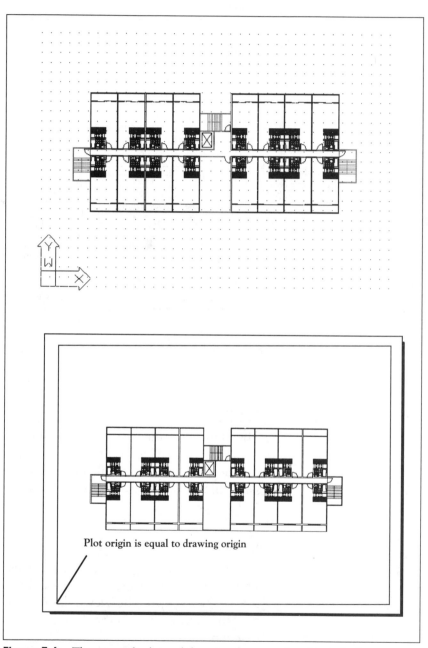

Plot origin is equal to drawing origin

Figure 7.6: The screen display and the printed output when Limits is chosen

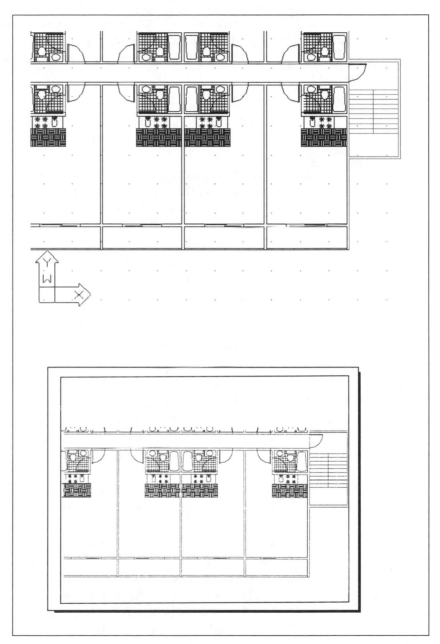

Figure 7.7: A comparison of the saved view and the printed output

If you let AutoCAD fit the drawing onto the sheet (by selecting Scaled to Fit), the plot will display exactly the same thing that you would see on the screen if you recalled the view you are plotting.

Window

Finally, the Window option allows you to use a window to indicate the area you wish to plot (see Figure 7.8). Nothing outside the window will print.

To use this option, click on the Window… button. Then enter the coordinates of the window in the appropriate input boxes. Or you can click on the Pick button to indicate a window in the drawing editor. The dialog box will temporarily close to allow you to select points. When you're done, click OK.

If you let AutoCAD fit the drawing onto the sheet using the Scaled to Fit check box, the plot will display exactly the same thing that you enclose within the window.

CONTROLLING SCALE AND LOCATION

The Scale, Rotation, and Origin button group is where you tell Auto-CAD the scale of your drawing, as well as how the image is to be rotated on the sheet, and the location of the drawing origin on the paper.

In the previous section, the descriptions of several options indicate that the Scaled to Fit check box must be checked. Bear in mind that, when you apply a scale factor to your plot, it changes the results of the Additional Parameters settings, and some subtle problems can arise. This is usually where most new users have difficulty.

For example, the apartment plan drawing fits nicely on the paper when you use Scaled to Fit. But if you tried to plot the drawing at a scale of 1″=1′, you would probably get a blank piece of paper, because, at that scale, hardly any of the drawing would fit on your paper. AutoCAD would tell you that it was plotting and then that the plot was finished. You wouldn't have a clue as to why your sheet was blank.

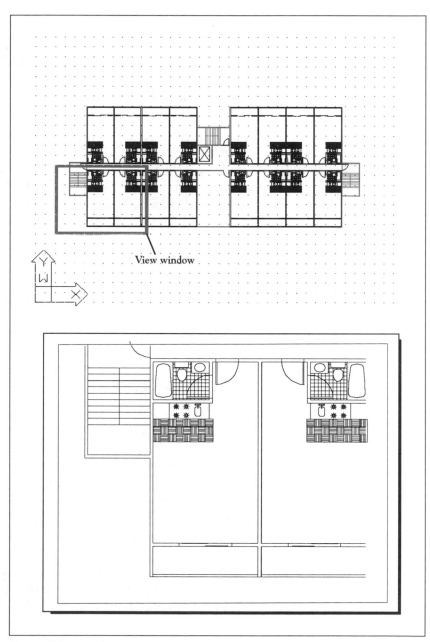

Figure 7.8: A selected window and the resulting printout

If an image is too large to fit on a sheet of paper because of improper scaling, the plot image will be clipped differently depending on whether the plotter uses the center of the image or the lower-left corner for its origin (see Figure 7.1). Keep this in mind as you specify Scale factors in this area of the dialog box.

SPECIFYING DRAWING SCALE

▼ NOTE

See *Chapter 3* for a discussion on unit styles and scale factors.

To indicate scale, two input boxes are provided in the Scale, Rotation, and Origin button group: Plotted Inches (or Plotted MM if you use metric units) and Drawing Units. For example, if your drawing is of a scale factor of 96, do the following:

1. Double-click on the Plotted Inches (or Plotted MM) input box, and enter **1** ↵.

2. Double-click on the Drawing Units input box, and enter **96**.

For a drawing set up using the Architectural unit style, you can enter a scale as a fraction of 1″ = 1′. For example, for a $\frac{1}{8}$″ scale drawing:

1. Double-click on the Plotted Inches (or Plotted MM) input box, and enter **1/8″**.

2. Double-click on the Drawing Units input box, and enter **1′**.

You can specify a different scale from the one you chose while setting up your drawing, and AutoCAD will plot your drawing to that scale. You are not restricted in any way as to scale, but entering the correct scale is important: If it is too large, AutoCAD will think your drawing is too large to fit on the sheet, though it will attempt to plot your drawing anyway.

The Scaled to Fit check box, as already described, allows you to avoid giving a scale altogether and forces the drawing to fit on the sheet. This works fine if you are doing illustrations that are not to scale.

SETTING THE OUTPUT'S ORIGIN AND ROTATION

To adjust the position of your drawing on the media, you enter the location of the view origin in relation to the plotter origin in x and y coordinates (see Figure 7.9).

For example, suppose you plot a drawing, then realize that it needs to be moved 1″ to the right and 3″ up on the sheet. You would replot the drawing by making the following changes:

1. In the Plot Configuration dialog box, click the Rotation and Origin… button in the Scale, Rotation, and Origin button group. The Plot Rotation and Origin dialog box appears.

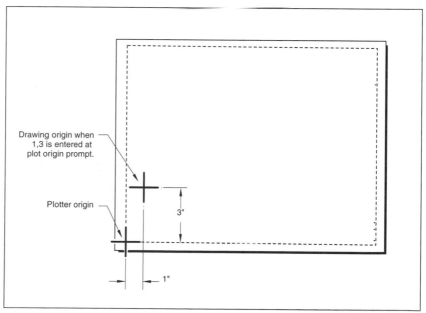

Drawing origin when 1,3 is entered at plot origin prompt.

Plotter origin

3″

1″

Figure 7.9: Adjusting the image location on a sheet

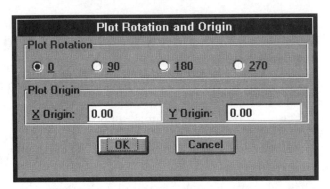

2. Double-click on the X Origin input box and type **1**.

3. Double-click on the Y Origin input box and type **3**.

4. Click on OK.

If you encounter problems with rotating plots, try setting up a UCS that is rotated 90° from the world coordinate system. Then use the Plan command (View ➤ 3D Viewport Presets ➤ Plan View) to view your drawing in the new rotated orientation. Next, save the view using the View command (View ➤ Named Views…). Once you do this, you can use the View button in the Additional Parameters group to plot the rotated view. See *Chapter 16* for more on UCS.

▼ **WARNING**

Now proceed with the rest of the plot configuration. With the above settings, when the plot is done, the image will be shifted on the paper exactly 1″ to the right and 3″ up.

The four radio buttons labeled 0, 90, 180, and 270 allow you to rotate the plot on the sheet. Each value indicates the number of degrees of rotation for the plot. The default is 0, but if you need to rotate the image to a different angle, click on the appropriate radio button.

ADJUSTING PEN PARAMETERS AND PLOTTER OPTIMIZATION

The Pen Parameters group of the Plot Configuration dialog box contains two buttons: Pen Assignments…, which helps you control line weight and color, and Optimization…, which lets you control pen motion in pen plotters.

WORKING WITH PEN ASSIGNMENTS AND LINE WEIGHTS

▼ **NOTE**

You can also control line weights through the use of polylines. See *Chapter 13* for details.

In most graphics programs, you control line weights by adjusting the actual width of lines in the drawing. In AutoCAD, you generally take a different approach to line weights. Instead of specifying a line weight in the drawing editor, you match plotter pen widths to colors in your drawing. For example, you might designate the color red to correspond to a fine line weight or the color blue to a very heavy line weight. To make these correlations between colors and line weights, you tell AutoCAD to plot with a particular pen for each color in the drawing.

The Pen Assignments... button in the Plot Configuration dialog box is the entry point to setting the drawing colors for the pens on your plotter. When you click on this button, the Pen Assignment dialog box appears.

▼ **NOTE**

This dialog box shows a listing for a Hewlett-Packard 7580 plotter.

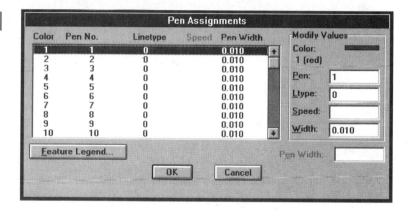

The predominant feature of this dialog box is the list of pen assignments. The color numbers in the first column of the list correspond to the colors in your drawing. The other columns show you what pen number, line type, pen speed, and pen width are assigned to those colors.

To change these settings, you click on the item in the list you want to change. The values for that selected item appear in the appropriate input boxes under Modify Values at the right. You can then change the values in the input boxes. You can highlight more than one color at a time with a Shift-click, to change the pen assignments of several colors at once.

Building on the Basics

II

▼ ISO PEN WIDTHS

You may have noticed a setting called ISO Pen Widths in the Select Linetype dialog box discussed in *Chapter 4* (Data ➤ Linetype...). This setting is in the form of a pull-down list. When you select a pen width from that list, the line-type scale is updated to conform to the ISO standard for that width. This setting has no effect on the actual plotter output, however. If you are using ISO standard widths, it is up to you to match the color of the lines to their corresponding widths in the Plot Configuration dialog box. Use the Pen Assignments dialog box to set the line colors to pen widths.

▼ NOTE

If you have a Hewlett Packard ink jet plotter, you can also control pen settings through the HPCONFIG command by typing **Hpconfig** ↵ at the command prompt.

Pen No.

You assign line weights to colors by entering a pen number in the Pen input box. The default for the color red, for example, is pen 1. If you have a pen plotter, you can then place a pen with a fine tip in the slot designated for pen 1 in your plotter. Then everything that is red in your AutoCAD drawing will be plotted with the fine pen. If you have an ink jet plotter, you can set the width of pens through the plotter's control panel.

Ltype

Some plotters offer line types independent of AutoCAD's line types. Using the Ltype input box, you can force a pen assignment to one of these hardware line types. If your plotter supports hardware line types, you can click on the Feature Legend button to see what line types are available and their designations. Usually line types are given numeric designations, so a row of dots might be designated as line type 1, or a dash-dot might be line type 5.

If your plotter can generate its own line types, you can also assign line types to colors. But this method is very seldom used, because it is simpler to assign line types to layers directly in the drawing.

Speed

The pen Speed setting lets you adjust the pen speed in inches per second. This is important because various pens have their own speed requirements. Refillable technical pens that use India ink generally require the slowest settings; roller pens are capable of very high speeds. Pen speeds will also be affected by the media you are using.

Selecting pens and media for your plotter can be a trial-and-error proposition. If you would like to learn more about the details of plotter pens and media, read *Appendix A*.

Width

AutoCAD uses this setting in conjunction with the Adjust Area Fill option under the Additional Parameters button group (discussed earlier). When AutoCAD draws solid fills, it draws a series of lines close together—much as you would do by hand (see Figure 7.10). To do this efficiently, AutoCAD must know the pen width. If the Width setting is too low, AutoCAD will take longer than necessary to draw a solid fill; if it is too high, solid fills will appear as cross-hatches instead of solids.

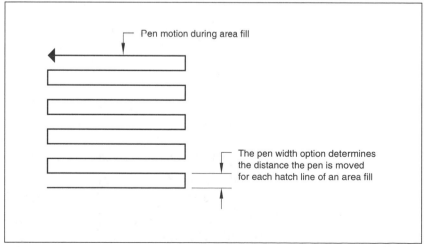

Pen motion during area fill

The pen width option determines the distance the pen is moved for each hatch line of an area fill

Figure 7.10:   How solid fill areas are drawn by a plotter

II

Building on the Basics

OPTIMIZING PLOTTER SPEED

AutoCAD does a lot of preparation before sending your drawing to the plotter. One of the things it does is optimize the way it sends vectors to your plotter, so your plotter doesn't waste time making frequent pen changes and moving from one end of the plot to another just to draw a single line.

The Optimization… button in the Pen Parameters group opens a dialog box that lets you control the level of pen optimization AutoCAD is to perform on your plots.

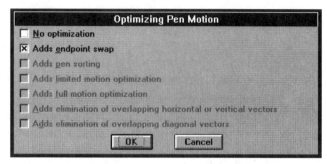

Here are brief descriptions of each setting:

No optimization   causes AutoCAD to plot the drawing just as it is regenerated on the screen.

Adds endpoint swap   forces the plotter to draw (as best it can) parallel lines in a back-and-forth motion, so that the pen moves the minimum distance between the end of one line and the beginning of another.

Adds pen sorting   sorts pens so that all of one color is plotted at once. This is fine if your plotter has a self-capping penholder, or if it is a single-pen plotter. You may not want to enable this option if you have a multipen plotter that does not cap the pens.

Adds limited motion optimization and **Adds full motion optimization**   further minimize pen travel over a plot.

Adds elimination of overlapping horizontal or vertical vectors does just what it says: It eliminates overlapping lines. With pen plotters, overlapping lines can cause the weight of the line to increase noticeably. This setting helps reduce line weight build-up when a drawing contains numerous line overlaps. This setting does not affect raster plotters or printers.

Adds elimination of overlapping diagonal vectors   performs a similar function as the previous option, but on diagonal lines.

OTHER PLOT CONTROLS

Here are a couple of other handy, timesaving features available to you in the Plot Configuration dialog box.

PREVIEWING A PLOT

If you are a seasoned AutoCAD user, you're probably all too familiar with the following scenario:

You're rushing to meet a deadline. You've got one hour to plot a drawing that you know takes 45 minutes to plot. You set up AutoCAD and start the plot, then run off to finish some paperwork. When you come back 45 minutes later, the plot image is half the size it is supposed to be.

You can avoid facing predicaments like this one with the Plot Preview feature. Once you've made all the settings you think you need for plotting your drawing, turn on the Full radio button in the Plot Preview group, and then click on Preview…. AutoCAD will show you what your drawing will look like according to the settings you've chosen. Preview also lists any warning messages that would appear during the actual plotting process.

While in the Full Preview, you can zoom in on an area and pan around, but be aware that each zoom and pan requires the Preview function to "replot" the image.

The Full Preview can take some time, though not as long as an actual plot. If you're just interested in seeing how the drawing fits on the sheet, you can choose Partial instead of Full before clicking on Preview. The Partial option shows the sheet edge, image orientation triangle, and the image boundary. The image itself is not shown. Using a small triangle in the corner of the drawing to indicate the lower-left corner of the drawing, AutoCAD shows you how the image is oriented on the sheet.

▼ **TIP**

You can press the Esc key to speed up the preview. Once the preview plot is done, you are immediately returned to the Plot Configuration dialog box. You can also press Ctrl-C to terminate the preview generation when you've seen enough.

II

Building on the Basics

▼
■
■
■
■

▼ REINITIALIZING YOUR INPUT/OUTPUT PORTS

If you are using two output devices (such as a printer and a plotter) on the same port, you may want to know about the REINIT command. This command lets you reinitialize a port for use by Auto-CAD after another program has used the port. For example, you may have a printer and a plotter connected to the same port through a switch box, and use the AutoCAD SHELL command (Tools ➤ External Commands ➤ Shell) to temporarily exit Auto-CAD to print out a document on your printer. When you return to AutoCAD to plot something, you will want to use REINIT to restore AutoCAD's connection to your plotter.

To use REINIT, enter **Reinit** at the command prompt or select Re-initialize... on the Tools menu. You will see a dialog box containing check boxes labeled Digitizer, Plotter, Display, and PGP File. You can check them all, if you like, or just check the items you are concerned most with.

REINIT can also be accessed using the Re-init system variable.

SAVING YOUR SETTINGS

At times, drawings will require special plotter settings, or you may find that you frequently use one particular setting configuration. Instead of trying to remember the settings every time you plot, you can store settings as files that you can recall at any time. Here's how to do this:

1. Set up the plotter settings exactly as you want them.

2. Click the Device and Default Selection... button.

3. In the Device and Default Selection dialog box, click on the Save Defaults To File... button. The Save to File dialog box appears.

4. Enter a name for the group of settings. The default name is the same as the current drawing name, with the .PCP file name extension.

5. Click on OK to create your .PCP file of settings.

To recall a settings file:

1. Click on File ➤ Print (or type **Plot** ↵ at the command line).

2. Click on the Device and Default Selection... button.

3. In the Device and Default Selection dialog box, click on the Get Defaults From File... button. The Obtain From File dialog box appears.

4. Click on the name of the desired plotter settings file.

5. Click on OK, and the settings will be loaded. You can then proceed with your plot.

The ability to store plotter settings in .PCP files gives you greater control over your output quality. It helps you to reproduce similar plots more easily when you need them later. You can store several different plotter configurations for one file, each for a different output device.

You can also open a .PCP file with a text editor. You can even create your own .PCP file by copying an existing one and editing it.

PLOTTING FROM THE COMMAND LINE

Many of you may be accustomed to the command-line method of plotting from AutoCAD and have devised methods for storing plotter settings. One common method is to use script files to plot from AutoCAD (see "Plotting from Scripts" just below). You can still use the older method of issuing the PLOT command from the command prompt and script files. To do this, you must first change the CMDDIA system variable to 0.

Here is the general procedure for the command-prompt method of configuring the plotter:

1. First set the CMDDIA system variable to 0.

2. Enter Plot ↵ at the command prompt.

3. When you see this prompt:

    What to plot—Display, Extents, Limits, View,
    or Window <D>:

    enter the desired option. The screen switches to text mode and you see a list similar to the following:

    Plot device is Hewlett-Packard (HPGL) ADI 4.2 by -
    Autodesk
    Description: HP 7585
    Plot Optimization level = 4
    Plot will NOT be written to a selected file
    Sizes are in Inches and the style is landscape
    Plot origin is at (0.00,0.00)
    Plotting area is 10.50 wide by 8.00 high (A)
    Plot is NOT rotated
    Area fill will NOT be adjusted for pen width
    Hidden lines will NOT be removed
    Plot will be scaled to fit available area
    Do you want to change anything?(No/Yes/File/Save)
    <N>

4. If you answer Y to the last prompt, you are asked,

    Do you want to change plotters? <N>:

5. If you answer Y again, you get a listing of the available plotters. (The following is a sample list. The list you see on your computer will depend on how you have configured the Auto-CAD plotter option.)

    1. Hewlett-Packard (HPGL) ADI 4.2 - by Autodesk
    Description HP 7585
    2. PostScript device ADI 4.2 - by Autodesk
    Description LaserWriter II
    Enter selection <1>:

6. If you answer N to the Do you want to change plotters? prompt and you have selected a multipen plotter, AutoCAD asks if you want to configure your plotter pen assignments.

7. If you answer Y, you get a list showing the current settings for pen assignments, as shown in Figure 7.11.

8. If you answer Y to the configuration question, you see the screen shown in Figure 7.12. Notice how this prompt duplicates the information on the first color listed in Figure 7.11. At the far right of the first line is a prompt to enter a pen number for the color. You can select a pen number corresponding to the color red, or accept the default pen number, 1.

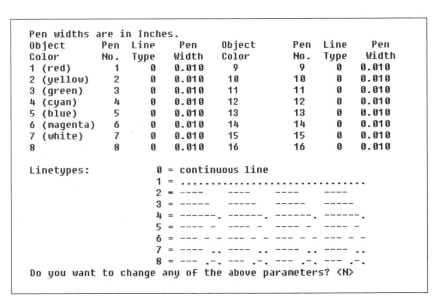

```
Pen widths are in Inches.
Object       Pen  Line   Pen      Object       Pen  Line   Pen
Color        No.  Type   Width    Color        No.  Type   Width
1 (red)      1    0      0.010    9            9    0      0.010
2 (yellow)   2    0      0.010    10           10   0      0.010
3 (green)    3    0      0.010    11           11   0      0.010
4 (cyan)     4    0      0.010    12           12   0      0.010
5 (blue)     5    0      0.010    13           13   0      0.010
6 (magenta)  6    0      0.010    14           14   0      0.010
7 (white)    7    0      0.010    15           15   0      0.010
8            8    0      0.010    16           16   0      0.010

Linetypes:           0 = continuous line
                     1 = ...............................
                     2 = ----    ----    ----    ----
                     3 = -----   -----   -----   -----
                     4 = ------. ------. ------. ------.
                     5 = ---- -  ---- -  ---- -  ---- -
                     6 = --- - - --- - - --- - - --- - -
                     7 = ---- .. ---- .. ---- .. ---- ..
                     8 = --- .-. --- .-. --- .-. --- .-.
Do you want to change any of the above parameters? <N>
```

Figure 7.11:   The pen assignments for a Hewlett-Packard 7585 plotter; other plotters will show different pen assignments.

Building on the Basics II

```
Enter values, blank=Next, Cn=Color n, Sn=Show n, X=Exit

Layer      Pen  Line  Line
Color      No.  Type  Width
1 (red)     1    0    0.010    Pen number <1>:
1 (red)     1    0    0.010    Line type <0>:
1 (red)     1    0    0.010    Pen width <0.010>:
2 (yellow)  2    0    0.010    Pen number <2>:
2 (yellow)  2    0    0.010    Line type <0>:
2 (yellow)  2    0    0.010    Pen width <0.010>:
3 (green)   3    0    0.010    Pen number <3>:
3 (green)   3    0    0.010    Line type <0>:
3 (green)   3    0    0.010    Pen width <0.010>:
.
.
.
```

Figure 7.12: This screen lets you change pen parameters.

9. Now the bottom line of the prompt changes to

   1 (red)   2   0   36   Line type <0>:

   which reflects the change in pen assignments you just made and asks you what line type you wish to use (unless your plotter does not offer built-in line types).

10. Finally, you are prompted for pen width. Once you have selected an option, the prompt changes to

    1 (red)   2   0   36   Pen speed <60>:

11. Now AutoCAD prompts you for pen speed (unless your plotter does not offer the pen speed option).

12. Once you supply this value, the prompt advances to display the settings for color number 2, yellow. You can now select pen number, pen speed, and line type for yellow just as you did for red.

13. Continue through all 15 colors.

14. At any time, you can enter one of the following options:

S	To review your settings.
C (*color number*)	To change the settings of another color. For example, enter **C4** ↵ to change the settings for color number 4.
X	To exit the pen assignments and move on to the next setting.

15. Once you've exited the pen assignments, you will get the series of prompts shown in Figure 7.13.

Once you've answered this series of prompts, you can start your plot.

```
Write the plot to a file? <N>
Size units (Inches or Millimeters) <I>:
Plot origin in Inches <0.00,0.00>:

Standard values for plotting size
Size      Width      Height
A         10.50       8.00
B         16.00      10.00
MAX       16.00      10.00

Enter the Size or Width,Height (in Inches) <E>:
Rotate plot clockwise 0/90/180/270 degrees <0>:
Remove hidden lines? <N>

Specify scale by entering:
Plotted Inches=Drawing Units or Fit or ? <F>:
```

Figure 7.13:   You are prompted for information on print options.

II

Building on the Basics

PLOTTING FROM SCRIPTS

▼ NOTE

See *Chapter 12* for more on script files and their use.

A popular method for automating plotting is to use *script files*. Script files act like DOS batch files. They are ASCII text files that contain the exact keystrokes used to perform some task.

To create a script file, use a text editor and create a file containing the exact keystrokes necessary to perform the plotter setup. Figure 7.14 shows a listing of a typical script file called Plotter.SCR for a Hewlett-Packard plotter. (Script files must always have the file name extension .SCR.) Once the file is created, you use Tools ➤ Run Script or the SCRIPT command to run the script.

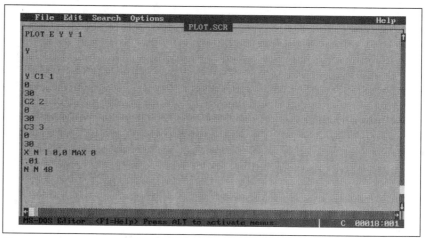

Figure 7.14:   A plotter script file

SENDING YOUR DRAWINGS TO A SERVICE BUREAU

Using a plotting service can be a good alternative to purchasing your own plotter. Or you might consider using a low-cost plotter for check plots, and then send the files to a service for your final product. Many reprographic services such as blueprinters offer plotting in conjunction with their other services. Quite often these services include a high-speed modem that allows you to send files over phone lines, eliminating the need for using courier services or regular mail.

Service bureaus will often use an *electrostatic plotter*—it's like a very large laser printer, and is often capable of producing color plots. These plotters are costly, and you probably won't want to purchase one yourself. However, they are excellent for situations requiring high volume and fast turnaround. The electrostatic plotter produces high-quality plots, often better than a laser printer, and it is fast: A 30″×42″ plot can take as little as two minutes. These plotters require special media, however, so you can't use your preprinted title blocks. Ask your prospective plotter service organization about the media limitations.

Another device used by service bureaus is the *laser photo plotter*. This device uses a laser to plot a drawing on a piece of film. The film negative is later enlarged to the finished drawing size by means of standard reprographic techniques. Laser photo plotters yield the highest-quality output of any device, and they offer the flexibility of reproducing drawings at any size.

Finally, many service bureaus can produce full E-size plots of PostScript files. With AutoCAD's full PostScript support, you can get presentation-quality plots from any AutoCAD drawing. See *Chapter 14* for more on PostScript and AutoCAD.

IF YOU WANT TO EXPERIMENT...

At this point, since you aren't rushing to meet a deadline, you may want to experiment with some of the plotter and printer variables and see firsthand what each one does. Figure 7.15 contains an exercise you can do to try printing a view and scale different from those used in the exercises.

1. Open the Bath file and use the Window option under the View command to create a view of the bath tub. Name the view BATH.

2. Start the Plot command. At the Plot dialog box click on the View... button and select the view named BATH.

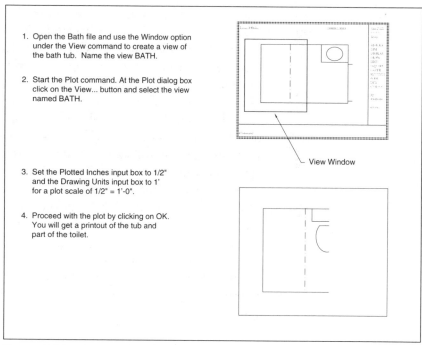

View Window

3. Set the Plotted Inches input box to 1/2" and the Drawing Units input box to 1' for a plot scale of 1/2" = 1'-0".

4. Proceed with the plot by clicking on OK. You will get a printout of the tub and part of the toilet.

Figure 7.15:   Printing the tub at $^1/_2{''}=1'{-}0''$ scale

8

ADDING TEXT TO DRAWINGS

Adding Text

Setting Justification of Text

Setting Text Scale

Selecting Fonts

Creating a Text Style

Editing Existing Text

Importing Text from Outside AutoCAD

Using the Spelling Checker

FAST TRACK

328 ▶ To enter text in a drawing

Click and drag Text from the Draw palette, then select Dtext, enter the desired height if you are prompted for it, enter a rotation angle, and then start typing. Use ↵ to start a new line. Use Backspace to back up as far as you like.

329 ▶ To set the justification of text you are about to enter

Click and drag Text from the Draw palette, then select Dtext. Enter the desired justification style, such as Center, Right, TL (top-left), Middle, and so forth. Answer the rest of the prompts, and then start typing.

330 ▶ To change the justification of text already entered

Click on Properties from the Object Properties toolbar, and then click on the text you want to modify. In the Modify Text dialog box, pull down the Justification list, and click on the desired justification style. Click on OK.

332 ▶ To find the appropriate height of text for a drawing according to its scale

Multiply the desired final text height by the scale factor. For example, if you want ⅛″ letters in a drawing that is to be plotted at ¼″=1′, multiply ⅛ times 48. (See *Chapter 3* for more on scale factors.)

335 ▶ To continue text where you left of

Start the DTEXT command (Dtext from the Draw palette). Press ↵ at all the prompts until you see the Text prompt. A text cursor will appear just below the last text line.

336 ▶ To include text in scripts and macros

Use the TEXT command instead of Dynamic Text or DTEXT.

338 ▶ To use PostScript fonts in your drawing

Enter **Style** ↵ at the command prompt, and then enter the name for your style. At the file list dialog box, locate and double-click the Post-Script .PFB file you want to use. Answer the prompts that follow.

344 ▶ To rename a text style

Choose Data ➤ Rename.... In the dialog box, choose Style in the Named Objects list box. In the Items list box, click on the old style name; then click on the input box next to the Rename To: button. Enter a new name, and click Rename To:.

349 ▶ To select a text style for use with the DTEXT command

Click on Data ➤ Object Creation.... At the Object Creation Modes dialog box, click on the Text Style button. At the Text Style dialog box, choose a style.

354 ▶ To change the style of existing text

Click on Properties from the Object Properties toolbar, and then click on the text whose style you want to change. In the Modify Text dialog box, open the Style pull-down list and click on the desired text style.

356 ▶ To edit text

Type **Ddedit** ↵ and click on the text you wish to edit. The Edit dialog box appears with the text, and you can use the standard input-box editing methods. When you are finished editing, click on OK, and then click on the next line to edit; or press ↵ when you are done.

357 ▶ To keep text from mirroring when included in a Mirror selection

Type **'Mirrtext** ↵ and then enter **0** ↵. From then on, the Mirror command and the ** MIRROR ** Grips option will not reverse text so it is unreadable, but rather will make copies of text mirroring their insertion points.

One of the more tedious drafting tasks is applying notes to your drawing. Anyone who has had to draft a large drawing containing lots of notes knows the true meaning of writer's cramp. AutoCAD not only makes this job go faster by allowing you to type your notes, it also helps you to create more professional-looking notes by using a variety of fonts, type sizes, and type styles. And with Release 13, you have some new features to further improve text handling—such as a spelling checker and word wrap for large blocks of text.

In this chapter you will add notes to your apartment house plan. In the process, you will explore some of AutoCAD's text creation and editing features. You will learn how to control the size, slant, type style, and orientation of text, and how to import text files.

LABELING A DRAWING

In this first section, you will add some simple labels to your Unit drawing to identify the general design elements: the bathroom, kitchenette, and living room.

1. Start AutoCAD and open the Unit file.

2. Turn off the Flr-pat layer. Otherwise, the floor pattern you added previously will obscure the text you will enter in this chapter.

3. Create a layer called **Notes** and make it the current layer. Notes is the layer on which you will keep all your text information.

4. Click and drag Text from the Draw palette then select Dtext or enter **Dtext** ↵ at the command prompt.

▼ **TIP**

It's a good idea to keep your notes on a separate layer, so you can plot drawings containing only the graphics information, or freeze the notes layer to save redraw/regeneration time.

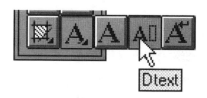

5. At the DTEXT Justify/Style/<Start point>: prompt, pick the starting point for the text you are about to enter, just below the kitchenette at coordinate 16′–2″, 21′–8″. By picking a point, you are accepting <Start point>, which is the default.

6. At the Height <0′–0 3/16″>: prompt, enter **6″** to indicate the text height.

7. At the Insertion angle <0>: prompt, press ↵ to accept the default, 0°. You can specify any angle other than horizontal if you want (for example, if you want your text to be aligned with a rotated object). You'll see a small square appear at the point you picked in step 5. This is your *text cursor*.

8. At the Text: prompt, enter the word **Kitchenette**. As you type, the word appears in the drawing.

9. Press ↵ to move the cursor down to start a new line.

10. This time you want to label the bathroom. Pick a point to the right of the door swing at coordinate 19′–11″, 26′–5″. The text cursor moves to that point.

11. Type **Bath** ↵. Figure 8.1 shows how your drawing should look now. (At this point, the text is in the default font, Txt; we'll discuss fonts later in this chapter.)

12. Press ↵ again to exit the Dynamic Text command.

As you have seen in the foregoing exercise, the Dynamic Text command (DTEXT) lets you enter a column of text by pressing ↵ at the end of each line. You can also click on a location for the next line, as you did in step 10.

JUSTIFYING TEXT

When you pick a point at the Dynamic Text's Justify/Style/<Start point>: prompt, your text is automatically justified to the left of the selected point, and the text uses that point as its *baseline* location. The *baseline* of text is an imaginary line on which the lowercase letters of the

▼ NOTE

Why make the text so high? Remember that you are drawing at full scale, and anything you draw will be reduced in the plotted drawing. We will discuss text height in more detail later in this chapter.

▼ TIP

If you make a typing error, back up to the error with the Backspace key and then retype the rest of the word. If you need to, you can backspace over several lines.

Building on the Basics

II

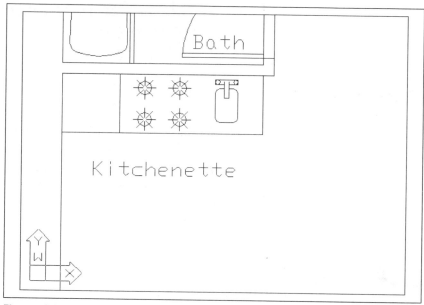

Figure 8.1: The Unit drawing with labels added for the kitchenette and bath

text sit. You can change the justification setting so that the text you enter will be justified either to the center or to the right. You can also specify whether the text baseline is on, above, or below the Start point prompt.

Here's how to change the justification setting:

▼ NOTE

If you are working through the tutorial, you can skip this exercise. It's here for reference only.

1. Click on Dtext from the Draw palette or enter **Dtext** ↵, just as you would to start entering text.

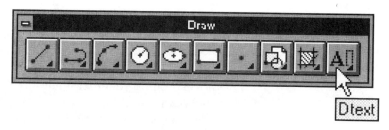

2. At the DTEXT Justify/Style/<Start point>: prompt, enter **J** ↵.

3. When you see this prompt:

   Align/Fit/Center/Middle/Right/TL/TC/TR/ML/MC/
   MR/BL/BC/BR:

   select the justification style you want by typing its name at the prompt. (All the elements of this prompt are described just below.)

4. Once you select a justification option, you are prompted for a point to locate your text. You can then start to enter your text.

When you start to enter text, it will first appear as though no change has been made to the justification. The text will come in using the default, left-justification. Don't be alarmed—the text will move into position after you've exited the Dynamic Text command.

Justification Options

Here are descriptions of each justification option (we've left Fit and Align until last).

Center causes the text to be centered on the start point, with the baseline on the start point.

Middle causes the text to be centered on the start point, with the baseline slightly below the start point.

Right causes the text to be justified to the right of the start point, with the baseline on the start point.

TL, **TC**, and **TR** stand for top left, top center, and top right. Text using these justification styles appears entirely below the start point and justified left, center, or right, depending on which of the three options you choose.

ML, **MC**, and **MR** stand for middle left, middle center, and middle right. These styles are similar to TL, TC, and TR, except that the start point will determine a location midway between the baseline and the top of the lowercase letters of the text.

II

Building on the Basics

BL, **BC**, and **BR**   stand for bottom left, bottom center, and bottom right. These styles, too, are similar to TL, TC, and TR, but here the start point determines the bottommost location of the letters of the text (the bottom of letters that have descenders, such as *p*, *q*, and *g*).

Figure 8.2 shows the relationship between the text start point and text justified with these options.

Fit and Align Options
With the Fit and Align justification options, you must specify a dimension within which the text is to fit. For example, suppose you want the word *Refrigerator* to fit within the 26″-wide box representing the refrigerator. You can use either the Fit or the Align option to accomplish this. With Fit, AutoCAD prompts you to select start and end points, and then stretches or compresses the letters

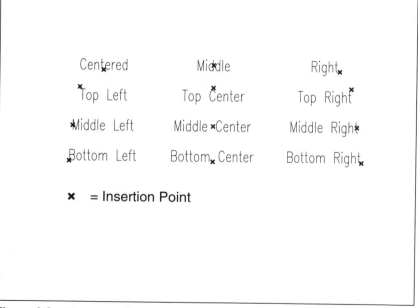

Figure 8.2:   Text inserted using the various Justify options

to fit within the two points you specify. You use this option when the text must be a consistent height throughout the drawing and you don't care about distorting the font. Align works like Fit, but instead of maintaining the current text style height, Align adjust the text height to keep it proportional to the text width, without distorting the font. Use this option when it is important to maintain the font's shape and proportion. Figure 8.3 demonstrates how Fit and Align work.

UNDERSTANDING TEXT AND SCALE

Text scale conversion is a concept many people have difficulty grasping. As you discovered in previous chapters, AutoCAD allows you to draw at full scale—that is, to represent distances as values equivalent to the actual size of the object. When you later plot the drawing, you tell AutoCAD at what scale you wish to plot and the program reduces the

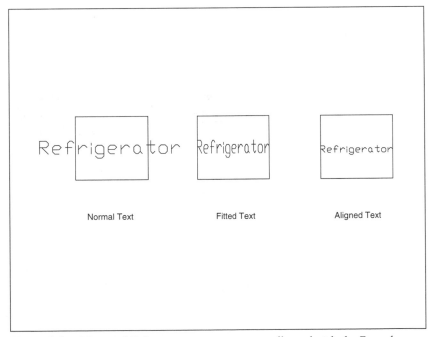

Figure 8.3: The word *Refrigerator* as it appears normally, and with the Fit and Align options selected

drawing accordingly. This allows you the freedom to input measurements at full scale and not worry about converting them to various scales every time you enter a distance. Unfortunately, this feature can also create problems when you enter text and dimensions. Just as you had to convert the plotted sheet size to an enlarged size equivalent at full scale in the drawing editor, you must convert your text size to its equivalent at full scale.

To illustrate this point, imagine you are drawing the unit plan at full size on a very large sheet of paper. When you are done with this drawing, it will be reduced to a scale that will allow it to fit on an $8^{1}/_{2}{\times}11''$ sheet of paper. So you have to make your text quite large to keep it legible once it is reduced. This means that if you want text to appear $^{1}/_{8}''$ high when the drawing is plotted, you must convert it to a considerably larger size when you draw it. To do this, you multiply the desired height of the final plotted text by a scale conversion factor.

If your drawing is at $^{1}/_{8}''{=}1'$ scale, you multiply the desired text height, $^{1}/_{8}''$, by the scale conversion factor of 96 (found in *Table 3.3*) to get a height of 12''. This is the height you must make your text to get $^{1}/_{8}''$-high text in the final plot. Table 8.1 shows you some other examples of text height to scale.

Table 8.1:   Text $^{1}/_{8}''$ High Converted to Size for Various Drawing Scales

Drawing Scale	Scale Factor	AutoCAD Drawing Height for $^{1}/_{8}$ High Text
1/16″ = 1′–0″	192	24.0″
1/8″ = 1′–0″	96	12.0″
1/4″ = 1′–0″	48	6.0″
1/2″ = 1′–0″	24	3.0″
3/4″ = 1′–0″	16	2.0″
1″ = 1′–0″	12	1.5″
1 1/2″ = 1′–0″	8	1.0″
3″ = 1′–0″	4	0.5″

ENTERING A COLUMN OF TEXT

You will often want to enter a note or description of an object that requires more than one line of text. You've already had a glimpse of how to do this. The next exercise will let you try it out.

CONTINUING TEXT
FROM WHERE YOU LEFT OFF

One feature of AutoCAD's Dynamic Text function is that it lets you stop to do something else and then return to add text in a column below the last line you entered. This exercise shows you the process.

1. Click on Dtext from the Draw palette or enter **Dtext** ↵.

2. Click on a point at coordinate 24'–0", 26'–5" to locate the beginning of your text.

3. Enter **6** ↵ for the height and press ↵ at the Angle prompt.

4. Type **Entry** ↵, and then press ↵ again to exit the Dynamic Text command.

   Now move to another part of the drawing to make changes. At this point, you've exited the Dynamic Text command, and will return now to pick up where you left off.

5. Zoom in to the area where you just added the text.

6. Start Dynamic Text again.

7. At the Justify/Style/<Start point>: prompt, press ↵. The Text prompt appears (skipping the prompts for height and insertion angle) and you see the Dtext cursor in the drawing area just below the word Entry.

8. Enter the entry dimensions **6'–0" x 7'–0"** ↵. The cursor moves down a line.

9. Type the words **to the kitchenette** ↵. You should now have something that looks like Figure 8.4.

10. Press ↵ to exit the Dynamic Text command.

II

Building on the Basics

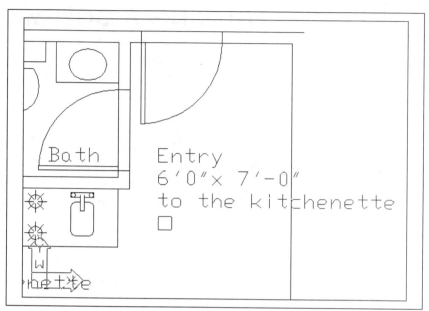

Figure 8.4: The column of text you entered from where you left off

WORKING WITH THE TEXT COMMAND

Another way of entering text is to use the TEXT command. Although the TEXT command is somewhat more difficult to use than Dynamic Text (DTEXT), the TEXT command can be incorporated into menus, scripts, and AutoLISP (see *Chapters 19* and *20*) macros, where the DTEXT command cannot. The TEXT command is best suited in menus and macros.

TEXT and DTEXT work almost identically, except for the following:

- ■ TEXT does not show your text in the drawing as you type.

- ■ TEXT requires you to press ↵ twice between lines in a column of text.

- ■ TEXT does not let you position text "on the fly" as DTEXT does.

To get a feel for how TEXT works, try the following exercise:

1. Zoom back to your previous view.

2. At the command prompt, enter **Text** ↵. You get the same prompt for a starting point as when you use Dynamic Text.

3. Pick a point on the balcony at coordinate 19′–8″, 4′–4″. Press ↵ twice to accept the default height and angle.

4. Type the word **Balcony**. As you type, the letters appear only in the prompt area. They do not appear in the drawing yet.

5. Press ↵. The word "Balcony" appears in the drawing (see Figure 8.5), and the command prompt reappears.

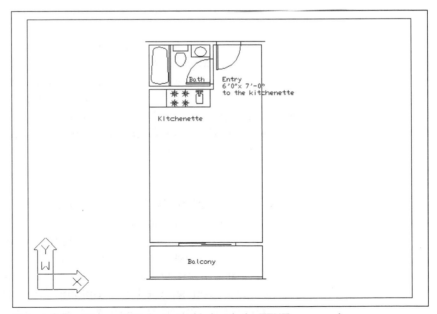

Figure 8.5:   The word "Balcony," added with the TEXT command

CHOOSING FONTS AND SPECIAL CHARACTERS

▼ NOTE

AutoCAD's fonts are contained in files with the .SHX extension in your AutoCAD directory. You can get other popular fonts, such as Helvetica and Times Roman, from third-party software companies. For more information, consult *Chapter 19*.

AutoCAD offers a wide choice of fonts that can be displayed in a number of different ways. The fonts include several specialized fonts, such as Greek and Cyrillic; symbols for astronomy, mapping, math, meteorology, and music are also provided. You can compress or expand these fonts and symbols, or modify them to create different type styles. Figure 8.6 shows you the fonts and symbols available with AutoCAD.

In addition, AutoCAD supplies a set of PostScript and TrueType fonts for applications in which you might want to use higher-quality display fonts. See "Using PostScript and TrueType Fonts" later in this chapter.

Bear in mind that the more complex the font, the longer it takes AutoCAD to regenerate your drawing. Before you choose a font for a particular job, consider how much text the drawing will contain. Use the Txt font if you like its look; it regenerates the fastest. Monotxt is a fixed-width font (like a typewriter font) that is useful for aligned columns of numbers or notes (see Figure 8.7). If you want something less boxy-looking, you can use the Romans font. Use the Romanc, Italicc, and other more complex fonts with discretion, as they will slow down the drawing regeneration considerably. Use the more complex fonts where you want a fancier type style, such as when drawing titles or labels in an exploded parts diagram (see Figure 8.8). You could use the Greeks font in conjunction with the Symath symbols for mathematical text.

CREATING A TYPE STYLE USING FONTS

Your drawings would look pretty boring if you used the same text style over and over. AutoCAD gives you the ability to create any number of text styles based on a set of predefined fonts. To create a style, you use Data ➤ Text Style and then select from the fonts available from Auto-CAD, or you can use PostScript and TrueType fonts if you have them. This next exercise will show you how to create a text style quickly from the predefined set of AutoCAD fonts.

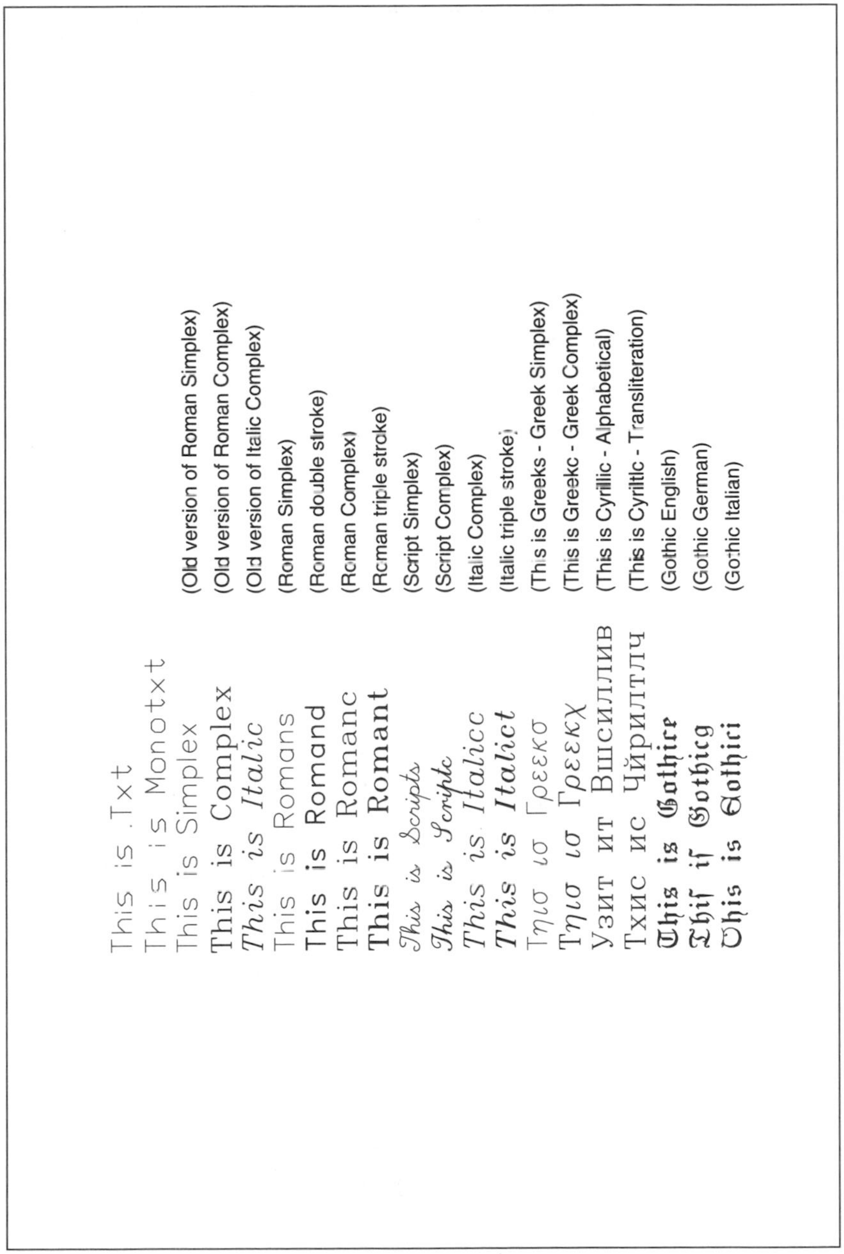

The AutoCAD script and symbol fonts are shown rotated within the figure box:

This is .Txt	
This is Monotxt	
This is Simplex	(Old version of Roman Simplex)
This is Complex	(Old version of Roman Complex)
This is Italic	(Old version of Italic Complex)
This is Romans	(Roman Simplex)
This is Romand	(Roman double stroke)
This is Romanc	(Roman Complex)
This is Romant	(Roman triple stroke)
This is Scripts	(Script Simplex)
This is Scripic	(Script Complex)
This is Italicc	(Italic Complex)
This is Italict	(Italic triple stroke)
Τηισ ιο Γρεεκο	(This is Greeks - Greek Simplex)
Τηισ ιτ Γρεεκχ	(This is Greekc - Greek Complex)
Уэит ит Вшсилиив	(This is Cyrillic - Alphabetical)
Тхис ис Чйрилтлч	(This is Cyriltic - Transliteration)
This is Gothice	(Gothic English)
This if Gothicg	(Gothic German)
This is Gothici	(Gothic Italian)

Figure 8.6A: The AutoCAD script and symbol fonts

II Building on the Basics

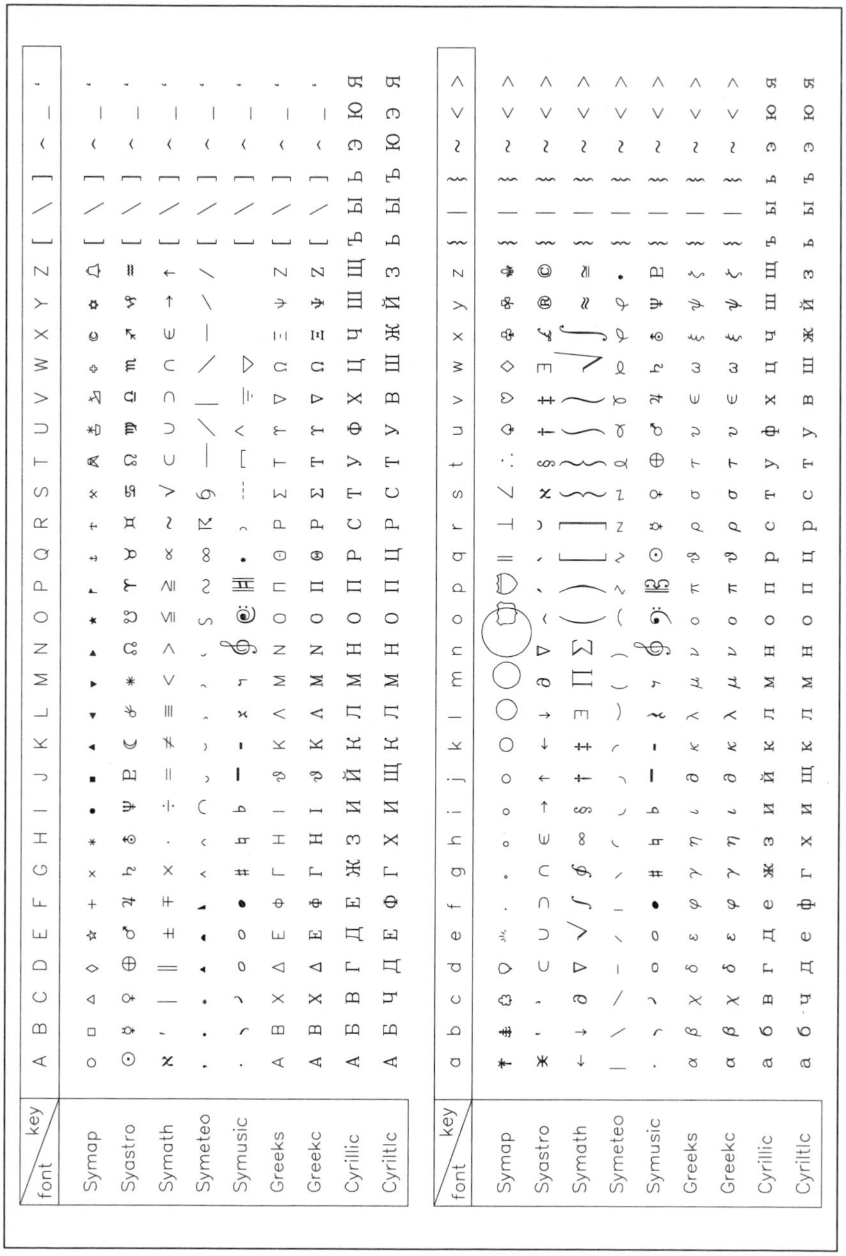

Figure 8.6B: The AutoCAD script and symbol fonts

Room #	Door #	Thick	Rate	Matrl	Const
116	116	1 3/4"	20 MIN	WOOD	SOLID CORE
114	114	1 3/4"	20 MIN	WOOD	SOLID CORE
112	112	1 3/4"	20 MIN	WOOD	SOLID CORE
110	---	1 3/4"	45 MIN	METAL	MINERAL CORE
108	108	1 3/4"	20 MIN	WOOD	SOLID CORE
106	106	1 1/2"	NO RATE	WOOD	HOLLOW
102	102	1 1/2"	NO RATE	WOOD	HOLLOW
104	104	1 3/4"	20 MIN	WOOD	SOLID CORE
107	107	1 3/4"	45 MIN	METAL	MINERAL CORE
105	105	1 3/4"	20 MIN	WOOD	SOLID CORE
101	101	1 3/4"	20 MIN	WOOD	SOLID CORE

Room #	Door #	Thick	Rate	Matrl	Const
116	116	1 3/4"	20 MIN	WOOD	SOLID CORE
114	114	1 3/4"	20 MIN	WOOD	SOLID CORE
112	112	1 3/4"	20 MIN	WOOD	SOLID CORE
110	---	1 3/4"	45 MIN	METAL	MINERAL CORE
108	108	1 3/4"	20 MIN	WOOD	SOLID CORE
106	106	1 1/2"	NO RATE	WOOD	HOLLOW
102	102	1 1/2"	NO RATE	WOOD	HOLLOW
104	104	1 3/4"	20 MIN	WOOD	SOLID CORE
107	107	1 3/4"	45 MIN	METAL	MINERAL CORE
105	105	1 3/4"	20 MIN	WOOD	SOLID CORE
101	101	1 3/4"	20 MIN	WOOD	SOLID CORE

Figure 8.7: Columns in the Txt and Monotxt fonts

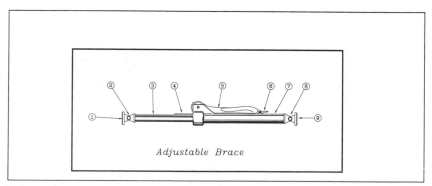

Adjustable Brace

Figure 8.8: Italicc (Italic Complex) is used as the title of this parts diagram.

II

Building on the Basics

1. Click on Data ➤ Text Style or type **Ddstyle** ↵. The Text Style dialog box appears.

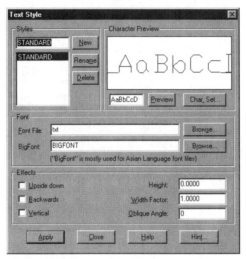

2. In the Styles input box in the upper-left corner, you will see the name STANDARD. STANDARD also appears in the list box just below the input box. This is the default text style of any new AutoCAD drawing. In the input box, change STANDARD to Romans, then click on the button labeled New. The name ROMANS appears in the list below the input box telling you you've created a new text style.

3. To select a font for your new style, first make sure the Romans style name is highlighted in the list box, then click on the Browse button to the right of the Font File input box that appears near the middle of the dialog box. This opens the Select Font File dialog box.

4. Double-click on the Font folder shown in the list box, then locate and double-click on the Romans.SHX font file. You can select from the standard AutoCAD fonts (.SHX), Post-Script fonts (.PFB), or TrueType fonts (.TTF). Once you select a font, you will be returned to the Text Style dialog box. The Character Preview window shows you what your style looks like.

5. In the Effects option group toward the bottom of the dialog box, locate the Height input box, then enter **6** for this option. This gives the Romans style a fixed 6-inch text height. If you enter a value other than 0 for the Height option, this value becomes the default height for this style; you will not be prompted for a text height in the future.

6. Locate the Width factor input box and enter **.8** for this option. Here you can compress or expand the font. Width factor values less than 1 will compress the font; values greater than 1 will expand the font. (You may find that you need a compressed font to fit into tight spaces. Or you may want to expand a font because of some design consideration. See Figure 8.9.)

This is the Simplex font expanded by 1.4
This is the simplex font using a width factor of 1
This is the simplex font compressed by .6

Figure 8.9:   Examples of compressed and expanded fonts

7. In the Character Preview section of the dialog box, click on Preview to see what the Effects options have done to your new style.

8. Click on Apply. You now have a new text style called Romans that uses the Romans.SHX font and has a height of 6 inches and a width factor of .8.

TURNING TEXT
UPSIDE DOWN AND BACKWARDS

In step 7 you got a preview of how the Width Factor option in the Effects button group affects the text style. The other Effects options—Oblique angle, Upside Down, Backwards, and Vertical—offer further modifications to the style. The Oblique angle option lets you slant the text to create an italic look (see Figure 8.10).

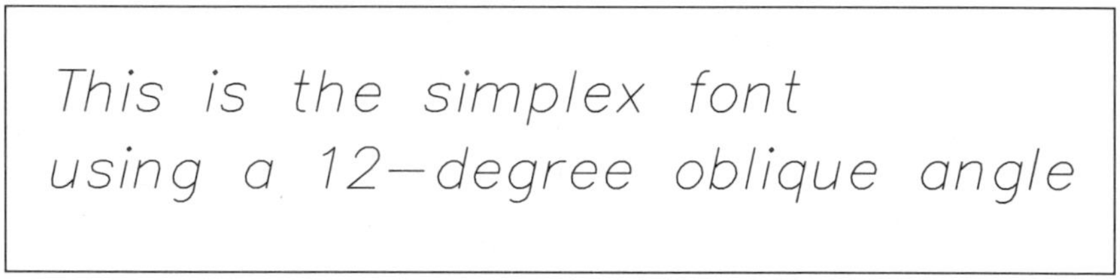

*This is the simplex font
using a 12—degree oblique angle*

Figure 8.10:   The Simplex font with a 12-degree oblique angle

The other check-box options do the following:

Backwards	Makes the text appear backwards, as if in a mirror
Upside-down	Sets the style to appear upside-down
Vertical	Arranges lines of text vertically

RENAMING A TYPE STYLE

In the last exercise, you named the new text style Romans—the same name as the font you selected. Giving the text style the same name as the font can help you remember what font you are using. But suppose you want to use another name for your newly created style. For example, you might want to create two styles of differing height using the same Romans font. Here's how you can change the style name:

1. Click on Data ➤ Rename... or enter **Ddrename** ↵ at the command prompt. The Rename dialog box appears.

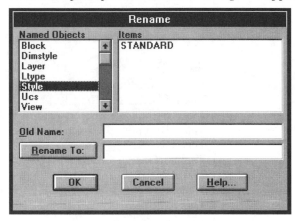

2. In the Named Objects list box, click on Style.

3. Click on the name ROMANS that appears in the Items list to the right; this makes ROMANS appear in the Old Name input box below the list.

4. In the input box next to the Rename To: button, enter the name **NOTE2**. Then click on the Rename To: button, and then on OK.

Now that you have renamed Romans to Note2, Note2 is your current style. You'll get a chance to see how this style will look in your drawing, but first, let's look at another way of creating a text style.

USING POSTSCRIPT AND TRUETYPE FONTS

Display fonts are fonts used in situations where appearances are important. In a typical architectural project, for example, display fonts are frequently used for presentation drawings of floor plans and building elevations. Traditionally, architects have used a device called a Kroy label machine to generate type for presentations. The Kroy machine is

II

Building on the Basics

slow and somewhat time-consuming to use, since you have to apply the lettering by hand to your art work. With PostScript and TrueType support, you can add display fonts (see Figure 8.11) directly to your CAD drawings, thereby saving time and gaining the ability to make multiple copies of your artwork. Here's how it's done.

This is CIBT_____.pfb
This is COBT_____.pfb
This is EUR_____.pfb
This is EURO_____.pfb
This is PAR.pfb
This is ROM_____.pfb
This is ROMB____.pfb
This is ROMI____.pfb
This is SAS_____.pfb
This is SASB_____.pfb
This is SASBO____.pfb
This is SASO_____.pfb
This is SUF.pfb
THIS IS TE_____.PFB
THIS IS TEB_____.PFB
THIS IS TEL_____.PFB
Τηισ ισ ΘMATH·ττφ
This is SWISSLI.ttf
This is VINET.ttf
This is SWISSL.ttf
This is SWISSEK.ttf
This is SWISSKO.ttf
This is SWISSEB.ttf
This is SWISSE.ttf
This is SWISSKI.ttf
This is SWISSK.ttf
This is SWISSI.ttf

This is SWISSCLI.ttf
This is SWISSEL.ttf
This is SWISSCL.ttf
THIS IS BGOTHL.TTF
THIS IS BGOTHM.TTF
.·%%® %® ′_′_÷ ★⊙™ ™ (compl.ttf)
This is COMPC.ttf
This is DUTCH.ttf
This is DUTCHB.ttf
This is DUTCHBI.ttf
This is DUTCHEB.ttf
This is DUTCHI.ttf
This is MONOS.ttf
This is MONOSB.ttf
This is MONOSBI.ttf
This is MONOSI.ttf
This is STYLU.ttf
This is SWISS.ttf
This is SWISSB.ttf
This is SWISSBI.ttf
This is SWISSBO.ttf
This is SWISSC.ttf
This is SWISSCB.ttf
This is SWISSCBI.ttf
This is SWISSCBO.ttf
This is SWISSCI.ttf
This is SWISSCK.ttf
This is SWISSCKI.ttf

Figure 8.11: PostScript and TrueType fonts supplied with AutoCAD

1. Select Data ➤ Text Style or enter **Style** ↵ at the command prompt.

2. At the Text style name (or ?) <NOTE2> prompt, enter **Note** ↵ for your text style name. The Select Font File dialog box appears.

3. Use the Files list to locate the PostScript font file TE_____.PFB, and double-click on it. (To quickly locate this file, use the List Files of Type pull-down list at the bottom of the dialog box to select Font(.PFB). This will cause the list box to display only the files with the .PFB file name extension.) The dialog box disappears.

4. At the height prompt, enter **6** ↵.

5. Complete the rest of the Style command just as you did in previous exercises.

▼ TIP

You can use the PSout command or File ➤ Export to export your drawings as fully PostScript-compatible files. Then download the file to a PostScript device for more accurate text reproduction (see *Chapter 14* for more on PSout).

The Textfill System Variable

Unlike the standard stick-like AutoCAD fonts, PostScript and True-Type fonts have filled areas. These filled areas take more time to generate, so if you have a lot of text in these fonts, your redraw and regen times will increase dramatically. To help reduce redraw and regen times, AutoCAD normally displays and plots these fonts as outline fonts, even though they are filled in their true appearance.

If you want, however, you can display and plot these fonts as solid filled fonts by adjusting the Textfill system variable. To change its setting, type **Textfill** ↵ and then type **1** ↵. This turns on text fill for PostScript and TrueType fonts. You can then plot your file with the text appearing as solid filled text instead of outlined. When you are editing your file, you will want to turn Textfill off.

USING A TYPE STYLE

Now let's see how to use the text styles you created. In the next exercise, you'll also get a change to use center justification for your text.

1. Click on Dtext from the Draw palette.

2. At the DTEXT Justify/Style/<Start point>: prompt, enter **C** ↵.

3. Pick a point near the center of the living room at coordinate 21′–11″, 15′–2″.

4. At the Rotation angle prompt, press ↵ to accept the default 0 angle.5. At the Text prompt, enter **Living room** ↵. (Your text will not be centered just yet.)

5. Press ↵ again. This ends the Dynamic Text command and executes the centering of your text on the selected point.

You might have noticed that in step 4 you got the Rotation angle prompt, skipping over the Height prompt. Remember that when you use a style with a height other than 0, AutoCAD doesn't bother to ask you what height you want. In this example, the text style has a preset height of 6″, so you are not prompted for a value.

▼
■
■
■
■

COMPILING POSTSCRIPT FONTS FOR SPEED

Some PostScript fonts may slow AutoCAD down because of the added overhead in translating PostScript font descriptions into a format AutoCAD can understand. To improve AutoCAD's performance, you can compile PostScript fonts into AutoCAD's native .SHX font format. Here's how it's done:

1. Click on Tools ➤ Compile…. The Compile Shape or Font File dialog box appears.

2. Double-click on the PostScript font you want to convert into the AutoCAD format. AutoCAD will work for a moment; then you'll see this message:

Compiling shape/font description file
Compilation successful. Output file
E:\ACADR13\COMMMON\FONTS\TE_____.shx
contains 59578 bytes.

When AutoCAD is done, you have a file with the same name as the PostScript font file, but with the .SHX file name extension. AutoCAD will use this compiled version of the font instead of the original PostScript .PFB file.

When you work with AutoCAD's .SHX font files, it is important to remember that

- License restrictions still apply to the AutoCAD-compiled version of the PostScript font.

- Like other fonts, compiled PostScript fonts can use up substantial disk space, so compile only the fonts you need.

- Some fonts may not load into AutoCAD at all, due to subtle differences in PostScript formatting.

▼ NOTE

When you use the STYLE command, your default style becomes the one you most recently edited or created.

In the last exercise, you entered text using the current default style. If you want to use a style other than the current one, you can use the Object Creation dialog box to change the current style.

1. Choose Data ➤ Object Creation…, or type **Ddemodes** ↵. The Object Creation dialog box appears.

Object Creation Modes	
Color... ▪	BYLAYER
Layer...	0
Linetype...	BYLAYER
Text Style...	STANDARD
Linetype Scale:	0'1"
Elevation:	0'0"
Thickness:	0'0"
OK Cancel	Help...

Building on the Basics

II

▼ **TIP**

If you want to quickly change
the text style and you already
know the name of the style
you want, you can type **S** ↵
style_name ↵ at the first
prompt of the DTEXT and
TEXT commands.

2. To change the current text style, click on Text Style.... The
   Select Text Style dialog box appears.

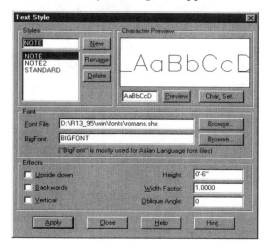

From here, you can choose from the list of styles available.
The list only shows styles you've already created. You can
also view the style's properties and see a sample.

3. Click on the STANDARD text style, and then on OK.

4. In the Object Creation Modes dialog box, click on OK.

5. Click on Dtext from the Draw palette or enter **Dtext** ↵.

6. Type **C** ↵.

7. Pick the point at coordinate 21′–11″, 14′–4″. This time the
   Height prompt appears, because you are now using a font
   whose height is set to 0. Notice how the default height is still
   at the last size you entered.

8. Press ↵ to accept the default height, and again to accept the
   default angle.

9. Enter **14′–0″ by 16′–5″** ↵.

10. Press ↵ again to exit Dynamic Text.

▼ **NOTE**

For more information on the
use of this dialog box, see
"Creating a Type Style Using
Fonts."

▼ **TIP**

If you remember all the justification options, you can enter
them directly at the Justify/
Style/<Start point> prompt
and skip the Justify prompt.

11. Zoom in to this group of text. Now you can see the Note and Standard styles, as shown in Figure 8.12. The words "Living room" use a smoother letterform than the dimensions "14′–0″ by 1–5″."

12. Start Dynamic Text again.

13. At the Starting point prompt, press ↵, and enter **230 square feet** ↵.

14. Press ↵ again to exit Dynamic Text.

15. Now zoom to your previous view.

Notice how the text you just entered is centered below the previously entered text (see Figure 8.13). AutoCAD remembers not only the location of the last text you entered, but the starting point you selected for it. If you had moved the last line of text, the new text would still appear below it.

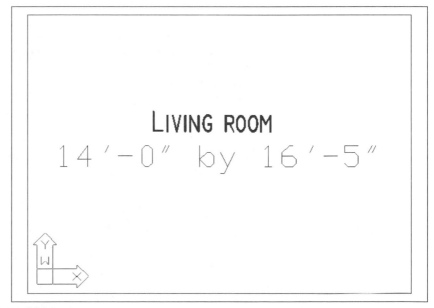

Figure 8.12: A close-up showing the Note and Standard styles

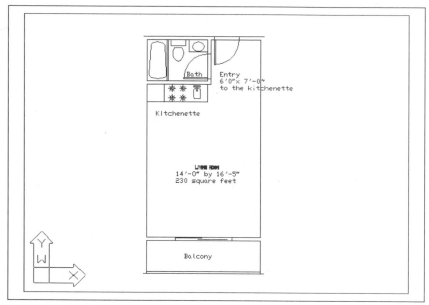

Figure 8.13:   The third line added to the column of text

▼ ■ ADDING SPECIAL CHARACTERS

You can add special characters to your text in AutoCAD. For example, you can place the degree symbol (°) after a number, or you can underscore (underline) text. To accomplish this, you use double percent (%%) signs in conjunction with a special code. For example, to underscore text, you enclose that text with the %% signs and follow it with the underscore code. So, to get this text:

This is <u>underscored</u> text.

you would enter this at the prompt:

> This is %%underscored%%u text.

Overscoring (putting a line above the text) operates in the same manner.

To insert codes for symbols, you just place the codes in the correct positions for the symbols they represent. For example, to enter 100.5°, you type **100.5%%d**.

Here is a list of the codes you can use:

Code	Special Characters
%%o	Toggles overscore on and off
%%u	Toggles underscore on and off
%%d	Places a degree sign (°) where the code occurs
%%p	Places a plus-minus sign where the code occurs
%%%	Forces a single percent sign; useful where you want a double percent sign to appear, or when you want a percent sign in conjunction with another code
%%nnn	Allows the use of extended ASCII characters when these characters are used in a text-definition file; nnn is the three-digit value representing the character

Building on the Basics

II

MODIFYING EXISTING TEXT

AutoCAD offers a variety of ways to modify text. Nearly every property associated with text can be edited. Of course, you can also edit the contents of the text. In this section, you will learn the various ways that text can be controlled to do exactly what you want it to do.

CHANGING THE PROPERTIES OF TEXT

Perhaps the simplest way to modify text is to use the Properties button in the Object Properties toolbar. This option gives you access to virtually all of the properties that control the appearance of text. Let's see how it works.

1. Zoom in to the entry area in the upper right corner of the floor plan again.

2. Click on Properties from the Object Properties toolbar.

3. At the Select object to modify prompt, click on the bottom line of the currently displayed text and then press ↵. The Modify Text dialog box appears; take a moment now to review the options.

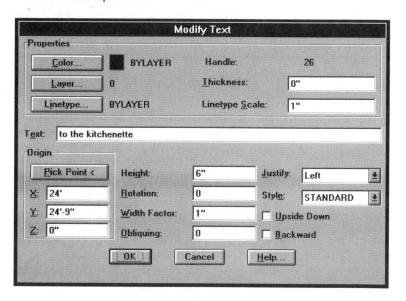

4. In the Modify Text dialog box, click on the arrow beside the Style pull-down list, which will then display all three text styles available in this file.

5. Click on NOTE, and the pull-down list closes.

6. Click on OK. The dialog box closes, and the text you selected changes to the new style (see Figure 8.14).

The Modify Text dialog box lets you change everything—from the text's justification style to its contents.

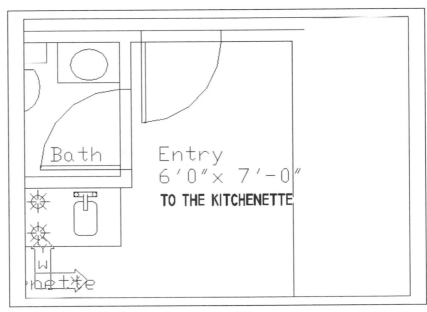

Figure 8.14: After changing the style to NOTE

TEXT EDITING SIMPLIFIED

When you want to change the contents of several lines of text, you may find the Modify Text dialog box a bit unwieldy. With the DDEDIT command, you can quickly edit several lines of text.

1. Click and drag Edit Polyline from the Modify palette then select Edit Text, or enter **Ddedit** ↵.

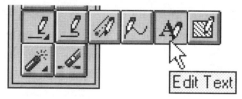

2. At the <Select a TEXT or ATTDEF object>/Undo: prompt, click on the second-to-last line of text displayed on the screen. A dialog box appears displaying that text.

3. Click on the space between the *x* and the *7*.

4. Press the Backspace key to delete the letter *x*, and then enter **by**.

5. Click on OK, and the text in the drawing reflects your modifications.

6. At the Select a TEXT... prompt, click on the next line down. The Edit Text dialog box appears again, allowing you to make more changes.

7. Click on OK.

8. Now click on Undo from the Standard toolbar or enter **U** ↵. The text you just edited changes back to its previous form, and the Select a TEXT... prompt remains.

9. Press ↵ to exit DDEDIT.

You can edit text in the DDEDIT dialog box just as you would in any other input box. Just double-click on the input box and proceed to enter an entirely new line of text. Or, as you have just seen, you can easily edit one or two letters within the current line of text.

Other Text Editing Utilities

Three other utilities are available on the companion CD that comes with this book:

> **EDSP.LSP** allows you to edit several lines of text as if they were a block of text.
>
> **ET.LSP** lets you quickly replace several lines of text with the same line that you enter.
>
> **ETS.LSP** lets you change a group of text objects into a sequence of numbers.

The ET.LSP and ETS.LSP utilities are especially useful when you are editing tables or schedules in which sets of numbers change or data is repeated in several places.

KEEPING TEXT FROM MIRRORING

At times you will want to mirror a group of objects that contain some text. This operation will cause the mirrored text to appear backward. You can change a setting in AutoCAD to make the text read normally, even when it is mirrored.

1. Enter **Mirrtext** ↵.
2. At the New value for MIRRTEXT <1>: prompt, enter **0** ↵.

Now any mirrored text that is not in a block will read normally. The text's *position*, however, will still be mirrored, as shown in Figure 8.15.

Text
Justified
Left

Text
Justified
Left

Mirrored Text

Original Text

Figure 8.15: Mirrored text, with MIRRTEXT set to 0

ENTERING LARGE BLOCKS OF TEXT

If you have a substantial amount of text in a drawing, or a sheet of general notes for a set of drawings, you can use the Multiline Text (MTEXT) command to enter text. MTEXT lets you enter and format entire paragraphs or lists. It offers features such as word wrapping to help you fit text in a specific area, variable text height, stacked fractions, and multiple styles. Here's how it works.

1. Click and drag Dtext from the Draw menu and select Text, or type **Mtext** ↵.

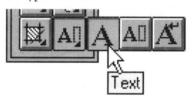

2. At the Attach/Rotation/Style/Height/Direction/<Insertion point> prompt, click on a point defining the upper-left corner of the area in which you want to place your word-wrapped text.

3. At the Other corner prompt, a window appears. Size the window to indicate the area within which you want to place your text. This text area is called the text boundary.

4. Once you've selected a text boundary, AutoCAD opens the Edit Mtext dialog box (see panel 1 of Figure 8.16).

5. Start typing your notes. As you type, the text appears in the window at the top of the dialog box in the layout that it will appear in the drawing. Notice that the text appears in the white area of the window. This white area represents the width of the area you selected in step 2 and 3 when you defined the area within which you want to place your text. This width will vary depending on the width of the area you select and the size of the text style you are currently using.

6. When you are done entering your note, Click on OK. The note appears in your drawing at the location you selected in step 2 (see panel 2 of Figure 8.16).

At any time while you are typing in step 5, you can make corrections to the text by moving the vertical bar text cursor to the location of your correction and making the appropriate changes. Just as with any text editor, you can highlight and replace whole blocks of text using your cursor.

As you can see from the prompt in step 2, you can set the rotation, style, height, and direction of the text before you enter it. You can also attach text to an existing text object. If you don't designate values for these other settings, AutoCAD will use the current default text settings.

EDITING AND FORMATTING MULTILINE TEXT

Multiline text offers many options for editing and formatting. In this section you'll take a closer look at that Edit Mtext dialog box and explore some of its other options.

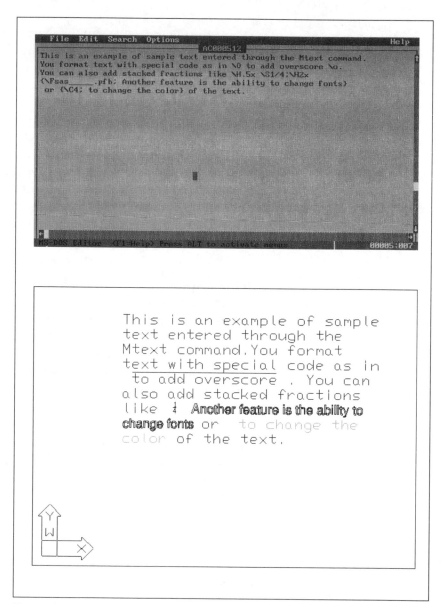

Figure 8.16: The Edit Mtext dialog box

The Edit Mtext dialog box doesn't only appear when you create new Multiline text. It also appears when you attempt to edit existing Multiline text. The following exercise demonstrates this.

1. Click on Properties from the Object Properties.

2. At the Select object prompt, click on the Multiline text.

3. In the Modify Mtext dialog box, click on Edit Contents….

4. The Edit Mtext dialog box appears with the selected text in it's edit window. At this point, you can make changes to your text, and then click on OK to exit the dialog box. The changes appear in your drawing and you return to the Modify Mtext dialog box.

While you are in the Edit Mtext dialog box, you have several options besides just revising text. Let's look at how you can use the Edit Mtext dialog box to control your text's appearance.

Stacking Fractions

Perhaps one of the oldest items on the AutoCAD wishlist is stacked fractions. You can now quickly add stacked fractions in the middle of your text without resorting to lots of tricks. Here's how it's done:

1. While in the Edit Mtext dialog box, highlight the fraction you want stacked using the text cursor. This operation will only work on fractions so the text you highlight must be in a form similar to 1/4 or 1/2.

2. Click on the button labeled Stack. The highlighted text will appear stacked in the text window.

Adjusting Text Size, Rotation Angle, and Width

You may decide that the multiline text is too large or that the text boundary is too narrow. The following describes another dialog box that lets you set text height and width on the fly.

1. While in the Edit Mtext dialog box, click on the Properties… button. The Mtext Properties dialog box appears.

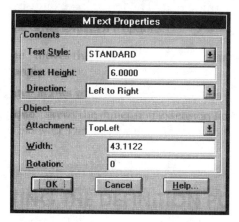

2. As an alternative, you can click on Properties from the Object Properties toolbar, select a single Multiline text object, then at the Modify Mtext dialog box, click on Edit Properties…. This also opens the Mtext Properties dialog box.

With this dialog box, you can make changes to the overall width or rotation angle of the text boundary using the Width and Rotation options in the Object group. The Attachment option lets you change the location of the text boundary in relation to the text boundary insertion point.

You can change the overall text style and text height using the Style and Height options in the Contents group. The Direction pop-up list is for languages that read vertically such as Japanese and Chinese.

Importing Text Files

With Multiline text objects, AutoCAD allows you to import standard ASCII text. Here's how you go about importing text files.

1. From the Edit Mtext dialog box, click on Import….

2. At the Import Text File dialog box, locate a valid text file. It must be a file in a raw text (ASCII) format such as a Notepad .TXT file.

3. Once you've highlighted the file you want, double-click on it or click on OK. The text appears in the Edit Mtext window.

4. You can then click on OK and the text will appear in your drawing.

In addition, you can use the Windows clipboard and Cut and Paste feature to add text to a drawing. To do this, take the following steps:

1. Use the Cut or Copy option in any other Windows program to place text into the Windows clipboard.

2. Go to AutoCAD, then choose Edit ➤ Paste. The text appears in the upper-left corner of the AutoCAD drawing window.

Since AutoCAD is an OLE client, you can also attach other types of documents to an AutoCAD drawing file. See *Chapter 14* for more on AutoCAD's OLE support.

EMBEDDING CODES FOR SPECIAL TEXT FORMATTING

Multiline text lets you format individual characters for style, with attributes such as italic, bold, underline, height, and font; you can also set the color of individual words. But before you can do this in the Windows version of AutoCAD, you must change the default text editor used with Multiline Text.

So far, you've been shown the Edit Mtext dialog box which is the internal text editor AutoCAD uses. You can, however, set up AutoCAD to use any text editor you choose. In the following example, we describe how you can set up AutoCAD to use the Windows Notepad in place of the AutoCAD internal text editor:

1. Choose Options ➤ Preferences.... The Preferences dialog box appears.

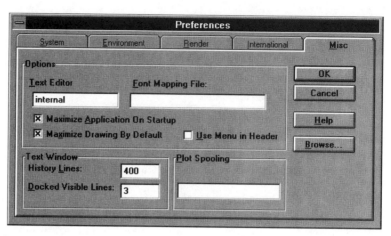

2. Click on the Misc tab at the top of the dialog box. A new set of options appears.

3. Double click on input box labeled Text Editor to highlight the word "internal."

4. Click on Browse…. The Select a File dialog box appears.

5. Locate the Notepad.EXE file in your Windows directory and double click on it.

6. At the Preferences dialog box, click on OK. From now on, whenever you create or edit Multiline text, you'll see the Windows Notepad application window in place of the Edit Mtext dialog box.

Once you've changed the text editor, you will be able to take advantage of special codes to format your text on a character-by-character basis. See the sidebar, "Embedding Format Codes in Multiple-Line Text," for details on format coding.

EMBEDDING FORMAT CODES IN MULTIPLE-LINE TEXT

Like Dynamic Text, the formatting of text inserted using the MTEXT command is also accomplished through the use of special codes. These codes differ somewhat from those used for single-line text inserted with DTEXT. Here are the codes and their uses:

\O	Start overline
\o	Stop overline
\U	Start underline
\u	Stop underline
\~	Nonbreaking spacc (keeps words together on a line)
\\	Literal backslash
\{	Literal opening brace
\}	Literal closing brace
\C*<number>*;	Change to color *<number>*
\F*<filename>*;	Change to font *<filename>*
\H*<size>*;	Change to text height *<size>*; to indicate a size relative to the main body of text, you can use an x (as in .75x)
\S*<string>*;	Stack two strings, as in fractions

To use these codes on blocks of text, you must enclose the coded text within braces. For example, to display this statement:

Include all new electrical equipment

with the words *all new* in red, you would type the following:

Include {\C1;all new} electrical equipment

Here C1 refers to the color number 1 (red); and the curly braces indicate the extent of text that is to be changed to red.

You can use these codes either within the MTEXT text window, or in text you intend to import through the MTEXT command.

II

Building on the Basics

CHECKING SPELLING

Although AutoCAD is primarily a drawing program, you will find that some of your drawings contain more text than graphics. At long last, Autodesk has recognized this and has included a spelling checker in AutoCAD Release 13. If you've ever used the spelling checker in a typical Windows word processor, such as Microsoft Word for Windows, the AutoCAD spelling checker's operation will be familiar to you. Here's how it works:

1. Choose Tools ➤ Spelling…, or type **Spelling** ↵ at the command prompt.

2. At the Select object prompt, select any text created with the Text, Dynamic Text (DTEXT), or Multiline Text (MTEXT) commands. When the spelling checker finds a word it does not recognize, the Check Spelling dialog box appears.

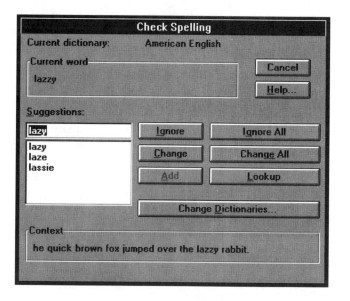

In the Check Spelling dialog box you'll see the word in question, along with the spelling checker's suggested alternate word in the Suggestions input box. If the spelling checker finds more than one suggestion, a list of suggested replacement words appears below the input box. You can then highlight the desired replacement and click on the Change button to change the misspelled word, or click on Change All to change all occurrences of the word in the selected text. If the suggested word is inappropriate, choose another word from the replacement list (if any), or enter your own spelling. Then choose Change or Change All.

Here are the other options available to you in the Check Spelling dialog box:

Ignore skips the word.

Ignore All skips all occurrences of the word in the selected text.

Add adds the word in question to the current dictionary.

Lookup checks the spelling of the word in the Suggestions box. This option is for the times when you decide to try another word that doesn't appear in the Suggestions input box.

Change Dictonaries lets you use a different dictionary to check spelling. This option opens the Change Dictionaries dialog box, described in the upcoming section.

Context displays the phrase in which the word in question was found.

CHOOSING A DICTIONARY

The Change Dictionaries option opens the Change Dictionaries dialog box, where you can select a particular main dictionary for foreign languages, or create or choose a custom dictionary. Main dictionary files have the .DCT extension. The Main dictionary for the U.S. version of AutoCAD is Enu.DCT.

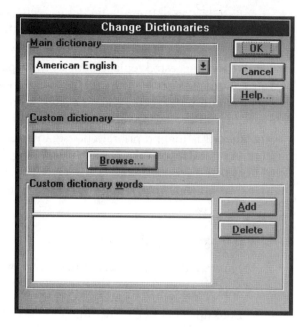

In this dialog box, you can also add or delete words from a custom dictionary. Custom dictionary files are ASCII files with the .CUS extension. Because they are ASCII files, they can be edited outside of AutoCAD. The Browse button lets you view a list of existing custom dictionaries.

If you prefer, you can also select a main or custom dictionary using the Dctust and Dctmain system variables. See *Appendix D* for more on these system variables.

SUBSTITUTING FONTS

There will be times when you will want to change all the fonts in a drawing quickly. For instance, you may want to convert PostScript fonts into a simple Txt.SHX font to help shorten redraw times while you are editing. Or you may need to convert the font of a drawing received from another office to a font that conforms to your own office standards. In AutoCAD Release 13, the Fontmap system variable works in conjunction with a font-mapping table, allowing you to easily substitute fonts in a drawing.

The font-mapping table is an ASCII file you create, containing one line for each font substitution you want AutoCAD to make. You can give this file any name you choose, as long as it has the .FMP extension.

A typical line in this file would read as follows:

romant; C:\acadr13\common\font\Txt.shx

In this example, AutoCAD is directed to use the Txt.SHX font in place of the Romant font. To execute this substitution, you would type

Fontmap ↵ *Fontmap_filename* ↵

where *Fontmap_filename* is the font-mapping table you've created. This tells AutoCAD where to look for the font-mapping information. Then you would issue the REGEN command to view the font changes. To disable the font mapping table, you type

Fontmap ↵ .↵

See *Appendix D* for more on Fontmap and other system variables.

See *Appendix D* for more on Fontmap and other system variables.

▼ **MAKING SUBSTITUTIONS**
■ **FOR MISSING FONTS**

■ Chances are, you will eventually have to work with unfamiliar files
   provided by another person or company. One of the most common
■ difficulties in this situation is encountering fonts you don't have.

■ When text styles are created, the associated fonts do not become
   part of the drawing file. Instead, AutoCAD loads the needed font
   file at the same time that the drawing is loaded. So if a text style in
   a drawing requires a particular font, AutoCAD looks for the font in
   the AutoCAD search path; if the font is there, it is loaded. Usually
   this isn't a problem if the drawing file uses the standard fonts that
   come with AutoCAD. But occasionally you will encounter a file
   that uses a custom font.

II

Building on the Basics

In earlier versions of AutoCAD, when you attempted to open such a file, you saw an error message. This missing-font message would often send the new AutoCAD user into a panic.

Fortunately, Release 13 offers a solution: AutoCAD now automatically substitutes an existing font for the missing font in a drawing. By default, AutoCAD substitutes the Txt.SHX font, but you can specify another one using the Fontalt system variable. Type **Fontalt** ↵ at the command prompt and then enter the name of the font you want to use as the substitute.

Be aware that the text in your drawing will change in appearance, sometimes radically, when you use a substitute font. If the text in the drawing must retain its appearance, you will want to substitute a font that is as similar in appearance to the original font as possible.

ACCELERATING ZOOMS AND REGENS WITH QTEXT

If you need to edit a drawing that contains lots of text, but you don't need to edit the text, you can use the QTEXT command to help accelerate redraws and regenerations when you are working on the drawing. QTEXT turns lines of text into rectangular boxes, saving AutoCAD from having to form every letter. This allows you to see the note locations so you don't accidentally draw over them.

To turn on QTEXT:

1. Select Options ➤ Drawing Aids… and turn on the Quick Text check box, or enter **Qtext** ↵ at the command prompt.

2. At the ON/OFF <OFF>: prompt, enter **ON** ↵.

3. To display the results of QTEXT, issue the REGEN command from the prompt.

▼ **TIP**

Selecting a large set of text objects for editing can be annoyingly slow. To improve the speed of text selection (and object selection in general), turn off the Highlight and Dragmode system variables. This will disable certain convenience features but may improve overall performance, especially on large drawings. See *Appendix D* for more information.

When QTEXT is off, text is generated normally. When QTEXT is on, rectangles show the approximate size and length of text, as shown in Figure 8.17.

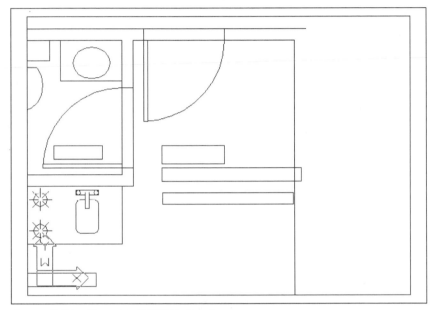

Figure 8.17:   Text with QTEXT off and on

IF YOU WANT TO EXPERIMENT...

At this point, you may want to try adding some notes to drawings you have created in other "If You Want to Experiment..." sections of this book. Try the exercise shown in Figure 8.18. You might also try importing a finish or door schedule from a word processor in the Monotxt font, to see how that works. If your application is mechanical, you might try importing a parts list.

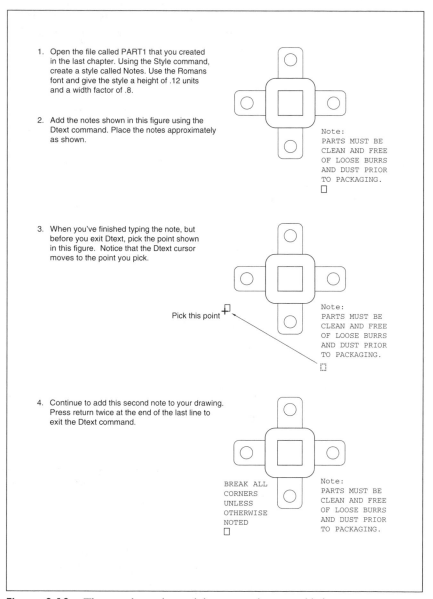

Figure 8.18: The sample mechanical drawing with notes added

9

USING DIMENSIONS

Setting Up a Dimension Style

Drawing Linear Dimensions

Continuing a Dimension String

Drawing Dimensions from a Common
Baseline

Appending Data to a Dimension's Text

Dimensioning Radii, Diameters, and Arcs

Using Ordinate Dimensions

Adding Tolerance Notation

FAST TRACK

377 ► ## To set up several dimension styles

Click on Data ➤ Dimensioning Style… and enter a name in the input box. Click on the Save button to make the name you entered into a style. Repeat these steps to create more styles. Once a style is defined, you can click on the labeled buttons to make adjustments to each style.

382 ► ## To open the Dimensioning Tool Palette

Click on Tools ➤ Toolbars ➤ Dimensioning.

382 ► ## To draw a vertical or horizontal dimension

Click on Linear Dimension from the Dimensioning palette, click on the two points you want to dimension, and then click on the location of the dimension line.

384 ► ## To add to a string of dimensions

Click on Continue Dimension from the Dimensioning palette, and then click on the next point you want to dimension.

388 ► ## To draw dimensions from a common baseline

Click on Baseline Dimension from the Dimensioning palette, and then click on the next point you want to dimension.

391 ► ## To append text to an existing dimension's text

Type **Dimedit** ↵ **N** ↵. Enter the appending text, and include the <> signs where the current text is to be placed in relation to the appending text. When you are done typing the text, press ↵, click on the text you wish to change, and press ↵ to finish your selection.

394 ▶ To ensure dimensions are updated when a drawing changes

Include a dimension's definition point with any edits you make on the drawing.

397 ▶ To move dimension text to a new location

Type **Dimoverride** ↵ **Dimfit** ↵ **4** ↵ ↵. Select the dimension you want to edit, then press ↵. With the Grips feature turned on, click on the dimension text you wish to move. Click on the grip located at the dimension text and move it into place.

407 ▶ To set up specific Osnap overrides as defaults when picking points

Click on Options ▶ Running Object Snap. Check any object snap settings that you want to be active at all times.

410 ▶ To draw a linear dimension at an angle

Click on Linear Dimension from the Dimensioning palette, click on the two points you want to dimension, enter **R** ↵ then enter the angle for the dimension. Then click on a point to locate the dimension line.

414 ▶ To dimension an arc

Click on Radius Dimension from the Dimensioning palette. Click on the Arc then pick a dimension location.

415 ▶ To add a note with a leader

Click on Leader from the Dimensioning palette, pick the arrow side of the leader, and pick points defining the leader lines. When you are done placing the leader lines, press ↵ and type the note.

Before you determine the dimensions of a project, your design is in flux and many questions may be unanswered. Once you begin dimensioning, you begin to see if things fit or work together. Dimensioning can be crucial to how well a design works and how quickly it develops. Communicating even tentative dimensions to others can accelerate design development.

With AutoCAD, you can easily add tentative or final dimensions to any drawing. AutoCAD gives you an accurate dimension without your having to take measurements. You simply pick the two points to be dimensioned and the dimension line location, and AutoCAD does the rest. AutoCAD's *associative dimensioning* capability automatically updates dimensions whenever the size or shape of the dimensioned object is changed. These dimensioning features can save you valuable time and reduce the number of dimensional errors in your drawings.

AutoCAD's dimensioning feature has a substantial number of settings. Though they give you an enormous amount of flexibility in formatting your dimensions, all these settings can be somewhat intimidating to the new user. We'll ease you into dimensioning by first showing you how to create a *dimension style*.

CREATING A DIMENSION STYLE

Dimension styles are similar to text styles. They determine the look of your dimensions as well as the size of dimensioning features, such as the dimension text and arrows. You might set up a dimension style to have special types of arrows, for instance, or to position the dimension text above or in line with the dimension line.

AutoCAD gives you a default dimension style called Standard, which is set up for mechanical drafting. You will doubtless add many other styles to suit the style of drawings you are creating. You can also create variations of a general style for those situations that call for only minor changes in the dimension's appearance.

In this first section you'll see how to set up a dimension style that is more appropriate for architectural drawings (see Figure 9.1).

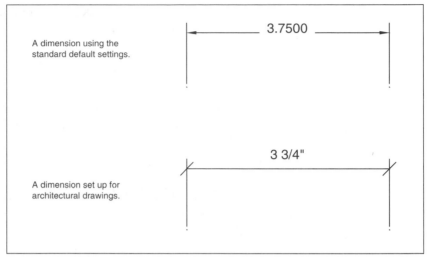

A dimension using the
standard default settings.

3.7500

A dimension set up for
architectural drawings.

3 3/4"

Figure 9.1: AutoCAD's standard dimension style compared with an
architectural-style dimension

1. Open the Unit file.

2. Click on Data ➤ Dimension Style…, or type **Ddim** ↵ at the
   command prompt. The Dimension Styles dialog box appears.

3. Double-click on the Name input box to highlight STAN-DARD, and then type in **architect**.

4. Click on Save.

You've just created a dimension style called Architect, but at this point, it is identical to the Standard style on which it is based. Nothing has happened to the Standard style, of course; it is still available if you need to use it.

SETTING THE DIMENSION UNIT STYLE

Now you need to modify the new Architect dimension style so that it conforms to the architectural style of dimensioning. Let's start by changing the unit style for the dimension text. Just as you changed the overall unit style of AutoCAD to a foot-and-inches style for your toilet and tub drawing in *Chapter 3*, you must do the same for your dimension styles.

1. In the Dimension Styles dialog box, click on the Annotation... button. The Annotation dialog box appears.

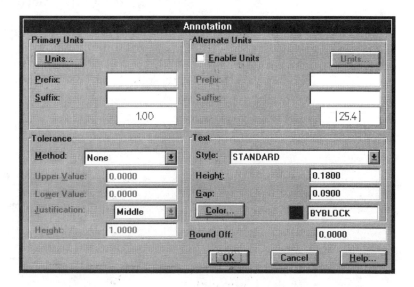

2. In the Primary Units group, click on the Units... button. The Primary Units dialog box appears.

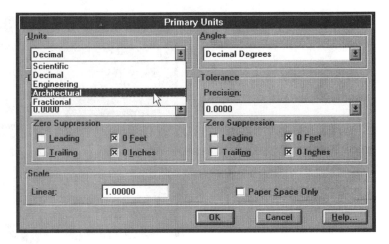

3. Open the Units drop-down list and choose Architectural. Notice that this drop-down list contains the same unit styles as the main Units dialog box (Data ➤ Units...).

4. In the Zero Suppression button group just below the Units list, click on 0 Inches to remove the x from this check box. If you leave it turned on, indications of 0 inches will be omitted from the dimension text. (In architectural drawings, 0 inches are shown as in this dimension: 12′–0″.)

5. Click on OK here and then again at the Annotation dialog box.

You have set up Architecture's dimension unit style to show dimensions in feet and inches, rather than inches and decimal inches.

SETTING THE LOCATION OF DIMENSION TEXT

AutoCAD's default setting for the placement of dimension text puts the text in line with the dimension line, as shown in the example at the top of Figure 9.1. However, we want the new Architectural style to put the text above the dimension line, as is done at the bottom of Figure 9.1. To do that, you will use the dimension style Format options.

1. In the Dimension Style dialog box, click on the Format...
   button. The Format dialog box appears.

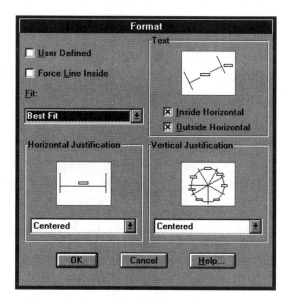

2. In the Vertical Justification box that occupies the lower-right
   corner of the dialog box, open the pull-down list and choose
   Above. The graphic changes to show you what this format
   will look like in your dimensions.

3. In the Text box (upper-right corner of the dialog box), click
   on the Inside Horizontal and Outside Horizontal check boxes
   to turn them both off. The graphic shows you the effect of
   these settings on your dimensions.

4. Now click OK to return to the Dimension Style dialog box.

CHOOSING AN ARROW STYLE
AND SETTING THE DIMENSION SCALE

Next, you will want to specify a different type of arrow for your new dimension style. For linear dimension in architectural drawings, a diagonal line or "tick" mark is typically used, rather than an arrow.

In addition, you will want to set the scale for the graphical components of the dimension, such as arrows and text. Recall from *Chapter 8* that text must be scaled up in size in order to appear at the proper size in the final output of the drawing. Dimensions, too, must be scaled so they look right when the drawing is plotted. For both the arrow and scale settings, you will use the Geometry settings.

1. In the Dimension Styles dialog box, click on the Geometry... button. The Geometry dialog box appears.

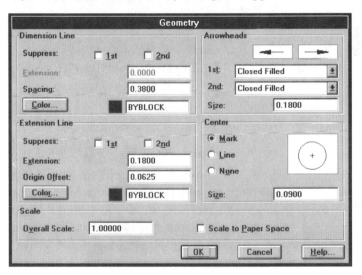

You can create your own arrowheads. See *Appendix D* for details.

Here's a simple way to figure out scale factors: Divide 12 by the decimal equivalent of the inch scale. So for $^1/_4''$, divide 12 by 0.25 to get 48. For $^1/_8''$, divide 12 by 0.125 to get 96. For $1^1/_2''$, divide 12 by 1.5 to get 8, and so on.

2. In the Arrowheads group, open the first pull-down list and choose Oblique. The graphic shows you what the arrow looks like. You can also cycle through all the arrow options by clicking on the graphic in the Arrowhead group.

3. Locate the Overall Scale input box at the lower-left of the dialog box, and change this value to 48. This is the scale factor for a $^1/_4''$ scale drawing.

4. Click on OK here and then again at the Dimension Style dialog box. Now you're ready to add architectural dimensions.

In this section, we've introduced you to the various dialog boxes that let you set the appearance of a dimension style. We haven't been able to discuss every option, of course, so if you want to learn more about the other dimension style options, consult *Appendix D*. There you'll find descriptions of all the items in the Dimension Styles dialog box, plus reference material covering the system variables associated with each option.

DRAWING LINEAR DIMENSIONS

The most common type of dimension you'll be using is the *linear dimension*, which is an orthogonal dimension measuring the width and length of an object. AutoCAD offers three dimensioning tools for this purpose, Linear (DIMLINEAR), Continue (DIMCONT), and Baseline (DIMBASE). These options are readily accessible from the Dimensioning tool palette.

FINDING THE DIMENSIONING PALETTE

Before you can apply any dimension, you'll want to open the Dimensioning palette. This palette contains nearly all the commands necessary to draw and edit your dimensions.

Choose Tools ➤ Toolbars ➤ Dimensioning, or click on Dimensioning from the Tools flyout on the Standard toolbar. The dimensioning toolbar appears.

Now you're ready to begin dimensioning.

PLACING HORIZONTAL AND VERTICAL DIMENSIONS

Let's start by looking at the basic dimensioning tool, Linear. In Release 13, the Linear Dimension button (the DIMLINEAR command) on the

Dimensioning palette accommodates both the horizontal and vertical dimensions.

In this exercise, you'll add a vertical dimension to the right side of the Unit plan.

1. To start either a vertical or horizontal dimension, click on Linear Dimension from the Dimensioning tool palette, or enter **Dimlinear** ⏎ at the command prompt.

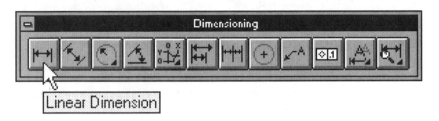

▼ NOTE

Notice that the prompt in step 2 gives you the option of pressing ⏎ to select an object. If you do this, you are prompted to pick the object you wish to dimension, rather than the actual distance to be dimensioned. We'll look at this method later.

2. The prompt, First extension line origin or RETURN to select:, is asking you for the first point of the distance to be dimensioned. An extension line is the line that connects the object being dimensioned to the dimension line. Use the Endpoint Osnap override and pick the upper-right corner of the entry, at the coordinate 29′–0″, 30′–10″.

3. At the Second extension line origin: prompt, pick the lower-right corner of the living room, at coordinate 29′–0″, 6′–10″.

4. In the next prompt,

   Dimension line location (Text/Angle/Horizontal/Vertical/Rotated):

   the dimension line is the line indicating the direction of the dimension and containing the arrows or tick marks. Move your cursor from left to right, and you see a temporary dimension appear. This allows you to visually select a dimension line location.

▼ NOTE

You have the option to append information to the dimension's text or change the dimension text altogether. You'll see how later in this chapter.

5. Enter **@4'<0** ↵ to tell AutoCAD you want the dimension line to be 4 feet to the right of the last point you selected. (You could pick a point using your cursor, but this doesn't let you place the dimension line as accurately.) After you've done this, the dimension is placed in the drawing as shown in Figure 9.2.

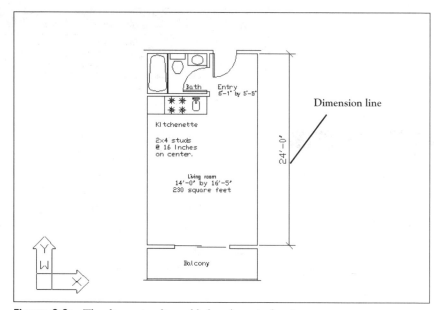

Figure 9.2: The dimension line added to the unit drawing

CONTINUING A DIMENSION

You will often want to input a group of dimensions strung together in a line. For example, you may want to continue dimensioning the balcony and have the continued dimension aligned with the dimension you just entered. To do this, you use the Dimensioning menu's Continue option.

1. Click on Continue Dimension from the Dimensioning pal-
    ette, or enter **Dimcont** ↵.

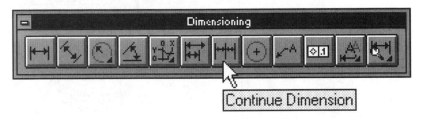

2. At the Second extension line origin or RETURN to Select:
    prompt, pick the upper-right corner of the balcony at coordi-
    nate 29′–0″, 6′–5″. See the top panel of Figure 9.3 for the
    results.

3. Pick the right end of the rail on the balcony, at coordinate
    29′–0″, 2′–8″. See the bottom panel of Figure 9.2 for the
    results.

4. Press ↵ twice to exit the DIMCONT command.

The Continue option adds a dimension from where you left off. The
last drawn extension line is used as the first extension line for the continued dimension. AutoCAD will keep adding dimensions as you
continue to pick points, until you press ↵.

Continuing a Dimension
from a Previous Dimension

If you need to continue a string of dimensions from a previous linear dimension, other than the most recently added one, press ↵ at the Second extension line origin or RETURN to Select prompt you saw in step
2 of the previous exercise. Then, at the Select continued dimension
prompt, click on the extension line from which you wish to continue.

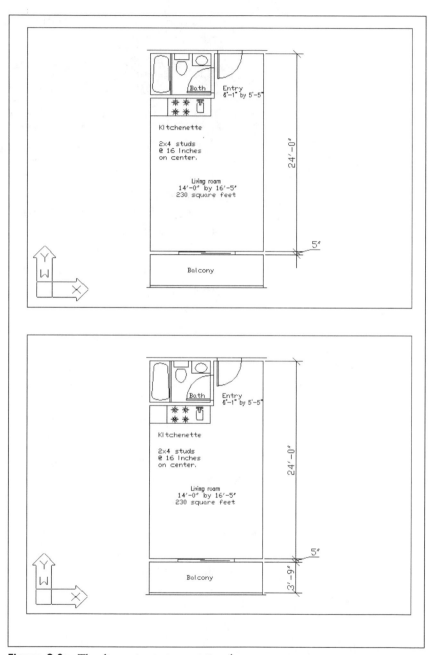

Figure 9.3: The dimension string continued

USING THE OLD STYLE DIMENSION COMMANDS

AutoCAD provides several commands for dimensioning that you can enter at the command prompt. Two of the commands not discussed specifically in this chapter are DIM and DIM1. These two commands are holdovers from earlier versions of AutoCAD and are maintained in Release 13 for compatibility. It is likely that they will disappear in later releases of AutoCAD.

The DIM command is like a self-contained program—once you enter it, you get the Dim: prompt instead of the familiar command prompt. Also, in DIM, you won't be able to use any other Auto-CAD commands (with the exception of transparent commands); only the commands that relate to dimensioning (listed below) are allowed. To exit the Dim: prompt, enter **Exit** ↵ or press Esc.

The DIM1 command allows you to enter a single dimension, then automatically returns you to the standard command prompt to enter other AutoCAD commands.

The DIM1 and DIM options are listed below, along with their command equivalents in Release 13. All of the DIM and DIM1 options can be issued using just the first three letters. For example, you can enter **Dim1** ↵ **Ver** ↵ to draw a vertical dimension.

DIM, DIM1 Option	Release 13 Command
Aligned	Dimaligned
Angular	Dimangular
Baseline	Dimbase
Center	Dimcenter
Continue	Dimcontinue
Diameter	Dimdiameter
Exit	*none*
Hometext	Dimedit/Home

DIM, DIM1 Option	Release 13 Command
Horizontal	Dimlinear
Leader	Leader
Newtext	Dimedit/Text
Oblique	Dimedit/Oblique
Ordinate	Dimordinate
Override	Dimoverride
Radius	Dimradius
Redraw	Redraw
Restore	Dimstyle/Restore
Rotate	Dimlinear
Save	Dimstyle/Save
Status	Dimstyle/Status
Style	Dimtxtsty
Tedit	Dimtedit
Trotate	Dimedit/Rotate
Undo	Undo
Update	*none*
Variables	Dimstyle/Variables
Vertical	Dimlinear

DRAWING DIMENSIONS FROM A COMMON BASE EXTENSION LINE

Another method for dimensioning objects is to have several dimensions originate from the same extension line. To accommodate this, AutoCAD provides the Baseline option on the Dimensioning menu. To see how this works, you will start another dimension—this time a horizontal one—across the top of the plan.

1. Click on Linear from the Dimensioning palette. Or, just as you did for the vertical dimension, you can type **Dimlinear** ⏎ to start the horizontal dimension.

2. At the First extension line... prompt, pick the upper-left corner of the bathroom, near coordinate 15′–0″, 30′–10″.

3. At the Second extension line... prompt, pick the upper-right corner of the bathroom, near coordinate 22′–6″, 30′–10″.

4. At the Dimension line... prompt, pick a point near coordinate 22′–5″, 33′–5″ (see Figure 9.4).

Now you're all set to draw another dimension continuing from the first extension line of the dimension you just drew.

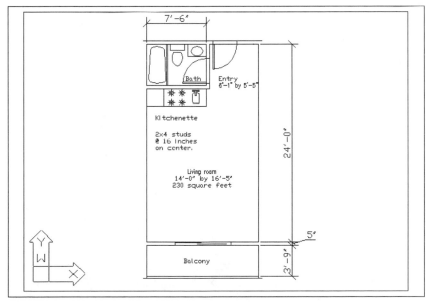

Figure 9.4: The bathroom with horizontal dimensions

5. Click on Baseline Dimension from the Dimensioning palette. Or you can type **Dimbase** ↵ at the command prompt to start a baseline dimension.

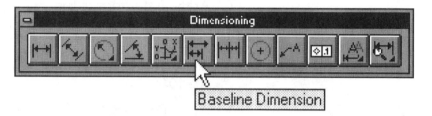

6. At the Second extension line... prompt, click on the upper-right corner of the entry as shown in Figure 9.5.

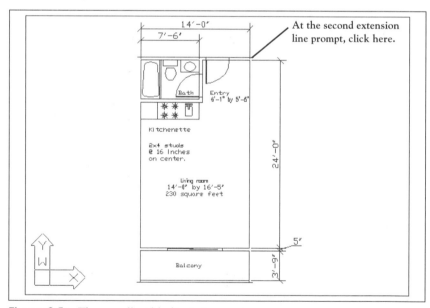

Figure 9.5: The overall width dimension

7. Click on View ➤ Zoom ➤ All to see the entire drawing with the continued dimension, as shown in Figure 9.5.

In this example, you see that the Baseline option is similar to the Continue option, except that Baseline allows you to use the first extension line of the previous dimension as the base for a second dimension.

Using a Previous Dimension   Just as with Continue Dimension(DIMCONT command), you can draw baseline dimension from a previous dimension by pressing ↵ at the Second extension line origin or RETURN to select prompt, and then selecting the dimension from which you want to draw the new baseline dimension.

EDITING DIMENSIONS

As you begin to add more dimensions to your drawings, you will find that AutoCAD will occasionally place a dimension text or line in an inappropriate location, or you may need to make a modification to the dimension text. You cannot edit the individual elements of a dimension with the standard set of editing tools. In this section, you'll take an indepth look at how dimensions can be modified to suit those special circumstances that always crop up.

APPENDING DATA TO DIMENSION TEXT

So far in this chapter, you've been accepting the default dimension text. You know you can append information to the default dimension value, if you need to. At the point when you see the temporary dimension dragging with your cursor, you enter **T** ↵. Then, by using the less than (<) and greater than (>) symbols, you can add text either before or after the default dimension. The Properties button on the Object Properties toolbar lets you modify existing dimension text in a similar way using the less than and greater than symbols. Let's see how this works by changing an existing dimension's text in your drawing.

1. Click and drag Edit Polyline from the Modify palette, then select Edit Text.

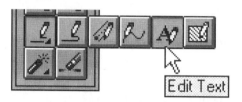

2. Next, click on the last horizontal dimension you added to the drawing at the top of the screen. The Edit Mtext dialog box appears. This is the same dialog box you saw in *Chapter 8* used for editing Multiline text. Notice the greater than and less than symbols (<>) in the window.

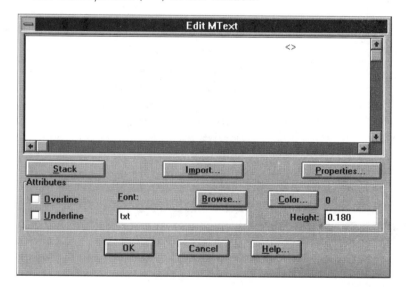

3. Move the cursor behind the <> sign, then type "**to face of stud**".

4. Click on OK. The dimension changes to read "14′–0′ to face of stud". The text you entered is appended to the dimension text.

5. Because you don't really need the new appended text for the tutorial, click on the undo button in the standard toolbar to remove the appended text.

Using the Edit Text command, you were able to combine the dimension text "14′–0″" with the text "to face of stud."

In this exercise, you were only able to edit a single dimension. To append text to several dimensions at once, you need to use the DIMEDIT command. See the sidebar entitled "Editing Multiple Dimension Text Using Dimedit" for more on this command.

You can also have AutoCAD automatically add a dimension suffix or prefix to all dimensions, instead of just a chosen few, by using the Annotation option in the Dimension Styles dialog box. See *Appendix D* for more on this feature.

EDITING MULTIPLE DIMENSION TEXT USING DIMEDIT

The DIMEDIT command offers a quick way to edit existing dimensions. It adds the ability to edit more than one dimension's text at one time. The following example shows an alternative to the Properties option for appending text to a dimension.

1. Type DIMEDIT ↵.

2. At this prompt:

   Dimension Edit (Home/New/Rotate/Oblique)<Home>:

   type **N** ↵ to use the New option, and then type **<> to face of stud** ↵.

3. At the Select object: prompt, pick the dimension you wish to add the new text to. The Select object: prompt remains, allowing you to select several dimensions.

4. Press ↵ to finish your selection. The dimension changes to include "to face of stud."

▼

■

■

■

■

DIMEDIT is useful in editing dimension text, but you can also use this command to make graphical changes to the text. Here is a listing of the other DIMEDIT options:

Home moves the dimension text to its standard default position and angle.

Rotate allows you to rotate the dimension text to a new angle.

Oblique skews the dimension extension lines to a new angle. See "Skewing Dimension Lines" later in this chapter.

LOCATING THE DEFINITION POINTS

AutoCAD provides the associative dimensioning capability to automatically update dimension text when a drawing is edited. Objects called *definition points* are used to determine how edited dimensions are updated.

The definition points are located at the same points you pick when you determine the dimension location. For example, the definition points for linear dimensions are the extension line origin and the intersection of the extension line/dimension line. The definition points for a circle diameter are the points used to pick the circle and the opposite side of the circle. The definition points for a radius are the points used to pick the circle, plus the center of the circle.

Definition points are actually point objects. They are very difficult to see because they are usually covered by the feature they define. You can, however, see them indirectly using grips. The definition points of a dimension are the same as the dimension's grip points. You can see them simply by clicking on a dimension. Try the following:

1. Make sure the Grips feature is turned on (see *Chapter 2* to refresh your memory on the Grips feature).

2. Click on the longest of the three vertical dimensions you drew in the earlier exercise. You will see the grips of the dimension, as shown in Figure 9.6.

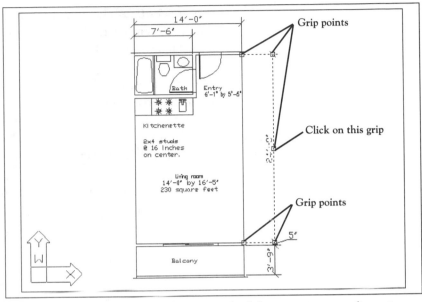

Figure 9.6: The grip points are the same as the definition points on a dimension.

▼ **TIP**

Since the Defpoints layer has the unique feature of being visible even when turned off, you can use it as a layer for laying out your drawing. While Defpoints is turned off, you can still see objects assigned to it, but the objects won't plot.

▼ **NOTE**

Here the entire dimension line moves, including the text. In a later exercise, you'll see how you can move the dimension text independently of the dimension line.

MAKING MINOR ADJUSTMENTS TO DIMENSIONS USING GRIPS

The definition points, whose location you can see through their grips, are located on their own unique layer called Defpoints. Definition points are displayed regardless of whether the Defpoints layer is on or off. To give you an idea of how these definition points work, try the following exercises, which show you how to directly manipulate the definition points.

1. With the grips visible, click on the grip near the dimension text.

2. Move the cursor around. Notice that when you move the cursor vertically, the text moves along the dimension line. When you move the cursor horizontally, the dimension line and text move together, keeping their parallel orientation to the dimensioned floor plan.

3. Enter **@9'<0** ↵. The dimension line, text, and the dimension extensions move to the new location to the right of the text (see Figure 9.7).

In step 3 of the last exercise you saw that you can specify an exact distance for the dimension line's new location, by entering a relative polar coordinate. Cartesian coordinates work just as well. You can even use object snaps to relocate dimension lines. Next, try moving the dimension line back using the Perpendicular Osnap override.

1. Click on the grip at the bottom of the dimension line.
2. Shift-click the right mouse button to pull down the Osnap overrides menu, and choose Perpendicular.

▼ TIP

If you need to move several dimension lines at once, select them all at the command prompt; then Shift-click on one set of dimension-line grips from each dimension. Once you've selected the grips, click on one of the hot grips again. You can then move all the dimension lines at once.

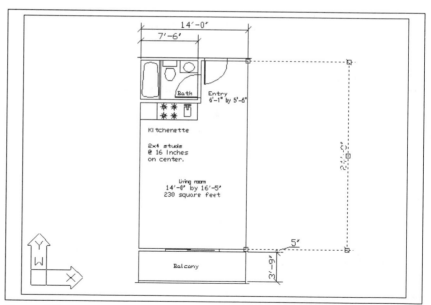

Figure 9.7: Moving the dimension line using its grip

3. Click on the vertical dimension line that dimensions the balcony. The selected dimension line moves to align with the other vertical dimension, back to its original location.

CHANGING STYLE
SETTINGS OF INDIVIDUAL DIMENSIONS

In some cases, you will have to make changes to an individual dimension's style setting in order to edit that dimension. For example, if you try to move the text of a typical linear dimension, you'll find that the text and dimension lines are inseparable. You need to make a change to the dimensions style setting that controls how AutoCAD locates dimension text in relation to the dimension line. This section describes how you can make changes to the style settings of individual dimensions to facilitate changes in the dimension.

Moving a Fixed Dimension Text

You may have noticed that AutoCAD automatically placed the wall dimensions 5″ dimension text away from the dimension line. This is done to avoid crowding the dimension between the extension lines. In some instances, you will want to manually move a dimension text away from the dimension line, but as you saw in an earlier exercise, this cannot be done with the current settings.

In the next exercise, you will make a change to a single dimension's style settings. Then you'll use grips to move the dimension text away from the dimension line.

1. Press Esc twice to cancel the grip selection from the previous exercise.

2. Click on Properties from the toolbar then click on the vertical dimension that measures the main room—the 24′–0″ dimension—and press ↵ to finish your selection. The Modify Dimension dialog box appears.

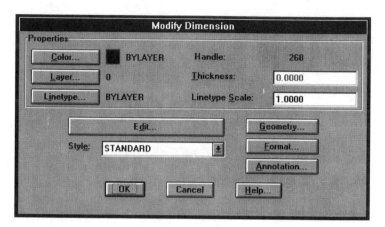

This dialog box contains the same three buttons, Geometry..., Format..., and Annotation..., that are in the Dimension Styles dialog box.

3. Click on Format.... The same Format dialog box appears that you saw in the early part of this chapter.

4. At the Format dialog box, choose Leader from the Fit drop-down list.

5. While still in the Format dialog box, change the Vertical Justification group setting to Centered. We'll explain why in the following paragraphs.

6. Click on OK here and then again at the Modify Dimension dialog box.

7. Now click on the 24′–0″ dimension to display its grips.

8. Click on the grip just below the dimension text and move the dimension text above and to the right of its current location as shown in the first panel of Figure 9.8. The dimension text is now horizontal and shows a leader from the text to the dimension line.

In the Format dialog box, the Leader option in the Fit pull-down list lets you move the dimension text independently of the dimension line. It also causes a leader to be drawn from the dimension line to the text. We asked you to change the Vertical Justification option to Centered because otherwise the leader line will be drawn through the dimension text.

In the previous exercise, you changed the format setting of a single dimension *after* it was placed. These settings can be made a standard part of your Architectural dimension style. To do this, choose Format from the Dimension Style dialog box, then choose Leader from the Fit pull-down list. In doing so, you will be able to move the text of all new dimensions you might add later. Don't change the Vertical Justification setting to centered, however, as this will cause all dimensions to appear centered on the dimension line—a format appropriate for mechanical drawings, but not architectural drawings. For existing dimensions, you will have to use the PROPERTIES command as shown in this exercise.

Both the Fit and Vertical Justification settings can be made using system variables. See *Appendix D* for more on these settings.

Rotating a Dimension Text

Both the 24′–0″ dimension and the 5″ dimension just below it are now oriented horizontally. In the case of the 5″ dimension, AutoCAD automatically places dimensions outside the dimension line with a leader when the dimension text is too large to fit between the dimension extension lines. The Best Fit Option in the Fit pull-down list of the Format dialog box produces this result. Unfortunately, these dimensions are not in the right location and are at the wrong angle for an architectural style drawing. They need to be rotated to a 90 degree angle, then moved into a position next to the dimension line. Here are the steps to do this:

1. First, click on the Undo button in the toolbar or type **U** ↵ to return the 24′–0″ dimension to its original location.

2. Click and drag Home from the Dimensioning palette, then select Rotate.

Building on the Basics

II

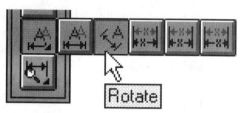

3. At the Select object prompt, click on the 5″ dimension text.

4. At the Enter text angle prompt, type **90** ↵ to rotate the text to a 90 degree angle.

Now, for the last operation, you will move the text next to its associated dimension line, aligning it with the other dimensions in the string.

1. Click on the dimension you just edited, so that its grips are displayed.

2. Click on the grip at the center of the dimension text and move the cursor around. Notice that the dimension text follows the cursor, and a leader line extends from the dimension text to the dimension line.

3. Click on a point above and to the left of the original dimension text location (see the second panel of Figure 9.8). The dimension text moves to its new location. The dimension itself remains highlighted, telling you that it is still available for editing.

4. Now save your drawing. You will use this drawing in its current condition in later chapters.

You may want to make other adjustments to the dimension text, such as its location along the dimension line and its rotation angle. Two other commands are available that allow you to rotate or move dimension text along the dimension line: DIMEDIT, which you've already used in previous exercises, and DIMTEDIT. DIMTEDIT works the same as DIMEDIT but doesn't offer the New option that lets you edit the dimension text.

▼ NOTE

You can use the Home option on the Dimensioning palette or the DIMEDIT and DIMTEDIT commands (discussed later in the chapter) to move a dimension text back to its original location.

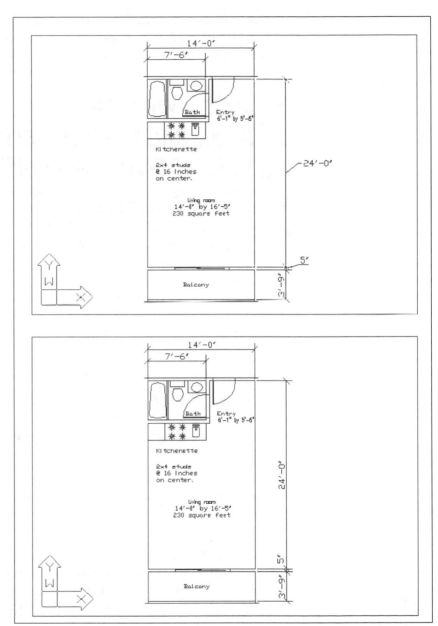

Figure 9.8: Moving the dimension text using grips. The first panel shows the dimension with the leader after making changes to the individual dimensions style setting. The second panel shows the dimension text moved to its new location.

As you have seen in this section, the Grips feature is especially well suited to editing dimensions. With grips, you can stretch, move, copy, rotate, mirror, and scale dimensions.

▼

■

■

■

■

MODIFYING THE DIMENSION STYLE SETTINGS FOR GROUPS OF DIMENSIONS

In the "Moving Dimension Text" section, you used the Properties button on the toolbar to facilitate the moving of the dimension text. You can also use the DIMOVERRIDE command to accomplish the same thing. DIMOVERRIDE is a command that allows you to make changes to an individual dimension's style settings. The advantage to DIMOVERRIDE is that it allows you to affect changes to groups of dimensions, not just one dimension. Here's an example showing how DIMOVERRIDE can be used in place of the Properties button in the first exercise of the "Moving Dimension Text" section.

1. Press the Escape key twice to make sure you are not in the middle of a command. Then type **Dimoverride** ↵.

2. At the next prompt:

Dimension variable to override (or Clear to remove overrides):

type **Dimfit**↵.

3. At the Current value <3>: prompt, enter **4** ↵. This has the same affect as selecting Leader from the Fit pop-up list of the Format dialog box.

4. The Dimension variable to override prompt appears again allowing you to enter another dimension variable. Press ↵ to move to the next step.

> **5.** At the Select object: prompt, select the dimension you
> want to change. You can selects a group of dimensions if
> you want to change several dimensions at once. Press ↵
> when you are done with your selection. The dimension set-
> tings will be changed for the selected dimensions.
>
> As you can see from this example, DIMOVERRIDE requires that
> you know exactly which dimension variable to edit in order to
> make the desired modification. In this case, setting the Dimfit vari-
> able to 4 will let you move the dimension text independently of the
> dimension line. If you find the DIMOVERRIDE command useful,
> consult *Appendix D* to find which system variable corresponds to the
> Dimension Style dialog box settings.

EDITING DIMENSIONS
AND OTHER OBJECTS TOGETHER

Certainly it's helpful to be able to edit a dimension directly using its
grips. But the key feature of AutoCAD's dimensions is their ability to
automatically adjust themselves to changes in the drawing. As long as
you include the dimension's definition points when you select objects
to edit, the dimensions themselves will automatically update to reflect
the change in your drawing.

To see how this works, try moving the living room closer to the bathroom wall. You can move a group of lines and vertices using the
STRETCH command and the Crossing option.

1. You won't need to save the changes you are about to make,
   so click on File ➤ Save before you do anything else.

2. Click on Stretch from the Modify palette, or type **Stretch** ↵
   and then **C** ↵. You will see the following prompt:

   At the Select objects to stretch by crossing-window or -
   polygon...
   Select objects: C
   First corner:

3. Pick a crossing window, as illustrated in Figure 9.9. Then press ↵ to confirm your selection.

4. At the Base point prompt, pick any point on the screen.

5. At the New point prompt, enter **@2'<90** to move the wall 2′ in a 90° direction. The wall moves, and the dimension text changes to reflect the new dimension, as shown in Figure 9.10.

6. When you are done reviewing the results of this exercise, exit the file without saving it.

When you selected the crossing window corners, you included the definition points of both vertical dimensions. This allowed you to move the dimension extension lines along with the wall, thereby updating the dimensions automatically.

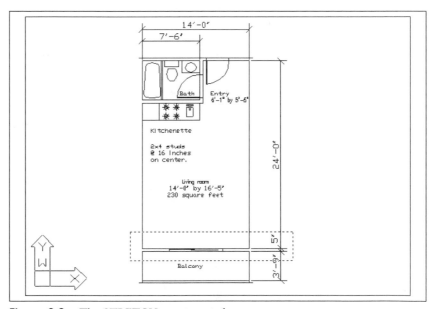

Figure 9.9: The STRETCH crossing window

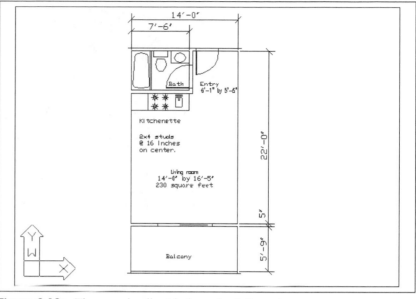

Figure 9.10: The moved wall, with the updated dimensions

Building on the Basics

II

▼ UNDERSTANDING
■ THE STRETCH COMMAND

The tool you used for moving the wall and the dimension line extensions is the STRETCH command. This is one of the most useful, yet least understood commands offered by AutoCAD. Think of STRETCH as a vertex mover: Its sole purpose is to move the vertices (or endpoints) of objects.

STRETCH actually requires you to do two things: select the objects you want to edit, and then select the vertices you wish to move. The crossing window and the Cpolygon window are convenient ways of killing two birds with one stone, because they select objects and vertices in one operation. But when you want to be more selective, you can click on objects and window vertices instead. For example, consider the exercise in this chapter where you moved a wall with the STRETCH command. If you wanted to move the walls but not the dimension-line extensions, you would do that as follows:

1. Enter **STRETCH** ↵ at the command prompt. (You enter STRETCH via the prompt because the STRETCH command in the Modify pull-down menu automatically uses the Crossing selection option.)

2. At the Select object: prompt, enter **W** ↵ (Window) or **WP** ↵ (Window Polygon).

3. Window the vertices you wish to move. Since the Window and Window Polygon selection options select objects completely enclosed within the window, most of the items you want to stretch will already be selected.

4. Click on the vertical walls to include them in the set of objects to be edited.

5. Press ↵ to finish your selection.

6. Indicate the base point and second point for the stretch.

You could also use the Remove selection option and click on the dimensions to deselect them in the previous exercise. Then, when you enter the base and second points, the walls would move but the dimensions would stay in place.

STRETCH will stretch only the vertices included in the last window, crossing window, crossing polygon, or window polygon (see *Chapter 2* for more on these selection options). Thus, if you had attempted to window another part of your drawing in the wall-moving exercise, nothing would have moved. Before STRETCH will do anything, objects need to be highlighted (selected) and their endpoints windowed.

The STRETCH command is especially well suited to editing dimensioned objects, and when you use it with the crossing polygon (CP) or window polygon (WP) selection options, you have substantial control over what gets edited.

You can also use the MIRROR, ROTATE, and STRETCH commands with dimensions. The polar arrays will also work, and Extend and Trim can be used with linear dimensions.

When editing dimensioned objects, be sure you select the dimension associated with the object being edited. As you select objects, using the Crossing or Cpolygon selection options (Assist ➤ Select Objects) will help you include the dimensions. See the sidebar in *Chapter 2,* "Other Options in the Object Selection Settings Dialog Box," for more on these selection options.

USING OSNAP WHILE DIMENSIONING

You may find that when you pick intersections and endpoints frequently, as during dimensioning, it is a bit inconvenient to use the Osnap overrides menu. In situations where your drawing is not too crowded and you want to set an Osnap override as a default, you can do so in the following two ways:

■ Click on Options ➤ Running Object Snap…. In the Running Object Snap dialog box, select the desired default mode. You can even pick more than one mode, for instance Intersec, Endpoint, and Midpoint, so that whichever geometry you happen to be nearest will be the point selected.

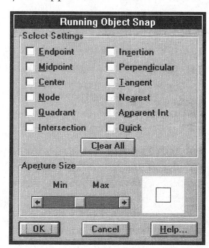

II

Building on the Basics

■ Another way of accomplishing this is to type **'osnap** ↵ and then enter the name of the Osnap modes you want to use. If you want to use more than one mode, enter their names separated by commas, as in

endpoint,midpoint,intersect

Then, to open the Running Object Snap dialog box, type **Ddosnap** ↵.

Once you've designated your defaults, the next time you are prompted to select a point, the selected Osnap modes will be automatically activated. You can still override the default settings using the Osnap drop-down menu (Shift-click the right mouse button) or the Osnap side menu (click the asterisks).

DIMENSIONING NONORTHOGONAL OBJECTS

So far, you've been reading about how to work with linear dimensions. You can also dimension nonorthogonal objects, such as circles, arcs, triangles, and trapezoids. In this section you will practice dimensioning nonorthogonal objects by drawing an elevation of a window in the set of plans for your studio apartment building. You'll start by drawing the window itself.

1. Open a new file called **Window**.

2. Set the file up as an architectural drawing at a scale of 3″=1′–0″ on an $8\frac{1}{2}{\times}11″$ sheet.

3. Click and drag Rectangle from the Draw menu to open the flyout, then click on Polygon. Or enter **Polygon** ↵.

4. At the Number of sides… prompt, enter **6** ↵.

5. At the Edge/<center of polygon> prompt, pick the center of the polygon at coordinate 1′–10″, 1′–6″. If you started the command with the keyboard, enter **C** ↵ at the Inscribe in circle/circumscribe… prompt.

6. At the Radius of circle: prompt, you will see the hexagon drag along with the cursor. You could pick a point with your mouse to determine its size.

7. Enter **8** ↵ to get an exact size for the hexagon.

8. Draw a circle with a radius of 7″ using coordinate 1′–10″, 1′–6″ as its center. Your drawing will look like Figure 9.11.

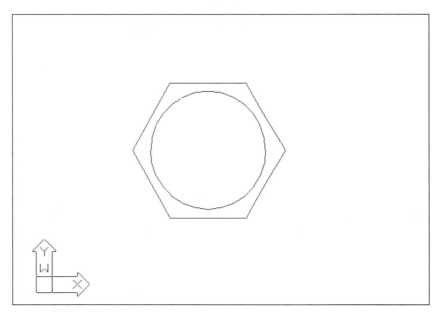

Figure 9.11: The window frame

DIMENSIONING NONORTHOGONAL LINEAR DISTANCES

Now you will dimension the window. The unusual shape of the window prevents you from using the horizontal or vertical dimensions you've used already. However, the Aligned option will allow you to dimension at an angle.

1. Start by setting the dimension scale to 4. A quick way to do this is by typing **Dimscale** ↵ **4** ↵.

2. Click on Aligned Dimension from the Dimensioning palette. You can also enter **Dimali** ↵ to start the aligned dimension.

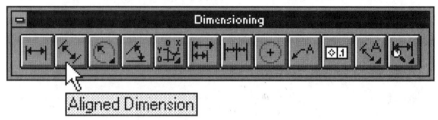

3. At the First extension line origin or RETURN to select: prompt, press ↵. You could have picked extension line origins as you did in earlier examples, but using the ↵ will show you firsthand how this option works.

4. At the Select object to dimension: prompt, pick the upper-right face of the hexagon near coordinate 2′–5″, 1′–10″. As the prompt indicates, you can also pick an arc or circle for this type of dimension.

5. At the Dimension line location (Text/Angle): prompt, pick a point near coordinate 2′–10″, 2′–2″. The dimension appears in the drawing as shown in Figure 9.12.

▼ TIP

Just as with linear dimensions, you can enter **T** ↵ at step 5 to enter specific text.

Next, you will dimension a face of the hexagon. Instead of its actual length, however, you will dimension a distance at a specified angle— the distance from the center of the face.

1. Click on Linear Dimension from the Dimensioning palette.

2. At the First extension line origin or RETURN to select: prompt, press ↵.

3. At the Select object to dimension prompt, pick the lower-right face of the hexagon near coordinate 2′–6″, 1′–4″.

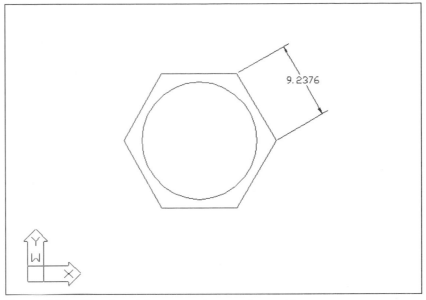

Figure 9.12:   The aligned dimension of a nonorthogonal line

4. At the Dimension line location (Text/Angle/Horizon-tal/Vertical/Rotated): prompt, type **R** ↵ to select the rotated option.

5. At the Dimension line angle <0> prompt, enter **30** ↵.

6. At the Dimension line location prompt, pick a point near coordinate 2′–11″, 0′–8″. Your drawing will look like Figure 9.13.

DIMENSIONING
RADII, DIAMETERS, AND ARCS

To dimension circular objects, you use the Angular Dimensioning option.

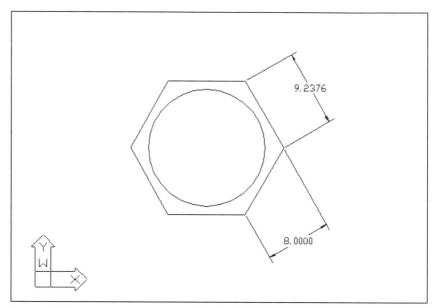

Figure 9.13: A linear dimension using the DIM1 rotated option

1. Click on Angular Dimension from the Dimensioning palette. Or you can enter **Dimang** ↵ to start the angular dimension.

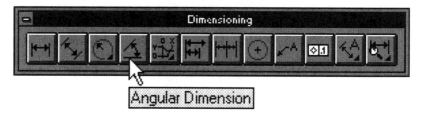

2. At the Select arc, circle, line, or RETURN: prompt, pick the upper-left face of the hexagon near coordinate 1'–3", 1'–10".

3. At the Second line: prompt, pick the top face at coordinate 1'–9", 2'–2".

4. At the Dimension line arc location (Text/Angle): prompt, notice how the dimension changes as you move the cursor. AutoCAD adjusts the dimension to fit the location.

5. Pick a point near coordinate 1′–8″, 1′–11″. The dimension is fixed in the drawing (see Figure 9.14).

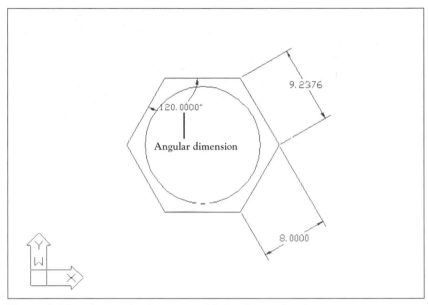

Figure 9.14:   The angular dimension added to the window frame

Now try the Diameter option, which shows the diameter of a circle.

1. Click and drag on Radius Dimension then select Diameter Dimension. Or you can enter **Dimdia** ↵ to start the diameter dimension.

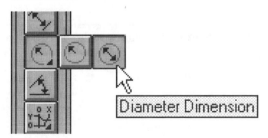

2. At the Select arc or circle: prompt, pick the circle near coordinate 2′–5″, 1′–6″.

3. At the Dimension line location (Text/Angle): prompt, you will see the diameter dimension drag with the cursor.

4. Adjust your cursor so that the dimension looks like Figure 9.15, and then click the mouse/pick button.

The Radius Dimension option on the Dimensioning palette gives you a radius dimension (see Figure 9.16) just as Diameter provides a circle's diameter. The Center Mark option on the Dimensioning palette just places a cross mark in the center of the selected arc or circle.

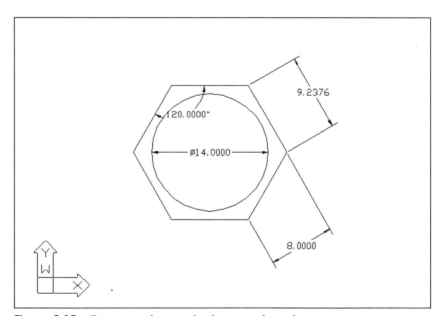

Figure 9.15: Dimension showing the diameter of a circle

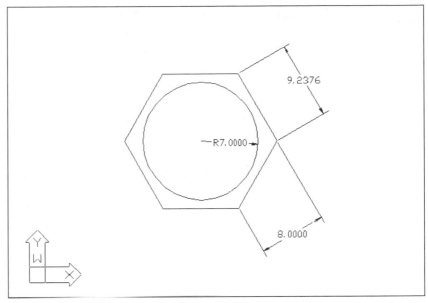

Figure 9.16: A radius dimension

ADDING A NOTE WITH AN ARROW

Finally, there is the Leader option, which allows you to add a note with an arrow pointing to the object the note describes.

1. Click on Leader from the Dimensioning palette, or enter **Leader** ↵.

2. At the Leader start: prompt, pick a point near coordinate 1'– 4", 2'–0".

3. At the To point: prompt, enter **@6<110** ↵. The leader appears.

4. At the To point (Format/Annotation/Undo)<Annotation>: prompt, you can continue to pick points just as you would draw lines. For this exercise, however, press ↵ to finish drawing leader lines.

▼ **TIP**

You can also add Multiline text at the leader. See the upcoming section.

5. At the Annotation (or RETURN for options): prompt, type **Window frame** ↵ ↵ as the label for this leader. Your drawing will look like Figure 9.17.

In this exercise, you used the default Annotation option in step 4 to add the text for the note. The Format option in this prompt lets you control the graphic elements of the leader. When you select the Format option by typing **F** ↵, you get the following prompt:

Spline/STraight/Arrow/None/<Exit>:

Choose Spline to change the leader from a series of line segments to a spline curve (see Figure 9.18). Often a curved leader shows up better than straight lines do. The STraight option changes the leader line to straight lines. None suppresses the arrowhead altogether, and Arrow restores it.

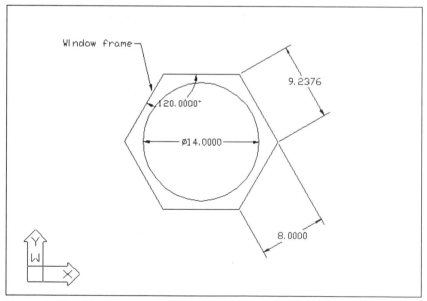

Figure 9.17: The leader with a note added

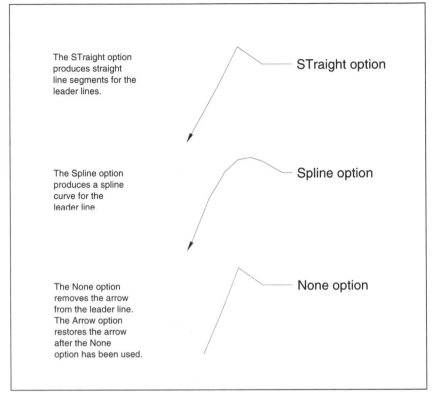

The STraight option produces straight line segments for the leader lines.

STraight option

The Spline option produces a spline curve for the leader line.

Spline option

The None option removes the arrow from the leader line. The Arrow option restores the arrow after the None option has been used.

None option

Figure 9.18:   The Leader format options

Using Multiline Text with Leaders

You also have the option to add Multiline text at the leader. Take another look at step 5 in the previous exercise. To add Multiline text, you would press ↵ at the Annotation (or RETURN for options): prompt in this step. The next prompt to appear is

Tolerance/Copy/Block/None/<Mtext>:

Press ↵ again, and you will see the standard Mtext prompt, which directs you to pick an insertion point and a second point indicating where the text goes. From there, the LEADER command acts just like the

MTEXT command (see *Chapter 8* for more on Mtext) by opening the Mtext dialog box.

The other options in the Annotation prompt are as follows:

Tolerance   lets you insert a tolerance symbol. A dialog box opens, where you specify the tolerance information (see *Appendix D* for more on the Tolerance feature).

Copy   lets you copy text from another part of the drawing. You are prompted to select a text object to copy to the leader text location.

Block   lets you insert a block. You are asked for a block name, and then the command proceeds to insert the block—just like the INSERT command (see *Chapter 3*).

Choose **None** if you don't want to do anything beyond drawing the leader arrow and line.

SKEWING DIMENSION LINES

At times, you may find it necessary to force the extension lines to take on an angle other than 90° to the dimension line. This is a common requirement of isometric drawings, where most lines are at 30° or 60° angles instead of 90°. To facilitate nonorthogonal dimensions like these, AutoCAD offers the Oblique option.

1. Click and drag on Dimension Styles from the Dimensioning palette then select Oblique Dimensions or type **Dimedit** ↵ **O** ↵.

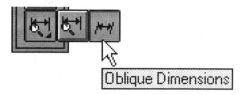

2. At the Select objects: prompt, pick the aligned dimension at the upper-right of the drawing and press ↵ to confirm your selection.

3. At the Enter obliquing angle (RETURN for none): prompt, enter **60** for 60°. The dimension will skew so that the extension lines are at 60°, as shown in Figure 9.19.

4. Now exit AutoCAD. You are done with the tutorials in this chapter.

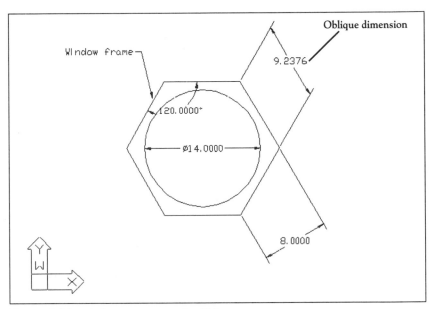

Figure 9.19: A dimension using the Oblique option

APPLYING ORDINATE DIMENSIONS

In mechanical drafting, *ordinate dimensions* are used to maintain the accuracy of machined parts by establishing an origin on the part. All major dimensions are described as x or y coordinates of that origin. The origin is usually an easily locatable feature of the part, such as a machined bore or two machined surfaces. Figure 9.20 shows a typical application of ordinate dimensions.

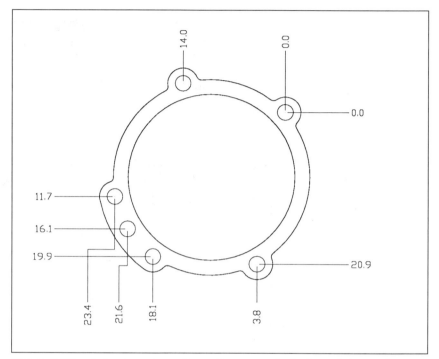

Figure 9.20:   A drawing using ordinate dimensions. In the lower-left, note the two dimensions whose leaders are jogged. Also note the origin location in the upper-right.

To use AutoCAD's Ordinate dimensioning command, follow these steps:

1. Click on View ➤ Set UCS ➤ Origin, or type **UCS** ↵ **Or** ↵.

2. At the Origin point <0,0,0>: prompt, click on the exact location of the origin of your part.

3. Toggle the ortho mode on.

4. Click on Automatic from the Dimensioning Palette. You can also enter **Dimord** ↵ to start the ordinate dimension.

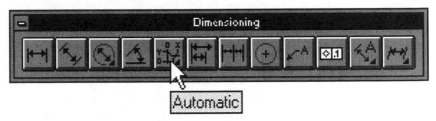

5. At the Select feature: prompt, click on the item you want to dimension.

6. At the Leader endpoint (Xdatum/Ydatum): prompt, indicate the length and direction of the leader. Do this by positioning the rubber-banding leader perpendicular to the coordinate direction you want to dimension, and then clicking on that point.

▼ NOTE

The direction of the leader will determine whether the dimension will be of the x datum or the y datum.

In steps 1 and 2, you used the UCS feature to establish a second origin in the drawing. The Automatic option (DIMORD) then uses that origin to determine the ordinate dimensions. You will get a chance to work with the UCS feature in *Chapter 16*.

The other two options in the Automatic flyout, Xdatum and Ydatum, force the dimension to be of the x coordinate or y coordinate no matter what direction the leader takes. The Automatic option (see step 4) will make the best guess at which direction you want dimensioned, based on the orientation of the leader.

If you turn ortho mode off, the dimension leader will be drawn with a jog, in order to maintain orthogonal lines (see Figure 9.20).

ADDING TOLERANCE NOTATION

In mechanical drafting, tolerances are a key part of a drawing's notation. To help facilitate tolerance notation, AutoCAD provides the

II

Building on the Basics

TOLERANCE command, which offers common ISO tolerance sym-
bols together with a quick way to build a standard *feature control* symbol.
Feature control symbols are industry standard symbols used to specify
tolerances. If you are a mechanical engineer or drafter, AutoCAD's tolerance notation options will be a valuable tool. A full discussion of
tolerances, however, requires a basic understanding of mechanical
design and drafting and is beyond the scope of this book.

To use the TOLERANCE command, choose Tolerance from the Dimensioning palette, or type **Tolerance** ↵ at the command prompt.

The Symbol dialog box appears.

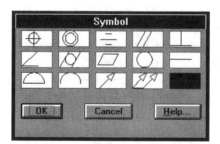

Figure 9.21 shows what each symbol represents.

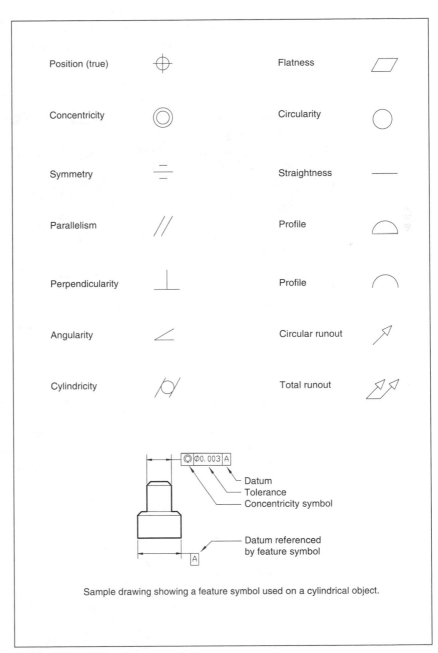

Position (true)	⊕	Flatness	▱
Concentricity	◎	Circularity	○
Symmetry	=	Straightness	—
Parallelism	//	Profile	⌓
Perpendicularity	⊥	Profile	⌒
Angularity	∠	Circular runout	↗
Cylindricity	⌭	Total runout	↗↗

⌾ | Φ0.003 | A

— Datum
— Tolerance
— Concentricity symbol

— Datum referenced
   by feature symbol

A

Sample drawing showing a feature symbol used on a cylindrical object.

Figure 9.21: The tolerance symbols

Building on the Basics

II

Once you select a symbol, you then see the Geometric Tolerance dialog box. This is where you enter tolerance and datum values for the feature control symbol. You can enter two tolerance values and three datum values. In addition, you can stack values in a two-tiered fashion.

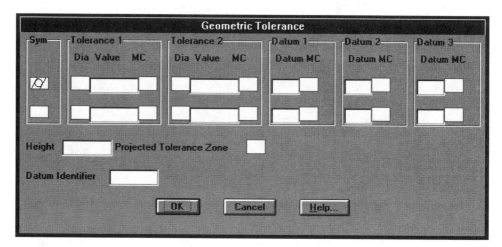

IF YOU WANT TO EXPERIMENT...

At this point, you might want to experiment with the settings described in this chapter to identify the ones that are most useful for your work. You can then establish these settings as defaults in a prototype file or the Acad.DWG file.

It's a good idea to experiment even with the settings you don't think you will need often—chances are you will have to alter them from time to time.

As an added exercise, try the steps shown in Figure 9.22. It will give you a chance to see how you can update dimensions on a drawing that has been scaled down.

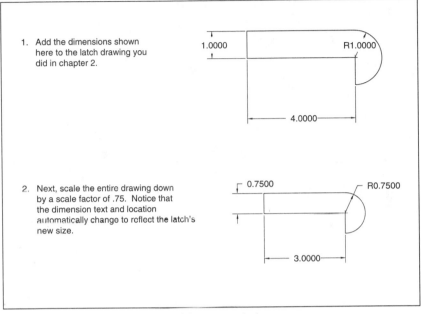

1. Add the dimensions shown here to the latch drawing you did in chapter 2.

2. Next, scale the entire drawing down by a scale factor of .75. Notice that the dimension text and location automatically change to reflect the latch's new size.

Figure 9.22:   A sample mechanical drawing with dimensions

PART THREE

BECOMING
■
AN
■
EXPERT

At this point, you are on the verge of becoming a real expert. The chapters in this part are designed to help you polish your present skills and give you a few new ones. *Chapter 10: Attributes—Storing Data with Graphics*, tells you how to attach information to drawing objects. In *Chapter 11: Copying Pre-Existing Drawings into AutoCAD*, you will learn three techniques for transferring paper drawings to AutoCAD. In *Chapter 12, Power Editing*, you will complete the apartment building tutorial, and in the process, will learn how to integrate what you've learned so far and gain some tips on working in groups. *Chapter 13, Drawing Curves and Solid Fills*, gives you an in-depth look at some special drawing objects, such as spline and fitted curves. *Chapter 14, Getting and Exchanging Data from Drawings*, will give you practice with getting information about a drawing, and you will learn how AutoCAD can interact with other applications, such as spreadsheets and desktop-publishing programs.

10

▼ ▼ ▼ ▼ ▼

ATTRIBUTES—
STORING DATA WITH GRAPHICS

Using Attributes to Store Data

Defining an Attribute and Adding It to
a Block

Entering Attribute Data

Editing Attribute Data, One Block at
a Time

Making Global Changes to Attribute
Values

Controlling Attribute Visibility

Exporting Attribute Data to Other
Programs

FAST TRACK

467 ▶ To open a database table from AutoCAD

Click on Administration on the External Database palette. At the Administration dialog box, choose an environment name from the Database Objects list box, then click on the Connect button. At the Connect to Environment dialog box, click on OK. Once connected, choose the Catalog radio button and click on the desired catalog name from the list. Click on the Schema radio button then select the desired schema name from the list. Finally, click on the Table radio button and select a table from the list. Click on OK to exit the dialog box.

469 ▶ To find a specific record in a database

Click on Rows on the External Database palette. At the Rows dialog box enter the search criteria in the Conditions input box. The records that match the search criteria appear in the list box.

471 ▶ To add a record to a database

Click on Rows on the External Database palette. At the Rows dialog box, click on the Updatable radio button, then click on Edit. Enter the record data, then click on Insert and Close.

472 ▶ To link an object to a database record

Click on Administration on the External Database palette. At the Administration dialog box, click on Link Path Names. Choose the columns you want to key by highlighting them and clicking on the On button. Enter a name for your link path then click on New. Click on Close then click on OK in the Administration dialog box.

478 ▶ To locate objects based on their links to a database

Click on Rows on the External Database palette. At the Rows dialog box locate the record that identifies the objects in your drawing you want to locate. Finally, click on Select <. The dialog box temporarily closes and the objects linked to the selected record are highlighted.

▼ NOTE

For some of the exercises in this chapter, you will need to know how to create and manipulate ASCII files. It is helpful, but not essential, for you to know how to use a database management program as well.

▼ TIP

You can even set up a default value for the attribute, such as *hollow core*, or *hc*. That way you only have to enter a value when it deviates from the default.

Attributes are unique to computer-aided design and drafting; nothing quite like them exists in traditional drafting. Because of this, they are often poorly understood. Attributes enable you to store information as text that you can later extract to use in database managers, spreadsheet programs, and word processors. By using attributes, you can keep track of virtually any object in a drawing.

Keeping track of objects is just one way of using attributes. You can also use them in place of text objects in situations where you must enter the same text, with minor modifications, in many places in your drawing. For example, if you are drawing a schedule that contains several columns of information, you can use attributes to help simplify your data entry.

Attributes can also be used where you anticipate global editing of text. For example, suppose a note that refers to a part number occurs in several places. If you think you will want to change that part number in every note, you can make the part a block with an attribute. Later, when you know the new part number, you can use the global editing capability of the Attribute feature to change the old part number for all occurrences in one step.

In this chapter you will use attributes for one of their more common functions: maintaining lists of parts. In this case, the parts are doors. We will also describe how to import these attributes into a database management program. As you go through these exercises, think about the ways attributes can help you in your particular application.

CREATING ATTRIBUTES

Attributes depend on blocks. You might think of an attribute as a tag attached to a block, with the tag containing information about the block. For example, you could have included an attribute definition with the door drawing you created in *Chapter 2*. If you had, then every time you subsequently inserted the door you would have been prompted for a value associated with that door. The value could be a number, a height or width value, a name, or any type of text information you want. When you insert the block, you get the usual prompts, followed by a prompt for an attribute value. Once you enter a value, it is stored as part of the block within the drawing database. This value can be displayed

III

Becoming an Expert

as text attached to the door, or it can be made invisible. You can even specify what the prompts say in asking you for the attribute value.

But suppose you don't have the attribute information when you design the door. As an alternative, you can add the attribute to a *symbol* that is later placed by the door when you know enough about the design to specify what type of door goes where. The standard door type symbol suits this purpose nicely because it is an object that can be set up and used as a block independent of the actual door block.

In the following exercises, you will create a door type symbol with attributes for the different values normally assigned to doors, namely, size, thickness, fire rating, material, and construction.

> **▼ NOTE**
>
> A door type symbol is a graphic code used to indicate special characteristics of the associated door. The code refers to a note on another drawing or in a set of written specifications.

FINDING THE ATTRIBUTE TOOL PALETTE

Before you start you will need to load the Attribute palette. This palette contains many of the commands you will use to add, redefine, and edit attributes. To load the Attribute palette, choose Tools ➤ Toolbars ➤ Attribute, or click on the Attribute icon on the Tools flyout on the Standard toolbar. The Attribute toolbar appears on the screen.

ADDING ATTRIBUTES TO BLOCKS

In this exercise, you will create a door type symbol, which is commonly used to describe the size, thickness, and other characteristics of any given door in an architectural drawing. The symbol is usually a circle, hexagon, or diamond, with a number in it. The number can be cross-referenced to a schedule that lists all the door types and their characteristics.

While in this exercise you will be creating a new file containing attribute definitions, you can also include such definitions in blocks you create using the BLOCK command or in files you create using the WBLOCK command. Just create the attribute definitions, then include them with the BLOCK or WBLOCK selections.

1. Open a new file and call it **S-door** (for symbol-door). Since the symbol will fit in the default limits of the drawing, you don't have to change the limits setting.

2. Draw a circle 0.25 units in diameter with its center at coordinate 7,5. Next, zoom into the circle.

3. Click on the Define Attribute button on the Attribute palette, or type **Ddattdef** ↵.

The Attribute Definition dialog box appears.

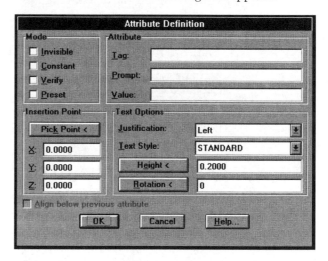

4. Click on the input box labeled Tag in the Attribute group. Enter **d-type**.

5. Click on the input box labeled Prompt, and enter **Door type**. Here you enter the text for the prompt that will appear when you insert the block containing this attribute. Often the prompt is the same as the tag, but it can be anything you like. Unlike the tag, the prompt can include spaces.

Use a prompt that gives explicit instructions so the user will know exactly what is expected. Consider including an example within the prompt. (Enclose the example in brackets to imitate the way AutoCAD prompts often display defaults.)

If an attribute is to contain a number that will later be used for making sorts in a database, use a default such as 000 to indicate the number of digits required. The zeros may also serve to remind the user that values less than 100 must be preceded by a leading zero, as in 099.

6. Click on the input box labeled Value. This is where you enter a default value for the door type prompt. Enter a hyphen.

7. Click on the arrow on the Justification pull-down list, then highlight Middle. This will allow you to center the attribute on the circle's center. You might notice several other options in the Text Options group. Since attributes appear as text, you can apply the same settings to them as you would to ordinary text.

8. Double-click on the input box next to the button labeled Height <, then enter **0.125**. This will make the attribute text 0.125 inches high.

9. Check the box labeled Verify in the Mode group. This option instructs AutoCAD to verify any answers you give to the attribute prompts at insertion time (you'll see later in this chapter how Verify works).

10. Click on the button labeled Pick Point < in the Insertion Point group. The dialog box closes momentarily to let you pick a location for the attribute.

11. Using the Center Osnap override, click to pick the center of the circle. The dialog box reappears.

12. Click on OK. You will see the attribute definition at the center of the circle (see Figure 10.1).

You have just created your first attribute definition. The attribute definition displays its tag in all uppercase to help you identify it. When you later insert this file into another drawing, you will see that the tag turns into the value you assign to it when it is inserted. If you only want one attribute, you can stop here and save the file. The next section shows you how you can quickly add several more attributes to your drawing.

III

Becoming an Expert

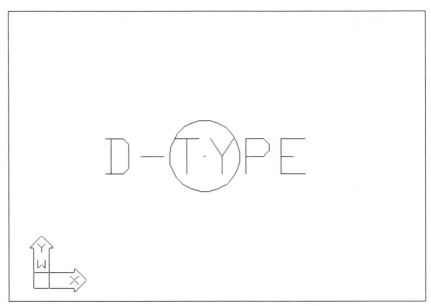

Figure 10.1: The attribute inserted in the circle and the second attribute added

CHANGING ATTRIBUTE SPECIFICATIONS

Next, you will add a few more attribute definitions, but instead of using the Attribute Definition dialog box, you will make an arrayed copy of the first attribute, then edit the attribute definition copies. This method can save you time when you want to create several attribute definitions that have similar characteristics. By making copies and editing them, you'll also get a chance to see first-hand how to make changes to an attribute definition.

1. Click on and drag on Copy Object from the Modify palette then select Rectangular Array from the flyout menu. You can also type **Array** ↵ **R** ↵ to start the ARRAY command.

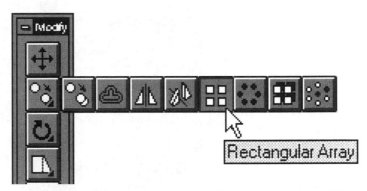

2. At the Select objects prompt, click on the attribute definition you just created, then press ↵.

3. At the Number of rows prompt, enter **7** ↵.

4. At the Number of columns prompt, press ↵.

5. At the Distance between rows prompt, enter **-.18** ↵. This is about 1.5 times the height of the attribute definition. Be sure to include the minus sign. This will cause the array to be drawn downward.

▼ TIP

You can type **DDmodify** ↵ and then continue from step 2. The DDEDIT command also lets you edit the tag, prompt, and default value of an attribute definition. It doesn't let you change an attribute definition's *mode*, however.

Now you are ready to modify the copies of the attribute definitions.

1. Click on the Properties button on the Object Properties toolbar.

2. At the Select object to modify: prompt, click on the attribute definition just below the original. The Modify Attribute Definition dialog box appears.

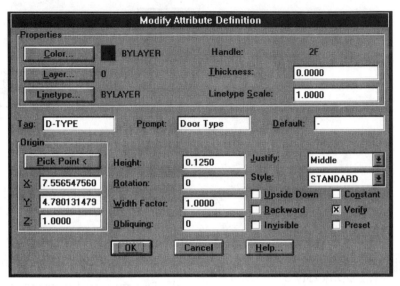

3. Click on the Invisible check box in the lower-right corner of the dialog box. This will cause this attribute to be invisible when the file is later inserted.

4. Double-click on the input box labeled Tag, then enter **d-size**.

5. Tab over to the Prompt input box, then type **Door size**.

6. Press Tab a second time to move to the Default input box, then enter a hyphen.

7. Click on OK. You will see the attribute definition change to reflect the new tag.

8. Continue to edit the rest of the attribute definitions using the attributes settings listed in Table 10.1. Make sure all but the original attributes have the Invisible option turned on.

9. After you have modified all the attributes, use the BASE command to change the base point of this drawing to center of the circle.

10. Now you have finished creating your door type symbol with attributes. Save the S-door file and open the Plan file.

Table 10.1: Attributes for the Door Type Symbol

Tag	Prompt
D-number	Door number
D-thick	Door thickness
D-rate	Fire rating
D-matrl	Door material
D-const	Door construction

When you later insert a file or block containing attributes, the attribute prompts will appear in the order that their associated definitions were created. If the order of the prompts at insertion time is important, you can control it by editing the attribute definitions so their creation order corresponds to the desired prompt order.

UNDERSTANDING ATTRIBUTE DEFINITION MODES

In the Attribute Definition dialog box, you saw several check boxes in the Mode group. I've briefly described what two of these modes do. You won't be asked to use any of the other modes in this tutorial, so the following set of descriptions is provided in case they might be useful for your work.

Invisible controls whether the attribute is shown as part of the drawing.

Constant creates an attribute that does not prompt you to enter a value. Instead the attribute simply has a constant, or fixed, value you give it during creation. *Constant* is used in situations where you know you will assign a fixed value to an object. Once they are set in a block, constant values cannot be changed using the standard set of attribute editing commands.

Verify causes AutoCAD to review the attribute values you enter at insertion time and asks you if they are correct.

Preset causes AutoCAD to automatically assign a default value to an attribute when its block is inserted. This saves time, since a preset attribute will not prompt you for a value. Unlike the Constant option, you can edit an attribute that has the Preset option turned on.

You can have all four modes on, all four off, or any combination of modes. With the exception of the Invisible mode, none of these modes can be altered once the attribute becomes part of a block. Later in this chapter we will discuss how to make an invisible attribute visible.

INSERTING BLOCKS CONTAINING ATTRIBUTES

In the last section, you created a door type symbol at the desired size for the actual plotted symbol. This means that whenever you insert that symbol, you have to specify an x and y scale factor appropriate to the scale of your drawing. This allows you to use the same symbol in any drawing, regardless of its scale. (You could have several door type symbols, one for each scale you anticipate using, but this would be inefficient.)

1. Use View ➤ Named View to restore view 1.

2. Be sure the Ceiling and Flr-Pat layers are off. Normally in a floor plan the door headers are not visible, and they will interfere with the placement of the door symbol.

3. Click and drag on the Block button on the Draw palette and select Insert Block on the flyout, or type **Insert** ⏎ **S-door** ⏎ to insert the S-door file.

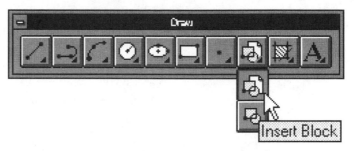

4. At the Insert dialog box, click on the File button.

5. Locate the S-door file in the file list and double-click on it.

6. Click on OK.

7. Insert the symbol at coordinate 41'-3", 72'-4".

8. At the X scale factor prompt, enter **96**.

9. Press ↵ at the Y scale factor prompt, and again at the Rotation angle prompt.

10. At the Door type <->: prompt, enter **A** ↵. Note that this prompt is the prompt you created. Note also that the default value is the hyphen you specified.

11. At the Door size <->: prompt, enter **7'-0"** ↵. This is also a prompt you created.

12. At the Door number <->: prompt, enter **116** ↵. Continue to enter the values for each prompt as shown in Table 10.2.

13. When you have finished entering the values, the prompts repeat themselves to verify your entry (because you selected Verify from the Modes group of the Attribute Definition dialog box). You can now either change an entry or just press ↵ to accept the original entry.

14. When you've finished and the symbol appears, the only attribute you can see is the one you selected to be visible: the door type.

15. Add the rest of the door type symbols for the apartment entry doors by copying or arraying the door symbol you just inserted. You can use the previously saved views to help you get around the drawing quickly. Don't worry that the attribute values won't be appropriate for each unit. I'll show you how to edit the attributes in a later section of this chapter.

Table 10.2: Attribute Values for the Typical Studio Entry Door

Prompt	Value
Door type	A
Door number	Same as room number
Door thickness	1 3/4″
Fire rating	20 min.
Door material	Wood
Door construction	Solid core

As a review exercise, you'll now create another file for the apartment number symbol (shown in Figure 10.2). This will be a rectangular box with the room number that you will place in each studio apartment.

1. Save the Plan file, then open a new file called **S-apart** (for *symbol apartment*).

2. Give the apartment number symbol attribute the tag name **A-number**, the prompt **Enter apartment number**, a default value of **000**, and a text height of **0.125** inches.

3. Make the base point of this drawing the lower-left corner of the rectangle.

4. Save S-apart.

5. Open the Plan file again and insert the apartment number symbol (using an x scale factor of **96**) into the lower-left unit. Give this attribute the value of **116**.

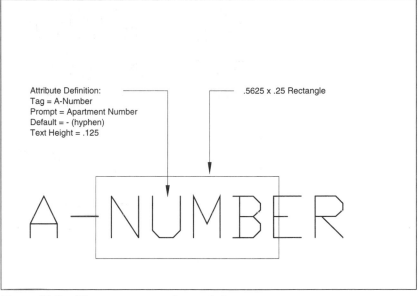

Attribute Definition:
Tag = A-Number
Prompt = Apartment Number
Default = - (hyphen)
Text Height = .125

.5625 x .25 Rectangle

A-NUMBER

Figure 10.2:   The apartment number symbol

6. Copy or array this room number symbol so that there is one symbol in each of the units. You'll learn how to modify the attributes to reflect their proper values in the following section, "Editing Attributes." Figure 10.3 shows what view 4 should look like once you've entered the door symbols and apartment numbers.

USING A DIALOG BOX TO ANSWER ATTRIBUTE PROMPTS

You can set up AutoCAD to display an Enter Attributes dialog box (instead of individual prompts) for entering the attribute values at insertion time. Since this dialog box allows you change your mind about a value before confirming your entry, the dialog box allows greater flexibility than individual prompts when entering attributes. You can also

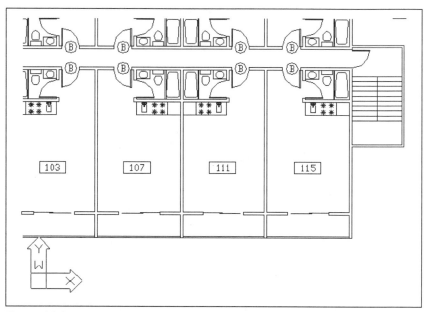

Figure 10.3: View 4 with door symbols and apartment numbers added

see all the attributes associated with a block at once, making it easier to
understand what information is required for the block.

To turn this feature on, do the following.

1. Enter **Attdia** ↵ at the command prompt.

2. At the New value for ATTDIA <0>: prompt, enter **1** ↵.

Attributes set with the Preset mode on will also appear in the dialog box and are treated no differently from other nonconstant attributes.

EDITING ATTRIBUTES

Because drawings are usually in flux even after actual construction or manufacturing begins, you will eventually have to edit previously entered attributes. In the example of the apartment building, many things can change before the final set of drawings is completed.

Attributes can be edited individually (one at a time) or globally (meaning you can edit several occurrences of a particular attribute tag all at one time). In this section you will make changes to the attributes you have entered so far, using both individual and global editing techniques, and you will practice editing invisible attributes.

EDITING ATTRIBUTES ONE AT A TIME

AutoCAD offers an easy way to edit attributes one at a time through a dialog box. The following exercise demonstrates this feature.

1. Use the View ➤ Named View option to restore view 1.

2. Click on Edit Attribute on the Attribute palette, or enter **Ddatte** ↵ at the command prompt.

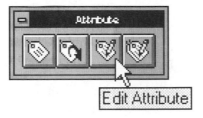

III

Becoming an Expert

3. At the Select block prompt, click on the apartment number attribute in the unit just to the right of the first unit in the lower-left corner. A dialog box appears, showing you the value for the attribute in an input box.

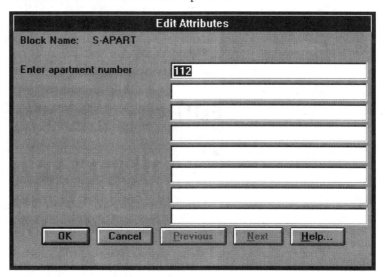

4. Highlight the attribute value in the input box and enter **112**, then click on OK to make the change.

5. Do this for each room number, using Figure 10.4 to assign room numbers.

EDITING SEVERAL ATTRIBUTES IN SUCCESSION

The Edit Attribute option is useful for reviewing attributes as well as editing them, because both visible and invisible attributes are displayed in the dialog box. This option is the same as the DDATTE command.

1. Click on Edit Attribute on the Attribute palette, or enter **Ddatte** ↵.

2. Click on a block containing attributes. The Edit Attributes dialog box appears as before.

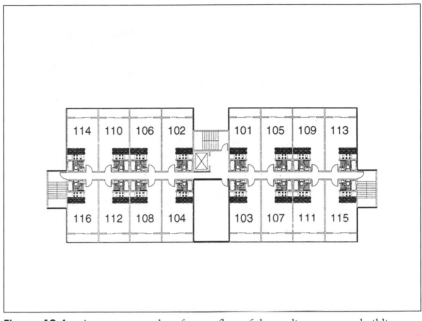

Figure 10.4: Apartment numbers for one floor of the studio apartment building

3. Click on OK. To review and edit other attributes, repeat steps 1–3.

MAKING MINOR CHANGES TO AN ATTRIBUTE'S APPEARANCE

Eventually, there will be situations where you will want to make a change to an attribute that doesn't involve its value, like moving the attribute's location relative to the block it's associated with, or changing its color, its angle, or even its text style. To make these types of changes, you must use the ATTEDIT command. Here's how to do it.

1. Click on the Edit Attribute Globally button on the Attribute palette, or type **Attedit** ↵ at the command prompt.

2. At the Edit attributes one at a time? <Y> prompt, press ↵ to accept the default **Y**.

3. At the Block name specification <*> prompt, press ↵. Optionally, you can enter a block name to narrow the selection to specific blocks.

4. At the Attribute tag specification <*> prompt, press ↵. Optionally, you can enter an attribute tag name to narrow your selection to specific tags.

5. At the Attribute value specification <*> prompt, press ↵. Optionally, you can narrow your selection to attributes containing specific values.

6. At the Select Attributes prompt, you can pick the set of blocks that contain the attributes you wish to edit. Once you press ↵ to confirm your selection, one of the selected attributes becomes highlighted, and an × appears at its base point (see Figure 10.5).

7. At the Value/Position/Height/Angle/Style/Layer/Color /Next <N>: prompt, you can enter the option that best describes the attribute characteristic you wish to change. After you make the change, the prompt returns, allowing you to make another change to the attribute. If you press ↵ to accept the default, **N**, another attribute highlights with an × at its base.

8. The Value/Position/Height prompt appears again, allowing you to make changes to the next attribute.

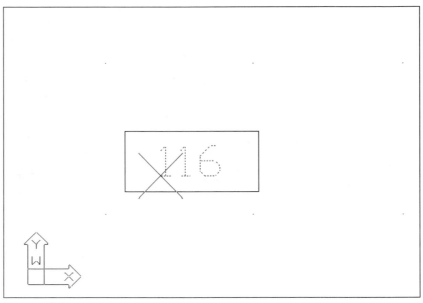

Figure 10.5:   Close-up of attribute with ✕

9. This process repeats until all the attributes have been edited or until you press Esc.

MAKING GLOBAL CHANGES TO ATTRIBUTES

There will be times when you'll want to change the value of several attributes in a file to be the same value. You can use the Edit Attribute Globally option to make any global changes to attribute values.

Suppose you decide you want to change all the entry doors to a type designated as B, rather than A. Perhaps door type A was an input error, or type B happens to be better suited for an entry door.

1. Use View ➤ Named Views to restore view 4.

2. Click on Edit Attribute Globally on the Attribute palette, or type **Attedit** ↵.

3. At the Edit attributes one at a time? <Y> prompt, enter **N** ↵ for *No*. You will see the message Global edit of attribute values. This tells you that you are in the global edit mode.

4. At the Edit only attributes visible on screen? <Y> prompt, press ↵. As you can see from this prompt, you have the option to edit all attributes, including those out of the view area. You'll get a chance to work with this option later in the chapter.

5. At the Block name specification <*> prompt, press ↵. Optionally, you can enter a block name to narrow the selection to specific blocks.

6. At the Attribute tag specification <*> prompt, press ↵. Optionally, you can enter an attribute tag name to narrow your selection to specific tags.

7. At the Attribute value specification <*> prompt, press ↵. Optionally, you can narrow your selection to attributes containing specific values.

8. At the Select Attributes prompt, select the door type symbols for units 103 to 115.

9. At the String to change prompt, enter **A** ↵.

10. At the New string prompt, enter **B** ↵. The door type symbols all change to the new value.

In step 8, you are asked to select the attributes to be edited. AutoCAD limits the changes to those attributes you select. If you know you need to change every single attribute in your drawing, you can do so by answering the series of prompts in a slightly different way, as in the following exercise.

1. Try the same procedure again, but this time enter **N** at the Edit only attributes visible on screen: prompt (step 4 in the previous exercise). The message Drawing must be regenerated afterwards appears. The display will flip to text mode.

2. Once again, you are prompted for the block name, the tag, and the value (steps 5, 6, and 7 in the previous exercise). Respond to these prompts as you did before. Once you have done that, you get the message 16 attributes selected. This tells you the number of attributes that fit the specifications you just entered.

3. At the String to change: prompt, enter **A** ↵ to indicate you want to change the rest of the A attribute values.

4. At the New string: prompt, enter **B** ↵. A series of B's appear, indicating the number of strings that were replaced.

You may have noticed that the Select Attribute prompt is skipped and you go directly to the String to change prompt. AutoCAD assumes that you want it to edit every attribute in the drawing, so it doesn't bother asking you to select specific attributes.

▼

■

■

■

■

USING SPACES
IN ATTRIBUTE VALUES

At times, you may want the default value to begin with a blank space. This enables you to specify text strings more easily when you edit the attribute. For example, you may have an attribute value that reads *3334333*. If you want to change the first 3 in this string of numbers, you have to specify **3334** when prompted for the string to change. If you start with a space, as in **_3334333** (I'm only using an underline here to represent the space—it doesn't mean you type an underline character), you can isolate the first 3 from the rest by specifying **_3** as the string to change (again, typing a space instead of the underline).

You must enter a backslash character (\) before the space in the default value to tell AutoCAD to interpret the space literally, rather than as a press of the spacebar (which is equivalent to pressing ↵).

MAKING INVISIBLE ATTRIBUTES VISIBLE

If an attribute has its invisible mode turned on, you cannot edit it using the global editing features described in the previous section. You can, however, make invisible attributes visible and *then* apply global edits to them. Here's how it's done.

1. Enter **Attdisp** ↲.

2. At the Normal/ON/OFF <Normal>: prompt, enter **ON** ↲. Your drawing will look like Figure 10.6. If Regenauto is turned off, you may have to issue the REGEN command. At this point you could edit the invisible attributes individually, as in the first attribute-editing exercise. For now, set the attribute display back to normal.

3. Enter **Attdisp** ↲ again; then at the Normal/ON/OFF prompt, enter **N** ↲ for normal.

▼ **TIP**

You may also use the Windows menu to change the display characteristics of attributes. Choose Options ➤ Display ➤ Attribute Display, then click on the desired option on the cascading menu.

▼ **NOTE**

You get a chance to see the results of the ON and Normal options. The OFF option will make all attributes invisible, regardless of the mode used when they were created.

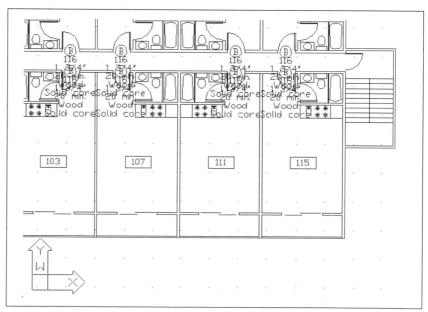

Figure 10.6: The drawing with all the attributes visible. Since the door type symbols are so close together, the attributes overlap.

REDEFINING BLOCKS CONTAINING ATTRIBUTES

Finally, you should be aware that attributes act differently from other objects when included in redefined blocks. Normally, blocks that have been redefined change their configuration to reflect the new block definition. But if a redefined block contains attributes, the attributes will maintain their old properties. This means that the old attribute position, style, etc., do not change even though you may have changed them in the new definition.

Fortunately, AutoCAD offers a tool specifically designed to let you update blocks with attributes. The following describes how you would go about updating attribute blocks.

1. Before you use the command to redefine an attribute block, you must first create the objects and attribute definitions that are going to make up the new replacement attribute block. The simplest way to do this is to explode a copy of the attribute block you wish to update. This ensures that you have the same attribute definitions in the updated block.

2. Make your changes to the exploded attribute block.

3. Click on the Redefine Attribute button on the Attribute toolbar.

4. At the Name of Block you wish to redefine: prompt, enter the appropriate name.

5. At the Select objects for new Block: prompt, select all the objects, including the attribute definitions, you want to include in the revised attribute block.

6. At the Insertion base point of new Block: prompt, pick the same location as used for the original block.

Once you pick the insertion point, AutoCAD will take a few seconds to update the blocks. The amount of time will vary depending on the complexity of the block and the number of times the block occurs in the drawing. If you include a new attribute definition with your new block, it too will be added to all the updated blocks, with its default value. Attribute definitions that are deleted from your new definition will be removed from all the updated blocks.

EXTRACTING AND EXPORTING ATTRIBUTE INFORMATION

▼ TIP

If you want to get a count of blocks in your drawing, check out the utility I've included on the bonus disk for just that purpose. See *Appendix C* for details.

▼ NOTE

Don't confuse this template file with the drawing prototype file you use to set up various default settings.

Once you have entered the attributes into your drawing, you can extract the information contained in them and use it in other programs. You may, for example, want to keep track of the door information in a database manager. This is especially useful if you have a project that contains thousands of doors, such as a large hotel.

The first step in extracting attribute information is to create a template file using a text editor like Windows Notepad. The template file used with attributes is an ASCII text file containing a list of the attributes you wish to extract and their characteristics. You can also extract information about the block an attribute is associated with. The block's name, x and y coordinates, layer, orientation, and scale are all available for extraction.

DETERMINING WHAT TO EXTRACT

In the template file, for every attribute you wish to extract, you must give the attribute's tag name followed by a code that determines whether the attribute value is numeric or text, how many spaces to allow for the value, and, if it is a numeric value, how many decimal places to give the number. If you are familiar with database management programs, you'll know these are typical variables you determine when you set up a database.

For example, to get a list of rooms containing the B door type, you would create a text file with the following contents.

```
D-ROOM N005000
D-TYPE C001000
```

The first item on each line (D-ROOM and D-TYPE in this example) is the tag of the attribute you want to list. This is followed by at least one space, then a code that describes the attribute. This code may look a little cryptic at first glance. The following list describes how the code is broken down from left to right:

■ The first character of the code is always a C or an N to denote a character (C) or numeric (N) value.

■ The next three digits are where you enter the number of spaces the value will take up. You can enter any number from 001 to 999, but you must enter zeros for null values. The D-ROOM example shows the value of 005 for five spaces. The two leading zeros are needed because AutoCAD expects to see three digits in this part of the code.

■ The last three digits are for the number of decimal places to allow if the value is numeric. For character values, these must always be zeros. Once again, AutoCAD expects to see three digits in this part of the code, so even if there are no decimal digits for the value, you must include 000.

Now you will use the Windows Notepad application to create a template file. If you like, you can use any Windows word processor that is capable of saving files in the ASCII format.

1. Switch over to the Program Manager, then locate and start up the Notepad application from the Accessories program group.

III

Becoming an Expert

2. Enter the following text as it is shown. Press ↵ at the end of *each* line, including the last.

    D-NUMBER C005000
    D-THICK C007000
    D-RATE C010000
    D-MATRL C015000
    D-CONST C015000

3. When you have finished entering these lines of text, click on File ➤ Save, then enter **Door.TXT** for the file name. For ease of access you should save this file to your current directory, the \ACADR13\WIN\ directory.

4. Close the Notepad, and return to AutoCAD.

You've just completed the setup for attribute extraction. Now that you have a template file, you can extract the attribute data.

Text Editor Line Endings It is very important that the last line of your file end with a single ↵. AutoCAD will return an error message if you either leave the ↵ off or have an extra ↵ at the end of the file. Take care to end the line with a ↵ and don't add an extra one.

EXTRACTING BLOCK INFORMATION USING ATTRIBUTES

▼ WARNING

A template file containing these codes must also contain at least one attribute tag, because AutoCAD must know which attribute it is extracting before it can tell what block the attribute is associated with. Code information for blocks works the same as for attributes.

I mentioned that you can extract information regarding blocks, as well as attributes. To do this you must use the following format.

BL:LEVEL	N002000
BL:NAME	C031000
BL:X	N009004
BL:Y	N009004
BL:Z	N009004
BL:NUMBER	N009000
BL:HANDLE	C009000
BL:LAYER	C031000

BL:ORIENT	N009004
BL:XSCALE	N009004
BL:YSCALE	N009004
BL:ZSCALE	N009004
BL:XEXTRUDE	N009004
BL:YEXTRUDE	N009004
BL:ZEXTRUDE	N009004

I have included some typical values for the attribute codes in this example. The following describes what each line in the above example is used for.

BL:LEVEL   returns the nesting level.

BL:NAME   returns the block name.

BL:X   returns the x coordinate of the insertion point.

BL:Y   returns the y coordinate of the insertion point.

BL:Z   returns the z coordinate of the insertion point.

BL:NUMBER   returns the order number of the block.

BL:HANDLE   returns the blocks handle. If no handle exists, a 0 is returned.

BL:LAYER   returns the layer the block is inserted on.

BL:ORIENT   returns the insertion angle.

BL:XSCALE   returns the x scale.

BL:YSCALE   returns the y scale.

BL:ZSCALE   returns the z scale.

BL:XEXTRUDE   returns the block's x extrusion direction.

BL:YEXTRUDE   returns the block's y extrusion direction.

BL:ZEXTRUDE   returns the block's z extrusion direction.

III

Becoming an Expert

PERFORMING THE EXTRACTION

AutoCAD allows you to extract attribute information from your drawing as a list in one of three different formats:

- CDF (comma-delimited format)

- SDF (space-delimited format)

- DXF (data exchange format)

Using the CDF Format

The CDF format can be read by many popular database management programs, as well as programs written in BASIC. This is the format you will use in this exercise.

1. Type **Ddattext** ↵. The Attribute Extraction dialog box appears.

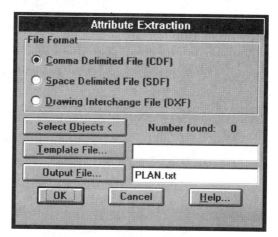

2. Click on the radio button labeled CDF.

3. Double-click on the Template File input box and enter **Door.TXT**.

4. Press the Tab key to move to the Output File input box, then enter **Plan.TXT**.

5. Click on OK. The computer will pause for several seconds, and when it is done, the message 16 records in extract file appears.

AutoCAD has created a file called Plan.TXT that contains the extracted list. Let's take a look at its contents.

1. Switch to the Program Manager and open the Notepad application from the Accessories.Program group.

2. Choose File ➤ Open to open **Plan.TXT** from the current directory. (In this exercise, the template file is located in the \ACADR13\WIN directory.) You will get the following list:

```
'116','1 3/4"','20 MIN','WOOD','SOLID CORE'
'114','1 3/4"','20 MIN','WOOD','SOLID CORE'
'112','1 3/4"','20 MIN','WOOD','SOLID CORE'
'110','1 3/4"','20 MIN','WOOD','SOLID CORE'
'108','1 3/4"','20 MIN','WOOD','SOLID CORE'
'106','1 3/4"','20 MIN','WOOD','SOLID CORE'
'102','1 3/4"','20 MIN','WOOD','SOLID CORE'
'104','1 3/4"','20 MIN','WOOD','SOLID CORE'
'107','1 3/4"','20 MIN','WOOD','SOLID CORE'
'105','1 3/4"','20 MIN','WOOD','SOLID CORE'
'101','1 3/4"','20 MIN','WOOD','SOLID CORE'
'103','1 3/4"','20 MIN','WOOD','SOLID CORE'
'111','1 3/4"','20 MIN','WOOD','SOLID CORE'
'109','1 3/4"','20 MIN','WOOD','SOLID CORE'
'113','1 3/4"','20 MIN','WOOD','SOLID CORE'
'115','1 3/4"','20 MIN','WOOD','SOLID CORE'
```

Since you picked the comma delimited format (CDF), AutoCAD placed commas between each extracted attribute value (or *field*, in database terminology).

The commas are used by some database management programs to indicate the separation of fields in ASCII files. This example shows everything in uppercase letters because that's the way they were entered when I inserted the attribute blocks in my own working sample. The extracted file maintains the case of whatever you enter for the attribute values.

III

Becoming an Expert

Using Other Delimiters with CDF Some database managers require the use of other symbols, such as double quotes and slashes, to indicate character values and field separation. AutoCAD allows you to use a different symbol in place of the single quote or comma. For example, if the database manager you use requires double-quote delimiters for text in the file to be imported, you can add the statement

c:quote ″

to the template file to replace the single quote with a double quote. A line from an extract file using *c:quote* ″ in the template file would look like this:

″115″,″1 3/4″ ″,″20 MIN″,″WOOD″,″SOLID CORE″

Notice that the single quote (′) is replaced by a double quote (″).
You can also add the statement

c:delim /

to replace the comma delimiter with the slash symbol. A line from an extract file using both *c:quote* ″ and *c:delim* / in the template file would look like this:

″115″/″1 3/4″ ″/″20 MIN″/″WOOD″/″SOLID CORE″

Here the comma is replaced by a forward slash. You can add either of these statements to the beginning or end of your template file.

Using the SDF Format

Like the CDF format, the space-delimited format (SDF) can be read by most database management programs. This format is the best one to use if you intend to enter information into a word-processed document, because it leaves out the commas and quotes. You can even import it into an AutoCAD drawing using the method described in *Chapter 8*. Now let's try using the SDF option to extract the same list we extracted a moment ago using CDF.

As an alternate, you can choose File ➤ Export, then at the Export Data dialog box, choose DXX Extract (*.DXX) from the List File of Type drop-down list. Enter a name for the extracted data file in the File name input box then click OK. Finally, in the drawing editor, select the attributes you want to extract.

1. Type **Ddattext** ↵ at the command prompt.

2. At the Attribute Extraction dialog box, use the same template file name, but for the attribute extract file name, use **Plan- SDF.TXT** to distinguish this file from the last one you created.

3. Click on the SDF radio button, then click on OK.

4. After AutoCAD has extracted the list, use the Windows Notepad to view the contents of the file. You will get a list similar to this one:

```
116 1 3/4" 20 MIN WOOD SOLID CORE
114 1 3/4" 20 MIN WOOD SOLID CORE
112 1 3/4" 20 MIN WOOD SOLID CORE
110 1 3/4" 20 MIN WOOD SOLID CORE
108 1 3/4" 20 MIN WOOD SOLID CORE
106 1 3/4" 20 MIN WOOD SOLID CORE
102 1 3/4" 20 MIN WOOD SOLID CORE
104 1 3/4" 20 MIN WOOD SOLID CORE
107 1 3/4" 20 MIN WOOD SOLID CORE
105 1 3/4" 20 MIN WOOD SOLID CORE
101 1 3/4" 20 MIN WOOD SOLID CORE
103 1 3/4" 20 MIN WOOD SOLID CORE
111 1 3/4" 20 MIN WOOD SOLID CORE
109 1 3/4" 20 MIN WOOD SOLID CORE
113 1 3/4" 20 MIN WOOD SOLID CORE
115 1 3/4" 20 MIN WOOD SOLID CORE
```

This format shows text without any special delimiting characters.

Using the DXF Format

The third file format is the data exchange format (DXF). There are actually two methods for DXF extraction. The Attribute Extraction dialog box you saw earlier offers the DXF option. This option extracts only the data from blocks containing attributes. Choose the File ➤ Export option then select .DXF from the List Files of Type: drop-box to convert an entire drawing file into a special format for data exchange between AutoCAD and other programs (for example, other PC CAD programs). I will discuss the DXF format in more detail in *Chapter 14*.

III

Becoming an Expert

USING EXTRACTED ATTRIBUTE DATA WITH OTHER PROGRAMS

You can import any of these lists into any word-processing program that accepts ASCII files. They will appear as shown in our examples.

As we mentioned earlier, the extracted file can also be made to conform to other data formats.

dBASE IV   Suppose you want to import the list you just created in the exercises above into dBASE IV by using the CDF option. First, you create a database file with the same field characteristics you entered for the template file (i.e., length of fields and character or number). Then enter:

Append from *AutoCAD directory*\\Plan.txt Delimited

where *AutoCAD directory* is the directory where the Plan.TXT file can be found.

To use the file created by the SDF option, replace **Delimited** in the line above with **SDF** and use **Plan-SDF.TXT** instead of **Plan.txt**.

If you are using a database manager other than dBASE IV, find out what its format requirements are for imported files and use the quote and delim options described earlier to make adjustments. You may also have to rename the file in order to import it into the database manager. Requirements for two of the more popular database managers are described here.

Lotus 1-2-3   You can also use the SDF format for importing files into Lotus 1-2-3. However, you must change the SDF file extension from .TXT to .PRN. Once you have done this, you can use Lotus' File Import command to create a spreadsheet from this file. Use the Numbers option on the Lotus Import submenu to ensure that the numeric values are entered as discrete spreadsheet cells. Any items containing text are grouped together in one cell. For example, the last three items in the Plan-SDF.TXT file are combined into one cell because each item contains text.

Excel If you want to export data to Excel, you will have to use the CDF format. There are no other special requirements for Excel, but importing into Excel is made somewhat easier if you give your export file an extension that begins with XL, as in **Plan.XLA**.

ACCESSING EXTERNAL DATABASES

▼ NOTE

The following tutorial is intended to give you an overview of the ASE capabilities, and by no means constitutes complete coverage of this feature.

AutoCAD offers a way to access an external database from within Auto-CAD. Through the *AutoCAD SQL Extension* (ASE) you can read and manipulate data from external database files. You can also use ASE to *link* parts of your drawing to an external database. There are numerous reasons for doing this. The most obvious is to keep inventory on parts of your drawing. If you are an interior designer doing office planning, you can link inventory data from a database to your drawing, with a resulting decrease in the size of your drawing file. If you are a facilities manager, you can track the movement of people and facilities using AutoCAD linked to a database file.

In this section I specifically avoid the more complex programming issues of database management systems, and I do not discuss the SQL language on which much of ASE is based. Still, you should be able to make good use of ASE with the information provided here.

I do assume a small degree of familiarity with databases in these exercises. For example, I will frequently refer to something called a *table*. A table is a SQL term referring to the row-and-column data structure of a typical database file. For the sake of this tutorial, you can think of a table as a dBASE III or IV database file. Other terms I'll use are *rows*, which are the records in a database, and *columns*, which refer to the database fields.

Finally, it is *very* important that you follow the instructions in these beginning exercises carefully. If anything is missed in the beginning, later exercises will not work properly.

▼
■   # DATABASE MANAGERS AND AUTOCAD
■
Chances are, you are already familiar with at least one database program. ASE provides support for dBASE III, dBASE IV, and the
■   DOS version of Borland's Paradox. But you needn't have these specific programs to work with ASE. Many other database and
■   spreadsheet programs can read and write to dBASE III files. If you are a Windows user, you can use Microsoft Excel to create database files for use with AutoCAD ASE.

SETTING UP ASE TO LOCATE DATABASE TABLES

ASE doesn't create new database files. You must use existing files or create them before you use ASE. In the first set of exercises below, you will use two files that come with AutoCAD. The two files are Employee.DBF and Inventry.DBF. The contents of the first of these database files are shown in Figure 10.7.

Before you start to work with databases, you must set up an *environment*. AutoCAD's SQL extension expects to work with a database environment that consists of *catalogs*, *schemas*, and *tables*. (See the sidebar entitled "What are Catalogs, Schemas, and Tables?")

Start by creating a special place for the database files.

▼ NOTE

The subdirectory name can be anything you like, but for this tutorial, you'll use DBF to remind you of the file type.

1. Check for the subdirectory called **DBF** under the \acadr13\common\sample subdirectory to make sure the .DBF files are there. The path should look something like this:

   Drive:\acadr13\common\sample\dbf

   You should replace *Drive* in this example with the drive letter where you have AutoCAD installed.

Next, you'll tell AutoCAD about this environment so that it can locate these files. This is done through the ASI.INI file.

EMP_ID	LAST_NAME	FIRST_NAME	DEPT	TITLE	ROOM	EXT
1000	Meredith	Dave	Sales	V.P.	101	8600
1001	Williams	Janice	Sales	Western Region Mgr.	102	8601
1003	Smith	Jill	Sales	Central Region Mgr.	104	8603
1004	Nelson	Kirk	Sales	Canadian Sales Mgr.	109	8640
1005	Clark	Karl	Sales	Educational Sales Mgr.	106	8605
1006	Wilson	Cindy	Accounting	Accountant	109	8606
1007	Ortega	Emilio	Accounting	Accountant	109	8607
1008	Benson	Adam	Accounting	Accountant	109	8608
1009	Rogers	Kevin	Accounting	Accountant	109	8609
1011	Thompson	Frank	Engineering	Mechanical Engineer	123	8611
1012	Simpson	Paul	Engineering	Mechanical Engineer	124	8612
1013	Debrine	Todd	Engineering	Design Engineer	125	8613
1014	Frazier	Heather	Engineering	Application Engineer	126	8614
1016	Taylor	Patrick	Engineering	Software Engineer	128	8616
1017	Chang	Yuan	Engineering	Software Engineer	129	8617
1018	Dempsy	Phil	Engineering	Application Engineer	112	8618
1019	Kahn	Jenny	Engineering	Programmer	113	8619
1020	Moore	George	Engineering	Programmer	114	8620
1021	Price	Mark	Engineering	Software Engineer	115	8621
1022	Quinn	Scott	Engineering	Software Engineer	116	8622
1023	Sanchez	Maria	Engineering	Mechanical Engineer	117	8623
1024	Ross	Ted	Engineering	Application Engineer	118	8624
1025	Saunders	Terry	Engineering	Software Engineer	119	8625
1026	Fong	Albert	Engineering	Programmer	120	8626

Figure 10.7: The contents of the Employee.DBF dBASE III file that comes with this book's companion CD

2. Locate the ASI.INI file in the \acadr13\win directory, then make a backup copy of the existing ASI.INI file. For example, while in the AutoCAD directory, type **Copy ASI.INI ASI-INI.BAK** ↵. This will make a backup copy of the ASI.INI file called ASI-INI.BAK.

3. Open the ASI.INI file using a text editor such as the Windows Notepad. You'll see a listing of data, most of which will be of no concern to you at this point.

4. Scroll down until you see the heading [ENVIRONMENTS. WinNT]. You'll see a list similar to the following:

```
DB3       =
FOX       =
ODBC      =
PDX40     =
```

III

Becoming an Expert

5. Add the line **DB3TUT** = to the end of the list. For added clarity, align the text with the other items in the list.

6. Scroll further down the file until you come to the heading [DB3]. This heading is followed by a list labeled Driver, Catalog, Schema, etc. You'll find out what these are shortly.

7. Just before the [DB3] heading, add the heading **[DB3TUT]** and the following list of information.

▼ NOTE

Replace the *Drive*: in the *CAT* = *item* line with the drive letter where you have AutoCAD installed.

```
Driver        = DB3DRV
Catalog       = CAT
Schema        = Tutorial
CAT           = Drive:\acadr13\common\sample
CAT.Tutorial  = dbf
```

This is where you tell AutoCAD where to find your dBASE III files. *Driver* tells AutoCAD which of its supplied database drivers to use. *Catalog* is an alias for the directory path that contains subdirectories for the database files. Here you supply a meaningful name for the actual directory path. In this case, the alias is CAT, which is just an abbreviation for Catalog. *Schema* is the alias for the subdirectory under Catalog that contains the actual database tables. Again, you would supply a name that conveys some meaning for the subdirectory. This sample uses Tutorial for the Schema alias.

Right after the Schema alias, you supply the actual path that the Catalog and Schema aliases represent. The line that reads CAT = *Drive*:\acadr13\common\sample indicates the location of the CAT catalog. The next line, CAT.Tutorial = dbf tells AutoCAD to look in the DBF subdirectory of the CAT catalog for the actual database tables. Here CAT.Tutorial is equivalent to *Drive*:\acadr13\common\sample\dbf.

You need to add one more item to ASI.INI before you can proceed.

1. Scroll down further until you come to the heading [ASE_CATALOG]. Add **DB3TUT = CAT** to the list that follows this heading.

2. Exit and save the ASI.INI file.

Now, lets take a look at how we can access the tables from AutoCAD.

LOADING THE EXTERNAL DATABASE PALETTE

First you need to locate the toolbar which accesses the ASE commands. Choose Tools ➤ Toolbars ➤ External Database, or click on External Database Toolbar on the Tools flyout on the Standard toolbar. The External Database tool bar appears.

OPENING A DATABASE FROM AUTOCAD

1. Start AutoCAD, then load the ASETUT file from the companion disk.

2. Click on the Administration button on the External Database palette, or type **Aseadmin** ↵.

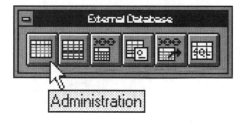

The Administration dialog box appears.

▼ WARNING

If ASE does not initialize, be sure that the \acadr13\winsup directory is included in the Support option of the Environment settings. This option can be found by clicking on Options ➤ Preferences, then at the Preferences dialog box, click on the tab labeled Environment. Be sure to close and restart AutoCAD after making the environment change.

III

Becoming an Expert

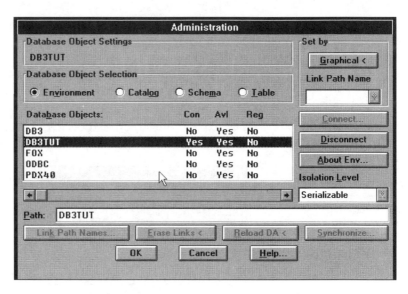

3. Click on DB3TUT from the Database Objects list. Notice that the Environment button is automatically selected.

4. Click on the Connect button to the right of the list. The Connect to Environment dialog box appears.

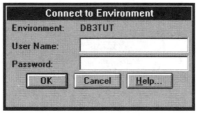

5. Click on OK, since the user name and password are not important to this tutorial.

6. Click on the Catalog button in the Database Object Selection group, then click on CAT, which appears in the Database Objects list. *CAT* is appended to the Database Object Settings at the top of the dialog box.

7. Click on the Schema button, then click on Tutorial from the list. *Tutorial* is added to the Database Object Settings at the top of the Dialog box.

8. Click on the Table button, then click on Employee from the list. *Employee* is appended to the Database Object Settings list at the top.

9. Finally, click on OK. You've just linked to the Employee.dbf file.

FINDING A RECORD IN THE DATABASE

Now that you are connected to the database, suppose you want to find the record for a specific individual. You might already know that the individual you're looking for is in the Accounting department.

1. Click on the Rows button on the External Database palette, or type **Aserows** ↵.

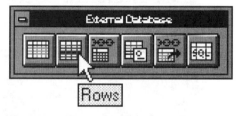

The Rows dialog box appears.

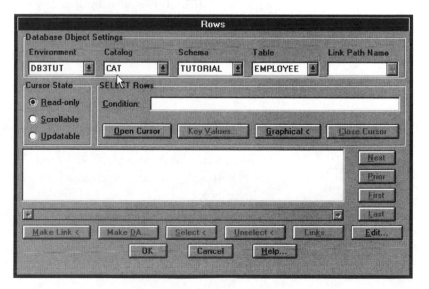

2. Click on the Condition input box and type **dept='Accounting'**.

3. Click on the Scrollable radio button in the Cursor State group, then click on the Open Cursor button below the Conditions input box. The first item that fulfills the Conditions criteria appears in the list box.

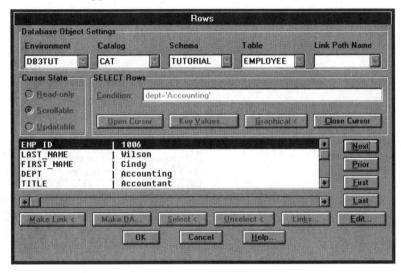

4. Click on the Next button to view the next row that meets the search criteria.

5. Click on Last to view the last row (the one with Kevin Rogers' name).

6. Click on OK to close the dialog box.

You can also click on Open Cursor without entering anything in the input box in step 2. This essentially tells ASE to select all the rows in the current database table. You would then be able to scan the entire table. To exit the list, you choose Close cursor or simply exit the Rows dialog box.

You've just seen how you can locate and view a record in a database. If you wanted to edit or delete that record, you would have clicked on the Editable radio button in step 3, instead of the Scrollable button. You could then make changes to the database item shown in the list box by clicking on the Edit button. The Edit button then opens another dialog box that allows you to edit individual items in a record. In the following section, you'll use the Edit Row dialog box, not to change a record, but to add one.

ADDING A ROW TO A DATABASE TABLE

Now suppose you have a new employee who will need to be set up in an office. The first thing you will want to do is add his or her name to the database. Here's how it's done.

1. Click on the Rows button on the External Database palette, or enter **Aserows** ↵.

2. Click on the Updatable button in the Cursor State group, then click on the Edit button toward the lower right corner of the dialog box. The Edit Row dialog box appears.

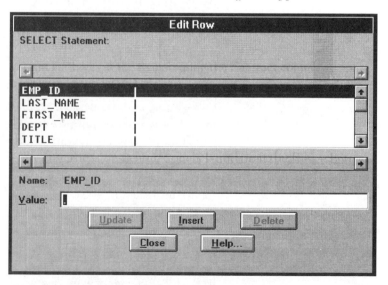

3. Enter the following data in the dialog box. To add an item, highlight the item in the list, then add the information in the input area at the bottom of the dialog box. After you type in each item, press ↵ to move to the next item.

EMP_ID ┊ **2000**
LAST_NAME ┊ **Ryan**
FIRST_NAME ┊ **Roma**
DEPT ┊ **Creative Resources**
TITLE ┊ **Producer/Lyricist**
ROOM ┊ **122**
EXT ┊ **8888**

3. When you've finished entering the list, click on Insert, then click on Close.

4. Click on OK at the Rows dialog box. You've just added a row to the database and it is the current one.

LINKING OBJECTS TO A DATABASE

So far, you've looked at ways you can access an external database file. You can also *link* specific drawing objects to elements in a database. But before you can link your drawing to data, you must *register* the table (i.e., database file) to which you want to link and then create a *link path*.

Registering a table is a way of naming a group of links between your drawing and the database file. You can register a table numerous times, allowing you to set up several different sets of links. For example, you may want to create a set of links between the Names column of your database table and the desks in your office plan. In another instance, you may want to link the phone extension numbers of the same database file to the room numbers in your office plan. To identify these different sets of links, you create a link path name, which is really just a name you give to each set of links.

Now let's see how you can create a link to the database by linking your new employee to one of the vacant rooms.

CREATING A LINK

In the following set of exercises, you will use a sample drawing of an office.

1. Click on the Administration button on the External Database palette.

2. With the Employee table selected, click on the Link Path Names button in the lower left corner of the Administration dialog box. The Link Path Names dialog box appears.

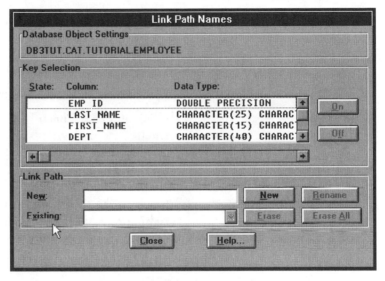

3. Highlight the item labeled LAST_NAME in the Key Selection dialog box, then click on the On button to the right. The word ON appears next to the name.

4. Repeat step 3 for the item labeled ROOM, which is lower down the list.

5. Click on the New input box in the Link Path group, just below the list then type **R-number**.

6. Click on New to the right of the New input box. The name R-NUMBER appears in the Existing pop-up list and the message Registered successfully appears in the lower left corner. At this point, you could select another set of items from the list and create another link path name.

7. Click Close and you return to the Administration dialog. Click on OK to exit this dialog box.

III

Becoming an Expert

You've just registered the Employee table and created a link path name. Now you are ready to add a link to room 122. The first step is to locate the record that is associated with room 122.

1. Open the Plan drawing and zoom into the area shown in Figure 10.8.

2. Click on Rows on the External Database palette.

3. Click on the Conditions input box, then type **ROOM='122'**.

4. Click on Open Cursor. The record for room 122 appears in the list.

5. Click on the button labeled Make Link <. The dialog box temporarily disappears.

6. Click on the room number (122) and the phone in the upper right corner of the room. Once you've done this, press ↵ to return to the Row dialog box.

7. Click on OK to exit the Rows dialog box.

Now you have a link established between the row for room 122 in the database and two objects in your drawing. Later, you can continue to build links between objects and database records, but for now, let's look at other things you can do with the link.

ADDING LABELS WITH LINKS

Once you've got a link established, you use it to perform a variety of editing tasks. For example, you can add labels to your drawing base on information in the database. The following shows you how you can add the employee name and telephone extension number to the drawing.

1. Click on Rows on the External Database palette. The Row dialog box appears.

2. Click on Graphical <. The dialog box disappears momentarily, allowing you to select an object.

▼ **NOTE**

The *DA* in *Make DA* stands for Displayable Attribute. Don't confuse this with the attributes we've discussed earlier in this chapter. They are not the same.

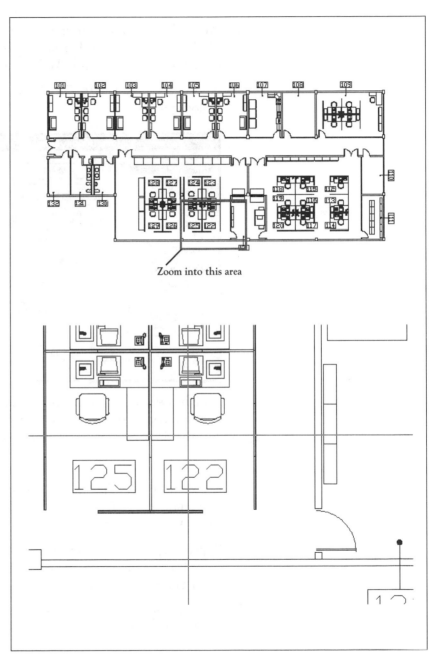

Figure 10.8: Enlarging your view of room 122

3. At the Select object prompt, click on the room number (122). The Row dialog box appears again and displays the record information that is linked to the number.

4. Now click on Make DA. The Make Displayable Attribute dialog appears.

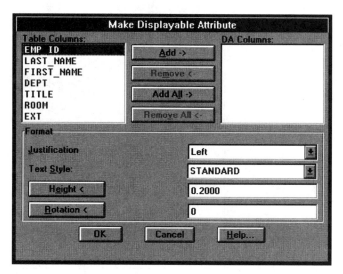

This dialog box shows two lists. The one on the left shows the items in the database record. The one on the right holds the records you want displayed in the drawing as labels. Right now the DA Columns list is empty.

5. Highlight the LAST_NAME item in the Table Columns list, then click on the Add –> button. The item is copied into the DA Columns list.

6. Repeat step 5 for the item labeled TITLE in the Table Columns list, then press OK. The dialog box disappears, and the Left Point prompt appears.

7. Pick a point just below and to the left of the chair. The Rows dialog box appears.

8. Click on OK. The Rows dialog box closes and you see a new label with the employee's name and title. This new label is also linked to the record in your database.

You may have noticed the Format group in the Make Displayable Attribute dialog box in step 4. These items allow you to control the graphic characteristics of the label, such as justification, style, height, and rotation. There is also a button labeled Add All. This copies all the columns from the row list to the DA Column list.

UPDATING ROWS AND LABELS

If a table is modified outside of AutoCAD, you must use the Synchronize button in the Administration dialog box to resynchronize the links between your drawing and the database the next time you open the linked drawing file.

Things are constantly changing, and chances are your database will change frequently. In the following exercise, you will get to change a database row and update one of the labels you just placed in your drawing. You will start by quickly setting the current row by selecting an object.

1. Click on Rows on the External Database palette, then, at the dialog box, click on the Updatable radio button in the Cursor State group.

2. Click on Graphical<. The dialog box closes and the Select object prompt appears.

3. Click on the label you just entered. The current row is now set to the one for your employee.

4. Click on the Edit button, then, at the Edit Row dialog box, highlight TITLE.

5. Change the Value input box to read **Chief Designer**, then press ↵. The ↵ is important; without it the Update button is not activated.

6. Click on Update. The Confirm Update or Erase Links dialog box appears.

III

Becoming an Expert

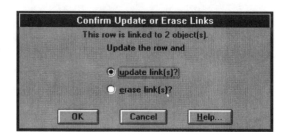

Click OK to update the database table and text in the drawing, then close the dialog boxes.

You have just edited a row in the database and updated the room label
at the same time.

FINDING AND SELECTING
GRAPHICS THROUGH THE DATABASE

You've just seen how you can use links to add and update labels to your
drawing. Links can also help you find and select objects in a drawing
that are linked to a database. The next exercise shows, in a simplified
way, how this works.

1. Click on Rows on the External Database palette, then type
   room ='122' into the Condition input box in the Select
   Rows group.

2. Click on Open Cursor. Once again, you see the familiar record we've been working with.

3. Click on Select <. The dialog box temporarily disappears,
   and you see all the items linked to this record highlighted in
   the drawing.

4. Press ↵ to return to the Row dialog box, then click on OK.

Once these steps have been taken, you can use the Previous Object
Selection option to select those objects that were highlighted in step 3.
   In this example, you only selected objects in one office. You can, how-
ever create a record called Vacant, then link all the vacant offices to

this one record. When a new employee is hired, you can then quickly locate all the vacant rooms in the floor plan to place the new employee. If you continue to link each database record with rooms in the drawing, you can then later locate a person's room through the same process.

DELETING A LINK

Earlier, you had to change a link that connected a room number and telephone in the drawing to an employee's database record. This next exercise shows you how you can delete the link to the telephone.

1. Click on Rows on the External Database palette, then, at the dialog box, click on Graphical <.

2. Click on the phone in room 122. The row assigned to that label is now the current row.

3. Click on Links.... The Links dialog box appears.

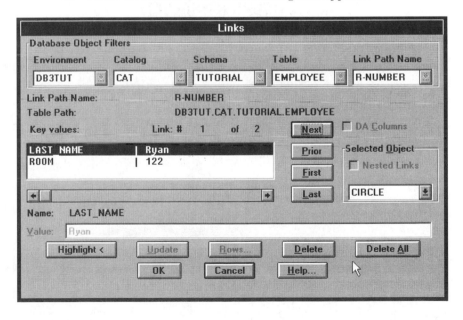

The Key Values list box shows the key values that were selected when you first created the link path name. Above the upper right side of the list, you see the statement Link: # 1 of 2. This tells you which object link in the drawing you are currently working with.

4. To see which object #1 is, click on the Highlight < button. The dialog box disappears and the drawing shows the room number 125 highlighted.

5. Press ↵, then click on the Next button to the right of the list. You are now on link #2.

6. Click on Highlight < to visually check that link #2 is in fact the telephone, then click on the Delete button at the bottom of the dialog box. The link between the record and the telephone are deleted.

FILTERING SELECTIONS AND EXPORTING LINKS

There are two options you didn't get a chance to try. They are Object Selection and Export Links. Object Selection offers a way to select objects based on a combination of graphical and database criteria. For example, suppose you want to select all the chairs of a certain description from one region of your office plan. Assuming you have already created links between your database table and your drawing, you could do the following:

1. Click on the Select Objects button on the External Database palette, or type **Aseselect** ↵.

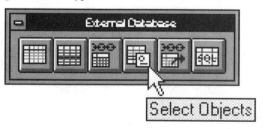

The Select Objects dialog box appears.

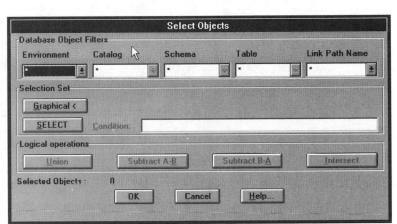

2. Select the appropriate environment, catalog, schema, and table. Under the Conditions input box, enter the search criteria for the chairs.

3. Under the Logical Operations group, choose the Intersection button, then choose Graphical <. The dialog box temporarily disappears to allow you to select objects.

4. Using a window, select the area in the drawing that includes the chairs you want, then press ↵.

5. Click OK to exit the dialog box. You can now use the Previous Selection option to select the specified chairs in the area you selected.

The Export Links feature lets you export information about the links between your drawing and your database. This can be useful when you are preparing reports from your database application, because database applications are unaware of the number of links that occur to your drawing. Once you export link information, you can then incorporate that information into your report. The exported information lists the object handles and the associated linked database value. Here's a description of how the Export Link function works.

1. Click on the Export Objects button on the External Database palette, or type **Aseexport** ↵. You are then asked to select an object.

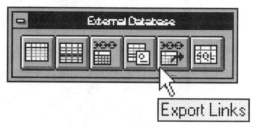

2. Select the objects that contain the links you wish to export. The Export Links dialog box appears.

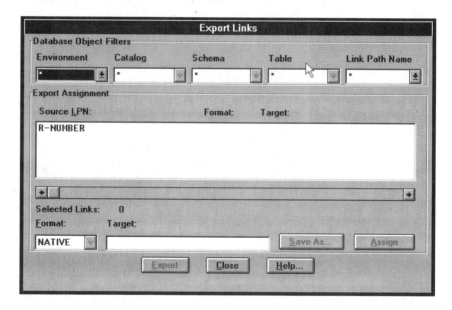

3. You can, at this point, reduce the scope of the link information you will export, by selecting a specific environment, catalog, schema, table, or link path name.

4. Select a link path name from the list box.

5. Select Native under the Format pull-down list, then enter a file name in the Target input box. This will be the name given to the table you want to create.

6. Click on Assign to assign the format and target to the link path name.

7. Choose Export to complete the export process.

You can export multiple link path names by repeating steps 3 through 6 before completing step 7.

USING SQL STATEMENTS

For those who are more familiar with SQL, AutoCAD offers a way that lets you access and manipulate database information with a greater degree of control. The SQL Editor can be accessed by clicking on the SQL Editor button on the External Database palette, or by typing **Asesqled** ⏎.

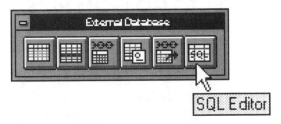

The SQL dialog box appears.

You can then enter a SQL statement in the edit box and click on Execute. Results of your query are displayed in the SQL Cursor dialog box.

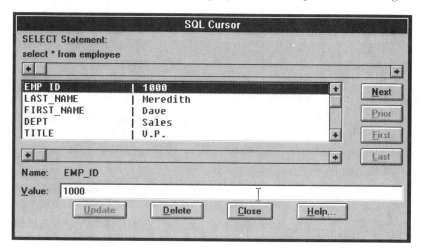

WHERE TO GO FROM HERE

You've seen how you can access and link your drawing to a database. I hope that in this brief tutorial, you can find the information you will need to develop your own database needs.

If you understand SQL, you can take advantage of it to perform more sophisticated searches. You can also expand the functionality of the basic ASE package included with AutoCAD. These topics are, unfortunately, beyond the scope of this book. For more detailed information about ASE and SQL, refer to the *AutoCAD SQL Extension* reference manual.

IF YOU WANT TO EXPERIMENT...

Attributes can be used to help automate data entry into drawings. To demonstrate this, try the following exercise.

Create a drawing file called **Record** with the attribute definitions shown in Figure 10.9. Note the size and placement of the attribute definitions as well as the new base point for the drawing. Save and exit the file, then create a new drawing called **Schedule** containing the schedule shown in Figure 10.10. Use the INSERT command and insert the Record file into the schedule at the point indicated. Note that you are prompted for each entry of the record. Enter any value you like for each prompt. When you are done, the information for one record is entered into the schedule.

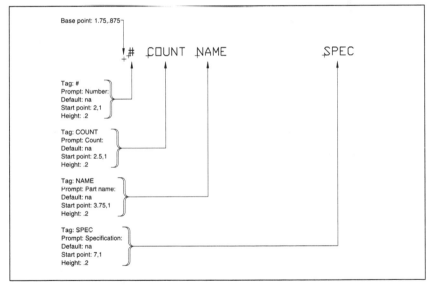

Figure 10.9: The Record file with attribute definitions

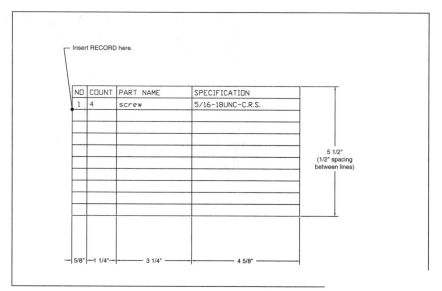

Figure 10.10: The Schedule drawing with Record inserted

11

▼ ▼ ▼ ▼ ▼

COPYING PREEXISTING DRAWINGS INTO AUTOCAD

Tracing a Drawing Using a Digitizer

Setting Up the Tablet for Digitizing

Cleaning Up the Digitized Drawing

Copying a Drawing Using a Scaling Technique

Scanning a Preexisting Drawing

Other Input Options

FAST TRACK

491 ▶ **To set up a drawing to be traced on a digitizer**

Secure the drawing on the digitizer. Enter **Tablet** ↵ **Cal** ↵ to calibrate the tablet. Then pick a known point on your drawing and enter its coordinates. Pick another point and enter its coordinates. Continue until you have selected all the points you want.

495 ▶ **To access the menus once you've calibrated your tablet**

Press F12 to toggle the tablet mode on and off.

496 ▶ **To trace a perspective view so it looks like an orthogonal one**

Secure the drawing or photograph on the digitizer. Enter **Tablet** ↵ **Cal** ↵ to calibrate the tablet. Calibrate the four corners of the facade. At the Orthogonal/Affine/Projective/<Repeat table> prompt, enter **P** ↵.

498 ▶ **To relocate a set of endpoints**

Turn on the Verb/Noun selection setting and the Grips feature. Select all the objects whose endpoints you want to relocate. Click on one grip, and then Shift-click on the rest of the grips you want to move. Click on one of the hot grips a second time, and stretch all the grips to their new location.

501 ▶ To straighten sets of lines

Turn on the ortho mode. Click and drag on the Resize button on the Modify palette, then select Point. Select the lines you want to straighten, and then click on a point indicating, roughly, their endpoint location.

507 ▶ To scale a drawing that contains curves without using a digitizer

Draw a grid in AutoCAD that conforms to the area of the drawing you intend to scale. Plot the grid; then overlay the grid onto the paper drawing. Locate key points on the grid, and transfer those points back into the grid drawing in AutoCAD.

511 ▶ To import a raster image into AutoCAD

Click on File ➤ Import to open the Import file dialog box. Choose PCX, GIF, or TIFF from the List files of Type drop-box, then select the file to be imported.

514 ▶ To import a PostScript image into AutoCAD

Click on File ➤ Import to open the Import file dialog box. Choose .EPS from the List Files of type drop-box, and select the file to be imported. Or enter **Psin** ↵ at the command prompt. Answer the prompts regarding insertion point, scale, and angle.

At times you will want to turn a hand-drafted drawing into an Auto-CAD drawing file. It may be that you are modifying a design you created before you started using AutoCAD, or that you are converting your entire library of drawings for future AutoCAD use. This chapter discusses three ways to enter a hand-drafted drawing: tracing, scaling, and scanning. Each of these methods of drawing input has its advantages and disadvantages.

Tracing with a digitizing tablet is the easiest method, but a traced drawing usually requires some cleaning up and reorganization. If dimensional accuracy is not too important, tracing is the best method for entering existing drawings into AutoCAD. It is especially useful for drawings that contain irregular curves, such as the contour lines of a topographical map.

Scaling a drawing is the most flexible method, since you don't need a tablet to do it and generally you are faced with less clean-up afterwards. Scaling also affords the most accurate input of orthogonal lines, because you can read dimensions directly from the drawing and enter those same dimensions into AutoCAD. The main drawback with scaling is that if the drawing does not contain complete dimensional information, you must constantly look at the hand-drafted drawing and measure distances with a scale. Also, irregular curves are difficult to scale accurately.

Of all the input methods, scanning produces a file that requires the most clean-up. In fact, you often spend more time cleaning up a scanned drawing than you would have spent tracing or scaling it. Even though some scanners can read straight text files, it is difficult to scan text in a drawing. Unfortunately, there is no easy way to transfer text from a hand-drafted drawing to an AutoCAD file. Scanning is best used for drawings that are difficult to trace or scale, such as complex topographical maps containing more contours than are practical to trace, or nontechnical line art.

TRACING A DRAWING

The most common and direct method for entering a hand-drafted drawing into AutoCAD is tracing. If you are working with a large drawing and you have a small tablet, you may have to cut the drawing into pieces

▼ TIP

Even if you don't plan to trace drawings into AutoCAD, be sure to read the tracing information anyway, because some of it will help you with your editing. For example, because traced lines often are not accurately placed, you will learn how to fix such lines in the course of cleaning up a traced drawing.

▼ NOTE

If you don't have a digitizing tablet, you can use scaling to enter the utility room drawing used in this section's tracing exercise. (You will insert the utility room into your apartment house plan in *Chapter 12*).

that your tablet can manage, trace each piece, and then assemble the completed pieces into the large drawing. The best solution is to have a large tablet to begin with, but many of us can't afford the five or ten thousand dollars these large-format tablets usually cost.

The following exercises are designed for an 11″×11″ or larger tablet. The sample drawings are small enough to fit completely on this size of tablet. You can use either a stylus or a puck to trace them, but the stylus will offer the most natural feel because it is shaped like a pen. A puck has crosshairs that you have to center on the line you want to trace, and this requires a bit more dexterity.

RECONFIGURING THE TABLET FOR TRACING

When you first installed AutoCAD, you configured the tablet to use most of its active drawing area for AutoCAD's menu template. Since you will need the tablet's entire drawing area to trace this drawing, you now need to reconfigure the tablet to eliminate the menu. Otherwise, you won't be able to pick points on the drawing outside the 4″×3″ screen pointing area AutoCAD normally uses (see Figure 11.1).

1. Start AutoCAD and open a new file called Utility.

2. Set up the file as a ¼″=1′–scale architectural drawing on an 8½×11″ sheet.

3. Choose Options ➤ Tablet ➤ Configure, or type **Tablet** ↵ **CFG** ↵.

4. At the Enter number of tablet menus desired (0-4): prompt, enter **0** ↵.

5. At the Do you want to respecify the screen pointing area? prompt, enter **Y** ↵.

6. At the Digitize lower left corner of Fixed screen pointing area: prompt, pick the lower-left corner of the tablet's active drawing area.

▼ TIP

You can save several different AutoCAD configurations that can be easily set at the DOS level by using batch files. See *Appendix B*.

▼ NOTE

When selecting points on the tablet, take care not to accidentally press the pick button twice, as this will give you erroneous results. Many tablets have sensitive pick buttons that can cause problems when you are selecting points.

▼ NOTE

On some tablets, a light appears to show you the active area; other tablets use a permanent mark, such as a corner mark. AutoCAD won't do anything until you have picked a point, so you don't have to worry about picking a point outside this area.

III

Becoming an Expert

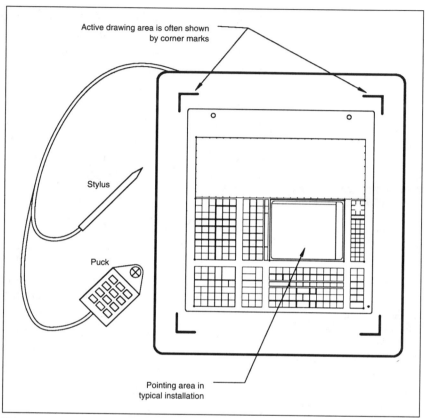

Figure 11.1: The tablet's active drawing area

7. At the Digitize upper right corner of screen pointing area: prompt, pick the upper-right corner.

8. At the Do you want to specify the Floating Screen pointing area prompt, press ⏎.

Now as you move your stylus or puck you will notice a difference in the relationship between your hand movement and the screen cursor. The cursor moves more slowly and it is active over more of the tablet surface.

CALIBRATING THE TABLET FOR YOUR DRAWING

Now make a photocopy of Figure 11.2, which represents a hand-drafted drawing of a utility room for your apartment building. Place the photocopied drawing on your tablet so that it is aligned with the tablet and completely within the tablet's active drawing area (see Figure 11.3).

Before you can trace anything into your computer, you must calibrate your tablet. This means you must give some points of reference so Auto-CAD can know how distances on the tablet relate to distances in the drawing editor. For example, you may want to trace a drawing that was drawn at a scale of $\frac{1}{8}''=1'-0''$. You will have to show AutoCAD two specific points on this drawing, as well as where those two points should

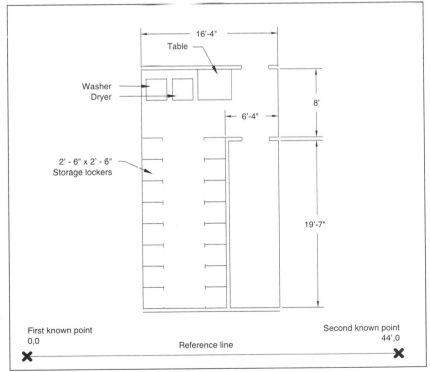

Figure 11.2: The utility room drawing

III

Becoming an Expert

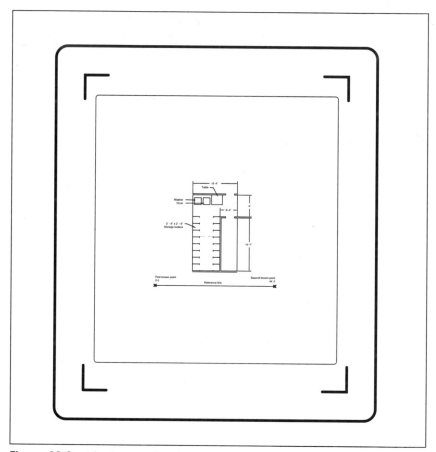

Figure 11.3: The drawing placed on the tablet

appear in the drawing editor. This is accomplished by using the TABLET command's Cal option.

In Figure 11.2, we have already determined the coordinates for two points on a reference line.

1. Choose Options ➤ Tablet ➤ Calibrate, or enter **Tablet** ↵ **Cal** ↵ at the command prompt.

2. The message "Calibrate tablet for use... Digitize first known point" appears, asking you to pick the first point for which

you know the absolute coordinates. Pick the X on the left end of the reference line.

3. At the Enter coordinates for first point: prompt, enter **0,0** ↵. This tells AutoCAD that the point you just picked is equivalent to the coordinate 0,0 in your drawing editor.

4. Next, the Digitize second known point: prompt asks you to pick another point for which you know the coordinates. Pick the X on the right end of the reference line.

5. At the Enter coordinates for second point: prompt, enter **44',0** ↵.

6. At the Digitize third known point (or RETURN to end): prompt, press ↵. The tablet is now calibrated.

The word Tablet appears on the status line to tell you that you are in tablet mode. While in tablet mode, you can trace the drawing but you cannot access the menus in Windows with some digitizers. (Check your digitizer manual for further information.) If you want to pick a menu item, you must toggle the tablet mode off by using the F12 function key. Or you can enter commands through the keyboard. (If you need some reminders of the keyboard commands, type **Help** ↵, and click on Commands from the Help dialog box to get a list.)

CALIBRATING MORE THAN TWO POINTS

In step 6 of the previous exercise, you bypassed the prompt that offered you the chance to calibrate a third point. In fact, you can calibrate as many as 31 points. Why would anyone want to calibrate so many points? Often the drawing or photograph you are trying to trace will be distorted in one direction or another. For example, blue-line prints are usually stretched in one direction because of the way prints are rolled through a print machine.

You can compensate for distortions by specifying several known points during your calibration. For example, we could have included a vertical distance on the utility room drawing to indicate a distance in the y-axis. You could have then picked that distance and calibrated its

III

Becoming an Expert

point. AutoCAD would then have a point of reference for the y distance as well as the x distance. If you calibrate only two points, as you did in the exercise, AutoCAD will scale x and y distances equally. Calibrating three points causes AutoCAD to scale x and y distances separately, making adjustments for each axis based on their respective calibration points.

Now suppose you want to trace a perspective view of a building, but you want to "flatten" the perspective so that all the lines are parallel. You can calibrate the four corners of the buildings facade to stretch out the narrow end of the perspective view to be parallel with the wide end. This is a limited form of what cartographers call "rubber-sheeting," where various areas of the tablet are stretched by specific scale factors.

When you select more than two points for calibration, you will get a message similar to that shown in Figure 11.4. Let's take a look at the parts of this message.

Across the top, you see the labels "Orthogonal," "Affine," and "Projective." These are the three major types of calibrations or Transformation types. The orthogonal transformation scales the x- and y-axes using the same values. Affine scales the x- and y-axes separately and requires at least three points. The projective transformation stretches the tablet coordinates differently, depending on where you are on the tablet. It requires at least four calibration points.

```
3 calibration points

Transformation type:            Orthogonal        Affine      Projective
--------------------------------------------------------------------------
Outcome of fit:                 Success           Exact       Impossible
RMS Error:                      0.0202
Standard deviation:             0.0042
Largest residual:               0.0247
At point:                             2
Second-largest residual:        0.0247
At point:                             3

Select transformation type...
Orthogonal/Affine/<Repeat table>:
```

Figure 11.4: AutoCAD's assessment of the calibration

Just below each label you will see either "Success," "Exact," or "Impossible." This tells you whether any of these transformation types are available to you. Since this example shows what you see when you pick three points, you get Impossible for the projective transformation.

The far-left column tells you what is shown in each of the other three columns.

Finally, the prompt at the bottom of the screen lets you select which transformation type to use. If you calibrate four or more points, the projective transformation is added to the prompt. The Repeat Table option simply refreshes the table.

Take care when you calibrate points on your tablet. Here are a few things to watch out for when calibrating your tablet:

- Use only known calibration points.

- Try to locate calibration points that cover a large area of your image.

- Don't get carried away—try to limit calibration points to only those necessary to get the job done.

TRACING LINES FROM A DRAWING

Now you are ready to trace the utility room. If you don't have a digitizer, you can skip this exercise. We've included a traced file on the companion CD that you can use for later exercises.

▼ **TIP**

Once a tablet has been calibrated, you can trace your drawing from the tablet, even if the area you are tracing is not displayed in the drawing editor.

1. Press the F12 function key, then click on the Line button on the Draw palette, or type **Line** ↵.

III

Becoming an Expert

2. Press the F12 function key again, then trace the outline of all the walls except the storage lockers.

3. Add the doors by inserting the Door file at the appropriate points and then mirroring them. The doors may not fit exactly, but you'll get a chance to make adjustments later.

4. Trace the washer and, since the washer and dryer are the same size, copy the washer over to the position of the dryer.

▼ NOTE

The raggedness of the door arc is the result of the way Auto-CAD displays arcs when you use the ZOOM command; see *Chapter 6* for details.

At this point, your drawing should look something like panel 1 of Figure 11.5—a close facsimile of the original drawing, but not as exact as you might like. Zoom in to one of the doors. Now you can see the inaccuracies of tracing. Some of the lines are crooked, and others don't meet at the right points. These inaccuracies are caused by the limited resolution of your tablet, coupled with the lack of steadiness in the human hand. The best digitizing tablets have an accuracy of 0.001 inch, which is actually not very good when you are dealing with tablet distances of $1/8''$ and smaller. In the following section, you will clean up your drawing.

CLEANING UP A TRACED DRAWING

In this section, you'll reposition a door jamb, straighten some lines, adjust a dimension, and add the storage lockers to the utility room.

In Figure 11.5, one of the door jambs is not in the right position (panel 2 gives you the best look). In this next exercise, you will fix this by repositioning a group of objects while keeping their vertices intact, using the Grips feature.

▼ NOTE

If you skipped the last exercise, open the 11trace.DWG file from the companion CD to do the next exercise.

1. With the Verb/Noun selection setting and the Grips feature both turned on, pick a crossing window enclosing the door jamb to be moved (see panel 1 of Figure 11.6).

2. Click on one of the grips at the end of the wall, and then Shift-click on the other grip. You should have two hot grips at the door jamb.

3. Click on the lower of the two hot grips, and drag the corner away to see what happens (see panel 2 of Figure 11.6).

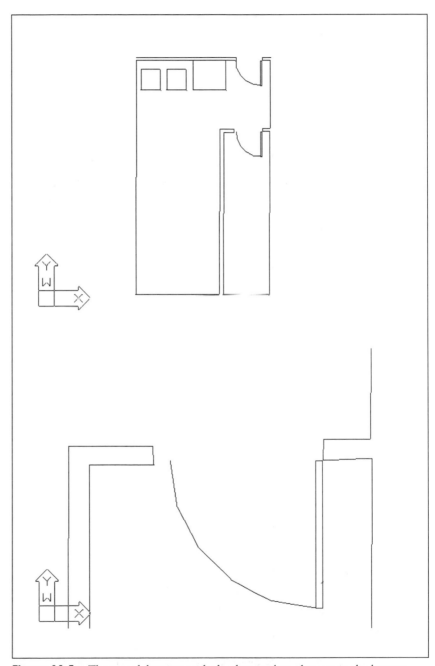

Figure 11.5: The traced drawing, with the door jamb in close-up in the bottom panel

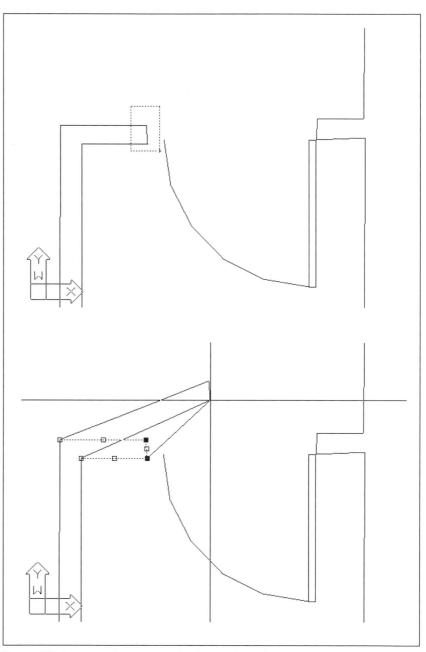

Figure 11.6: A window crossing the door jamb, and the door jamb being stretched (bottom panel)

4. Use the Endpoint Osnap override to pick the endpoint of the arc. The jamb repositions itself, and all the lines follow (see Figure 11.7).

Another problem in this drawing is that some of the lines are not orthogonal. To straighten them, use the Point option from the Resize flyout on the Modify palette or the CHANGE command, together with the ortho mode.

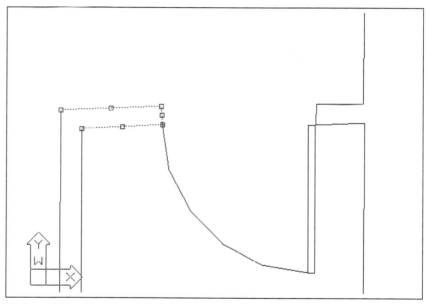

Figure 11.7:   The repositioned door jamb

1. Toggle the ortho mode on.

2. Press the F12 Function key, then click and drag the Resize button from the Modify palette, then select Point from the flyout. Or you can type **Change** ↵ at the command prompt to start this operation.

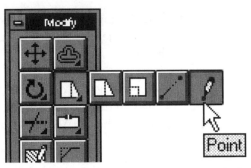

3. At the object-selection prompt, pick the two lines representing the wall just left of the door, and press ↵ to confirm your selection.

4. At the Properties/<Change point> prompt, use the Perpendicular Osnap override and pick the wall to the left of the lines you just selected. The two lines straighten out, and their endpoints align with the wall to the left of the two lines (see Figure 11.8).

▼ **WARNING**

The CHANGE command's Change Point option changes the location of the endpoint closest to the new point location. This can cause erroneous results when you are trying to modify groups of lines.

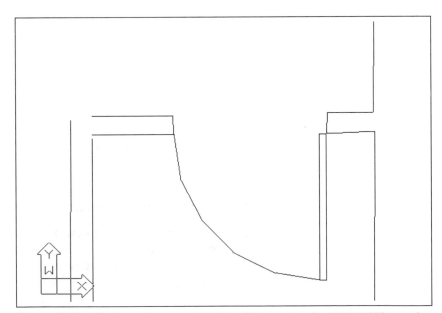

Figure 11.8: The lines after using the Resize/Point option (or CHANGE) is used

As you have just seen, you can use the Point option not only to straighten lines, but to make them meet another line at a perpendicular angle. This only works with the ortho mode on, however. To extend several lines to be perpendicular to a nonorthogonal line, you have to rotate the cursor to that line's angle (see panels 1 and 2 of Figure 11.9), using the Snapang system variable. (You can also use the Snap Angle input box in the Options ➤ Drawing Aids dialog box to rotate the cursor.) Then you use the process just described to extend or shorten the other lines (see panel 3 of Figure 11.9).

The overall interior dimension of the original utility room drawing is 16′–4″×28′–0″. Chances are the dimensions of the drawing you traced will vary somewhat from these.

1. Click and drag the Inquiry button on the Object Properties palette, then select Distance from the flyout to find your drawing's dimensions.

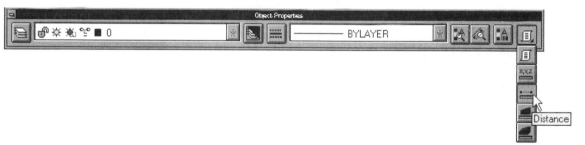

2. To adjust the walls to their proper positions (see Figure 11.11), either use the Grips feature, or click and drag the Resize button on the Modify palette, then select Stretch on the flyout.

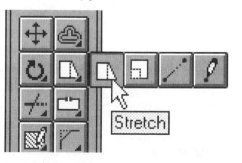

III

Becoming an Expert

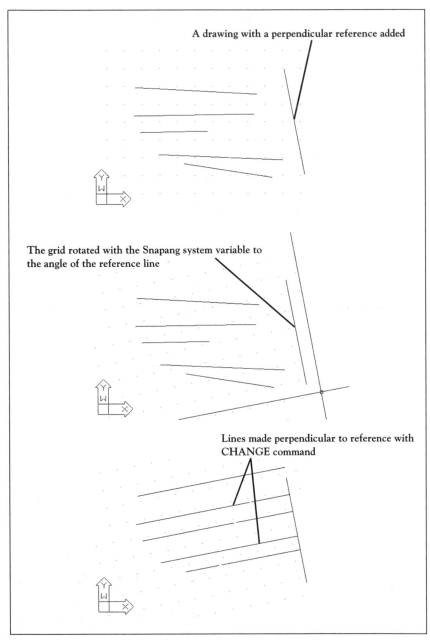

Figure 11.9:   How to change lines at an angle other than 0° or 90°

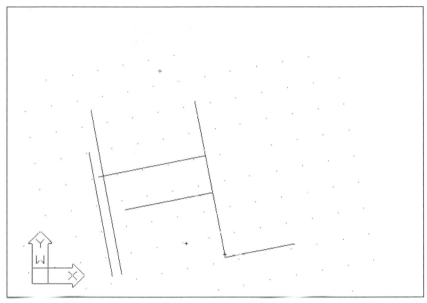

Figure 11.10:   Lines accidentally made perpendicular to the wrong point

When changing several lines to be perpendicular to another line, you must be careful not to select too many lines. If the overall width of the group of lines is greater than the distance between the ends of the lines and the line to which they will be perpendicular, some of the lines will not change properly (see Figure 11.10). Once the lines have been straightened out, you can use the FILLET command to make the corners meet.

3. Use the BASE ↵ command to make the base point the upper-left corner of the utility room, near coordinate 13′,30′.

4. To add the storage lockers, begin by drawing one locker accurately, using the dimensions provided on the traced drawing.

5. Use the MIRROR and ARRAY commands to create the other lockers. Both of these commands are available on the Modify palette. (For entering objects repeatedly, this is actually a faster and more accurate method than tracing. If you traced each locker, you would also have to clean up each one.)

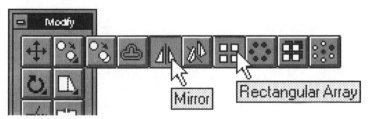

III

Becoming an Expert

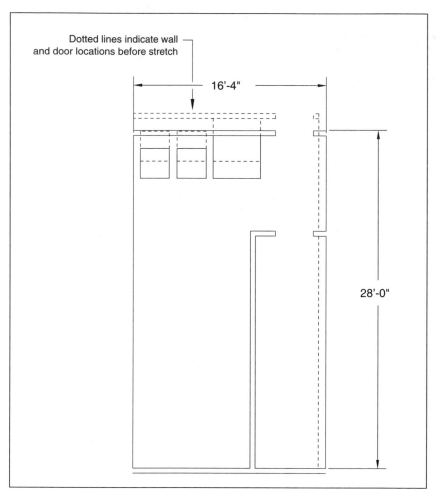

Figure 11.11:   The walls stretched to the proper dimensions

Finally, you may want to add the dimensions and labels shown earlier in Figure 11.2.

1. Create a layer called Notes to contain the dimensions and labels.

1. Create a layer called Notes to contain the dimensions and labels.

2. Set the Dimscale dimension setting to 48 before you start dimensioning. This can be done by clicking on Dimension Style from the Dimensioning palette, opening the Geometry dialog box, then entering 48 in the Overall Scale input box (see *Chapter 9* for details on this process).

3. Set the text height to 6″.

4. When you are done, save the file and exit AutoCAD.

> **▼ NOTE**
>
> You can also set the Dimscale dimension setting by typing **Dimscale** ↵ then entering the desired scale of 48.

WORKING SMARTER WITH DIGITIZERS

In the first exercise of this chapter, you traced the entire drawing; however, you could have just traced the major lines with the ortho mode on, and then use the OFFSET command to draw the wall thickness (Click and drag on the Copy objects button on the Modify palette, then select Offset). Fillet and Trim (see *Chapter 5*) could then be used to "clean up" the drawing where lines cross or where they don't meet.

> **▼ TIP**
>
> If you have only a small 12×12 format digitizer, but you need to digitize large drawings, consider hiring a finish carpenter to cut a hole in your table to accommodate the digitizer. You can then recess your digitizer into the table, so you can lay drawings flat over it.

If you are a civil engineer, you would take a different approach. In laying out a road, for instance, you might first trace in the center lines, then use the Offset option on the Modify palette to place the curb and gutter. You could trace curved features using arcs (just to see what the radius of the curve is), and then redraw the arc accurately, joining straight line segments. The digitizer can be a great tool if it is used with care and a touch of creativity.

SCALING A DRAWING

When a hand-drafted drawing is to scale, you can read the drawing's own dimensions or measure distances using an architect's or engineer's

III

Becoming an Expert

scale, and then enter the drawing into AutoCAD as you would a new drawing using these dimensions. Entering distances through the keyboard is slower than tracing, but you don't have to do as much clean-up because you are entering the drawing accurately.

When a drawing contains lots of curves, you'll have to resort to a different scaling method that is actually an old drafting technique for enlarging or reducing a drawing. First, draw a grid in AutoCAD to the same proportions as your hand-drafted drawing. Plot this grid on translucent media and place it over the drawing. Then place points in the AutoCAD grid file relating to points on the grid overlay that intersect with the hand-drafted drawing (see Figure 11.12). Once you have positioned these points in your AutoCAD file, you can connect them to form the drawing by using polylines. This method is somewhat time-consuming and not very accurate, so if you plan to enter many drawings containing curves, it's best to purchase a tablet and trace them, or consider scanning or using a scanning service.

SCANNING A DRAWING

No discussion of drawing input can be complete without mentioning scanners. Imagine how easy it would be to convert an existing library of drawings into AutoCAD drawing files by simply running them through a scanning device. Unfortunately, scanning drawings is not quite that simple.

In scanning, the drawing size can be a problem. Desktop scanners are generally limited to an $8^{1}/_{2} \times 14''$ sheet size. Many low-cost hand-held scanners will scan a $22'' \times 14''$ area. Larger-format scanners are available but more expensive; they can cost five thousand dollars or more.

Once the drawing is scanned and saved as a file, it must be converted into a file AutoCAD can use. This conversion process can be time consuming and requires special translation software. Finally, the drawing usually requires some clean-up, which can take even longer than cleaning up a traced drawing. The poorer the condition of the original drawing, the more clean-up you'll have to do.

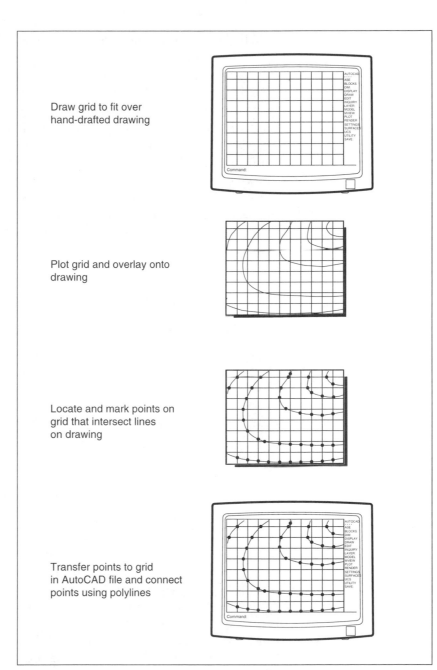

Figure 11.12: Using a grid to transfer a hand-drafted drawing that contains curves

Whether a scanner can help you depends on your application. If you have drawings that would be very difficult to trace—large, complex topographical maps, for example—a scanner may well be worth a look. You don't necessarily have to buy one; some scanning services offer excellent value. And if you can accept the quality of a scanned drawing before it is cleaned up, you can save a lot of time. On the other hand, a drawing composed mostly of orthogonal lines and notes may be more easily traced by hand with a large tablet or entered directly by using the drawing's dimensions.

Despite the drawbacks of scanning, it can be an excellent document management tool for your existing paper drawings. You might consider scanning your existing paper drawings for archiving purposes. You can then use portions or all of your scanned drawings later, without committing to a full-scale, paper-to-AutoCAD scan conversion.

▼ HYBRID SCANNING SYSTEMS

A few software products use scanner technology to let you place a grayscale scanned image behind your drawing. With one such product, *CAD Overlay* from Softdesk, you can view a scanned image as a background while in AutoCAD. A drawing is first scanned using any one of several popular scanners. The file generated by the scanner is then translated into a form that the CAD Overlay software can read. This file is imported into AutoCAD as a background that you can trace over for your final drawing. The background image always remains in place in relation to your AutoCAD drawing, even when you perform a pan or zoom.

The conversion from scanned image to background is considerably faster than from scanned image to an AutoCAD file, and you can build an intelligent drawing using the standard AutoCAD drawing entities. You usually have to do the work of converting a scanned drawing into an intelligent CAD drawing anyway, so products such as CAD Overlay offer a faster and more direct conversion method for many types of drawings. Or, if you need to, you can combine scanned images with AutoCAD drawing for output—for example, in civil applications where aerial photos are combined with roadway, site development, or parcel drawings.

IMPORTING AND TRACING RASTER IMAGES

If you have a scanner and you would like to use it to import drawings into AutoCAD, you can use AutoCAD's raster import capabilities. The File ➤ Import option in the pull-down menu opens the Import File dialog box which in turn allows you to import .TIF, .GIF, and .PCX files.

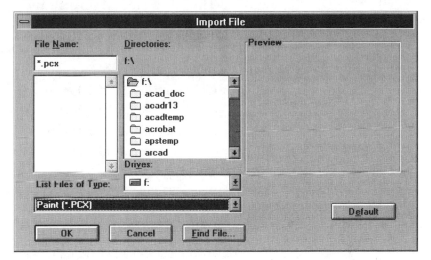

Use the List Files or Type pull-down list at the bottom of the dialog box to specify the file .TIF, .GIF or .PCX file name extension. Most scanners have facilities to store scanned images in at least one of these formats.

But before you get too excited, there are some definite drawbacks to the raster import commands. The biggest problem with importing scanned bitmap files is that the AutoCAD file to which you are importing becomes enormous. A simple $8\frac{1}{2} \times 11''$ line drawing scanned at 200 dpi can become a 2 MB AutoCAD file. Another issue is that some files simply won't import, for one technical reason or another. TIFF files are particularly troublesome because there are so many versions of TIFF in the marketplace.

If the drawing you want to scan is not too complicated and is a fairly clean drawing, then the raster import commands can be helpful. Following are step-by-step instructions on using raster import for tracing

III

Becoming an Expert

purposes, using a .PCX file as an example. If you have a .PCX file, you can try this. Or better yet, if you have a scanner (a hand-scanner will do) scan Figure 11.2 and try importing it.

1. At the command prompt, enter **Riedge** ⏎.

2. At the Raster input edge detection <0>: prompt, enter 1. This tells AutoCAD to draw the image into AutoCAD using the bounding edges of filled areas.

3. Select File ➤ Import, or enter **Import** ⏎ ⏎ to open the Import File dialog box.

4. Click on Paint (*.PCX) in the List Files of Type pull-down list, then select the PCX file you want to import.

5. Click on OK. AutoCAD will seem to pause as it works to convert the .PCX file into an AutoCAD image.

6. At the Insertion point prompt, you'll notice a square at the cursor. This is a schematic representation of the imported image, intended to help you place it. Pick a point for the lower-left corner of the image.

7. At the Scale factor prompt, you can enter a scale or use the cursor to indicate the size you want the image to be. (You can scale it again more accurately later if you need to.) Once you select a scale factor, the image will gradually appear on your screen.

The method for importing .TIF and .GIF images is the same as for .PCX files, but rather than selecting .PCX from the List File or Type drop-down list in step 4, you would select .TIF or .GIF. Then you may browse and select the appropriate file to import

Once the image is in, you can use it as a background to trace over, and then discard the image when you are done. As mentioned earlier, the file size is greatly increased when importing raster images. You will have to try it out to see how large a file your system can tolerate.

In addition, there are several system variables that let you control how the image gets translated. One of these system variables, Riedge (used in the foregoing exercise), is useful for importing line drawings. Here are descriptions of these settings:

Riaspect allows you to modify the aspect ratio of imported .TIF and .GIF files. For example, if you are importing a 320×200-mode .GIF file from 3D Studio or Autodesk Animator, you may want to set Riaspect to 0.8333.

Ribackg controls the background color of the imported image. The default background color is 0. If your background is another color, change Ribackg's setting to match that color number.

Riedge controls the detection of boundary edges between colors in an image. Turn this feature on (set it to 1) when you want to import an image for tracing. Leave it at the default setting (0) for importing full images for viewing.

Rigamut controls the number of colors used when importing images. The default is 256, but you can set it to 16 or 8 to reduce the size of the imported image or to make the image conform to your display limitations.

Rigrey allows you to import an image in shades of gray. The default setting is off (0). AutoCAD has a limited palette of grays, so you can turn on Rigrey when you want to reduce the size of the imported image.

Rithresh controls what gets translated into AutoCAD based on a brightness threshold. The default setting is off (0). The raster import commands use higher values to determine what level of brightness to accept for translation into the AutoCAD file. The higher the value, the brighter the import threshold.

III

Becoming an Expert

You will have to experiment with these settings to determine which is best for your needs. Here are a few points you should consider if you plan to use raster import for tracing drawings:

- Scan in your drawing using a grayscale scanner, or convert your black-and-white scanned image to grayscale using your scanner software.

- Use a paint program or your scanner software to clean up unwanted gray or spotted areas in the file before importing into AutoCAD.

- If your scanner software or paint program has a de-speckle or de-spot routine, use it. It can help clean up your image and ultimately reduce AutoCAD file size and import time.

- Scan at a reasonable resolution. Remember that the human hand is usually not more accurate than a few thousandths of an inch, so scanning at 150 to 200 dpi may be sufficient.

- If you plan to make heavy use of raster import, upgrade your computer to the fastest processor you can afford and don't spare the memory.

If you can get past some of the annoying features of raster importing, you'll find it a tool that is indispensable for some applications. In addition to tracing scanned drawings, the raster import commands can incorporate paper maps or plans into 3D AutoCAD drawings for presentations. We know of one architectural firm that produces some very impressive presentations with very little effort, by combining 2D scanned images with 3D massing models for urban design studies. If you have the memory capacity, you can include raster images on 3D surfaces to simulate storefronts, people, or other surface features.

IMPORTING POSTSCRIPT IMAGES

In addition to raster import, you can use the built-in PostScript import feature to import PostScript files. This feature can be accessed by clicking on File ➤ Import or by typing **Import** ↵ ↵. The Import File dialog box lets you easily locate the file to be imported. Select Encapsulated PostScript (.EPS) from the List Files of Type pull-down list, then browse to find the file you want. Once you select a file, the rest of the program works just like the raster import commands. You are asked for an insertion point, a scale, and a rotation angle. Once you've answered all the prompts, the image appears in the drawing.

You can make adjustments to the quality of imported PostScript files by using the Psquality system variable (accessed via File ➤ Options ➤ PostScript Quality, or by typing **Psquality** ↵). This setting takes an integer value in the range −75 to 75, with 75 being the default. The absolute value of this setting is taken as the ratio of pixels to drawing units. If, for example, Psquality is set to 50 or −50, then Psin will convert 50 pixels of the incoming PostScript file into 1 drawing unit. You use negative values to indicate that you want outlines of filled areas rather than the full painted image. Using outlines can save drawing space and improve readability on monochrome systems or systems with limited color capability.

Finally, if Psquality is set to 0, only the bounding box of the imported image is displayed in the drawing. Though you may only see a box, the image data is still incorporated into the drawing and will be maintained as the image is exported (using Psout).

Another system variable you will want to know about is Psdrag, which controls how the imported PostScript image appears at the insertion point prompt. Normally, Psdrag is set to 0, so Psin displays just the outline (bounding box) of the imported file as you move it into position. To display the full image of the imported PostScript file as you locate an insertion point, you can set Psdrag to 1. Access Psdrag from the pull-down menus by choosing File ➤ Options ➤ PostScript Display.

IF YOU WANT TO EXPERIMENT...

If you want to see firsthand how the PostScript import and export commands work, you can try the following exercise:

1. Open the Plan file.

2. Then choose File ➤ Export to open the Export Data dialog box. Select Encapsulated PostScript (.EPS) in the List files of

III

Becoming an Expert

Type pull-down list. You can also type **Psout** ↵ at the command line. This will open the Create PostScript File dialog box and allow you to select or enter a file name.

3. Click on OK to accept the suggested PostScript file name of Plan.EPS.

4. At the What to plot -- Display, Extents, Limits, View, Window,<D> prompt, press ↵ to accept the default of Display. You will then get the next series of prompts; press ↵ at all of these prompts to accept the following defaults:

   Include a screen preview image in the file?
   (None/EPSI/TIFF) <None>:
   Size units (Inches or Millimeters) <Inches>:
   Specify scale by entering:
   Output Inches=Drawing Units or Fit or ? <Fit>:
   Standard values for output size
   Size Width Height
   (a list of sizes are shown here)
   Enter the Size or Width,Height (in Inches) <USER>:

5. AutoCAD will begin to write the PostScript file. When the plot is complete, close the Plan file and open a new file. It can be an unnamed file.

6. Click on File ➤ Import to open the Import File dialog box.

7. Select encapsulated PostScript in the List Files of Type pull-down list. Locate the Plot file you just created and double-click on it. The file appears in your drawing. You will be prompted for Insertion point and Scale factor. Position and size the image as required.

▼ TIP

You may notice that arcs, circles and curves are not very smooth when you use this method to export, then import PostScript files. To improve the appearance of arcs and curves, specify a large sheet size at the Enter the Size or Width,Height (in Inches) <USER>: prompt.

12

POWER EDITING

Taking Advantage of Previous Work

Using Grips: Some Examples

Understanding the Entity Sort Methods
Available

Using Cross-Reference Files (Xrefs)

Using Paper Space

Using Viewports

Selecting Specific Types of Objects
Using the Filter Tools

Finding Drawing Locations Using the
Calculator

FAST TRACK

521 ► To copy a set of lines using the Grips feature

Select the lines, Shift-click on the midpoint grips, click again on one of the hot grips, type **C** ↵, and enter a relative coordinate for the location of the copies.

536 ► To rotate an object using Grips

Select the object or objects, click on a grip point close to the rotation point, press ↵ twice, and then enter a rotation angle or indicate an angle using the cursor.

538 ► To scale an object using Grips

Select the object or objects, click on a grip point close to a scale center point, press ↵ three times, and then enter a scale factor or indicate a new scale using the cursor.

541 ► To select an object that is overlapped by another

Hold the Ctrl key down while clicking on the object. If the wrong object is highlighted, click again. The next object will highlight. If there are several objects overlapping, continue to click until the desired object is selected.

547 ► To open the External Reference Palette

Choose Tools ➤ Toolbars ➤ External Reference.

547 ► To insert an Xref drawing

Click on Attach from the External Reference palette. At the dialog box, locate the file you wish to cross-reference and double-click on it. Answer the prompts for insertion point, scale, and angle.

552 ▶ To import a named element (layer or block) from an Xref

Click and drag on All from the External Reference palette then select the type of element you want to import from the flyout menu. Enter the name of the element, including the file name prefix.

555 ▶ To enter Paper Space

Click on View ➤ Paper Space to place a check mark on this menu item, or type **Tilemode** ↵ **0** ↵.

556 ▶ To create a Paper Space viewport

While in Paper Space, click on View ➤ Floating Viewports; then select the type or number of desired viewports. You can also type **Mview** ↵ while in Paper Space and then answer the prompts.

560 ▶ To return to Model Space

Click on View ➤ Tiled Model Space to place the check mark on this menu item, or type **Tilemode** ↵ **1** ↵.

561 ▶ To accurately scale a view in a Paper Space viewport

While in paper space, enter **MS** ↵, click on the viewport to be set, type **Zoom** ↵, and then type the inverse of the desired scale factor of the view, followed by **XP**. For example, for a ¼″=1′ scale view, you would enter **1/48XP**.

565 ▶ To freeze a layer in a particular viewport

While in paper space, enter **MS** ↵, click on the viewport to be set, and then click on Data ➤ Layers.... Click on the layer you wish to freeze. Then click on the FRZ button across from the Cur PV: label.

Because you may not know all of a project's requirements when it begins, you usually base the first draft of a design on projected needs. As the plan goes forward, you make adjustments for new requirements as they arise. As more people enter the project, additional design restrictions come into play and the design is further modified. This process continues throughout the project, from first draft to final product.

In this chapter you will review much of what you've already learned. In the process, you will look at some techniques for setting up drawings to help manage the continual changes a project undergoes. You will also discover some steps you can take to minimize duplication of work. AutoCAD can be a powerful timesaving tool if used properly. In this chapter, we'll examine methods of harnessing that power.

EDITING MORE EFFICIENTLY

The apartment building plan you've been working on is currently incomplete. For example, you need to add the utility room you created in *Chapter 11*. In the real world, this building plan would also undergo innumerable changes as it was developed. Wall and door locations would change, and more notes and dimensions would be added. In the space of this book's tutorials, we can't develop these drawings to full completion. However, we can give you a sample of what is in store while using AutoCAD on such a project.

In this section, you will add a closet to the Unit plan (you will update the Plan file later in this chapter). In the editing you've already done, you've probably found that you use certain commands frequently: Move, Offset, Fillet, Trim, Grips, and the Osnap overrides. Now you will learn some ways to shorten your editing time by using them more efficiently.

▼
■
■
■
■

QUICK ACCESS TO YOUR FAVORITE COMMANDS

As you continue to work with AutoCAD, you'll find that you use a handful of commands 90% of the time. You can collect your favorite commands in a single palette using AutoCAD's palette customization feature. This way, you can have ready access to your most frequently used commands.

In addition, if you find yourself using one particular flyout menu over and over, you can easily turn it into a stand-alone floating palette for quick access. *Chapter 21* gives you all the information you need to open flyouts as floating palettes and create your own custom palette.

EDITING AN EXISTING DRAWING

First, let's look at how you can add a closet to the unit plan. You'll begin by copying existing objects to provide the basis for the closet.

1. Open the Unit plan, and freeze the Notes and Flr-pat layers. This will keep your drawing clear of objects you won't be editing.

2. If they are not already on, turn on Noun/Verb Selection and the Grips feature.

3. Click on the right side wall, and then on its midpoint grip.

4. Enter **C** ⏎ to start the Copy mode; then enter **@2'<180** (see Figure 12.1).

5. Zoom in to the entry area.

III

Becoming an Expert

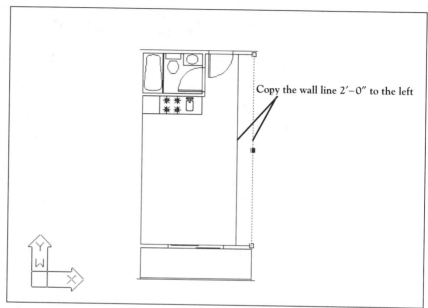

Copy the wall line 2'–0" to the left

Figure 12.1: Where to copy the wall to start the closet

6. Issue the **Offset** command (click and drag Copy from the draw palette then select Offset). At the Offset *distance or through* prompt, use the Nearest Osnap override and pick the outside wall of the bathroom near the door, as shown in Figure 12.2.

7. At the *Second point:* prompt, use the Perpendicular Osnap override and pick the other side of that wall (see Figure 12.2).

8. Click on the copy of the wall line you just created, and then on a point to the left of it.

In steps 7 and 8 above, you determined the offset distance by selecting existing geometry. If you know you want to duplicate a distance, but don't know what that distance is, you can often use existing objects as references.

Next, use the same idea to copy a few more lines for the other side of the closet.

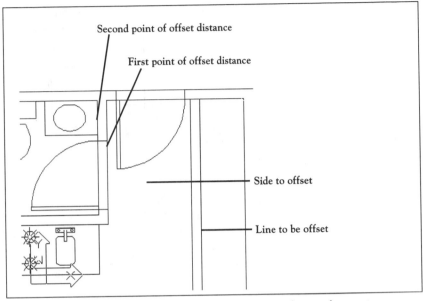

Figure 12.2: How to use an existing wall as a distance reference for copying

1. Zoom back to see the kitchenette in your screen view.

2. Click to highlight the two lines that make up the wall at the top of your view.

3. Shift-click on the midpoint grips of these lines (see Figure 12.3).

4. Click again on one of the midpoint grips, and then enter **C** ↵ to select the Copy option.

5. Enter **B** ↵ to select a base point option.

6. Use the upper-right corner of the bathroom for the base point, and the lower-right corner of the kitchenette as the second point.

Now you've got the general layout of the closet. The next step is to clean up the corners. First, you'll have to do a bit of prep work and break the wall lines near the wall intersections, as shown in Figure 12.4.

III

Becoming an Expert

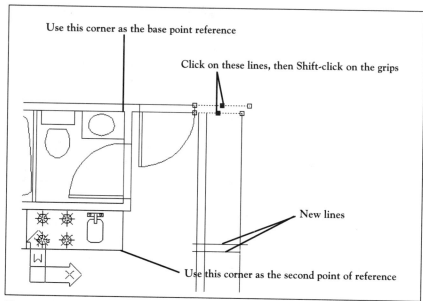

Figure 12.3: Adding the second closet wall

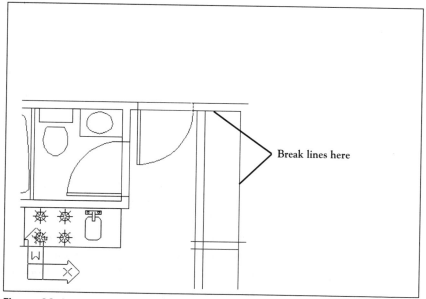

Figure 12.4: Where to break the wall lines

1. Click on 1 Point from the Modify palette. This tool breaks a line at a point on the object

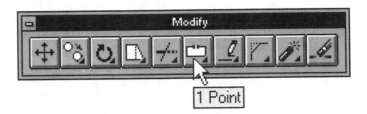

2. Click on the vertical wall to the far right at a point near the location of the new wall (see Figure 12.4).

3. Click on 1 Point again; then click on the horizontal line just below the topmost line on the screen (see Figure 12.4).

4. Click and drag Chamfer from the modify palette, then select Fillet, or type **Fillet** ↵ to join the wall lines that don't meet (see Figure 12.5).

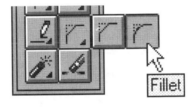

▼ NOTE

When you click on an object in steps 2 and 3, nothing seems to happen. Since the lines are broken at a point, no gap appears, so you really can't see any change—but the lines are, in fact, broken into two line segments. The 1 Point Select option on the 1 Point fly-out performs the same function as the 1 Point option but also allows you to select the break point with more accuracy.

In steps 2 and 3, you didn't have to be too exact about where to pick the break points, because Construct ➤ Fillet takes care of joining the wall lines exactly. Now you are ready to add the finishing touches.

1. At the closet door location, draw a line from the midpoint of the interior closet wall to the exterior (see Figure 12.6). Make sure this line is on the Jamb layer.

2. Offset the new line 3' in both directions. These new lines are the closet door jambs.

Becoming an Expert

III

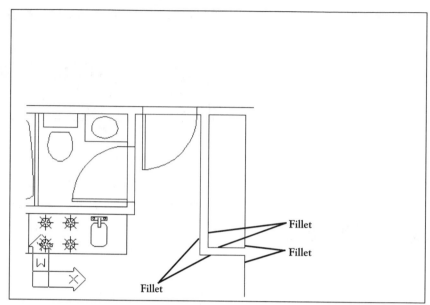

Figure 12.5: Where to fillet the corners

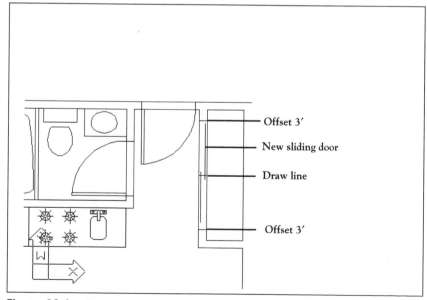

Figure 12.6: Constructing the closet door jambs

3. Click on Trim from the Modify palette, then click on the two jambs, and then press ↵.

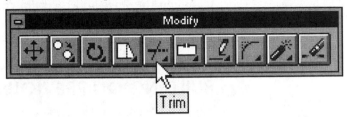

4. Click on the two vertical lines between the jambs.

5. Add door headers and the sliding doors as shown in Figure 12.7.

6. Use File ➤ Save to save the file.

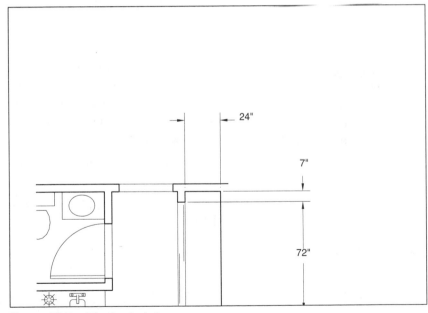

Figure 12.7: The finished closet

Sometimes it's easier to trim lines back and then draw them back in, as in steps 4 and 5 above. At first this may seem counterproductive, but trimming the lines and then drawing in headers actually takes fewer steps and is a less tedious operation than some other routes. And the end result is a door that is exactly centered on the closet space.

BUILDING ON PREVIOUSLY DRAWN OBJECTS

Suppose your client decides your apartment building design needs a few one-bedroom units. In this exercise, you'll use the studio unit drawing as a basis for the one-bedroom unit. To do so, you'll double the studio's size, add a bedroom, move the kitchenette, rearrange and add closets, and move the entry doors. In the process of editing this new drawing, you will see how you can build on previously drawn objects.

Start by setting up the new file. As you work through this exercise, you'll be using commands that you've seen in previous exercises, so we won't bother describing every detail. But do pay attention to the process taking place, as shown in Figures 12.8 through 12.12.

> **▼ NOTE**
>
> Although you could be more selective in step 4 about the objects you erase, and then add line segments where there are gaps in walls, this is considered bad form. When editing files, it's wise to keep lines continuous rather than fragmented. Adding line segments increases the size of the drawing database and slows down editing operations.

1. Open a new file called **Unit2** and use the Unit file as a prototype. (Reminder: To use another drawing as a prototype, click on the Prototype… button in the Create New Drawing dialog box, and then use the Prototype Drawing File dialog box to locate the prototype drawing.)

2. Later you will move the kitchenette, so erase its floor pattern.

3. MOVE the dimension string at the right of the unit, 14′–5″ further to the right, and copy the unit the same distance to the right. Your drawing should look like Figure 12.8.

4. Now erase the bathroom, kitchenette, door, closet, and wall lines, as shown in Figure 12.9.

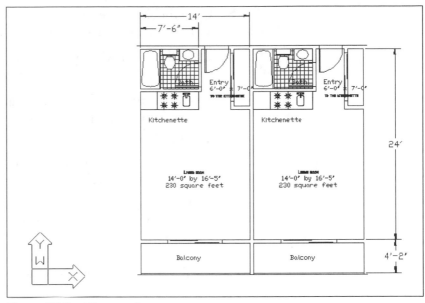

Figure 12.8: The copied unit

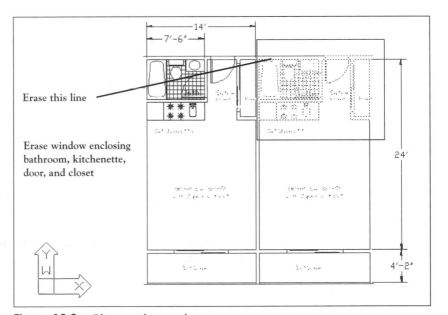

Figure 12.9: Objects to be erased

5. Copy the short interior wall of the closet to the right about 4′, to replace that side of the wall (see Figure 12.10).

6. Use Fillet in the Modify palette to join and extend walls where they have been broken (see Figure 12.10).

7. Extend the topmost line so its endpoint is 5″ beyond the right interior wall line. (You've already done this once before in *Chapter 5*.)

8. MOVE the kitchenette to the opposite corner of the unit, as shown in Figure 12.11.

9. MOVE the remaining closet down 5′–5″, as shown in Figure 12.12. You can use the corners of the bathroom as reference points.

Next, you'll work on finishing the new bedroom door and entry.

1. Zoom in to the area that includes the closet and the two doors.

2. Copy the existing entry door downward, including header and jambs (see Figure 12.13).

3. Clean up the walls by adding new lines and filleting others, as shown in Figure 12.14.

4. Mirror the door you just copied so it swings in the opposite direction.

5. Use STRETCH (click on Stretch from the Modify palette) to move the entry door from its current location to near the kitchenette, as shown in Figure 12.15.

6. Once you've moved the entry door, mirror it in the same way you mirrored the other door.

In the foregoing exercise, you once again used parts of the drawing instead of creating new parts. In only a few instances are you adding new objects.

▼ TIP

Use the midpoint of the door header as the first axis endpoint.

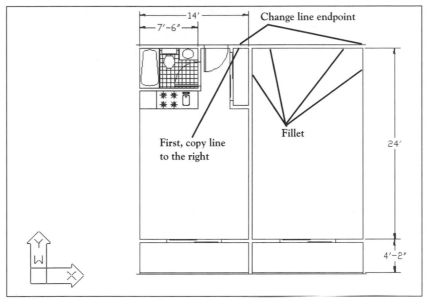

Figure 12.10:   Replacing erased walls

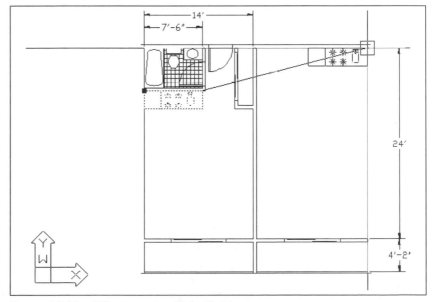

Figure 12.11:   Where to move the kitchenette

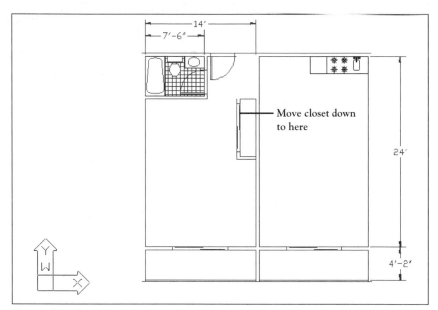

Figure 12.12: The closet's new location

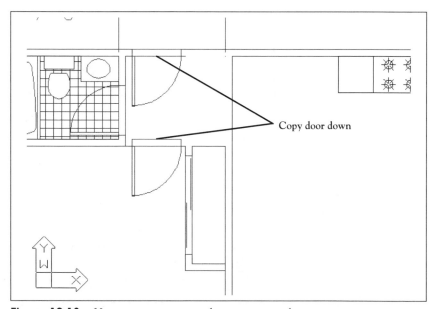

Figure 12.13: How to use an existing door to create a door opening

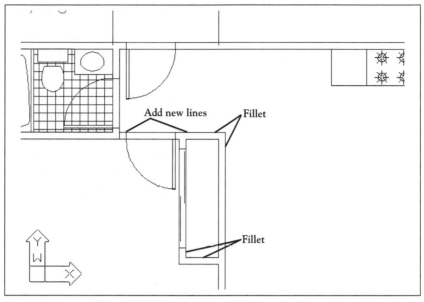

Figure 12.14:   Cleaning up the walls

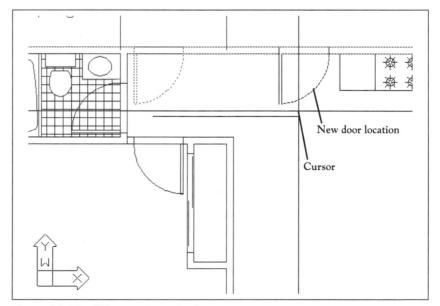

Figure 12.15:   Where to move the door

III

Becoming an Expert

1. Now set the view of your drawing so it looks similar to Figure 12.16.

2. Click and drag Trim from the Modify palette then select Extend, or type **Extend** ↵ at the command prompt.

3. At the Select boundary edge(s)... Select object: prompt, pick the wall at the bottom of the screen, as shown in Figure 12.16, and press ↵. Just as with Trim, Extend requires that you first select a set of objects to define the boundary of the extension, and then select the objects you wish to extend.

4. At the Select object to extend: prompt, you need to pick the two lines just below the closet door. To do this, first enter **F** ↵ to use the Fence selection option.

5. At the First Fence point prompt, pick a point just to the left of the lines you want to extend.

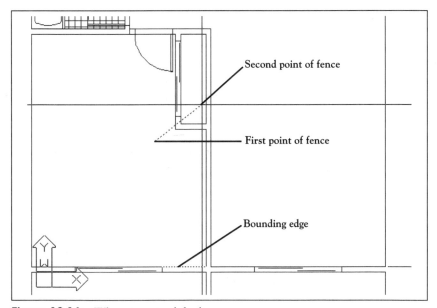

Figure 12.16: Where to extend the lines

6. At the Undo/<Endpoint of line> prompt, pick a point to the right of the two lines, so the fence crosses over them (see Figure 12.6).

7. Press ↵. The two lines extend to the wall.

8. Use a combination of Trim and Fillet to clean up the places where the walls meet.

9. Add another closet door on the right side of the new closet space you just created. Your drawing should look like Figure 12.17.

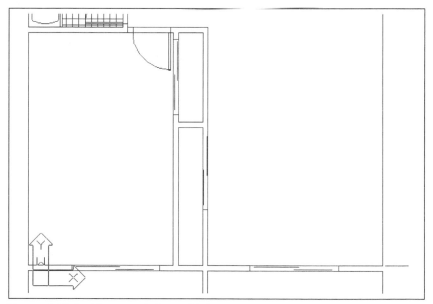

Figure 12.17: The second closet added

USING GRIPS TO SIMPLIFY EDITING

Now suppose you want to change the location and orientation of the kitchenette. You will use the Grips feature to do just that.

1. Set up a view similar to the one in Figure 12.18.

2. Click on the kitchenette.

3. Click on the grip in the upper-left corner to make it a hot grip. The grip changes from hollow to solid.

4. Press the ↵ key two times until you see the *** ROTATE *** message at the prompt.

5. Enter –90.

6. Click on the kitchenette's grip again; then, using the End-point Osnap override, click on the upper-right corner of the room. Your drawing should look like Figure 12.19.

▼ TIP

Remember that the Spacebar acts the same as the ↵ key for most commands, including the Grips... modes.

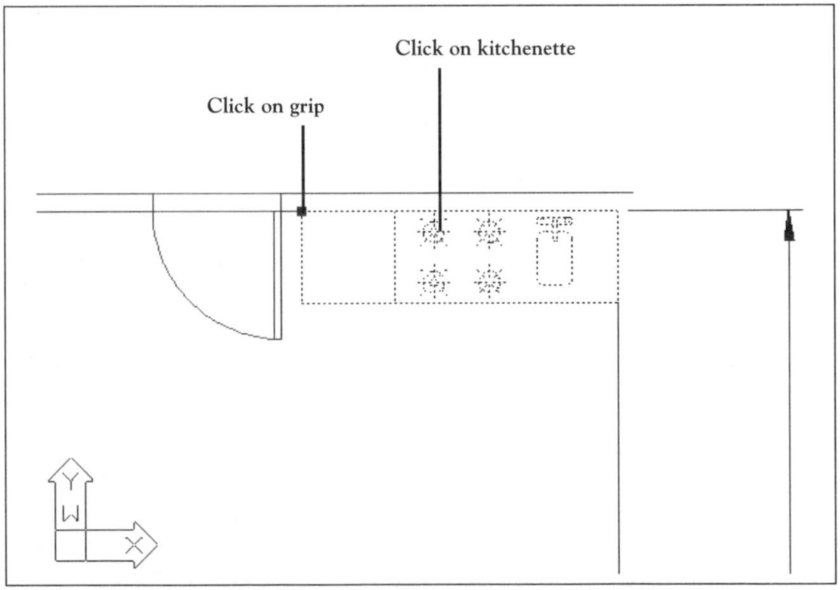

Click on kitchenette

Click on grip

Figure 12.18: The rotation base point

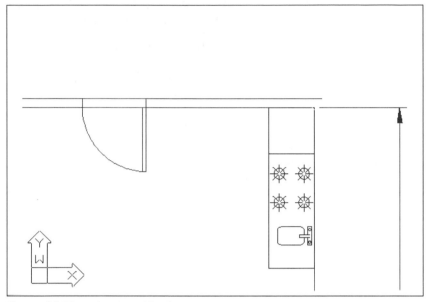

Figure 12.19:   The revised kitchenette

Since the kitchenette is a block, its grip point is the same as its insertion point. This makes the kitchenette block—as it does all blocks—a great candidate for grip editing. Remember that the door, too, is a block.

Now suppose you want to widen the entrance door from 36″ to 42″. Try the following exercise involving a door and its surrounding wall.

1. Use a crossing window to select the door jamb.

2. Shift-click on both of the door jamb's grips.

3. Click on one of the grips again. It is now a hot grip.

4. At the ** Stretch ** prompt, enter **@6<180**. The door should now look like Figure 12.20.

Notice that in step 4 you don't have to specify a base point to stretch the grips. AutoCAD assumes the base to be the original location of the selected hot grip.

III

Becoming an Expert

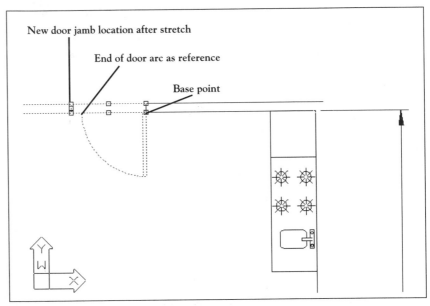

Figure 12.20: The widened door opening

Now you can enlarge the door using the GRIPS command's Scale mode. Scale allows you to change the size of an object or a group of objects. You can change the size visually, by entering a scale value, or by using an object for reference. In this exercise, you will use the current door width as a reference.

1. Press the Escape key to clear your selection set.

2. Click on the door, and then on the door's grip point.

3. Press ⏎ three times to get to the Scale mode.

4. At the <Scale factor>/Base point/Copy/Undo/Reference/eXit: prompt, enter **R** ⏎ to select the Reference option.

5. At the Reference length <0'-1">: prompt, click on the door's grip point.

6. At the Second point: prompt, click on the endpoint of the door's arc at the wall line. As you move the cursor, the door changes in size relative to the distance between the grip and the end of the arc.

7. At the <New length>/Base point/Copy/Undo/Reference/eXit: prompt, use the Endpoint Osnap override and click on the door jamb directly to the left of the arc endpoint. The door enlarges to fit the new door opening (see Figure 12.21).

8. Save the file.

You could have used the Scale option on the stretch flyout of the Modify palette to accomplish the operation performed in the above exercise with the Scale hot-grip command. The advantage to using grips is that you don't need to use the Osnap overrides to select exact grip locations, thereby reducing the number of steps you must take to accomplish this task.

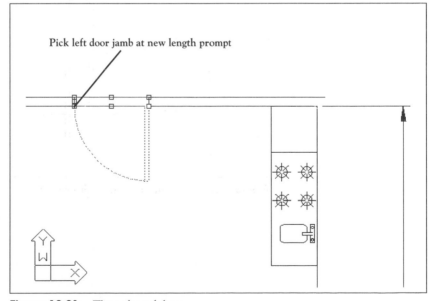

Figure 12.21: The enlarged door

In the next section, you will update the Plan file to include the revised studio apartment and the one-bedroom unit you have just created (see Figure 12.22). You will be making changes such as these throughout the later stages of your design project. As you have seen, AutoCAD's ability to make changes easily and quickly can ease your work and help you test your design ideas more accurately.

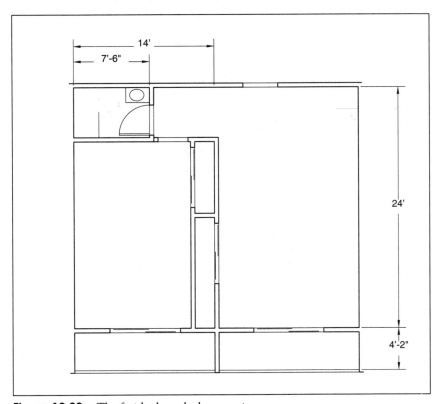

Figure 12.22: The finished one-bedroom unit

SINGLING OUT PROXIMATE OBJECTS

In *Chapter 3*, we mentioned that you will encounter situations where you need to select an object that is overlapping or very close to another object. In Release 12 of AutoCAD, this was a difficult task; you had no control over what would be selected when you clicked on two overlapping objects.

Selection Cycling

Release 13 comes with a feature that eliminates the hassle of selecting overlapping objects. *Selection cycling* lets you cycle through objects that overlap until you select the one you want. To use this feature, simply hold down the Ctrl key while clicking on an object. If the first object highlighted is not the one you want, click again. When several objects are overlapping, just keep clicking until the right object is highlighted and selected.

Object Sorting

If you are a veteran AutoCAD user, you may have grown accustomed to clicking on the most recently created object of two overlapping objects. Unfortunately, with Release 12, AutoCAD changed the method of selecting overlapping objects so that you didn't always get to the most recently drawn object. Now, with Release 13, you can make a simple setting change and revert to the old selection method. This setting is buried in the Object Selection Settings dialog box, as a subdialog box called Object Sort Method. To get there, click on Options ➤ Selection... and then click on the Object Sort Method... button.

Object Sort Method

Sort Objects for

☐ **O**bject Selection

☐ Object **S**nap

☐ **R**edraws

☐ S**l**ide Creation

☐ Re**g**ens

☒ **P**lotting

☒ PostS**c**ript Output

[**OK**] [Cancel]

III

Becoming an Expert

This dialog box lets you set the sort method for a variety of operations. If you enable any of the operations listed, AutoCAD will use the pre-Release 12 sort method for that operation. You will probably not want to change the sort method for object snaps or regens. But by checking Object Selection, you can control which of two overlapping lines are selected when you click on them. For plotting and for PostScript output, you can control the overlay of screened or hatched areas.

These settings can also be controlled through system variables. See *Appendix D* for details.

USING CROSS-REFERENCES (XREFS)

We mentioned in *Chapter* 6 that careful use of blocks, cross-references, and layers can help you improve your productivity. In this section you will see firsthand how to use these elements to help reduce design errors and speed up delivery of an accurate set of drawings. You do this by controlling layers in conjunction with blocks and cross-referenced files (Xrefs) to create a common drawing database for several drawings.

PREPARING EXISTING DRAWINGS FOR CROSS-REFERENCING

▼ NOTE

If you prefer, you can skip this exercise. For the later exercises that call for the elements created here you can use the Plan, Col-gr, Floor1, Floor2, and Common files (supplied on the companion disk).

In *Chapter* 6 we discussed using the Freeze option of the Layer Control dialog box to control layers. Think of layers as being z-coordinate locations in your drawing. For example, you can create a layer for each of the three floors of your apartment building and then insert the Unit blocks on the appropriate layers. A fourth layer can contain the blocks common to all the floors, such as the lobby, stairs, utility room, and some of the units (see Figure 12.23). To display or plot a particular floor, you freeze all the layers except that floor and the layer containing the common information. The following exercise shows you how to do all of this.

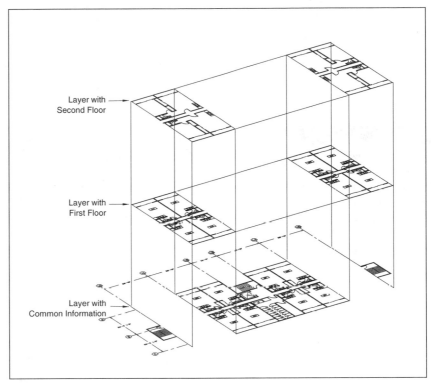

Figure 12.23: A 3D representation of layers

1. Open the Plan file.

2. Create a layer called **Gridline,** and add the grid and dimension information shown in Figure 12.24.

3. Use Properties from the toolbar and assign a Center line type to the gridlines. This is a typical center-line composed of a long line, then a short dash, then another long line, usually used to denote the center of an object—in this case, a wall. Be sure Ltscale is set to 96 (click on Options ➤ Linetypes ➤ Global Linetype Scale, and specify 96).

III

Becoming an Expert

▼ NOTE

Gridline and related dimensions are used in architectural drawings as a system to establish references from which accurate dimensions can be taken. They are usually based on key structural elements, such as columns and foundation wall locations.

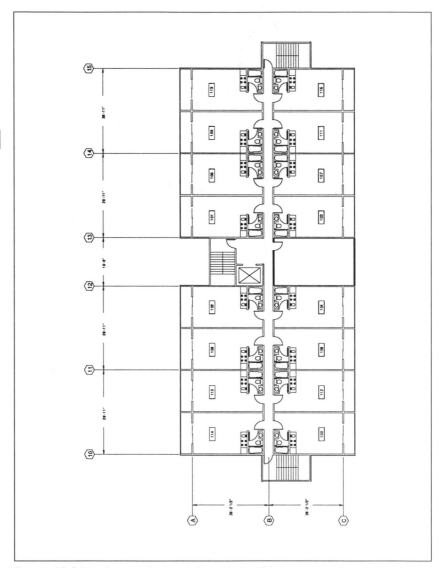

Figure 12.24: The overall plan with grid lines added

4. Use the WBLOCK command (File ➤ Export) to write the gridlines and other grid information to a file named **Col-gr.DWG**. Remember to enter the full name including the .DWG extension. Use the drawing origin, 0,0, for the insertion base point.

5. Use the WBLOCK command again, and write the eight units in the corners of your plan to a file called **Floor1.DWG** (see Figure 12.25). When you select objects for the WBLOCK, be sure to include the door symbols for those units. Use 0,0 again for the WBLOCK insertion base point.

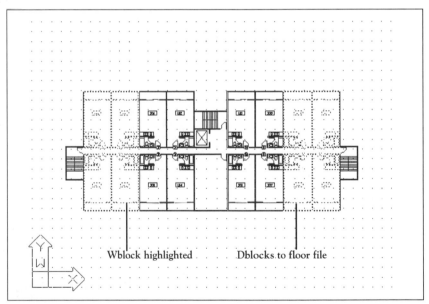

Figure 12.25:   Units to be exported to the Floor1 file

III

Becoming an Expert

6. Using Figure 12.26 as a guide, insert Unit2 into the corners where the other eight units previously appeared.

7. Once you've accurately placed the corner units, use the WBLOCK command to write these corner units to a file called **Floor2.DWG**. Again, use the 0,0 coordinate as the insertion base point for the WBLOCK.

8. Now use the WBLOCK command to turn the remaining set of unit plans into a file called **Common.DWG**. Remember that you can select everything in the drawing by entering **ALL** ↵ at the Select objects prompt.

You've just created four files: Col-gr, Floor1, Floor2, and Common. Each of these files contains unique information about the building. Next, you'll use the XREF command to re-combine these files for the different floor plans in your building.

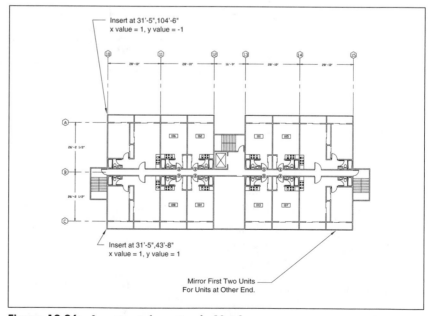

Figure 12.26: Insertion information for Unit2

ASSEMBLING CROSS-REFERENCES TO BUILD A DRAWING

Next, you will create composite files for each floor, using cross-references of only the files needed for the individual floors. You will use the Attach option of the XREF command to insert all the files you exported from the Plan file.

1. Close the Plan file (don't save the changes) and open a new file called **Xref-1**.

2. Set up this file as an architectural drawing 18″×24″ with a scale of $\frac{1}{8}$″=1′.

3. Use options ➤ Linetypes ➤ Global Linetype scale to set LTSCALE to 96.

4. Open the External Reference tool palette by choosing Tools ➤ Toolbars ➤ External Reference.

5. Click on Attach from the External Reference toolbar.

The Select File to Attach dialog box appears.

6. Double-click on the COMMON.DWG file name.

7. At the Insertion point prompt, enter **0,0** ↵.

8. Press ↵ at the x and y Scale factor prompts and the rotation angle prompt.

9. Repeat the Attach option to insert the Floor1 file and the Col-gr file. You now have the plan for the first floor.

10. Save this file.

III

Becoming an Expert

11. Create a new file called **Xref-2**. Repeat steps 2 through 9 (you won't have to repeat step 4), but in step 9, insert the Floor2 file, instead. This new file represents the plan for the second floor.

12. Save this file.

Now when you need to make changes to Xref-1 or Xref-2, you can edit the individual cross-referenced files that they comprise. Then, the next time you open either Xref-1 or Xref-2, the updated Xrefs will automatically appear in their most recent forms.

Cross-references need not be permanent. You can attach and detach them easily at any time. This means, if you need to get information from another file—to see how well an elevator core aligns, for example—you can temporarily cross-reference the other file to quickly check alignments, and then detach it when you are done.

Think of these composite files as final plot files that are only used for plotting and reviewing. Editing can then be performed on the smaller, more manageable cross-referenced files. Figure 12.27 diagrams the relationship of these files.

The combinations of cross-references are limited only by your imagination, but avoid multiple cross-references of the same file.

Updating Blocks in Cross-References

There are several advantages to using cross-referenced files. Since the cross-references don't become part of the drawing file's database, these composite files remain quite small. Also, because cross-referenced files are easily updated, work can be split up among several people in a workgroup environment or on a network. One person can be editing the Common file while another works on Floor1, and so on. The next time the composite file is opened, it will automatically reflect any new changes made in the cross-referenced files. Now let's see how to set this up.

1. Open the Common file and, once the drawing starts to appear, press the Esc key to stop the drawing regeneration. Don't be alarmed if only part of the drawing appears on the screen; the drawing is still there.

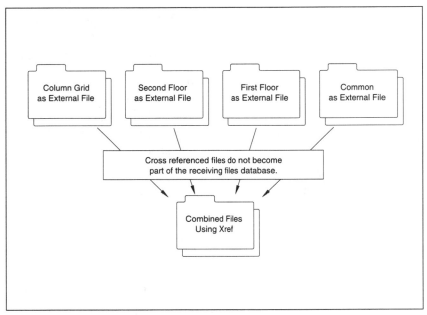

Figure 12.27: Diagram of cross-referenced file relationships

2. Now you need to update the Unit plan you edited earlier in this chapter. Click on Insert Block from the Draw palette.

3. At the Insert dialog box, click on the File button and click on the UNIT file name. Then click on OK here, and again in the Insert dialog box.

4. At the warning message, click on OK.

5. At the Insertion point: prompt, press Esc.

III

Becoming an Expert

6. Enter **Regen** ⏎ to regenerate the drawing. You will see the new Unit plan in place of the old one (see Figure 12.28). You will also see all the dimensions and notes for each unit.

7. Open the Layer Control pop-up list in the Object Properties toolbar and locate the Notes layer. Click on the Freeze/Thaw icon (it looks like a sun) to freeze this layer and keep the notes from interfering with the drawing. The Sun icon turns into a snowflake icon showing you that the layer is now frozen.

8. Click in the drawing area to close the list. Your drawing should now look like Figure 12.29.

9. Using Insert Block in the Draw palette again, replace the empty room across the hall from the lobby, with the utility room you created in *Chapter 11* (see Figure 12.30). If you didn't create the utility room drawing, use the Util.DWG file from the companion disk.

10. Save the Common file.

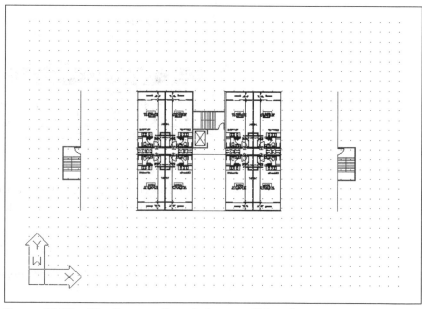

Figure 12.28:   The Common file with the revised Unit plan

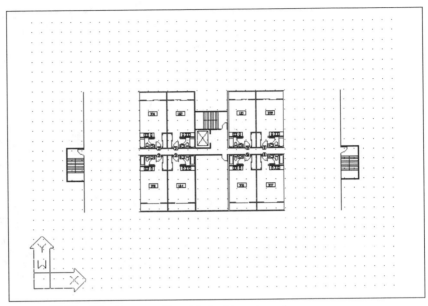

Figure 12.29:   The Common file with the Notes layer frozen

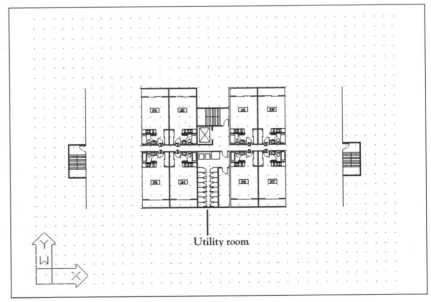

Figure 12.30:   The utility room installed

11. Now open the Xref-1 file. You will see the utility room and the typical units in their new form. Your drawing should look like Figure 12.31.

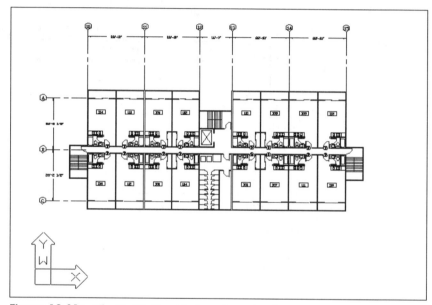

Figure 12.31: The Xref-1 file with the units updated

▼ TIP

You can set the Visretain system variable to 1 to force AutoCAD to remember layer settings of cross-referenced files (see *Appendix E* for details). You can also use the Lrestore.LSP AutoLISP utility, supplied on the companion disk and discussed in *Appendix C*, to re

IMPORTING NAMED ELEMENTS FROM CROSS-REFERENCES

In *Chapter 5*, we discussed how layers, blocks, line types, and text styles—called *named elements*—are imported along with a file that is inserted into another. Cross-referenced (Xref) files, on the other hand, do not import named elements. You can, however, review their names and use a special command to import the ones you want to use in the current file. AutoCAD renames named elements from Xref files by giving them the prefix of the file name from which they come. For example, the Wall layer in the Floor1 file will be called Floor1 | wall in the Xref-1 file;

the Toilet block will be called Floor1 | toilet. You cannot draw on the layer Floor | wall, nor can you insert Floor1 | toilet; but you can view cross-referenced layers in the Layer Control dialog box, and you can view cross-referenced blocks using the Insert dialog box.

Next you'll look at how AutoCAD identifies layers and blocks in cross-referenced files, and you'll get a chance to import a layer from an Xref.

▼ NOTE

You can also open the Layer Control pop-up list to view the layer names.

1. While in the Xref-1 file, click on Data ➤ Layers. Notice that the names of the layers from the cross-referenced files are all prefixed with the file name and the | vertical bar character. Exit the Layer dialog box.

2. Click and drag on All from the External Reference palette then select Layer, or enter **Xbind** ↵ **LA** ↵.

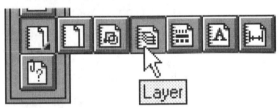

3. At the Dependent Layer Name(s): prompt, enter **Floor1 | Wall** ↵. You then see the next message, Scanning... 1 Layer(s) bound. You have now imported the Wall layer from the Floor1 file. However, AutoCAD maintains the imported layer's uniqueness by giving it another name.

4. Click on Data ➤ Layers again.

5. Scroll down the list of layer names until you get to the ones that start with the Floor1 prefix. Notice that Floor1 | wall no longer exists. In its place is a layer called Floor1$0$wall.

As you can see, when you use XBIND to import a named item, such as the Floor1 | wall layer, the vertical bar (|) is replaced by two dollar signs surrounding a number, which is usually zero. (If for some reason the imported layer name Floor1$0$wall already exists, then the zero in that name is changed to 1, as in *Floor1$1$wall*.) Other named items are also renamed in the same way, using the 0 replacement for the vertical bar.

III

Becoming an Expert

NESTING CROSS-REFERENCES AND USING OVERLAYS

Cross-references can be nested. For example, the COMMON.DWG file created in this chapter might use the UNIT.DWG file as a cross-reference rather than an inserted block, and you would still get the same result in the Xref-1.DWG file. That is, you would see the entire floor plan, including the unit plans, when you open Xref-1.DWG. In this situation, UNIT.DWG is nested in the COMMON.DWG file, which is in turn cross-referenced in the Xref-1.DWG file.

Though nested Xrefs can be helpful, there will be times when you won't want this to occur. For example, you might cross-reference the COMMON.DWG file into the Floor1.DWG file as a means of referencing walls and other features of the COMMON.DWG file. You might also reference the COMMON.DWG file into the Floor2.DWG file for the same reason. Once you do this, however, you will have three versions of the Common plan in the Xref-1.DWG file, since each Xref now has COMMON.DWG attached to it. And because AutoCAD would dutifully load COMMON.DWG three times, Xref-1.DWG would occupy substantial computer memory, slowing your computer down when you edit the Xref-1.DWG file.

To avoid this problem, you can use the Overlay option on the External Refernce palette (**Xref↵ 0↵**). An Overlayed cross-reference cannot be nested. For example, even if you Overlayed the COMMON.DWG file into the Floor1.DWG and Floor2.DWG files, the nested COMMON.DWG file would be ignored when you opened the Xref-1.DWG file, thereby eliminating the redundant occurrence of COMMON.DWG. In another example, if you Overlayed the UNIT.DWG file into the COMMON.DWG file and then XREF'd COMMON.DWG into Xref-1.DWG, you would not see the unit plan in Xref-1.DWG. The nested UNIT.DWG drawing would be ignored (see Figure 12.32).

SWITCHING TO PAPER SPACE

Your set of drawings for this studio apartment building would probably include a larger-scale, more detailed drawing of the typical unit plan. You already have the beginnings of this drawing in the form of the Unit file.

As you have seen, the notes and dimensions you entered into the Unit file can be frozen in the Plan file so they don't interfere with the graphics of the drawing. The Unit file can be part of another drawing file that contains more detailed information on the typical unit plan at a larger scale. To this new drawing you can add other notes, symbols, and dimensions. Whenever the Unit file is altered, you update its occurrence in the large-scale drawing of the typical unit as well as in the Plan file (see Figure 12.32). The units are thus quickly updated, and good correspondence is ensured among all the drawings for your project.

Now suppose that you want to combine drawings having different scales in the same drawing file—for example, the overall plan of one floor plus an enlarged view of one typical unit. This can be accomplished by using the Paper Space mode first discussed in *Chapter 6*. First, let's see how to get into Paper Space.

Your gateway to Paper Space is the setting of the Tilemode system variable. When Tilemode is set to 1 (On), the default setting, you

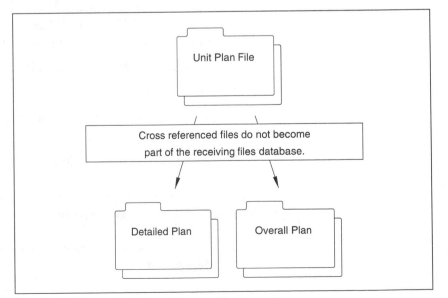

Figure 12.32:   Relationship of drawing files in a project

cannot enter Paper Space; when it is set to 0 (Off), you can freely move from Paper Space to Model Space.

1. If it isn't already open, open the Xref-1 file, making sure your display shows all of the drawing.

2. Click on View ➤ Paper Space, or enter **Tilemode** ↵ **0** ↵. Your screen goes blank and your UCS icon changes to a triangular shape. Also note the word PAPER in the status bar; this tells you at a glance that you are in Paper Space.

The new UCS icon tells you that you are in Paper Space. But where did your drawing go? Before you can view it, you must create the windows, or *viewports*, that let you see into Model Space. But before you do that, let's explore Paper Space.

1. Click on Data ➤ Drawing Limits or enter **Limits** ↵ at the command prompt. Then note the default value for the lower-left corner of the Paper Space limits. It is 0'–0", 0'–0".

2. Press ↵ and note the current default value for the upper-right corner of the limits. It is 1'–0", 9", which is the standard default for a new drawing. This tells us that the new Paper Space area is 12" wide by 9" high—an area quite different from the one you set up originally in this drawing.

3. Click on Data ➤ Drawing Limits again.

4. At the ON/OFF: prompt, press ↵.

5. At the upper-right corner: prompt, enter **42,30** ↵ to designate an area that is 42"×30".

6. Click on View ➤ Zoom ➤ All.

Now you have your Paper Space set up. The next step is to create viewports so you can begin to paste up your views.

7. Click on View ➤ Floating Viewports ➤ 3 Viewports, or type **Mview** ↵ **3**.

8. At the Horizontal/Vertical/Above/Below/Left/<Right>: prompt, enter **A** ↵ for Above. This option creates one large viewport along the top half of the screen, with two smaller viewports along the bottom.

9. At the Fit/<first point>: prompt, enter **F** ↵ for the Fit option. Three rectangles appear in the formation shown in Figure 12.33. Each of these is a viewport to your Model Space.

Now you need to get access to the viewports in order to display and edit your drawing.

10. Click on View ➤ Floating Model Space. This gives you control over Model Space. (You can also enter **MS** ↵ as a keyboard shortcut to entering Model Space mode.)

11. Be sure the top viewport is the current one (if not, click on it); then click on View ➤ Zoom ➤ Extents. The view enlarges to fill in the current active viewport.

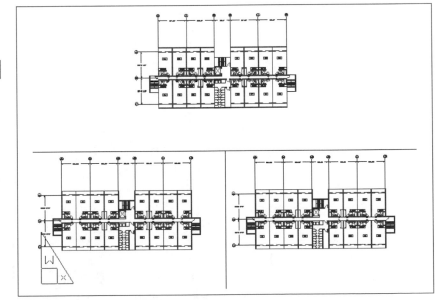

Figure 12.33: The newly created viewports

12. Click on the lower-left viewport to activate it.

13. Click on View ➤ Zoom ➤ Window and select the elevator area.

14. Click on the lower-right viewport and use View ➤ Zoom ➤ Window to enlarge your view of a typical unit.

When you use View ➤ Floating Model Space to move into Model Space mode, the UCS icon again changes shape—instead of one triangular-shaped icon, you have three arrow-shaped ones, one for each viewport on the screen. Also, as you move your cursor into the currently active viewport, the cursor changes from an arrow into the usual crosshair. Another way to tell which viewport is the active one is by its double border.

You can move from viewport to viewport even while you are in the middle of most commands. For example, you can issue the LINE command, then pick the start point in one viewport, then go to a different viewport to pick the next point, and so on. To activate a different viewport, you simply click on it (see Figure 12.34).

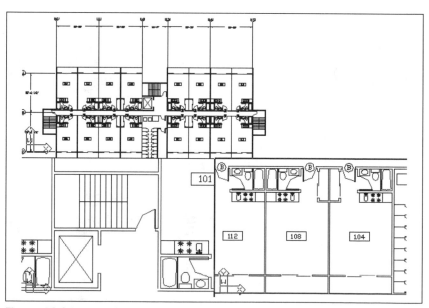

Figure 12.34: The three viewports with the plan in view

▼

■

■

■

■

USING MVSETUP
TO SET UP PAPER SPACE

If you prefer, you can use a feature that automates the Paper Space setup. The AutoLISP utility called MVSetup automatically establishes viewports in paper space and offers a set of title blocks. The following describes MVSetup and how to use it.

1. Click on View ➤ Paper Space to switch to Paper Space. (You can also set the Tilemode system variable to 0 to switch to Paper Space.)

2. Click on View ➤ Floating Viewports ➤ MV Setup, or type **Mvsetup** ↵. You see the following prompt:

   Align/Create/Scale viewports/Options/Title block/Undo:

Here are descriptions of the Paper Space options:

Align lets you align features of one viewport to those of another, or rotate a viewport view.

Create lets you create a set of viewports by choosing from a set of predefined viewport layouts.

Scale viewports lets you set the view scale of each viewport individually or globally.

Options lets you adjust several preferences for the MVsetup utility, such as default limits, default layers for title blocks, units, and whether title blocks are inserted or cross-referenced.

Title Block inserts a title block from a set of predefined title blocks. You can add your own custom title blocks to this set.

Undo undoes the last MVsetup option you selected.

III

Becoming an Expert

GETTING BACK TO MODEL SPACE

Once you've created viewports, you can then reenter Model Space through the viewport using View ➤ Floating Model Space. But what if you want to quickly get back into the old full-screen Model Space you were in before you entered Paper Space? The following exercise demonstrates how this is done.

1. Click on View ➤ Tiled Model Space, or enter **Tilemode** ↵ **1** ↵. Your drawing returns to the original full-screen view—everything is back to normal.

2. Click on View ➤ Paper Space, or enter **Tilemode** ↵ **0** ↵. You are back in Paper Space. Notice that all the viewports are still there when you return to Paper Space. Once you've set up Paper Space, it remains part of the drawing until you delete all the viewports.

You may prefer doing most of your drawing in Model Space and using Paper Space for setting up views for plotting. Since viewports are retained, you won't lose anything when you go back to Model Space to edit your drawing.

WORKING WITH PAPER SPACE VIEWPORTS

Paper Space is intended as a page-layout or composition tool. You can manipulate viewports' sizes, scale their view independently of one another, and even set layering and line-type scale independently. Let's try manipulating the shape and location of viewports, using the MODIFY command options.

1. Click on View ➤ Paper Space and get back into the Paper Space mode. (You can also enter **PS** ↵ as a keyboard shortcut to return to Paper Space mode.)

2. Click on Stretch from the Modify palette and stretch the two viewport corners, as shown in Figure 12.35. Notice how the view within each viewport changes.

▼ **TIP**

You can also click on the viewport frames and then stretch their corners using their grips. A viewport remains rectangular even when you try to stretch only one corner of it.

3. Click on Erase from the Modify Palette, then click on the frame of the lower-right viewport.

4. Use the MOVE command to move the lower-left viewport to a new position, as shown in Figure 12.35.

Viewports are actually objects, so they can be manipulated by all the editing commands just like any other object. In the foregoing exercise you moved, stretched, and erased viewports. Next, you'll see how layers affect viewports.

1. Create a new layer called **Vport**.

2. Use Properties button on the toolbar to change the viewport borders to the Vport layer.

3. Finally, turn off the Vport layer. The viewport borders will disappear.

A viewport's border can be assigned a layer, color, or line type. If you put the viewport's border on a layer that has been turned off, that border will become invisible, just like any other object on such a layer. Making the borders invisible is helpful when you want to compose a final sheet for plotting. Even when turned off, the active viewport will show a heavy border around it to simplify editing, and all the viewports will still display their views.

SCALING VIEWS IN PAPER SPACE

▼ NOTE

While in Paper Space, you cannot edit objects in Model Space, and vice versa. You must use View ➤ Floating Model Space and View ➤ Paper Space to move from one mode to the other. Paper Space and Model Space each have separate scales, just as they have separate objects.

Paper Space has its own unit of measure. You have already seen how you can set the limits of Paper Space independently of Model Space. When you first enter Paper Space, regardless of the area your drawing occupies in Model Space, you are given limits that are 12 units wide by 9 units high. This may seem incongruous at first, but if you keep in mind that Paper Space is like a paste-up area, then this difference of scale becomes easier to comprehend. Just as you might paste up photographs and maps representing several square miles onto an 11″×17″ board, so can you use paper Space to paste up views of scale drawings representing city blocks or houses.

III

Becoming an Expert

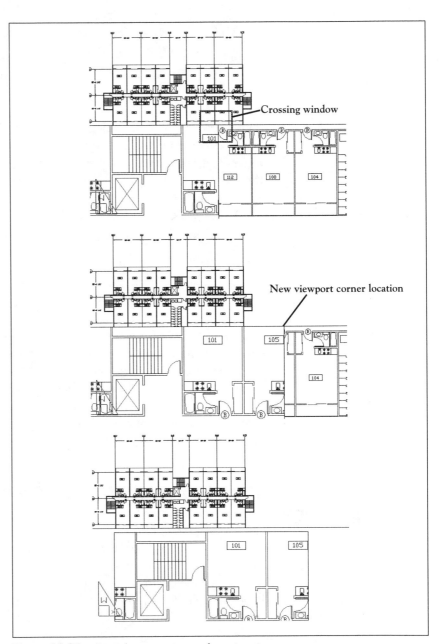

Figure 12.35: Stretching, erasing, and moving viewports

You must carefully consider scale factors when composing your Paper Space paste-up. Let's see how to put together a sheet in Paper Space and still maintain accuracy of scale.

1. Click on View ➤ Floating Model Space or enter **MS** ↵ to return to Model Space.

2. Click on the top view to activate it.

3. Pan the view so that the plan is centered in the viewport (see Figure 12.36).

4. Click on View ➤ Zoom ➤ Scale or enter **Zoom** ↵ (or **Z** ↵).

5. At the All/Center/Dynamic/Extents... prompt, enter **1/96xp** ↵. The **xp** suffix appended to the **1/96** tells Auto-CAD that the current view should be scaled to $\frac{1}{96}$ of the Paper Space scale. You get the **1/96** simply by taking the inverse of the drawing's scale factor, 96.

6. Click on the lower viewport.

7. Pan the view so that two of the typical units are centered in the viewport (see Figure 12.36).

8. Choose View ➤ Zoom ➤ Scale again, and enter **1/24xp** ↵ at the All/Center/Dynamic prompt. Your view of the unit will be scaled to $\frac{1}{4}''=1'$ in relation to Paper Space.

It's easy to adjust the width, height, and location of the viewports so that they display only the parts of the unit you want to see; just go back to the Paper Space mode and use the STRETCH, MOVE, or SCALE commands. The view within the viewport itself will remain at the same scale and location, while the viewport changes in size. You can use these commands on a viewport with no effect on the size and location of the objects within the view.

You can also overlap viewports. Use the Osnap overrides to select geometry within each viewport, even while in Paper Space. This allows you to align one viewport on top of another at exact locations.

You can also add a title block at a 1:1 scale to frame your viewports, and then plot this drawing while still in Paper Space at a scale of 1:1. Your plot will appear just as it does in Paper Space.

III

Becoming an Expert

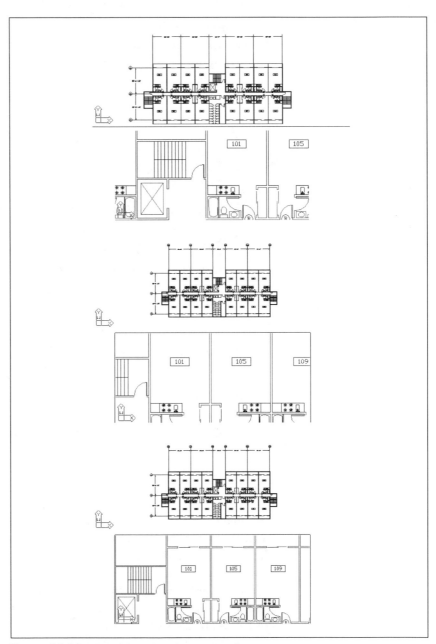

Figure 12.36: Setting viewport views to scale

SETTING LAYERS IN INDIVIDUAL VIEWPORTS

Another unique feature of Paper Space viewports is their ability to freeze layers independently. You could, for example, display the usual plan information in the overall view of a floor but show only the walls in the enlarged view of one unit.

1. Activate the lower viewport.

2. Click on Data ➤ Layers….

3. Click on FLOOR1 | DOOR in the list of layers to highlight it.

4. Click on the FRZ button next to the Cur VP: label.

5. Click on OK. The active viewport will regenerate, with the Door layer invisible in the current viewport. Door remains visible in the other viewport, however (see Figure 12.37).

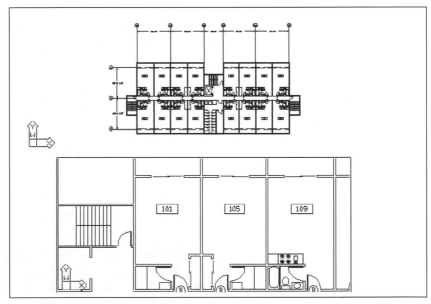

Figure 12.37:   The drawing editor with the Door layer turned off in the active viewport

Becoming an Expert

III

You might have noticed the other two similar buttons next to the label New VP. These two buttons control layer visibility in any new viewports you might create next, rather than controlling existing viewports.

If you prefer, you can also use the Layer Control pop-up list in the toolbar to freeze layers in individual viewports. Select the layer from the list, then click on the Sun icon with the small rectangle below it. This is the equivalent to the FRZ and Thw buttons in the Layer Control dialog box.

Now save and exit the Xref-1 file.

▼
■
■
■
■

MASKING OVER PARTS OF A DRAWING

In *Chapter* 6, we described a method for using 3D faces to hide floor patterns under equipment or furniture in a floor layout. You can use a similar method to hide irregularly shaped areas in a paper space viewport. This would be desirable for plotting site plans, civil plans, or floor plans that require portions of the drawing to be masked out.

Instead of using a 3D face, you use an object called a Region. Here's how it's done.

1. Draw a closed polyline outlining the area you want to mask out of your plot.

2. Click and drag Rectangle from the Draw palette, then select Region or type **Region** ↵.

3. At the select objects prompt, select the polyline outline you just drew, then press ↵. You've just created a region.

4. Click on the Region, then click on one of it's grip. Press ↵ to set up to move the region.

5. Enter **@0,0,1**. This moves the region 1 unit in the z-axis (see *Chapter 15* for more on the z-axis). The region will appear to have not moved since the movement was in your line of sight.

6. Create a layer called **Mask** and change the region to that layer.

7. When you are ready to plot, make sure the Mask layer is off and that the Hideplot setting (View ➤ Floating Viewpoints ➤ Hideplot) is on for the viewport showing your view with the mask. Or, if you have created the mask in paper space, make sure the Hidden lines check box is checked in the Plot Configuration dialog box.

When you plot your view, the area enclosed by the region will be hidden. To check your view, use the Preview option in the Plot Configuration dialog box.

There are a few more points you should be aware of when using Regions for masks:

• Text will always show through the region, even when hidden lines are removed, unless the text is given a 3-dimensional thickness (see *Chapter 15* for more on giving objects thickness).

• You can control the visibility of objects by placing them above or below the Region in the z-axis (see *Chapter 15* for more on z-axis placement).

• You can cut holes in the Region using the Subtract command (see *Chapter 18* for details).

• You can turn off the layer the Region resides on to hide its outline at plot time. Leave the layer on if you want the outline to appear in the drawing.

This section concludes the apartment building tutorial. Although you haven't drawn the complete building, you've already learned all the commands and techniques you need to do so. Figure 12.38 shows you a completed plan of the first floor; to complete your floor plans and get some practice using AutoCAD, you may want to add the symbols shown in this figure to your Plan file.

III

Becoming an Expert

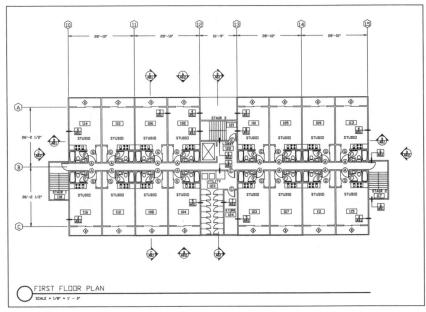

Figure 12.38: A completed floor of the apartment building

Since buildings like this one often have the same plans for several floors, the plan for the second floor can also represent the third floor. Combined with the first floor, this will give you a three-level apartment building. This project might also have a ground-level garage, which would be a separate file. The Gridline file you created earlier can be used in the garage file as a reference for dimensions. The other symbols can be blocks stored as files that can be retrieved in other files.

ADVANCED TOOLS: SELECTION FILTER AND CALCULATOR

Before ending this chapter, you will want to know about two other tools that are extremely useful in your day-to-day work with AutoCAD: Selection Filters on the Assist menu, and the Calculator in the Tools menu. We've saved the discussion of these tools for this chapter because you won't really need them until you've become accustomed to the way AutoCAD works. Chances are you've already experimented with some of AutoCAD's menu options not yet discussed in the tutorial. Many of the pull-down menu options and their functions are self-explanatory. Selection filters and the Calculator, however, require some further explanation.

We'll start with selection filters.

FILTERING SELECTIONS

Suppose you need to take just the walls of your drawing and isolate them in a separate file. One way would be to turn off all the layers except the Wall layer; then you could use the WBLOCK command and select the remaining walls, using a window to write the wall information to a file. Filters can simplify this operation by allowing you to select groups of objects based on their properties.

1. Open the Unit file.

2. Start the WBLOCK command by clicking on File ➤ Export. In the Create Drawing File dialog box, enter **unitwall.DWG** in the File input box, and click OK.

3. Press ↵ at the prompt for a block name, and then enter **0,0** at the Insertion base prompt.

4. At the object-selection prompt, click and drag Select Window from the toolbar, then select Selection Filters, or type **'Filter** ↵ at the command prompt.

The Object Selection Filters dialog box appears.

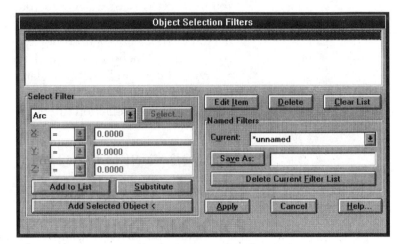

5. Open the pull-down list in the Select Filter button group.

6. Scroll down the list, and find and highlight the Layer option.

7. Click on the Select... button next to the pop-up list to get a list of layers, and double-click on the Wall layer.

8. At the Object Selection Filters dialog box, click on the Add to List button toward the bottom of the Select Filter button group. Layer = Wall is added to the list box.

9. Click on Apply. The dialog box closes.

10. Use a window to select the entire unit plan. Only the objects assigned to the Wall layer are selected.

11. Press ↵, and you'll see the message Exiting Filtered selection. 14 found.

12. Press ↵ again to complete the WBLOCK command. All the walls are written out to a file called **Unitwall**.

In this exercise, you filtered out a layer using the Selection Filters option in the Select Window toolbar flyout. Once a filter is designated, you then select the group of objects you want AutoCAD to filter through. AutoCAD finds the objects that match the filter requirements and passes those objects to the current command.

As you've seen from the previous exercise, there are many options to choose from in this utility. Let's take a closer look.

Working with the Object Selection Filters Dialog Box

To use the Object Selection Filters dialog box, you first select the criteria for filtering from the pull-down list. If the criteria you select is a named item (layers, line types, colors, or blocks), you can then click on the Select button to choose specific items from a list. If there is only one choice, the Select button is grayed out.

Once you've determined what to filter, you must add it to the list by clicking on the Add to List button. The filter criteria then appear in the list box at the top of the dialog box. Once you have added something to the list box, you can then apply it to your current command or to a later command.

Saving Filter Criteria

If you prefer, you can preselect a filter criteria. Then, at any Select objects prompt, you can click on Selection Filters from the toolbar (or type **'Filter** ⏎), highlight the appropriate filter criteria in the list box, and click on Apply. The specifications in the Object Selection Filters box remain in place for the duration of the current editing session.

You can also save a set of criteria by entering a name in the input box next to the Save As button and then clicking the button. The criteria list data is saved in a file called Filter.NFL. You can then access the criteria list at any time by opening the Current pop-up list and choosing the name of the saved criteria list.

Filtering Objects by Location

Notice the X, Y, and Z pull-down lists just below the main Select Filters pull-down list. These lists become accessible when you select a criteria that describes a geometry or a coordinate (such as an arc's radius or center point, for instance). You can use these lists to define filter selections even more specifically, using greater than (>), less than (<), equal to (=), or not equal to (!=) comparisons (called *relational operators*).

For example, suppose you want to grab all the circles whose radii are greater than 4.0 units. To do this, choose Circle Radius from the Select Filters pop-up list; then, in the X list, select the >. Enter **4.0** in the input box to the right of the X list, and click on Add to List. You see the item

Circle Radius > 4.0000

added to the list box at the top of the dialog box. You have thus used the > to indicate a circle radius greater than 4.0 units.

Creating Complex Selection Sets

There will be times when you will want to create a very specific filter list—say you need to filter out all the door blocks on the layer floor2 *and* all arcs with a radius equal to 1. To do this, you use the *grouping operators* found at the bottom of the Select Filters pull-down. You'll need to build a list as follows:

```
** Begin OR
** Begin AND
Entity = Block
Layer = Floor2
** End AND
** Begin AND
Entity = Arc
Arc Radius = 1.0000
** End AND
** End OR
```

Notice that the Begin and End operators are balanced; that is, for every Begin OR and Begin AND, there is an End OR and an End AND.

This list may look rather simple, but it can get confusing—mostly because of the way we normally think of the terms *and* and *or*. If a criteria is bounded by the AND grouping operators, then the objects must fulfill *both* criteria before they are selected. If a criteria is bounded by the OR grouping operators, then the objects fulfilling *either* criteria will be selected.

Here are the steps to build the list shown just above:

1. In the Select Filters pull-down list, choose **Begin OR, and click on Add to List. Then do the same for **Begin AND.

2. Click on Block from the Select Filters list, and then on Add to List.

3. For the layer, click on Layer from the Select Filters list. Then click Select…, choose the layer name, and click Add to List.

4. In the Select Filters list, choose **End AND and click on Add to List. Then do the same for **Begin AND.

5. Select Arc from the Select Filters list and click Add to List.

6. Select Arc Radius from the Select Filters list, and enter **1.0** in the input box next to the X pop-up. Be sure the = shows in the X pull-down, and then click on Add to List.

7. Choose **End AND and click on Add to List. Then do the same for **End OR.

If you make an error in any of the above steps, just highlight the item, select an item to replace it, and click on the Substitute button instead of the Add to List button. If you only need to change a value, click on Edit Item near the center of the dialog box.

FINDING GEOMETRY WITH THE CALCULATOR

Another useful AutoCAD tool is the geometry Calculator. Like most calculators, it adds, subtracts, divides, and multiplies. If you enter an arithmetic expression such as 1 + 2, the calculator returns 3. This is useful for doing math on the fly, but the Calculator does much more than arithmetic, as you will see in the next examples.

Finding the Midpoint between Two Points

One of the most common questions heard from AutoCAD users is, "How can I locate a point midway between two objects?" With previous versions of AutoCAD, you first had to draw a construction line between

III

Becoming an Expert

the two objects, and then use the Midpoint override to select the midpoint of the construction line. Starting with Release 12, however, this operation has been greatly simplified.

In the following exercise, you start a line midway between the center of an arc and the endpoint of a line. Draw a line and an arc and try this out.

▼ TIP

You can also type **'Cal** ↵ at the command prompt to start the Calculator.

1. Start the LINE command, and at the First point prompt, click on Tools ➤ Calculator.

2. At the >> Expression: prompt, enter **(end + cen)/2** ↵.

3. At the >> Select entity for END snap: prompt, click on the endpoint of a line.

4. At the >> Select entity for CEN snap: prompt, click on an arc. The line will start midway between the arc's center and the endpoint of the line.

Using Osnap Modes in Calculator Expressions

In the foregoing exercise, you used Osnap modes as part of arithmetic expressions. The Calculator treats them as temporary placeholders for point coordinates until you actually pick the points (at the prompts shown in steps 3 and 4).

The expression

(end + cen)/2

finds the average of two values. In this case, the values are coordinates, so the average is the midpoint between the two coordinates. You can take this one step further and find the centroid of a triangle using this expression:

(end + end + end)/3

Note than only the first three letters of the Osnap mode are entered in Calculator expressions. Table 12.1 shows what to enter in an expression for Osnap modes.

Table 12.1:   The Geometry Calculator's Osnap Modes

Calculator Osnap	Meaning
End	Endpoint
Ins	Insert
Int	Intersection
Mid	Midpoint
Cen	Center
Nea	Nearest
Nod	Node
Qua	Quadrant
Per	Perpendicular
Tan	Tangent
Rad	Radius
Cur	Cursor Pick

I've included two items in the table that are not really Osnap modes, though they work similarly when they are used in an expression. The first is Rad. When you include Rad in an expression, you get the prompt

Select circle, arc or polyline segment for RAD function:

You can then select an arc, polyline arc segment, or circle, and its radius is used in place of Rad in the expression.

The other item, Cur, prompts you for a point. Instead of looking for specific geometry on an object, it just locates a point.

Finding a Point Relative to Another Point

Another common task in AutoCAD is starting a line at a relative distance from another line. The following steps describe how to use Calculator to start a line from a point that is 2.5″ in the x-axis and 5.0″ in the y-axis from the endpoint of another line.

1. Start the LINE command. At the First point prompt, click on Tools ➤ Calculator.

2. At the >> Expression: prompt, enter **end + [2.5,5.0]** ↵.

3. At the >> Select entity for END snap: prompt, pick the endpoint. The line starts from the desired location.

In this example, you used the Endpoint Osnap mode to indicate a point of reference. This is added to Cartesian coordinates in square brackets, describing the distance and direction from the reference point. You could have entered any coordinate value within the square brackets. You could also have entered a polar coordinate in place of the Cartesian coordinate, as in the following:

end + [5.59<63]

You don't have to include the @, because Calculator assumes you want to add the coordinate to the one indicated by the Endpoint Osnap mode. Also, it's not necessary to include every coordinate in the square brackets. For example to indicate a displacement in only one axis, you can leave out a value for the other two coordinates, as in the following examples:

[4,5] = [4,5,0] [,1] = [0,1,0]
[,,2] = [0,0,2]
0 = [0,0,0]

Adding Foot and Inch Distances on the Fly

One of the more frustrating situations you may have run across is having to stop in the middle of a command to find the sum of two or more distances. Say you start the MOVE command, select your objects, and pick a base point. Then you realize you don't know the distance for the move, but you do know that the distance is the sum of two values—unfortunately, one value is in feet and the other is in inches. Usually in this situation you would have to reach for pen and paper (or, if you've got one, a foot and inch calculator), then figure out the distance, and then return to your computer to finish the task. AutoCAD's geometry Calculator puts an end to this runaround.

Here's what to do if you want to move a set of objects a distance that is the sum of 12′ 6⅝″ and 115¾″:

1. Issue the MOVE command, select objects, and pick a base point.

2. At the Second point prompt, start the Calculator.

3. At the >> Expression: prompt, enter

   [@12′6" + 115" < 45]

   Then press ↵, and the objects move into place at the proper distance.

In this example, you are mixing inches, and feet—under normal circumstances, a time-consuming calculation. Notice that the foot-and-inch format follows the standard AutoCAD syntax (no space between the foot and inch values). The coordinate value in square brackets can have any number of operators and values, as in the following:

[@4 * (22 + 15) - (23.3 / 12) + 1 < 13 + 17]

This expression demonstrates that you can also apply operators to angle values.

Guidelines for Working with the Calculator

You may be noticing some patterns in the way expressions are formatted for the calculator. Here are some guidelines to remember:

- Coordinates are enclosed in square brackets.

- Nested or grouped expressions are enclosed in parentheses.

- Operators are placed between values, as in simple math equations.

- Object snaps can be used in place of coordinate values.

III

Becoming an Expert

Table 12.2 lists all the operators and functions available in the Calculator. You may want to experiment with these other functions on your own.

Table 12.2:   The Geometry Calculator's Functions

Operator/ Function	What It Does	Example
+ or −	Add or subtract numbers or vectors	2 − 1 = 1 [a,b,c] + [x,y,z] = [a+x, b+y, c+z]
* or /	Multiply or divide numbers or vectors	a*[x,y,z] = [a*x, a*y, a*z] 8.4/2 = 4.2
^	Exponentiation of a number	3^2 = 9
sin	Sine of angle	sin (45) = 0.707107
cos	Cosine of angle	cos (30) = 0.866025
tang	Tangent of angle	tang (30) = 0.57735
asin	Arcsine of a real number	asin (0.707107) = 45.0
acos	Arccosine of a real number	acos (0.866025) = 30.0
atan	Arctangent of a real number	atan (0.57735) = 30.0
ln	Natural log	ln (2) = 0.693147
log	Base-10 log	log (2) = 0.30103
exp	Natural exponent	exp (2) = 7.38906
exp10	Base-10 exponent	exp10 (2) = 100
sqr	Square of number	sqr (9) = 81.0
abs	Absolute value	abs (−3.4) = 3.4
round	Rounds to nearest integer	round (3.6) = 4
trunc	Drops decimal portion of real number	trunc (3.6) = 3
r2d	converts radians to degrees	r2d (1.5708) = 90.0002

Table 12.2: The Geometry Calculator's Functions (continued)

Operator/ Function	What It Does	Example
d2r	Converts degrees to radians	d2r (90) = 1.5708
pi	The constant pi	3.14159
vec	Vector between two points	vec ([2,2],[4,4]) = (2.0,2.0,0.0)
vec1	1 unit vector between two points	vec1 ([2,2],[4,4]) = (0.707107,0.707107,0.0)

The geometry Calculator is capable of much more than the typical uses you've seen here and extends beyond the scope of this text. Still, the processes described in this section will be helpful as you use Auto-CAD. If you want to know more about the Calculator, consult the *AutoCAD Command Reference* and the *User's Guide* that come with Release 13.

IF YOU WANT TO EXPERIMENT...

You may want to experiment further with Paper Space in order to become more familiar with it. Try the following exercise. In it you will add two more viewports using the View ➤ Floating Viewports options (MVIEW) and COPY commands.

1. Open the Plan file you used for the earlier Paper Space exercise.

2. At the command prompt, type **Pspace** ↵ to go to Paper Space.

3. Turn on the Vport layer, and STRETCH the lower viewport so that it occupies the lower-right third of the screen (see panel 1 of Figure 12.39).

III

Becoming an Expert

4. To create a new viewport, choose View ➤ Floating Viewports ➤ 1 Viewport or type **Mview** ↵.

5. At the OFF/ON/Hideplot prompt, pick the lower-left corner of the screen.

6. At the Other corner prompt, size the viewport so that it is similar to the viewport on the right, as shown in panel 1 of Figure 12.39.

7. Press Esc to stop the drawing regeneration.

8. Use the COPY command to copy the lower-right viewport to the left. This time, let the drawing regeneration occur. Notice that the view in the copied viewport is identical to that in the original.

9. At the command prompt, type **Mspace** ↵ to switch over to Model Space.

10. Pick the lower-left viewport.

11. Type **Regen** ↵. Notice that only the current viewport regenerates.

12. Issue the ZOOM command and use the Dynamic option to move your view to the elevator area. You get a miniature version of the Dynamic Zoom view.

13. Arrange the views in the other viewport to look like panel 2 of Figure 12.39.

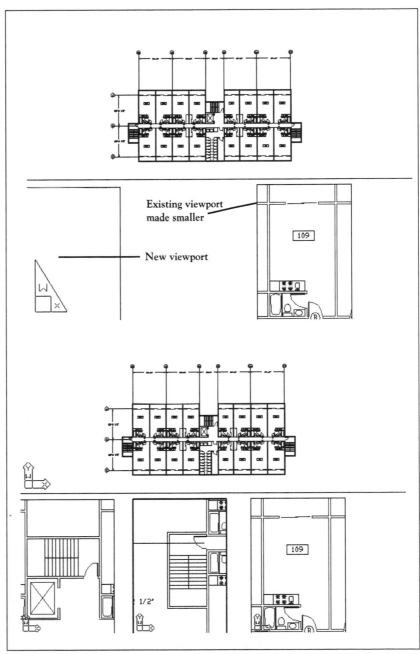

Figure 12.39: Creating new viewports in Paper Space

13

DRAWING CURVES
AND SOLID FILLS

Drawing Smooth Curves

Tracing Curves with a Digitizer

Editing Polylines and Curves

Marking Divisions on Curves

Drawing Filled Areas

Controlling Filled Area Visibility

FAST TRACK

586 ▶ To draw a polyline arc

Click and drag the Polyline button on the Draw palette, and then select Polyline on the flyout. Pick a start point, and then enter **A** ↵. You can then specify a center point, direction, second point, or endpoint for the arc—similar to the way you do for the Arc command.

592 ▶ To join a polyline with another object

First make sure that the polyline and the other object meet exactly end to end. Click and drag the Special Edit button on the Modify palette, select Edit Polyline on the flyout, and then click on the polyline. Enter **J** ↵ and select the object you want to join. Press ↵ to confirm your selection.

593 ▶ To change the width of a polyline

Click and drag the Special Edit button on the Modify palette, select Edit Polyline on the flyout, and then click on the polyline you wish to widen. Enter **W** ↵ and then enter the new width.

594 ▶ To smooth out a polyline

Click and drag the Special Edit button on the Modify palette, and then select Edit Polyline on the flyout. Click on the polyline to be smoothed, and then enter **F** ↵. Press ↵ to exit the PEDIT command.

597 ▶ To convert a line or arc into a polyline

Click and drag the Special Edit button on the Modify palette, select Edit Polyline on the flyout, and then click on the line or arc you wish to convert. Press ↵ at the next prompt.

597 ▶ To turn a polyline into a spline curve

Click and drag on the Special Edit button on the Modify palette, select Edit Polyline on the flyout, and then click on the polyline you wish to turn into a curve. Enter **S** ↵.

604 ▶ To vary the width of a polyline

Click and drag the Special Edit button on the Modify palette, select Edit Polyline on the flyout, and then click on the polyline you wish to change. Enter **E** ↵, and then press ↵ until the X marker is on the vertex of the polyline where you want to start varying the width. Enter the width you want at the current point, then enter the width you want at the next vertex. Enter **R** ↵ to see the resulting new widths. Press ↵ to go to the next vertex, or **X** ↵ ↵ to exit the PEDIT command.

621 ▶ To mark an object into equal divisions

Click and drag the Point button on the Draw palette, and select Divide on the flyout. Click on the object you want to mark, and then enter the number of divisions you want.

623 ▶ To make equally spaced copies of an object along a curved path

First, select the object you want to copy and turn it into a block. Next, click and drag the Point button on the Draw palette, and then select Divide on the flyout. Click on the object defining the curved path, enter **B** ↵, and then enter the name of the block you just created. Finally, specify the number of divisions along the path.

625 ▶ To sketch with AutoCAD

Click on the Sketch button on the Miscellaneous toolbar. Click on a point to start the temporary sketch line and then click on a point to stop the sketch line. Press **R** to make the temporary sketch line permanent. Enter **X** ↵ to exit the sketch mode.

630 ▶ To solid-fill a circular area

Click and drag the Circle button on the Draw palette, and then select Donut on the flyout. Enter the diameter of the center hole, enter the overall diameter, and then pick points placing the solid-filled circle.

So far in this book, you've been using basic lines, arcs, and circles to create your drawings. In this chapter, it's time to add polylines and spline curves to your repertoire. Polylines offer many options for creating forms, including solid fills. Spline curves are perfect for drawing smooth, nonlinear objects. The Splines are true NURBS curves. NURBS stands for Non-Uniform Rational B-Splines—but all you really need to know about the meaning of NURBS is that their curve information is mathematically accurate, unlike previous versions of AutoCAD, which created approximations of curves through short line segments.

INTRODUCING POLYLINES

Polylines are like composite line segments and arcs. A polyline may look like a series of line segments, but it acts like a single object. This characteristic makes polylines useful for a variety of applications, as you'll see in the upcoming exercises.

DRAWING A POLYLINE

First, to introduce you to the polyline, you will begin a drawing of the top view of the joint in Figure 13.1.

1. Open a new file called **Joint2d**. Don't bother to make special setting changes, as you will do this drawing with the default settings.

2. Click on the Polyline button on the Draw palette. You may also type **Pline** ↵ at the command prompt.

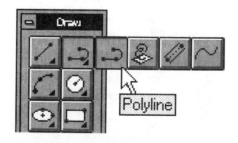

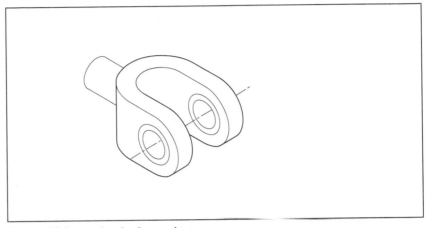

Figure 13.1:   A sketch of a metal joint

III

Becoming an Expert

▼ NOTE

You can draw polylines just as you would with the LINE command. Or you can use the other PLINE options to enter a polyline arc, specify polyline thickness, or add a polyline segment in the same direction as the previously drawn line.

▼ NOTE

The Arc option allows you to draw an arc that starts from the last point you selected. Once selected, the Arc option offers additional options. The default Save option is the endpoint of the arc. As you move your cursor, an arc follows it in a tangent direction from the first line segment you drew.

3. At the From point prompt, enter a point at coordinate 3,3 to start your polyline.

4. At the prompt,

   Arc/Close/Halfwidth/Length/Undo/Width/<Endpoint of line>:

   enter **@3<0** ↵ to draw a horizontal line of the joint.

5. At the Arc/Close/Halfwidth... prompt, enter **A** ↵ to continue your polyline with an arc.

6. At the prompt,

   Angle\CEnter\CLose\Direction\Halfwidth\Line\Radius\Second pt\Undo\Width\<Endpoint of arc>:

   enter **@4<90** ↵ to draw a 180° arc from the last point you entered. Your drawing should now look like Figure 13.2.

7. Continue the polyline with another line segment. To do this, enter **L** ↵.

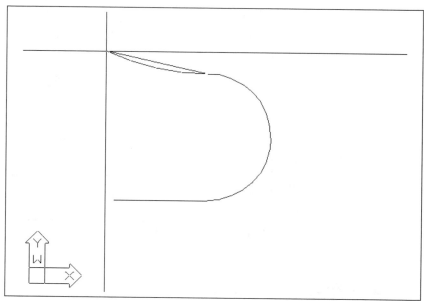

Figure 13.2: A polyline line and arc

8. At the Arc\Close\Halfwidth... prompt, enter **@3<180** ↵. Another line segment continues from the end of the arc.

9. Press ↵ to exit PLINE.

You now have a sideways, U-shaped polyline that you will use in the next exercise to complete the top view of your joint.

POLYLINE OPTIONS

Let's pause from the tutorial to look at some of the Polyline options you didn't use.

> **Close**   draws a line segment from the last endpoint of a sequence of lines to the first point picked in that sequence. This works exactly like the Close option on the Draw ➤ Line menu.

Length enables you to specify the length of a line that will be drawn at the same angle as the last line entered.

Halfwidth creates a tapered line segment or arc by specifying half its beginning and ending widths (see Figure 13.3).

Width creates a tapered line segment or arc by specifying the full width of the segment's beginning and ending points.

Undo deletes the last line segment drawn.

If you want to break down a polyline into simple lines and arcs, you can use the Explode option on the Modify palette, just as you would with blocks. Once a polyline is exploded, it becomes a set of individual line segments or arcs.

To turn off the filling of solid polylines, click on Options ➤ Display and turn off the Solid Fill option. (The Display options are explained in detail later in this chapter, in the section on solid fills.)

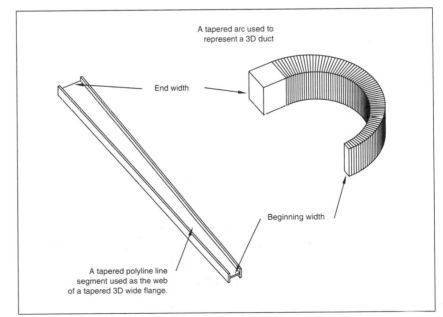

A tapered arc used to represent a 3D duct

End width

Beginning width

A tapered polyline line segment used as the web of a tapered 3D wide flange.

Figure 13.3: Tapered line segment and arc created with Halfwidth

III

Becoming an Expert

EDITING POLYLINES

You can edit polylines with many of the standard editing commands. To change the properties of a polyline, click on the Properties button on the Object Properties palette (DDMODIFY). The STRETCH command on the Modify palette can be used to displace vertices of a polyline, and the Trim, Extend, and Break commands on the Modify palette also work with polylines.

In addition, there are many editing capabilities offered only for polylines. For instance, later you will see how you can smooth out a polyline using the Fit option under the PEDIT command (Modify ➤ Edit Polyline). Let's take a closer look at some of the other PEDIT options, by continuing the work on our top view of the joint.

In the following exercise, you'll use the OFFSET command on the Modify palette to add the inside portion of the joint.

1. Click and drag the Copy button on the Draw palette and select Offset or type **Offset** ↵.

2. At the Offset distance prompt, enter **1**.

3. At the Select object prompt, pick the U-shaped polyline you just drew.

4. At the Side to offset prompt, pick a point toward the inside of the U. A concentric copy of the polyline appears (see Figure 13.4).

The concentric copy of a polyline made with Construct ➤ Offset can be very useful when you need to draw complex parallel curves like the ones in Figure 13.5.

Next, complete the top view of the joint.

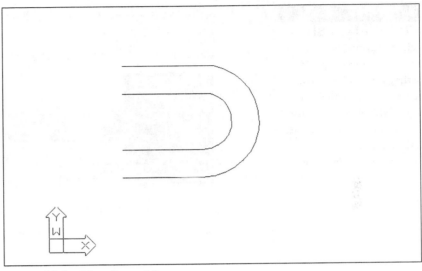

Figure 13.4:   The offset polyline

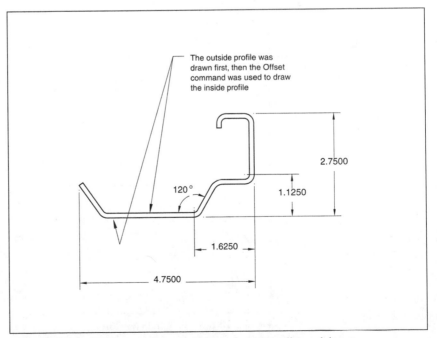

Figure 13.5:   Sample complex curves drawn by using offset polylines

▼ WARNING

The objects to be joined must touch the existing polyline exactly endpoint to endpoint, or else they will not join. To ensure that you place the endpoints of the lines exactly on the endpoints of the polylines, use the Endpoint Osnap override to select each polyline endpoint.

1. Connect the ends of the polylines with two short line segments (see Figure 13.6).

2. Click on Edit Polyline from the Modify Palette, or type **Pedit** ↵.

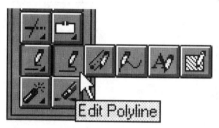

3. At the Select polyline prompt, pick the outermost polyline.

4. At the Close/Join/Width... prompt, enter **J** ↵ for the Join option.

5. At the Select objects prompt, pick all the objects you have drawn so far.

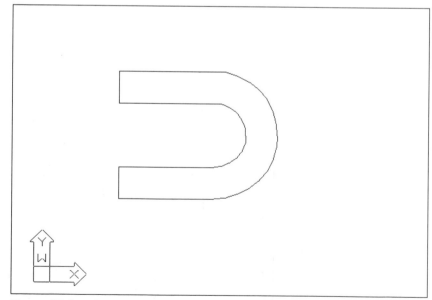

Figure 13.6: The joined polyline

6. Once all the objects are selected, press ↵ to join them all into one polyline.

By using the Width option under Edit Polyline, you can change the thickness of a polyline. Let's change the width of your polyline, to give some thickness to the outline of the joint.

1. Click on the Edit Polyline button from Modify palette again.

2. At the Close/Join/Width… prompt, enter **W** ↵ for the Width option.

3. At the Enter new width for all segments: prompt, enter **.03** ↵ for the new width of the polyline. The line changes to the new width (see Figure 13.7), and you now have a top view of your joint.

4. Press ↵ to exit the PEDIT command.

5. Save this file.

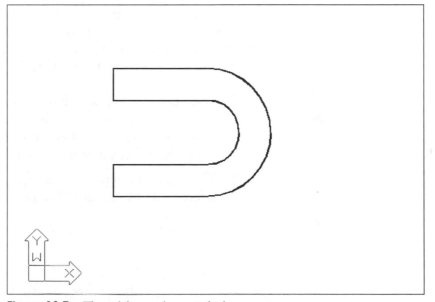

Figure 13.7: The polyline with a new thickness

Now here's a brief look at a few of the PEDIT options you didn't try firsthand.

Close connects the two endpoints of a polyline with a line segment. If the polyline you selected to be edited is already closed, this option changes to Open.

Open removes the last segment added to a closed polyline.

Spline/Decurve smooths a polyline into a Bézier curve (discussed in detail later in this chapter).

Edit Vertex lets you edit each vertex of a polyline individually (discussed in detail in the next section).

Fit turns polyline segments into a series of arcs.

Ltype Gen controls the way noncontinuous line types pass through the vertices of a polyline. If you have a fitted or spline curve with a noncontinuous line type, you will want to turn this option on.

SMOOTHING POLYLINES

There are many way to create a curve in AutoCAD. If you don't need the representation of a curve to be exactly accurate, you can use a polyline curve. In the following exercise, you will draw a polyline curve to represent a contour on a topographical map.

1. Open the TOPO.DWG drawing that is included on the CD that comes with this book. You will see the drawing of survey data shown in panel 1 of Figure 13.8. Some of the contours have already been drawn between the data points.

2. Zoom in to the upper-right corner of the drawing, so your screen looks like panel 2 of Figure 13.8.

3. Click on the Polyline button in the Draw palette. Using the Center Osnap mode, draw a polyline that connects the points labeled "254.00" in the upper-right corner of the drawing. Your drawing should look like panel 3 of Figure 13.8.

4. When you have drawn the polyline, press ↵.

Next you will convert the polyline you just drew into a smooth contour line.

1. Click on Edit Polyline from the Modify palette, or type **Pedit** ↵.

2. At the PEDIT Select objects: prompt, pick a contour line.

3. At the prompt,

   Close/Join/Width/Edit vertex/Fit/Spline/Decurve/Ltype gen/Undo/eXit:

   press **F** ↵ to select the Fit option. This causes the polyline to smooth out into a series of connected arcs that pass through the data points.

4. At the prompt,

   Close/Join/Width/Edit vertex/Fit/Spline/Decurve/Ltypegen/Undo/eXit:

   press ↵ to end the PEDIT command.

Your contour is now complete. The Fit curve option under the PEDIT command causes AutoCAD to convert the straight-line segments of the polyline into arcs. The endpoints of the arcs pass through the endpoints of the line segments, and the curve of each arc depends on the direction of the adjacent arc. This gives the effect of a smooth curve. Next, you'll use this polyline curve to experiment with some of the editing options unique to the PEDIT command.

III

Becoming an Expert

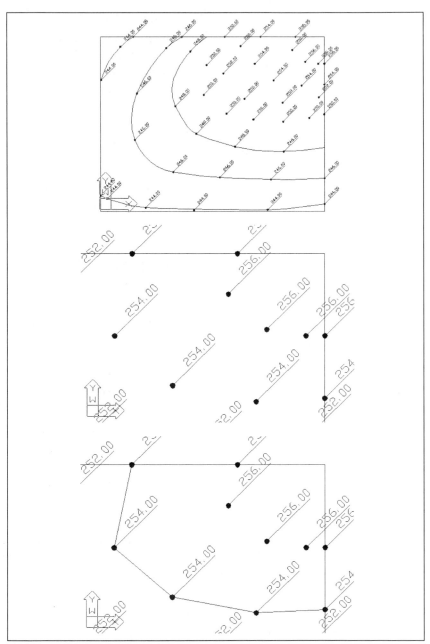

Figure 13.8: The TOPO.DWG drawing shows survey data portrayed in an AutoCAD drawing. Notice the dots indicating where elevations were taken. The actual elevation value is shown with a diagonal line from the point.

▼ **TURNING OBJECTS**
■ **INTO POLYLINES AND**
■ **POLYLINES INTO SPLINES**

There may be times when you will want to convert regular lines, arcs, or even circles into polylines. You may want to change the width of lines, or join lines together to form a single object such as a boundary. Here are the steps to take to convert lines, arcs, and circles into polylines.

1. Click and drag the Polyline button on the Modify palette, and select Edit Polyline on the flyout. You can also type **Pedit** ↵ at the command prompt.

2. At the Select polyline prompt, pick the object you wish to convert. If you want to convert a circle to a polyline, you must first break the circle (Break option on the Modify palette) so that it becomes an arc of 359°.

3. At the prompt,

    Object selected is not a polyline. Do you want to turn it into one? <Y>

    press ↵. The object is converted into a polyline.

If you have a polyline you would like to turn into a true spline curve, do the following:

1. Click and drag the Polyline button on the Modify palette and then click on Edit Polyline, or type **Pedit** ↵. Select the polyline you want to convert.

2. Type **S** ↵ to turn it into a polyline spline; then type **X** ↵ to exit the PEDIT command.

3. Click and drag the Polyline button on the Draw palette, then select Spline on the flyout, or type **Spline** ↵.

4. At the Object/<Enter first point>: prompt, type **O** ↵ for the Object option.

5. At the Select object prompt, click on the polyline. Though it may not be apparent at first, the polyline is converted into a spline.

III

Becoming an Expert

EDITING VERTICES

One of the PEDIT options we haven't yet discussed, Edit Vertex, is almost like a command within a command. Edit Vertex has numerous suboptions that allow you to fine-tune your polyline by giving you control over its individual vertices. We'll discuss this command in depth in this section.

1. First, turn off the Data and Border layers to hide the data points and border.

2. Click on the Edit Polyline button in the Modify palette. Then select the polyline you just drew.

3. Type **E** ↵ to enter the Edit Vertex mode. An X appears at the beginning of the polyline, indicating the vertex that will be affected by the Edit Vertex options.

Edit Vertex Suboptions

When you select Edit Vertex, you get the prompt

> Next/Previous/Break/Insert/Move/Regen/Straighten/Tangent/Width/eXit <N>:

Next and Previous   The Next and Previous options enable you to select a vertex for editing. When you started the Edit Vertex option, an X appeared on the selected polyline to designate its beginning. As you select Next or Previous, the X moves from vertex to vertex to show which one is being edited. Let's try this out.

1. Press ↵ a couple of times to move the X along the polyline. (Since Next is the default option, you only need to press ↵ to move the X.)

2. Type **P** ↵ for Previous. The X moves in the opposite direction. Notice that now the default option becomes P.

Break   The Break option breaks the polyline between two vertices.

▼ **NOTE**

You can also use the Break and Trim options on the Modify palette to break a polyline anywhere, as you did when you drew the toilet seat in *Chapter 3*.

1. Position the X on one end of the segment you want to break.

2. Enter **B** ↵ at the command prompt.

3. At the Next/Previous/Go/eXit <N>: prompt, use Next or Previous to move the X to the other end of the segment to be broken.

4. When the X is in the right position, pick Go from the Edit Vertex menu or enter **G** ↵, and the polyline will be broken (see Figure 13.9).

Insert   Next, try the Insert option, which inserts a new vertex:

▼ **TIP**

If a curve is not smooth enough or does not conform to a particular shape, you can use the Edit Vertex/Insert option to add vertices to a polyline, thereby giving you more control over its shape.

1. Type **X** ↵ to temporarily exit the Edit Vertex option. Then type **U** ↵ to undo the break.

2. Type **E** ↵ to return to the Edit Vertex option, and position the X before the new vertex.

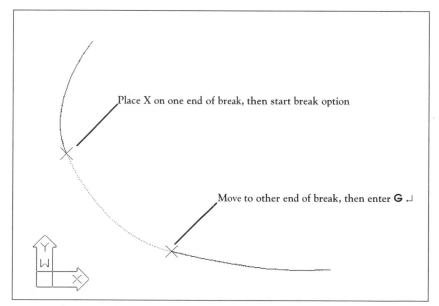

Figure 13.9:   How the Break option works

Becoming an Expert

3. Enter **I** ↵ to select the Insert option.

4. When the prompt Enter location of new vertex: appears, along with a rubber-banding line originating from the current X position (see Figure 13.10), pick a point indicating the new vertex location. The polyline is redrawn with the new vertex.

Notice that the inserted vertex appears between the currently marked vertex and the *next* vertex, so this Insert option is sensitive to the direction of the polyline. If the polyline is curved, the new vertex will not immediately be shown as curved (see panel 1 of Figure 13.11). You must smooth it out by exiting the Edit Vertex option and then using the Fit option, as you did to edit the site plan (see panel 2 of Figure 13.11). You can also use the STRETCH command (on the Modify palette) to move a polyline vertex.

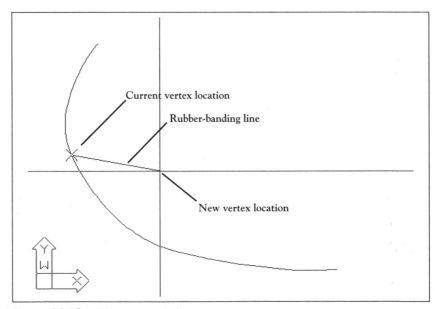

Figure 13.10:   The new vertex location

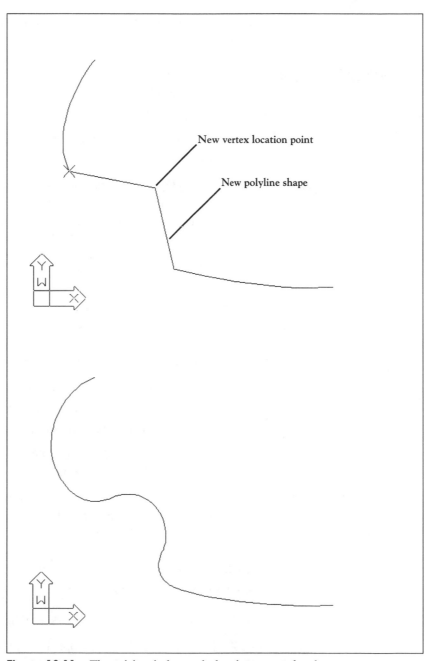

Figure 13.11: The polyline before and after the curve is fitted

Move   In this brief exercise, you'll use the Move option to move a vertex.

1. Undo the inserted vertex by exiting the Edit Vertex option (**X** ↵) and typing **U** ↵.

2. Restart the Edit Vertex option, and use the Next or Previous option to place the X on the vertex you wish to move.

3. Enter **M** ↵ for the Move option.

4. When the Enter new location: prompt appears, along with a rubber-banding line originating from the X (see panel 1 of Figure 13.12), pick the new vertex. The polyline is redrawn (see panel 2 of Figure 13.12). Again, if the line is curved, the new vertex appears as a sharp angle until you use the Fit option (see panel 3 of 13.12).

Straighten   The Straighten option straightens all the vertices between two selected vertices, as shown here:

1. Undo the moved vertex (from previous exercise).

2. Start the Edit Vertex option again, and select the starting vertex for the straight line.

3. Enter **S** ↵ for the Straighten option.

4. At the Next/Previous/Go/eXit: prompt, move the X to the other end of the straight line.

5. Once the X is in the proper position, enter **G** ↵ for the Go option. The polyline straightens between the two selected vertices (see Figure 13.13).

Tangent   Next is the Tangent option, which alters the direction of a curve on a curve-fitted polyline.

1. Undo the straightened segment from the previous exercise.

2. Restart the Edit Vertex option, and position the X on the vertex you wish to alter.

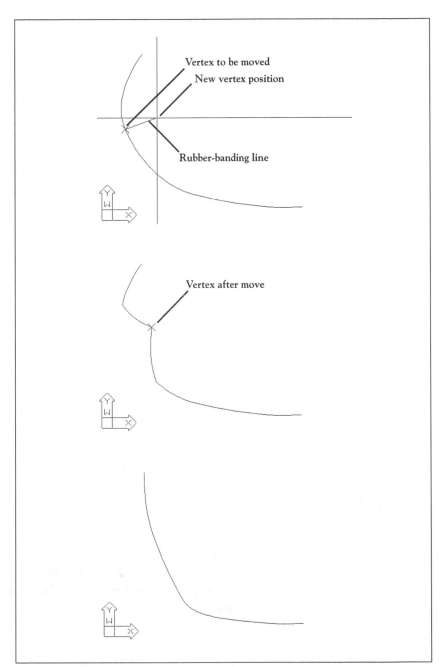

Figure 13.12: Picking a new location for a vertex, with the polyline before and after the curve is fitted

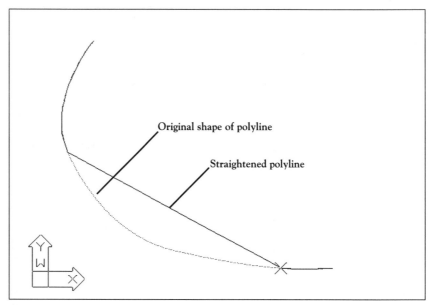

Figure 13.13: A polyline before and after straightening

3. Enter **T** ↵ for the Tangent option. A rubber-banding line appears (see panel 1 of Figure 13.14).

4. Point the rubber-banding line in the direction for the new tangent, and click the mouse. An arrow appears, indicating the new tangent direction (see panel 2 of Figure 13.14).

Don't worry if the polyline shape does not change. You must use Fit to see the effect of Tangent (see panel 3 of Figure 13.14).

Width   Finally, try out the Width option. Unlike the PEDIT command's Width option, Edit Vertex/Width enables you to alter the width of the polyline at any vertex. Thus you can taper or otherwise vary polyline thickness.

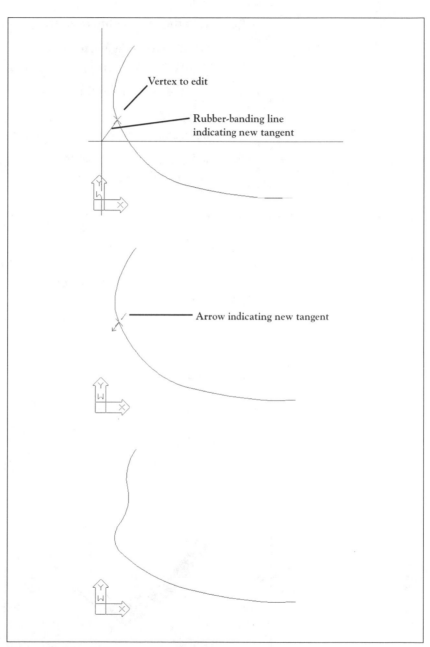

Figure 13.14: Picking a new tangent direction

1. Undo the tangent arc from the previous exercise.

2. Return to the Edit Vertex option, and place the X at the beginning vertex of a polyline segment.

3. Pick Width from the Edit Vertex menu or enter **W** ↵.

4. At the Enter starting width prompt, enter a value, 3' for example, indicating the polyline width desired at this vertex.

5. At the Enter ending width prompt, enter the width, 8' for example, for the next vertex.

Again (as with Straighten), don't be alarmed if nothing happens after you enter this Width value. To see the result, you must exit the Edit Vertex command (see Figure 13.15).

As you have seen throughout these exercises, you can use the Undo option to reverse the last Edit Vertex option used. And you can use the eXit option to leave Edit Vertex at any time. Just enter **X** ↵, and this brings you back to the PEDIT Close/Join/Width... prompt.

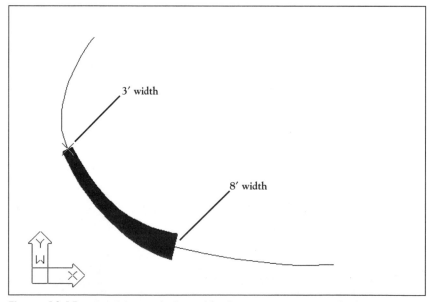

Figure 13.15: A polyline with the width of one segment increased

CREATING A POLYLINE SPLINE CURVE

▼ **NOTE**

A polyline spline curve does not represent a mathematically true curve. See "Using True Spline Curves" later in this chapter to learn how to draw a more accurate spline curve.

The PEDIT command's Spline option (named after the spline tool used in manual drafting) offers a way to draw smoother and more controllable curves than those produced by the Fit option. A polyline spline does not pass through the vertex points as a fitted curve does. Instead, the vertex points act as weights pulling the curve in their direction. The polyline spline only touches its beginning and end vertices. Figure 13.16 illustrates this concept.

Let's see how using a polyline spline curve might influence the way you edit a curve.

1. Undo the width changes you made in the previous exercise.

2. To change the contour into a polyline spline curve, click on Edit Polyline from the Modify palette. Then pick the polyline to be curved.

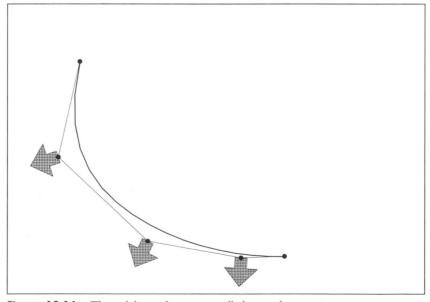

Figure 13.16:   The polyline spline curve pulled toward its vertices

III

Becoming an Expert

3. At the Close\Join\Width... prompt, enter **S** ↵. Your curve will change to look like Figure 13.17.

4. Press ↵ to exit Edit Polyline.

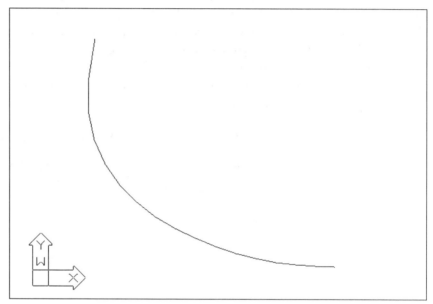

Figure 13.17:   A spline curve

The curve takes on a smoother, more graceful appearance. It no longer passes through the points you used to define it. To see where the points went and to find out how spline curves act, do the following:

1. Make sure the Noun/Verb Selection mode and the Grips feature are turned on.

2. Click on the curve. You'll see the original vertices appear as grips.

3. Click on the grip that is second from the top of the curve, and move the grip around. Notice how the curve follows, giving you immediate feedback on how the curve will look.

4. Pick a point as shown in the bottom panel of Figure 13.18. The curve is fixed in its new position.

USING TRUE SPLINE CURVES

So far, you've been working with polylines to generate spline curves. The advantage to using polylines for curves is that they can be enhanced in other ways—you can modify their width, for instance, or join several curves together. But at times you will need a more exact representation of a curve. The Spline object, created with Draw ➤ Spline, offers a more accurate model of spline curves, as well as more control over its shape.

DRAWING A SPLINE

The next exercise demonstrates the creation of a spline curve.

1. Turn the Data layer on so you can view the data points.

2. Adjust your view so you can see all the data points with the elevation of 250.00 (see Figure 13.19).

3. Click and drag on the Polyline button on the Draw palette, and then select the Spline button on the flyout.

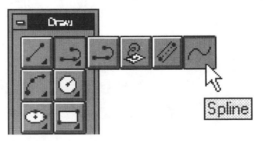

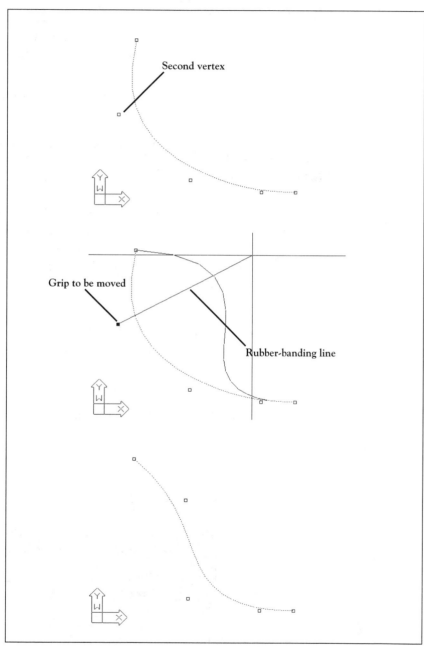

Figure 13.18: The fitted curve changed to a spline curve, with the location of the second vertex and the new curve

4. At the Object/<Enter first point>: prompt, use the Center Osnap override to start the curve on the first data point in the lower-right (see Figure 13.19). The prompt changes to Close/Fit Tolerance/<Enter point>:.

5. Continue to select the 250.00 data points until you reach the last one. Notice that as you pick points, a curve appears, and bends and flows as you move your cursor.

6. Once you've selected the last point, press ↵.

Notice that the prompt changes to Enter start tangent:. Also, a rubber-banding line appears from the first point of the curve to the cursor. As you move the cursor, the curve adjusts to the direction of the rubber-banding line. Here, you can set the tangency of the first point of the curve (see the top panel of Figure 13.20).

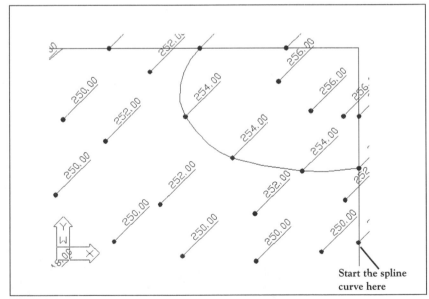

Figure 13.19: Starting the Spline curve at the first data point

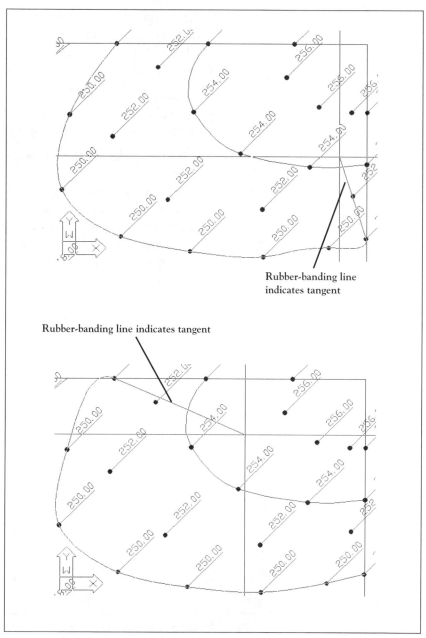

Figure 13.20: The last two prompts of the Spline command let you determine the tangent direction of the spline.

7. Press ↵. This causes AutoCAD to determine the first point's tangency based on the current shape of the curve. A rubber-banding line appears from the last point of the curve. As with the first point, you can indicate a tangent direction for the last point of the curve (see bottom panel of Figure 13.20).

8. Press ↵ to exit the Spline command without changing the endpoint tangent direction.

▼ TIP

See *Chapter 2* for more information on grip editing.

You now have a smooth curve that passes through the points you selected. These points are called the *control points*. If you click on the curve, you'll see the grips appear at the location of these control points, and you can adjust the curve simply by clicking on the grip points and moving them.

You may have noticed two other options—Fit Tolerance and Close—as you were selecting points for the spline in the last exercise. Here is a description of these options:

Fit Tolerance lets you change the curve so that it doesn't actually pass through the points you pick. When you select this option, you get the prompt Enter Fit Tolerance <0.0000>:. Any value greater than 0 will cause the curve to pass close to, but not to the points. A value of 0 causes the curve to pass through the points. (You'll see how this works in a later exercise.)

Close lets you close the curve into a loop. If you choose this option, you are prompted to indicate a tangent direction for the closing point.

FINE-TUNING SPLINE CURVES

Spline curves are different from other types of objects, and many of the standard editing commands won't work on splines. AutoCAD offers the Edit Spline option on the Modify palette (SPLINEDIT command) for making changes to splines. The following exercise will give you some practice with this command. You'll start by focusing on Splinedit's Fit Data option, which lets you fine-tune the spline curve.

III

Becoming an Expert

Controlling the Fit Data of a Spline

The following exercise will demonstrate how the Fit Data option lets you control some of the general characteristics of the curve.

1. Click and drag on the Edit Polyline button on the Modify palette, and select Edit Spline on the flyout, or type **Splinedit** ↲ at the command prompt.

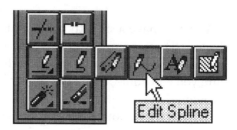

2. At the Select Spline prompt, select the spline you drew in the previous exercise.

3. At the prompt,

   Fit Data/Close/Move Vertex/Refine/rEverse/Undo/eXit <X>:

   type **F** ↲ to select the Fit Data option.

▼ NOTE

The Fit Data option is similar to the Edit Vertex option of the PEDIT command, in that Fit Data offers a subset of options that let you edit certain properties of the spline.

4. At the next prompt,

   Add/Close/Delete/Move/Purge/Tangents/toLerance/eXit <X>:

   type **T** to select the Tangents option. Move the cursor, and notice that the curve changes tangency through the first point, just as it did when you first created the spline (Figure 13.20).

5. Press ↲. You can now edit the other endpoint tangency.

6. Press ↲ again. You return to the Add/Close/Delete... prompt.

7. Now add another control point to the spline curve. At the Add/Close/Delete... prompt, type **A** ↲ to access the Add option.

8. At the Select point prompt, click on the second point from the bottom end (see panel 1 of Figure 13.21). A rubber-banding line appears from the point you selected. That point and the next point are highlighted. The two highlighted points tell you that the next point you select will fall between these two points.

9. Click on a new point. The curve changes to include that point. In addition, the new point becomes the highlighted point, indicating that you can continue to add more points between it and the other highlighted point (see panel 2 of Figure 13.21).

10. Press ↵. The Select point prompt appears, allowing you to add another point if you so desire.

11. Press ↵ again to return to the Add/Close/Delete… prompt.

Before we end our examination of the Fit Data options, let's look at how toLerance works.

1. At the Add/Close/Delete… prompt type **L** ↵ to select the toLerance option. This option sets the tolerance between the control point and the curve.

2. At the Enter fit tolerance <0.0000>: prompt, type **30** ↵. Notice how the curve no longer passes through the control points, except for the beginning and endpoints (see Figure 13.22). The fit tolerance value you enter determines the maximum distance away from any control point the spline can be.

3. Type **X** ↵ to exit the Fit Data option.

You've seen how you can control many of the shape properties of a spline through the Fit Data option. Here are descriptions of the other Fit Data options you didn't try in these exercises:

Delete removes a control point in the spline.

Close lets you close the spline into a loop.

III

Becoming an Expert

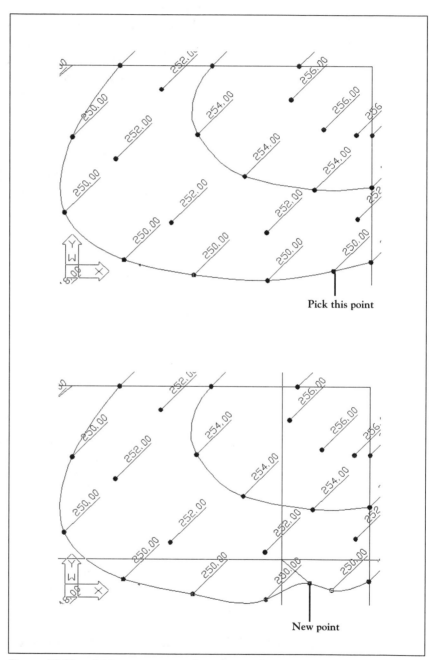

Figure 13.21: Adding a new control point to a spline

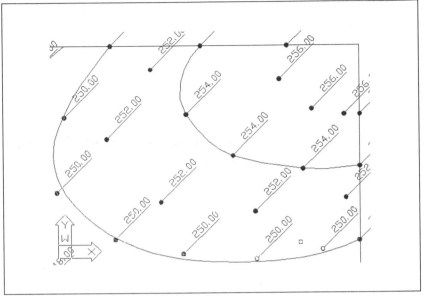

Figure 13.22: The spline after setting the control point tolerance to 1

Move lets you move a control point.

Purge deletes the fit data of the spline, thereby eliminating the Fit Data option for the purged spline. (See "When *Can't* You Use Fit Data?" just below.)

When Can't You Use Fit Data?

The Fit Data option of the SPLINEDIT command offers many ways to edit a spline; however, this option is not available to all spline curves. When you invoke certain of the other SPLINEDIT options, a spline curve will lose its fit data, thereby disabling the Fit Data option. These operations are as follows:

- Fitting a spline to a tolerance (SPLINE/Fit Tolerance) and moving its control vertices

- Fitting a spline to a tolerance (SPLINE/Fit Tolerance) and opening or closing it

- Refining the spline

III

Becoming an Expert

■ Purging the spline of its fit data using the Purge option
(SPLINEDIT/Fit Data/Purge)

Also, note that the Fit Data option is not available when you edit
spline curves that have been created from polyline splines. See the sidebar, "Turning Objects into Polylines and Polylines into Splines."

Adjusting the Control Points with the Refine Option

While you are still in the SPLINEDIT command, let's look at another
of its options—Refine—with which you can fine-tune the curve.

1. At the Fit Data/Open/Move Vertex/Refine... prompt, type
R ↵. The Refine option lets you control the "pull" exerted on
a spline by an individual control point. This isn't quite the
same effect as the Fit Tolerance option you used in the previous exercise.

2. At the prompt,

Add Control Point/Elevate Order/Weight/eXit <X>:

type **W** ↵. The first control point is highlighted.

3. At the next prompt,

Next/Previous/Select Point/eXit/<Enter new
weight><1.0000> <N>:

press ↵ to move the highlight to the next control point.

4. Type **25** ↵. The curve not only moves closer to the control
point, it also bends around the control point in a tighter arc
(see Figure 13.23).

You can use the Weight value of SPLINEDIT's Refine option to pull
the spine in tighter. Think of it as a way to increase the "gravity" of the
control point, causing the curve to be pulled closer and tighter to the control point.

Continue your look at the SPLINEDIT command by adding more
control points—without actually changing the shape of the curve. You
do this using Refine's Add Control Point and Elevate Order options.

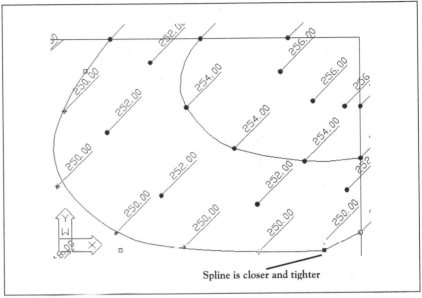

Spline is closer and tighter

Figure 13.23: The spline after increasing the Weight value of a control point

1. Type **X** ↵ to exit the Refine/Weight option; then type **A** ↵ to select the Add Control Point option.

2. At the Select a point on the spline: prompt, click on the second-to-last control point toward the top end of the spline (see panel 1 of Figure 13.24). The point you select disappears and is replaced by two control points roughly equidistant from the one you selected (see panel 2 of Figure 13.24). The curve remains unchanged. Two new control points now replace the one control point you selected.

3. Now type **E** ↵ to select the Elevate Order option.

4. At the Enter new order <4>: prompt, type **6** ↵. The number of control points increases, leaving the curve itself untouched.

5. Type **X** ↵ twice to exit the Refine option and then the SPLINEDIT command.

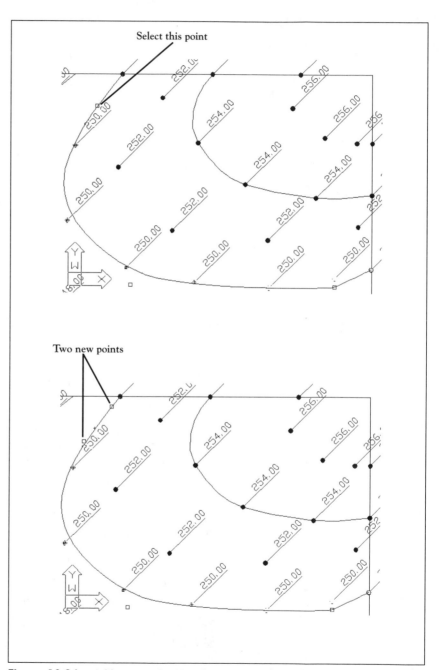

Figure 13.24: Adding a single control point using the Refine option

You would probably never edit contour lines of a topographical map in quite the way these exercises have shown. But by following this tutorial you have explored all the potential of the AutoCAD's spline object. Aside from its usefulness for drawing contours, it can be a great tool for drawing freeform illustrations. It is an excellent tool for mechanical applications, where precise, nonuniform curves are required, such as drawings of cams or sheet metal work.

MARKING DIVISIONS ON A CURVE

▼ NOTE

The use of DIVIDE and MEASURE are discussed here in conjunction with polylines, but you can use these commands on any object except blocks and text.

Perhaps one of the most difficult things to do in manual drafting is to mark regular intervals on a curve. AutoCAD offers the DIVIDE and MEASURE commands to help you perform this task with speed and accuracy.

DIVIDING OBJECTS INTO SEGMENTS OF EQUAL LENGTH

DIVIDE can be used to divide an object into a specific number of equal segments. For example, suppose you needed to mark off the contour you've been working on in this chapter, into nine equal segments. One way to do this is to first find the length of the contour by using the LIST command, and then sit down with a pencil and paper to figure out the exact distances between the marks. But there is another, easier way.

DIVIDE will place a set of point objects on a line, arc, circle, or polyline, marking off exact divisions. This next exercise shows how it works.

1. Click and drag the Point button on the Draw palette, and select Divide on the flyout, or type **Divide** ↵ at the command prompt.

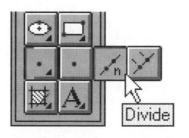

III

Becoming an Expert

2. At the Select objects to divide: prompt, pick the contour line.

3. The <Number of segments>/Block: prompt that appears next is asking for the number of divisions you want on the selected object. Enter **9** ↵.

The command prompt now returns, and it appears that nothing has happened. But AutoCAD has placed several points on the contour indicating the locations of the nine divisions you have requested. To see these points more clearly, do the following:

4. Click on Options ➤ Display ➤ Point Style. The Point Style dialog box appears.

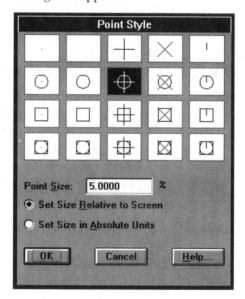

5. Click on the X point style in the upper-right side of the dialog box, click on the Set Size Relative to Screen radio button, and then click on OK.

6. Enter **Regen** ↵. A set of Xs appear, showing the nine divisions (see Figure 13.25).

▼ TIP

To snap to point objects, you can use the Nodes Osnap override.

The DIVIDE command uses *Point* objects to indicate the division points. Point objects are created by using the POINT command; they usually appear as dots. Unfortunately, such points are nearly invisible when placed on top of other objects. But, as you have seen, you can alter their shape using the Point Style dialog box. You can use these X points to place objects or references to break the object being divided. (DIVIDE does not actually cut the object into smaller divisions.)

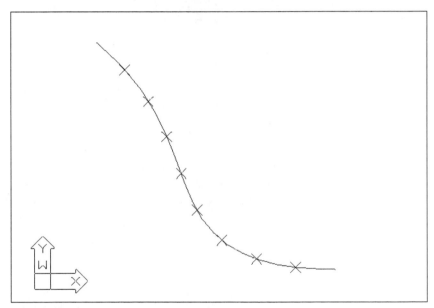

Figure 13.25:   Using the DIVIDE and MEASURE commands on a polyline

▼ NOTE

MEASURE is AutoCAD's equivalent of the divider tool in manual drafting. A divider is a V-shaped instrument, similar to a compass, used to mark off regular intervals along a curve or line.

DIVIDING OBJECTS INTO SPECIFIED LENGTHS

The MEASURE command acts just like DIVIDE; however, instead of dividing an object into segments of equal length, MEASURE marks intervals of a specified distance along an object. For example, suppose you need to mark some segments exactly 5′ apart along the contour. Try the following exercise to see how MEASURE is used to accomplish this.

1. Click and drag the Point button on the Draw palette, and select Measure on the flyout.

2. At the Select object to measure: prompt, pick the contour

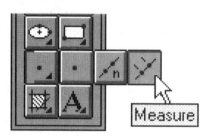

at a point closest to its lower endpoint. We'll explain shortly why this is important.

3. At the <Segment length>/Block: prompt, enter **5′** ↵. The X points appear at the specified distance.

4. Now exit this file.

Bear in mind that the point you pick on the object to be measured will determine where MEASURE begins measuring. In the last exercise, for example, you picked the contour near its bottom endpoint. If you had picked the top of the contour, the results would have been different, because the measurement would have started at the top, not the bottom.

▼ MARKING OFF INTERVALS
▪ USING BLOCKS INSTEAD OF POINTS

You can also use the Block option under the DIVIDE and MEASURE commands to place blocks at regular intervals along a line, polyline, or arc. Here's how to use blocks as markers:

1. First be sure the block you want to use is part of the current drawing file.

2. Start either the DIVIDE or MEASURE command (Click and drag the Point button on the Draw palette, then select Divide or Measure from the flyout).

3. At the Number of segments: prompt, enter **B**.

4. At the Block name to insert: prompt, enter the name of a block.

5. At the Align block with object? <Y> prompt, press ↵ if you wish the blocks to follow the alignment of the selected object. (Entering **N** ↵ causes each block to be inserted at a 0 angle.)

6. At the Number of segments: prompt, enter the number of segments. The blocks appear at regular intervals on the selected object.

One example of using DIVIDE's or MEASURE's Block option is to place a row of sinks equally spaced along a wall. Or you might use this technique to make multiple copies of an object along an irregular path defined by a polyline.

SKETCHING WITH AUTOCAD

No discussion of polylines would be complete without mentioning the Draw ➤ Sketch option. Though AutoCAD isn't a sketch program, you *can* draw "freehand" using the SKETCH command. With SKETCH, you can rough in ideas in a free-form way, and later overlay a more formal drawing using the usual lines, arcs, and circles. You can use sketch with a mouse, but it makes more sense to use this command with a digitizing tablet that has a stylus. The stylus affords a more natural way of sketching.

FREEHAND SKETCHING WITH AUTOCAD

The SKETCH command is located on the Miscellaneous toolbar. You can load this toolbar from the Tools menu.

III

Becoming an Expert

Here's a step-by-step description of how to use SKETCH:

1. Make sure the Ortho and Snap modes are turned off. Then type **Skpoly** ⏎ **1** ⏎. This sets the SKETCH command to draw using polylines.

2. Choose Tools ➤ Toolbars ➤ Miscellaneous, and click on the SKETCH button, or type **Sketch** ⏎ at the command prompt.

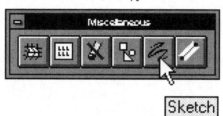

3. At the Record increment <0.1000>: prompt, enter a value that represents the smallest line segment you will want SKETCH to draw. Remember that this command approximates a sketch line by drawing a series of short line segments. So the value you enter here determines the length of those line segments.

4. At the Sketch. Pen eXit Quit Record Erase Connect . prompt, press the pick button and then start your sketch line. Notice that the message <Pen down> appears, telling you that AutoCAD is recording your cursor's motion.

5. Press the pick button to stop drawing. The message <Pen up> tells you AutoCAD has stopped recording your cursor motion. As you draw, notice that the line is green. This indicates that you have drawn a temporary sketch line and have not committed the line to the drawing.

6. A line drawn with SKETCH is temporary until you use Record to save it, so turn the sketch line into a polyline now by typing **R**.

7. Type **X** ⏎ to exit the SKETCH command.

Here are some of the other SKETCH options we weren't able to cover in this brief description:

Connect allows you to continue a line from the end of the last temporary line drawn. Type **C** and then move the cursor to the endpoint of the temporary line. AutoCAD automatically starts the line, and you just continue to draw. This only works in the <Pen up> mode.

Period (.) allows you to draw a single straight line segment by moving the cursor to the desired position and then pressing the period key. This only works in the <Pen up> mode.

Record, **Erase**, **Quit**, and **Exit** control the recording of lines and exiting from the SKETCH command. Record is used to save a temporary sketched line; once a line has been recorded, you must edit it as you would any other line. With Erase you can erase temporary lines before you record them. Quit ends the SKETCH command without saving unrecorded lines. On the other hand, the Exit option on the Sketch menu automatically saves all lines you have drawn, and then exits the SKETCH command.

FILLING IN SOLID AREAS

You have learned how to create a solid area by increasing the width of a polyline segment. But suppose you want to create a simple solid shape or a very thick line. AutoCAD provides the SOLID, TRACE, and DO-NUT commands to help you draw simple filled areas. The TRACE command acts just like the LINE command (with the added feature of drawing wide line segments), so only SOLID and DONUT are discussed here.

DRAWING LARGE SOLID AREAS

We've seen people use hatch patterns to fill in solid areas—and that's a great way to fill an irregular shape. However, hatches tend to increase

III

Becoming an Expert

the size of a file dramatically, thereby increasing loading and regeneration time. To keep file size down, use solids and polylines to do solid fills whenever possible.

Solids are four-sided polygons that are filled solid. They also plot as solid fills. Following are the steps for drawing a solid.

1. Click and drag the Rectangle button on the Draw palette, and select 2D Solid from the flyout, or type **Solid** ↵ at the command prompt.

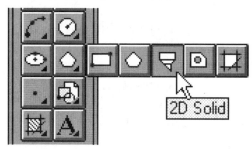

2. The SOLID command draws a four-sided solid area, so the first point you pick will be one of the area's corners. At the First point: prompt, pick a point indicating the first corner of the solid filled area.

3. At the Second point: prompt, pick the next corner of your solid area.

4. Selecting the third point is where things get a little tricky. In this exercise, you are drawing a square first, so your third point is the corner diagonal to the last corner you picked (see Figure 13.26). At the Third point: prompt, pick the point that is diagonal to second point you picked for the rectangular area you are filling. (Imagine that you are drawing a Z pattern.)

5. At the Fourth point: prompt, pick the final corner of your fill. A solid area appears between the four points you selected.

6. When the Third point: prompt appears again, you have an opportunity to continue your fill pattern. You can select a sequence of points in a Z pattern again.

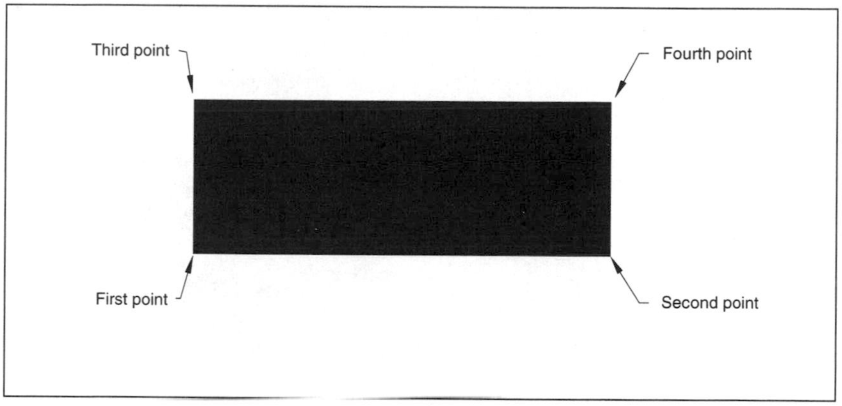

Figure 13.26:   Points for a solid square

If you were to pick points in a circular rather than a Z pattern, you would end up with a filled area shaped like a bow tie (see Figure 13.27). You can create solid filled areas with more than four sides by entering more points in a Z pattern (see Figure 13.28). There is no limit to the number of points you can select.

To end the SOLID command, press ↵ without picking a point.

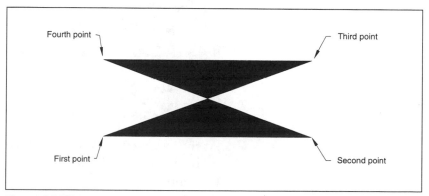

Figure 13.27:   An area filled by picking points in a clockwise pattern

III

Becoming an Expert

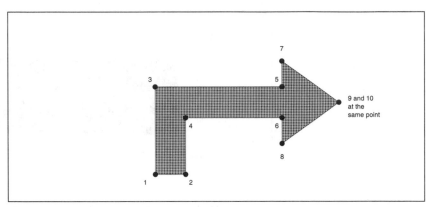

Figure 13.28: How to use SOLID to fill in an odd shape

DRAWING FILLED CIRCLES

If you need to draw a thick circle like an inner tube, or a solid filled circle, take the following steps:

1. Click and drag the Circle button on the Draw palette and select Donut on the flyout, or enter **Donut** ↵ at the command
   prompt.

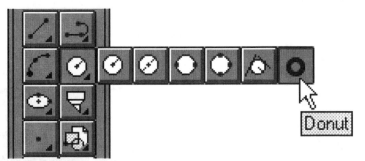

2. At the Inside diameter: prompt, enter the desired diameter
   of the donut "hole." This value determines the opening at
   the center of your circle.

3. At the Outside diameter: prompt, enter the overall diameter of the circle.

4. At the Center of doughnut: prompt, click on the desired location for the filled circle. You can continue to select points to place multiple donuts (see Figure 13.29).

5. Press ↵ to exit this process.

If you need to fill only a part of a circle, such as a pie slice, you can use the DONUT command to draw a full circle, and then use the Trim or Break options on the Modify palette to cut out the portion of the donut you don't need.

TOGGLING SOLID FILLS ON AND OFF

Once you have drawn a solid area with the PLINE, SOLID, TRACE, or DONUT commands, you can control whether the solid area is actually displayed as filled in. When Options ➤ Display ➤ Solid Fill does

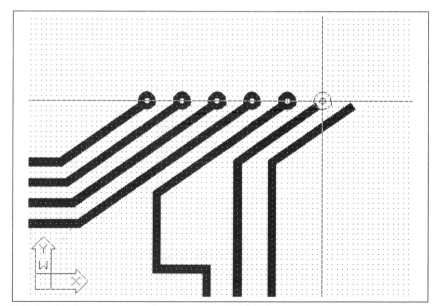

Figure 13.29: Drawing wide circles using the DONUT command

III

Becoming an Expert

▼ WARNING

If REGENAUTO is turned off, you will have to issue the RE-GEN command to display the effects of the FILL command.

not show a check mark, thick polylines, solids, traces, and donuts appear as outlines of the solid areas (see Figure 13.30).

Turning the solid filled areas on and off is easy. Just select Options ➤ Display ➤ Solid Fill to toggle solid fills on and off. Or you can enter **Fill** ↵ at the command prompt; then, at the ON/OFF <ON>: prompt, enter your choice of **on** or **off**.

You can also control the visibility of solid fills by using the Solid Fill check box in the Drawing Aids dialog box (Options ➤ Drawing Aids...).

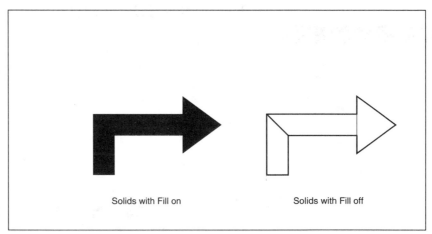

Solids with Fill on   Solids with Fill off

Figure 13.30: A solid displayed with the Fill option turned on and turned off

OVERLAPPING SOLID LINES AND SHADED FILLS

If you use a raster plotter or laser printer that can convert solid areas into screened or gray-shaded areas, you may encounter the problem of shading areas overlapping lines and hiding them. This problem may not be apparent until you actually plot the drawing; it frequently occurs when a gray area is bounded by lines (see Figure 13.31).

Most other graphics programs have specific tools to handle this difficulty. These tools are commonly named Move To Front or Move To

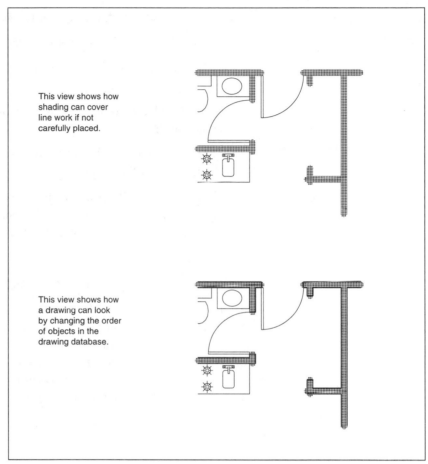

This view shows how
shading can cover
line work if not
carefully placed.

This view shows how
a drawing can look
by changing the order
of objects in the
drawing database.

Figure 13.31: Problems that occur with overlapping lines and gray areas

Back, indicating that you move an object in front of or behind another object. Although AutoCAD does not have a specific command to perform a "move to front," there is hope. Here is how to bring one object in front of another:

1. Select the objects that you want to move in front of the gray surfaces.

2. Click on Copy Objects on the Modify palette.

3. At the Base point: prompt, enter **@**.

4. At the Second point: prompt, enter **@** again.

5. Click on the Erase button on the Modify palette.

6. At the Select objects: prompt, enter **P** ↵ **to select the previously selected objects, and then press** ↵ **to complete the command.**

7. Before you plot, click on Options ➤ Selection… and then click on the Object Sort Method… button.

8. Make sure the Plotting check box is checked. If you are sending your plots to a PostScript device, make sure the PostScript Output check box is checked.

IF YOU WANT TO EXPERIMENT…

There are many valuable uses for polylines beyond those covered in this chapter. We encourage you to become familiar with this unique object so you can take full advantage of AutoCAD.

To further explore the use of polylines, try the exercise illustrated in Figure 13.32. It will give you an opportunity to try out some of the options discussed in this chapter that weren't included in exercises.

1. Open a new file called PART13. Set the snap mode to .25 and be sure the snap mode is on. Use the Pline command to draw the object shown to the right. Draw it in the direction indicated by the arrows and start at the upper left corner. Use the Close option to add the last line segment.

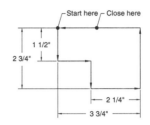

2. Start the Pedit command then pick the Edit Vertex option. At the Next/Previous/Break prompt, press return until the X mark moves to the first corner shown in the figure to the right. Enter an S for the Straighten option. At the Next/Previous/Go prompt, press return twice to move the X to the other corner shown in the figure. Press G for Go to straighten the polyline between the two selected corners.

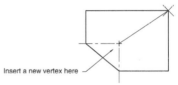

3. Press return twice to move the X to the upper right corner then enter I for Insert. Pick a point as shown in the figure. The polyline changes to reflect the new vertex. Enter an X to exit the Edit Vertex option then press return to exit the Pedit command.

4. Start the Fillet command and use the Radius option to set the fillet radius to .30. Press return to start the Fillet command again but this time use the Polyline option and pick the polyline you just edited. All the corners fillet to the .30 radius. Add the .15 radius circles as shown in the figure and exit the file with the End command.

Figure 13.32:   Drawing a simple plate with curved edges

14

GETTING AND EXCHANGING
DATA FROM DRAWINGS

Finding Areas of a Drawing

Getting the Drawing Status and Settings

Keeping Track of Time in a Drawing

Saving System Data in a File

Accessing Files on a Network

Using the Windows Clipboard to Import
and Export Data

Importing and Exporting Drawings to
Other Programs

FAST TRACK

640 ▶ **To find the area of a simple shape**

Click and drag List from the Object Properties toolbar then select Area, and then click on points defining the outline of the area.

644 ▶ **To find the area of a complex shape**

Enter **Boundary** ↵ at the command prompt. At the Boundary dialog box, click inside the areas that figure into the area calculation, and press ↵. Select Assist ➤ Inquiry ➤ Area; then enter **A** ↵ and then **O** ↵. Click on the polylines defining the gross areas, press ↵, enter **S** ↵ **O** ↵, and then click on the areas to be subtracted from the gross areas.

652 ▶ **To get an overall view of a drawing's status**

Click on Data ➤ Status. A listing of the drawing's status will appear.

654 ▶ **To determine the amount of time spent on a drawing**

Select Data ➤ Time or enter **Time** ↵ at the command prompt.

656 ▶ **To retrieve the last area calculation value**

Enter é**Setvar** ↵ **Area** ↵ at the command prompt.

660 ▶ To unlock a file you know is currently not being used

Select File ➤ Management ➤ Unlock file…. Click on Unlock File from the File Utilities dialog box, then in the File(s) to Unlock dialog box, locate and double-click on the name of the file you wish to unlock.

663 ▶ To export a .DXF file

Select File ➤ Export…. At the dialog box, enter the name for your .DXF file including the .DXF file name extension. At the Enter decimal place… prompt, press ⏎.

663 ▶ To import a .DXF file

Select File ➤ Import…. At the dialog box, select .DXF from the pop-up list near the bottom, then double-click on the file name to import.

664 ▶ To export a PostScript .EPS file

Select File ➤ Export…. Enter a name for your .EPS file in the dialog box including the .EPS file name extension.

AutoCAD drawings contain a wealth of data. In them you can find graphic information such as distances and angles between objects, as well as precise areas and the properties of objects. But as you become more involved with AutoCAD, you will find that you also need data of a different nature. For example, as you begin to work in groups, the various settings in a drawing become important. Statistics on the amount of time you spend on a drawing are needed when you are billing computer time. As your projects become more complex, file maintenance requires a greater degree of attention. To take full advantage of AutoCAD, you will want to exchange much of this data with other people and other programs.

In this chapter, you will explore the ways in which all types of data can be extracted from AutoCAD and made available to you, your coworkers, and other programs. First, you will discover how to get specific data on your drawings. Then you will look at ways to exchange data with other programs—such as word processors, desktop publishing software, and even other CAD programs.

GETTING INFORMATION ABOUT A DRAWING

AutoCAD can instantly give you precise information about your drawing, such as the area, perimeter, and location of an object; the base point, current mode settings, and space used in a drawing; and the time at which a drawing was created and last edited. In this section you will practice extracting this type of information from your drawing, using options on the Assist ➤ Inquiry menu.

FINDING THE AREA OR LOCATION OF AN OBJECT

Architects, engineers, and facilities planners often need to know the square-foot area of a room or a section of a building. A structural engineer might want to find the cross-sectional area of a beam. In this section you will practice determining the areas of both regular and irregular objects.

▼ TIP

To find absolute coordinates in a drawing, use the ID command. Choose Locate Point on the List flyout on the Object Properties Toolbar, or type **ID** ↵. At the prompt ID Point, use the Osnap overrides to pick a point, and its x, y, and z coordinates will be displayed on the prompt line.

First you will find out the square-foot area of the living room and entry of your studio unit plan.

1. Start AutoCAD and open the Unit file you created earlier, or use the Unit file from the companion CD.

2. ZOOM into the living room and entry area.

3. Click and drag List from the Object Properties toolbar, then select Area, or type **Area** ↵ at the command prompt.

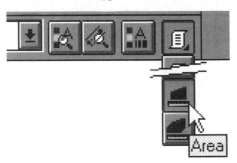

4. At the <First point>/Object/Add/Subtract: prompt, pick the lower-left corner of the living room near coordinate 15′– 0″,6′–10″ (see Figure 14.1).

5. At the Next point: prompt, pick the upper-left corner of the kitchenette near coordinate 15′–0″, 25′–5″.

6. Continue to pick the corners, as shown in Figure 14.1, outlining the living room and entry area until you have come full circle to the first point. You don't need to pick the first point a second time.

7. When you complete the circuit, press ↵. You get the message

   Area = 42209.00 sq in (293.1181 sq ft), Perimeter = 76′–0″

There is no limit to the number of points you can pick to define an area. This means you can obtain the areas of very complex shapes.

III

Becoming an Expert

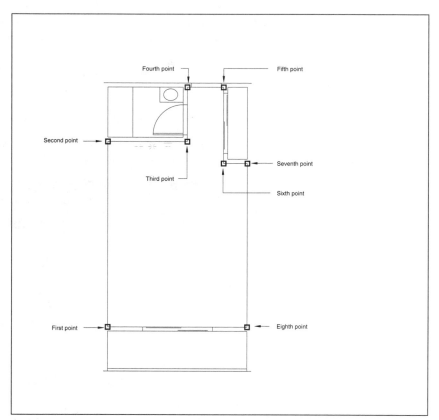

Figure 14.1: Selecting the points to determine the area of the living room and entry

Using Boundary

Using the Object option of the AREA command, you can also select circles and polylines for area calculations. Using this option in conjunction with another AutoCAD utility called Boundary, you can quickly get the area of a bounded space. You will recall from the discussion on hatch patterns in *Chapter* 6 that a region polyline is drawn when you use the Boundary Hatch (BHATCH) function; Boundary works similarly. Where Bhatch generates a hatch pattern that conforms to the outline of a boundary, Boundary generates a polyline outline without adding the hatch. Here's how to use it.

1. Set the layers so the doors are turned off and the door headers are on.

2. Click and drag Rectangle on the Draw palette, then select Boundary to get the Boundary Creation dialog box.

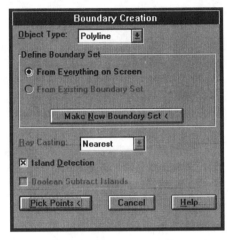

3. Click on the Pick Points button. The dialog box closes.

4. At the Select internal point prompt, click on the interior of the unit plan. The outline of the interior is highlighted (see Figure 14.2).

5. Press ↵. Nothing seems to have happened, but Boundary has drawn an outline of the floor area using a polyline.

6. Select any line that bounds the interior area, using a crossing window. The boundary is highlighted, showing you where the new polyline occurs.

7. Click on Area from the Object Properties toolbar, or type **Area** ↵ at the command prompt, and then enter **O** ↵ for the Object option.

8. Ctrl-click on the boundary; when it is highlighted, press ↵. You get the same Area... message as in the previous exercise.

III

Becoming an Expert

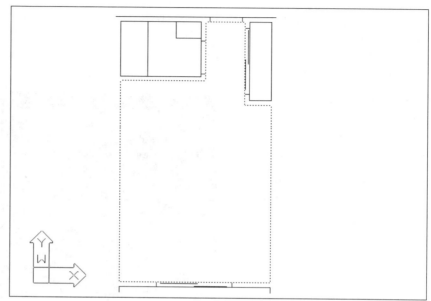

Figure 14.2: Once you select a point on the interior of the plan using Boundary, an outline of the area is highlighted.

The BOUNDARY command creates a polyline that conforms to the boundary of an area. This feature, combined with the ability of the AREA command to find the area of a polyline, makes short work of area calculations.

FINDING THE AREA OF COMPLEX SHAPES

The BOUNDARY command works well if the shape or the area you want to find is not complex. For complex objects, you must also enlist the aid of the other AREA command options: Object, Add, and Subtract. Using Add and Subtract, you can maintain a running total of several separate areas being calculated. This gives you flexibility in finding areas of complex shapes.

The exercise in this section guides you through the use of these options. First, you'll look at how you can keep a running tally of areas. In preparation for the exercise, follow these steps:

1. Exit the Unit file, and open the file named **Flange** from the companion CD. Don't bother to save changes in the Unit File.

2. Use the Edit Polyline option on the Modify palette (PEDIT command is described in *Chapter 13*) to turn the arcs into polyline arcs before you start the AREA command (see Figure 14.3).

Now study the shape to see what rectangular areas can be selected first. Figure 14.4 shows the areas that can be determined by selecting points. Then you must determine the areas to be subtracted from the area calculation. When AutoCAD calculates a polyline area, it automatically connects the endpoints. In our flange example, the entire

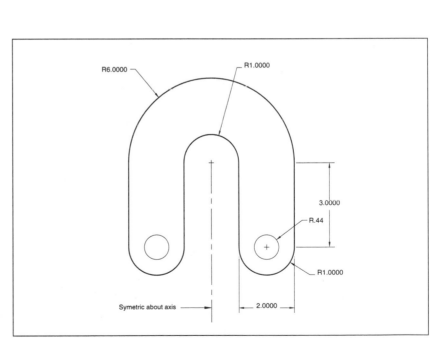

Figure 14.3: A flange to a fictitious mechanical device

III

Becoming an Expert

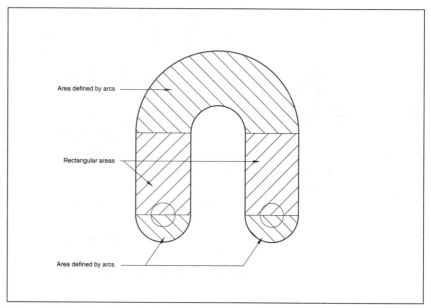

Figure 14.4: The flange, broken down into types of areas

area of the large arc in the flange will be calculated, including the area covered by the smaller concentric arc defining the inside of the flange (see Figure 14.5). This means the area of the smaller arc will have to be subtracted from the overall area calculation.

Finding the Gross Area

Once you have made these determinations, you can proceed to use the AREA command to find the gross area. First, take the areas of the rectangular shapes.

1. Click on Area from the Object Properties toolbar to start the Area command again.

2. Type **A** ⏎ for the Add option.

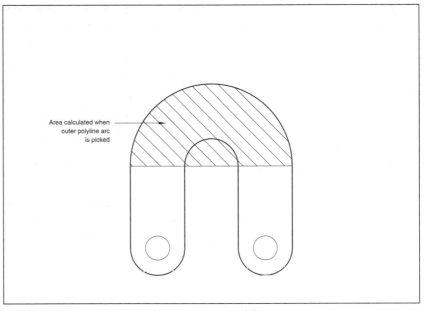

Figure 14.5: Area calculated when selecting polyline arcs

3. Pick the four corners of one rectangle and press ↵. This causes AutoCAD to calculate the area of that rectangle:

   Area = 6.0000, Perimeter = 10.0000
   Total area = 6.0000
   <First point> /Object/Subtract:

4. Pick the corners of the other rectangle and press ↵ again.

Once you have picked the second set of corners, the area value in the prompt changes:

   Area = 6.0000, Perimeter = 10.0000
   Total area = 12.0000
   <First point> /Object/Subtract:

III

Becoming an Expert

The new area is twice the first area calculated, because AutoCAD adds the previously calculated area to the current area and both rectangular areas measured are the same (see Figure 14.6).

You may have noticed that as you selected points in step 3, the prompt said (ADD mode) Next point:. This prompt helps remind you that you are in Add mode. Also, if you were to press ↵ without selecting a point, you would remain in the AREA command. While you are in Add or Subtract mode, AutoCAD assumes you want to continue to add to or subtract from your area count. Whenever you enter either of these modes, AutoCAD maintains a running count of the areas you are selecting and leaves you in the AREA command, so you can continue to add areas to or subtract them from your running total.

We are still in the AREA command, so let's continue by adding the area defined by the polyline arcs.

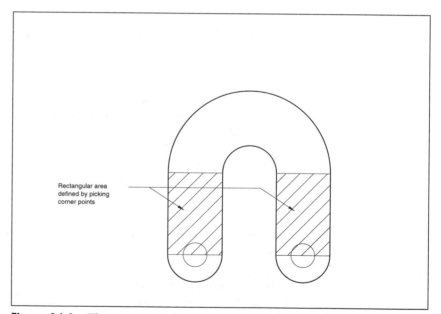

Rectangular area
defined by picking
corner points

Figure 14.6: The two rectangular areas selected for the area calculation

5. Enter **O** ↵ to select the Object option.

6. At the <ADD mode> Select objects: prompt, pick the outer polyline arcs (see Figure 14.7). As you pick the arcs, the running total area is displayed above the prompt, along with the area and perimeter of the object selected.

7. When you are done selecting the arcs, press ↵. This brings you back into the point-selection mode.

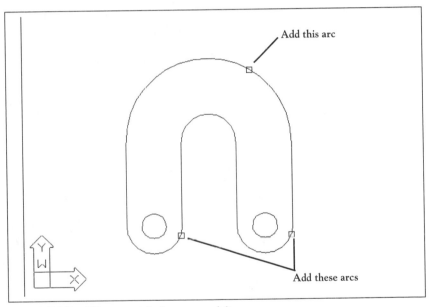

Add this arc

Add these arcs

Figure 14.7:   Where to pick the outer polyline arcs

Some area geometries make it impossible to obtain the gross area first. In these situations, you can use the Subtract option first to find the negative areas, and then use Add to find the gross areas.

Subtracting Unwanted Areas from the Area Calculation

Now that you have the gross area, you must take the areas that you don't want to include as part of the area count and subtract them from the current running total area.

III

Becoming an Expert

▼ NOTE

Now that you are in Subtract mode, Add is the current area-selection option.

1. At the First point/Object/Subtract: prompt, enter **S** ↵ or pick Subtract from the Area menu.

2. At the <First point>/Object/Add: prompt, pick the Object option again, since you are going to subtract the area defined by one polyline arc and the circles.

3. At the <SUBTRACT mode> Select objects: prompt, pick the two circles and the arc defining the inside of the flange, as shown in Figure 14.8. As you pick the objects, the running total is displayed again above the prompt.

4. Once you are done, you see the final total area above the prompt line:

   Total area = 26.4940
   <SUBTRACT mode> Select object:

5. To exit the AREA command, press ↵ twice.

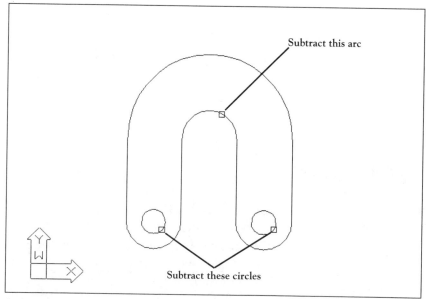

Figure 14.8: Where to pick the subtractive objects

It is important to remember that whenever you press ⏎ during an area calculation, AutoCAD automatically connects the first and last points and returns the area calculated. You can continue to select points or objects defining areas, but the additional areas will be calculated from the *next* point you pick.

This last exercise was intended to give you practice in using some of the other AREA command options. Looking back, note that you could have used the BOUNDARY command to first outline the main area of the part, and then used the AREA command's Add, Subtract, and Object options to quickly get an area count. You could have then saved the Boundary polyline for future reference or erased it.

In this example, you obtained the area of a mechanical object. However, the same process works for any type of area you want to calculate. It can be the area of a piece of property on a topographical map, or the area of a floor plan. For example, you can use the Entity option to find an irregular area like the one shown in Figure 14.9, as long as it is a polyline. Remember: If the polyline is not closed, the AREA command assumes the first and last points picked are connected, and calculates the area accordingly.

Recording Area Data in a Drawing File

Once you find the area of an object, you'll often need to record it somewhere. You can write it down in a project log book, but this is easy to overlook. A more dependable way to store area information is to use *attributes*.

For example, in a building project, you can create a block that contains attributes for the room number, room area, and the date when the room area was last taken. You might make the area and date attributes invisible, so only the room number appears. This block could then be inserted into every room. Once you find the area, you can easily add it to your block attribute with the DDATE command. In fact, such a block could be used with any drawing in which you wished to store area data.

▼ TIP

Appendix C describes an AutoLISP program on your companion disk that lets you easily record area data in a drawing file.

III

Becoming an Expert

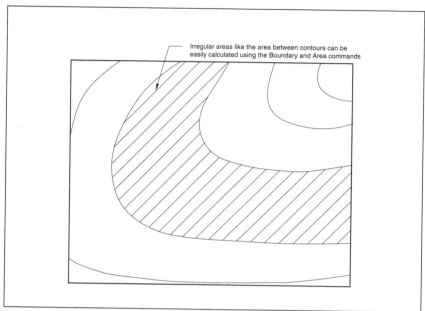

Irregular areas like the area between contours can be easily calculated using the Boundary and Area commands

Figure 14.9: The site plan with an area to be calculated

DETERMINING THE DRAWING'S STATUS

When you work with a group of people on a large project, keeping track of a drawing's setup becomes crucial. The STATUS command enables you to obtain some general information about the drawing you are working on, such as the base point, current mode settings, and workspace or computer memory use. STATUS is especially helpful when you are editing a drawing someone else has worked on, because you may want to identify and change settings for your own style of working. When you pick Status from the Data menu, you get a list like the one shown in Figure 14.10.

Here is a brief description of each item on the status screen:

154 entities in C:\ACADr13\win\Drawing: The number of entities or objects in the drawing.

Model space limits are: The coordinates of the Model Space limits (see *Chapter 3* for more details on limits).

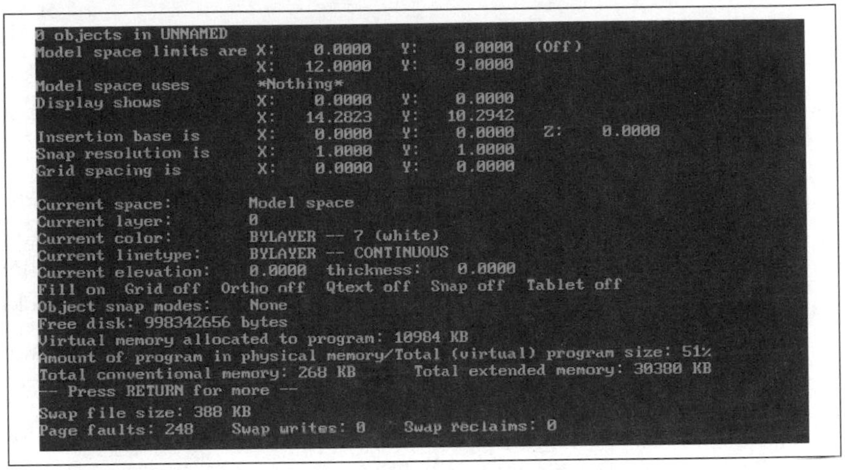

```
0 objects in UNNAMED
Model space limits are X:      0.0000   Y:      0.0000   (Off)
                       X:     12.0000   Y:      9.0000
Model space uses         *Nothing*
Display shows          X:      0.0000   Y:      0.0000
                       X:     14.2823   Y:     10.2942
Insertion base is      X:      0.0000   Y:      0.0000   Z:      0.0000
Snap resolution is     X:      1.0000   Y:      1.0000
Grid spacing is        X:      0.0000   Y:      0.0000

Current space:         Model space
Current layer:         0
Current color:         BYLAYER -- 7 (white)
Current linetype:      BYLAYER -- CONTINUOUS
Current elevation:     0.0000   thickness:     0.0000
Fill on  Grid off  Ortho off  Qtext off  Snap off  Tablet off
Object snap modes:     None
Free disk: 998342656 bytes
Virtual memory allocated to program: 10984 KB
Amount of program in physical memory/Total (virtual) program size: 51%
Total conventional memory: 268 KB      Total extended memory: 30380 KB
-- Press RETURN for more --
Swap file size: 388 KB
Page faults: 248     Swap writes: 0     Swap reclaims: 0
```

Figure 14.10: The Status screen

Model space uses: The area the drawing occupies; equivalent to the extents of the drawing.

**Over: If present, means that part of drawing is outside the limit boundary.

Display shows: The area covered by the current view.

Insertion base, Snap resolution, and Grid spacing lines: The current default values for these mode settings.

Current space: Model Space or Paper Space.

Current layer: The current default layer.

Current color: The color assigned to new objects.

Current linetype: the line type assigned to new objects.

Current elevation/thickness: The current default z coordinate for new objects, plus the default thickness of objects; these are both 3D-related settings (see *Chapter 15* for details).

Fill, Grid, Ortho, Qtext, Snap, and Tablet: The status of these options.

Object snap modes: The current default Osnap setting.

▼ **NOTE**

For more information on memory use, see *Appendix A*.

Free disk: The amount of space you have left on your hard disk for AutoCAD's temporary files.

Virtual memory allocated to program: The amount of RAM AutoCAD has reserved for itself.

Amount of program in physical memory/Total (virtual) program size: The percentage of available RAM AutoCAD is using for the program and, if greater than the RAM capacity, the total amount of RAM being used in kilobytes.

Total conventional memory: The amount of base 640K DOS memory that is available.

Total extended memory: The amount of available extended memory.

Available free memory: The amount of free memory available in both physical memory (RAM present in the computer) and virtual memory (hard-disk page space used to temporarily store data from RAM).

Swap file size/Swap file size limit: The current swap-file size will vary depending on the drawing size and on what external AutoLISP or ADS applications you are using. Includes a reading on the limit of the swap-file size that is set using Auto-CAD's Cfig386.EXE utility. See *Appendix A* for more on Cfig386.EXE.

In addition to being useful in understanding a drawing file, STATUS is an invaluable tool for troubleshooting. Frequently, problems with a file can be isolated by a technical support person using the information provided by the STATUS command.

KEEPING TRACK OF TIME

The TIME command allows you to keep track of the time spent on a drawing, for billing or analysis purposes. You can also use TIME to check the current time and find out when the drawing was created and most recently edited. Because the AutoCAD timer uses your computer's time, be sure the time is set correctly in Windows.

To access the TIME command, enter **Time** ↵ at the command prompt, or select Data ➤ Time. You get a message like the one in Figure 14.11.

The first three lines tell you the current date and time, the date and time the drawing was created, and the last time the drawing was saved or ended.

The fourth line shows the total time spent on the drawing from the point of its creation. This elapsed timer lets you time a particular activity, such as changing the width of all the walls in a floor plan or redesigning a piece of machinery. You can turn the elapsed timer on or off or reset it, by entering **on, off,** or **reset** at the prompt shown as the last line of the message. The timer will not show any time spent on a drawing between the last time it is saved and the time a QUIT command is issued.

The last line tells you when the next automatic save will be.

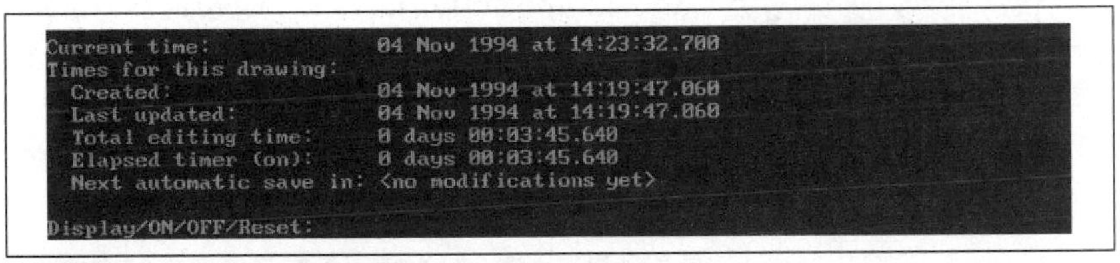

```
Current time:           04 Nov 1994 at 14:23:32.700
Times for this drawing:
  Created:              04 Nov 1994 at 14:19:47.060
  Last updated:         04 Nov 1994 at 14:19:47.060
  Total editing time:   0 days 00:03:45.640
  Elapsed timer (on):   0 days 00:03:45.640
  Next automatic save in: <no modifications yet>

Display/ON/OFF/Reset:
```

Figure 14.11: The Time screen

GETTING INFORMATION FROM SYSTEM VARIABLES

If you've been working through this book's tutorial, you'll have noticed occasional mentions of a *system variable* in conjunction with a command. You can check the status or change the setting of any system variable while you are in the middle of another command. To do this, you simply type an apostrophe ('), followed by the name of the system variable, at the command prompt.

III

Becoming an Expert

For example, if you have started to draw a line, and you suddenly decide you need to rotate your cursor 45°, you can do the following:

1. At the To point prompt, enter **'snapang**.

2. At the New value for SNAPANG prompt, enter a new cursor angle. Once you have entered an angle value, you are returned to the LINE command with the cursor in its new orientation.

You can also recall information such as the last area or distance calculated by AutoCAD. Since the Area system variable duplicates the name of the AREA command, you must enter **'Setvar ⏎ Area ⏎** to read the last area calculation. The SETVAR command lets you list all the system variables and their status, as well as access each system variable individually.

Many of the system variables give you direct access to detailed information about your drawing. They also let you fine-tune your drawing and editing activities. In *Appendix D* you'll find all the information you need to familiarize yourself with the system variables available. Don't feel that you have to memorize them all at once; just be aware that they are available.

STORING SYSTEM DATA FOR LATER RETRIEVAL

If you are working in groups, it is often quite helpful to have a record of the status, editing time, and system variables for particular files, readily available to other group members. It is also convenient to keep records of block and layer information, so you can see if a specific block is included in a drawing or what layers are normally on or off.

The following exercise demonstrates how you can get a record of the information displayed by many of the AutoCAD commands:

▼ TIP

As a shortcut, you can quickly turn the Log File feature on and off by typing **Logfileon** ⏎ and **Logfileoff** ⏎ at the command prompt in AutoCAD.

1. Click on Options ➤ Preferences..., then at the Preferences dialog box, click on the tab labeled Environment at the top of the dialog box. A new set of options appears.

2. Click on the check box labeled Log File in the File group toward the lower left corner of the dialog box, then click on OK.

3. Click on Data ➤ Status.

4. Return to the Preferences dialog box again, select the environment tab, then click on Log File check box again remove the X from the check box. Click OK to exit the dialog box.

5. Switch over to the program manager and start the Notepad application or any text editor.

6. With the text editor, open the file called Acad.LOG in the \Acadr13\Win directory. This is the file that stores the text data from the command prompt whenever the Log File option is turned on. You must turn off the Log File feature before you can actually view this file in AutoCAD.

Since Acad.LOG is a standard text file, you can easily send it to other members of your workgroup, or print it out for a permanent record.

▼
■
■
■
■

EASY ACCESS FOR THE ACAD.LOG FILE

If you want to have easy access to the Acad.LOG file, place it in your AutoCAD r13 program group. Here's how it's done:

1. Open the File manager, then locate and highlight the Acad.LOG file.

2. Click on File ➤ Associate from the File Manager menu.

3. At the Associate dialog box, click on Browse.

4. At the Browse dialog box, locate the text editor you want to use with the Acad.LOG file. Typically, this would be the Notepad.EXE application found in the Windows directory.

5. Click OK at each dialog box, then once you've returned to the File Manager, click and drag Acad.LOG from the File Manager to the AutoCAD r13 program group. A Notepad icon appears with Acad.LOG as its label.

Once this is done, you can open the Acad.LOG file by double-clicking on the Notepad icon in your AutoCAD program group.

III

Becoming an Expert

MANAGING FILES IN AUTOCAD

As your projects become more complex and your library of drawings and symbols expands, you will find yourself devoting a good deal of effort to organizing your files. Backing up, deleting, renaming, and even just searching for files begins to take more of your time. Fortunately, Auto-CAD offers a variety of ways to let you keep up your file housekeeping with a minimum of hassle.

USING THE FILE UTILITIES

You can perform a series of simple file operations directly from AutoCAD by selecting an option from the File ➤ Management cascading menu.

The function of the these options are described here.

> **Unlock** includes the following set of options:
>
> > *List files*   simply lists the files in any directory. You can also filter the list using the Pattern input box.
> >
> > *Copy file*   copies a file to the new location you select using the directory list, with the new name you enter in the input box.
> >
> > *Rename file*   renames a file after you locate the source file using the two list boxes, and then enter a new file name in the input box.
> >
> > *Delete file*   works in the usual way, first displaying a warning message appears asking you to confirm your action.
> >
> > *Unlock files*   unlocks drawing or password files that have been locked (see next section).
> >
> > *Help*   opens AutoCAD's main Help screen.

Audit   checks the current file for any errors and displays the results in the text window.

Recover   attempts to recover damaged or corrupted AutoCAD files. The current file is closed in the process as Recover attempts to open the file to be recovered.

▼
■
■
■
■

EXCHANGING FILES WITH EARLIER RELEASES

One persistent dilemma that has plagued AutoCAD users is how to exchange files between earlier versions of the program. In the past, if you upgraded your AutoCAD, you would find that you were locked out from exchanging your drawings with people using earlier versions. Release 12 alleviated this difficulty by making Release 12 files compatible with Release 11 files.

Now, with Release 13, we have a file structure that is radically different from earlier versions of AutoCAD. Fortunately, you can still exchange files with earlier versions of the program, using the Saveasr12 command. Type **Saveasr12** ↵ at the command prompt. You get the Save Release 12 Drawing As dialog box, which is a typical file dialog box. From here, the command acts like the standard File ➤ Save As command.

You don't get something for nothing, however; there are certain things you will lose when you save a Release 13 file in Release 12 format. Bear these considerations in mind when using the SAVEASR12 command:

- Splines become polyline splines.

- 3DSolids become polylines representing the wireframe of the solid.

- Multilines become polylines.

- Line types with embedded shapes are separated into lines and shapes.

- Dimension styles are not completely translated.

- Line styles are not completely translated.

- TrueType fonts are not supported in Release 12 or earlier versions.

When you invoke SAVEASR12, you will receive a message telling you how the file is being modified to accommodate the limited Release 12 format. You may want to use the LOGFILEON command to store this conversion message for future reference.

UNLOCKING FILES ON A NETWORK

Drawing files are not the only files that are locked. Nearly all types of AutoCAD files—from menu files to font files—are locked while they are being read from disk. They are un-locked, however, once file ac-cess has been completed and the file in question has been loaded.

On a network, there is always the potential for more than one person to access a file at the same time. If more than one person tries to edit the same file at the same time, it can be disastrous to file integrity. For this reason, AutoCAD provides file-locking capability.

Whenever a file is opened for editing, AutoCAD creates a small lock file that exists only during the time the drawing file is being edited; once the file is closed, the lock file is erased. If you try to edit this drawing at the same time someone else is editing it, AutoCAD will detect the lock file and return a message like the following:

```
Waiting for file: Plan1.DWG
Locked by John Doe at 11:55 am on 12/25/95
Press Esc to cancel
```

AutoCAD repeatedly attempts to access the file every five seconds, until either the drawing file is closed by the other user, or you cancel the operation by pressing Esc. If you cancel, you get the following message and must then wait your turn to access this file:

```
Access denied: Plan1.DWG
Press RETURN to continue:
```

Sometimes, however, a lock file may exist even though its associated drawing file has been closed. This can occur when someone aborts an editing session by using the Ctrl-Alt-Del key-combination. When such an orphaned lock file exists, you must manually unlock the file by using File ➤ Management ➤ Unlock file. (You can also delete the lock file using the Windows File Manager.)

You can recognize a lock file by its file name extension; Table 14.1 lists lock file extensions and their AutoCAD file counterparts.

Table 14.1: AutoCAD Filename Extensions and Their Lock File Counterparts

File Description	Standard Extension	Lock File Extension
Audit files	.ADT	.ADK
Drawing backup	.BAK	.BKK
AutoCAD configuration	.CFG	.CFK
Drawing	.DWG	.DWK
Binary data exchange	.DXB	.DBK
DXF drawing interchange	.DXF	.DFK
Attribute data in DXF format	.DXX	.DXK
AutoShade filmroll	.FLM	.FLK
Line type definition	.LIN	.LIK
Compiled menu	.MNX	~MNK
Converted old drawing	.OLD	.OLK
Plot configuration parameters	.PCP	.PCK
Plot file	.PLT	.PLK
Login file	.PWD	.PWK
Mass properties	.MPR	.MPK
Multiline styles	.MLN	.MLK
ACIS file	.SAT	.SAK
Shape and font	.SHX	.SXK
Slides	.SLD	.SDK
Stereolithography file	.STL	.STK
Attribute template	.TXT	.TXK
Xref log	.XLG	.XLK

III

Becoming an Expert

EXCHANGING CAD DATA WITH OTHER PROGRAMS

AutoCAD offers many ways to share data with other programs. Perhaps the most common type of data exchange is to simply share drawing data with other CAD programs. In this section, you'll look at how you can export and import CAD drawings using the DXF file format. You'll also look at how you can use bitmap graphics, both to and from AutoCAD, through the Windows clipboard.

Other types of data exchange involve text, spreadsheets, and databases. We cover database links in *Chapter 10*, but here, we'll look at how you can include text, spreadsheet, and database files in a drawing or include AutoCAD drawings in other program files using a Windows feature called Object Linking and Embedding.

USING THE .DXF FILE FORMAT

A .DXF file is a text file containing all the information needed to reconstruct a drawing. It is often used to exchange drawings created with other programs. Many micro-CAD programs, including some 3D perspective programs, can generate or read files in .DXF format. You may want to use a 3D program to view your drawing in a perspective view, or you may have a consultant who uses a different CAD program that accepts .DXF files. There are many 3D rendering programs that read .DXF files, on both the IBM PC and compatibles and on Apple Macintosh computers. Most 2D drafting programs also read and write .DXF files.

▼ NOTE

AutoCAD no longer supports the IGES standard for CAD data translation.

You should be aware that not all programs that read .DXF files will accept all the data stored therein. Many programs that claim to read .DXF files will "throw away" much of their information. Attributes are perhaps the most commonly ignored objects, followed by many of the 3D objects, such as meshes and 3Dfaces. But .DXF files, though not the most perfect medium for translating data, have become something of a standard.

Exporting .DXF Files

To export your current drawing as a .DXF file, try the following:

▼ NOTE

You can also click on File ➤ Export…, then enter the name of your export file including the .DXF file name extension. AutoCAD will skip the prompt in step 3 and proceed to create the DXF file.

1. Enter **DXFout** ↵. The Create .DXF File dialog box appears.

2. In the File input box, enter the name you wish to give your .DXF file, and click OK.

3. At the next prompt,

   Enter decimal places of accuracy (0 to 16)/Objects/Binary <6>:

   press ↵ to accept the default, or enter a value to increase or decrease the decimal accuracy of your .DXF file.

In step 3 above, you have two additional options:

- To specify that your .DXF file be written in a binary format, enter **B** ↵ (for Binary). This helps make the file smaller, but some other CAD programs are unable to read the binary version of .DXF files.

- To select specific objects for export, enter **O** ↵. You are then prompted to select objects. Once you are done, you see the Enter decimal places of accuracy prompt again.

Importing .DXF Files

To import .DXF files, follow these steps:

1. Click on File ➤ Import…, or enter **DXFin** ↵. A typical file dialog box appears.

2. Choose .DXF from the pop-up list at the bottom of the dialog box (you don't need to do this if you enter **DXFin** at the command prompt).

3. Locate and select the .DXF file you wish to import.

4. Double-click on the file name to begin importing it.

III

Becoming an Expert

If the import drawing is large, AutoCAD may take several minutes to complete the process.

USING AUTOCAD IN DESKTOP PUBLISHING

As you probably know, AutoCAD is a natural for creating line art, and because of its popularity, most desktop publishing programs are designed to import AutoCAD drawings in one form or another. Those of you who employ desktop publishing software to generate user manuals or other technical documents will probably want to be able to use AutoCAD drawings in your work. In this section, we will examine ways to output AutoCAD drawings for use by the two most popular desktop publishing programs available for the IBM PC: Page-Maker and Ventura.

EXPORTING DRAWINGS TO DESKTOP PUBLISHING PROGRAMS

▼ TIP

If you are a circuit board de-signer or drafter, you will want to use the PostScript Out op-tion to output your layout to li-notronic typesetting devices. This will save time and file size since this option converts AutoCAD entities into true PostScript descriptions.

There are two methods for transferring AutoCAD drawings to a desk-top publishing program. Since most of these programs accept HPGL and PostScript files, you can either have AutoCAD plot to a file using an HPGL plotter configuration, or you can use the PostScript Out op-tion found under File ➤ Export ➤ PostScript.

HPGL Output

First, let's look at how you export an HPGL file.

1. Configure your plotter setting for a Hewlett-Packard plotter (HPGL). Just about any of the Hewlett-Packard plotter op-tions will work.

2. Click on File ➤ Print. Then use the Device and Default Selection dialog box to set the default plotter to Hewlett-Packard.

3. PLOT your drawing to a file.

PostScript Output

Another method for file transfer is to use the Encapsulated Post-Script (EPS) format. If you use PostScript fonts in your drawing, then the PostScript output file will contain the proper code to utilize the true PostScript fonts in your output device.

▼ TIP

You can also choose File ➤ Export, then select Encapsulated PS (*.EPS) from the List file of Type drop-down list in the Export Data dialog box. Enter a name for your file, then click on OK. AutoCAD will skip steps 2 through 7 and immediately starts to write the drawing to an .EPS file.

1. At the command prompt, type **Psout** ↵.

2. Enter a name for your file and include the file name extension, then click OK.

3. At the What to plot... prompt, select an option.

4. At the Include a screen preview image in the file? (None/EPSI/TIFF) <None>: prompt, press ↵.

5. At the Size units (Inches or Millimeters) <Inches>: prompt, press ↵.

▼ TIP

You can increase the "resolution" and accuracy of your exported drawings by using the larger output sizes.

6. At the Output Inches=Drawing Units or Fit or ? <Fit>: prompt, press ↵. You then see the following list:

Standard Values for Output Size

Width	Height	Size
A	8.0000	10.5000
B	10.0000	16.0000
C	16.0000	21.0000
D	21.0000	33.0000
E	33.0000	43.0000
F	28.0000	40.0000
G	11.0000	90.0000
H	28.0000	143.0000
J	34.0000	176.0000
K	40.0000	143.0000
A4	7.8000	11.2000
A3	10.7000	15.6000
A2	15.6000	22.4000

III

Becoming an Expert

Standard Values for Output Size

Width	Height	Size
A0	32.2000	45.9000
USER	7.50	10.50

7. At the Enter the Size or Width,Height (in Inches) <A>: prompt, enter the appropriate sheet size. Chances are, if you are importing AutoCAD documents into PageMaker or Ventura, you'll want the A size, or you can enter a custom width and height at this prompt.

8. AutoCAD displays the message

   Effective plotting area: X.XX wide by Y.YY high

   where X.XX and Y.YY are the width and height of the output image. AutoCAD will take a moment to generate the file and then return to the command prompt.

▼ NOTE

You can also use File ➤ Export... (Export) to export .EPS files. When the Export Data dialog box appears, enter the desired name of your file including the .EPS file name extension. Export will skip over all the prompts shown in here and go directly to creating the .EPS file.

If you choose to enter **EPSI** or **TIFF** when you are asked if you want a preview image (at step 2 above), you will get this prompt:

   Screen preview image size (128x128 is standard)? (128/256/512) <128>:

In this case, you can enter a value for the image size in pixels. The preview image is somewhat crude but is only provided to allow easy identification of the art when it is pasted into a document. For this reason, you may not need to increase the size unless the image cannot be identified easily using the default value.

ADDING SOUND, MOTION, AND PHOTOS TO YOUR DRAWINGS

Perhaps the most exciting addition to AutoCAD in release 13 is its ability to include data from other Windows sources. These include scanned photographs in the form of bitmap files, sound files, and even live action video and animation. Imagine how you might be able to enhance your drawings with photographs, sound and full motion video. You can include voice annotation, or, if the file is to go to a client, an animated video clip of your building or mechanical design. The potential for this feature is enormous.

You can also insert more typical types of data like spreadsheets and databases into your AutoCAD drawing. A spreadsheet inserted into an AutoCAD drawing can be set up to automatically reflect changes in the original spreadsheet document, in much the same way that cross-reference drawings are automatically updated.

Here's a step-by-step description of how to import data from an Excel spreadsheet:

1. With AutoCAD open, start Excel and open the spreadsheet file you want to import.

2. Highlight the cells you want to bring into AutoCAD, then choose Edit ➤ Copy from the Excel menu bar.

3. Return to AutoCAD, then choose Edit ➤ Paste Special. The Paste Special dialog box appears. You can use this dialog box to choose how the spreadsheet data is imported.

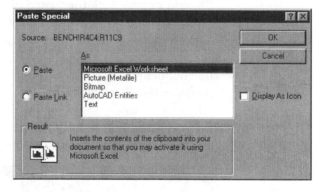

4. Click on the Paste Link radio button on the left side of the dialog box. This option causes the pasted spreadsheet data to be linked to the source file (the next section, "Choosing Between Linking and Embedding," describes the difference between a simple Paste and a Paste Link).

5. Select the Excel Worksheet option, then click on OK. The spreadsheet will appear in the AutoCAD drawing area.

III

Becoming an Expert

You can also use the Windows 95 drag-and-drop feature to insert objects into AutoCAD. To do this, locate the file using the Windows Explorer or the Drive icon in the My Computer icon on your Desktop. Once you've located the file, drag it into AutoCAD. By using the Ctrl and Shift keys, you can control how the file is pasted into AutoCAD:

Drag only	Result determined by target and source
Shift+drag	Move the file
Ctrl+drag	Copy the file
Shift+Ctrl+drag	Link the file

If AutoCAD is minimized to a button, drag the file over the button, wait until AutoCAD opens, then drop the file into the AutoCAD Window. If the pasted object is an image file, such as a TIFF or Targa file, the image will appear. If it's not an image data file like a spreadsheet or database, the data will appear as it does in the application it came from. A sound file will appear as an icon representing the application you have associated with the sound file. Video files display their first frame.

To edit or play back the pasted object, double click on it. The application associated with the object will start up and the object will appear in the application. You can make your changes, then select File ➤ Update to return to AutoCAD (Update replaces the usual Save option in the File menu of the object's application). Sound and video play back when you double click on the sound icon or video image.

If you want to create a new spreadsheet and paste it into AutoCAD, you can choose Edit ➤ Insert Object... (Insertobj) from the AutoCAD pull-down menu bar. The Insert Object dialog box appears.

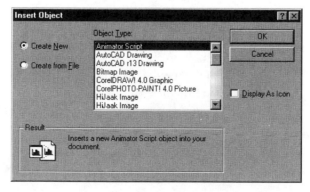

This shows a list of the types of files on your system that support OLE. The contents of this list will depend on the applications you have installed in your system and whether they support OLE. From here, you can choose an item on the list to create a new object to paste into Auto-CAD. If you select Microsoft Excel Worksheet, for example, Excel will open with a blank worksheet into which you can add data. If you choose a bitmap image, the Windows Paint application will open and, simultaneously, a bitmap image will appear in the AutoCAD drawing area. As you begin to draw in Window Paint, the image is replicated in the AutoCAD pasted image.

Choosing Between Linking or Embedding

When you paste a data object into your AutoCAD file, you have the option to have it *linked* to the source file or to *embed* it. If you link it to the source file, then the pasted object can be updated whenever the source file is modified. This is similar to an AutoCAD cross-referenced file (see *Chapter 12* for more on cross-referenced files).

If a file is not linked to its source file, then it is considered an embedded object. You can still open the application associated with the object by double clicking on the object, but the object is no longer associated with the source file. This is similar to a drawing inserted as a block where changes in the source drawing file have no effect on the inserted block.

You can control whether an object is linked or embedded by choosing the Paste Link (linked) or Paste (embedded) radio button from the Paste Special dialog box.

Editing Links

Once you've pasted an object with links, you can make changes to the object by right-clicking on it. You'll see a pop-up menu with the options Cut, Copy, Clear, Undo, and, if it's an Excel worksheet, Worksheet Object. Cut, Copy, and Clear perform the standard Windows Clipboard functions. For example, if you want to delete a pasted object, right-click on it and choose Clear from the pop-up menu. The Undo option will undo the last command or option chosen. Click on Worksheet Object; you'll see Edit, Open, and Convert options. Both Edit and Open let you make changes to the source file. The Convert option opens the Convert dialog box.

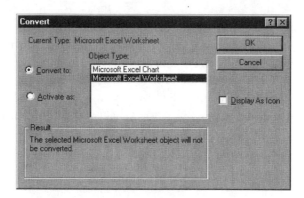

The list box offers conversion options. In addition, you can change the pasted spreadsheet into an icon, if you prefer.

Other types of objects will offer a different option at the bottom of the pop-up menu. Bitmap images, for example, will show the option Bitmap Image Option instead of Worksheet Object. The suboptions of Edit, Open, and Convert are the same, however.

USING THE CLIPBOARD TO EXPORT AUTOCAD DRAWINGS

Just as you can cut and paste data into AutoCAD from applications that support OLE, you can also cut and paste AutoCAD images to other applications. This can be useful as a way of including AutoCAD images into word processed documents, spreadsheets, or desktop publishing documents. It can also be useful in creating background images for visualization programs like 3D Studio, or paint programs like Fractal Painter.

▼ **NOTE**

If you cut and paste an Auto-CAD drawing to another file using OLE, then send the file to someone using another computer, they must also have AutoCAD Release 13 installed before they can edit the pasted AutoCAD drawing.

The receiving application need not support OLE, but if it does, then the exported drawing can be edited with AutoCAD and will maintain it's accuracy as a CAD drawing. Otherwise, the AutoCAD image will be converted to a bitmap graphic.

To use the clipboard to export a specific view from your AutoCAD drawing, use the Edit ➤ Copy View (Copylink) option. Here's an example of the steps to take.

1. While in AutoCAD, set up the view you want exported.

2. Choose Edit ➤ Copy View or type **Copylink** ↵. AutoCAD will pause for a second then the command prompt returns.

3. Open the receiving application and file, then choose the Paste Special… from the Edit pull-down menu to paste and link the AutoCAD image to the file.

The receiving file and application must support OLE in order to link or embed the AutoCAD image. Otherwise, the image will be pasted as a simple bitmap image with no links to AutoCAD.

If you want to be more selective about what you are copying to the clipboard, you can choose Edit ➤ Copy or Edit ➤ Cut from the Auto-CAD menu bar in step 2. You are then prompted to select objects. You can then select specific objects you want to copy to the clipboard.

COPYING AND PASTING IN THE TEXT WINDOW

We've described how you can record the text from the AutoCAD text window using the Log File feature. You can also record the entire contents of the text window to the Windows clipboard. Here's how it's done:

1. Move the arrow cursor to the command prompt window at the bottom of the AutoCAD window.

2. Right-click on the mouse. A pull-down menu appears.

3. Click on Copy History. The entire contents of the text window is copied to the clipboard.

By default, the text window stores 400 lines of text. You can change this number by changing the options in the Text Window group in the Misc tab of the Preferences dialog box.

If you only want to copy a portion of the text window to the clipboard. do the following:

1. Press the F2 function key to open the text window.

2. Using the I-beam text cursor, highlight the text you wish to copy to the clipboard.

III

Becoming an Expert

▼

■

■

■

■

> **3.** Right click on your mouse, then click on Copy from the pop-up menu. You can also click on Edit ➤ Copy from the text window's menu bar. The highlighted text is copied to the clipboard.
>
> You may notice two other options on the pop-up menu: Paste and Preferences…. Paste will paste the first line of the contents of the clipboard into the command line. This can be useful for entering re-petitive text or for storing and retrieving a frequently used com-mand. Preferences… will open the Preferences dialog box.

EXPORTING TIFF, GIF, PCX, AND FAX FILES

In *Chapter 11*, you read about ways to import TIFF, GIF, PCX, and Post-Script files into AutoCAD. You can also export to these formats, as well as to a wide variety of other raster-format files, including FAX group III.

There are numerous situations that require output in one of these ras-ter formats. You may want to use a raster format for your desktop pub-lishing program, instead of HPGL or PostScript. Or you may want to use one of your drawings in a paint or rendering program—to add a texture map to 3D Studio, for example. If you're putting together a presenta-tion, you may want to have slides made of some of your CAD drawings. For a multimedia presentation, you will most likely prefer to use raster images. With AutoCAD's raster output capabilities, you won't have to resort to an intermediate translator for obtaining raster files.

Here are the steps for accessing this feature:

1. Click on Options ➤ Configure.

2. As suggested by the prompt at the bottom of the screen, press ↵ to get through the opening screen.

3. At the configuration list menu, enter **5** ↵ to select the Configure Plotter option.

4. At the Plotter Configuration menu, enter **1** ↵ to add a plotter to your configuration.

5. Press ↵ twice to get a list of plotter options. Enter the number that corresponds with the item labeled

   Raster file export ADI 4.2 - by Autodesk

   You will then see the following list:

   Supported models:
   1. 320 × 200 (CGA/MCGA Colour)
   2. 640 × 200 (CGA Monochrome)
   3. 640 × 350 (EGA)
   4. 640 × 400
   5. 640 × 480 (VGA)
   6. 720 × 540
   7. 800 × 600
   8. 1024 × 768
   9. 1152 × 900 (Sun standard)
   10. 1600 × 1280 (Sun hi-res)
   11. User-defined
   Enter selection, 1 to 11 <1>:

6. Enter the number corresponding to the resolution you want. Next, you'll see this list:

   1. GIF (CompuServe Graphics Interchange Format)
   2. X Window dump (xwd compatible)
   3. Jef Poskanzer's Portable Bitmap Toolkit Formats
   4. Microsoft Windows Device-independent Bitmap (.BMP)
   5. TrueVision TGA Format
   6. Z-Soft PCX Format
   7. Sun Rasterfile
   8. Flexible Image Transfer System (FITS)
   9. Encapsulated PostScript image (Adobe-2.0; EPSF-2.0)
   10. TIFF (Tag Image File Format)
   11. FAX Image (Group 3 Encoding)
   12. Amiga IFF / ILBM Format

III

Becoming an Expert

7. Enter the number that corresponds to the type of file you want to export. A series of prompts will then ask you questions pertaining to the option you choose.

8. When you are done answering the prompts, you return to AutoCAD's drawing editor. At the Plot Configuration dialog box, select the raster format.

The range of raster output options is quite comprehensive. Chances are, if you need raster output from AutoCAD, at least one of the options from the previous list should fill your needs. The FAX Image format is perhaps the most interesting option, offering the ability to plot to a remote location via a fax machine.

TAKING ADVANTAGE OF STEREOLITHOGRAPHY

Stereolithography is a process that generates resin models of 3D computer solid models. It offers the mechanical designer a method of rapidly prototyping designs directly from AutoCAD drawings. The process requires special equipment that will read computer files in a particular format.

AutoCAD supports stereolithography through the STLOUT command. This command generates an .STL file, which can be used with Stereolithograph Apparatus (STA) to generate a model. You must first create a 3D solid model in AutoCAD (see *Chapter 18* for details); then you can proceed with the following steps to create the .STL file:

1. Type **Stlout** ↵ at the command prompt.

2. At the Select a single object for STL output prompt, select a solid or a set of solids, and press ↵. All solids must reside in the positive x, y, and z coordinates of the world coordinate system.

3. At the Create a binary STL file? <Y> prompt, press ↵ to create a binary file, or enter **N** ↵ for an ASCII file.

4. At the Create STL File dialog box, enter a name for your file.

The AutoCAD 3D solids are translated into a set of triangular-faceted meshes in the .STL file. You can use the Facetress system variable to control the fineness of these meshes.

IF YOU WANT TO EXPERIMENT...

If you use a desktop publishing program in your work, you may want to experiment with various ways of exporting AutoCAD files to that program. Add a Hewlett-Packard plotter to your plotter configuration and try the following exercises:

1. Open the Unit plan.
2. Start the PLOT command.
3. Click on Device and Default Selection, and click on the Hewlett-Packard plotter listed.
4. Check the Plot to File check box.
5. Use the Size button in the Paper Size and Orientation group to set the size to 11×17.
6. Enter **1/2"** in the Plotted Inches input box and **1'** in the Drawing Units box.
7. Accept the default settings for the rest of the plotter prompts.
8. When the plotting is done, exit AutoCAD.
9. Open your desktop publishing program. Start a new file called **Unitdtp**.

If you are using PageMaker:

1. Choose Place from the Files menu.
2. At the Place File dialog box, enter the appropriate path and file name to access the Unit plot file.
3. You may get another dialog box asking for a file format type. If this happens, pick HPGL.

III

Becoming an Expert

4. When your cursor changes to an icon reflecting the type of drawing file you are importing, pick the upper-right corner of your page, and your drawing will appear. You may have to resize it to fit on the page.

Try adding a few notes to your drawing, and then print out the file.

In this chapter, you have seen how AutoCAD allows you to access information ranging from the areas of objects to information from other programs. You may never use some of these features, but knowing they are there may at some point help you to solve a production problem.

You've just completed Part III of our tutorial. If you've followed the tutorial from the beginning, this is where you get a diploma. You have reached Expert status in 2D drawing and have the tools to tackle any drawing project thrown at you. You need only to log in some time on a few real projects to round out your experience.

From now on, you won't need to follow the book's chapters in order. If you're interested in 3D, continue to Part IV, where you'll get thorough instructions on 3D drawing and imaging with AutoCAD. Otherwise, you can skip to Part V to become a full-fledged AutoCAD power-user.

Also, don't miss the appendices—they are packed with information that will answer many of your specific questions or problems. Of course, the entire book is a ready reference to answer questions as they arise or to refresh your memory about specific commands.

Good luck!

PART FOUR

MODELING ■ AND ■ IMAGING ■ IN 3D

While 2D drafting is AutoCAD's workhorse application, AutoCAD's 3D capabilities give you a chance to expand your ideas and look at them in a new light. *Chapter 15, Introducing 3D*, covers AutoCAD's basic features for creating three-dimensional drawings. *Chapter 16, Using Advanced 3D Features*, introduces you to some of the program's more powerful 3D capabilities. *Chapter 17, Rendering and Animating 3D Drawings*, shows how you can use the AutoCAD Renderer for this purpose. *Chapter 18, Mastering 3D Solids*, is a guided tour of AutoCAD Release 13's new solid modeling feature.

15

▼ ▼ ▼ ▼ ▼

INTRODUCING 3D

Creating a 3D Object

Getting a 3D View

Getting a Hidden Line View

Getting a Shaded View

Using Special 3D Shapes

Converting a 3D View into a
2D Drawing

Using Slides to Save Shaded or
Hidden Line Images

FAST TRACK

682 ▶ To extrude 2D lines to form vertical surfaces

Click on the Properties button on the Object Properties toolbar, and then select the objects you want to extrude. At the dialog box, enter the height you want in the Thickness input box.

687 ▶ To move or copy objects in the z-axis

Click on the Move or Copy Objects button on the Modify palette, select the objects you want to edit, and press ↵. At the Base point prompt, pick any point. At the Second point prompt, enter a relative Cartesian coordinate and include the z coordinate (@0,0,8', for example). You can also use grips to copy and move objects in the z-axis. Or, if 3D geometry already exists in the drawing, you can use Osnap overrides to grab 3D geometry to indicate displacements.

690 ▶ To view your drawing in 3D

Click on View ➤ 3D Viewpoint Presets ➤ SW Isometric. This will place your viewpoint below and to the left of the drawing, looking downward at a 35° angle. You can then use View ➤ 3D Viewpoint ➤ Vector to make adjustments to your view.

705 ▶ To turn your wireframe view into a hidden-line view

Set up the 3D view you want; then click on the Hide button on the Render palette.

707 ▶ To shade your view to show volume

Set up the 3D view you want; then click on the Shade button on the Render palette. If you want to shade the surfaces so they have more depth, enter **Shadedge** ↵ **1** ↵ before you shade the view.

713 ▶ To select points in 3D space relative to existing geometry

When prompted to pick a point, enter **.xy** ↵ and then select an Osnap mode. Click on the geometry you want to locate the point in the x- and y-axes. You are then free to specify a z coordinate, either by using the Osnap modes again or by entering a z value. You can also use this method to align points to other geometry in 2D.

721 ▶ To draw basic 3D shapes such as spheres, wedges, and cones

Click on the desired object icon on the Surfaces palette. Answer the set of prompts that follow to describe the shape and size of the object.

722 ▶ To convert a 3D view into a 2D drawing

Type **Psout** ↵ to export your drawing as an .EPS file. Open a new file, and type **Psin** ↵ to import the .EPS file.

723 ▶ To save a hidden line or shaded view for later retrieval

After you have created the hidden-line view or shaded view, choose Tools ➤ Slide ➤ Save... or enter **Mslide** ↵ at the command prompt. At the Create Slide File dialog box, enter the name for the saved view. Your view becomes a slide file that you can retrieve at any time while in AutoCAD.

724 ▶ To retrieve a saved hidden line or shaded view

Choose Tools ➤ Slide ➤ View... or enter **Vslide** ↵ at the command prompt. At the Select Slide File dialog box, locate and double-click on the slide file you wish to retrieve.

725 ▶ To automate a slide presentation

Using a text editor, create a file that contains the exact sequence of keystrokes needed to view each slide in your presentation. Between each *Vslide* statement, insert a line that reads *Delay 3000*. This pauses the VSLIDE command between slides. Save the file; then click on Tools ➤ Run Script..., or enter **Script** ↵. At the Select Script File dialog box, locate and double-click on the script file name you created.

Viewing an object in three dimensions lets you have a sense of its true shape and form. It also helps you conceptualize the design, which results in better design decisions. Finally, using three-dimensional objects helps you communicate your ideas to those who may not be familiar with the plans, sections, and side views of your design.

A further advantage to drawing in three dimensions is that you can derive 2D drawings from your 3D model, which might otherwise take considerably more time with standard 2D drawing methods. For example, you could model a mechanical part in 3D and then quickly derive its top, front, and right-side views using the techniques discussed in this chapter.

AutoCAD allows you to turn any drawing you create into a 3D model by changing the properties of the objects making up the drawing. Auto-CAD does this through a combination of two types of objects: *extruded 2D objects* and *3Dfaces*. A 3Dface is an object created by AutoCAD that acts like a three-dimensional surface.

In this chapter, you will use AutoCAD's 3D capabilities to see what your studio apartment looks like from various angles.

CREATING A 3D DRAWING

One way AutoCAD creates three-dimensional forms is by *extruding* two-dimensional objects. For example, to draw a cube using this process, you first draw a square, and then extrude the square by giving its lines a *thickness* (see Figure 15.1). This thickness is a value given as a z coordinate. Imagine that your screen's drawing area is the drawing surface. A z coordinate of 0 is on that surface. A z coordinate greater than 0 is a position closer to you and above that surface. Figure 15.2 illustrates this concept.

When you draw an object with thickness, you don't see the thickness until you view the drawing from a different angle. This is because normally your view is perpendicular to the imagined drawing surface. At that angle, you cannot see the thickness of an object because it projects toward you—just as a sheet of paper looks like a line when viewed from one end. Thus, to view an object's thickness, you must change the angle at which you view your drawing.

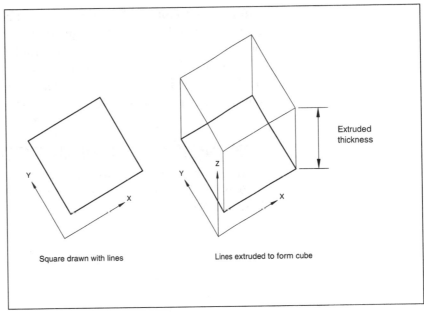

Square drawn with lines   Lines extruded to form cube

Figure 15.1: How to create a cube using extrusion

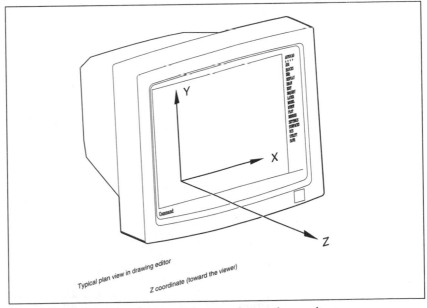

Typical plan view in drawing editor

Z coordinate (toward the viewer)

Figure 15.2: The z coordinate in relation to the x and y coordinates

You can set AutoCAD so that everything you draw has an *elevation*. Normally, you draw on the imagined surface, but you can set the z coordinate for your drawing elevation so that whatever you draw is above that surface. An object with an elevation value other than 0 rests not *on* the imagined drawing surface but *above* it (or *below* it if the z coordinate is a negative value). Figure 15.3 illustrates this concept.

CHANGING A 2D PLAN INTO A 3D MODEL

In this exercise, you will turn the 2D studio unit drawing into a 3D drawing by changing the properties of the wall lines. You will also learn how to view the 3D image.

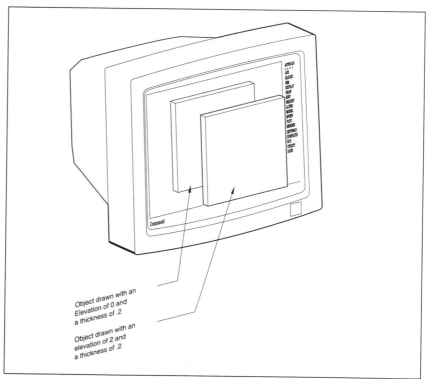

Object drawn with an
Elevation of 0 and
a thickness of .2

Object drawn with an
elevation of 2 and
a thickness of .2

Figure 15.3: Two identical objects at different z coordinates

1. Start AutoCAD and open the Unit file.

2. Set the current layer to Wall, and turn off all the other layers except Jamb.

3. Turn on the grid (if it isn't on already). Your screen should look like Figure 15.4.

4. Click on View ➤ 3D Viewpoint ➤ Vector, or type **Vpoint** ↵ at the command prompt. This starts the VPOINT command that allows you to view the studio unit in 3D.

5. At the Rotate/<viewpoint><0'-0",0'-0",0'-1">: prompt, enter **-1,-1,1** ↵. The default value is a list of the x, y, and z coordinates of your last viewing location relative to your object. Your view looks as if you are standing below and to the left of your drawing, rather than directly above it (see Figure 15.5). The grid shows you the angle of the drawing surface.

▼ TIP

You can also use View ➤ 3D Viewpoint Presets ➤ SW Isometric and skip step 5.

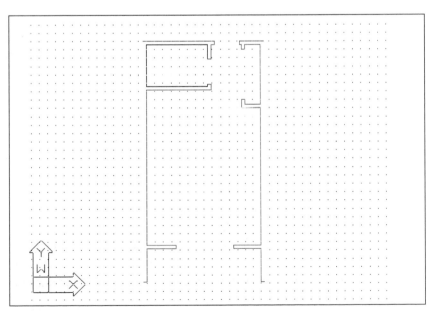

Figure 15.4: The plan view of the walls and door jambs

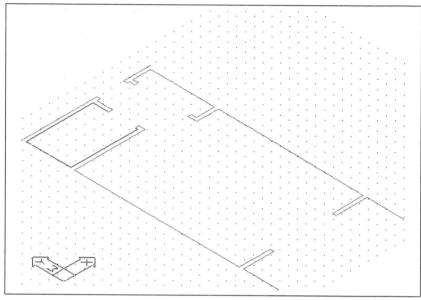

Figure 15.5: A 3D view of the floor plan

6. Click on the Properties button on the Object Properties toolbar, or type **Ddmodify** ↵.

7. At the object-selection prompt, use a crossing window to pick the entire drawing and press ↵.

8. At the Change Properties dialog box, double-click on the Thickness input box, enter **8′**, and click on OK. The walls and jambs now appear to be 8′ high.

Figure 15.6 shows the extruded wall lines. You are able to see through the walls because this is a *wireframe view*. A wireframe view shows the volumes of a 3D object by showing the lines representing the intersections of surfaces. Later we will discuss how to make an object's surfaces opaque in order to facilitate a particular point of view for a drawing.

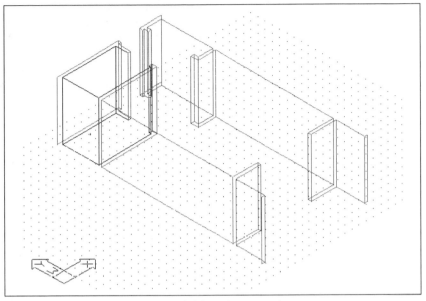

Figure 15.6: The wall lines, extruded (wireframe view)

Next you will change the elevation of the door headers by moving them in the z-axis using grips.

1. Turn on the Ceiling layer. The door headers appear as lines on the floor where the door openings are located.

2. Click on the two magenta lines representing the header over the balcony door.

3. Shift-click on the midpoint grips of these two lines.

4. Click again on one of the hot grips.

5. At the ** STRETCH ** prompt, enter **@0,0,7'** ↵. The lines move to a new position 7' above the floor (see Figure 15.7).

6. Click on the Properties button on the Object Properties toolbar and change the thickness of the header to 1' using the Thickness input box. Click on OK.

▼▼▼▼▼

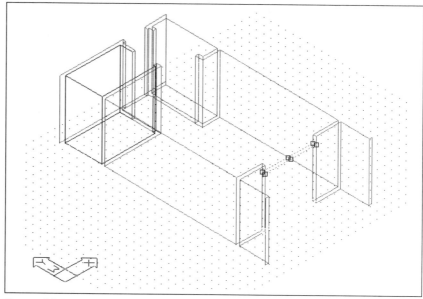

Figure 15.7:   The header lines at the new elevation

7. Click on the four lines representing the door header for the closet and entry.

8. Repeat steps 3 through 6. Your drawing will look like Figure 15.8.

You could have used the MOVE command to move the lines to their new elevation, entering the same **@0,0,7'** at the Second point prompt for MOVE. Since you must select objects to edit them using grips, with MOVE you save a step by not having to select the lines a second time for the DDMODIFY command (Properties button on the Object Properties palette).

CREATING A 3D OBJECT

Though you may visualize a design in 3D, you will often start sketching it in 2D and later generate the 3D views. When you know from the start what the thickness and height of an object will be, you can set these

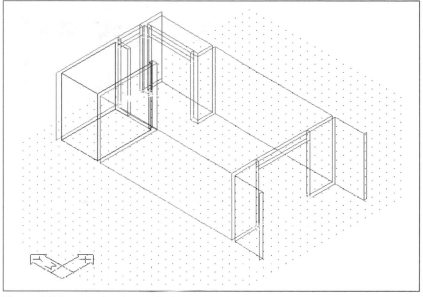

IV

Modeling and Imaging in 3D

Figure 15.8: The headers with the new thickness

values so that you don't have to extrude the object later. The following exercise shows you how to set elevation and thickness before you start drawing.

1. Click on the Object Creation button on the Object Properties toolbar.

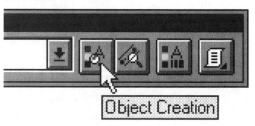

The Object Creation Modes dialog box appears.

Object Creation Modes	
Color... ■	BYLAYER
Layer...	0
Linetype...	BYLAYER
Text Style...	STANDARD
Linetype Scale:	1.0000
Elevation:	0.0000
Thickness:	0.0000
OK	Cancel	Help...

2. Enter **3"** in the Elevations input box.

3. Enter **12"** in the Thickness input box.

4. Click on OK. The grid changes to the new elevation. Now as you draw objects, they will appear 12" thick at an elevation of 3".

5. Draw a circle representing a planter at one side of the balcony (see Figure 15.9). Make it 18" in diameter. The planter appears as a 3D object with the current thickness and elevation settings.

Extruding forms is a very simple process, as you have seen. You just have to keep track of thicknesses and elevations. With these two properties, you can create nearly any three-dimensional form you need. Next you will discover how to control your view of your drawing.

VIEWING A 3D DRAWING

Your first 3D view of a drawing is a wireframe view. It appears as an open model made of wire; none of the sides appear solid. This section describes how to manipulate this wireframe view so you can see your drawing from any angle. We will also describe how, once you have selected your view, you can view the 3D drawing as a solid object with the hidden lines removed. And we will cover methods for saving views for later recall.

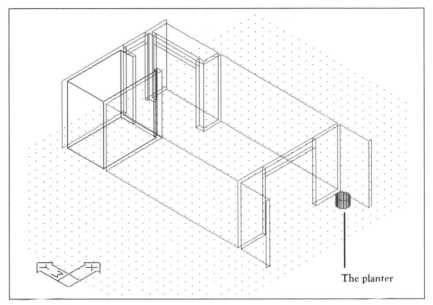

The planter

Figure 15.9:   The planter

1. Click on View ➤ 3D Viewpoint ➤ Tripod, or enter **Vpoint** ↵ ↵ at the command prompt. You get a screen that helps you visually select your 3D view (see Figure 15.10). The three lines converging at one point compose the *coordinate tripod*.

2. Move your mouse around, and watch how the tripod rotates to show your orientation *in relation to the x-, y-, and z-axes of your drawing*. Each line is labeled to indicate which axis it represents. Above and to the right of the tripod is a target with a small cursor. As you move your mouse, the cursor follows, staying near or within the target.

3. Move the cursor around the center of the target. Note how the tripod appears to rotate, indicating your changing view (see Figure 15.11). This target shows you *your viewpoint in relation to the drawing*.

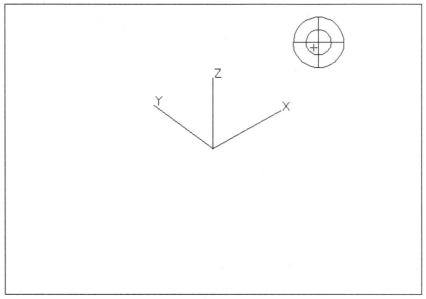

Figure 15.10:   The coordinate tripod and target

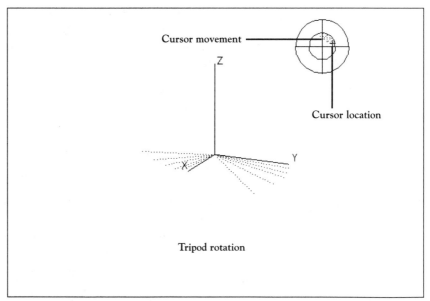

Figure 15.11:   The tripod rotates as you move the cursor around the target's center.

4. If it isn't on already, toggle on the dynamic coordinate read-out. As you move the cursor, the readout tells you *your x,y co-ordinates in relation to the target's center.*

5. Move the cursor closer to the center. The coordinate readout approaches 0,0, and the z-axis of the tripod begins to fore-shorten until it is no longer visible (see Figure 15.12). This shows that you are almost directly above the drawing, as you would be in a 2D view.

6. Position the cursor as shown in Figure 15.12 and pick the point indicated. Your drawing will look something like Fig-ure 15.13. Now you can see that your view does indeed look like a plan view. The closer to the target's center you move the cursor, the higher in elevation your view will be.

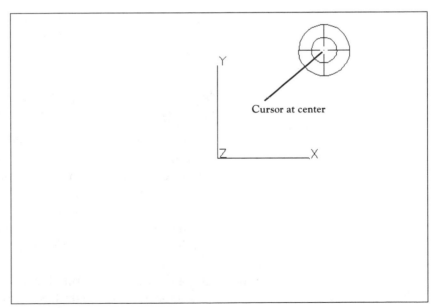

Figure 15.12:   The z-axis foreshortened

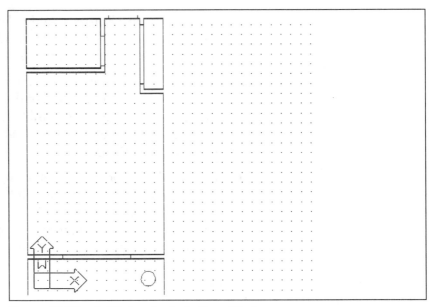

Figure 15.13: A 3D view that looks like a 2D view

UNDERSTANDING COORDINATE VALUES AND THE VIEWPOINT PROMPT

Let's take a moment to study the relationship between coordinate values entered at the Enter view point prompt, and the coordinate tripod. In an earlier exercise, when you entered a coordinate value at the Viewpoint prompt, what you were specifying were the x, y, and z values for your position in relation to the origin of the coordinate tripod. The coordinate tripod graphically shows your orientation to the drawing. The coordinate values are not meaningful in themselves, but only in relation to each other.

The origin of the coordinate tripod, in this case, is your entire drawing—not the actual drawing origin (see Figure 15.14).

In addition, the coordinate readout offers some additional help when using the coordinate tripod. The following list describes how positive and negative coordinate values affect your view.

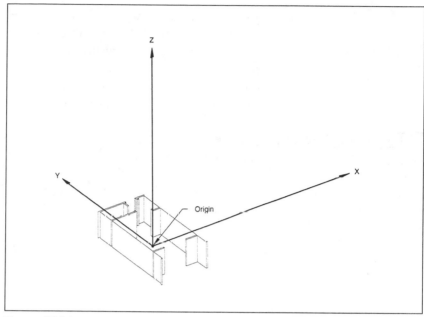

Figure 15.14: The coordinate tripod, superimposed on the plan

- The negative x value places your viewing position to the left of your drawing.

- The negative y places your position 270° in relation to your drawing.

- The positive 1 value for the z-axis lifts your view above the surface.

As you go through the exercise in the next section, you will see more clearly the relationship between your view and these coordinates.

UNDERSTANDING THE VIEWPOINT AXES TARGET

The cursor's position in relation to the target's center represents your viewpoint in relation to your drawing. You might think of the target as a schematic-plan view of your drawing, with the cursor being your position in relation to the plan (see Figure 15.15). For example, if you place the cursor just below and to the left of the center, your view will be from the lower-left corner of your overall drawing, like your view of the floor plan in the first exercise. If you place the cursor above and to the right of the center, you will view your drawing from the upper-right corner.

In the following exercise, you'll see first-hand how the tripod cursor affects your 3D views.

1. Click on View ➤ 3D Viewpoint ➤ Tripod. The tripod and target appear.

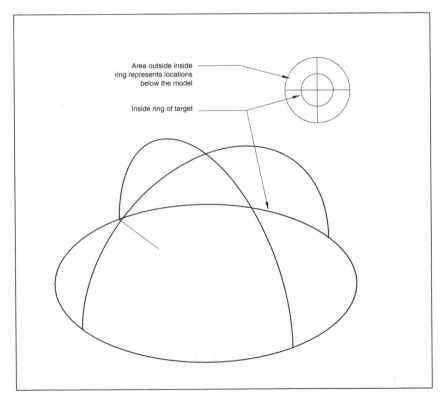

Area outside inside ring represents locations below the model

Inside ring of target

Figure 15.15: This diagram shows how the viewpoint axes target relates to your drawing.

IV

Modeling and Imaging in 3D

2. Look at the target. As you move the cursor closer to its inner ring, the x and y lines begin to flatten until, as you touch the circle, they are parallel (see Figure 15.16). This first ring represents a directly horizontal position on your drawing surface.

3. Position the cursor as shown in Figure 15.16 and click on this position. Your drawing will look as if you are viewing the drawing surface edge-on, and the walls from the side (see Figure 15.17).

4. Click on View ➤ 3D Viewpoint ➤ Tripod again.

5. Move the cursor to the outermost ring of the target. The z-axis line foreshortens again. This ring represents a view located underneath your drawing, as if you are looking at the back of the screen.

▼ NOTE

VPOINT Defaults: This time the x and y values are high, while the z value is 0 or close to it. This indicates the previous view was from an elevation of 0.

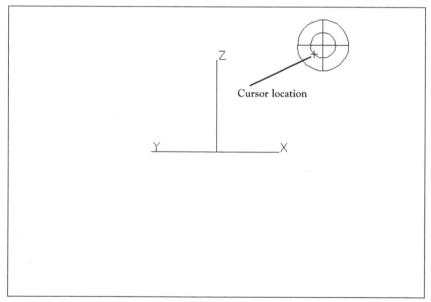

Figure 15.16: The parallel x- and y-axes

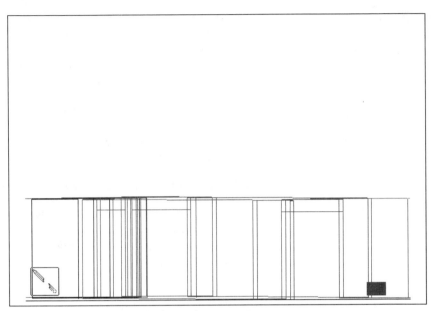

Figure 15.17: View of walls from side

If you find it a little difficult to tell what is going on because you can see right through the walls, don't worry—as you work with 3D, you will become more accustomed to this type of view.

If you want to get back to a plan view of your drawing, click on View ➤ 3D Viewpoint Presets ➤ Plan View ➤ Current, or type **Plan** ⏎. You will notice that your 2D view looks just the way it did before you extruded the walls. This is because you are viewing the wall lines edge-on.

You can save and recall a 3D view just as you can any other view. Simply set it up and then click on the Named Views button on the Standard toolbar, or choose View ➤ Named Views. At the View Control dialog box, click on New. Enter a name, then click on Save View.

6. Pick a point just inside this outer ring, as shown in Figure 15.18. You will get a view something like Figure 15.19.

At first you might think that your view (as shown in Figure 15.19) is just another view from above the drawing. However, if you look carefully at the position of the bathroom in relation to the rest of the unit, you will notice that it appears to be mirrored, just like any drawing viewed from the back of the drawing sheet.

Now let's return to the view you used to edit the Unit drawing.

1. Click on View ➤ 3D Viewpoint ➤ Vector, or type **Vpoint** ⏎.

2. Enter **-1,-1,1** ⏎. You will see the drawing from a viewpoint similar to the one you started with.

3. Using View ➤ Named Views…, save this view, and give it the name **3D**.

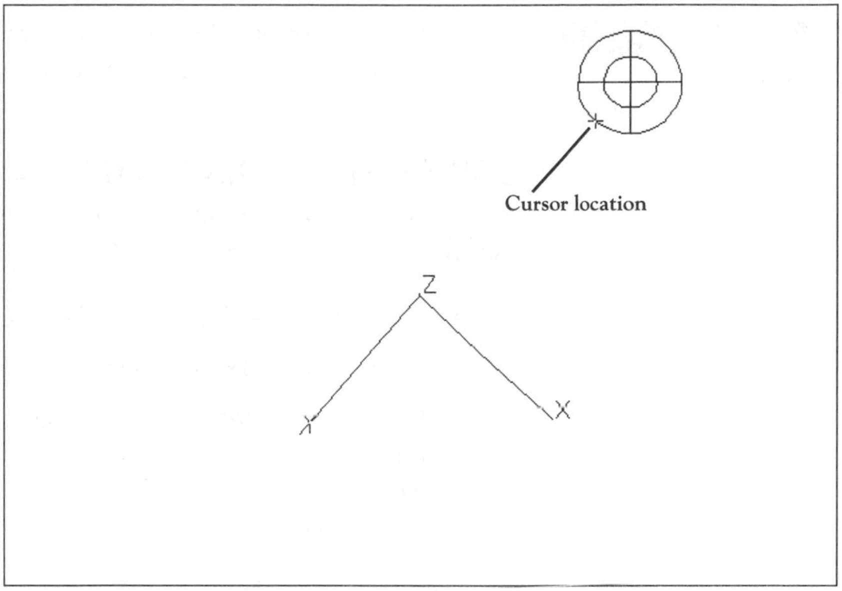

Cursor location

Z

X   X

Figure 15.18: The cursor location for an underside view

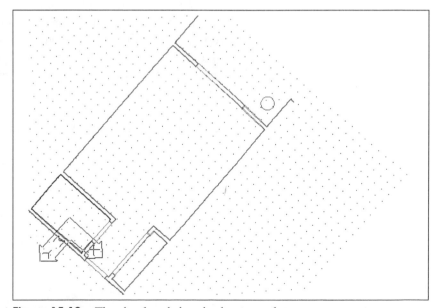

Figure 15.19: The plan from below the drawing surface

▼ NOTE

If you have forgotten how to redefine a block, refer to *Chapter 6*.

4. Finally, turn on all the layers except Notes. You will see the rest of the drawing still in a 2D form.

USING THE VPOINT ROTATE OPTION

A more direct way of obtaining a view from a 3D drawing is by using the VPOINT command's Rotate option.

1. Turn off all the layers except Wall and Ceiling.

2. Click on View ➤ 3D Viewpoint ➤ Vector, and then type **R** ↵.

3. Look at the Enter angle in X-Y plane in X axis <225>: prompt. The number in brackets tells you the rotational angle for the current view. If you imagine looking at a 2D view of the apartment, as in Figure 15.4, this value represents a position toward the lower-left of the view. Enter **45** ↵ now to get a view at the opposite side of the apartment.

4. Now look at the number in brackets in the Enter angle from X-Y plane <35>: prompt. It tells you the angle of the current view above the current floor elevation. If you imagine looking at the side of the apartment as in Figure 15.17, this value represents the direction of your point of view above the floor. Press ↵ to accept the default value. You get a new view of the apartment from the opposite side of your current view (see Figure 15.20).

Figure 15.21 illustrates what these view values represent.

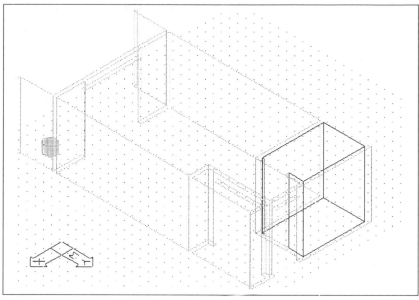

Figure 15.20:   The new view of the apartment

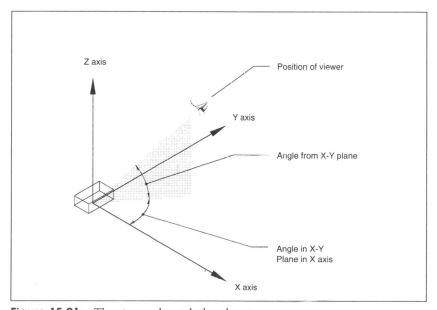

Figure 15.21:   The view angles and what they represent

If you like, you can visually choose the rotational angle of your view. To do this, follow these steps:

▼ **NOTE**

Using the ID command lets you set up a new last point, which can be accessed by using the @ during any point prompt.

1. Click and drag the Inquiry button on the Object Properties palette, and select Locate Point on the flyout. You can also type **ID** ↵ and pick a point at the center of the apartment.

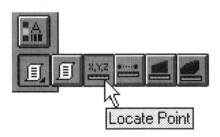

▼ **NOTE**

The position of the cursor determines your view position. With the Osnap modes you can even use part of your apartment model as a reference.

2. Start the VPOINT command and select the Rotate option as you did in the previous exercise. A rubber-banding line will appear, with one end at the point you selected and the other end on the cursor (see Figure 15.22).

3. At the Enter angle from XY plane from X Axis prompt, pick a point indicating the position from which you wish to view the model.

▼ **WARNING**

You cannot use the rubber-banding line to select the view height; you must enter a value.

4. At the Enter angle from the x,y plane prompt, enter a value indicating the angle above the floor plane.

Your view will change to reflect your new view angle.

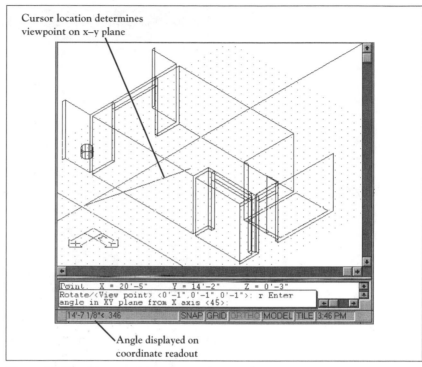

Figure 15.22:   How to select a view angle using the cursor

USING A DIALOG BOX TO SELECT 3D VIEWS

A third way to select 3D views is by indicating an angle from the x-axis
and from the floor plane using a dialog box graphic.

1.   Click on View ➤ 3D Viewpoint ➤ Rotate…. The Viewpoint
     Presets dialog box appears. The square dial to the left lets you
     select a viewpoint location in degrees relative to the x-axis,
     similar to the target you used earlier. The semicircle to the
     right lets you select an elevation for your viewpoint.

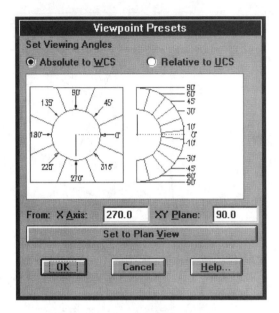

2. Click on the number 135 in the upper-left of the square dial. Then click on the box labeled 60 in the right-hand semicircle.

3. Click on OK. Your view changes according to the new settings you just made.

Other settings in this dialog box let you determine whether the selected view angles are relative to the world coordinate system or to the current User Coordinate System (UCS is discussed in *Chapter 16*). You can also go directly to a plan view.

VISUALIZING YOUR MODEL

From time to time, you will want to get an idea of how your model looks with hidden lines removed. This is especially true of complex 3D models. Frequently, object intersections and shapes are not readily apparent until you can see what object lies in front of others.

AutoCAD provides two helpful viewing commands, both on the Tools menu, for this situation. First, the HIDE command allows you to quickly view your drawing with hidden lines removed. You can then assess where surfaces are and get a better feel for the model. HIDE is also an option at plot time, allowing you to create hard copy line drawings of a 3D model. You can then render the hard copy using manual techniques if you want.

The second command, SHADE, lets you add a sense of solidity to the image by adding color to surfaces. Shade has a variety of settings for controlling how colors are applied. This option is better suited to presentations, and as a visualization tool when HIDE proves inadequate. Unfortunately, you cannot plot a view generated by the SHADE command. You can, however, store the view as a slide file for independent viewing.

Let's begin by looking at the HIDE command; we'll discuss Slides in more detail later in this chapter.

LOADING THE RENDER PALETTE

Both HIDE and SHADE are located on the Render palette. Choose Tools ➤ Toolbars ➤ Render, or click on Render on the Tools flyout on the Standard toolbar. The Render toolbar will appear.

REMOVING HIDDEN LINES

You'll start by getting a quick hidden line view.

▼ TIP

You can also plot a view with hidden lines removed by checking the Hide Lines check box in the Plot Configuration dialog box before you start your plot. Using the Hide Lines option will generally add only a few minutes to your plot time.

1. Restore the view you saved earlier with the name 3D.

2. Click on the Hide button on the Render palette, or enter **Hide** ↵ at the command prompt. AutoCAD will display this message:

   HIDE Regenerating drawing
   Hiding lines *value*% done

where *value%* changes as the command calculates the hidden line removal. (On a very fast computer, such as a 486/50, you won't notice the value change.) When AutoCAD is done, the *value%* reads 100% and the image appears with hidden lines removed (see Figure 15.23).

This hidden-line view will remain until your drawing is regenerated. Note that you cannot use the VIEW command to save a hidden-line view. You can, however, save this view as a slide.

Although it did not take much time to perform a hidden-line removal on this drawing, the more complex the 3D drawing, the longer the HIDE command will take. But since Release 12, even the most complex model you create will not take much more than several minutes. This is a vast improvement over earlier releases of AutoCAD, which took hours to perform this task.

▼ NOTE

HIDE does not hide text objects unless the text is given a thickness; SHADE, however, does.

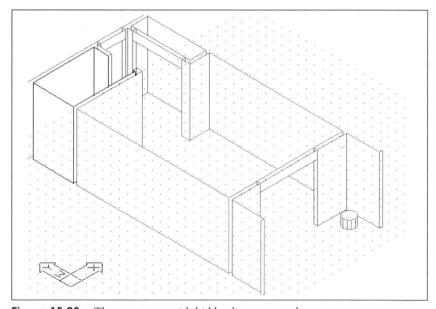

Figure 15.23:   The apartment with hidden lines removed

IV

Modeling and Imaging in 3D

SHADING YOUR 3D MODEL

If you're used to looking at wireframe 3D images, the HIDE command is usually good enough to give you an idea of how your model looks. But when you want to get an even better visualization of the form your model is taking on, it's time for the SHADE command. To see how it works, try the following exercise:

1. Click on View ➤ 3D Viewpoint ➤ Vector.

2. At the prompt, enter **-2,-4,3**. This changes the view so you have a different line of sight to each wall surface.

3. Click on the Shade button on the Render palette, or enter **Shade** ↵ at the command prompt. Just as with the HIDE command, AutoCAD displays a message telling you that it is regenerating the drawing. In a short time, the shaded view appears.

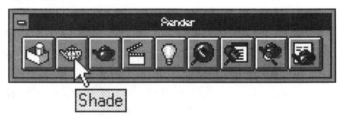

4. Enter **Shadedge** ↵ at the command prompt.

5. At the New value for SHADEDGE prompt, enter **1** ↵.

6. Click again on the Shade button on the Render palette, and notice that the shaded image now looks more realistic and less like a cartoon (see Figure 15.24).

7. Enter **Shadedge** ↵ again, this time with the value **0** ↵ at the New value for SHADEDGE prompt.

8. Render the drawing a third time. Now only the surfaces appear, with no edges showing.

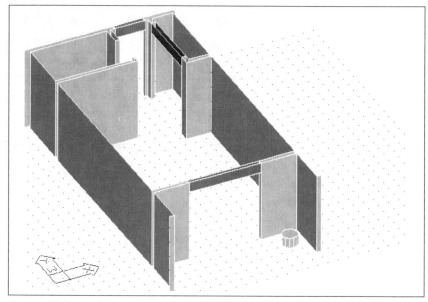

Figure 15.24: The Unit plan shaded with Shadedge system variable set to 1

In step 2, you changed your view slightly so your line of sight to the various walls was at a different angle. Had you not changed your view, the SHADE command would have shaded all the walls with the same intensity in steps 6 and 8. This is because SHADE renders a view as if a light source emanates from the same direction as the viewer. Thus, when all the walls are at the same angle to the view, they all receive and reflect the same amount of light. With the model slightly turned, however, light then reflects off each surface differently.

You used the Shadedge system variable to change the way surfaces were rendered. Here are descriptions of the four Shadedge settings:

0	Shades the surfaces with no edge highlighting
1	Shades the surfaces and highlights the edges
2	Shades the surfaces with the background color and the edges with the surface color
3	Shades the surface with the object color and the edges with the background color

Another system variable, Shadedif, influences the contrast of colors among different surfaces. A higher Shadedif number increases contrast; a lower number decreases contrast. The value can range from 0 to 100, with a default setting of 70. You may want to experiment with this setting on your own.

There is a third method for visualizing your model that allows you to place varying light sources in your drawing. The AutoCAD rendering functions on the Render palette let you adjust light reflectance of surfaces, smooth out faceted surfaces such as spheres and cylinders, and place light sources accurately. You'll get a chance to work with the rendering functions in *Chapter 16*. For now, let's look at some other factors that affect how a 3D model will look when it is shaded or when hidden lines are removed.

GETTING THE 3D RESULTS YOU WANT

Working in 3D is tricky because you can't see exactly what you are drawing. You must alternately draw and then hide or shade your drawing from time to time to see exactly what is going on. Here are a few tips on how to keep control of your 3D drawings.

MAKING HORIZONTAL SURFACES OPAQUE

To make a horizontal surface appear opaque, you must draw it with a wide polyline, a trace, a solid, or a 3Dface. Consider a table, for example: You might represent the table top with a rectangle and give it the appropriate thickness, but the top would appear to be transparent when the lines were hidden. Only the sides of the table top would become opaque. To make the entire table top opaque, you can use the SOLID command (or a wide trace or polyline) to draw a filled rectangle and give it the appropriate thickness. When the lines are hidden, the table top appears to be opaque (see Figure 15.25). This technique works even with the Fill setting off.

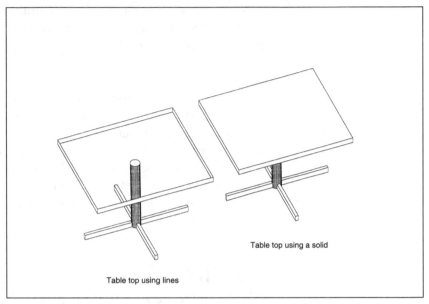

Table top using lines

Table top using a solid

Figure 15.25: One table using lines for the top, and another using a solid

When a circle is used as an extruded form, the top surface appears opaque when you use the HIDE command. Where you want to show an opening at the top of a circular volume, as in a circular chimney, you can use two 180° arcs (see Figure 15.26).

For complex horizontal surfaces, you can use a combination of wide polylines, solids, and 3Dfaces to create them. For example, a sidewalk on a street corner would use a donut for the rounder corner, then solids or 3Dfaces at either side for the straight portion of the sidewalk. It's OK to overlap surfaces to achieve the effect you want.

SETTING LAYERS CAREFULLY

Bear in mind that the HIDE command hides objects that are obscured by other objects on layers that are turned off. For example, if a couch in the corner of the studio unit is on a layer that is off when you use HIDE, the lines behind the couch are hidden even though the couch does not

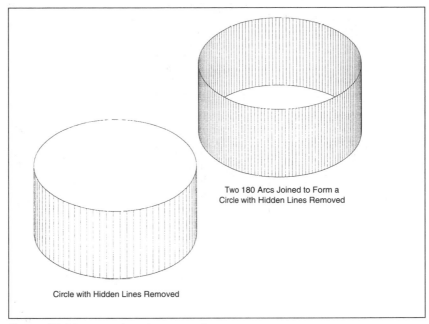

Two 180 Arcs Joined to Form a
Circle with Hidden Lines Removed

Circle with Hidden Lines Removed

Figure 15.26: A circle and two joined arcs

appear in the view (see Figure 15.27). You can, however, freeze any layer containing objects that you do not want affected by the hidden-line removal process. You can also use AutoCAD's solid modeler (described in *Chapter 18*) to draw complex 3D surfaces with holes.

DRAWING 3D SURFACES

In your work with 3D so far in this chapter, you have simply extruded existing forms, or you have set AutoCAD to draw extruded objects. But extruded forms have their limitations. Using just extruded forms, it's hard to draw diagonal surfaces in the z-axis. AutoCAD provides the 3Dface object to give you more flexibility in drawing surfaces in three-dimensional space. The 3Dface produces a 3D surface where each corner can be given an x, y, and z value. By using 3Dfaces in conjunction

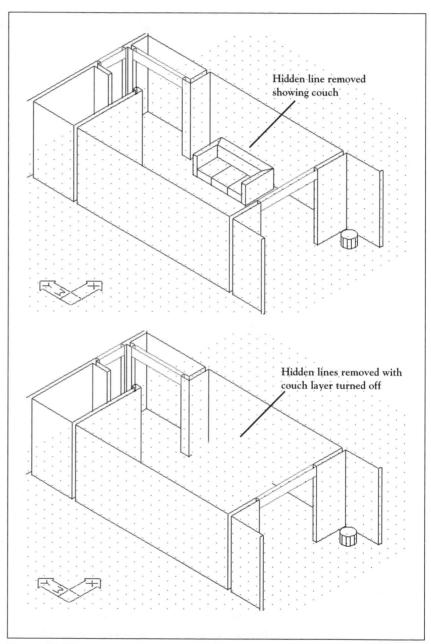

Figure 15.27: A couch hiding a line, when the layer is turned on and turned off

IV

Modeling and Imaging in 3D

with extruded objects, you can create a 3D model of just about anything. When you view these 3D objects in a 2D plan view, you will see them as 2D objects showing only the x and y positions of their corners or endpoints.

USING FILTERS

Before you start working with 3D surfaces, you should have a good idea of what the z coordinate values are for your model. The simplest way to construct surfaces in 3D space is to first create some layout lines to help you place the endpoints of 3Dfaces.

AutoCAD offers a method for 3D point selection, called *filtering*, that simplifies the selection of z coordinates. Filtering allows you to enter an x, y, or z value by picking a point on the screen and telling AutoCAD to use only the x, y, or z value of that point, or any combination of those values. If you don't specify a z coordinate, the current elevation setting is assumed.

In the following exercises, you will add a stair rail to the studio apartment. In doing this, you will practice using 3Dfaces and filters. You'll start by doing some setup, so you can work on a copy of the Unit file and keep the old Unit plan for future reference.

1. Restore the view you saved earlier as a 3D view, using View ➤ Named Views....

2. Save the Unit file, and create a new file called **Unitloft** using the Unit file as a prototype. You can also use the Unitloft.DWG file supplied on the companion disk.

3. Click on the Object Creation button on the Object Properties palette. At the Object Creation Modes dialog box, set the Thickness and Elevation to 0. Click on OK.

4. Set the current layer to Wall.

Now you are ready to lay out your stair rail.

▼ NOTE

Notice the .X, .Y, and .Z options on Object Snap menu (Shift–right-click). These are the 3D filters. By picking one of these options as you select points in a 3D command, you can filter an x, y, or z value, or any combination of values, from that selected point. You can also enter filters through the keyboard.

1. Click on Line on the Draw palette.

2. At the From point prompt, Shift-click the right mouse button to bring up the Osnap menu, then pick .xy; or enter **.xy** ↵. (By doing this you are telling AutoCAD that you are going to first specify the x and y coordinates for this beginning point, and then later indicate the z coordinate.)

3. At the From point: .xy of prompt, pick a point along the same axis as the bathroom wall, 3′– 6″ from the right side wall of the unit near coordinate 25′– 6″,25′–5″. This will be the first line at the bottom of the stair rail.

4. At the .xy of (need Z): prompt, enter **9′** ↵ (the z coordinate).

5. At the to point prompt, pick .xy again from the Osnap menu or enter **.xy** ↵.

6. Enter **@12′ <270**.

7. At the (need Z): prompt, enter **0** ↵.

8. Press ↵ to end the LINE command. Your drawing should look like Figure 15.28.

▼ TIP

Filters can also be used in a 2D drawing to select an x or y component of an object to which you want to align a point.

Now you will copy the line vertically to draw the top of the stair rail.

1. Click on the Copy Objects button on the Modify palette.

2. Select the 3D line you just drew, and press ↵.

3. At the base point prompt, pick any point on the screen.

4. At the second point prompt, enter **.xy** ↵, and then enter **@** ↵. This tells AutoCAD that your second point will maintain the x,y coordinates of the first point.

5. At the (need Z): prompt, enter **3′6″** ↵ to place the copy 3′–6″ on the z-axis. A copy of the 3D line appears 3′–6″ above the original.

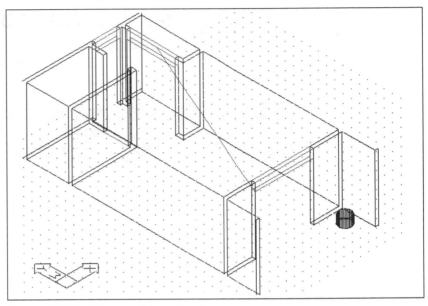

Figure 15.28: 3D view of the stair rail

In step 4 you specified that the second point used the same x and y coordinates of the base point, so you only needed to enter the z value for the second point. In the earlier exercise, you used a relative coordinate to move door headers to a position 7′ higher than their original location. You could have used the same method here to copy the line vertically, but in this exercise you got a chance to see how the .xy filter works.

CREATING IRREGULAR 3D SURFACES

Sometimes you will want to draw a solid surface so that when you remove hidden lines, objects will appear as surfaces rather than wireframes. If you were to continue drawing the side of the stair rail using lines, the side of the stair rail would appear transparent. So the next step is to fill in the side using 3Dfaces.

LOADING THE SURFACES TOOLBAR

The 3Dface command and AutoCAD's 3D shapes are located on the Surfaces tool palette. Choose Tools ➤ Toolbars ➤ Surfaces, or click on Surfaces on the Tools flyout on the Standard toolbar.

ADDING A 3D FACE

Now that you've opened the Surfaces palette, you can begin to draw 3D Faces.

1. ZOOM in to the two lines you just created, using the zoom window shown in Figure 15.29.

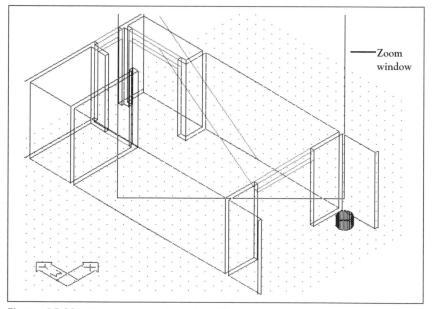

Figure 15.29: Zooming in to the stair rail lines

2. Click on the 3D Face button on the Surfaces palette or type **3dface** ↵.

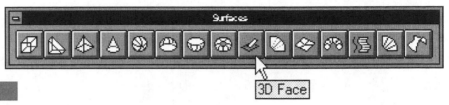

3. At the First point: prompt, use the Osnap overrides to pick the first of the four endpoints of the 3D lines you drew. Be sure the ortho mode is off.

4. As you continue to pick the endpoints, you will be prompted for the second, third, and fourth points.

5. When the Third point: prompt appears again, press ↵ to end the 3DFACE command. A 3Dface appears between the two 3D lines. It is difficult to tell if they are actually there until you use the HIDE command, but you should see vertical lines connecting the endpoints of the 3D lines. These vertical lines are the edges of the 3Dface (see Figure 15.30).

6. COPY the 3Dface you just drew 5″ horizontally in the 0 angle direction.

7. Use the 3DFACE command to put a surface on the top and front sides of the rail, as demonstrated in panel 1 of Figure 15.31.

8. Use the Intersection Osnap override to snap to the corners of the 3Dfaces.

9. Use the HIDE command on the Render palette to get a view that looks like panel 2 of Figure 15.31.

Now you can save the Unitloft file. You won't be using it in any future exercise, but you can keep it around to experiment with 3Dfaces, if you like. Try adding some stair treads: Use 3D Face on the Surfaces palette

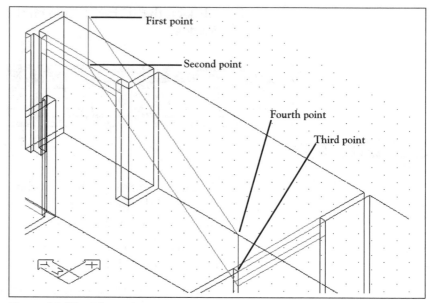

First point

Second point

Fourth point

Third point

Figure 15.30: The 3Dface

(3DFACE) to draw the first tread, then array it, and use the Properties command (DDMODIFY)on the Object Properties palette to alter each stair tread's elevation.

HIDING UNWANTED SURFACE EDGES

When using the 3DFACE command, you are limited to drawing surfaces with four sides. You can, however, create more complex shapes by simply joining several 3Dfaces. Figure 15.32 shows an odd shape constructed of three joined 3Dfaces. Unfortunately, you are left with extra lines that cross the surface; but you can hide those lines by using the Invisible option under the 3DFACE command, in conjunction with the Splframe Setvar variable.

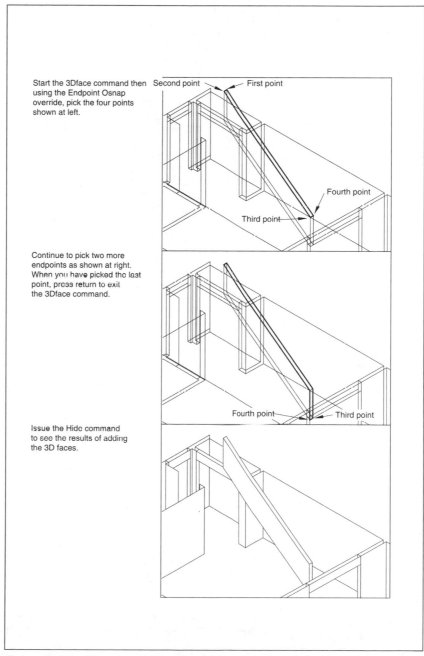

Start the 3Dface command then using the Endpoint Osnap override, pick the four points shown at left.

Second point   First point

Fourth point

Third point

Continue to pick two more endpoints as shown at right. When you have picked the last point, press return to exit the 3Dface command.

Fourth point   Third point

Issue the Hide command to see the results of adding the 3D faces.

Figure 15.31: The top and front faces of the stair rail, and the stair rail with the hidden lines removed

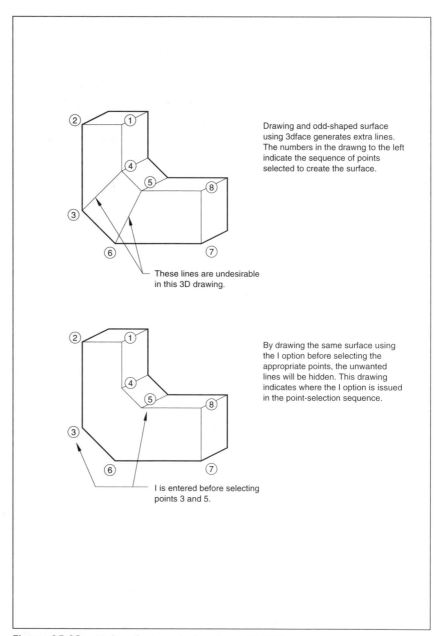

Drawing and odd-shaped surface using 3dface generates extra lines. The numbers in the drawng to the left indicate the sequence of points selected to create the surface.

These lines are undesirable in this 3D drawing.

By drawing the same surface using the I option before selecting the appropriate points, the unwanted lines will be hidden. This drawing indicates where the I option is issued in the point-selection sequence.

I is entered before selecting points 3 and 5.

Figure 15.32: Hiding the joined edge of multiple 3Dfaces

To make an edge of a 3Dface invisible, start the 3DFACE command as usual. While selecting points, just before you pick the first point of the edge to be hidden, enter I ↵ . When you are drawing two 3Dfaces sequentially, only one edge needs to be invisible to hide their joining edge.

You can make invisible edges visible for editing by setting the Splframe system variable to 1. Setting Splframe to 0 will cause Auto-CAD to hide the invisible edges.

Bear in mind that the Splframe system variable can be useful in both 3D and 2D drawings. You can use 3DFACE in place of the SOLID command when you want to draw a surface with a complex shape but don't want the surface to be a solid fill.

▼ TIP

The Edge option on the Surfaces toolbar (EDGE) lets you change an existing visible 3Dface edge to an invisible one. Click on the Edge button then select the 3Dface edge to be hidden.

USING PRE-DEFINED 3D SURFACE SHAPES

You may have noticed that the surfaces toolbar offers several 3D surface objects, among them cones, spheres, and torus shapes. All are made up of 3Dfaces. To use them, click on the appropriate button on the Surfaces tool palette. When you select an object, AutoCAD will prompt you for the points and dimensions that define that 3D object. Then AutoCAD will draw the object. This provides quick access to shapes that would otherwise take substantial time to create.

▼

■ # THINGS TO WATCH OUT
■ # FOR WHEN EDITING 3D OBJECTS

■ You have seen how you can use the COPY command on 3D lines
and 3Dfaces. You can also use the Move and Stretch commands on
■ 3D lines, 3Dfaces, and 3D shapes to modify their z coordinate values—but you have to be careful with these commands when editing
■ in 3D. Here are a few tips to keep in mind:

■ The Scale command will scale an object's z coordinate
value, as well as the standard x and y coordinates.(Click
and drag the Resize button on the Modify palette and select Scale on the flyout.) Suppose you have an object with
an elevation of two units. If you use the Scale command to

enlarge that object by a factor of 4, the object will have a new elevation of 2 units times 4, or 8 units. If, on the other hand, that object has an elevation of 0, its elevation will not change, because 0 times 4 is still 0.

- ARRAY, MIRROR, and ROTATE (on the Modify palette) can also be used on 3D lines, 3Dfaces, and 3D shapes, but these commands won't affect their z coordinate values. Z coordinates can be specified for base and insertion points, so take care when using these commands with 3D models.

- Using the MOVE, STRETCH, and COPY commands (on the Modify palette) with object snaps can produce some unpredictable and unwanted results. As a rule, it is best to use point filters when selecting points with Osnap overrides. For example, to move an object from the endpoint of one object to the endpoint of another on the same z coordinate, invoke the .xy filter at the Base point and Second point prompts *before* issuing the endpoint override. Proceed to pick the endpoint of the object you want; then enter the z coordinate, or just pick any point to use the current default z coordinate.

- When you create a block, the block will use the UCS that is active at the time the block is created to determine its own local coordinate system. When that block is later inserted, it will orient its own coordinate system with the current UCS. (UCS is discussed in more detail in *Chapter 16*.)

▼ TIP

If you need more accuracy in the conversion, configure the AutoCAD Plotter for an ADI plotter. Set it up to plot a .DXB file. Your plots will then generate .DXB files, which you can import using the DXBIN command. Type **Dxbin** ↵ to open the Select DXB File dialog box and select the appropriate .DXB file.

TURNING A 3D VIEW INTO A 2D AUTOCAD DRAWING

We know of one company that uses AutoCAD 3D models to study their designs. Once a specific part of a design is modeled and approved, they convert the model into 2D elevations, ready to plug into their elevation drawing. Here is how that can be done:

1. Type **Psout** ↵ to export your drawing as an encapsulated PostScript file (.EPS). This will open the Create PostScript File

dialog box. See "PostScript Output" in *Chapter 14* for details on how this is done. For greater accuracy in the conversion, use the largest Output Sheet Size possible.

2. Open a new file and type **Psin** ⏎ to import the .EPS file you just created.

CREATING AND USING SLIDES

3D graphics are often handy for presentations, and 3D AutoCAD images are frequently used for that purpose, as well as for producing drafted 2D drawings. You may want to show off some of your 3D work directly from the computer screen. If your drawings are complicated, however, your audience may get impatient waiting for the hidden lines to be removed. Fortunately, AutoCAD provides two commands on the Tools ➤ Slide menu that let you save a view from your screen in a form that will display quickly.

The MSLIDE and VSLIDE commands will save a view as a file on disk. Such a view is called a slide. You can display a slide any time you are in the AutoCAD drawing editor. Slides display at redraw speed, no matter how complex they may be. This means you can save a slide of a hidden-line view of your 3D drawing and recall it quickly at any time.

Slides can also be used for reference during editing sessions, instead of panning, zooming, or viewing. A slide cannot be edited, however, nor will it be updated when you edit the drawing.

CREATING SLIDES

In the following exercise, you will make a few slides of the Unit file.

1. Open the Unit file and click on the Hide button on the Render palette to get a hidden-line view of the unit.

2. Choose Tools ➤ Slide ➤ Save..., or type **Mslide** ⏎ at the command prompt.

3. At the File dialog box, click OK to accept the default file name, Unit SLD. (The default slide name is the same name as the current drawing, with the extension .SLD.) The actual drawing file is not affected.

4. ZOOM in to the bathroom, and use MSLIDE to save another view called **Unitbath**, this time without the hidden lines removed.

5. When the File dialog box appears, highlight the File input box at the bottom of the dialog box, enter **Unitbath** ↵, and click OK.

VIEWING SLIDES

Now that you've saved two views, let's see how to view them.

1. ZOOM back to the previous view and choose Tools ➤ Slide ➤ View..., or enter **Vslide** ↵.

2. At the File dialog box, enter **unitbath** and click on OK. The slide of the bathroom appears. You can move the cursor around the view and start commands in the normal way, but you cannot edit or obtain information from this slide.

3. Start VSLIDE again.

4. This time, click on OK at the dialog box to accept the default slide file name, Unit. The 3D view of the unit appears with its hidden lines removed. Since slides display at redraw speed, you don't have to wait to view the unit without its hidden lines.

▼ **NOTE**

Any command that performs a redraw will also return you to the current drawing.

5. Click on View ➤ Redraw View to return to the drawing being edited.

6. Open the Plan file and use the VSLIDE command to view the Unitbath slide again. As you can see, you are able to call up the slide from any file, not just the one you were in when you created the slide.

7. Now create a slide of the Plan file and call it **Plan1**.

Next, you'll get to see how you might automate a slide presentation using the slides you just created.

AUTOMATING A SLIDE PRESENTATION

As mentioned in *Chapter 7*, SCRIPT (Tools ➤ Run Script...) can be used like the batch file in DOS, to run a sequence of commands automatically. Let's create a script file to automatically show the slides you made in the last exercise.

First you'll create a script file that you will use later to run a slide show. You'll add the DELAY command to the script. DELAY's function is to pause a script for a specific length of time.

1. Open a new file called **Show.**

2. Use a text editor to create a file called **Show.SCR**, and insert the following lines into this file, pressing ↵ at the end of each.

   ```
   vslide
   unit
   delay 3000
   vslide
   unitbath
   delay 3000
   vslide
   Plan1
   ```

These lines are a sequence of predetermined instructions to Auto-CAD that can be played back later. When you play this script file, each line is entered at the AutoCAD command prompt, just as you would enter it through the keyboard. Notice that the VSLIDE command is executed before each slide, which is then followed by the line delay 3000, which tells AutoCAD to pause roughly 3,000 milliseconds after each VSLIDE command is issued (you can substitute another value if you like). If no delay is specified, the next slide will come up as soon as the previous slide is completed.

You can also have the slides repeat themselves continuously by adding the RSCRIPT command at the very end of the Show.SCR file. You may want to do this in a presentation intended for casual viewing as an exhibit in a display area with people passing through. To stop a repeating script, press the Backspace key.

Now try playing the script.

1. Return to AutoCAD, then click Tools ➤ Run Script... or enter **Script** ↵.

2. At the Select Script File dialog box, highlight and pick the file you just created (Show.SCR) from the file list, and then click OK.

The slides you saved will appear on the screen in the sequence in which you entered them in the Show.SCR file.

CREATING A SLIDE LIBRARY

You can group slide files together into one file to help keep your slides organized—for example, by project or by drawing type. Slide libraries also save disk space, since they often require less space than the total consumed by the individual slide files.

Slide libraries are also used to create image menus in the DOS version, (though in release 13 for windows, such menu's are not used).

The tool you use to create a slide library is the Slidelib.EXE utility that comes with AutoCAD. This utility can be found in the \acadr13\common\support subdirectory. To create a slide library, follow these steps:

1. Use a word processor and make a list of the slides you want to include in the library. For the slides you created earlier, it would look like the following:

    plan1
    unit
    unitbath

    Notice that you do not include the .SLD extension in the file names in your list.

IV

Modeling and Imaging in 3D

2. Save this list as an ASCII file, with an appropriate name. For this example, call it **Slide1.LST**. Be sure it is saved in the same directory as your slide files.

3. Use the Slidelib.EXE program. If you set up a support directory, you should find it in \acadr13\common\support. Be sure your Slidelib.EXE file is in the same directory as your slide list file and slide files. Unless you have created a different working directory, they will be in \acadr13\win\.

4. Open a DOS window, then at the DOS prompt, enter **slidelib Myslides < slide1.lst** ↵. A file named Myslides.SLB will be created. The library name can be any legal DOS file name.

Do not include the file name extension; the Slidelib utility program automatically adds the file extension .SLB. For example, if you use Plans as the library name in step 4, a slide library file called Plans.SLB is created.

Now let's test your slide library. To view a slide from a slide library, you use the VSLIDE command. This time, however, you will specify the file name differently. Instead of picking a slide name from the dialog box, you must enter the name at the prompt line in a special format. The name must be entered with the library name first, followed by the individual slide name in parentheses.

1. Open a new temporary file called **Temp**, and at the Auto-CAD command prompt, click on Tools ➤ Slide ➤ View… and enter **Vslide** ↵.

2. At the File dialog box, click the Type It button. This causes the dialog box to close and lets you complete the command from the command line.

3. At the Slide file< current file name>: prompt, enter **Myslides(plan1)** ↵. The slide will appear in the drawing area.

If you placed the slide library file in a directory other than the current one, be sure you enter the directory name before the slide library name in step 3.

To use slide libraries from scripts, you use the slide library and slide name following the VSLIDE command, as in the following example:

```
vslide
myslides(unit)
delay 3000
vlside
myslides(unitbath)
```

```
delay 3000
vslide
myslides(plan1)
delay 3000
rscript
```

You've seen how you can save and display 3D views quickly and how you can automate a presentation of slides using scripts. With these tools, you can create an impressive, fast-paced presentation.

IF YOU WANT TO EXPERIMENT...

Don't forget that 3D modeling can be fun, as well as productive. You get to see your ideas take shape. 3D helps you visualize concepts more clearly, and in some cases can show you things that a traditional 3D chipboard model cannot.

The following exercise is really just for fun. It shows you how to do a limited form of animation, using View ➤ 3D Viewpoint, the Mslide command, and scripts.

1. Open the Unit plan.

2. Do a hidden-line removal; then use MSLIDE to create a slide called **V1**.

3. Click and drag the Inquiry button on the Object Properties palette, the select Locate Point on the flyout. Pick a point in the center of the floor plan. This marks the view center for the next step.

4. Enter **Vpoint** ↵ **R** ↵ at the command prompt.

5. At the Enter angle at XY plane prompt, enter **235** ↵; at the next prompt, press ↵.

6. Do another hidden-line removal, and use MSLIDE again to create a slide called **V2**.

7. Repeat steps 4 through 6, but this time increase by 10 the angle value you entered at step 5 (to **245**). At step 6, increase the slide name by 1 (to **V3**).

8. Keep repeating steps 4 through 6, increasing the angle value by 10 each time and increasing the slide file name by 1. Repeat these steps at least five more times.

9. Use a text editor to create a script file called **Animate.SCR,** containing the following lines, pressing ↵ at the end of each.

```
Vslide v1
Vslide v2
Vslide v3
Vslide v4
Vslide v5
Vslide v6
Vslide v7
Vslide v8
Rscript
```

10. Return to AutoCAD. At the command prompt, enter **Script** ↵ and click on Animate at the File dialog box. Then click OK and watch the show.

11. Press Esc or Backspace to end the show.

You might also want to try creating an animation that moves you completely around the unit plan.

Here's another suggestion for experimenting: To practice drawing in 3D, turn the kitchenette of your 3D unit drawing into a 3D object. Make the cooking top 30″ high and add some cabinet doors.

IV

Modeling and Imaging in 3D

16

USING ADVANCED 3D FEATURES

Defining a New UCS

Getting an Overhead (Plan) View

Controlling the UCS Icon

Laying Out a 3D Form

Creating a 3D Surface

Extruding and Rotating 2D Shapes
into 3D

Aligning Objects in 3D Space

Rotating Objects in 3D Space

FAST TRACK

739 ▶ To get a plan view of any UCS

Click on View ➤ 3D Viewpoint Presets ➤ Plan View, and then click on the desired UCS from the last cascading menu. Choose the current UCS, the world coordinate system, or select a saved UCS from a dialog box.

745 ▶ To change the display of the UCS icon

Click on Options ➤ UCS, and then select the desired setting for the UCS icon from the cascading menu. You can turn it on or off, or set it so it shows the location of the current UCS's origin.

746 ▶ To divide the screen into tiled viewports for easy 3D editing

Click on View ➤ Tiled Viewports. At the Tiled Viewports cascading menu, click on the desired viewport layout.

763 ▶ To draw a nonlinear 3D surface

First, use lines and 3D polylines to lay out your surface. Use arcs, lines, and polylines to define the edges of the surface. Be sure the objects defining the edges touch end-to-end. Finally, click on the Edge Surface button on the Surfaces palette, and select the edge objects, one at a time in a circular fashion.

766 ▶ To save a UCS

Click on the Named UCS button on the UCS palette. At the dialog box, highlight the *No Name* UCS. In the input box, enter the new name and click on the Rename To button. (You cannot do this with either *WORLD* or *PREVIOUS*, as these are names reserved for the world coordinate system and the UCS command's Previous option.

766 ▶ To recall a UCS

Click on Named UCS button on the UCS palette. At the dialog box, click on the name of the UCS you wish to recall. Click on the Current button and then on OK.

770 ▶ To set the number of segments in a 3Dmesh

Enter **Surftab1** or **Surftab2** at the command prompt, and enter the number of segments you want per surface axis.

774 ▶ To draw a surface that is "stretched" over two objects

Draw two objects that define the two sides of the 3D object you want to create. Click on the Ruled Surface button on the Surfaces palette, and then click on the two objects.

777 ▶ To extrude a shape in a circular fashion, like a lath

First draw the profile of the object to be extruded in a circular motion. Then draw a line representing the center axis of the circular motion. Click on the Revolved Surface button on the Surfaces palette. Click on the profile, and then click on the line.

781 ▶ To create a UCS that is perpendicular to the current UCS or WCS

Click on the X-Axis Rotate UCS button on the UCS palette, and enter **90** ↵.

788 ▶ To draw a pre-defined shape such as a cone or sphere

Click on the desired shape icon on the Surfaces palette. Answer the prompts that follow. You can then edit the basic shape to your exact needs.

AutoCAD's extended set of tools for working with 3D drawings lets you create 3D objects with few limitations on shape and orientation. This chapter focuses on the use of these tools, which help you easily generate 3D forms and view them in both the perspective and orthogonal modes.

MASTERING THE USER COORDINATE SYSTEM

The User Coordinate System (UCS) allows you to define a coordinate system in 3D space. All the same commands used in 2D drawings can be applied to 3D drawings.

By now you are familiar with the L-shaped icon in the lower-left corner of the AutoCAD screen, containing the letters W, X, and Y. The W indicates that you are currently in what AutoCAD calls the World Coordinate System (WCS); the X and Y indicate the positive directions of the x- and y-axes. WCS is a global system of reference from which you can define other user coordinate systems.

It may help to think of these AutoCAD user coordinate systems as different drawing surfaces, or two-dimensional planes. You can have several user coordinate systems at any given time. By setting up these different UCSs, you are able to draw as you would in the WCS in 2D, yet draw a 3D image. Let's say you want to draw a house in 3D with doors and windows on each of its sides. You can set up a UCS for each of the sides; then you can move from UCS to UCS to add your doors and windows (see Figure 16.1). Within each of these UCSs, you draw your doors and windows as you would in a typical 2D drawing. You can even insert elevation views of doors and windows that you have created in other drawings.

In this chapter you will be experimenting with a number of different views and UCSs. All of the commands you will use are available both at the command line and also via the Windows menus. Additionally, a number of the View and UCS commands can be accessed from the UCS and View tool palettes. The first thing to do is to open these palettes to have access to their buttons.

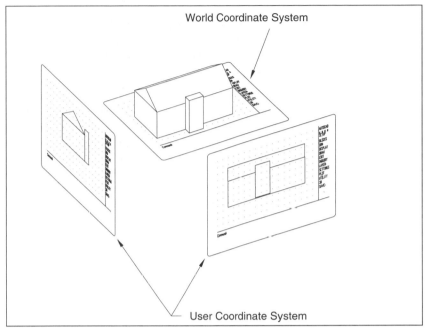

World Coordinate System

User Coordinate System

Figure 16.1:   Different user coordinate systems in a 3D drawing

LOADING THE VIEW AND UCS PALETTES

To display the View and UCS palettes, choose Tools ➤ Toolbars ➤
View and Tools ➤ Toolbars ➤ UCS. When the palettes appear on the
screen, you may drag them to a convenient location to the side. Both
of these palettes are also available as flyouts on the Standard toolbar.

DEFINING A UCS

In the first set of exercises, you will draw a chair that you can later add to your 3D Unit drawing. In drawing this chair, you will be exposed to the use of the UCS, as well as to some of the other 3D capabilities available in AutoCAD.

Begin the chair by drawing the seat and legs.

1. Start AutoCAD and open a new file called **Barcelon**.

2. Set up your drawing as an architectural drawing with a scale of 1"=1'–0" on an 8$\frac{1}{2}$×11" sheet. Then click the Zoom All button on the Standard toolbar.

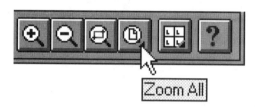

3. To draw the seat of the chair, click Rectangle on the Draw palette. Draw a rectangle measuring 20" in the x-axis and 30" in the y-axis. Position the rectangle so the lower-left corner is at the coordinate 2'–0",2'–0" (see Figure 16.2).

4. To draw the back of the chair, draw another rectangle 17" in the x-axis and 30" in the y-axis, just to the right of the previous rectangle(see Figure 16.2).

5. Click on the Properties button on the Object Properties palette.

6. At the Select objects: prompt, select the two rectangles.

7. At the Change Properties dialog box, enter **3** in the Thickness input box and click on OK. This gives the seat and back a thickness of 3".

8. Click on View ➤ 3D Viewpoint ➤ Vector and enter **-1,-1,1** ↵ in response to the prompt. (See *Chapter 15* if you need to refresh your memory on this command.) This gives you a 3D view from the lower-left of the rectangles.

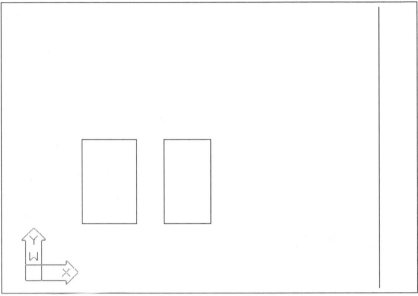

IV

ling and Imaging in 3D

Figure 16.2: The chair seat and back in plan view

9. Enter **Zoom** ↵ **.7x** ↵ to zoom out a bit and give yourself some room to work.

Notice that the UCS icon appears in the same plane as the current co-ordinate system. The icon will help you keep track of which coordinate system you are in. Now you can see the chair components as 3D objects. Next, you will define a UCS based on one side of the seat.

1. Click on the 3 Point UCS button on the UCS palette. You may also choose View ➤ Set UCS ➤ 3 Point, or type **UCS** ↵ **3** ↵. This option allows you to define a UCS based on three points that you select.

2. At the Origin point <0,0,0>: prompt, use your cursor and the Endpoint Osnap override to pick the bottom of the lower-left corner of the rectangle representing the seat (see label 1 in Figure 16.3). This is the origin point of your UCS.

3. At the next prompt:

   Point on positive portion of the X axis <2′–1″,2′– 0″,0′– 0″>:

   use your cursor and the Endpoint Osnap override to pick the bottom of the lower-right corner of the rectangle (see label 2 in Figure 16.3). (The default value for the prompt in this step, 2′–1″,2′–0″,0′–0″, indicates the positive direction of the x-axis of the current coordinate system.)

4. At the next prompt:

   Point on positive - Y portion of the UCS X-Y plane <2′– 0″,2′–0″,2′–1″>:

   pick the top of the left-hand corner of the rectangle, just above the corner you picked for the origin of the UCS (see label 3 in Figure 16.3). The screen regenerates, and both the cursor and the UCS icon change to indicate your new UCS.

5. Now that you have defined a UCS, you may want to save it so that you can return to it in a later editing session. Click on Save UCS from the UCS palette or choose View ➤ Set UCS ➤ Save. You can also type **UCS** ↵ **S** ↵.

6. At the ?/Name of UCS: prompt, enter the name **Side**.

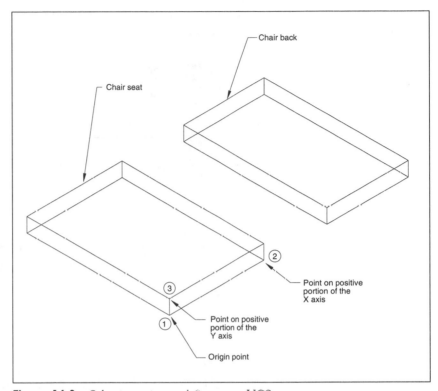

Figure 16.3: Selection points to define a new UCS

Now you can issue the UCS command and use the Restore option whenever you want to return to this UCS. You'll get a chance to use the Restore option in the later section called "Creating a 3D Surface."

VIEWING A UCS IN PLAN

Next, you will want to arrange the seat and back and draw the legs of the chair. All of this will be easier to accomplish by viewing the chair from the side. To do this, you need to view your newly created UCS as if it were a 2D view. First, save the current 3D view so you can return to it easily later on.

1. Click on Named Views from the View palette, or use View ➤ Named Views.... You can also type **Ddview** ↵.

The View Control dialog box appears.

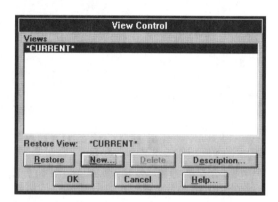

2. Click on the New button to save this view. The Define New View dialog box opens.

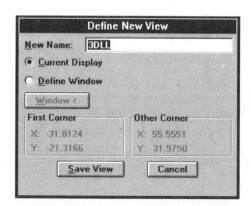

3. Give the new view the name **3DLL**, and then click on the Save View button.

4. Click on OK to return to the drawing.

5. Click on View ➤ 3D Viewpoint Presets ➤ Plan View ➤ Current. You can also type **Plan** ↵ ↵ to issue the PLAN command. The view changes to show the two objects from their sides (see Figure 16.4).

6. Enter **Zoom** ↵ **.7x** ↵ to view more of the drawing and to give yourself some room to work.

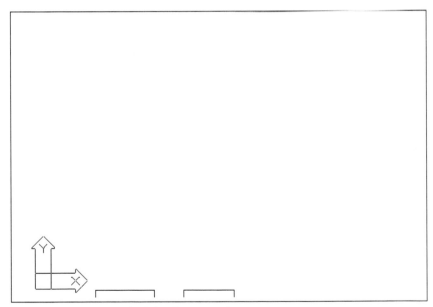

Figure 16.4:   The newly defined UCS in plan view

WORKING IN A UCS

You could have given these rectangles a different elevation to lift them off the WCS plane. Instead, you will change their elevation by using the standard MOVE command while viewing them edge-on. In this exercise you will see how you can use standard editing commands to draw in 3D.

1. Click on the Move button on the Modify palette, or type Move ↵. Use a crossing window to select the chair seat and back.

2. MOVE them vertically in the current UCS y-axis 8.5″, just as you would if you were moving any object in 2D. Your screen should look like Figure 16.5.

Now you need to move the chair seat and back to their proper locations. Grips will make quick work of this operation.

3. Window the rectangle that represents the seat back.

4. Click on the lower-left grip, and then press ↵ twice to get to the ** ROTATE ** mode.

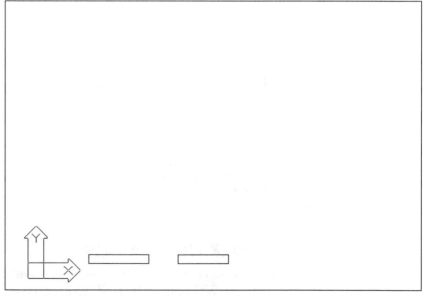

Figure 16.5: Elevating the chair seat and back

▼ TIP

If this exercise doesn't seem to be working, check to see if Grips and Noun/Verb Selection are both turned on (see *Chapter 2* if you need help).

5. At the Rotation angle prompt, enter **80** ↵ for a rotation angle of 80°. You can also select a rotation angle visually using your cursor.

6. Click on the same grip again, and this time press ↵ once to get to the ** MOVE ** mode.

7. Using the Endpoint Osnap override, click on the upper-right corner of the other rectangle to the left, as shown in Figure 16.6.

8. Select both rectangles; then click on the same grip point that you used previously, at the intersection of the two rectangles.

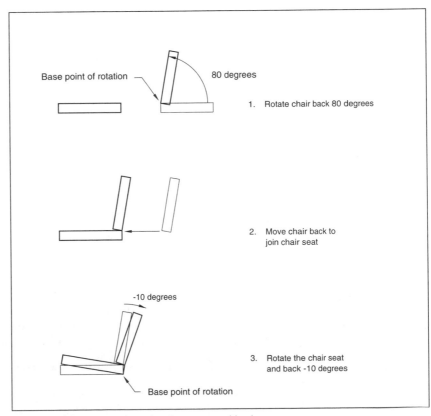

Figure 16.6:   Positioning the chair seat and back

9. Press ↵ twice to get to ** ROTATE ** mode, and then enter −10 to rotate both rectangles −10°. Use Figure 16.6 as a guide.

10. To get a 3D view of the chair to see your progress, click on the Named Views button on the Views palette, or choose View ➤ Named Views... to restore the view you saved earlier as 3DLL. Your screen should look like Figure 16.7.

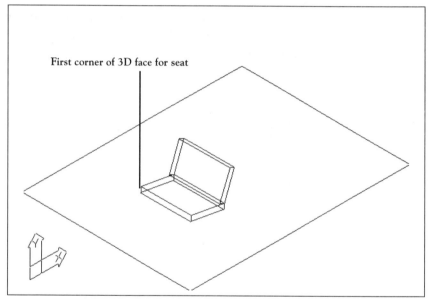

First corner of 3D face for seat

Figure 16.7: The 3D view of your drawing so far, showing where to pick points for the 3Dface

▼ NOTE

To display the Surfaces palette, choose Tools ➤ Toolbars ➤ Surfaces. If you need some help with the 3DFACE command, see *Chapter 15*.

11. Click on the 3D Face button on the Surfaces palette (3DFACE) to draw a surface over the top sides of the seat and back. Start the 3Dface in the leftmost corner of the seat and work in a counterclockwise fashion.

12. ZOOM in on the chair so you can pick points more easily.

Normally, when picking points for 3Dfaces, it doesn't matter where you start selecting points. But for the purpose of this tutorial, we had you select points for the seat's 3Dface starting at the leftmost corner and work in a counterclockwise fashion. The way you create the chair seat will influence the action of some UCS command options that you'll use later in this chapter.

CONTROLLING THE UCS ICON

So far, you have used only the UCS 3 Point option (View ➤ Set UCS ➤ 3 Point) to create other coordinate systems. There are several other options available to allow easy creation of and access to the UCS function. In the following section, "Using Viewports to Aid in 3D Drawing," you will want to set the UCS icon to show the current UCS origin location as well as its orientation.

Make sure your view is similar to the one in Figure 16.7, then click on Options ➤ UCS ➤ Icon Origin, or type **Ucsicon** ↵ **OR** ↵. Do this now in your current drawing, and the UCS icon will move to a location below the chair.

Now, whenever a new UCS is defined, the UCS icon will shift its location to show you not only the orientation of the UCS but also its origin. This will be useful in later exercises.

The Options ➤ UCS cascading menu actually represents several options of a single command: UCSICON. Let's take a moment to look at the options offered by the UCSICON command.

> **Origin**   (the option you used just above as Options ➤ UCS ➤ Icon Origin) forces the UCS icon to appear at the location of the current UCS's 0,0,0 origin point. If the UCS's origin is off-screen, the UCS icon appears in the screen's lower-left corner.
>
> **On** and **Off**   control whether the UCS icon is displayed or not. These options appear as Options ➤ UCS ➤ Icon. When this option is checked the icon is displayed; when it is not checked the icon is turned off.
>
> **Follow**   sets a system variable called UCSfollow. When checked, Follow causes the display to always show a plan view of the current UCS.

All doesn't actually appear on the Options ➤ UCS menu, but it lets you set the UCS icon's appearance in all the viewports on your screen at once. This option has no significance if you only have one viewport on the screen. To use this option, type **Ucs-icon** ⏎ **A** ⏎.

USING VIEWPORTS TO AID IN 3D DRAWING

In *Chapters* 6 and 12, you were introduced to AutoCAD's viewports. In this next section, you will use viewports to see your 3D model from several sides at the same time. This is helpful in both creating and editing 3D drawings, since it allows you to refer to different portions of the drawing without having to change views. In *Chapter 12*, you created viewports from Paper Space. This time, you'll create viewports directly in Model Space.

1. Click on View ➤ Tiled Viewports ➤ 3 Viewports.

2. At the Horizontal/Vertical/Above/Below/Left <Right>: prompt, press ⏎ to accept the default Right option. This causes the right viewport to occupy half the screen, while the left half is divided into two smaller viewports.

Now you see three of the same images in each viewport. Each viewport can display a different view of your drawing. In step 2, the prompt gives you the option to divide the screen horizontally in three equal viewports (Horizontal) or vertically into three equal viewports (Vertical). Above, Below, and Left each divide the screen into unequally sized viewports, with the option name indicating where the larger of the three viewports is placed.

3. Click on the upper-left viewport to activate it. Then click on View ➤ 3D Viewpoint Presets ➤ Plan View ➤ World, or type **Plan** ⏎ **W** ⏎. (The W is the World option of the PLAN command—it sets your view up as a plan view of the WCS.) The view changes to a plan view of your chair.

4. Use the ZOOM command to make some room in your view. Do this by entering **Z** ⏎ **.7x** ⏎.

5. Activate the lower-left viewport.

6. Click on View ➤ 3D Viewpoint Presets ➤ Plan View ➤ Current to get a plan view of the current UCS. The side view of your chair will appear in this viewport.

7. Enter **Z** ⏎ **.7x** ⏎ again to allow some room in this view.

8. PAN this view up so you can draw the legs of the chair more easily.

9. Switch to the 3D view on the right and enlarge it to get a better look at the chair in 3D. You should have a screen similar to Figure 16.8.

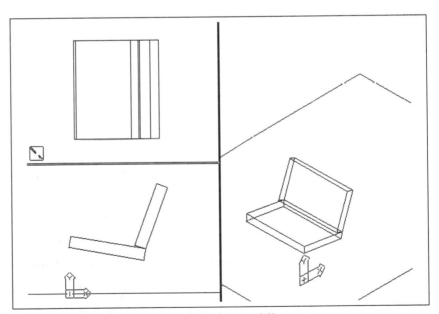

Figure 16.8:   Three viewports, each displaying a different view

Adding the Legs

Now let's finish off the chair by adding legs.

1. Go to the side view of the chair and draw two curved polylines as shown in Figure 16.9. You may have to adjust your view so you can draw the legs more easily. You don't have to be absolutely perfect about placing or shaping these lines either.

2. Use the grips of the polylines to adjust their curve, if necessary.

3. Using the Edit Polyline command from the Modify palette, give the polylines a width of 0.5″.

4. Use the Properties button on the Object Properties palette to open the Modify polyline dialog box and give the polylines a thickness of −2″. Notice that as you draw and edit a polyline, it appears in both the plan and 3D views.

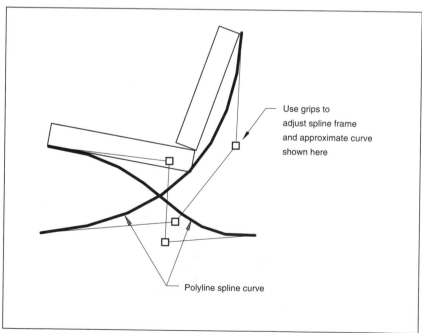

Figure 16.9: Drawing the legs of the chair

5. Go to the plan view, and click on the upper-left viewport.

6. Click on the Named UCS button on the UCS palette.

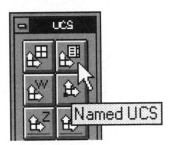

7. At the UCS Control dialog box, click on *WORLD*, then on the Current button, and finally on OK.

8. Toggle the ortho mode on and MIRROR the polylines representing the chair legs to the opposite side of the chair in roughly the same location. Your screen should look similar to Figure 16.10.

▼ NOTE

Notice that the broken-pencil UCS icon has shifted to the viewport in the lower-left corner. This icon tells you that the current UCS is perpendicular to the plane of that view.

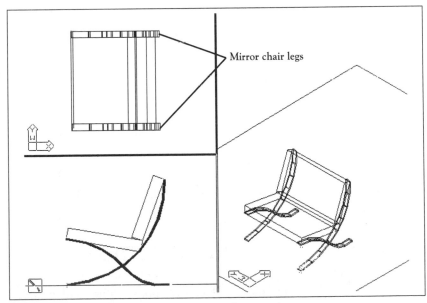

Figure 16.10: Copying the legs from one side to another

Your chair is now complete. Let's finish up by getting a better look at it.

1. Click on the viewport to the right.

2. Type Hide ↵ to see what the chair actually looks like when it is viewed as a solid (see Figure 16.11). You can also use Tools ➤ Toolbars ➤ Hide.

3. Click on View ➤ Tiled Viewports, and choose 1 Viewport in the cascading menu.

4. Click on OK. The 3D view fills the screen in preparation for the next set of exercises.

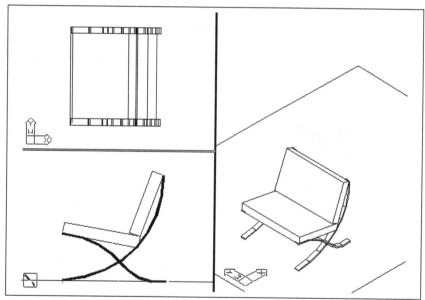

Figure 16.11: The chair in 3D with hidden lines removed

CONTROLLING THE UCS

There are a number of other ways to define a UCS. You can, for example, use the 3Dface of your chair as the definition for a UCS. In the following set of exercises, you will get some practice moving your UCS around. Learning how to move effortlessly between UCSs is crucial to your mastering the creation of 3D models, so you'll want to pay special attention to the command options shown in these procedures. You'll be using the options of the UCS command (**UCS** ↵). These options are also accessible either via the View ➤ Set UCS cascading menu or the UCS tool palette.

Orienting a UCS in the View Plan

Before you begin with the exercises, you'll need to define a UCS in the current view plane. To do this, click on the View UCS button on the UCS palette or choose View ➤ Set UCS ➤ View. You can also type **UCS** ↵ **V** ↵. The UCS icon changes to show that the UCS is aligned with the current view.

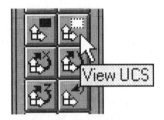

AutoCAD uses the current UCS origin point for the origin of the new UCS. By defining a view as a UCS, you can enter text to label your drawing, as you would in a technical illustration. Text entered in a plane created in this way will appear normal (see Figure 16.12).

UCS Based on Object Orientation

You can also define a UCS based on the orientation of an object. This is helpful when you want to work on a predefined object to fill in detail on its surface plane.

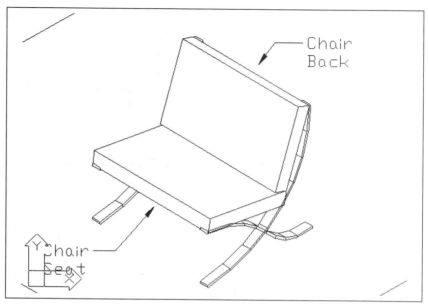

Figure 16.12: You can add text to a 3D view using the View option of the UCS command

1. Click on the Object UCS button on the UCS palette, or choose View ➤ Set UCS ➤ Object. You can also type **UCS** ↵ **OB** ↵ at the command prompt.

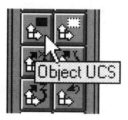

2. At the Select object to align UCS: prompt, pick the 3Dface used to define the top surface of the chair seat. The UCS icon shifts to reflect the new coordinate system's orientation (see Figure 16.13).

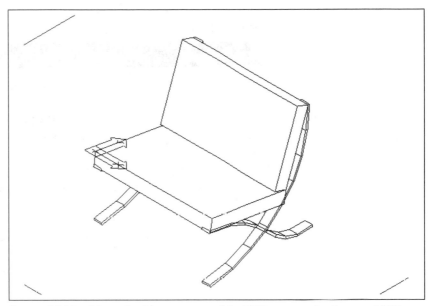

Figure 16.13:   Using the Object option of the UCS command to locate a UCS

Orientation of the UCS Origin   Remember earlier when we asked you to draw the 3Dface for the seat in a specific way? Well, the location of the UCS origin and its orientation are dependent on how the 3Dface was created. If you had drawn it other than as instructed, the UCS you defined using the Object option in the above exercise would not have been generated as described.

Table 16.1 describes how an object will determine the orientation of a UCS.

UCS Based on an Offset Orientation

There may be times when you want to work in a UCS that has the same orientation as the current UCS but is offset. For example, you may be making a drawing of a building that has several parallel walls offset with a sawtooth effect (see Figure 16.14). You can easily hop from one UCS to another, parallel UCS by using the Origin option.

Table 16.1: Collapsing directory levels

Object Type	UCS Orientation
Arc	The center of the arc establishes the UCS origin. The x-axis of the UCS passes through the pick point on the arc.
Circle	The center of the circle establishes the UCS origin. The x-axis of the UCS passes through the pick point on the circle.
Dimension	The midpoint of the dimension text establishes the origin of the UCS origin. The x-axis of the UCS is parallel to the x-axis that was active when the dimension was drawn.
Line	The endpoint nearest the pick point establishes the origin of the UCS, and the x,z plane of the UCS contains the line.
Point	The point location establishes the UCS origin. The UCS orientation is arbitrary.
2D Polyline	The starting point of the polyline establishes the UCS origin. The x-axis is determined by the direction from the first point to the next vertex.
Solid	The first point of the solid establishes the origin of the UCS. The second point of the solid establishes the x-axis.
Trace	The direction of the trace establishes the x-axis of the UCS with the beginning point setting the origin.
3Dface	The first point of the 3Dface establishes the origin. The first and second points establish the x-axis. The plane defined by the face determines the orientation of the UCS.
Shapes, Text, Blocks, Attributes, and Attribute Definitions	The insertion point establishes the origin of the UCS. The object's rotation angle establishes the x-axis.

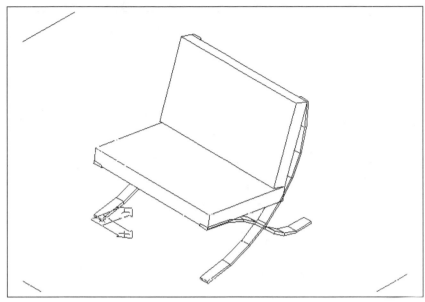

Figure 16.14:   Using the Origin option to shift the UCS

1. Click on the Origin UCS button on the UCS palette, or choose View ➤ Set UCS ➤ Origin. You can also type **UCS** ⏎ **O** ⏎ at the command prompt.

2. At the Origin point <0,0,0>: prompt, pick the bottom end of the chair leg, just below the current UCS origin. The UCS icon shifts to the end of the leg, with its origin at the point you picked (see Figure 16.15).

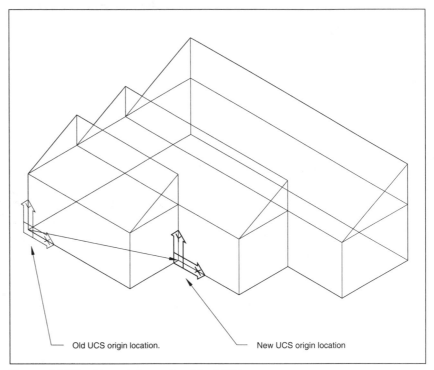

Old UCS origin location.   New UCS origin location

Figure 16.15: Moving the origin of the UCS

UCS Rotated around an Axis

Now suppose you want to change the orientation of the x-, y-, or z-axis of the current UCS. You can accomplish this by using the X, Y, or Z options of the UCS command. Let's try rotating the UCS about the z-axis to see how this works.

1. Click on the Z Axis Rotate UCS button on the UCS palette or choose View ➤ Set UCS ➤ Z Axis Rotate. You can also type **UCS** ⏎ **Z** ⏎. This will allow you to rotate the current UCS about the z-axis.

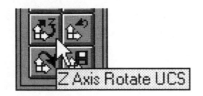

2. At the Rotation angle about Z axis <0>: prompt, enter **90** for 90°. The UCS icon rotates to reflect the new orientation of the current UCS (see Figure 16.16).

Similarly, the X and Y options allow you to rotate the UCS about the current x- and y-axis, respectively, just as you did for the z-axis just above. Finally, you can skew the UCS by using the Z Axis Vector option. This is useful when you need to define a UCS based on a z-axis determined by two objects.

1. Click on the Z Axis Vector UCS button on the UCS palette, or choose View ➤ Set UCS ➤ Z Axis Vector. You can also type **UCS ⏎ ZA ⏎.**

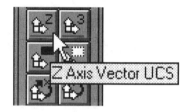

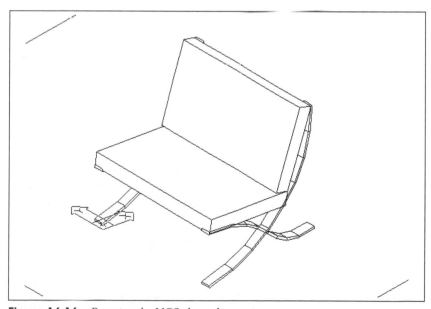

Figure 16.16: Rotating the UCS about the z-axis

2. At the Origin point <0,0,0>: prompt, press ↲ to accept the default, which is the current UCS origin. You can shift the origin point at this prompt if you like.

3. At the next prompt,

   Point on positive portion of Z-axis <0'–0",0'– 0",0'–1">:

   use the Endpoint Osnap override and pick the other chair leg end, as shown in Figure 16.17. The UCS twists to reflect the new z-axis of the UCS.

Now we've finished our tour of the UCS command. Set the UCS back to the world coordinate system and Exit and Save this file.

USING 3DMESHES

In the previous example, you drew a chair composed of objects that were mostly straight lines or extruded curves. All the forms in that chair

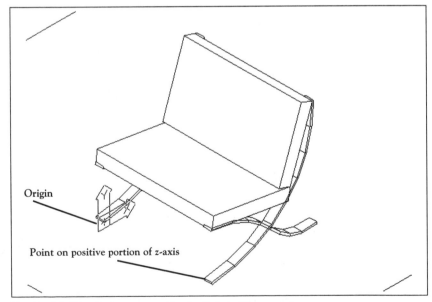

Figure 16.17: Picking points for the Z-Axis Vector option

were defined in planes perpendicular to each other. At times, however, you will want to draw objects that do not fit so easily into perpendicular or parallel planes. The following exercise demonstrates the creation of more complex forms using some of AutoCAD's other 3D commands.

LAYING OUT A 3D FORM

In this next group of exercises, you will draw a butterfly chair. This chair has no perpendicular or parallel planes to work with, so you will start by setting up some points that you will use for reference only. This is similar in concept to laying out a 2D drawing. These points will define the major UCSs needed to construct the drawing. As you progress through the drawing construction, notice how the reference points are established to help create the chair.

1. Open a new file called **Btrfly.** Set up an architectural drawing at $1'' = 1'-0''$ scale on an $8\frac{1}{2}\times11''$ sheet.

2. Click Rectangle on the Draw palette. Draw a rectangle 20″ square with its first corner at coordinate 36,36.

3. Use the OFFSET command (on the Copy flyout of the Modify palette) to offset the square 4″ out, so you have two concentric squares with the outer square measuring 28″.

4. MOVE the larger of the two squares, the 28″ square, to the left 2″. Your screen should look similar to Figure 16.18.

5. Choose View ➤ 3D Viewpoint ➤ Vector, or type **Vpoint** ↵ to start the VPOINT command.

6. At the Rotate/<viewpoint> prompt, enter **-1,-.75,.5**. This will give you a view from the lower-left side of the rectangles.

7. Now you need to move the outer rectangle in the z-axis so that its elevation is 30″. To do this, first click on the outer rectangle, then click on one of its grips. Press ↵ to enter the ** MOVE ** mode, and then enter **@0,0,30** ↵. This tells AutoCAD to move the rectangle a 0 distance in both the x- and y-axes and 30″ in the z-axis.

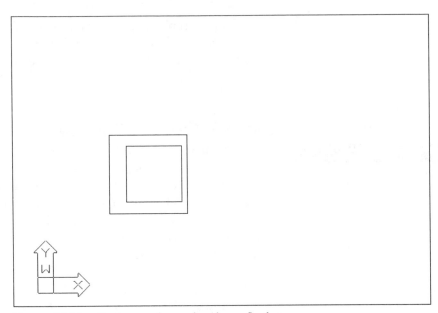

Figure 16.18:   Setting up a layout for a butterfly chair

8. Use the LINE command and draw lines from the corners of the outer square to the corners of the inner square, as shown in Figure 16.19. This is the layout for your chair.

Spherical and Cylindrical Coordinate Formats

In the foregoing exercise, you used relative Cartesian coordinates to locate the second point for the MOVE command. For commands that accept 3D input, you can also specify displacements by using the *spherical* and *cylindrical coordinate formats*.

The spherical coordinate format lets you specify a distance in 3D space while specifying the angle in terms of degrees from the x-axis of the current UCS and degrees from the x–y plane of the current UCS (see panel 1 of Figure 16.20). For example, to specify a distance of 4.5″ at a 30° angle from the x-axis and 45° from the x–y plane, you'd enter **@4.5<30<45**. This is the direct distance, followed by a < symbol; then

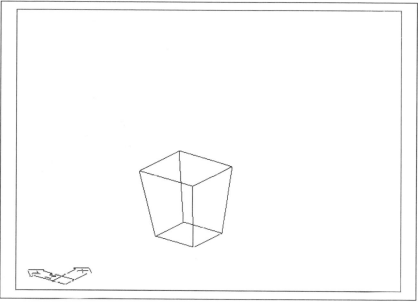

Figure 16.19: The finished layout

the angle from the x-axis of the current UCS followed by another <symbol; then the angle from the x–y plane of the current UCS. To use the spherical coordinate format to move the rectangle in the exercise, you would enter **@30<0<90** at the Second point prompt.

The cylindrical coordinate format, on the other hand, lets you specify a location in terms of a distance in the plane of the current UCS and a distance in the z-axis. You also specify an angle from the x-axis of the current UCS (see panel 2 of Figure 16.20). For example, to locate a point that is a distance of 4.5″ in the plane of the current UCS, at an angle of 30° from the x-axis, and a distance of 3.3″ in the z-axis, you'd enter **@4.5<30,3.3**. This is the distance of the displacement as it relates to the plane of the current UCS, followed by the < symbol; then the angle from the x-axis, followed by a comma; then the distance in the z-axis. Using the cylindrical format to move the rectangle, you would enter **@0<0,30** at the Second point prompt.

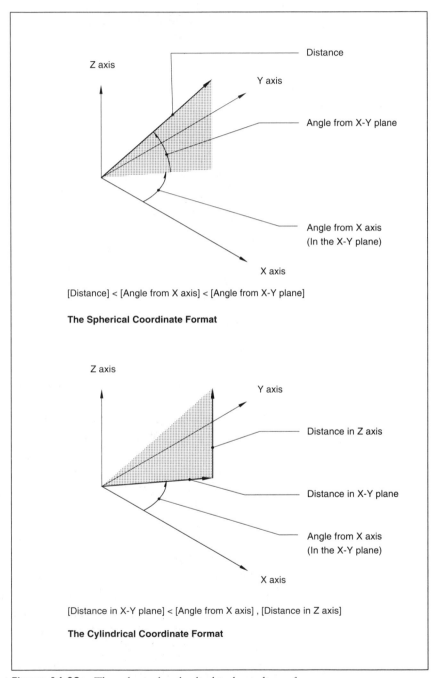

Figure 16.20: The spherical and cylindrical coordinate formats

USING A 3D POLYLINE

Now you will draw the legs for the butterfly chair, using a 3D polyline. This is a polyline that can be drawn in 3D space.

1. Zoom in to the frame so you can select the points on the frame more easily.

2. Click and drag on the Polyline button on the Draw palette, and select 3D Polyline from the flyout, or enter **3Dpoly** ↵ at the command prompt.

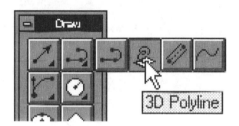

3. At the First point: prompt, pick a series of points as shown in Figure 16.21, using the Endpoint and Midpoint Osnap overrides.

4. Draw another 3D polyline in the mirror image of the first (see Figure 16.21).

5. ERASE the rectangles and connecting lines that make up the frame.

CREATING A 3D SURFACE

Next, you will draw the seat of the chair. The seat of a butterfly chair is usually made of canvas and drapes from the four corners of the chair legs. You will first define the perimeter of the seat using arcs, and then use the Edge Surface option (EDGESURF) on the Surfaces palette to form the shape of the draped canvas. Edge Surface creates a surface based on four objects defining the edges of that surface. In this example, you will use arcs to define the edges of the seat.

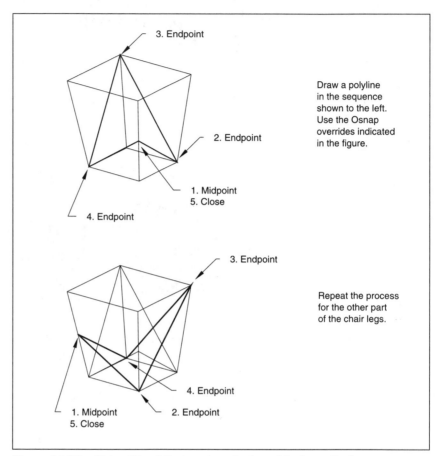

Figure 16.21: Using 3D polylines to draw the legs of the butterfly chair

To draw the arcs defining the seat edge, you must first establish the UCSs in the planes of those edges. Remember that in the last example you created a UCS for the side of the chair before you could draw the legs. In the same way, you must create a UCS defining the planes that contain the edges of the seat.

Click on the 3 Point UCS button on the UCS palette, or choose View ➤ Set UCS ➤ 3 Point, to create a UCS using the three points shown in the top view of Figure 16.22.

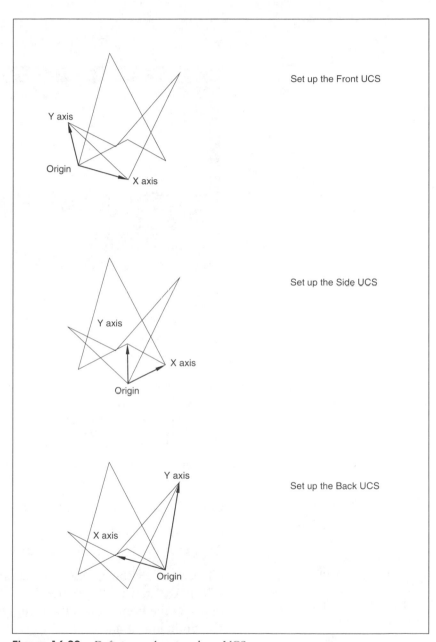

Figure 16.22:   Defining and saving three UCSs

2. Click on the Named UCS on the UCS palette, or choose View ➤ Named UCS.... The UCS Control dialog box appears.

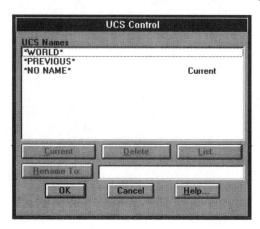

3. Highlight the *NO NAME* item in the list box; in the input box, change the name to **Front**.

4. Click on the Rename To button, and then on OK. The new current UCS is now named Front.

5. Define a UCS for the side of the chair, and use the UCS Control dialog box to rename this UCS **Side**, just as you did for Front in steps 1 through 4. Remember that you rename the *No Name* UCS.

6. Repeat these steps again for a UCS for the back of the chair, named **Back**. Use Figure 16.22 for reference.

7. Open the UCS Control dialog box again and highlight FRONT.

8. Click on the Current button below the list, and then on OK. This activates Front as the current UCS.

9. Click and drag the 3 Points button on the Draw palette, and select Arc Start End Direction from the flyout. Draw the arc defining the front edge of the chair (see Figure 16.23). Use the Endpoint Osnap override to pick the top endpoints of the chair legs as the endpoints of the arc. (If you need help with the ARC command, refer to *Chapter 3*.)

▼ WARNING

Don't skip step 8. If you do, you will not get the results you want when you start picking the arc's endpoints in step 9. AutoCAD only draws arcs in the current UCS. Remember: Only lines, 3D polylines, and other 3D objects can be drawn in three-dimensional space. All other objects can be drawn only in the current UCS.

IV

Modeling and Imaging in 3D

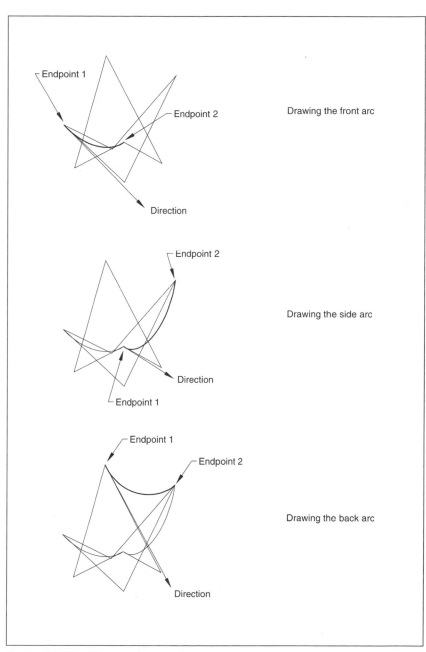

Figure 16.23: Drawing the seat edge using arcs

10. Repeat steps 7 through 9 for the UCS named Side, and then again for the UCS named Back—each time using the top endpoints of the legs for the endpoints of the arc.

Next, you will mirror the side-edge arc to the opposite side. This will save you from having to define a UCS for that side.

1. Click on the Named UCS button on the UCS palette, and use the UCS Control dialog box to activate the world coordinate system (*WORLD*). The reason for doing this is that you want to mirror the arc along an axis that is parallel to the plane of the WCS. Remember: You must go to the coordinate system that defines the plane you wish to work in.

2. Click on the arc you drew for the side of the chair (the one drawn on the Side UCS).

3. Click on the midpoint grip of the arc; then press ↵ or the right mouse button four times to get to the ** MIRROR ** mode.

4. Enter **B** ↵ to select a new base point for the mirror axis.

5. Enter **C** ↵ to select the Copy option.

6. At the Base point prompt, use the Intersection Osnap override to pick the intersection of the two legs in the Front plane.

7. Next, use the Intersection override (Shift-click ➤ Intersection) to pick the intersection of the two legs in the Back plane. Refer to Figure 16.24 for help. The arc should mirror to the opposite side, and your chair should look like Figure 16.25.

8. Press Esc twice to clear the grips.

Finally, let's finish off this chair by adding the mesh representing the chair seat.

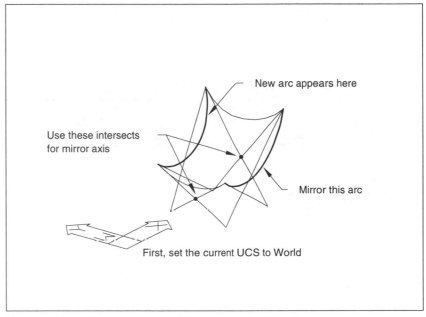

Figure 16.24:   Mirroring the arc defining the side of the chair seat

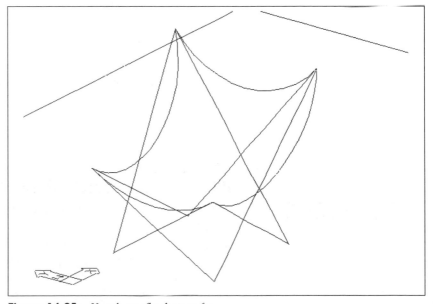

Figure 16.25:   Your butterfly chair so far

▼ NOTE

To display the Surfaces palette, choose Tools ➤ Toolbars
➤ Surfaces.

1. Click on the Edge Surface button on the Surfaces palette, or enter **Edgesurf** ↵ at the command prompt.

▼ WARNING

In order for the command to
work properly, the arcs—or
any set of objects—used to define the boundary of a mesh
with the Edge Surface option
must be connected exactly
end-to-end.

2. At the Select edge 1: prompt, pick the arc on the Front UCS.

3. At the Select edge 2: prompt, pick the next arc on the Side UCS.

4. Continue to pick the other two arcs in succession. (The arcs must be picked in a circular fashion, not crosswise.) A mesh will appear, filling the space between the four arcs. Your chair is now complete.

5. Use the HIDE command to get a better view of the butterfly chair. You should have a view similar to Figure 16.26.

6. Save this file.

At this point, you've been introduced to one of the options on the Surfaces palette. You'll get a chance to use a few more options later in this chapter. Next, you'll learn how to edit mesh objects like the Butterfly chair's seat.

ADJUSTING THE SETTINGS THAT CONTROL MESHES

▼ NOTE

See *Chapters 13* and *14* and
Appendix D for more on system variables.

As you can see, the seat is made up of rectangular segments. If you want to increase the number of segments in the mesh (to get a look like that in Figure 16.27), you can change the Surftab1 and Surftab2 system variables. Surftab1 controls the number of segments along edge 1, the first edge you pick in the sequence; and Surftab2 controls the number of segments along edge 2. AutoCAD refers to the direction of edge 1 as *m* and

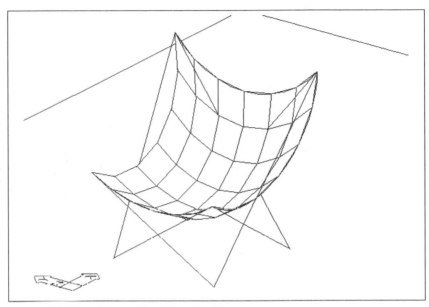

Figure 16.26: The completed butterfly chair

the direction of edge 2 as *n*. These two directions can be loosely described as the x- and y-axes of the mesh, with *m* being the x-axis and *n* being the y-axis.

In Figure 16.27 the setting for Surftab1 is 24, and for Surftab2 is 12. The default value for both settings is 6. If you would like to try different Surftab settings on the chair mesh, you must erase the existing mesh, change the Surftab settings, and then use the EDGESURF command again to define the mesh.

EDITING A MESH

You can use Edit Polyline (PEDIT) on the Modify palette to edit meshes in a way similar to editing polylines. When you start PEDIT and pick a mesh, you get this prompt:

```
Edit vertex/Smooth surface/Desmooth/Mclose/
\close/Undo/eXit <X>:
```

Modeling and Imaging in 3D

IV

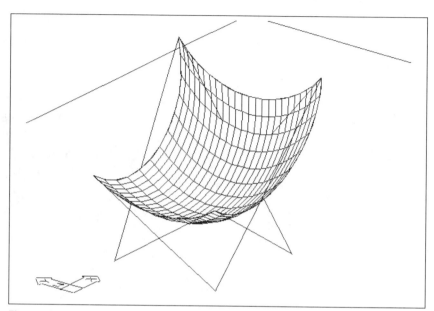

Figure 16.27:   The chair with different Surftab settings

Here are descriptions of these options:

Edit vertex   allows you to relocate individual vertices in the mesh. (You'll find a detailed discussion of this option in the following section.)

Smooth surface   is similar to the Spline option for polylines. Rather than having the mesh's shape determined by the vertex points, Smooth surface adjusts the mesh so that mesh vertices act as control points that pull the mesh—much as a spline frame pulls a spline curve.

Desmooth   reverses the effects of Smooth surface.

Mclose and **Nclose**   allow you to close the mesh in either the m or n direction. When either of these options is used, the prompt line will change, replacing Mclose or Nclose with Mopen or Nopen, allowing you to open a closed mesh.

▼ TIP

You can adjust the amount of pull the vertex points exert on a mesh by using Smooth surface in conjunction with the Surftype system variable. If you'd like to know more about these settings, see *Appendix D*.

EDITING VERTICES IN A MESH

If you want to move a specific vertex in the mesh, you can use the Edit vertex option of the PEDIT command, as follows:

1. Click Edit Polyline on the Modify palette, or enter **Pedit** ↵.

2. Select the Mesh you want to edit.

3. Enter **E** ↵. You then see this prompt:

   Vertex (0,0): Next/Previous/Left/Right/Up
   /Down/Move/REgen/eXit <N>:

   and an X appears on the vertex to be edited.

Here are descriptions of the Edit vertex options:

Next and **Previous**   move the X quickly along the n-axis to another vertex.

Left and **Right**   move the X one vertex at a time along the n-axis.

Up and **Down**   move the X along the m-axis one vertex at a time.

Move   lets you relocate a vertex once you have placed the X on the vertex you want to edit.

Regen   regenerates the mesh to show the effects of any changes you make to a mesh.

The m- and n-axes mentioned above are like the mesh's own local coordinate. Their direction depends on how the mesh is created.

Now that you've explored meshes, let's move on and try out some of the other 3D surface drawing commands.

OTHER USES FOR SURFACE DRAWING COMMANDS

In the last example, you used the EDGESURF command to create a 3D surface. There are several other 3D surface commands available that allow you to generate surface shapes easily.

CREATING A 3DMESH BY GIVING COORDINATES

If you need to draw a mesh like the one in the previous example, but you want to give exact coordinates for each vertex in the mesh grid, you can use the 3DMESH command. Suppose you have data from a survey of a piece of land; you can use 3DMESH to convert your data into a graphic representation of its topography. Another use of 3DMESH is to plot mathematical data to get a graphic representation of a formula.

Because you must enter the coordinate for each vertex in the mesh, 3DMesh is better suited in scripts or AutoLISP programs, where a list of coordinates can be applied automatically to the 3DMESH command in a sequential order.

USING TWO OBJECTS TO DEFINE A SURFACE

The Ruled Surface (RULESURF) button on the Surfaces palette draws a surface between two 2D objects, such as a line and an arc or a polyline and an arc. This command is useful for creating extruded forms that transform from one shape to another along a straight path. Let's see firsthand how this command works.

1. Open a new file called **Table**.

2. Set up this drawing in the same way as the other two drawings, Barcelon and Btrfly.

3. Now you need to draw two objects that you will use with the Ruled Surface option. While in the WCS, draw an arc forming a semicircle with a radius of 12″.

4. Draw a line connecting the two endpoints of the arc (see Figure 16.28).

5. Change your viewpoint to view the drawing in 3D.

6. Move the line 10″ in the z-axis.

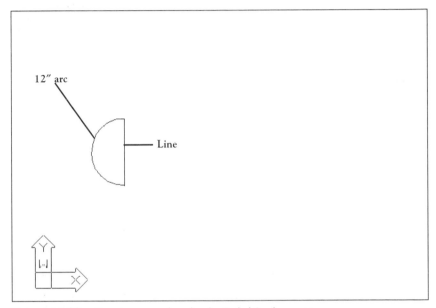

12″ arc

Line

Figure 16.28:   Drawing two edges for the Ruled Surface option

7. Now you are ready to connect the two objects with a 3D surface. Click on the Ruled Surface button on the Surfaces toolbar, or type **Rulesurf** ↵ at the command prompt.

Surfaces

Ruled Surface

8. At the Select first defining curve prompt, move the cursor toward the lower end of the arc and click on it.

9. At the Select second defining curve prompt, move the cursor toward the upper end of the line and click on it. The surface will appear as shown in Figure 16.29.

▼ WARNING

The position you use to pick the second object will determine how the surface is generated.

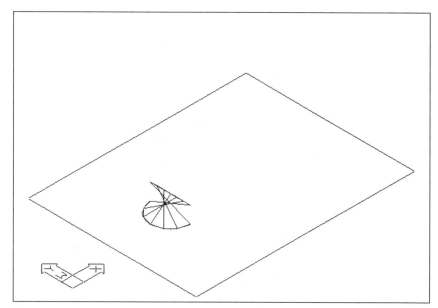

Figure 16.29: The RULESURF surface

Notice that the segments defining the surface cross each other. This crossing effect is caused by picking the defining objects near opposite endpoints. The arc was picked near its lower end, and the line was picked toward the top end.

1. ERASE the surface you just drew.

2. Click on the Ruled Surface button on the Surfaces palette again, but this time pick the defining objects at or near the

▼ **NOTE**

You may have noticed that each of the surfaces you just drew was made up of six segments. You can control the number of segments that appear by adjusting the Surftab1 system variable, just as you can for Edge Surfaces.

same end. You will get a surface similar to the one in Figure 16.30.

3. Now finish the table by following the instructions in Figure 16.31, and save the file.

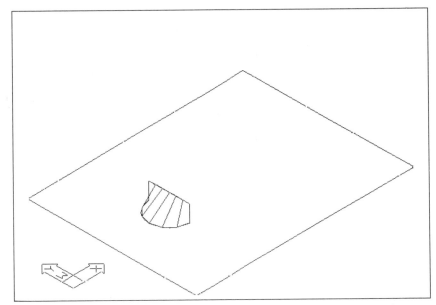

Figure 16.30:   The ruled surface redrawn by using different points to select the objects

DRAWING EXTRUDED AND ROTATED 3D FORMS

In *Chapter 15*, you learned how you can extrude objects in the z-axis by using the Change Properties button on the Object Properties toolbar to change an object's thickness. The Revolved Surface option (REVSURF) on the Surfaces palette lets you extrude an object in a linear or circular fashion in any direction in space. In the following example, you will draw a simple lever-type door handle to see how these other extrusions can be accomplished.

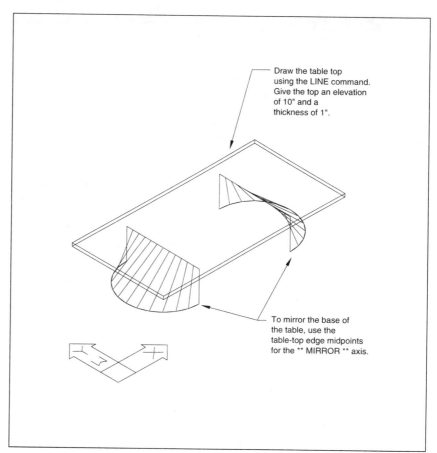

Draw the table top
using the LINE command.
Give the top an elevation
of 10" and a
thickness of 1".

To mirror the base of
the table, use the
table-top edge midpoints
for the ** MIRROR ** axis.

Figure 16.31: Completing the table drawing

1. Open a new file called **Handle,** and set it up as an architectural drawing at full scale on an $8^{1}/_{2}\times11''$ sheet.

2. Draw a circle to the left of the center of the screen with
   a 0.4" radius.

3. Draw a vertical line 0.5" to the right of the circle. This line
   will be the axis about which you will extrude the circle to
   form the curved portion of the handle.

4. Choose View ➤ 3D Viewpoint ➤ Vector, or type **Vpoint** ↵.

5. Enter **-1,-1,1** to get a 3D view of your circle from the lower-left of the WCS.

6. Click on the Revolved Surface button on the Surfaces palette, or type **Revsurf** ↵ at the command prompt. Revolved Surface allows you to extrude an object in an arc or circle.

7. At the Select path curve prompt, select the circle. (The *path curve* is an object that defines the shape to be extruded; in this case, a circle.)

8. At the Select axis of revolution prompt, pick the line to the right of the circle, below its midpoint. (The *axis of revolution* is the axis about which the path curve will be rotated to form the extrusion.)

9. At the Start angle prompt, press ↵. This allows you to enter the beginning angle of the circular extrusion; this angle is in relation to the object you selected for extrusion. The default, 0, starts the extrusion at the position of the object. A greater or lesser value would offset the beginning of the extrusion.

10. At the Included angle (+=ccw, -=cw) <Full circle>: prompt, enter **90** ↵ for a 90° extrusion. The circle will extrude in a 90° arc toward the screen (see Figure 16.32).

The Included angle prompt (step 10) allows you to control the distance of the extrusion. If you press ↵ without entering anything, the object will be extruded a full 360°. A value in degrees—180, for example—results in an extrusion in a partial circle. You can also control the direction of the extrusion by entering either a plus or a minus sign before the degree value, or by selecting one of the ends of the line defining the axis of revolution. In the previous exercise, you selected a

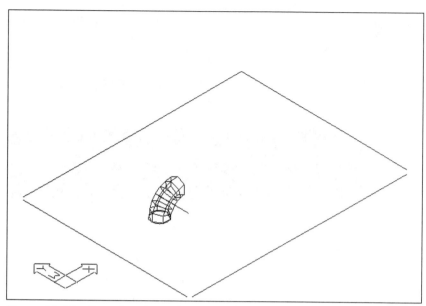

Figure 16.32:   Extruding the circle in a circular fashion

point below the middle of the line so the extrusion would be in a direction
toward you. Had you picked a point above the midpoint, the extrusion
would have taken a path in the opposite direction, or away from you.

You can use circles, arcs, lines, and polylines for your extruded shape,
and lines or polylines for your axes. To control the number of segments
in the extrusion, set Surftab1 to a higher or lower value; Surftab2 will
control the number of segments in the object. For example, if you set
Surftab1 to 24, you will have 24 segments in the extrusion arc, giving
the arc a smoother appearance. Set Surftab2 to 24, and the circle making up the extruded shape will be composed of 24 segments. This gives
your handle a rounded appearance rather than a hexagonal one (see
Figure 16.33). Bear in mind, however, that the more segments you use,
the larger your drawing file becomes, so keep the Surftab settings as low
as possible without sacrificing appearance.

Let's continue by drawing the straight part of the door handle. First,
you will have to set up a new UCS in preparation for the next 3D object

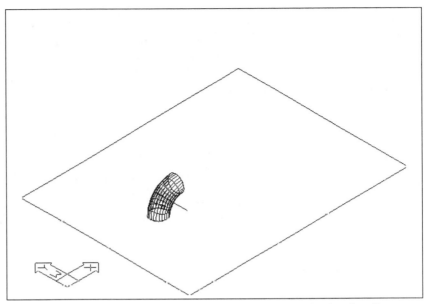

Figure 16.33: Using a higher Surftab2 value when drawing the door handle

command. You'll create a UCS perpendicular to the WCS, with its x-axis aligned with the x-axis of the WCS.

1. Click on the X Axis Rotate UCS button on the UCS palette, or choose View ➤ Set UCS ➤ X Axis Rotate.

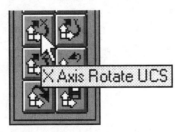

2. At the Rotation angle about the X axis prompt, enter **90** ↵. This rotates the UCS 90° in the positive direction. The right-hand rule (described in the tip above) applies here also.

With your UCS icon changed to reflect the orientation of your new UCS, you are ready to draw the straight part of the handle using the Extruded Surface option (TABSURF) in the Surfaces palette. To prepare to extrude a surface, you will have to rotate the circle −90° in the current UCS.

1. ZOOM in to the circle.

2. Select the circle, and then click on its center grip.

3. Press ↵ twice to get to the ** ROTATE ** mode.

4. Enter **B** ↵ to select a different base point for the rotation axis. Then use the Endpoint Osnap override to pick the end of the line you used earlier when you used the Revolved Surface option.

5. Enter **-90** ↵ to rotate the circle −90°.

6. Draw a line 5″ long in the x–y plane of the WCS, just above the original circle (see Figure 16.34). This line will be used by the next command, TABSURF, to define the direction and distance you want the rotated circle to be extruded.

7. Click on the Extruded Surface button on the Surfaces palette, or enter **Tabsurf** ↵ at the command prompt. Extruded Surface extrudes objects in a straight line.

8. At the Select path curve: prompt, pick the circle. Here, you are being asked to select the object you want to extrude. If you need to, zoom in close to the circle so you can pick it more easily.

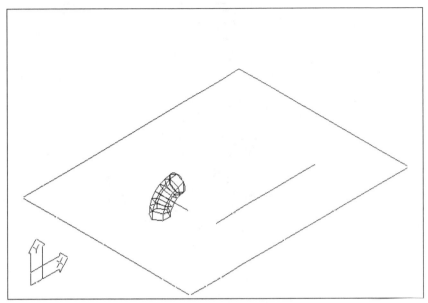

Figure 16.34:   Adding the line representing the direction vector

9. At the Select direction vector: prompt, pick the line you
    drew to define the path of the extrusion. The point you pick
    on the line will determine the direction of the extrusion.
    The endpoint closest to your pick point on the direction vec-
    tor will be the base point of the extrusion. The opposite end
    of the direction vector will indicate the direction of the ex-
    trusion. So, if you pick a point on the line closest to the cir-
    cle, the extrusion will occur toward the line in the positive x
    direction. If you pick a point on the line farthest from the cir-
    cle, the extrusion will occur away from the line (see Fig-
    ure 16.35).

10. Finish the drawing by adding the escutcheon plate for the
    door handle (see Figure 16.36), then close the file.

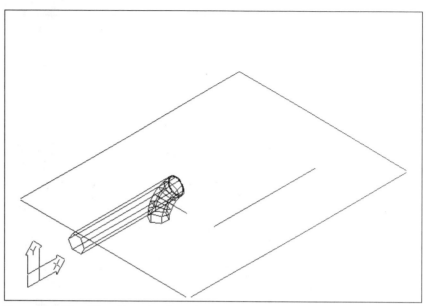

Figure 16.35: The effect of picking the direction vector end away from the extruded object

Surftab1 controls the number of segments that are used for the path curve. The higher the Surftab setting, the smoother the circle will be. You can use either a line or polyline as the direction vector, and you can use circles, arcs, lines, or polylines as objects to extrude. Two other command options, 3D AR-RAY and 3D MIRROR (both on the Copy flyout of the Modify palette) offer 3D versions of the ARRAY and MIR-ROR commands.

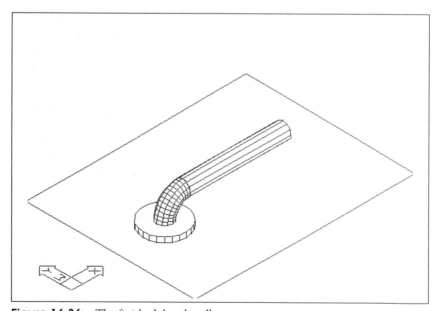

Figure 16.36: The finished door handle

EDITING IN 3D

AutoCAD provides two utilities for moving objects in 3D space: ALIGN and 3DROTATE. Both of these commands are found on the Rotate flyout of the Modify palette. They help you perform some of the more common moves associated with 3D editing.

ALIGNING OBJECTS IN 3D SPACE

In mechanical drawing you often create the parts in 3D, and then show an assembly of the parts. The ALIGN option can greatly simplify the assembly process. The following exercise describes how ALIGN works.

1. Click and drag the Rotate button on the Modify palette, then select Align on the flyout, or type **Align** ↵.

2. At the Select objects prompt, select the 3D source object you want to align to another part. (The *source object* is the object you want to move.)

3. At the 1st source point prompt, pick a point on the source object that is the first point of an alignment axis—such as the center of a hole or the corner of a surface.

4. At the 1st destination point prompt, pick a point on the destination object to which you want the first source point to move. (The *destination object* is the object with which you want the source object to align.)

5. At the 2nd source point prompt, pick a point on the source object that is the second point of an alignment axis—such as another center point or other corner of a surface.

6. At the 2nd destination point prompt, pick a point on the destination object indicating how the first and second source points are to align in relation to the destination object.

7. At the 3rd source point prompt, you can press ↵ if two points are adequate to describe the alignment. Otherwise, pick a third point on the source object that, along with the first two points, best describes the surface plane you want aligned with the destination object.

8. At the 3rd destination point prompt, pick a point on the destination object that, along with the previous two destination points, describes the plane with which you want the source object to be aligned. The source object will move into alignment with the destination object.

Figure 16.37 gives some examples of how the Align utility works.

ROTATING AN OBJECT IN 3D

If you just want to rotate an object in 3D space, the 3D Rotate option on the Modify palette can simplify the operation. Click and drag the Rotate button on the Modify palette, select 3D Rotate from the flyout and select the required objects. Once you've selected the objects, you get the following prompt:

Axis by Entity/Last/View/Xaxis/Yaxis/Zaxis/<2points>

This prompt is asking you to describe the axis of rotation. Here are descriptions of the options presented in the prompt:

Entity   allows you to indicate an axis by clicking on an object. When you select this option, you are prompted to pick a line, circle, arc, or 2D polyline segment. If you click on a line or polyline segment, the line is used as the axis of rotation. If you click on a circle, arc, or polyline arc segment, AutoCAD uses the line passing through the center of the circle or arc and perpendicular to its plane.

Last   uses the last axis that was used for a 3D rotation. If no previous axis exists, you are returned to the Axis... prompt.

View   uses the current view direction as the direction of the rotation axis. You are then prompted to select a point on the view direction axis to specify the exact location of the rotation axis.

IV

Modeling and Imaging in 3D

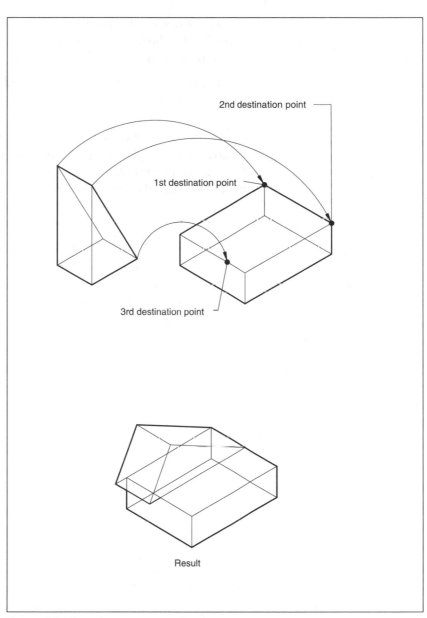

2nd destination point

1st destination point

3rd destination point

Result

Figure 16.37: Aligning two 3D objects

Xaxis/Yaxis/Zaxis   uses the standard x-, y-, or z-axis as the direction for the rotation axis. You are then prompted to select points on the x-, y-, or z-axis to locate the rotation axis.

<2points>   uses two points you provide as the endpoints of the rotation axis.

This completes our look at creating and editing 3D objects. You have had a chance to practice using nearly every type of object available in AutoCAD. You might want to experiment on your own with the predefined 3D shapes offered on the Surfaces palette.

IF YOU WANT TO EXPERIMENT...

You've covered a lot of territory in this chapter, so it may be a good idea to play with these commands to help you remember what you've learned. Try the exercise shown in Figure 16.38.

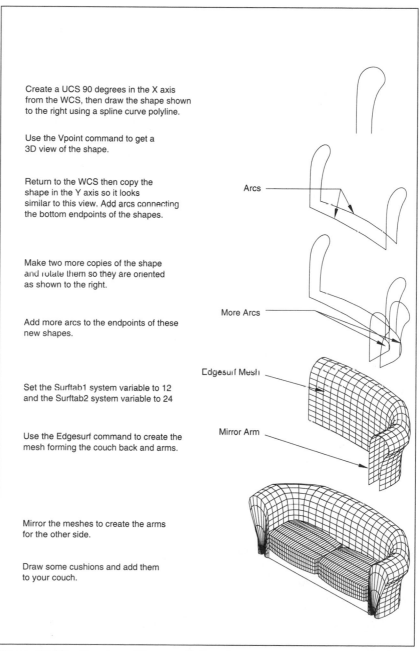

Create a UCS 90 degrees in the X axis from the WCS, then draw the shape shown to the right using a spline curve polyline.

Use the Vpoint command to get a 3D view of the shape.

Return to the WCS then copy the shape in the Y axis so it looks similar to this view. Add arcs connecting the bottom endpoints of the shapes.

Make two more copies of the shape and rotate them so they are oriented as shown to the right.

Add more arcs to the endpoints of these new shapes.

Set the Surftab1 system variable to 12 and the Surftab2 system variable to 24

Use the Edgesurf command to create the mesh forming the couch back and arms.

Mirror the meshes to create the arms for the other side.

Draw some cushions and add them to your couch.

Arcs

More Arcs

Edgesurf Mesh

Mirror Arm

Figure 16.38: Drawing a 3D overstuffed couch

17

CREATING YOUR FIRST DRAWING

Setting up a Perspective View with DVIEW

Adjusting the Distance between Your Object and Your Viewpoint

Fine-Tuning Your View

Setting Up Your Drawing to Get a Rendered View

Adding Light Sources

Saving Your Light and View Setup

Adding Surface Reflectance Data

Saving a Rendered View as an Image File

Saving Files in 3D Studio Format

FAST TRACK

794 ▶ **To get a perspective view from a plan view**

Click on View ➤ 3D Dynamic View, and then select parts of your drawing that will help you get your bearings. Enter **PO** ↵, and pick a target and camera location. Finally, enter **D** ↵ and use the slide bar to select a distance.

798 ▶ **To pan to another part of your model**

Click on View ➤ 3D Dynamic View, and then select parts of your drawing that will help you get your bearings. Enter **TA** ↵. Move your cursor until you get the desired view and click the mouse/pick button.

802 ▶ **To change your view so you are looking down at your model**

Click on View ➤ 3D Dynamic View, and then select parts of your drawing that will help you get your bearings. Enter **CA** ↵, then **T** ↵ ↵. Move your cursor until you get the camera angle you want, and click the left mouse button.

805 ▶ **To change the focal length to get more of your model in the view**

Click on View ➤ 3D Dynamic View. Then select parts of your drawing that will help you get your bearings. Enter **Z** ↵. Enter a new focal length value or move the cursor until you get a view you like, and then click the mouse/pick button.

809 ▶ **To cut out portions of your model in the foreground that obscure your view**

Click on View ➤ 3D Dynamic View, and then select parts of your drawing that will help you get your bearings. Enter **CL** ↵. Move the slide bar to the far left, and then gradually move it toward the right until the part of the foreground you want removed disappears. Click the mouse/pick button when you are done.

811 ▶ To open the render tool palette

Choose Tools ➤ Toolbars ➤ Render.

813 ▶ To add lights to your model

While in a plan view, click on Lights from the Render palette. Click on New, and select the type of light you want to add. Enter a light name, click on Modify, and select the location of the light.

821 ▶ To add gradient and smooth shading

Click on Render Preferences from the Render palette, and click on Smooth Shading in the dialog box.

825 ▶ To ensure that all surfaces are rendered

Click on Render Preferences from the Render palette, and then on Other Options. Make sure the Discard Back Faces option is turned off.

829 ▶ To add a finish to a surface

Click on Materials from the Render Palette. Click on Materials Library, choose the finish you want, and then click on Import. Click on Attach, and select the objects to which you want to attach the finish.

834 ▶ To store an image of a rendered view

Click on Render from the Render palette, then select File from the Destination pop-up list. Click on Render Scene, then enter a name for the image if it is to be different from the default. You can determine the type of image file to save by clicking on Other Options in the Destination group of the Render or Render Configuration dialog boxes.

So far, your views of 3D drawings have been in *parallel projection*. This means parallel lines appear parallel on your screen. Though this type of view is helpful while constructing your drawing, you will want to view your drawing in true perspective from time to time, to get a better feel for what your 3D model actually looks like. In the first part of this chapter, you will explore the use of the DVIEW command (View ➤ 3D Dynamic View), which allows you to see your drawing in *true perspective*.

Once you're familiar with DVIEW, you'll be ready to take advantage of AutoCAD's rendering capabilities, which are introduced in the second half of the chapter. This is perhaps the only chapter where you will need a system capable of displaying 256 colors. Most computers set up for AutoCAD use an SVGA display with at least 800×600 display resolution and 256 colors, so for most readers this chapter's requirements aren't a problem. But if your renderings don't look like the ones in the figures, it's possible your system doesn't support 256 colors. Check your display card manual if you have difficulties.

GETTING PERSPECTIVE VIEWS

DVIEW is a complex command, so this chapter's exercises are brief, presenting the use of each DVIEW option in turn. With this in mind, you may want to begin these exercises when you know you have an hour or so to complete them all at one sitting.

Now let's begin!

1. Open the Barcelon file you created in the first part of *Chapter 16*, or use the copy of this file supplied on your companion CD. Be sure you are in the world coordinate system, and issue the PLAN command (View ➤ 3D Viewpoint Presets ➤ Plan View ➤ World) so you have a plan view of the chair.

2. Use View ➤ Zoom ➤ All to get an overall view of the drawing.

3. Click on View ➤ 3D Dynamic View, or enter **Dview** ↵ at the command prompt.

4. At the object selection prompt, pick the chair seat and back. You will use these objects as references while using the DVIEW command.

5. Next you will see the DVIEW prompt:

CAmera/TArget/Distance/POints/PAn/Zoom/T-Wist/CLip/Hide/Off/Undo/<eXit>:

at which you can select the appropriate option. (These options are discussed in the remaining exercises in this chapter.) Then the screen will change to show only the objects you selected.

DVIEW uses *dynamic dragging,* which allows you to preview your perspective view. For this reason, you are asked to select objects that will allow you to get a good idea of your view without slowing the dynamic-dragging process. If you had selected the whole chair, view selection would be much slower, because the whole chair would have to be dragged during the selection process.

SETTING UP YOUR PERSPECTIVE VIEW

AutoCAD uses the analogy of a camera to help determine your perspective view. As with a camera, your perspective view is determined by the distance from the object, camera position, view target, and lens type.

Follow these steps to determine the camera and target positions:

1. At the DVIEW prompt, enter **PO** ↵ for the Points option.

2. At the Enter target point <current point>: prompt, pick the center of the chair. This will allow you to adjust the camera target point, which is the point at which the camera is aimed.

3. At the Enter camera point <current point>: prompt, pick the lower-left corner of the screen. This places the camera location (the position from which you are looking) below and to the left of the chair, on the plane of the WCS (see Figure 17.1).

▼ WARNING

When selecting views in this set of exercises using DVIEW and its options, be sure you click the mouse/pick button as indicated in the text. If you press the ↵ key (or click the ↵ button on the mouse), your view will return to the default orientation, which is usually the last view selected.

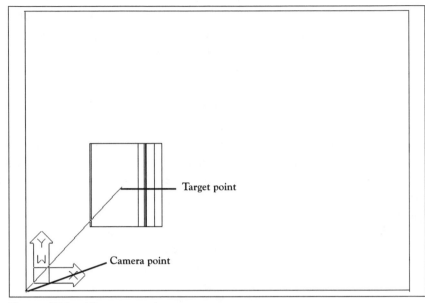

Figure 17.1:   The target and camera points

▼ NOTE

Make Dviewblock as simple as possible, but without giving up the detail necessary to distinguish its orientation.

Your view now changes to reflect your target and camera locations, as shown in Figure 17.2. The DVIEW prompt returns, allowing you to further adjust your view.

If you like, you can press ↵ at the object-selection prompt without picking any object, and you will get the default image, a house, to help you set up your view (see Figure 17.3). Or you can define a block and name it **Dviewblock**. Dviewblock should be defined in a one-unit cubed space. AutoCAD will search the current drawing database, and if it finds Dviewblock, will use it as a sample image to help you determine your perspective view.

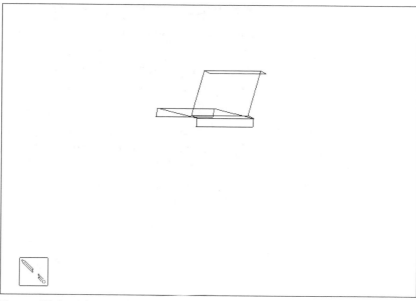

Figure 17.2: The view with the camera and target positioned

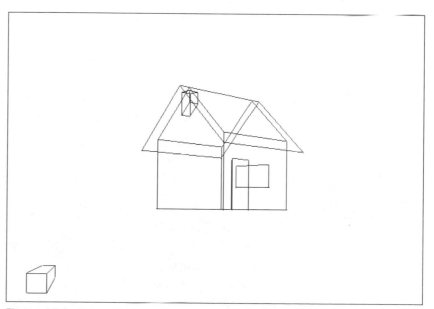

Figure 17.3: The default sample image used with DVIEW

ADJUSTING DISTANCES

Next, you will adjust the distance between the camera and target.

1. At the DVIEW prompt, enter **D** ↵ for the Distance option. A slide bar appears at the top of the screen.

2. At the New camera/target distance <current distance>: prompt, move your cursor from left to right. The chair appears to enlarge and reduce. You can also see that the position of the diamond in the slide bar moves. The slide bar gives you an idea of the distance between the camera and the target point in relation to the current distance.

3. As you move the diamond, you see lines from the diamond to the 1× value (1× being the current view distance). As you move the cursor toward the 4× mark on the slide bar, the chair appears to move away from you. Move the cursor toward 0×, and the chair appears to move closer.

4. Move the cursor further to the left; as you get to the extreme left, the chair appears to fly off the screen. This is because your camera location has moved so close to the chair that the chair disappears beyond the view of the camera—as if you were sliding the camera along the floor toward the target point. The closer to the chair you are, the larger and farther above you the chair appears to be (see Figure 17.4).

5. Adjust your view so it looks like Figure 17.5. To do this, move the diamond to between 1× and 4× in the slide bar.

6. When you have the view you want, click the mouse/pick button. The slide bar disappears and your view is fixed in place. Notice that you are now viewing the chair in perspective.

▼ NOTE

The Distance option actually serves two functions: Aside from allowing you to adjust your camera to target distance, it also turns on the perspective view mode. The Off option of DVIEW changes the view back to a parallel projection.

ADJUSTING THE CAMERA AND TARGET POSITIONS

Next, you will want to adjust your view so you can see the whole chair. You are still in the DVIEW command.

IV

Modeling and Imaging in 3D

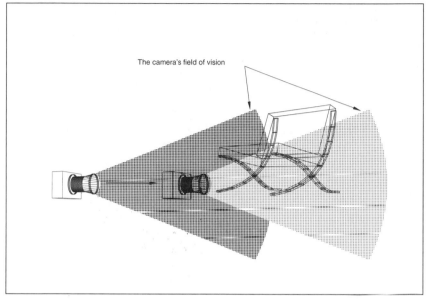

Figure 17.4: The camera's field of vision

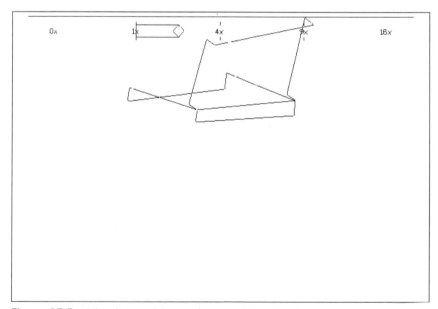

Figure 17.5: The chair and diamond cursor while using the Distance option

1. At the DVIEW prompt, enter **TA** ↵ for the Target option. The chair will temporarily disappear from view.

2. At the prompt,

   Toggle angle in/Enter angle from X-Y plane <.00>:

   move your cursor very slowly in a side-to-side motion. Keep the cursor centered vertically otherwise you may not be able to find the chair. The chair moves in the direction of the cursor in an exaggerated manner. The sideways motion of the cursor simulates panning a camera from side to side across a scene (see Figure 17.6).

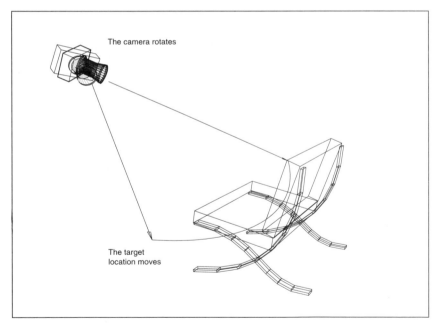

The camera rotates

The target location moves

Figure 17.6: Adjusting the target option is like panning your camera across a scene.

3. Center the chair in your view, and then move the cursor slowly up and down. The chair moves in the opposite direction to the cursor. The up-and-down motion of the cursor simulates panning a camera up and down.

4. Watch the coordinate readout as you move the cursor up and down. It displays the camera's vertical angle as you move the cursor. Moving the cursor down causes the readout to list increasing negative numbers; moving the cursor up causes the readout to list increasing positive numbers. This coincides with the prompt that asks for an angle from the x–y plane. If you knew the exact camera angle you wanted from the x–y plane, you could enter it now.

▼ TIP

If you lose your view of the chair but remember your camera angle, you can enter it at the Enter angle in X-Y plane prompt to help relocate your view.

5. When you're ready, enter **T** ↵ to select the Toggle angle option. The prompt changes to

   Toggle angle from/Enter angle in X-Y plane from X axis <*current angle*>:

6. Move your cursor from left to right; now the coordinate readout displays the angle of the camera relative to the x-axis of the horizontal (x–y) plane. As you move the cursor from left to right, the coordinate readout shows the direction the camera is pointing relative to the x-axis. If you knew the exact camera angle you wanted from the x-axis of the x–y plane, you could enter it now.

7. Position the view of the chair so it looks like Figure 17.7, and click the mouse/pick button. You've now fixed the target position.

In steps 4 and 6 above, we mentioned that you could enter an angle value indicating either the vertical or horizontal angle to the target. Once you enter that value (or just press ↵), the angle becomes fixed in either the vertical or horizontal direction. Then, as you move your cursor, the view's motion will be restricted to the remaining unfixed direction.

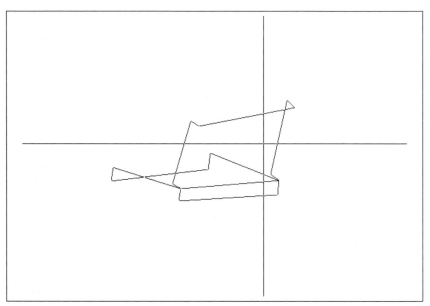

Figure 17.7:   While in the DVIEW Target option, set up your view so it looks like this figure.

CHANGING YOUR POINT OF VIEW

Next, you will want to adjust the camera location to one that is higher in elevation.

1. At the DVIEW prompt, enter **CA** ↵ to select the Camera option.

2. At the prompt,

   Toggle angle in/Enter angle from XY plane <11>:

   move your cursor slowly up and down. As you move the cursor up, your view changes as if you were rising above the chair (see Figure 17.8). The coordinate readout displays the camera's angle from the horizontal x–y plane as you move the cursor. If you know the angle you want, you could enter it now.

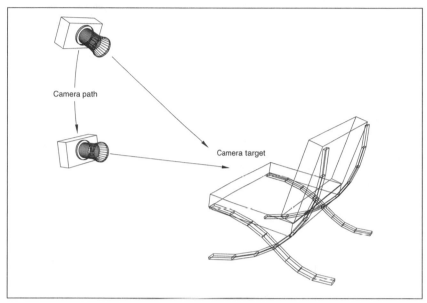

Camera path

Camera target

Figure 17.8: While in the Camera option, moving the cursor up and down is like moving your camera location up and down in an arc.

3. Move the cursor down so you have a view that is roughly level with the chair, and then move the cursor from side to side. Your view changes as if you were walking around the chair, viewing it from different sides (see Figure 17.9).

4. When ready, enter **T** ↵ to choose the Toggle angle in/Enter angle from XY plane option. The prompt changes to

    Toggle angle from/Enter angle in XY plane from *x* axis <–144>:

5. Now when you move the cursor from side to side, the coordinate readout lists the camera's angle to the target point relative to the x-axis. If you know the horizontal angle you want, you can enter it now.

6. Position your view of the chair so it is similar to the one in Figure 17.10, and click the mouse/pick button.

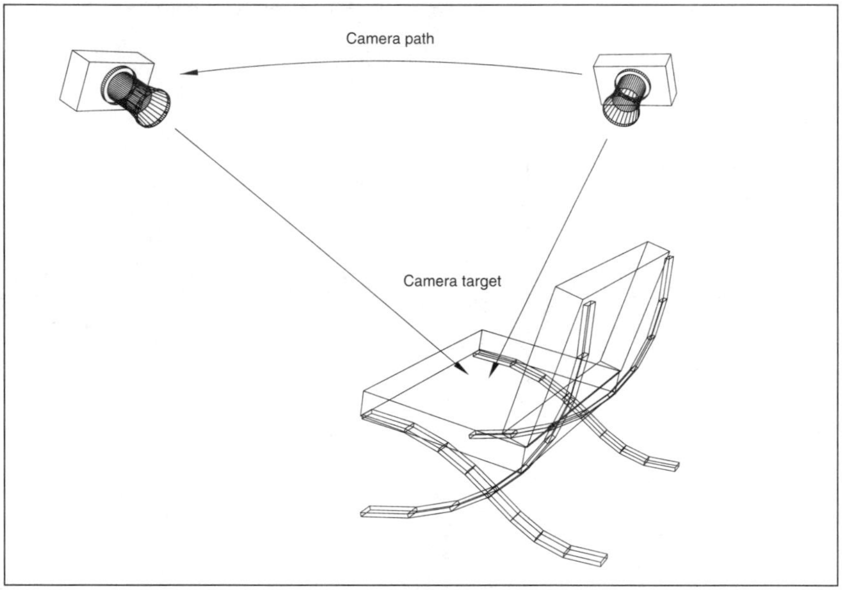

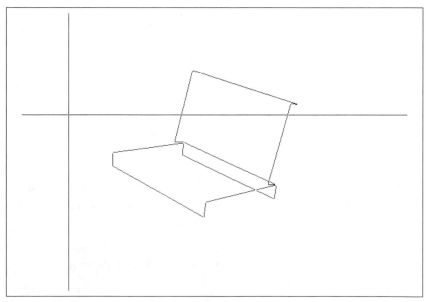

Figure 17.9: Moving the cursor from side to side is like walking around the target position.

Figure 17.10: Set up your camera location so you have a view similar to this one.

In steps 2 and 5, we mentioned that you could enter an angle value indicating either the vertical or horizontal angle to the camera. Once you indicate a value, either by entering a new one or by pressing ↵, the angle becomes fixed in either the vertical or horizontal direction. Then, as you move your cursor, the view's motion will be restricted to the remaining unfixed direction.

USING THE ZOOM OPTION AS A TELEPHOTO LENS

The Zoom option of DVIEW allows you to adjust your view's cone of vision, much like a telephoto lens in a camera. You can expand your view to include more of your drawing, or narrow the field of vision to focus on a particular object.

> ▼ NOTE
>
> When you don't have a perspective view (obtained by using the Distance option) and you use the Zoom option, you will get the prompt Adjust zoom scale factor <1>: instead of the Adjust lenslength prompt. The Adjust zoom… prompt acts just like the standard ZOOM command.

1. At the DVIEW prompt, enter **Z** ↵ for the Zoom option. Move your cursor from side to side, and notice that the chair appears to shrink or expand. You also see a slide bar at the top of the screen, which lets you see your view in relation to the last Zoom setting, indicated by a diamond. You can enter a value for a different focal length, or you can visually select a view using the slide bar.

2. At the Adjust lenslength <50.000mm>: prompt, press ↵ to accept the 50.000mm default value.

TWISTING THE CAMERA

The Twist option lets you adjust the angle of your view in the view frame—like twisting the camera to make your picture fit diagonally across the frame.

1. At the DVIEW prompt, enter **TW** ↵ for the Twist option. Move your cursor, and notice that a rubber-banding line emanates from the view center; the chair also appears to rotate, and the coordinate readout changes to reflect the twist angle.

2. At the New view twist <0>: prompt, press ↵ to keep the current 0° twist angle.

3. Press ↵ again to exit the DVIEW command, and the drawing regenerates, showing the chair in perspective (see Figure 17.11).

In the next section, you will look at one special DVIEW option—Clip—that lets you control what is included in your 3D views.

USING CLIP PLANES TO HIDE PARTS OF YOUR VIEW

At times, you may want a view that would normally be obscured by objects in the foreground. For example, if you try to view the interior of your Unit drawing, the walls closest to the camera obscure your view. The DVIEW command's Clip option allows you to eliminate objects in either the foreground or the background, so you can control your views

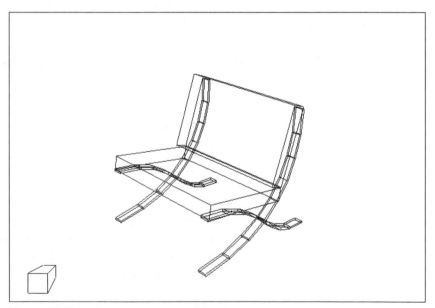

Figure 17.11: A perspective view of the chair

more easily. In the case of the apartment unit, you can set the Clip/Front option to delete any walls in the foreground that might obscure your view of its interior (see Figure 17.12).

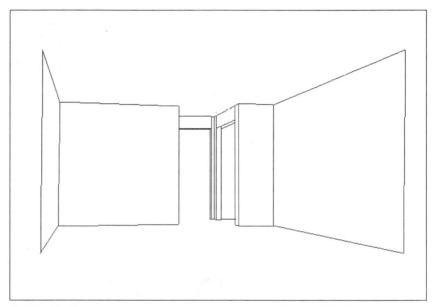

Figure 17.12:   A view of an apartment unit interior using the Clip/Front plane

1. Open the Unit file that you turned into a 3D model in *Chapter 15*, and set up a perspective view using Figure 17.13 as a guide. You can also use the 3Dunit.DWG file from the companion CD.

2. Click on View ➤ 3D Dynamic View or enter **Dview** ↵ at the command prompt.

3. At the Object-selection prompt, select the entire drawing.

4. Using the Points option (**PO** ↵), first place the target at the center of the room, then place the camera location toward

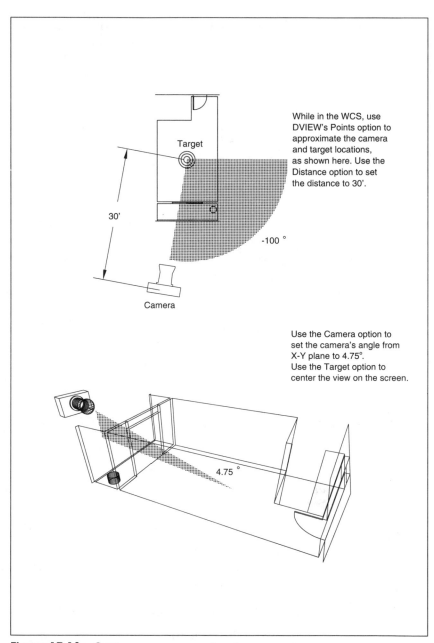

While in the WCS, use
DVIEW's Points option to
approximate the camera
and target locations,
as shown here. Use the
Distance option to set
the distance to 30'.

Target

30'

-100 °

Camera

Use the Camera option to
set the camera's angle from
X-Y plane to 4.75°.
Use the Target option to
center the view on the screen.

4.75 °

Figure 17.13: Setting up your perspective view

the bottom of the screen at a slight angle, as shown at the top of Figure 17.13. Use the dynamic coordinate readout to help you locate the camera in relation to the target point.

5. Use the Distance option (**D** ↵) and enter **30′** to set the target-to-camera distance accurately.

6. Use the Camera option (**CA** ↵) and enter **4.75** at the Toggle angle in/Enter angle from XY plane <0.0000>: prompt to place the camera angle at 4.75° from the floor.

7. When the Camera option's Toggle angle from/Enter angle in XY plane from X axis: prompt appears, press ↵ to accept the default.

8. Use the Target option (**TA** ↵) to center the room on the screen. Remember to move the cursor slowly to center the view in the screen. When your view looks roughly like Figure 17.12, press the left mouse button.

With this view, the walls between the interior of the unit and the balcony obscure the interior. Next you will learn how to make the wall invisible, using DVIEW's Clip option.

1. While still in the DVIEW command, enter **CL** ↵ for the Clip option.

2. At the Back/front<off>: prompt, enter **F** ↵ for the Front option. A slide bar appears at the top of the screen.

3. As you move the diamond on the slide bar from left to right, the walls in the foreground begin to disappear, starting at the point closest to you. Moving the diamond from right to left brings the walls back into view. You can select a view either by using the slide bar or by entering a distance from the target to the Clip plane.

4. At the Eye/<distance from target>< current distance>: prompt, move the slide bar diamond until your view looks similar to Figure 17.12. Then click the mouse/pick button to fix the view.

5. To make sure the Clip plane is in the correct location, pre-view your perspective view with hidden lines removed. Enter **H** ↵ at the DVIEW prompt. The drawing regenerates, with hidden lines removed.

There are several other DVIEW Clip options that let you control the location of the Clip plane. These option are described as follows:

Eye   places the Clip plane at the position of the camera itself.

Back   operates in the same way as the Front option, but it clips the view behind the view target instead of in front (see Figure 17.14).

Off   turns off any Clip planes you may have set up.

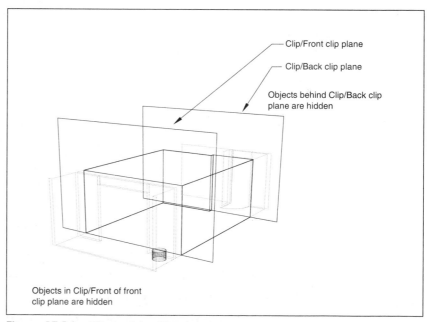

Figure 17.14:   Effects of the Clip planes

You've now completed the DVIEW command exercises and should have a better understanding of how DVIEW can be used to get exactly the image you want.

If you like, you can use View ➤ Named Views to save your perspective views. This is helpful when you want to construct several views of a drawing to play back later as part of a presentation. You can also use the Hide and Shade options on the Tools pull-down menu to help you visualize your model.

In the next section, we'll examine the rendering functions built into AutoCAD. These functions take the Tools ➤ Shade command one step further, to let you control lights and surface reflectance.

▼ **TIP**

The quickest and easiest way to establish a perspective view is to first use VPOINT (View ➤ 3D Viewpoint ➤ Vector) to set up your 3D view orientation; then start DVIEW, and use the Distance option right off the bat to set your camera-to-target distance. Once this is done, you can easily use the other DVIEW options as needed, or exit DVIEW to see your perspective view.

RENDERING A 3D MODEL

The render functions (Tools ➤ Render) use the analogy of a movie set to help you set up various rendered views. Each "set" contains lights and camera locations. The lights can be point sources, such as light bulbs or directed sources, which act like spotlights. Camera locations are determined through the DVIEW and VIEW commands.

OPENING THE RENDER PALETTE

The first step is to get access to the rendering functions. Virtually all the rendering commands are available in the Render palette. To open it, choose Tools ➤ Toolbars ➤ Render. The Render Palette appears.

Now you're ready to proceed with the rest of the exercises.

SETTING UP THE RENDERER

Before you begin to set up your lights, you will want to make some minor adjustments to the renderer's preference settings.

1. Click on Render Preferences from the Render palette, or enter **Rpref** ↵.

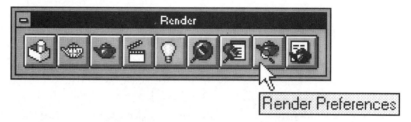

The Rendering Preferences dialog box appears.

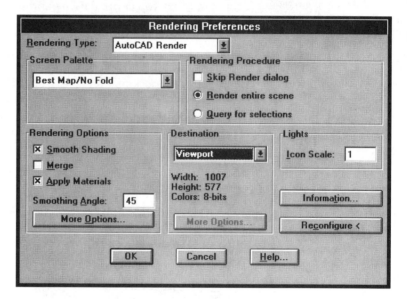

2. Double-click on the Icon Scale input box in the Settings button group, and enter **24**. As you start to insert lights into the model, you will see icons that indicate the location of your light sources. This setting tells AutoCAD how large to make those icons so they will be visible in the model.

3. Click on OK to close the dialog box.

You will return to this dialog box a bit later. Now you are ready to add some lights.

ADDING A POINT-LIGHT SOURCE

With your rendering preferences established, here's how to set up some lighting:

1. First, choose View ➤ Named Views and use the View Control dialog box to save the current perspective view as **pers1**.

2. Change your view to a plan view, so it looks like Figure 17.15.

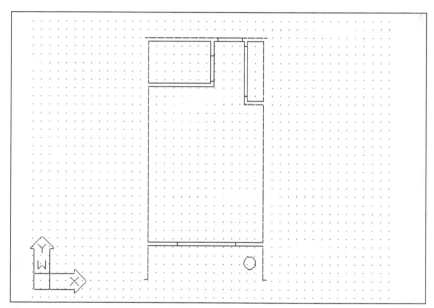

Figure 17.15:   A plan view of the apartment unit

3. In the View Control dialog box, save the plan view as **Plan,** so you can easily return to it as you work.

4. Click on Lights from the Render palette, or enter **Light** ↵.

The Lights dialog box appears. Notice the pop-up list next to the New... button. This list lets you choose from three types of light sources: Point Light, Distant Light, and Spotlight (described in more detail later in this chapter).

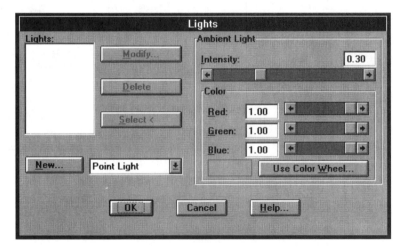

5. Make sure Point Light is selected in the pull-down list, then click on the New button. The New Point Light dialog box appears.

New Point Light

Light **N**ame: [   ]

Intensity: [237.40]

[◄]————————[ ]————————[►]

Attenuation
- ○ N**o**ne
- ◉ Inverse **L**inear
- ○ Inverse S**q**uare

Position

[**M**odify <]　[**S**how...]

Color

Red: [1.00]　[◄]————————[►]

Green: [1.00]　[◄]————————[►]

Blue: [1.00]　[◄]————————[►]

[   ]　[Use Color **W**heel...]

[OK]　[Cancel]　[Help...]

In step 7, the graphic is automatically inserted into a layer called Ashade. If this layer does not exist, AutoCAD will create one before it inserts the graphic, so you can isolate the graphic by either freezing or turning off the Ashade layer. You can save the lighting and any other information that appears on this layer without the graphic interfering with your drawing.

If you need help using the 3D filters, review the section "Using Filters" in *Chapter 15*.

6. In the Light Name input box, enter **lite1** for the light name. Render allows you to use several light sources for a scene, and many scenes can use the same light source. You must give each light source a name so you can distinguish among them. (We have named the light **lite1** for this exercise, but you can give it any name you like.)

7. Click on the Modify button. The dialog box temporarily closes to reveal the plan, with a graphic added to represent the point-light source (see Figure 17.16).

8. At the Enter light location prompt, enter **.xy** ↵ and pick a point in the center of the unit (see Figure 17.16).

9. At the (need Z) prompt, enter **8'**↵. Using the .xy filter allows you to place the light at a specific location in the plan, and specify the light's height, as well. Once you enter the z value, the dialog box returns.

10. Click on OK. You return to the Lights dialog box, and you see Lite1 in the list box. You've just created your first point-source light. Click on OK to exit the dialog box.

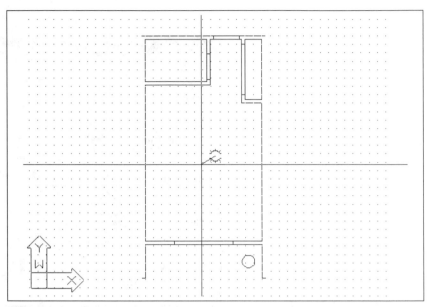

Figure 17.16: Picking the location for the point-light source

You now see the word LITE1 inside the point-light graphic. This is the name you gave this light source earlier in this command. The graphic itself is actually a block containing the attributes needed to generate your shaded view. These attributes hold information such as the name and coordinates of the light source, information that will be used by the renderer to determine how to shade your model.

UNDERSTANDING THE TYPES OF LIGHT SOURCES

In step 5 of the "Adding a Point-Light Source" exercise, you had the opportunity to choose from three different light sources. Here are brief descriptions of the available light sources and their uses:

Ambient Light   is general lighting in the model. It has no specific source or direction. Think of it as the kind of light you get on an overcast day—such lighting casts no shadows, and the light is evenly distributed.

> **Distant Light** is similar to ambient light, in that it is used as general lighting. But unlike ambient light, directed light emits light in a specific direction. Perhaps its most common use is to simulate sunlight. Use it to differentiate the effects of light on planar surfaces that lie in different directions.
>
> **Point Light** is similar to a light bulb. It is a well-defined light source whose light is emitted radially in all directions away from its center. The intensity of point light diminishes or "falls off" as you move further away from the source.

ADDING A DISTANT LIGHT SOURCE

You can also add a distant light source. A distant light source is one that acts like the sun. It can be used to vary the lighting on the different surfaces of your model. You can add as many point or directed light sources as you want to achieve the kind of lighting you require for your shaded model.

▼ NOTE

The two graphics in the right half of the New Distant Light dialog box show you the *azimuth* or direction and the altitude of the light source and target. If you prefer, you can adjust these values by entering values in the input boxes above the graphic, or by clicking and dragging the indicators on the graphics themselves. For now, use the settings you made in steps 4 through 6 of the previous exercise.

1. Click on Lights from the Render palette once again, and choose Distant Light from the Lights pull-down list.

2. Click on New....

3. In the New Distant Light dialog box, enter **1D** for the light name.

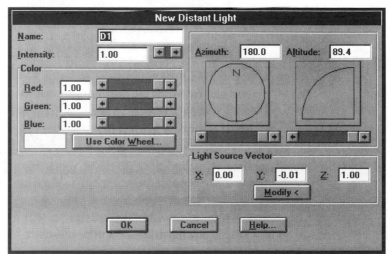

4. Click on Modify to place the light. The dialog box temporarily closes.

5. At the Enter light direction To prompt, enter **.xy** ↵ and pick a point in the middle of the wall at the left of the unit (see Figure 17.17).

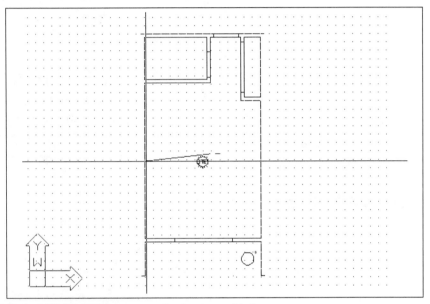

Figure 17.17:   The aim point for the directed light source

6. At the (need Z) prompt, enter **4'**↵ for the height of the target point.

7. At the Enter light direction FROM prompt, use the .xy filter to pick a point in the upper-right of the drawing area (see Figure 17.18). Enter **20'** ↵ for the z value or height of the directed source. The New Distant Light dialog box returns.

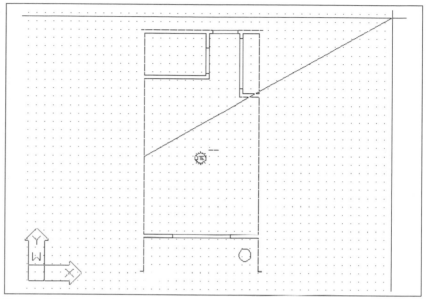

Figure 17.18:   The location of the directed light source

8. In the New Distant Light dialog box, click on OK, then
    again in the Light dialog box. You now see the distant light
    source graphic in the upper right-corner of your drawing as
    shown in Figure 17.19. You're now ready to set up your view.

SETTING UP AND ADJUSTING A VIEW

For the final step, set up a view that will let you see the overall effect of
your lighting.

1. Click on View ➤ 3D Dynamic View and select the entire
    unit plan.

2. At the DVIEW prompt, enter **PO** ↵ to select the target and
    view point.

3. At the Enter target point prompt, pick a point at the center
    of the unit.

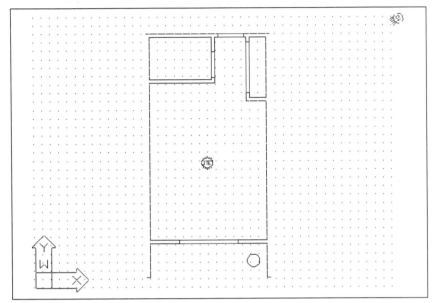

Figure 17.19: The directed light source graphic

4. At the Enter camera point prompt, enter **.xy** and pick a point in the extreme lower-right corner of the screen.

5. At the (need Z) prompt, enter **30′** ↵.

6. Using the DVIEW Distance and Target options, adjust your view of the unit so it is centered in the screen and looks roughly like Figure 17.20. Press ↵ to exit the DVIEW command.

7. Click on Render from the Render palette.

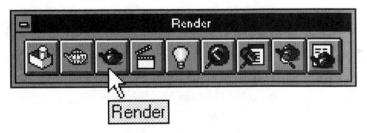

The Render dialog box appears.

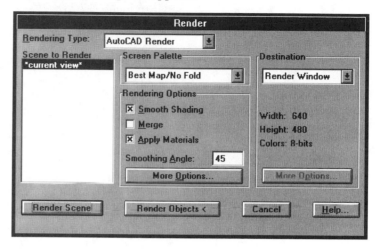

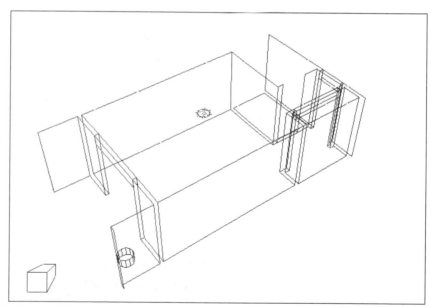

Figure 17.20: Set up your view of the unit to look like this

8. Click on the Render Scene button. You will get a view similar to Figure 17.21.

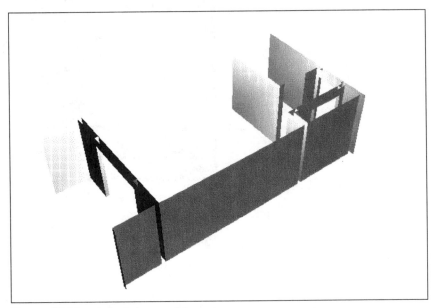

Figure 17.21: A shaded view of the unit

ADJUSTING LIGHTING CONDITIONS

Due to the high intensity of the LITE1 light source, many of the surfaces seem to have disappeared. You can adjust the lighting in your shaded model using settings in the Lights dialog box.

1. Click on Lights from the Render palette. At the Lights dialog box, highlight lite1 in the list.

2. Click on the Modify button to display the Modify Point Light dialog box, which is identical to the New Point Light dialog box you saw when you first created this light.

IV

Modeling and Imaging in 3D

3. Move the Intensity slide bar toward the left until the Intensity input box shows a value of about 100.

4. Click on OK here and then again in the Lights dialog box.

5. Render the view again. Now all the wall surfaces appear.

Here you turned down the intensity of the point-source light located in the middle of the unit. This allows the walls to show more subtle reflectance properties. Now let's refine the walls in the foreground, which seem a bit dark. To increase the general lighting of a rendering, you increase the Ambient lighting.

1. Open the Lights dialog box again and move the Ambient slide bar up to the middle of the bar.

2. Render the scene again.

Now the darker walls aren't so dark, and you can begin to see more of its form (see Figure 17.22).

ADJUSTING SMOOTH SHADING

To add a final touch of realism, you can set the renderer to shade surfaces using a shading method called phong shading (see the "Additional Preference Settings" Sidebar for more information).

1. Click on Render Preferences from the Render palette.

2. Click on the More Options… button in the Rendering Options button group, the AutoCAD Render Options dialog box appears.

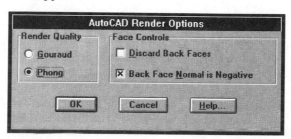

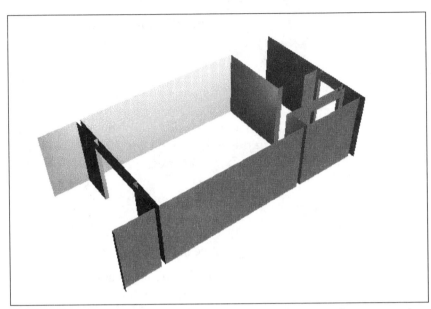

Figure 17.22:   A shaded view of the unit obtained by decreasing the intensity of LITE1 and increasing the Ambient light setting

3. Click on the Phong radio button, then click O.K.

4. Render the model again. Notice that the interior walls now appear to have more variation in light intensity.

The Unit plan doesn't really show off the Smooth Shading feature as it applies to meshes. Later in the "Applying Materials to Objects" section, You'll look at another 3D model to see how smooth shading can improve the look of faceted surfaces.

ADDITIONAL PREFERENCE SETTINGS

Other options in the More Options dialog box of the Rendering Preferences dialog box allow you to control render quality versus render time. Here are descriptions of those settings:

Gouraud is a smooth-shading method that looks at the difference of colors at the corners of two planes and then interpolates or gradates the colors across the two planes. This option only works when Smooth Shading is turned on.

Phong is a method that offers smooth shading superior to Gouraud's, though it takes more time. Phong often yields better highlights or metallic appearance. As with Gouraud, Phong only works with Smooth Shading turned on.

Discard Back Faces can help speed up rendering time if your drawing's orientation and surface normals coincide. *Surface normals (or "normals")* refer to the direction in which a surface, such as a 3Dface, points. A normal is described as a vector that is perpendicular to the plane of a surface. This vector describes the direction of that surface. Think of a surface normal as its face. It would be somewhat difficult to ensure that all surface normals are oriented the same way for any given view, so this option is usually left turned off.

Back Face Normal is Negative works in conjunction with the Discard Back Faces option. When Back Face Normal is Negative, you can determine which side of a face is rendered. If you render a scene and nothing appears, try changing this setting.

SAVING YOUR LIGHT AND VIEW COMBINATIONS

Once you have found the perfect combination of lights and view, you can save these settings together as *scenes*. You can then recall them later for further rendering or editing.

1. Click on Scenes from the Render palette, or enter **Scene** ↵.

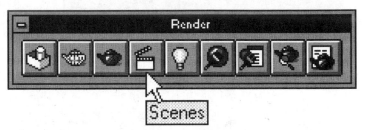

The Scenes dialog box appears. The list box contains any existing saved scenes in the file. Right now, there are none. You can create a new scene, modify an existing one, or delete a scene from this list box.

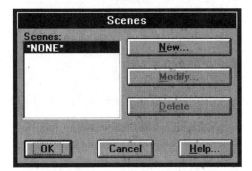

2. Click on New… to display the New Scene dialog box. To create your scene, you highlight the desired combination of lights and saved views from the list, and then enter a name in the input box at the upper-right corner of the dialog box.

3. You won't save a scene here, so click on Cancel here and again in the Scene dialog box.

UNDERSTANDING THE PREFERENCES OPTIONS

You've used the Preferences dialog box (Render Preferences from the Render palette) a few times now, so you know what some of its options do. You won't get to use all of them in this tutorial, so here is a review for your future reference:

Rendering Type   lets you choose from the following:

> *AutoCAD Render*, the rendering system you've been using.
>
> *Autovision*, a photorealistic renderer that uses ray tracing to generate an image. Autovision is an add-on that you must purchase separately from Autodesk.

Rendering Options   let you control whether smooth shading is applied and whether finishes are applied or ignored (see the next section for more on finishes).

> *Smooth Shading*   smoothes out facets in meshes and gives gradient shading on flat surfaces.
>
> *Smoothing Angle*   lets you determine the condition Auto-CAD will use to apply smoothing.
>
> *Merge*   is for compositing images in a frame buffer and can only be used if you have selected a frame buffer in your renderer configuration.
>
> *Apply Materials*   lets you control whether or not the materials applied to objects are rendered. This will influence the time it takes to render your model (you'll learn more about materials in the next section).
>
> *More Options*   offers advanced rendering options (see the sidebar, "Additional Preferences Settings").

Destination   lets you choose the destination of your rendering.

> *Viewport*   sends the output to the screen.
>
> *File*   lets you store your image as a file on disk.
>
> *Hardcopy*   is available only if you have configured the renderer for a hardcopy device.
>
> *More Options...*   is active only if you choose File from the Destination pop-up list, and presents a dialog box that lets you select the file type and compression.

Rendering Procedure   lets you control what gets rendered when you render the drawing.

> *Skip Render dialog*   does just that; it causes the Render command to begin the rendering process without opening the Render dialog box.
>
> *Render the entire scene*   is self-explanatory.
>
> *Query for selections*   lets you select specific objects to render.

Screen Palette   lets you choose the method AutoCAD uses to select colors for the rendering. AutoCAD will try to use all 256 colors, though the first 16 are reserved for parts of the Auto-CAD screen.

> *Best Map/No Fold*   causes AutoCAD to use the top 240 colors only.
>
> *Best Map/Fold*   causes AutoCAD to make a best-fit attempt at using all available 256 colors.
>
> *Fixed ACAD Map*   forces AutoCAD to use all the 256 colors in a fixed way.

Information…   displays information on the current configuration of the renderer.

Reconfigure…   lets you reconfigure the renderer to use various display and output devices.

APPLYING MATERIALS TO OBJECTS

One of the main features of the AutoCAD's rendering function is its ability to assign *materials* to objects individually. The Materials feature of the renderer lets you designate how object surfaces reflect light. You can make an object shiny or dull, or you can make an object reflect a particular range of colors. The next set of exercises introduce you to the Materials feature.

1. Open the Sextant file in the \acadr13\common\sample directory.

2. Click on Render Preferences from the Render palette, and make sure Smooth Shading is checked.

3. Click on More Options … then click on the Phong radio button. Choose OK twice to exit the Preferences dialog box.

4. Click on Lights from the Render palette, and choose Point Light from the pop-up list.

5. Click on New….

6. Enter **lite1** for the Light Name and click on the Modify button. The dialog box will momentarily disappear.

7. At the Enter light location prompt, enter **100,35,240** ↵. (This locates the light for you, but you can place your own later if you like.)

8. In the Modify Point Light dialog box, move the Intensity Slider all the way to the right, then click OK.

9. In the Lights dialog box, set the Ambient light slide bar so the Ambient input box reads 0.75.

10. Render the model.

The rendered sextant will appear in a few seconds. This image shows you what the sextant looks like without any special reflectance applied. Next, set up part of the sextant to reflect light like a metallic object.

1. Click on Materials from the Render palette.

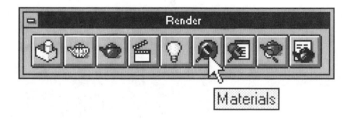

The Materials dialog box appears.

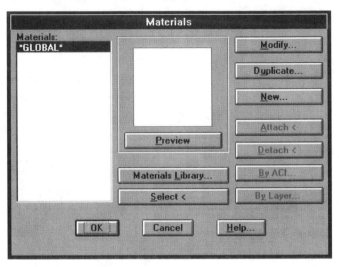

2. Click on Materials Library to display the Materials Library dialog box. This set of predefined materials comes with Auto-CAD. You can also create your own and store them for later retrieval.

3. In the list of materials on the right, locate and highlight Stainless Steel.

4. Click on the Import button. Notice that Stainless Steel is now listed in the list box on the left.

5. Click on OK to exit the Materials Library dialog box.

6. Make sure that Stainless Steel is highlighted in the Materials list, and then click on the Modify button. The Modify Standard Material dialog box appears next, in which you control the reflectance characteristic of a finish setting.

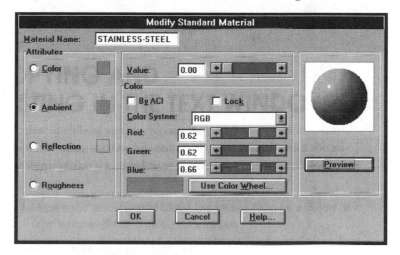

7. Click on the Ambient radio button, and then move the Value slider to the left, to 0.

8. Click on the Preview button. A sphere appears, showing you how a surface will be rendered with this finish. Click on OK when you've examined it.

9. In the Materials dialog box, click on Attach <. The dialog box closes temporarily.

10. At the Select object to attach STAINLESS STEEL to: prompt, click on all the yellow components of the sextant, and press ↵ to finish your selection.

11. Click on OK, and render the sextant again.

This time, the yellow components of the sextant have a shiny appearance.

THE MODIFY FINISH DIALOG BOX OPTIONS

Take a moment to look at the Modify Standard Material dialog box; play with the settings, and click on the Preview button to see their effect. Here are brief descriptions of the Modify Finish components:

Color   controls the color of the material.

Ambient   controls the amount of ambient light the finish reflects. If Ambient is set high, the finish gains in overall brightness.

Reflection   controls the shininess of a finish. A high specular value causes light to reflect off a surface with little or no scattering of light.

Roughness   controls the "spread" of a light source reflection. A high roughness value causes the reflection to disperse over a greater area, like a satin finish on metal. If Reflection is set to 0, then Roughness has no effect.

Use Color Wheel   opens another dialog box that lets you choose color characteristics from a color wheel.

By ACI   lets you choose a color based on the AutoCAD Color Index. Another dialog box appears, listing the colors by their number index.

THE MATERIALS DIALOG BOX OPTIONS

You've just seen how a material can be applied to a surface. You can import, modify, and save any number of materials to get your model looking just the way you want. The vehicle for retrieving materials is the Materials dialog box, which you used briefly in the previous exercise. Here is a listing of the other components you didn't get to try out:

New   opens a dialog box identical to the Modify Standard Material dialog box just described. You can then create a finish with the exact settings you want.

Modify   lets you modify the finish that is highlighted in the list box on the left (you saw this work in the exercise).

Duplicate   lets you copy an existing material and give it a different name.

Materials Library   lets you select a material definition from a list. Materials are stored in a file with the .MLI extension. You can access these files from this dialog box.

Attach/Detach   lets you apply or remove a material from an object.

By ACI   lets you attach a finish to objects in your model based on their AutoCAD Color Index (ACI). Another dialog box appears, showing you the colors listed by their number index.

By Layer   lets you assign materials by layer. Another dialog box appears, listing layer names and materials. You then match materials to layers.

Select   lets you choose a material by clicking on an object that already has a material assigned to it. This is useful when you want to edit an object's material definition but you don't know what that material is.

SAVING AND VIEWING RENDERED VIEWS

When you have the image you want to keep, you will want to store it as a bitmap file, or you may want to view it in another way. AutoCAD offers several output options for your rendering, each controlled by the Destination group of the Render or Rendering Preferences dialog box.

This group lets you determine the destination of your rendered image. So far, you've been rendering to a viewport. You also have the option to render to a file, for later retrieval, or to a separate render window. Let's first look at how you would render to a file.

RENDERING DIRECTLY TO A FILE

Here is a step-by-step description of what to do to render to a file.

1. Click on Render from the Render palette.

2. In the Destination group of the Render dialog box, select File from the pop-up list.

3. Click on More Options…. The File Output Configuration dialog box appears. This is where you can set up your output file to store your rendering. Once you make your settings in this dialog box, you can proceed with your rendering. Before AutoCAD starts to render, you will be prompted for a file name.

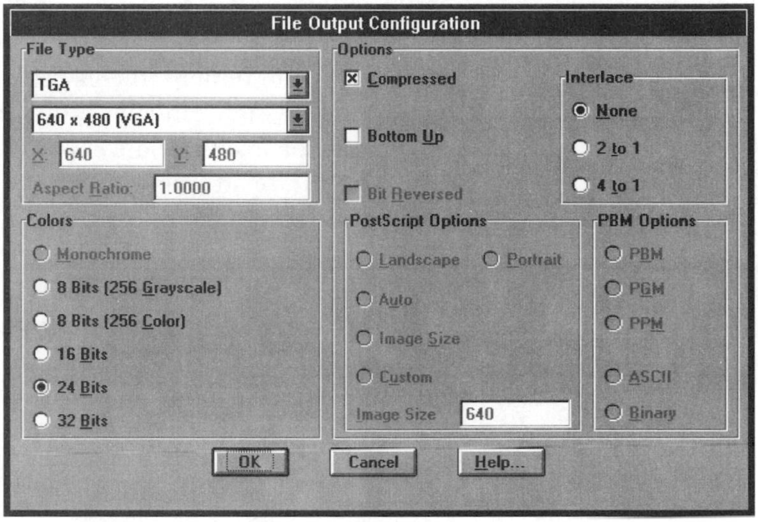

The File Output Configuration dialog box offers a wealth of options for your output file. Here's a rundown of those options by button groups:

File Type   You can set the type of file and its resolution in this group. You can choose from the more popular file types like TGA, PCX, TIFF, and PostScript, as well as other format such as FITS and Fax Group III. A set of predefined standard resolutions are offered in a pull-down list, or you can set a custom resolution using the User Defined option in the pop-up list in conjunction with the input boxes. You can even set the aspect ratio for the image file.

Colors   This group lets you select the color depth for your output. Most of the file types offered in the File Type group allow color, though the range of color depth may vary between file types. Choose a low value, 8 bit for example, if you want a smaller file size and image realism isn't of great concern. Choose higher values for smoother shading.

Options   In this group, you can choose to compress the files, reverse the scan line direction, or enable bit reversing for modem transmission. As with the color options, these options are not valid with some types of files. Compression can reduce the size of the file by half, but some programs are unable to read compressed files. (This shouldn't be confused with third-party file compression programs such as Lharc and Pkzip.) Bottom Up will reverse the scan line direction.

PostScript Options   These options are only valid for PostScript file output. These setting control the image size and orientation. Landscape and Portrait control the image orientation. If Auto is selected, AutoCAD automatically sizes the image. Image Size uses the image size set in the File Type group. Custom uses the size indicated in the Image Size input box.

Interlace   The Interlace option is only valid for Targa files, so unless you select TGA in the File Type group, these options are grayed out. Since the Targa format allows for output to TV Video monitors, these options allow you to select an interlace value (TV monitors display images by "Interlacing" scan lines).

PBM Options   These options are only valid for the Portable Bit Map (PBM) file type. You can choose from three encoding methods and whether the file is in ASCII or Binary format.

RENDERING TO A SEPARATE RENDER WINDOW

If you prefer, you can have AutoCAD render to a separate window. This separate render window offers some additional options not found when rendering to the AutoCAD window. As with rendering to a file, you use the Destination group of the Render dialog box to direct the rendered view to a separate window. Here is a step-by-step description of what to do to render to a separate window.

1. Click on Render from the Render palette.

2. In the Destination group of the Render dialog box, select Render Window from the pull-down list.

3. Proceed to render the drawing by clicking on the Render Scene button. A window appears with the rendered image (see Figure 17.23).

You can render several views and each view will appear as a window within the Render Window. You can save your rendered views as .BMP files using the File ➤ Save menu option. You can also retrieve and view saved .BMP files from this window. File ➤ Print lets you print the image to your system printer. The Edit ➤ Copy option copies the image to the Windows Clipboard for transfer to another program.

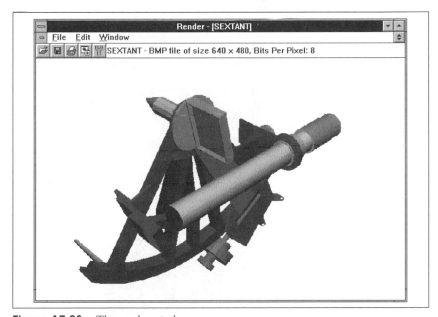

Figure 17.23:   The render window

In addition to saving, retrieving, printing, and copying to the clipboard, the Render Window lets you control color depth and image resolution. When you choose File ➤ Options, you get the Window Render Options dialog box.

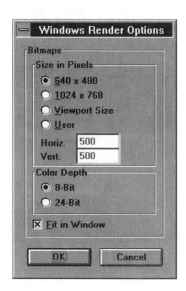

The following list describes the function of the button groups in this dialog box. Be aware that radio button options take effect the next time you render.

Size in Pixels lets you set the size of the image based on pixels. You can set it to two standard sizes or the size of the AutoCAD Viewport. In addition, the User option lets you set a custom size.

Color Depth lets you control whether the file is to be saved as an 8-bit (256 colors) or 24-bit (16 million colors) file. Even if your display is only 8 bit, you can still save the rendering as a 24-bit color image. Note that 24-bit color increases the file size.

Fit in Window sizes the image to fit in the window.

Finally, you'll notice the buttons in the toolbar of the render window.

These buttons duplicate the Open, Save, Print, Copy, and Options functions found in the pull-down menus. You may want to click on these buttons to familiarize yourself with their functions.

INTERACTING WITH 3D STUDIO

3D Studio is an important 3D rendering companion to AutoCAD. With it you can produce photorealistic renderings as well as animations. You can also easily montage computer models on scanned photographs, to create "what-if" images of proposed projects.

If you're already a 3D Studio user, you'll be glad to know that AutoCAD now reads and writes 3D Studio files directly. So if you like using AutoCAD for modeling, you'll have more flexibility to edit your 3D Studio models. You'll find the 3D Studio capabilities in the File ➤ Import and File ➤ Export options. If you prefer using the command line, **3dsin** ↵ imports a 3D Studio file, and **3dsout** ↵ exports it.

IMPORTING FROM 3D STUDIO

To import a 3D Studio file, take the following steps:

1. Choose File ➤ Import….

2. Choose 3D Studio (*.3DS) from the pull-down list at the bottom of the Import File dialog box.

3. Select a 3D Studio file from the list box or enter a file name in the File input box.

4. Make the appropriate selections from the 3D Studio File Import Options Dialog box that appear next.

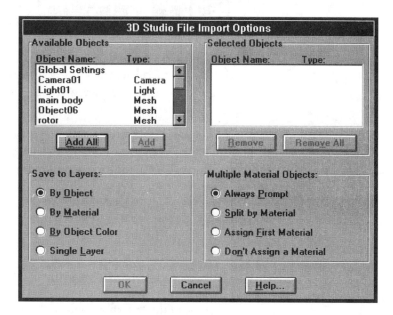

This dialog box lets you determine how to handle 3D Studio objects. You begin by selecting the objects you want to import (click Add All to select all the objects in the 3D Studio file, or highlight only the objects you want to import, then click on Add). The selected objects will be added to the list on the right.

Once you've selected the objects, you then decide how to represent them in AutoCAD. The Save to Layers button group lets you control how the objects are categorized in AutoCAD. Since 3D Studio objects have no equivalent in AutoCAD, you have the option to keep them separated by layers. Here's a breakdown of the buttons in this group:

By Object creates a separate layer for each 3D Studio object. The layers are given the names of the objects they contain.

By Material creates a separate layer for each object, based on its material assignment. The layers are given the name of the material they contain.

IV

Modeling and Imaging in 3D

By Object Color   creates a layer for each different object color in the 3D Studio file. Layers are named using the 3D Studio color index number.

Single Layer   imports everything into a single layer that Auto-CAD will create, called Avlayer.

The Multiple Material Objects button group lets you control the interaction between AutoCAD and AutoVision. 3D Studio is capable of assigning multiple materials to single objects. AutoVision does not have this capability, so the Multiple Material Objects button group is needed to help determine how AutoCAD translates the 3D Studio file for AutoVision. Here are descriptions of these options:

Always Prompt   causes AutoCAD to stop at every 3D Studio object that has multiple materials assigned to it, and prompt you for an action. You have three options:

- Split the object into many objects based on the various materials

- Have the first material encountered by AutoCAD be assigned to the entire object

- Assign a single material to the object by choosing from a list

Split by Material   splits a single object into multiple objects, based on its material assignment.

Assign First Material   assigns the first material encountered for an object to the whole object, regardless of other material assignments the object may have.

Don't Assign a Material   means just that; it ignores material assignments from 3D Studio. These material assignments are then lost.

EXPORTING TO 3D STUDIO

You can export your AutoCAD 3D models directly to a 3D Studio file format by following these steps:

1. Choose File ➤ Export.... (As an alternate, you can type **3DSout** ↵ then skip to step 3.)

2. At the Export Data dialog box, enter the name for your 3D Studio file including the .3DS file name extension.

3. Click on OK and you are prompted to select objects. Select the parts of the drawing you want to export to 3D Studio, then press ↵. You then get the 3D Studio File Export Options dialog box.

The operation of exporting AutoCAD files to 3D Studio format is similar to how 3D Studio itself imports AutoCAD's .DXF files. The 3D Studio File Export Dialog box offers the following options:

Layer, AutoCAD Color Index (ACI), and AutoCAD Object Type   let you control whether 3D Studio objects are created based on layer, color, or object type.

Override causes AutoCAD blocks to be converted into single 3D Studio objects.

Auto-Smoothing applies 3D Studio Auto-smoothing feature to exported objects.

Degrees controls the threshold angle below which smoothing is applied.

Auto-Welding helps improve 3D Studio model efficiency by combining or "Welding" congruent vertices into one vertex.

Threshold determines the distance (in world coordinates) at or below which Welding will occur.

Finally, here are a few guidelines to watch when importing and exporting 3D Studio files:

- Smoothing groups are lost when you import files. This usually isn't a significant problem unless you have a large number of smoothed objects in 3D Studio.

- AutoCAD only exports objects that have surface characteristics, such as 3Dfaces, solids, and 3Dmeshes. Circles are exported as surfaces, as are lines, polylines, and arcs with thicknesses greater than 0. Wide polylines are also recognized.

- AutoCAD views and lights are converted to 3D Studio-equivalent cameras and lights; distant lights become spotlights in 3D Studio.

IF YOU WANT TO EXPERIMENT...

You've covered a lot of ground in this chapter, so it might be a good idea to play with the commands you've explored here to help you remember what you've learned.

To test what you've learned about DVIEW, try the following exercise:

1. Make a copy of the Unit plan. Insert the chairs and other objects you created earlier in this chapter. Use Figure 17.24 as a guide.

2. Once you have inserted the furnishings, use the DVIEW command to create an interior view. Repeat the DVIEW Clip exercise (in "Using Clip Planes to Hide Parts of Your View") to get a view similar to the one in Figure 17.24.

3. Once you have the view on screen, save it. Then use the rendering features to set up some lights and finishes.

4. Render the scene, and save the rendered scene as a .TGA file.

Figure 17.24: Inserting the furniture into the Unit plan

18

MASTERING 3D SOLIDS

FAST TRACK

884 ▶ To quickly create several paper space viewports

On the status bar, double-click on the Paper/Model button to switch to Paper Space. Click on View ➤ Floating Viewports ➤ MV Setup, and press ↵ at the prompt. Next, enter **C** ↵ ↵ to create the viewport layout in Paper Space. Enter **2** at the text screen. Select two points defining the area for the four viewports, and then specify the spacing between viewports.

894 ▶ To generate a cross-section of a solid

While in Model Space, click on the Section button on the Solids palette. Indicate the orientation of the cross section's plane, and then the origin of the cross section.

896 ▶ To use Boolean subtraction on 2D objects

First create a closed 2D polyline outline of the object. Also, draw 2D polyline representations of areas you want to subtract from the outline (circles and polygons will also work). Click and drag on the Polygon button on the Draw palette, select Region on the flyout, then select the polylines. Click and drag on the Explode button on the Modify menu, and select Subtract on the flyout. Then select the main outline. Next, select the objects you want to subtract from the main outline. Other Boolean operations are also possible.

899 ▶ To find the geometric properties of a solid model

Click and drag on the Inquiry button on the Object Properties toolbar, select Mass Properties on the flyout, and then click on the solid.

So far, you have been creating 3D models according to a method called *surface modeling*: As you drew, you used 3Dfaces to give your models form and the appearance of solidity. But there is another method that you can use to create 3D computer models: *solid modeling.*

With surface models, drawing a simple cube requires several steps; with solids, you can create a cube with one command. Once created, you can assign materials to a solid model and have the computer find physical properties of the model, such as weight and center of mass. It is easier to create models by using solid modeling, and there are many advantages to the technique, especially in mechanical design and engineering.

Solid modeling was once thought to require more computational power than most personal computers could offer, but with today's microcomputer hardware, solid modeling is well within the reach of most PC users. And with Release 13, AutoCAD now offers built-in solid modeling functions.

UNDERSTANDING SOLID MODELING

Solid modeling is a way of defining 3D objects as solid forms rather than as wire frames with surfaces attached. When you create a 3D model using solid modeling, you start with the basic forms of your model—cubes, cones, and cylinders, for instance. These basic solids are called *primitives*. Then, using more of these primitives, you begin to add to or subtract from your basic forms. For example, to create a model of a tube, you first create two solid cylinders, one smaller in diameter than the other. Then you align the two cylinders so that they are concentric, and you tell AutoCAD to subtract the smaller cylinder from the larger one. The larger of the two cylinders then becomes a tube whose inside diameter is that of the smaller cylinder, as shown in Figure 18.1.

Several primitives are available for modeling solids in AutoCAD (see Figure 18.2).

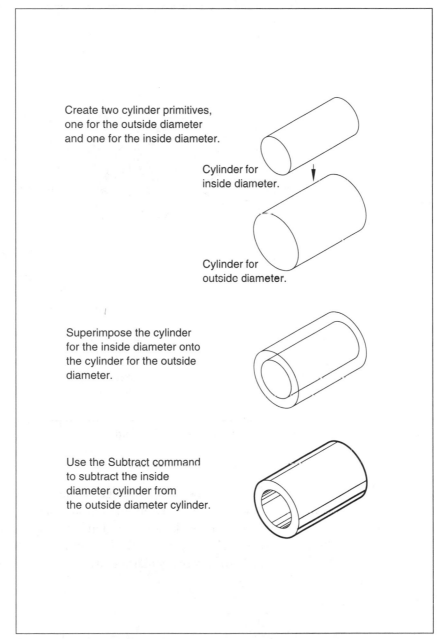

Create two cylinder primitives,
one for the outside diameter
and one for the inside diameter.

Cylinder for
inside diameter.

Cylinder for
outside diameter.

Superimpose the cylinder
for the inside diameter onto
the cylinder for the outside
diameter.

Use the Subtract command
to subtract the inside
diameter cylinder from
the outside diameter cylinder.

Figure 18.1: Creating a tube using solid modeling

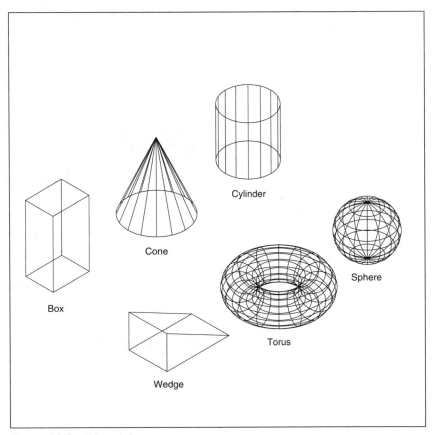

Figure 18.2: The solids primitives

These shapes—box, wedge, cone, cylinder, sphere, and donut or *torus*—can be joined in one of four ways to produce secondary shapes. The first three, demonstrated in Figure 18.3 using a cube and a cylinder as examples, are called *Boolean operations*. (The name comes from the nineteenth-century mathematician George Boole.)

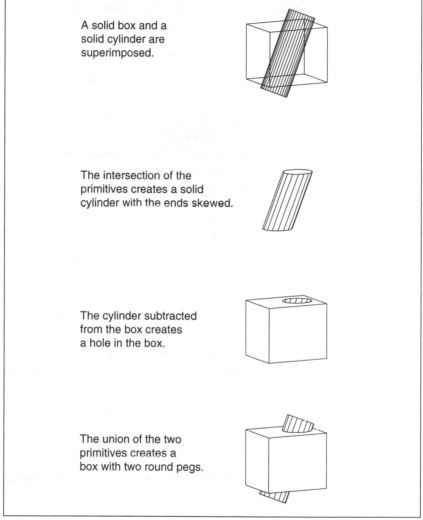

A solid box and a
solid cylinder are
superimposed.

The intersection of the
primitives creates a solid
cylinder with the ends skewed.

The cylinder subtracted
from the box creates
a hole in the box.

The union of the two
primitives creates a
box with two round pegs.

Figure 18.3:   The Intersection, Subtraction, and Union of a cube and a cylinder

- ■ **Intersection**   uses only the intersecting region of two objects to define a solid shape.

- ■ **Subtraction**   uses one object to cut out a shape in another.

- ■ **Union**   joins two primitives so that they act as one object.

A fourth option, **Interference,** lets you find exactly where two or more solids coincide in space, similar to the results of a Union. You can have AutoCAD either show you the shape of the coincident space or create a solid based on the coincident space's shape.

Joined primitives are called *composite solids*. You can join primitives to primitives, composite solids to primitives, and composite solids to other composite solids.

Now let's take a look at how these concepts let us create models in AutoCAD.

CREATING SOLID FORMS

In this section, you will begin to draw the object shown in Figure 18.4. In the process, you will explore the creation of solid models by creating primitives and then setting up special relationships between them.

DISPLAYING THE SOLIDS PALETTE

All of the commands you will use to create the solids primitives, and many of the commands you can use for editing solids, are accessible on the Solids palette. Choose Tools ➤ Toolbars ➤ Solids, or click on Solids on the Tools flyout on the Standard toolbar. The Solids palette will appear.

Now you're ready to begin creating basic solids.

Figure 18.4:   The steel bracket from the following exercises. This image was created in AutoCAD and rendered in 3D Studio.

CREATING PRIMITIVES

Primitives are the basic building blocks of solid modeling. At first, it may seem limiting to have only six primitives to work with, but consider the varied forms you can create with just a few two-dimensional objects. Let's begin by creating the basic mass of our fictitious part.

1. Open a new file called **Bracket**.

2. Set the Snap spacing to 0.5 (using Options ➤ Drawing Aids…), and turn on the grid and the snap mode.

3. Turn on the dynamic coordinate readout by pressing F6. We'll use the readout to help guide you in selecting points in the exercises that follow.

4. Click on the Box button on the Solids palette, and select the Corner option on the flyout; or enter **Box** ↵.

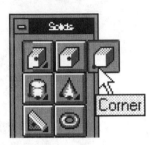

5. At the Center/<Corner of box><0,0,0> prompt, pick a point at coordinate 3,2.5.

6. At the Cube/Length/<Other corner>: prompt, enter **@7,5** ↵ to create a box with a length of 7 and a width of 5.

7. The Height: prompt that appears next is asking for the height of the box in the z-axis. Enter **1** ↵.

You've now drawn your first primitive, a box that is 7″ long by 5″ wide by 1″ deep. Let's change the view now, so we can see the box more clearly. Use the VPOINT command to shift your view so that you are looking at the WCS from the lower left.

8. Click on View ➤ 3D Viewpoint ➤ Vector, or type **Vpoint** ↵ at the command prompt.

9. At the Rotate/<viewpoint>: prompt, enter **–1,–1,.5**.

10. Enter **Z** ↵. At the All/Center/Dynamic prompt, enter **.6x**. Your screen will look like Figure 18.5.

TURNING A 2D POLYLINE INTO A 3D SOLID

Now let's add another box to form the lower lip of the bracket. This time, you'll create a box primitive from a polyline.

1. Click and drag on the Polyline button on the Draw palette, and select Polyline on the flyout.

2. At the From point prompt, start the polyline from the coordinate **.5,2.5**.

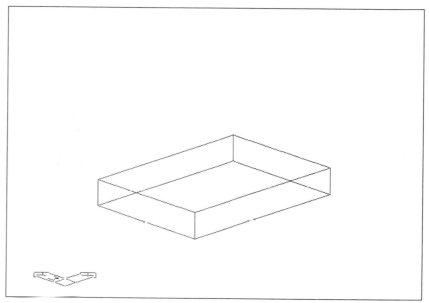

Figure 18.5:   The first stage of the bracket

3. Continue the polyline around to create a rectangle that is 1″ in the x-axis and 3″ in the y-axis. Do this by entering the following set of polar coordinates: **@1<0** ↵ **@3<90** ↵ **@1<180** ↵ **C** ↵. The last **C** closes the polyline. Your drawing will look like Figure 18.6.

4. Click on the Extrude button on the Solids palette, or type **EXTRUDE** ↵.

5. At the Select objects prompt, pick the polyline and press ↵.

Figure 18.6: The polyline drawn in place

6. At the Path/<Height of extrusion>: prompt, type **1** ↵.

7. At the Extrusion taper angle <0>: prompt, press ↵ to accept the default taper of 0°. (You'll get to see what the taper option does in a later exercise.) The polyline now extrudes in the z-axis to form a bar, as shown in Figure 18.7.

8. Type **R** ↵ to redraw the screen.

You've now drawn two box primitives using the Box and the Extrude options on the Solids palette. Just for variety's sake, we had you create the smaller box by converting a polyline into a solid, but you could just as easily have used Box for that as well. Extrude will convert polylines, circles, and traces into solids. (Regular lines, 3D lines, 3Dfaces, and 3D polylines cannot be extruded.)

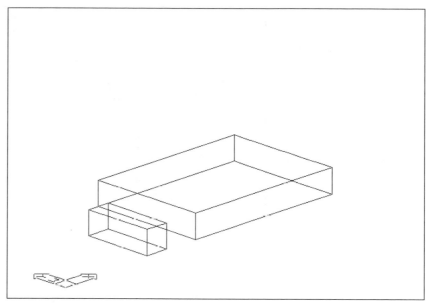

Figure 18.7: The converted polyline box

Other Solids Options

Before you continue, let's examine the commands for primitives that you haven't had a chance to use yet. Refer to Figures 18.8 through 18.11 to understand the terms used with these other primitives.

> **Cone ↲ (Cone icon on the Solids palette)** draws a circular cone or a cone with an elliptical base. Drawing a circular cone is much like drawing a circle, with an added prompt asking for a height. The Ellipse option acts like the ELLIPSE command (on the Draw palette), with an additional prompt for height.

> **Sphere ↲ (Sphere icon on the solids palette)** acts like the CIRCLE command, but instead of drawing a circle it draws a sphere.

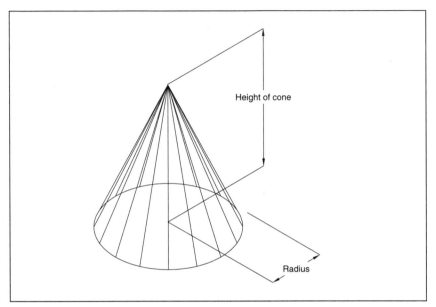

Figure 18.8: Drawing a solid cone

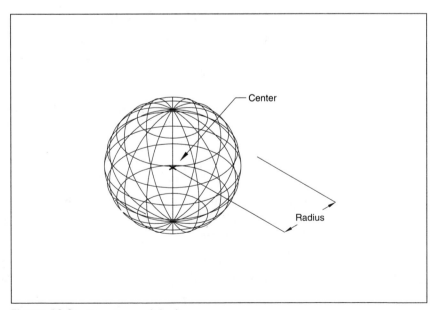

Figure 18.9: Drawing a solid sphere

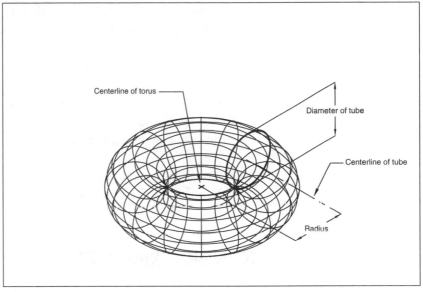

Figure 18.10: Drawing a solid torus

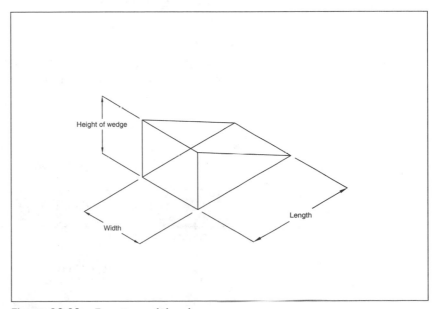

Figure 18.11: Drawing a solid wedge

Torus ⏎ (Torus icon on the Solids palette)   creates a torus (a donut-shaped solid). You are prompted for two diameters or radii, one for the diameter or radius of the torus and another for the diameter or radius of the tube portion of the torus.

Wedge ⏎ (Wedge icon on the Solids palette)   creates a wedge-shaped solid. This command acts much like the BOX command you used to draw the bracket. You have the choice of defining the wedge by two corners or by its center and a corner.

In the following exercises you will be creating and combining solid primitives. The commands required to create complex solids are available on the Explode flyout of the Modify palette.

JOINING PRIMITIVES

Now let's see how the two box objects you created are joined. First you'll move the new box into place, and then join the two boxes to form a single solid.

1. Start the MOVE command, pick the smaller of the two boxes, and press ⏎.

2. At the Base point prompt, use the Midpoint Osnap override and pick the middle of the upper-left edge of the smaller box facing the front, as shown in panel 1 of Figure 18.12.

3. At the Second point prompt, pick the middle of the bottom edge of the larger box, as shown in panel 2 of Figure 18.12.

4. Click and drag on the Explode button on the Modify palette and select Union or type **Union** ⏎.

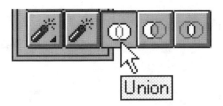

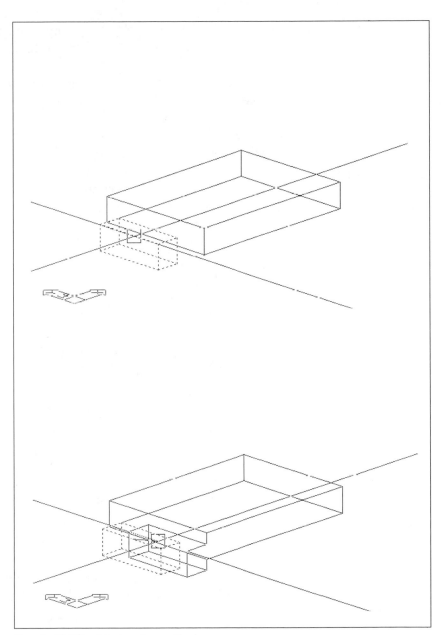

Figure 18.12:   Moving the smaller box

5. At the Select objects prompt, pick both boxes and press ⏎. Your drawing looks like Figure 18.13.

As you can see in Figure 18.13, the form has joined to appear as one object. It also acts like one object when you select it. You now have a composite solid made up of two box primitives.

Now let's place some holes in the bracket. In this next exercise, you will discover how to create negative forms to cut portions out of a solid.

1. Click on the Center button on the Solids palette, or type **Cylinder** ⏎.

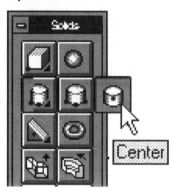

2. At the Elliptical/<center point>: prompt, pick a point at the coordinate 9,6.5.

3. At the Diameter/<radius>: prompt, enter **.25**.

4. At the Center of other end/<Height> prompt, enter **1.5** ⏎. The cylinder is drawn, as shown in Figure 18.14.

5. Copy the cylinder 3 units in the negative direction of the y-axis, so your drawing looks like Figure 18.14.

You now have the cylinder primitive, but you still need to define its relationship to the composite solid you created from the two boxes.

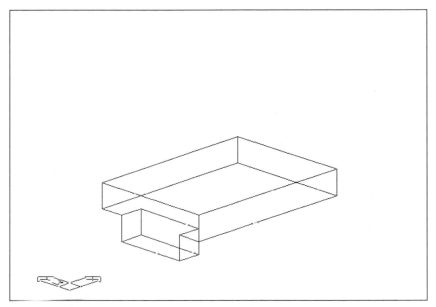

Figure 18.13:   The two boxes joined

1. Click and drag on the Union button on the Modify palette, and select Subtract on the flyout, or type **Subtract** ↵.

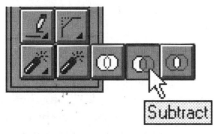

2. At the Select solids and regions to subtract from... Select objects: prompt, pick the composite solid of the two boxes and press ↵.

3. At the Solids and regions to subtract... Select objects: prompt, pick two of the cylinders and press ↵. The cylinder has now been subtracted from the bracket.

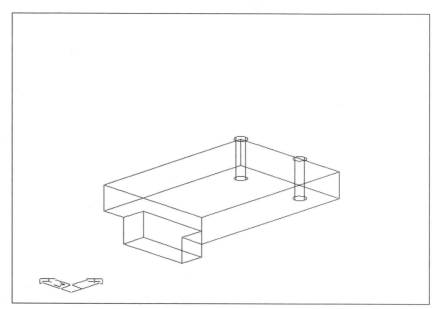

Figure 18.14: The cylinders added to the drawing

4. To view the solid, click on Hide on the Render palette, or type **Hide** ↵. You'll see a hidden-line image of the solid, as shown in Figure 18.15.

As you've learned in the earlier chapters in *Part IV*, wireframe views such as the one in step 3 above are somewhat difficult to decipher. Until you use Hide (step 4), you cannot tell for sure that the subtracted cylinder is in fact a hole. Using the HIDE command frequently will help you keep track of what's going on with your solid model.

In step 3 of the previous exercise, you may have noticed that the cylinders changed shape to conform to the depth of the bracket. You'll also recall that we asked you to draw the cylinder at a height of 1.5″, not 1″, which is the thickness of the bracket. Having drawn the cylinder taller than needed, you can see that AutoCAD, when it performed the subtraction, ignored the portion of the cylinder that doesn't affect the bracket. AutoCAD will always discard the portion of a primitive that isn't used in a Subtract operation.

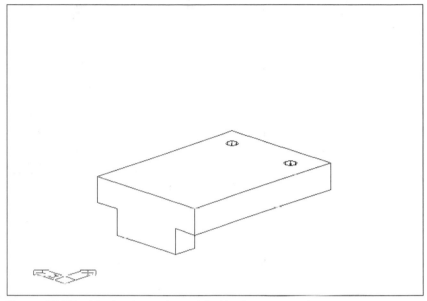

Figure 18.15: The bracket so far, with hidden lines removed

CREATING COMPLEX PRIMITIVES

As you learned earlier, you can convert a polyline into a solid by using the Extrude option on the Solids palette. This process lets you create more complex primitives. In addition to the simple straight extrusion you've already tried, you can also extrude shapes into curved paths, or you can taper an extrusion.

TAPERING AN EXTRUSION

Next, you'll take a look at how you can taper an extrusion to create a fairly complex solid with very little effort.

▼ **WARNING**

Remember to use the Close option to create the last side of the box.

1. Draw a 4″×4″ closed polyline at the top of the current solid. Start at the back-left corner of the bracket at coordinate 3.5,3,1, and then draw the 4″×4″ square to fit in the top of the composite solid, as shown in Figure 18.16.

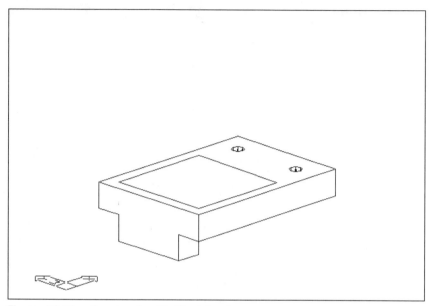

Figure 18.16: Drawing the 4″×4″ polyline box

2. Click on Fillet on the Chamfer flyout on the Modify palette. At the Polyline/Radius/Trim/<Select first line> prompt, type **R** ↵ to set the radius of the fillet.

3. At the prompt for the fillet radius, type **.5** ↵.

4. At the command prompt, press ↵ to again issue the Fillet command, and then type **P** ↵ to tell the FILLET command that you want to chamfer a polyline.

5. Click on the polyline. The corners become rounded.

6. Click on the Extrude button on the Solids palette, or enter **Extrude** ↵ at the command prompt.

7. At the object-selection prompt, pick the polyline you just drew and press ↵. (As the prompt indicates, you can pick polylines or circles.)

8. At the Path/<Height of extrusion>: prompt, enter **4** ↵.

▼ NOTE

In step 9, you can indicate a taper for the extrusion. Specify a taper in terms of degrees from the z-axis, or enter a negative value to taper the extrusion outward. Or press ↵ to accept the default, 0°, to extrude the polyline without a taper.

9. At the Extrusion taper angle from Z <0>: prompt, enter **4** for 4° of taper. The extruded polyline looks like Figure 18.17.

10. Now join the part you just created with the original solid. To do this, click and drag on the Explode button on the Modify palette and select Union on the flyout. Then click on both the tapered solid and the base and press ↵.

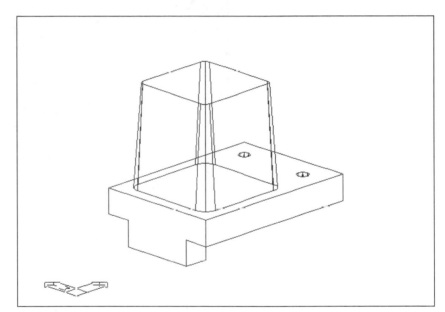

Figure 18.17:   The extruded polyline

EXTRUDING ON A CURVED PATH

As demonstrated in the following exercise, the EXTRUDE command lets you extrude virtually any polyline shape along a path that is defined by a polyline, arc, or 3D polyline.

1. Start by placing the UCS on a vertical plan perpendicular to the back of the part. Do this by clicking on the Preset UCS

button on the Standard toolbar. You may also choose View ➤ Preset UCS ... or type **Dducsp** ⏎. The UCS Orientation dialog box appears:

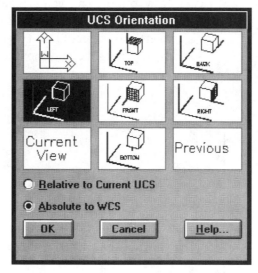

2. Click on the graphic labeled Left toward the middle left of the dialog box, then click OK. The UCS will shift to the back of the part as shown in the top panel of Figure 18.18.

3. Start a polyline at the point shown in panel 1 of Figure 18.18. After you locate the first point, enter the following coordinates. When you are done, your drawing should look like panel 2 of Figure 18.18.

   @2.6<180
   @1<270
   @1.5<180

4. Click and drag on Edit Polyline on the Modify palette, then click on the polyline you just drew.

5. At the Close/Join/WIdth... prompt, type **S** ⏎. The polyline turns into a curve. Press ⏎ to exit the PEDIT command. This is the path you will use to extrude the circle.

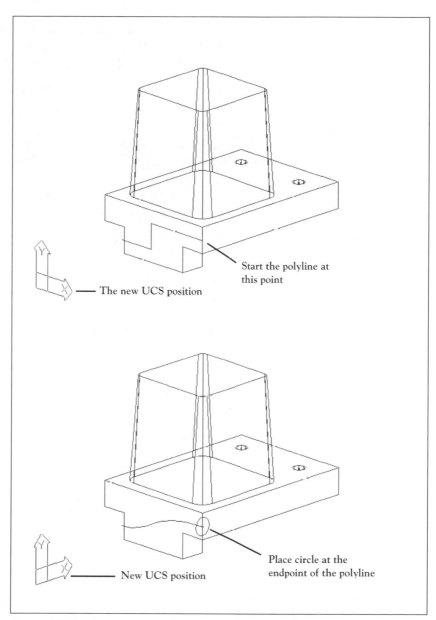

Figure 18.18:   Setting up your drawing to create a curved extrusion

6. Return to the WCS by choosing View ➤ Set UCR ➤ World, then choose View ➤ Preset UCS… and double-click on Front from the UCS Orientation dialog box.

7. Draw a circle with a 0.35″ radius at the beginning end of the polyline. See the location shown in panel 2 of Figure 18.18.

At this point, you've created the components needed to do the extrusion. Next, you'll finish the extruded shape.

8. Click on the Extrude button on the Solids palette, then click on the circle, and press ↵.

9. At the Path/<Height of Extrusion>: prompt, type **P** ↵ to enter the Path option.

10. At the Select path prompt, click on the polyline curve. AutoCAD will pause a moment and then generate a solid "tube" that follows the path. Though it isn't obvious at first, you can detect the "tube" by the single curved line that is parallel to the curved polyline you drew earlier.

11. Click and drag on the Explode button on the Modify palette and select Subtract, or type Subtract ↵. At the Select object prompt, select the solid you created earlier.

12. Press ↵, and at the Select object prompt, click on the curved solid and press ↵. The curved solid is subtracted from the tapered solid. Your drawing will look like Figure 18.19.

In this exercise, you used a curved polyline for the extrusion path, but you can use any type of 2D or 3D polyline, as well as lines and arcs, for an extrusion path.

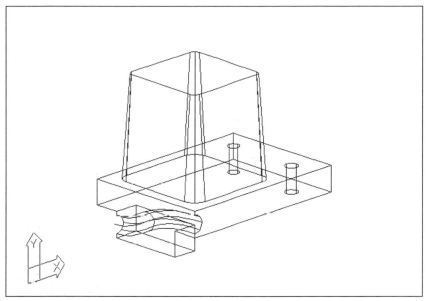

Figure 18.19: The solid after subtracting the curve

REVOLVING A POLYLINE

When your goal is to draw an object that is circular, the REVOLVE command on the Solids palette is designed to let you create a solid that is revolved, or swept in a circular path. Think of REVOLVE's action as similar to a lathe that lets you carve a shape from a spinning shaft. In this case, the spinning shaft is a polyline, and rather than carving it, you define the profile and then revolve the profile about an axis.

In the following exercise, you will draw a solid that will form a slot in the tapered solid.

1. ZOOM in to the top of the tapered box, so that you have a view similar to Figure 18.20.

2. Turn the snap mode off.

3. Return to the WCS by choosing View ➤ Set UCS ➤ World.

4. Choose View ➤ Set UCS ➤ Orgin to move the UCS origin.

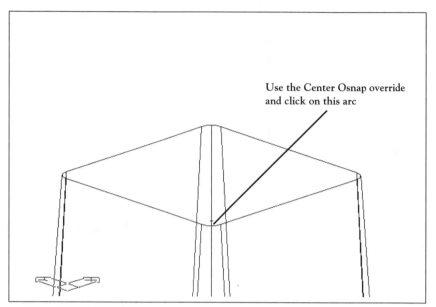

Use the Center Osnap override and click on this arc

Figure 18.20:   An enlarged view of the top of the tapered box, and the new UCS location

5. At the Origin prompt, use the Center Osnap override and pick the center of the arc closest to the bottom of the view, as shown in Figure 18.20.

6. Set the Snap distance to 0.125, and with the coordinate read-out turned on, draw a polyline using the following coordinates:

   −0.375, 1.75
   @1.25<270
   @.875<0
   @1<30
   @0.625<0
   @1<330
   @1.25<0
   @1.25<90

7. When you've finished, type **C** ↵ to close the polyline. Auto-CAD will not revolve an open polyline. Your drawing should look like Figure 18.21.

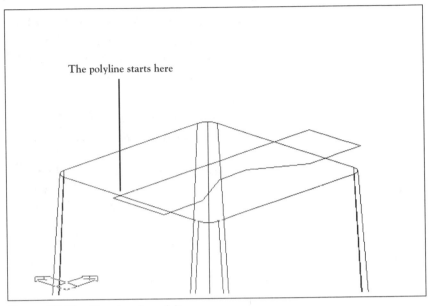

The polyline starts here

Figure 18.21: Drawing the polyline

8. Click on the Revolve button on the Solids palette, or type **Revolve** ↵ at the command prompt.

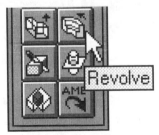

9. At the Select objects: prompt, pick the polyline you just drew and press ↵.

10. When you see the next prompt,

   Axis of revolution – Object/X/Y/<Start point of axis>:

   use the Endpoint Osnap override and pick the beginning end-point of the polyline you just drew.

11. Turn on the ortho mode (press F8), and turn off the snap mode (press F9). Then pick a point to the far left of the screen, so that the rubber-banding line is parallel with the x-axis of the current UCS.

12. At the Angle of revolution <full circle>: prompt, press ↵ to sweep the polyline a full 360°. The revolved form will appear, as shown in Figure 18.22.

You have just created a revolved solid that will be subtracted from the tapered box to form a slot in the bracket. But before you subtract it, you need to make a slight change in the orientation of the revolved solid.

1. Click and drag on the Rotate button on the Modify palette and select 3D Rotate on the flyout.

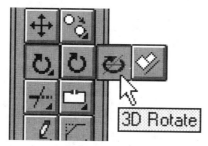

2. At the Select objects prompt, select the revolved solid and press ↵.

3. At the prompt,

   Axis by Entity/Last/View/Xaxis/Yaxis/Zaxis/<2point>

   use the Endpoint Osnap override and click on the right side of the smaller circle of the revolved solid, as shown in Figure 18.23.

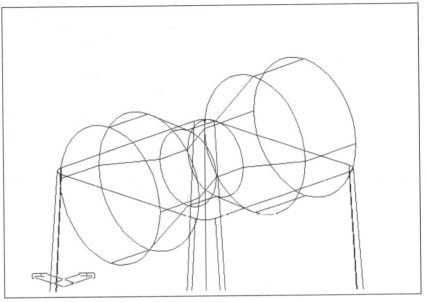

Figure 18.22: The revolved polyline

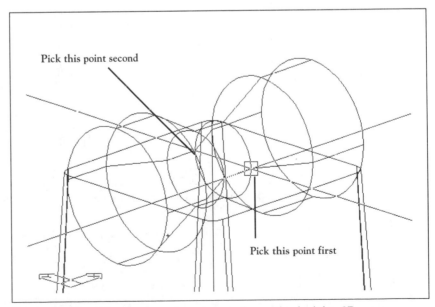

Pick this point second

Pick this point first

Figure 18.23: Selecting the points to rotate the revolved solid in 3D space

4. At the 2nd point on axis prompt, use the Endpoint Osnap override again and click on the opposite side of the circle, as shown in Figure 18.23.

5. At the <Rotation angle>/Reference: prompt, type **5** ↵. The solid rotates 5°.

6. Click and drag on the Explode button on the Modify palette and select Subtract on the flyout, or type **Subtract** ↵. Click on the tapered box, and press ↵.

7. At the object-selection prompt, click on the revolved solid and press ↵. Your drawing looks like Figure 18.24.

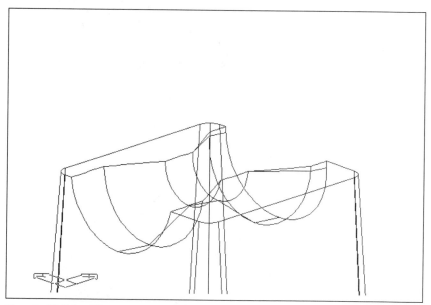

Figure 18.24:   The composite solid, after subtracting the revolved solid from the tapered solid

EDITING SOLIDS

Though solids are fairly easy to create, there are only a handful of commands for editing them. In this section you will examine the commands that will be most useful to you for these editing chores. They include the SLICE command and its options on the Solids palette; and the FILLET and CHAMFER commands on the Modify palette.

SPLITTING A SOLID INTO TWO PIECES

Unfortunately, although reworking a part of your solid may be a common task for you, there aren't any simple ways to make changes to solids. You can, however, slice a solid into two parts, an action that can facilitate the enlargement of solids, or simplify the creation of models by letting you create one monolithic shape to then slice into smaller components. The next exercise shows you how to use the SLICE command.

1. Zoom to the previous view and return to the World Coordinate System.

2. Click on the Slice button on the Solids palette, or type **Slice** ↵.

3. At the object selection prompt, click on the part you've been working on and press ↵.

4. At the next prompt,

    Slicing plane by Object/Zaxis/View/XY/YZ/ZX/<3points>:

    type **XY** ↵. This will let you indicate a slice plane parallel to the XY plane.

5. Type **0,0,.5** ↵. This places the slice plane at the z coordinate of .5 units.

▼ **NOTE**

In step 2, you could select more than one solid. The SLICE command would then slice all the solids through the plane indicated in steps 3 and 4.

▼ **NOTE**

If you want to delete one side of the sliced solid, you can indicate the side you want to keep by clicking on it in step 5, instead of entering **B** ↵.

6. At the Both sides/<Point on desired side of the plane>: prompt, type **B** ↵ to keep both sides of the solid. AutoCAD will divide the solid horizontally, one half inch above the base of the part as shown in Figure 18.25.

The Slice Options

There were several options in step 3 of the foregoing exercise that are worth discussing here. Here are descriptions of those options:

Object lets you select an object to define the slice plane.

Zaxis lets you select two points defining the z-axis of the slice plane. The two points you pick will be perpendicular to the slice plane.

View generates a slice plane that is perpendicular to your current view. You are prompted for the coordinate through which the slice plane must pass—usually a point on the object.

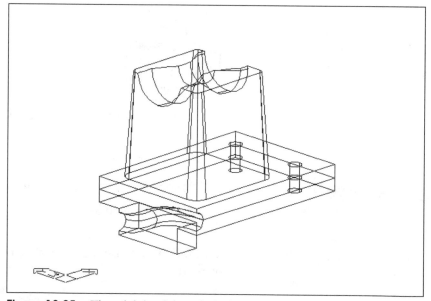

Figure 18.25: The solid sliced through the base

IV

Modeling and Imaging in 3D

<3point> is the default, and lets you select three points defining the slice plane. Normally, you would pick points on the solid.

XY/YZ/ZX Pick one if these to determine the slice plane based on the x-, y-, or z-axis. You are prompted to pick a point through which the slice plane must pass.

ROUNDING CORNERS WITH FILLET

Your bracket has a few sharp corners that you may want to round in order to give the bracket a more realistic appearance. You can use the Construct menu's FILLET and CHAMFER commands to add these rounded corners to your solid model.

1. Click and drag on the Chamfer button on the Modify palette and select Fillet on the flyout.

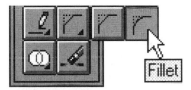

2. At the <Select first object> prompt, pick the edge indicated in Figure 18.26.

3. At the Enter radius prompt, type **.2** ↵.

4. At the Chain/Radius/<Select edge> prompt, type **C** ↵ for the Chain option. Chain lets you select a series of solid edges to be filleted.

5. Select the other three edges at the base of the tapered form, and press ↵ when you are done.

6. Choose Hide on the Render palette, or type **Hide** ↵ to get a better look at your model.

As you saw in step 5 above, Fillet acts a bit differently when you use it on solids. The Chain option lets you select a set of edges, instead of just two adjoining objects.

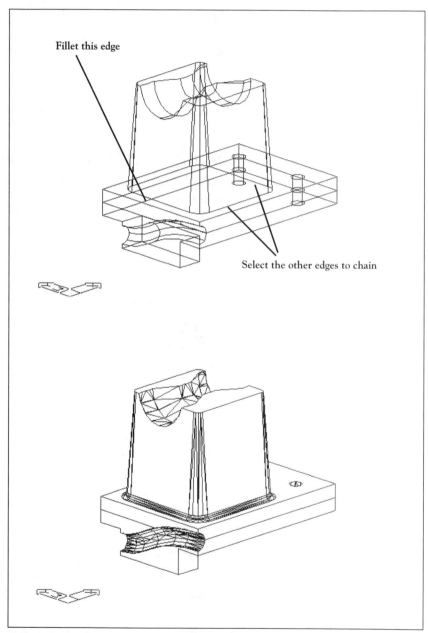

Figure 18.26: Filleting solids

BEVELING CORNERS WITH CHAMFER

Now let's try chamfering a corner. To practice using Chamfer, you'll add a countersink to the cylindrical hole you created in the first solid.

1. Type **Regen** ↵ to return to a wire frame view of your model.

2. Click and drag on the Fillet button on the Modify palette and select Chamfer on the flyout, or type **Chamfer** ↵.

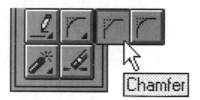

3. At the prompt,

   Polyline/Distance/Angle/Trim/Method/<select first line>:

   Pick the edge of the hole, as shown in Figure 18.27. Notice that the top surface of the solid is highlighted, and the prompt changes to Next/ok. The highlighting indicates the base surface, which will be used as a reference in step 5. (You could also type **N** ↵ to choose the other adjoining surface, the inside of the hole, as the base surface.)

4. Press ↵ to accept the current highlighted face.

5. At the Enter base surface distance: prompt, type **.125** ↵. This indicates that you want the chamfer to have a width of .125 across the highlighted surface.

6. At the Enter other surface distance <0.1250>: prompt, type **.2** ↵.

7. At the Loop <select edge> prompt, click on the edge of both holes and then press ↵. When it is done, your drawing will look like Figure 18.28.

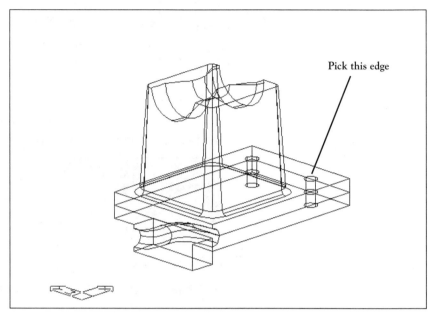

Figure 18.27:   Picking the edge to chamfer

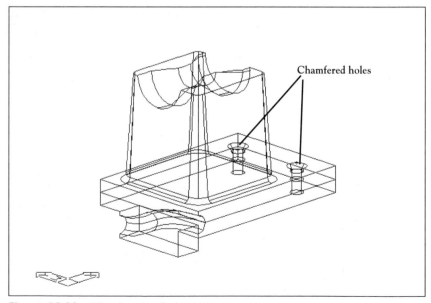

Figure 18.28:   The chamfered edges

ENHANCING THE 2D DRAWING PROCESS

Using solids to model a part such as the example used in this chapter may seem a bit on the exotic side, but there are definite advantages to modeling in 3D—even if you want to draw the part in only 2D as a page in a set of manufacturing specs.

The following exercises show you how to quickly generate a typical mechanical drawing from your 3D model using the MVsetup command. You will also examine techniques for dimensioning and including hidden lines.

DRAWING A STANDARD TOP, FRONT, AND RIGHT-SIDE VIEW

▼ NOTE

If you need to refresh your memory about using Paper Space, refer to the sidebar in chapter 12 entitled "Using MV Setup to set up Paper Space."

One of the more common types of mechanical drawings is the *orthogonal projection*. This style of drawing shows the top, front, and right-side view of an object. Sometimes a 3D image is also added for clarity. You can derive such a drawing within a few minutes, once you have created your 3D solid model. The first step is to select a sheet title block. The title block consists of a border and place in the lower right corner for notes and other drawing information. You'll use the MVsetup command to do create the title block.

1. Click on View ➤ 3D Viewpoint Presets ➤ Plan View ➤ World or type **Plan** ↵ to get a top view of your model. Then click on the Zoom Out button on the Standard toolbar.

2. Create a layer called **Title**, and activate it as the current layer. This will be the layer for your title block.

3. On the Status Bar, double-click on the MODEL button to turn on Paper Space. Alternatively you can choose View ➤ Paper Space or type **Tilemode** ↵ **0** ↵.

Now you are ready to use the MVsetup command. Steps 4 through 8 guide you through one of its options.

4. Click on View ➤ Floating Viewports ➤ MV Setup. This command offers a variety of options that simplify your work in laying out a mechanical drawing.

5. At the Align/Create/Scale viewport/Options/Title block/Undo prompt, enter **T** ↵ to select the Title block option.

6. At the Delete objects/Origin/Undo/<Insert Title Block> prompt, press ↵. The screen flips to text mode, and you see a numbered list of sheet sizes.

7. At the Add/Delete/Redisplay/<Number of entry to load> prompt, enter **9** for a C-size sheet. AutoCAD flips to graphics mode and draws a title block.

8. At the Create a drawing called ansi-c.dwg prompt, enter **N** ↵, and then press ↵ again to exit MVSetup.

You now have an industry standard title block. The next step is to place your drawing with the title block.

Setting Up a Set of Standard Views

As you can see in step 6, MVsetup offers a range of predefined engineering sheets for you to use. The next step is to get your viewport set up.

1. Create a new layer called **Views** and make it the current layer. This will be the layer for the new viewports MVSetup will create.

2. Click on View ➤ Floating Viewports ➤ MV Setup again.

3. At the Align/Create/Scale viewports prompt, enter **C** ↵ to use the Create option.

4. At the Delete objects/Undo/<Create viewports> prompt, press ↵ to accept the default. A list of four viewport options appears on the screen.

5. Next you'll see the Redisplay/< Number of entry to load> prompt. Enter **2** ↵ to select the Std. Engineering option. This option generates four viewports with special characteristics, as you will see in a moment.

6. At the Bounding area for viewports. First point prompt, pick a point toward the lower-left corner of the title block (see Figure 18.29).

7. At the Other corner prompt, pick a point as shown in Figure 18.29 to locate the opposite corner of the set of viewports.

8. At the Distance between viewports in X prompt, enter **.5** ↵. Here you are telling MVsetup how much space to put between each viewport horizontally.

9. At the Distance between viewports in Y prompt, press ↵. (Notice that the default is the same as the x distance you just entered.) This tells MVsetup how much space to leave between the viewports vertically.

10. AutoCAD works for a moment to set up the top, front, right-side, and SE Isometric views of your 3D part. When you are ready, press ↵ to exit MVsetup. Your drawing should look like Figure 18.30.

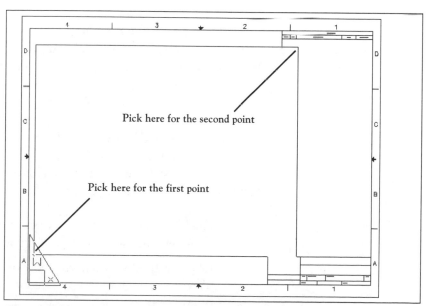

Figure 18.29: Where to pick points to place the viewports

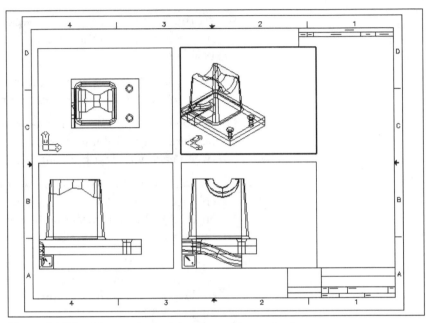

Figure 18.30: The top, front, right side, and isometric view

Setting Up the Top, Front, and Right Side View Manually

In the last exercise, you saw how MVsetup automatically changes each viewport to conform to the standard top, front, and right side view of a typical mechanical drawing. You may, however, find yourself in a situation where you cannot use MVsetup to create your views. Or you may find that you need a different set of views, a set that MVsetup does not provide. The following steps describe how you might set up the top, front, and right side view manually. These steps assume you have a top view showing in all four viewports to start with.

1. Click on View ➤ Floating Model Space. This lets you work in modelspace within each viewport.

2. Click on the lower left viewport then click on View ➤ 3D Viewport Preset ➤ Front. The view changes to front orientation.

3. Click on the lower right viewport, then click on View ➤ 3D Viewport Preset ➤ Right. The view changes to a right side view.

4. Click on the upper right viewport then click on View ➤ 3D Viewport Preset ➤ SE Isometric. The view changes to an Isometric view from the "south east" direction approximately – 45 degrees in the XY plane. Your drawing should look like Figure 18.30.

As you can see from the View ➤ Viewport Preset cascading menu, you can choose from top, bottom, left, right, front and back views. You can also select from four typical isometric views.

Scaling Viewports Uniformly

Now you have a title block and your view's layout. The next step is to scale your drawing to the appropriate size for this sheet. Once again, you'll use MVSetup.

1. Click on View ➤ Floating Viewports ➤ MV Setup.

2. At the Align/Create/Scale viewports prompt, enter **S** ↵ for Scale viewports.

3. At the Select objects prompt, click on the four viewports and then press ↵.

4. At the next prompt,

   Set zoom scale factor for viewports Interactively/<Uniform>

   press ↵ to accept the Uniform default. This causes all viewports to be scaled to the same scale factor.

5. At the Number of paper space units prompt, enter **.5** ↵.

6. At the Number of model space units prompt, press ↵ to accept the default value of 1. The two prompts in steps 5 and 6 combine to give your drawing a scale of $\frac{1}{2}''=1''$.

7. Press ↵ to exit the MVsetup option.

▼ **NOTE**

Remember, to select a viewport, you click on its border.

8. Change the current layer to 0, then turn off the Views layer to hide the viewport borders. Your drawing will look like Figure 18.31. The borders of the viewports will disappear but their views will remain.

REMOVING HIDDEN LINES IN PAPER SPACE VIEWPORTS

As a final step, with viewports set up, you will want to make sure that each viewport will do a hidden-line removal at plot time. Here's how you turn on hidden-line removal for each viewport in Paper Space.

1. Turn the Views layer on again, then choose View ➤ Floating Viewports ➤ Hideplot, or type **Mview** ↵ **H** ↵.

2. Type **On** ↵.

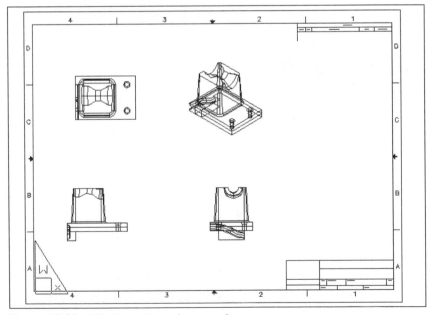

Figure 18.31: The Paper Space layout so far

3. At the Select objects prompt, select all four viewports and press ↵.

Although nothing seems to have changed, you have in fact set all the viewports to perform a hidden-line removal at plot time. You can check to make sure hidden lines are removed by using the Preview option in the Plot dialog box. Let's continue with that task.

4. Double-click on the MODEL button on the Status bar to go to Paper Space. This is a crucial step because if you are not in Paper Space, your Plot will be of your Model Space view.

5. Choose File ➤ Print, or type **Plot** ↵.

6. At the Plot Configuration dialog box, make sure the Scale to Fit check box is checked, and that the Full option in the Plot Preview button group is on. Also make sure the Extents radio button is selected.

7. Click on the Preview button. AutoCAD will calculate on its own for a few seconds and then display a preview of your plot, as shown in Figure 18.32. Notice that the views of the solid model are shown with hidden lines removed.

USING DASHED LINES TO SHOW HIDDEN LINES

You have just about everything complete at this point. The views are in place and in scale. But mechanical drawings often represent hidden geometry by means of dashed lines. The next exercise suggests a method to add dashed lines for hidden lines in Paper Space.

1. While in Paper Space, zoom into the front view in the lower-left corner of your sheet layout.

2. Create a layer called **Hidden,** and give that layer the Hidden2 line type. You may also want to give this layer a color that will contrast with the 3D solid. Make Hidden the current layer.

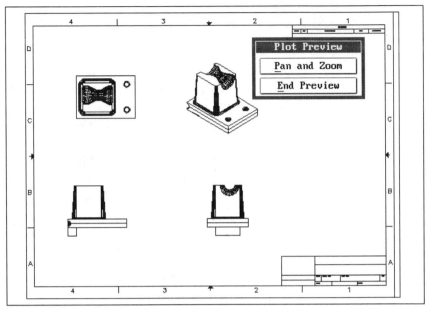

Figure 18.32: A plot preview of the Paper Space layout with hidden lines removed

3. Now trace over the parts of the 3D solid that would normally be shown as hidden lines in a mechanical drawing.

4. To check your work, switch to Floating Model Space by double-clicking on the PAPER button on the Status bar, or type **MS** ⏎. This puts you in a mode where you can edit Model Space through your Paper Space viewport.

5. Click on the inside of your viewport.

6. Choose Hide on the Render palette, or type **Hide** ⏎ at the command prompt. AutoCAD does a hidden-line removal on the objects in Model Space. The Paper Space lines you just added will remain unchanged. You will have a view similar to Figure 18.33.

IV

Modeling and Imaging in 3D

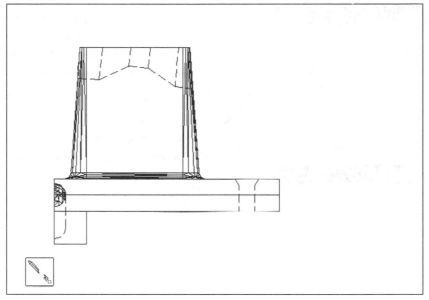

Figure 18.33:   Dashed lines are drawn over a Model Space view

The idea here is to overlay lines that *are* hidden during plot time with lines that are *not* hidden. These new lines will appear as dashed lines in the final plot. Since these lines on the Hidden layer are not part of the model, you will have to revise them whenever your 3D model is updated or changed. Still, to generate a typical engineering drawing, this method is much faster than manual drafting.

If you have a fairly complex mechanical drawing, you may want to pursue a course that does not require you to trace all of the hidden geometry. Consider using the 3D-to-2D conversion process outlined in *Chapter 15* to generate the hidden-line portion of your drawing. Here's a step-by-step description of how to do that:

1. In Paper Space again, zoom out to view the whole drawing and turn off the Hideplot setting of your viewports, using View ➤ Floating Viewports ➤ Hideplot.

▼ TIP

If arcs and circles seem too rough in the imported Post-Script file, specify a very large sheet size when you export the PostScript file. This has the effect of increasing the overall resolution of the PostScript file.

▼ TIP

See the sections on using Grips in *Chapter 12* for more on scaling objects.

2. Enter **Psout** ↵ to create a PostScript file of your drawing. (At this point, you might want to window the viewports, so you don't get the title block in the PostScript output file. Remember also to specify a screen preview image.)

3. Enter **Psin** ↵ to import the exported file back into your drawing.

4. Scale the imported drawing to match your Paper Space views. Do this by matching a feature of the imported image—say, a corner of the solid in one of the views—to its corresponding location in the drawing. Then use the Reference option of the SCALE command to match another point of the imported image to its corresponding point in the drawing. (The SCALE command is located on the Resize flyout on the Modify palette.)

5. Change the imported drawing to appear as dashed lines. The easiest way to do this is to create a layer and assign it the Hidden2 line type, and then assign the imported file to this layer.

6. Turn the viewports' Hideplot setting back on.

If you prefer, you could explode the imported file, and then erase all the extraneous line work, leaving only the hidden lines. You will want to keep this imported file on its own layer, so you can turn it off when you add dimensions (discussed in the upcoming section). If you try to dimension your drawing in Paper Space with the imported file visible, you may get erroneous dimensions, because the imported file won't have the accuracy of your Model Space solid model.

ADDING DIMENSIONS AND NOTES IN PAPER SPACE

▼ NOTE

See *Chapters 8 and 9* for a more detailed discussion of notes and dimensions.

Though I don't recommend adding dimensions in Paper Space for architectural drawings, it may be a good idea for mechanical drawings like the one in this chapter. By maintaining the dimensions and notes separate from the actual model, you keep these elements from getting in the way of your work on the solid model. You also avoid the confusion of having to scale the text and dimension features properly to ensure that they will plot at the correct size.

As long as you set up your Paper Space work area to be equivalent to the final plot size, you can set dimension and text to the sizes you want at plot time. If you want text ¼″ high, you set your text styles to be ¼″ high.

To dimension, just make sure you are in Paper Space (View ➤ Paper Space), and then use the dimension commands in the normal way. There is one thing you do have to be careful of, however: If your Paper Space viewports are set to a scale other than 1 to 1, you must set the Annotation Units option in the Dimension Style dialog box to a proper value. Here's how:

1. Click on the Dimension Styles button on the Dimensioning palette, or type **Ddim** ↵.

2. At the Dimension Styles dialog box, make sure you have selected the style you want to use, and click on Annotation.

3. In the Annotation dialog box, click on the Units button.

4. In the Scale input box, enter the value by which you want your Paper Space dimensions multiplied. For example, if your Paper Space views are scaled at one-half the actual size of your model, you would enter **2** in this box, to multiply your dimensions' values by 2.

5. Once you have entered a scale value, make sure the Paper Space Only check box is checked. This ensures that your dimension is scaled only while you are adding dimensions in Paper Space. Dimensions added in Model Space are not affected.

You've had to complete many steps to get the final drawing you have now, but, compared to having to draw these views by hand, you have doubtless saved a great deal of time. In addition, as you will see later in this chapter, what you have is more than just a 2D drafted image. With what you have created now, further refinements are now quite easy.

▼ TIP

To make sure the value you need in step 4 is correct, just determine what scale factor you would need for your Paper Space drawing to get its actual size; that's the value you need to enter.

DRAWING A CROSS SECTION

One element of your drawing that is missing is a cross section. Auto-CAD will draw a cross section through any part of the solid model. In the following exercise, you will draw a cross section.

1. First, save your drawing so you can return to this stage (in case you don't want to save the results of the following steps).

2. Click on View ➤ Tiled Modelspace, or type **Tilemode** ⏎ **1** ⏎.

3. Click on the Section button on the Solids palette.

4. At the Select object prompt, click on the solid model you have drawn and press ⏎.

5. At the next prompt,

    Section plane by Obect/
    Last/Zaxis/View/XY/YZ/ZX/<3points>

    enter **ZX** ⏎. This tells AutoCAD you want to cut the solid in the plane defined by the x- and z-axes.

6. At the Point on ZX plane prompt, pick the midpoint of the top-left surface of the base plate (see panel 1 of Figure 18.34). The section cut appears as shown in panel 2 of Figure 18.34.

7. Move the section cut outline away from the solid.

8. If you like, use the HATCH command to hatch the section cut, and then place it in a convenient place so you can add it to your finished drawing later.

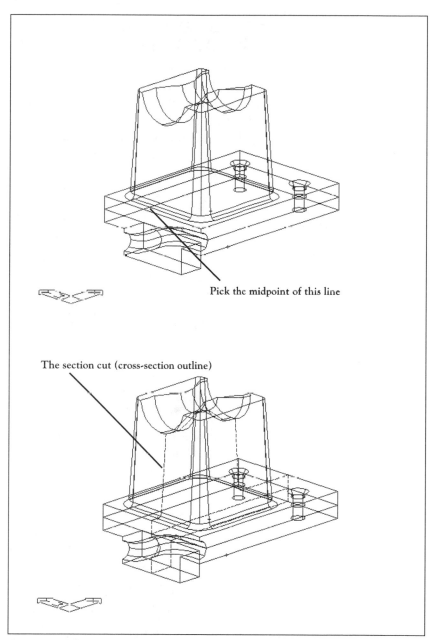

Pick the midpoint of this line

The section cut (cross-section outline)

Figure 18.34:   Selecting the point on the z–x plane to define the section cut outline

USING 3D SOLID OPERATIONS ON 2D DRAWINGS

You can apply of some of the features described in this chapter to 2D drafting by taking advantage of AutoCAD's *region* object. Regions are two-dimensional objects to which you can apply Boolean operations.

Try the following optional exercise, which demonstrates how two Boolean operations, Union and Subtract, work on 2D objects:

1. If you have been working through the tutorial on 3D solids, save the bracket drawing now.

2. Open the Region.DWG drawing supplied on the companion CD. You will see the drawing shown in panel 1 of Figure 18.35.

3. Click and drag on the Polygon button on the Draw palette and select Region on the flyout, or type **Region** ↵.

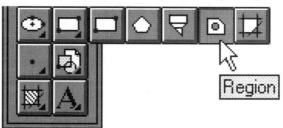

4. At the object-selection prompt, click on all the objects in the drawing and press ↵. AutoCAD now regards all the objects as belonging to the same region, and all together they compose a single region object.

5. Move the two circles and the hexagons into the positions illustrated in panel 2 of Figure 18.35. (For this demonstration exercise, you don't have to worry about matching the positions exactly.)

6. Click and drag on the Explode button on the Modify palette, and select Union on the flyout.

7. At the Select objects: prompt, click on the rectangle and the two circles. The circles merge with the rectangle to form one object.

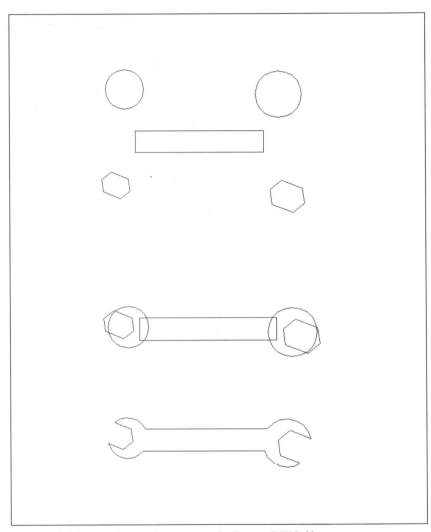

Figure 18.35: Working with regions in the Region.DWG file

8. Click and drag on the Union button on the Modify palette, and select Subtract on the flyout. At the first object-selection prompt, click on the newly created region and press ↵.

9. At the next object-selection prompt, click on the two hexagons. Now you have a single, 2D solid object in the shape of a wrench.

You can use regions to generate complex surfaces that might include holes or unusual bends (see Figure 18.36). Two things to keep in mind:

- Regions act like surfaces; when you remove hidden lines, objects behind the regions are hidden.

- You can explode regions to edit them. (You can't do this with solids.) Exploding a region causes the region to lose its surface-like quality, however, and objects will no longer hide behind its surface(s).

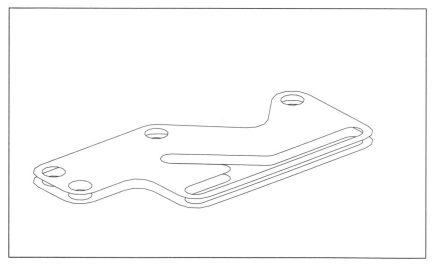

Figure 18.36: You can use the regional model to create complex 2D surfaces for use in 3D surface modeling.

FINDING THE PROPERTIES OF A SOLID

All of this effort to create a solid model isn't just to create a pretty picture. Once your model is drawn and built, you can obtain information about its physical properties. In this section, you will look at a few of the commands that let you gather such information.

FINDING A MODEL'S MASS PROPERTIES

You can find the volume, moment of inertia, and other physical properties of your model by using the MASSPROP command. Such properties can also be recorded as a file on disk so you can modify your model without worrying about losing track of its original properties.

1. Open the Bracket drawing you worked on through most of this chapter.

2. Click and drag on the List button on the Object Properties toolbar, and select Mass Properties on the flyout, or enter **Massprop** ↵.

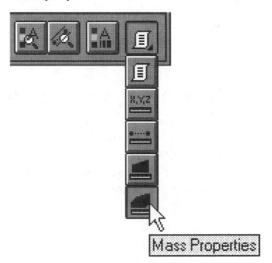

3. At the object-selection prompt, pick the composite solid you created. AutoCAD will calculate for a moment, and then it will display a list of the object's properties as shown in Figure 18.37.

```
----------------   SOLIDS   ----------------
Mass:                67.7492
Volume:              67.7492
Bounding box:     X: 2.9970  --  10.0000
                  Y: 2.4990  --   7.5000
                  Z: 0.1619  --   5.0000
Centroid:         X: 5.7432
                  Y: 4.9842
                  Z: 2.2433
Moments of inertia: X: 2232.2202
                  Y: 2824.5544
                  Z: 4154.1523
Products of inertia: XY: 1939.3657
                  YZ: 754.5816
                  ZX: 846.7649
Radii of gyration: X: 5.7401
                  Y: 6.4569
                  Z: 7.8305
Principal moments and X-Y-Z directions about centroid:
                  I: 192.6175 along [0.8579 0.0269 -0.5132]
                  J: 247.5423 along [-0.2720 0.8710 -0.4090]
                  K: 253.4072 along [0.4360 0.4905 0.7545]
```

Figure 18.37:   The Mass Properties listing derived from the solid model

IF YOU WANT TO EXPERIMENT...

This chapter has focused on a mechanical project, but you can of course use solids to help simplify the construction of 3D architectural forms. If your interest lies in architecture, try drawing the window in Figure 18.38. (Imagine trying to create this window without the solid modeling capabilities of AutoCAD!)

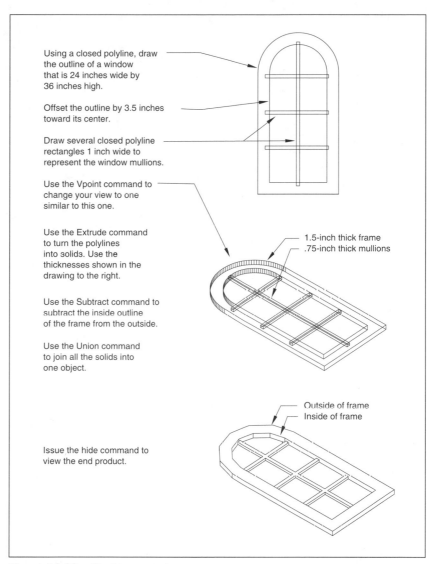

Using a closed polyline, draw the outline of a window that is 24 inches wide by 36 inches high.

Offset the outline by 3.5 inches toward its center.

Draw several closed polyline rectangles 1 inch wide to represent the window mullions.

Use the Vpoint command to change your view to one similar to this one.

Use the Extrude command to turn the polylines into solids. Use the thicknesses shown in the drawing to the right.

Use the Subtract command to subtract the inside outline of the frame from the outside.

Use the Union command to join all the solids into one object.

Issue the hide command to view the end product.

1.5-inch thick frame
.75-inch thick mullions

Outside of frame
Inside of frame

Figure 18.38: Drawing a window

PART FIVE

CUSTOMIZATION—
■
TAKING
■
AUTOCAD
■
TO THE
■
LIMIT

In this last part of the book, you will learn how you can take full control of AutoCAD. *Chapter 19, Introduction to Customization*, gives you a gentle introduction to the world of AutoCAD customization. You'll learn how to load and use existing utilities that come with AutoCAD. You'll also be introduced to the world of third-party add-ons. *Chapter 20, Exploring AutoLISP*, shows you how to tap the power of this programming language to add new functions to AutoCAD. *Chapter 21, Integrating AutoCAD into Your Projects and Organization*, shows you how to adapt AutoCAD to your own work style. You will want to consult *Appendix E* when you get to this chapter.

19

INTRODUCTION TO CUSTOMIZATION

Locating and Loading AutoLISP Utilities

Understanding the Applications
Dialog Box

Loading Your Favorite AutoLISP
Utilities Automatically

Creating Keyboard Macros

Creating Keyboard Abbreviations of
Your Most Commonly Used Commands

Understanding Third-Party Software

Exploring Online Services

FAST TRACK

909 ▶ To load an AutoLISP program

Click on Tools ➤ Applications..., and then on the Files button. In the Load AutoLISP and ADS Files dialog box, locate and double-click on the AutoLISP program you want to load. Highlight the program name in the list box and click on OK.

915 ▶ To have AutoCAD load your favorite AutoLISP programs automatically at startup

With your favorite text editor, open a new text file and call it **Acad.LSP**. Enter the line **(load "*filename*")**, where *filename* is the name of the AutoLISP file you want to load. If the file is not in the current DOS path, include drive and path information with the file name. In place of the backslash (\ ) for DOS directory listings, use a forward slash (/). Do this for each utility you want loaded automatically.

915 ▶ To create a keyboard macro

Switch to text mode. Enter **(defun c:*progname* ()** ↵, where *progname* is the name you want to give your macro. Next, enter **(command "*comname*" "*key1*" "*key2*" "*key3*"...)** ↵ where *comname* is the name of the command you want to use, and *key1*, *key2*, etc. are the exact keystrokes you need to execute your macro. Be sure you add the closing parenthesis. Finally, enter **)** ↵ to finish the macro. To use your macro, enter the name you entered for the *comname* and press ↵.

920 ▶ To create keyboard abbreviations for your favorite commands

Using your favorite text editor, open the Acad.PGP file, found in the /acadr13/common/support subdirectory. Locate the list that starts with A,*ARC. In the same format as the other abbreviations, enter the key(s) you want to use as the shortcut for the command, followed by a comma and several spaces, then the name of the command preceded by an asterisk. Place your macro at the end of the list.

AutoCAD offers a wealth of features that you can use to improve your productivity. But even with these aids to efficiency, there are always situations that can use some further automation. In this chapter, you'll be introduced to the different ways AutoCAD can be customized and enhanced. First, you'll load and run several handy AutoLISP utilities. Next, you'll learn how to add keyboard shortcuts to improve access to your favorite commands. Finally, you'll finish the chapter by taking a look at how third-party applications and online services can enhance AutoCAD's role in your workplace.

PUTTING AUTOLISP TO WORK

Most high-end CAD packages offer a macro or programming language to help users customize their systems. AutoCAD has *AutoLISP*, which is a pared-down version of the popular Common LISP artificial intelligence language. There is also the Autodesk Development System (ADS) that allows C programmers to develop utilities and full applications that work with AutoCAD. Chances are you won't get too involved with ADS, except as an end user. AutoLISP, however, offers the intermediate and advanced AutoCAD user many advantages.

Don't let AutoLISP scare you. In many ways, an AutoLISP program is just a set of AutoCAD commands that help you build your own features. The only difference is that you have to follow a different set of rules when using AutoLISP. But this isn't unusual. After all, you had to learn some basic rules about using AutoCAD commands, too—how to start commands, for instance, and how to use command options.

If the thought of using AutoLISP is a little intimidating to you, bear in mind that you don't really need substantial computer knowledge to use this tool. In this section, you will see how you can get AutoLISP to help out in your everyday editing tasks, without actually doing any programming at all.

LOADING AND RUNNING AN AUTOLISP PROGRAM

As mentioned, AutoCAD comes with several AutoLISP programs ready to use. These programs are in the form of ASCII text files with the extension .LSP. Before you can use .LSP files, you must load them while in the drawing editor. Here's how:

1. Start AutoCAD and open the Unit file.

2. Click on Tools ➤ Applications. The Load AutoLISP and ADS Files dialog box appears.

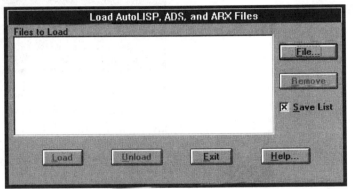

3. Click on the File button.

4. In the Directories list, locate the \acadr13\common\sample directory. From the file list, double-click on Chroma.LSP. The Files dialog box closes, and you next see the Load ADS and AutoLISP Files dialog box, with Chroma.LSP in the list box.

5. Highlight Chroma.LSP, and click on the Load button. You will see the message C:COlor loaded.

6. Now enter **CO** ↵. The Color dialog box appears. (This dialog box is similar to the one you see when you pick Set Color from the Layer Control dialog box.)

Customization—Taking AutoCAD to the Limit

V

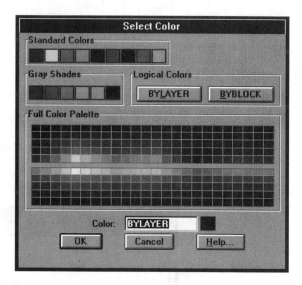

7. From here, you can click on a color to make it the default color for any new objects you create. Two other buttons, Bylayer and Byblock, let you set the color to these options. See the sidebar "Understanding Colors and Linetypes" in *Chapter 4* for information on these two options. Click on Cancel to exit this dialog box.

You have just loaded and used an AutoLISP utility. As you saw in the file dialog box, there are several other utilities you can load and try out. You'll be introduced to a few more of these utilities later on, but for now, let's look more closely at the Load AutoLISP and ADS Files dialog box.

WORKING WITH THE LOAD AUTOLISP AND ADS FILES DIALOG BOX

The Load AutoLISP and ADS Files dialog box gives you plenty of flexibility in managing your favorite AutoLISP and ADS utilities. As you saw from the previous exercise, you can easily find and select utilities using this dialog box. Once you locate a file, it becomes part of the list, saving you from having to hunt down your favorite utility every time you want to use it.

Even when you exit AutoCAD, the dialog box retains the name of any AutoLISP or ADS files you select. This is because, by default, the Save List check box in the dialog box is checked. (If you don't want to retain items in the list, turn this option off.)

To remove an item from the list, just highlight it and click on the Remove button. As with any other list box, you can select multiple items and load them all at once.

ENHANCEMENTS STRAIGHT FROM THE SOURCE

As you've already seen, there is much more to AutoCAD than meets the eye. If you've followed the tutorial in this book, you've already used a few of the AutoLISP programs that come with AutoCAD, perhaps without even being aware that they were AutoLISP programs. In this section we'll describe a few more of these AutoLISP tools.

UTILITIES FROM THE SUPPORT AND SAMPLE SUBDIRECTORIES

Here are a few programs that are not found in the AutoCAD menu. A full tutorial on each of these programs would make this chapter prohibitively long, and you should feel comfortable enough with AutoCAD by now to experiment with them on your own. It's likely you'll find them useful in your day-to-day work. Remember—before you can use them, you must first load them individually as described in the first section of this chapter.

Edge.LSP

Located in the \acadr13\common\support directory, Edge.LSP allows you to easily change the visibility of edges on a 3Dface.

Type **Edge** ↵ to start the utility. At the Display/<Select edge> prompt, click on the 3Dface edge that you want to hide. To redisplay edges that you have previously hidden, type **D** ↵ at the Display/<Select edge> prompt. At the next prompt, Select/<All>, press ↵ to view all the hidden edges, or type **S** ↵ to select individual 3Dfaces to view.

Julian.LSP

Located in the \acadr13\common\sample directory, Julian.LSP displays the date and time at the command prompt. This program is called Julian because it uses the Julian date format that AutoCAD uses, and converts that format into one that is more easily read.

Once the program is loaded, you simply type **Date** ↵ at the command prompt to start it.

Xplode.LSP

Located in the \acadr13\common\support directory, Xplode.LSP performs the same function as the EXPLODE command (Modify ➤ Explode), with some enhancements. Xplode lets you explode multiple objects at once. You can specify the layer, color, or line type of objects contained in the blocks. It also lets you explode a block so that the objects contained therein will inherit the block's layer assignment.

Once it's loaded, type **XP** ↵ or **Xplode** ↵ to start the program. At the object-selection prompt, select the objects you want to explode and press ↵. The next prompt offers the following options:

XPlode Individually/<Globally>: appears when you select more than one object. Here, you can choose to explode all of the selected objects the same way, or you can type **I** to explode each object separately.

All lets you specify color, line type, and layer for all the objects.

Color lets you specify just the color for all the objects.

LAyer lets you designate the layer to be assigned to the exploded objects.

LType presents choices for assigning a line type to the exploded objects.

Inherit from parent block assigns the original objects' properties to the exploded objects.

Explode simply explodes all the selected objects.

Xdata.LSP

Located in the \acadr13\common\sample directory, Xdata.LSP attaches extended data types to selected objects. It also lets you retrieve or read this data. This can be used to attach information to objects for later retrieval.

Once Xdata is loaded type **Xdata** ↵ to attach data to an object. At the Select object prompt, click on the object to which you want to attach data. At the Application name prompt you must enter a name (any one you want). This option lets third-party developers store data using a name unique to their application. Once you enter a name, you see a prompt containing a set of options that help you to enter data according to the following types:

3Real   stores three real numbers. The most common use for this data type would be a 3D coordinate, such as 1.0,2.2,4.5.

DIR   stores a 3D coordinate; the DIR value is adjusted when the object is rotated or mirrored.

DISP   stores a 3D coordinate; the DISP value is adjusted when the object is rotated, scaled, or mirrored.

DIST   stores a real value that is adjusted when the object is scaled.

Hand   stores an object's handle, which is a hexadecimal value.

Int   stores an integer.

Layer   stores the layer associated with the extended object data.

LOng   stores a 32-bit integer.

Pos   stores a coordinate that is adjusted when the object is moved, scaled, mirrored, or rotated.

Real   stores any real value.

SCale   stores a value that is scaled along with the associated object.

STr   stores a text string.

To read the extended object data from an object, you type **Xdlist** ↵. You are then presented with a list of the data that has been stored as extended object data.

UTILITIES AVAILABLE FROM OTHER SOURCES

The utilities listed in the previous section are just a few samples of the many available for AutoCAD. Other sources for AutoLISP utilities are the AutoCAD journals *Cadence* and *Cadalyst*. Both offer sections that list utilities written by readers and editorial staff. If you don't already have a subscription to one of these publications and want to know more about them, their addresses are as follows:

> *Cadence*
> Miller Freeman Inc.
> 600 Harrison St.
> San Francisco, CA 94107

> *Cadalyst*
> Advanstar Communications
> 859 Willamette St.
> P.O. Box 10460
> Eugene, OR 97440-2460

Finally, there is the companion CD included with this book. It contains some free and shareware utilities.

If you find the shareware utilities useful, please don't neglect to register them. This will encourage the authors of this and other shareware to continue their efforts in providing such low-cost programs.

I have also included my own AEC software offering basic architectural utilities, such as a symbols library, automatic door and window insertion program, and reference symbols. In addition, a DXF-to-Post-Script translation utility has been included on the CD.

LOADING AUTOLISP PROGRAMS AUTOMATICALLY

If you find some of the above AutoLISP programs useful, you can combine them into a single file called **Acad.LSP**. Once you place Acad.LSP in your AutoCAD directory, the programs you have included in that file will be loaded automatically every time you open a drawing file.

Your Acad.LSP file should contain only the command-line entries you would normally use to load the utilities you want to use. Use the Windows Notepad text editor to create this file, and save it as **Acad.LSP** in your AutoCAD directory. For example, to have Auto-CAD automatically load the Xdata.LSP, Plud.LSP, and Edge.LSP utilities, you would create an Acad.LSP file that contains the following lines:

```
(load "Xdata")
(load "Xplode")
(load "Edge")
```

If you haven't set a path in DOS to the location of these AutoLISP files, you will want to include the path in the file names in the Acad.LSP file.

CREATING KEYBOARD MACROS WITH AUTOLISP

You can write some simple AutoLISP programs of your own, to create what are called *keyboard macros*. Macros—like script files—are strings of predefined keyboard entries. They are invaluable for shortcuts to commands and options you use frequently. For example, you might find that, while editing a particular drawing, you often use the Modify ➤ Rotate command to rotate objects 90°. Here are the steps for quickly creating a macro for this task, while in AutoCAD.

1. Open the Unit file and, at the command prompt, enter the following. Be sure you enter the line exactly as shown here. If you make a mistake while entering this line, use Backspace to remove your entry and start over.

   (defun C:R90 () (command "_rotate" pause "" "@" "90"))

2. Next, enter **R90** ↲. The ROTATE command will start and you will be prompted to select an object.

3. Click on the entry door. The door immediately rotates 90°, as shown in Figure 19.1.

You've just written and run your first AutoLISP macro! Let's take a closer look at this very simple program (see Figure 19.2). It starts out with an opening parenthesis, as do all AutoLISP programs, followed by the word *DEFUN*. Defun is an AutoLISP function that lets you create commands; it is followed by the name you want to give the command (R90 in this case). The command name is preceded by C:, telling Defun

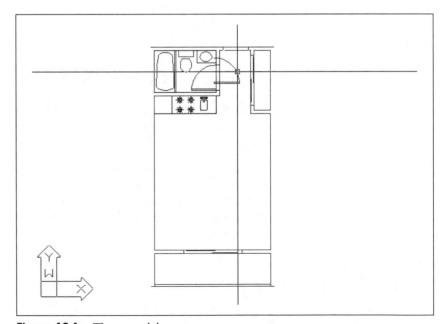

Figure 19.1: The rotated door

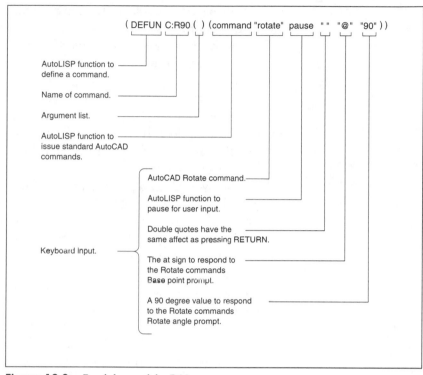

(DEFUN C:R90 ( ) (command "rotate" pause " " "@" "90"))

AutoLISP function to
define a command.

Name of command.

Argument list.

AutoLISP function to
issue standard AutoCAD
commands.

AutoCAD Rotate command.

AutoLISP function to
pause for user input.

Double quotes have the
same affect as pressing RETURN.

Keyboard Input.

The at sign to respond to
the Rotate commands
Base point prompt.

A 90 degree value to respond
to the Rotate commands
Rotate angle prompt.

Figure 19.2: Breakdown of the R90 macro

V

Customization—Taking
AutoCAD to the Limit

to make this command accessible from the command prompt. If the C: were omitted, you would have to start R90 using parentheses, as in **(R90)**.

After the command name is a set of open and closing parentheses. This encloses what is called the *argument list*. We won't go into detail about it here (you'll learn more about argument lists in *Chapter 20*); just be aware that these parentheses must follow the command name.

Finally, a list of words follows, enclosed by another set of parentheses. This list starts with the word *command*. Command is an AutoLISP function that tells AutoLISP that whatever follows should be entered just like regular keyboard input. Only one item in the R90 macro—the word *pause*—is not part of the keyboard input series. Pause is an AutoLISP function that tells AutoLISP to pause for input. In this particular macro, AutoLISP pauses to let you pick an object to rotate.

▼ NOTE

Notice that the rest of the program is nearly the exact set of keyboard entries needed to rotate a single object 90°.

Notice that most of the items in the macro are enclosed in quotation marks. Literal keyboard input must be enclosed in quotation marks in this way. The Pause function, on the other hand, does not require quotation marks, because it is a proper function, one that AutoLISP can recognize.

Finally, the program closes with two closing parentheses. All parentheses in an AutoLISP program must be in balanced pairs, so these two parentheses close the opening parenthesis at the start of the Command function and then the opening parenthesis way back at the beginning of the Defun function.

When you create a program at the command prompt, such as you did with this macro, AutoCAD remembers it only until you exit the current file. Unless you want to recreate this macro the next time you use Auto-CAD, you can save it by copying it into an ASCII text file with a .LSP extension, as shown in the following example, where I've saved the R90 macro along with some others I use often.

Figure 19.3 shows the contents of a file I've named Keycad.LSP. This file contains the macro you used above along with several others. The other macros are commands that include optional responses. For example, the third item, DEFUN C:ZP, would cause AutoCAD to return to a previous view by issuing the ZOOM command then automatically enter a P for the Previous option. Table 19.1 shows the command abbreviations and what they do.

```
(DEFUN C:R90 () (command "rotate" pause "" "@" "90"))
(DEFUN C:ZW () (command "zoom" "w"))
(DEFUN C:ZP () (command "zoom" "p"))
(DEFUN C:ZM () (command "zoom" "v"))
(DEFUN C:ST () (command "stretch" "c"))
(DEFUN C:FL () (command "fillet" "r" "0" "fillet"))
(DEFUN C:BR () (command "break" pause "F"))
(DEFUN C:MV (/ gp) (setq gp (ssget)) (command "move" gp "" "@"))
(DEFUN C:CO (/ gp) (setq gp (ssget)) (command "copy" gp "" "@"))
(DEFUN C:CH (/ gp) (setq gp (ssget)) (command "change" gp "" "P" "LA"))
(DEFUN C:MI (/ gp) (setq gp (ssget)) (command "mirror" gp "" pause pause "Y"))
```

Figure 19.3: The contents of Keycad.LSP

Table 19.1: The Shortcut Key (Command Abbreviations) Macros Provided by the Keycad.LSP File

Abbreviation	Command or Action Taken
R90	ROTATE object 90°
ZW	ZOOM Window
ZP	ZOOM Previous
MO	MOVE @
CO	COPY @
ST	STRETCH
FL	FILLET 0 radius
BR	BREAK F
CH	CHANGE Layer
MI	MIRROR Delete

Use your word processor and copy the listing in Figure 19.3. Give this file the name **Keycad.LSP,** and be sure you save it as an ASCII file. Then, whenever you want to use these macros you don't have to enter each one at the command prompt; instead, you load the Keycad.LSP file the first time you want to use one of the macros, and they're all available for the rest of the session. You load the macros file just as you loaded the sample AutoLISP files earlier in this chapter—that is, by entering

(load "keycad")

Once it is loaded, you can use any of the macros contained within it just by entering the macro name. For example, entering **CH** will start the CHANGE command.

Macros loaded in this manner will be available to you until you exit AutoCAD. Of course, you can have these macros loaded automatically every time you start AutoCAD by including the statement **(load "keycad")** in your Acad.LSP file. That way, you don't have to remember to load it in order to use it.

Now that you have some firsthand experience with AutoLISP, we hope these examples will encourage you to try learning more about this powerful tool. *Chapter 20* will continue our look at AutoLISP in more detail, but first let's explore some of AutoCAD's other hidden features.

NEW NAMES
FOR OLD COMMANDS

AutoCAD includes a file (Acad.PGP in the \acadr13\common\support subdirectory) that provides keyboard abbreviations or shortcuts, also known as *command aliases*—alternative names for commands. The ZOOM command, for example, has the alias of Z—you can enter **Z** at the command prompt, and ZOOM will start just as if you had entered the full name of the command or selected it from the menu.

You can easily create your own command aliases by editing the Acad.PGP file. Acad.PGP already has several aliases built into it. These are shown in Table 19.2.

Table 19.2: Standard Command Aliases in the Acad.PGP File

Standard Commands	
Alias	**Full Command Name**
A	ARC (Draw ➤ Arc)
C	CIRCLE (Draw ➤ Circle)
CP	COPY (Construct ➤ Copy)
DV	DVIEW (View ➤ 3D Dynamic View)
E	ERASE (Modify ➤ Erase)
L	LINE (Draw ➤ Line)
LA	LAYER (Data ➤ Layers)
M	MOVE (Modify ➤ Move)
MS	MSPACE (View ➤ Tiled Model Space)
P	PAN (View ➤ Pan)

Table 19.2: Standard Command Aliases in the Acad.PGP File (continued)

Standard Commands

Alias	Full Command Name
PS	PSPACE (View ➤ Paper Space)
PL	PLINE (Draw ➤ Polyline)
R	REDRAW (View ➤ Redraw View)
Z	ZOOM (View ➤ Zoom)
3DLINE	LINE (Draw ➤ Line)
SERIAL	_Pkser (*no pull-down equivalent*)

Dimensioning Commands

Alias	Full Command Name
DIMALI	DIMALIGNED
DIMANG	DIMANGULAR
DIMBASE	DIMBASELINE
DIMCEN	DIMCENTER
DIMCONT	DIMCONTINUE
DIMDIA	DIMDIAMETER
DIMED	DIMEDIT
DIMTED	DIMTEDIT
DIMLIN	DIMLINEAR
DIMORD	DIMORDINATE
DIMRAD	DIMRADIUS
DIMSTY	DIMSTYLE
DIMOVER	DIMOVERRIDE
LEAD	LEADER
TOL	TOLERANCE

V

Customization—Taking
AutoCAD to the Limit

You can modify the existing aliases or add some of your own to the Acad.PGP file by following the simple format presented there. First the alias is entered, followed by a comma and several spaces, and then the full command name preceded by an asterisk. Here is an example, using the ZOOM alias:

Z, *ZOOM

If you find you use some commands frequently, you may want to use this feature of AutoCAD to simplify your access to them. You cannot, however, create macros with Acad.PGP. For that, you will need to use AutoLISP or you will need to create custom palette buttons (see *Chapter 21* for more on customizing palettes and buttons).

USING THIRD-PARTY SOFTWARE

One of the most significant reasons for AutoCAD's popularity is its strong support for third-party software. AutoCAD is like a chameleon; it can change to suit its environment. Out of the box, AutoCAD may not fulfill the needs of some users. But by incorporating one of the over 300 third-party add-ons, you can tailor AutoCAD to your specific needs.

This section discusses a few of the third-party add-ons that are popular today, so you'll know about some of the possibilities open to you while using AutoCAD. Don't be discouraged if you don't see exactly what you need; covering all the different add-on programs is far beyond the scope of this text.

AUTOCAD-SPECIFIC FILE VIEWERS

Although there are several notable general-purpose file managers you can use with AutoCAD, the ones discussed here are aimed directly at AutoCAD users. These programs not only list drawing files but also let you view files without having to start up AutoCAD. Most AutoCAD viewing utilities offer direct plotting of files, multiple windows so you can view several files at once, block viewers that allow you to view blocks within drawings, zooming and panning of viewed files, file conversion, and much more.

▼ NOTE

The prices for these products range from $100 to $300. One product, *AutoManager* (Figure 19.4), is offered for OS/2 and Unix as well as MS-DOS.

Perhaps one of the greatest sources of resistance to using AutoCAD and CAD in general in an office environment is the fact that people not using the program directly are locked out from using and viewing drawing files. This is a source of concern especially for project managers and design firm principals who, with manual drafting techniques, can normally look over the shoulder of someone doing the drawing. With CAD, these people have less access to drawings, and therefore feel they have less control over the drawing production process.

AutoCAD file viewers remove the barriers between the drawings and the non-AutoCAD users. These applications allow non-AutoCAD users to examine AutoCAD files without having to learn AutoCAD. Because many viewers are, in fact, easy to learn, casual and non-AutoCAD users are no longer locked out of the AutoCAD world (see Figure 19.4).

V

Customization—Taking AutoCAD to the Limit

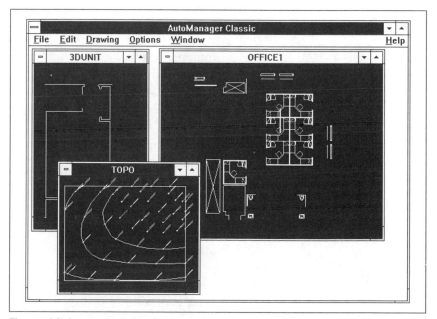

Figure 19.4: A sample screen from *Automanager* (Cyco International, Atlanta, Georgia)

A thorough discussion of all the AutoCAD viewers would require a chapter's worth of information, so we won't attempt that here. Many of the AutoCAD-related journals such as *Cadence* and *Cadalyst* have reviewed these products, so you can contact them for further details if you are interested. Here is a list of some of these viewers and their manufacturers' addresses.

Automanager
Cyco International
1908 Cliff Valley Way #2000
Atlanta, GA 30307
(404) 634-3302

Autoview
Marcomp
13 Laurienn #100
Parkton, MD 21120
(410) 343-2743

Autovue
Cimmetry Systems, Inc.
1430 Massachusetts Ave. #306
Cambridge, MA 02138-3810
(514) 735-3219

Drawing Librarian
SoftSource
301 W. Holly
Bellingham, WA 98225
(206) 676-0999

Fastlook for Windows
Kamel Software, Inc.
2822 Forsyth Rd., Ste. J101
Winter Park, FL 32792
(407) 672-0202

Quick-See
The Great Softwestern Co., Inc.
919 S. Carroll Blvd. #203
Denton, TX 76201
(817) 383-4434

Slick!
CAD Systems Unlimited, Inc.
5201 Great America Pkwy #443

Santa Clara, CA 95054
(408) 562-5762

ADDING FONTS TO AUTOCAD

Perhaps one of the first things AutoCAD users do to customize their systems is to add a set of fonts to replace AutoCAD's standard ones. There are probably more vendors of AutoCAD fonts than of any other type of add-on. Let's take a look at a few of the offerings.

Some third-party vendors offer a wide range of fonts, including Helvetica, Times Roman, and monospaced versions of Roman fonts. Two notable products, *Letterease* from CAD Lettering Systems and *Xfonts* from Autograf Utilities, offer accurate renditions of popular fonts in both out-line and solid forms. These fonts provide the near-typeset-quality text you need for applications in which the text appearance is important, in such elements as title blocks or special labels.

You can also obtain high-quality text by entering it with a desktop-publishing program, such as PageMaker or Ventura (see *Chapter 14*). Keep in mind, however, that your drawing size will be limited by the output size used by the desktop-publishing program.

As mentioned in *Chapter 8*, you can also use the hundreds of PostScript fonts offered by Adobe and other font foundries. There are even some public-domain and shareware PostScript fonts available on CompuServe.

▼ **NOTE**

If you would like more information on these products, contact *CAD Lettering Systems*, P.O. Box 850, Oldsmar, FL 34677; or *Autograf*, 608 Sonora Ave., Glendale, CA 91201.

V

Customization—Taking
AutoCAD to the Limit

CUSTOM-TAILORING AUTOCAD

▼ TIP

The companion CD includes a basic AEC add-on called *On-Screen AEC*. This add-on provides the basic tools for creating architectural CAD drawings, as well as some great utilities for your everyday use.

In addition to the third-party products we've described that are useful to virtually all AutoCAD users, some available products are aimed at specific types of AutoCAD applications. The needs of an architect, for example, are far different from those of a mechanical designer. Developers have created some specialized tools that help users of specific types of AutoCAD applications.

Most of these add-ons come complete with libraries of parts or symbols, AutoLISP and ADS programs, and menus—all integrated into a single package. These packages offer added functions to AutoCAD that simplify and speed up the AutoCAD user's work. For example, most AEC (architectural or engineering construction) add-ons offer utilities for drawing walls, inserting doors and windows, and creating schedules. These functions can be performed with the stock AutoCAD package but usually require a certain amount of effort. Certainly, you can create your own system of symbols, AutoLISP programs, and menus, and often this is the best way of molding AutoCAD to your needs, but when users want a ready-made solution, these add-ons are invaluable.

Specialized third-party add-ons are available for AEC, mechanical, civil engineering, piping, mapping, finite element analysis, numeric control, GIS, and many other applications. They can save you a good deal of frustration and time, especially if you find just the right one for your environment. Like so many things, however, third-party add-ons can't be all things to all people. It is likely that no matter what add-on you purchase, you will find something lacking. When you're considering custom add-ons, make sure that there is some degree of flexibility in the package, so if you don't like something, you can change it or add to it later.

THIRD-PARTY PRODUCT INFORMATION ON THE COMPANION CD

If you want to learn more about third-party offerings, the companion CD included with this book is a good place to start. There you'll find the complete *AutoCAD Resource Guide* from ICP Inc. This guide contains listings and information on virtually all the third-party products available for AutoCAD as of this book's publication. You can search for products using a variety of criteria and it's presented in a typical Windows Help format so you'll find it easy to use.

I've also included some convertible software from some of the third-party vendors that offer them. Convertible software is software that can be used for a limited time on a trial basis, or that has some features locked. You can try out the software, then if you decide you like it, you can purchase a code from the developer to unlock it. You also receive hardcopy documentation. So take some time to check out the CD. You may find the software you need, right at your fingertips!

AUTODESK'S OWN OFFERINGS

Autodesk itself offers products that can enhance your use of AutoCAD. In fact, a trial version of *AutoVision Release 2* is packaged with Auto-CAD. Here is a brief description of the Autodesk products aimed specifically at AutoCAD users.

AUTOVISION

AutoVision is a 3D rendering tool that offers photorealistic images from your 3D AutoCAD models. This product has a wide range of uses, from architectural rendering to mechanical design. Some of the features include:

- Camera-target-path animation

- Render-Crop Window

- Quick preview

- Controllable backgrounds

- Fog and depth Queing

- Animation players for both DOS and Windows

You get a trial version of AutoVision with your AutoCAD package. This trial version will work for 30 days, then you must purchase a registration code to continue to use it.

V

Customization—Taking
AutoCAD to the Limit

DESIGNER

Designer is package for the mechanical engineer. It is a parametric, feature-based solid modeling tool that automates the mechanical design process and simplifies the creation of 2D drafted documents. Designer features include:

- Design and editing through dimension control

- Automated creation of working drawings

- Association between solid models and working drawings

- Sketch mode to let you "rough in" your ideas

AUTOCAD DATA EXTENSION

The *AutoCAD Data Extension* or ADE is a unique product that extends AutoCAD functions into the realm of data management. Facilities managers can use it to isolate layers, blocks, or other objects in a set of drawing files. Civil engineers and cartographers can use it to greatly improve the time it takes to load drawing files and locate information. AEC professionals can use it to coordinate the different diciplines involved in large projects. Here are some further benefits of using ADE:

- Access multiple AutoCAD drawings simultaneously—make changes to several drawings at once

- Extract information from multiple drawings through a database query

- Combine features from several drawings to create a new drawing

- Isolate portions of a set of drawings

- Link AutoCAD graphics and database files easily

ADE is not the most glamorous Autodesk product, but it offers the tools that can use to open AutoCAD to a much bigger world that includes non-CAD information managers.

GETTING THE LATEST INFORMATION FROM ONLINE SERVICES

There are many resources available for the AutoCAD user. Perhaps the most useful can be found on today's popular online services. If you don't already subscribe to one, you would do well to get a modem and explore the AutoCAD newsgroups, departments, or "forums" in online services.

The Autodesk forum on *CompuServe* is an excellent source of useful AutoCAD-related utilities, as well as information about AutoCAD and other Autodesk products. You can often get the latest information on new products, updates, bug fixes, and more. To get to the Autodesk forum, type **GO ADESK** at the CompuServe ! prompt. Or, if you use WINCIM, choose Services ➤ Go... and enter **Adesk** at the Go dialog box. Once you are logged on, you will have a choice of the Autodesk AutoCAD, Multimedia, or Retail Products forums. You can also enter **Acad** at the Go dialog box to go directly to the AutoCAD forum.

Cadence offers its own forum on CompuServe. To access the Cadence forum on CompuServe, type **GO CADENCE** at CompuServe's ! prompt. Or, if you use WINCIM, choose Service ➤ Go... and then type **Cadence** at the Go dialog box. (Cadence also offers its own download only BBS which you can access without a CompuServe account. Connect to (415) 905-8130.)

Another online service that offers help to AutoCAD users is *America Online* (AOL). Although it doesn't offer a direct line to Autodesk, there is a forum for AutoCAD users to exchange ideas and troubleshooting tips. AOL also offers a library of AutoCAD-related utilities. To get to the AutoCAD folder in AOL, click on the Computing button at the Main menu after you have logged on. Then, in this order as the various windows appear, click on Computing, then Graphics & Animation, and then the Software Libraries button or the Message Board. The final step is to choose CAD from the list box.

IF YOU WANT TO EXPERIMENT...

Just for fun, you may want to try the AutoLISP program in Figure 19.5. This program is an AutoCAD version of a mathematical game used to

```
;function to find the midpoint between two points
(defun mid (a b)
 (list (/ (+ (car a)(car b)) 2)
       (/ (+ (cadr a)(cadr b)) 2)
 )
)

;function to generate random number
(defun rand (pt / rns rleng lastrn)
 (setq rns (rtos (* (car pt)(cadr pt)(getvar "tdusrtimer"))))
 (setq rnleng (strlen rns))
 (setq lastrn (substr rns rnleng 1))
 (setq rn (* 0.6 (atof lastrn)))
 (fix rn)
)

;The Chaos game
(defun C:CHAOS (/ pta ptb ptc rn count lastpt randn key)
 (princ "\nPick 3 points at random: ")
 (setq pta (getpoint))                              ;define point a
 (setq ptb (getpoint))                              ;define point b
 (setq ptc (getpoint))                              ;define point c
 (setq lastpt (getpoint "Pick a start point:"))     ;pick a point to start
 (while (/= key 3)                                   ;while pick button not pushed
  (setq randn (rand lastpt))                         ;get random number
  (cond                                              ;find midpoint to a b or c
   ( (= randn 0)(setq lastpt (mid lastpt pta)) )     ;use corner a if 0
   ( (= randn 1)(setq lastpt (mid lastpt pta)) )     ;use corner a if 1
   ( (= randn 2)(setq lastpt (mid lastpt ptb)) )     ;use corner b if 2
   ( (= randn 3)(setq lastpt (mid lastpt ptb)) )     ;use corner b if 3
   ( (= randn 4)(setq lastpt (mid lastpt ptc)) )     ;use corner c if 4
   ( (= randn 5)(setq lastpt (mid lastpt ptc)) )     ;use corner c if 5
  );end cond
  (grdraw lastpt lastpt 5)                           ;draw midpoint
  (setq key (car (grread T)))                        ;test for pick
 );end while
);end Chaos
```

Figure 19.5:   The Chaos.LSP program listing

determine how seemingly random events can create very nonrandom patterns. The game is described in Figure 19.6.

Carefully copy the program from the companion disk into your Auto-CAD directory. Load Chaos.LSP as you would load any other AutoLISP utility, and enter **Chaos**. You will be asked to pick a starting point. Pick any point on the screen and watch the pattern unfold. To exit the program, enter Esc or Ctrl-Break.

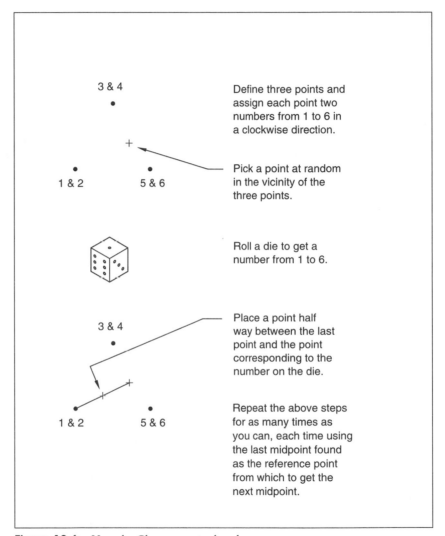

3 & 4

Define three points and
assign each point two
numbers from 1 to 6 in
a clockwise direction.

Pick a point at random
in the vicinity of the
three points.

1 & 2   5 & 6

Roll a die to get a
number from 1 to 6.

Place a point half
way between the last
point and the point
corresponding to the
number on the die.

3 & 4

Repeat the above steps
for as many times as
you can, each time using
the last midpoint found
as the reference point
from which to get the
next midpoint.

1 & 2   5 & 6

Figure 19.6:   How the Chaos game is played

20

▼ ▼ ▼ ▼ ▼

EXPLORING AUTOLISP

Using the AutoLISP Interpreter

Using Variables to Store Coordinates

Understanding Expressions and Arguments

Writing a Simple Program

Getting Input Interactively

Manipulating Data

Selecting Objects

Adding Decision-Making Functions

FAST TRACK

▽

937 ▶ To define a variable

Use the Setq function, followed by the variable name, and then the value you wish to assign to the variable. Example: **(setq *myvariable* 108)**.

942 ▶ To assign text to a variable

When assigning text to a variable, be sure to use double quotes (*""*) to enclose the text. Example: **(setq *myvariable* "This is text")**.

943 ▶ To assign coordinates to a variable

Enclose the coordinates in parentheses and precede the first (opening) parenthesis with a single quote. Example: **(setq *myvariable* '(1.0,2.0,3.0))**.

946 ▶ To set up a program to get point input from the user

Use the Getpoint function. For example, to prompt the user to select a point and store that point in a variable, use **(setq *myvariable* (getpoint "Select a point: "))**. The item enclosed in double quotes becomes the prompt. The point the user selects is assigned to *myvariable*.

948 ▶ To extract a coordinate from a coordinate list

Use the Nth function. For example, to extract the y coordinate from a variable that contains a coordinate list, use **(nth 1 *mycoordinate*)**, where *mycoordinate* is a varible that has been assigned a coordinate value. If *mycoordinate* equals (1.0 2.0 3.0), you will get the number 2.0 as the result of the sample expression. The 1 in the example indicates the second element of the coordinate list.

949 ▶ To combine elements into a list

Use the List function. For example, to combine three numbers into a coordinate list, use **(list 1.0 2.0 3.0)**, where each number following the List function is an x, y, or z coordinate. This will create the list (1.0 2.0 3.0). Text can also be combined into a list, but each text string must be enclosed in double quotes.

950 ► To set up a program to obtain text input from the user

Include the Getstring function. For example, to prompt the user to enter his or her name, use **(setq *username* (getstring "Enter your name: "))**, where *username* is the variable used to hold the person's name.

953 ► To set up a program to obtain a selection set from the user

Use the Ssget function. For example, to assign a set of objects to a variable, use **(setq *selections* (ssget))**. When AutoCAD executes this expression, the user is prompted to select objects. The user can then use all the standard selection options. Whenever the *selections* variable is called, the selected items will be used.

957 ► To have your program execute one expression or another based on a condition

Use the If function. For example, if you want to have AutoCAD start a line at a point only if a particular coordinate variable exists, use **(if *point1* (command "line" *point1*))**, where *point1* is the variable to be tested for.

960 ► To have your program repeat an expression or several expressions while a condition exists

Use the While function. For example, to have AutoCAD continue to obtain points from the user until the user presses ↵, use **(while *point1* (setq *point1* (getpoint "Pick a point: ")))**. When the user presses ↵, the variable *point1* is assigned a nil value, and While stops evaluating its arguments. You can include more than one expression within a While expression.

In the last chapter, you were introduced to AutoLISP, AutoCAD's macro and programming language. You learned that you can take advantage of this powerful tool without really having to know anything about its internal workings. In this chapter you'll see how you can take more control of AutoLISP and have it do the things you want to do for your own AutoCAD environment. You will learn how to store information such as text and point coordinates, how to create smart macros, and how to optimize AutoLISP's operation on your computer system.

A word of advice as you begin this chapter: Be prepared to spend lots of time with your computer—not because programming in AutoLISP is all that difficult, but because it is so addicting! You've already seen how easy it is to use AutoLISP programs. We won't pretend that learning to program in AutoLISP is just as easy as using it, but it really isn't as hard as you may think. And once you've created your first program, you'll be hooked.

UNDERSTANDING THE INTERPRETER

You access AutoLISP through the AutoLISP *interpreter*, which is a little like a hand-held calculator. When you enter information at the command prompt, the interpreter *evaluates* it and then returns an answer. *Evaluating* means performing the instructions described by the information you provide. You could say that evaluation means "find the value of." The information you give the interpreter is like a formula—called an *expression* in AutoLISP.

Let's examine the interpreter's workings in more detail.

1. Start AutoCAD and open a new file called **Temp20a**. You'll use this file just to experiment with AutoLISP, so don't worry about saving it.

2. At the command prompt, enter **(+ 2 2)** ↵. The answer, 4, appears on the prompt line. AutoLISP has *evaluated* the formula (+ 2 2) and returned the answer, 4.

By entering information this way, you can perform calculations or even write short programs on the fly.

The plus sign you used in step 2 represents a *function*—an instruction telling the AutoLISP interpreter what to do. In many ways it is like an AutoCAD command. A very simple example of a function is the math function, Add, represented by the plus sign. AutoLISP has many built-in functions, and you can create many of your own.

DEFINING VARIABLES WITH SETQ

Another calculator-like capability of the interpreter is its ability to remember values. You probably have a calculator that has some memory. This capability allows you to store the value of an equation for future use. In a similar way, the AutoLISP interpreter lets you store values using *variables*.

A variable is like a container that holds a value. That value can change many times in the course of a program's operation. You assign values to variables by using the *Setq* function. For example, let's assign the numeric value 1.618 to a variable named Golden. This value, often referred to as the *golden section*, is the ratio of a rectangular area's height to its width. Aside from having some interesting mathematical properties, the golden section is said to represent a ratio that occurs frequently in nature.

1. At the command prompt, enter **(setq Golden 1.618)** ↵. The value 1.618 appears just below the line you enter. The value of the Golden variable is now set to 1.618. Let's check it to make sure.

2. Enter **!Golden** ↵ at the command prompt. As expected, the value 1.618 appears at the prompt.

The exclamation point (!) acts as a special character that extracts the value of an AutoLISP variable at the prompt. From now until you quit AutoCAD, you can access the value of Golden at any time, by preceding the variable name with an exclamation point.

In addition to using math formulas as responses to prompts, you can also use values stored as variables in the same way. Let's see how we can use the variable Golden as the radius for a circle.

1. Click on the Circle Button on the Draw palette and select the Circle Center Radius Button.

2. At the center point prompt, pick a point in the center of your screen.

3. At the radius prompt, enter **!Golden** ↵. A circle appears with the radius of 1.618. Check this using the List option on the Object Properties toolbar (see Figure 20.1).

Numbers aren't the only things that can be stored with Setq. Let's take a look at the variety of other types of data that variables can represent.

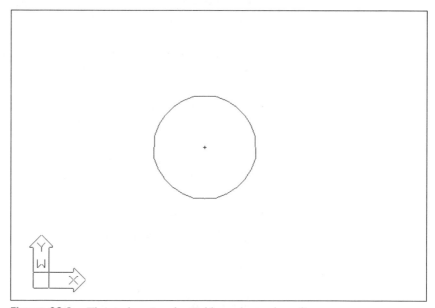

Figure 20.1:   The circle, using the Golden value as the radius

UNDERSTANDING DATA TYPES

Variables are divided into several categories called *data types*. Categorizing data into types lets AutoLISP determine precisely how to evaluate

It is important to understand the various data types and how they differ, because they can be a source of confusion if not carefully used. Remember that you cannot mix data types in most operations, and quotes and parentheses must always be used in open-and-closed pairs.

the data and keep programs running quickly. Your computer has different ways of storing various types of data, so the use of data types helps AutoLISP communicate with the computer more efficiently. Also, data types aid your programming efforts by forcing you to think of data as having certain characteristics. The following sections describe each of the available data types.

Integers

Integers are whole numbers. When a mathematical expression contains only integers, only an integer will be returned. For example, the expression

(/ 2 3)

means two divided by three (the forward slash is the symbol for the division function). This expression returns the value 0, because the answer is less than one. Integers are best suited for counting and numbering. The numbers 1, −12, and 144 are all integers.

Real Numbers

Often referred to as *reals*, *real numbers* are numbers that include decimals. When a mathematical expression contains a real number, a real number will be returned. For example, the expression

(/ 2.0 3)

returns the value 0.66667. Real numbers are best suited for situations where accuracy is important. Examples of real numbers are 0.1, 3.14159, and −2.2.

Strings

Strings are text values. They are always enclosed in double quotes. Here are some examples of strings: "1", "George", and "Enter a value".

Lists

Lists are groups of values enclosed in parentheses. Lists offer a convenient way to store whole sets of values in one variable. There are actually two classes of lists: those meant to be evaluated, and those intended as repositories for data. In the strictest sense, AutoLISP programs are lists, as they are enclosed in parentheses. Here are some examples of lists: (6.0 1.0 0.0), (A B C D), and (setq golden 1.618).

Elements

Finally, there are two basic elements in AutoLISP: *atoms* and *lists*. We have already described lists. An atom is an element that cannot be taken apart. Atoms are further grouped into two categories: *numbers* and *symbols*. A number can be a real number or an integer. A symbol, on the other hand, is often a name given to a variable, such as *point1* or *dx2*. As you can see, a symbol can use a number as part of its name; however, its name must always start with a letter. Think of a symbol as a name given to a variable or function as a means of identifying it.

USING ARGUMENTS AND EXPRESSIONS

In the previous exercise, you used the Setq function to store variables. The way you used Setq is a typical usage of all functions.

Functions act on *arguments* to accomplish a task. An argument can be a symbol, a number, or a list. A simple example of a function acting on numbers is the addition of 0.618 and 2. In AutoLISP, this function is entered as

(+ 0.618 2)

which returns the value 2.618.

This formula—the function followed by the arguments—is called an *expression*. It starts with the left (opening) parenthesis first, then the function, then the arguments, and finally the right (closing) parenthesis.

Arguments can also be expressions, which means you can *nest* expressions. For example, here is how to assign the value returned by 0.618 + 2 to the variable Golden:

(setq Golden (+ 0.618 2))

▼ NOTE

An expression is actually a list that contains a function and arguments for that function.

This is called a *nested expression*. Whenever expressions are nested, the deepest nest is evaluated first, then the next deepest, and so on. In this example, the expression adding 0.618 to 2 is evaluated first.

Arguments to functions can also be variables. For example, suppose you use Setq to assign the value 25.4 to a variable called Mill. You could then find the result of dividing Mill by Golden, as follows:

1. Enter **(setq Mill 25.4)** ↵ to create a new variable called Mill.

2. Next, enter **(/ Mill Golden)** ↵. (As mentioned earlier, the forward slash is the symbol for the division function.) This returns the value 15.698393. You can assign this value to yet another variable.

3. Enter **(setq B (/ Mill Golden))** ↵ to create a new variable, B. Now you have three variables—Golden, Mill, and B—which are all assigned values that you can later retrieve, either within an AutoCAD command (by entering an ! followed by the variable), or as arguments within an expression.

WATCHING PARENTHESES AND QUOTES

You must remember to close all sets of parentheses when using nested expressions. Take the same care to enter the second " in each pair of "" used to enclose a string.

If you get the prompt showing a number followed by the > symbol, for example,

        2>

you know you have an incomplete AutoLISP expression. This is the *AutoLISP prompt*. The number indicates the number of parentheses (or quotes) that are missing in your expression. If you see this prompt, you must type the closing parenthesis (or quotes) the number of times indicated by the number. AutoCAD will not evaluate an AutoLISP program that has the wrong number of parentheses or quotes.

USING TEXT VARIABLES WITH AUTOLISP

Our examples so far have shown numbers being manipulated, but text can also be manipulated in a similar way. Variables can be assigned text strings that can later be used to enter values in commands requiring text input. For text variables, you must enclose text in quotation marks, as in the following example:

    (setq text1 "This is how text looks in AutoLISP")

This example shows a sentence being assigned to the variable *text1*.

Strings can also be *concatenated*, or joined together, to form new strings. Here is an example of how two pieces of text can be added together:

    (setq text2 (strcat "This is the first part and " "this is the second part"))

Here, the AutoLISP function *strcat* is used to join the two strings. The result is

    "This is the first part and this is the second part"

Strings and numeric values cannot be evaluated together, however. This may seem like a simple rule, but if not carefully considered it can lead to confusion. For example, it is possible to assign the number 1 to a variable as a text string, by entering

    (setq foo "1")

Later, you may accidentally try to add this string variable to an integer or real number, and AutoCAD will return an error message.

The Setq and the addition and division functions are but three of many functions available to you. AutoLISP offers all the usual math functions, plus many others used to test and manipulate variables. Table 20.1 shows some commonly used math functions.

Table 20.1: Math Functions Available in AutoLISP

Functions That Accept Multiple Arguments	
Function	**Operation**
(+ *number number* ...)	Add
(− *number number* ...)	Subtract
(* *number number* ...)	Multiply
(/ *number number* ...)	Divide
(Max *number number* ...)	Find largest number in list
(Min *number number* ...)	Find smallest number in list
(Rem *number number* ...)	Find the remainder of numbers

Functions That Accept Single Arguments	
Function	**Operation**
(1+ *number*)	Add 1 to number
(1− *number*)	Subtract 1 from number
(Abs *number*)	Find the absolute value of number
(Atan *angle in radians*)	Arc tangent of angle
(Cos *angle in radians*)	Cosine of angle
(Exp *n*)	*e* raised to the nth power
(Expt *number n*)	*Number* raised to the nth power
(Gcd *integer integer*)	Find greatest common denominator
(Log *number*)	Find natural log of number
(Sin *angle in radians*)	Sine of angle
(Sqrt *number*)	Find the square root of number

STORING POINTS AS VARIABLES

Like numeric values, point coordinates can also be stored and retrieved. But since coordinates are actually sets of two or three numeric values, they have to be handled differently. AutoLISP provides the *Getpoint* function to handle the acquisition of points. Try the following to see how it works.

1. At the command prompt, enter **(getpoint)** ↵. The command prompt will go blank momentarily.

2. Pick a point near the middle of the screen. In the prompt area, you'll see the coordinate of the point you picked.

Here, Getpoint pauses AutoCAD and waits for you to pick a point. Once you do, it returns the coordinate of the point you pick in the form of a list. The list shows the x-, y-, and z-axes enclosed by parentheses.

You can store the coordinates obtained from Getpoint using the Setq function. Try the following to see how this works.

1. Enter **(setq point1 (getpoint))** ↵.

2. Pick a point on the screen.

3. Enter **!point1** ↵.

Here you stored a coordinate list in a variable called *point1*. You then recalled the contents of point1 using the !. Notice that the value of the coordinate is in the form of a list with the x, y, and z values appearing as real numbers separated by spaces, instead of the commas you've been used to.

CREATING A SIMPLE PROGRAM

So far, you have learned how to use AutoLISP to do some simple math and to store values as variables. Certainly, AutoLISP has enormous value with these capabilities alone, but you can do a good deal more. In this section, you'll examine how to combine these three capabilities—math calculations, variables, and lists—to write a simple program for drawing a rectangle.

1. First, use the F2 key to flip to a text display.

2. At the command prompt, enter **(defun c:rec ()** ↵. You will get a new prompt that looks like this:

    1>

This is the AutoLISP prompt. It tells you, among other things, that you are in the AutoLISP interpreter. While you see this prompt, you can enter instructions to AutoLISP. You will automatically exit the interpreter when you have finished entering the program. A program is considered complete when you've entered the last parenthesis, thereby balancing all the parentheses in your program.

▼ **WARNING**

While you're entering lines in AutoLISP, once you press ↵, you cannot go back to change a line.

3. Now, very carefully, enter the following several lines. If you make a mistake while typing a line, back up using Backspace and retype the line. Once you press ↵, you cannot go back to fix a line. Each time you enter a line and press ↵, you will see the AutoLISP prompt appear.

```
(setq Pt1 (getpoint "Pick first corner point:" )) ↵
(setq Pt3 (getpoint "Pick opposite corner:" )) ↵
(setq Pt2 (list (nth 0 Pt3) (nth 1 Pt1))) ↵
(setq Pt4 (list (nth 0 Pt1) (nth 1 Pt3))) ↵
(command "Pline" Pt1 Pt2 Pt3 Pt4 "C") ↵
) ↵
```

▼ **NOTE**

AutoLISP is not *case sensitive*. It doesn't matter if you type entries in upper- or lowercase letters. They will work either way. The only time you must be careful with upper- and lowercase is when you use string data types.

Once you enter the last parenthesis, you return to the standard AutoCAD command prompt.

4. Check the lines you have entered against the listing in step 3, and make sure you entered everything correctly. If you find you made a mistake, start over from the beginning and reenter the program.

▼ **TIP**

You can use AutoLISP programs transparently, as long as the program doesn't contain an embedded AutoCAD command.

When you are done, you get the message C:REC. This confirms that you have the rectangle drawing program stored in memory. Let's see it in action.

1. Enter **Rec** ↵ at the command prompt.

2. At the Pick first corner point prompt, pick a point at coordinate 1,1.

3. At the Pick opposite corner prompt, pick a point at 6,4. A box appears between the two points you picked (see Figure 20.2).

V

Customization—Taking
AutoCAD to the Limit

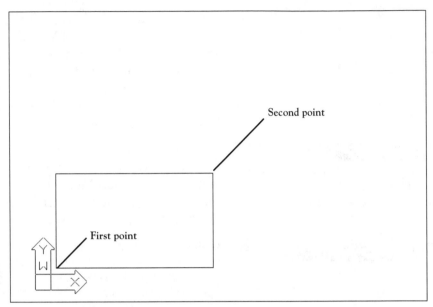

Figure 20.2: Using the rectangle drawing program

DISSECTING THE RECTANGLE PROGRAM

The Rectangle drawing program incorporates all the things you've learned so far. Let's see exactly how it works. First, it finds the two corner coordinates of a rectangle, which it gets from you as input, and then extracts parts of those coordinates to derive the coordinates for the other two corners of the rectangle. Once it knows all four coordinates, the program can draw the lines connecting them. Figure 20.3 illustrates what the Rectangle program does. Next, we'll look at the program in more detail.

Getting Input from the User

In the foregoing exercise, you started out with the line

```
(defun c:rec ()
```

You may recall from *Chapter 19* that the Defun function lets you create commands. The name that follows the Defun function is the name of

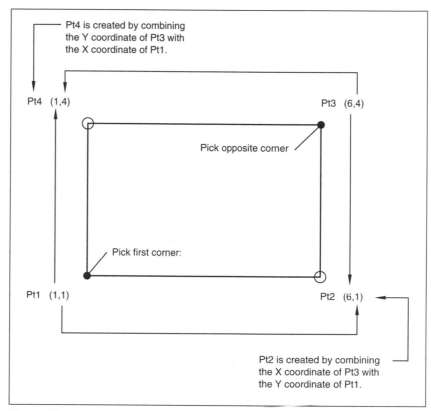

Figure 20.3: The Rectangle program draws a rectangle by getting two corner points of the rectangle from you, and then re-combining coordinates from those two points to find the other two points of the rectangle.

the command as you enter it through the keyboard. The c: tells AutoLISP to make this program act like a command. If the c: is omitted, you would have to enter **(rec)** to view the program. The set of empty parentheses is for an argument list, which we'll discuss later.

In the next line, the variable Pt1 is assigned a value for a point you enter using your cursor. Getpoint is the AutoLISP function that pauses the AutoLISP program and allows you to pick a point using your cursor, or to enter a coordinate. Once a point is entered, Getpoint returns the coordinate of that point as a list.

Immediately following Getpoint is a line that reads

"Pick first corner point:"

Getpoint allows you to add a prompt in the form of text. You may recall that when you first used Getpoint, it caused the prompt to go blank. Instead of a blank, you can use text as an argument to the Getpoint function to display a prompt describing what action to take.

The third line is similar to the second. It uses Getpoint to get the location of another point, and then assigns that point to the variable Pt3:

```
(setq Pt3 (getpoint "Pick opposite corner:" ))
```

Once AutoLISP has the two corners, it has all the information it needs to find the other two corners of the rectangle.

Taking Apart Lists

The next thing AutoLISP must do is take Pt1 and Pt3 apart to extract their x and y coordinates, and then re-assemble those coordinates to get the other corner coordinates. AutoLISP must take the x coordinate from Pt3, and the y coordinate from Pt1, to get the coordinate for the lower-right corner of the rectangle (see Figure 20.3). To do this, you use two new functions: *Nth* and *List*.

Nth extracts a single element from a list. Since coordinates are lists, Nth can be used to extract an x, y, or z component from a coordinate list. In the fourth line of the program, you see

```
(nth 0 Pt3)
```

Here the zero immediately following the Nth function tells Nth to take element number 0 from the coordinate stored as Pt3. Nth starts counting from 0 rather than 1, so the first element of Pt3 is considered item number 0. This is the x component of the coordinate stored as Pt3.

To see firsthand how Nth works, try the following:

1. Enter **!point1** ↵. You see the coordinate list you created earlier using Getpoint.

2. Enter **(nth 0 point1)** ↵. You get the first element of the coordinate represented by point1.

Immediately following the first Nth expression is another Nth expression similar to the previous one:

(nth 1 Pt1)

Here, Nth extracts element number 1, the second element, from the coordinate stored as Pt1. This is the y component of the coordinate stored as Pt1. If you like, try the previous exercise again, but this time, enter **(nth 1 point1)** and see what value you get.

Combining Elements into a List

AutoLISP has extracted the x component from Pt3, and the y component of Pt1. They must now be joined together into a new list. This is where the List function comes in. The List expression looks like this:

(list (nth 0 pt3) (nth 1 pt1))

You know that the first Nth expression extracts an x component, and the second extracts a y component, so the expression can be simplified to look like this:

(list X Y)

Here X is the value derived from the first Nth expression, and Y is the value derived from the second Nth expression. The List function simply recombines its arguments into another list, in this case another coordinate list.

Finally, the outermost function of the expression uses Setq to create a new variable called Pt2, which is the new coordinate list derived from the List function. The following is a schematic version of the fourth line of the Rectangle program, so you can see what is going on more clearly.

(setq pt2 (list X Y))

You can see that Pt2 is a coordinate list derived from combining the x component from Pt3 and the y component from Pt1.

Try the following exercise to see how List works.

1. Enter **(list 5 6)** ↲. You see the list (5 6) appear in the prompt.

2. Enter **(list (nth 0 point1) (nth 1 point1))** ↲. You see the x and y coordinates of point1 in a list, excluding the z coordinate.

The fifth line is similar to the fourth. It creates a new coordinate list using the x value from pt1 and the y value from pt2:

    (setq Pt4 (list (nth 0 Pt1) (nth 1 Pt3)))

The last line tells AutoCAD to draw a polyline through the four points to create a box:

    (command "Pline" Pt1 Pt2 Pt3 Pt4 "c")

The Command function issues the PLINE command and then inputs the variables Pt1 through Pt4. Finally, it enters **c** to close the polyline. Note that within this expression, keystrokes entries, like "PLINE" and "c", are enclosed in quotes.

GETTING OTHER INPUT FROM THE USER

In your Rectangle program, you were able to prompt the user to pick some points by using the Getpoint function. There are several other functions that allow you to pause for input and instruct the user what to do. Nearly all of these functions begin with the Get prefix.

Table 20.2 shows a list of these Get functions. They accept single values or, in the case of points, a list of two values.

In Getstring, string values are case sensitive. This means that if you enter a lowercase letter in response to Getstring, it will be saved as a lowercase letter; uppercase letters will be saved as uppercase letters. You can enter numbers in response to the Getstring function, but they will be saved as strings and cannot be used in mathematical operations. Also, AutoLISP will automatically add quotes to string values it returns, so you don't have to enter any.

Table 20.2: Functions That Pause to Allow Input

Function	Description
Getint	Allows entry of integer values
Getreal	Allows entry of real values
Getstring	Allows entry of string or text values
Getkword	Allows filtering of string entries through a list of keywords
Getangle	Allows keyboard or mouse entry of angles based on the standard AutoCAD compass points (returns values in radians)
Getorient	Allows keyboard or mouse entry of angles based on UNITS command setting for angles (returns values in radians)
Getdist	Allows keyboard or mouse entry of distances (always returns values as real numbers, regardless of unit format used)
Getpoint	Allows keyboard or mouse entry of point values (returns values as coordinate lists)
Getcorner *	Allows selection of a point by using a window
Initget	Allows definition of a set of keywords for the Getkword function; keywords are strings, as in (initget " Yes No ")

* This function requires a base point value as a first argument. This base point defines the first corner of the window. A window appears, allowing you to select the opposite corner.

Just as with Getpoint, all these Get functions allow you to create a prompt by following the function with the prompt enclosed by quotation marks, as in the expression

(getpoint "Pick the next point:")

This expression causes the prompt Pick the next point to be displayed while AutoCAD waits for your input.

Customization—Taking
AutoCAD to the Limit

V

The functions Getangle, Getorient, Getdist, Getcorner, and Getpoint allow you to specify a point from which the angle, distance, or point is to be measured, as in the expression

(getangle Pt1 "Pick the next point:")

where Pt1 is a previously defined point variable. A rubber-banding line appears from the coordinate defined by Pt1 (see Figure 20.4).

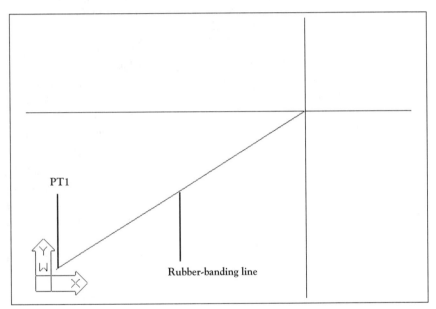

Figure 20.4:   Using Getangle

Once you pick a point, the angle defined by Pt1 and the point you pick are returned in radians. You can also enter a relative coordinate through the keyboard in the unit system currently being used in your drawing. Getangle and Getdist prompt you for two points if a point variable is not provided. Getcorner always requires a point argument and will generate a window rather than a rubber-banding line (see Figure 20.5).

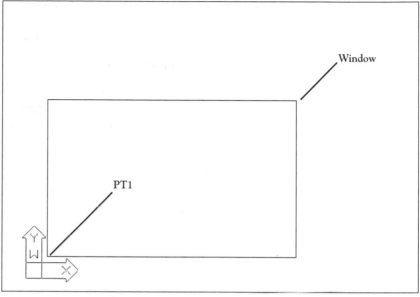

Figure 20.5: Using Getcorner

SELECTING OBJECTS WITH AUTOLISP

In *Chapter 19*, you worked with a simple AutoLISP macro that rotated a single object 90°. While it did the job, the macro was limited—you could only select a single object to rotate. What if you wanted to have that macro rotate a set of objects instead of just one? At this point, you know enough to create a program to do just that. The only part missing is how to get AutoLISP to select several objects instead of just one. For this, you need Ssget.

THE SSGET FUNCTION

So far, you know you can assign numbers, text, and coordinates to variables. Ssget is a function that assigns a set of objects to a variable, as demonstrated in the following exercise:

1. Draw a few random lines on the screen.

2. Enter **(setq ss1 (ssget))** ↲.

3. At the Select objects prompt, select the lines using any standard selection method. Notice that you can select objects just as you would at any object-selection prompt.

4. When you are done selecting objects, press ↲. You get the message <Selection set: *n*> where *n* is an integer value.

5. Start the MOVE command, and at the object-selection prompt, enter **!ss1** ↲. The lines you selected previously will be highlighted.

6. Press ↲, then pick two points to finish the MOVE command.

In this exercise, you stored a selection set as the variable Ss1. You can recall this selection set from the command prompt, using the !, just as you did with other variables.

USING SSGET IN AN EXPRESSION

You can also use the Ss1 variable in an AutoLISP expression. For example, the R90 macro you created in *Chapter 19* could be modified to accommodate the selection of several objects. In the following exercise, it is rewritten to include the Ssget function:

1. Enter **(defun c:R90 (/   ss1)** ↲. The AutoLISP prompt appears.

2. To complete the macro, enter

   (setq ss1 (ssget))(command "rotate" ss1 "" pause "90"))

   and press ↲.

3. Enter **R90** ↲ to start the macro.

4. At the Select objects prompt, select a few of the random lines you drew earlier.

5. Press ↵ to confirm your selection, and then pick a point near the center of the screen. The lines you selected rotate 90°.

This macro starts out in the same way as the one in *Chapter 19*. The Defun function tells AutoLISP this is to be a command called R90. A list follows the name of the macro—it's called an *argument list*. We'll look at argument lists a bit later in this chapter.

Following the argument list is the (setq ss1 (ssget)) expression you used in the previous exercise. This is where the new macro stops and asks you to select a set of objects to be applied later to the ROTATE command.

The next expression uses the Command function described in *Chapter 19*. Command lets you include standard command line input within an AutoLISP program. In this case, the input starts by issuing the ROTATE command. Then it applies the selection set stored by Ss1 to the ROTATE command's object-selection prompt. Next, the two "" marks indicate a ↵. The *pause* lets the user select a base point for the rotation. Finally, the value of 90 is applied to the ROTATE command's angle prompt. The entire expression when entered at the command prompt might look like the following:

```
Command: Rotate ↵
Select objects: !Ss1 ↵
Select objects: ↵
Base point: (pause for input)
< Rotation angle >/Reference: 90 ↵
```

In this macro, the Ssget function adds flexibility by allowing the user to select as many objects as desired. (You could use the Pause function in place of the variable SS1, but with Pause, you cannot anticipate whether the user will use a window, pick points, or select a previous selection set.)

MEMORY
LIMITATIONS OF SELECTION SETS

Although you can have virtually an unlimited number of variables in a program, you are limited to 128 selection-set variables. If the number exceeds 128, AutoCAD will not allow further selection of objects. If this situation occurs, you must set some of the selection-set variables to nil, and then use the GC (Garbage Collection) function to clear the unused variables from memory. Here is a sample line of AutoLISP code that will free selection sets from memory:

```
(setq ss1 nil ss2 nil ss3 nil...) (GC) ↵
```

This example demonstrates three things: First, you can assign values to more than one variable using the Setq function. In this example, several selection-set variables are set to nil. This is done by alternating the variables and values in the Setq expression. Second, you can assign a variable the nil value. Finally, the GC function has no arguments at all. Its sole purpose is to free your system of unused memory segments, called *nodes*. A full discussion of nodes is beyond the scope of this book. Just be aware that GC, used in conjunction with setting selection-set variables to nil, will free up memory.

CONTROLLING MEMORY
CONSUMPTION WITH LOCAL VARIABLES

Selection sets are memory hogs in AutoLISP. You don't want to create too many of them or you will end up draining AutoLISP's memory reserves. To limit the memory used by selection sets, you can turn them into *local variables*. Local variables are variables that only exist while the program is executing its instructions. Once the program is finished, local variables are discarded.

The vehicle for making variables local is the argument list. Let's look again at the set of empty parentheses that immediately follow the program name in the Rectangle program:

(defun c:rec ()...)

If you include a list of variables between those parentheses, those variables become local. In the new R90 macro you just looked at, the Ss1 selection set variable is a local variable:

(defun c:R90 (/ ss1)...)

Notice that the argument list starts with a forward slash, then a space, followed by the list of variables. Once the R90 program is done with its work, any memory assigned to Ss1 can be recovered.

Sometimes you will want a variable to be accessible at all times by all AutoLISP programs. Such variables are known as *global variables*. You can use global variables to store information in the current editing session. You could even store a few selection sets as global variables. To control memory consumption, however, use global variables sparingly.

V

Customization—Taking
AutoCAD to the Limit

CONTROLLING THE FLOW OF AN AUTOLISP PROGRAM

A typical task for a program to perform is to execute one function or another depending on some existing condition. This type of operation is often called an *if-then-else conditional statement:* "If a condition is met, then perform computation A, else perform computation B." AutoLISP offers the If function to facilitate this type of operation.

USING THE IF FUNCTION

The If function requires two arguments. The first argument must be a value that returns a True or a False—in the case of AutoLISP, *T* for true or *nil* for false. It is like saying "If True then do A." Optionally, you can supply a third argument, which is the action to take if the value returned is nil. ("If True then do A, else do B.")

Here is an example of an If expression:

(if Exst (+ a b) (* a b))

Here, the value of the Exst variable determines which of the two following expressions is evaluated. If Exst has a value, then it returns T for true; that is, when AutoLISP evaluates Exst, the value returned is T. The expression then evaluates the second argument, (+ a b), which is itself an expression. If Exst does not have a value or is nil, then the expression evaluates the third argument, (* a b).

Several special AutoLISP functions test variables for specific conditions. For example, you can test a number to see if it is equal to, less than, or greater than another number, as in the following:

(if (= A B) (+ A B) (* A B))

In this expression, if A equals B, then the second argument is evaluated:

(if (> A B) (+ A B) (* A B))

In this expression, if A is greater than B, then the second argument is evaluated.

The functions that test for T or nil are called *predicates* and *logical operators*. Table 20.3 shows a list of these functions.

Let's see how conditional statements, predicates, and logical operators work together. Suppose you want to write a program that either multiplies two numbers or simply adds the numbers together. You want the program to ask the user which action to take depending on which of the two values is greater.

1. Enter the following program at the command prompt, just as you did for the Rectangle program.

   ```
   (defun c:mul-add () ↵
   (setq A (getreal "Enter first number:" )) ↵
   (setq B (getreal "Enter second number:" )) ↵
   (if (< A B) (+ a b) (* a b)) ↵
   ) ↵
   ```

Table 20.3: A List of Predicates and Logical Operators

Function	Returns T (True) If...
<	One numeric value is less than another
>	One numeric value is greater than another
<=	One numeric value is less than or equal to another
>=	One numeric value is greater than or equal to another
=	Two numeric or string values are equal
/=	Two numeric or string values are not equal
eq	Two values are exactly the same
equal	Two values are the same (approximate)
atom	A symbol represents an atom (as opposed to a list)
listp	A symbol represents a list
minusp	A numeric value is negative
numberp	A symbol is a number, real or integer
zerop	A symbol evaluates to zero
and	All of several expressions or atoms return non-nil
not	A symbol is nil
nul	A list is nil
or	One of several expressions or atoms returns non-nil

2. Now run the program by entering **Mul-add** ↵.

3. At the Enter first number prompt, enter **3** ↵.

4. At the Enter second number prompt, enter **4** ↵. The value 7.0 is returned.

5. Try running this program again, but this time enter **4** at the first prompt and **3** at the second prompt. This time, you get the returned value 12.0.

In this program, the first two Setq expressions get two numbers from you. The conditional statement that follows, (< A B), tests to see if the first number you entered is less than the second. If this predicate function returns T for true, then (+ a b) is evaluated. If it returns nil for false, then (* a b) is evaluated.

You will often find that you need to perform not just one, but several steps depending on some condition. Here is a more complex If expression that evaluates several expressions at once:

(if (= A B) (progn (* A B)(+ A B)(- A B)))

In this example, the function Progn tells the If function that several expressions are to be evaluated if (= A B) returns True.

REPEATING AN EXPRESSION

Sometimes you will want your program to repeatedly evaluate a set of expressions until a particular condition is met. If you are familiar with BASIC or Fortran, you know this function as a *loop*.

You can repeat steps in an AutoLISP program by using the While function in conjunction with predicates and logical operators. Like the If function, While's first argument must be one that returns a T or nil. You can have as many other arguments to the While function as you like, just as long as the first argument is a predicate function.

(while test (expression 1) (expression 2) (expression 3)...)

The While function isn't the only one that will repeat a set of instructions. The Repeat function causes a set of instructions to be executed several times, but unlike While, Repeat requires an integer value for its second value, as in the following:

(Repeat 14 (expression 1)(expression 2)(expression 3)...)

In this example, Repeat will evaluate each expression 14 times.

A third function, Foreach, evaluates an expression for each element of a list. The arguments to Foreach are first a variable, then a list whose elements are to be evaluated, then the expression used to evaluate each element of the list.

(foreach var1 (list1) (expression var1))

Foreach is a bit more difficult to understand at first, since it involves a variable, a list, and an expression, all working together.

USING OTHER BUILT-IN FUNCTIONS

▼ NOTE

In many of the examples in this section, you'll see numeric values or lists as arguments. As in all AutoLISP functions, you can use variables as arguments, as long as the variable's value is of the proper data type.

At this point, you have seen several useful programs created with just a handful of AutoLISP functions. Although we can't give you a tutorial showing you how to use every available AutoLISP function, in this final section we'll demonstrate a few more. This is far from a complete list, but it should be enough to get you well on your way to making AutoLISP work for you. Experiment with the functions at your leisure—but remember, using AutoLISP can be addicting!

GEOMETRIC OPERATIONS

These functions are useful for manipulating geometric data. (And don't forget the Get functions listed earlier, in Table 20.2.)

Angle

▼ NOTE

Notice that in some examples an apostrophe precedes a list. This apostrophe tells AutoLISP not to evaluate the list, but to treat it as a repository of data.

The Angle function finds the angle between two points, and returns a value in radians. For example,

    (angle '(6.0 4.0 0.0) '(6.0 5.0 0.0))

returns 1.57. This example uses two coordinate lists for arguments, but point variables can also be used.

Distance

The Distance function finds the distance between two points. The value returned is in base units. Just like Angle, Distance requires two coordinates as arguments. This expression

    (distance '(6.0 4.0 0.0) '(6.0 5.0 0.0))

returns 1.0.

V

Customization—Taking
AutoCAD to the Limit

Polar

The Polar function returns a point in the form of a coordinate list based on the location of a point, an angle, and a distance. This expression

(polar '(1.0 1.0 0.0) 1.5708 1.0)

returns (0.999996 2.0 0.0). The first argument is a coordinate list; the second is an angle in radians; and the third is a distance in base units. The point must be a coordinate list.

Inters

The Inters function returns the intersection point of two vectors, with each vector described by two points. The points must be in this order: the first two points define the first vector, and the second two points define the second vector. This expression

```
(inters
'(1.0 4.0 0.0)'(8.0 4.0 0.0)'(5.0 2.0 0.0)'(5.0 9.0 0.0)
)
```

returns (5.0 4.0 0.0). If the intersection point does not lie between either of the two vectors, you can still obtain a point, provided you include a non-nil fifth argument.

STRING OPERATIONS

These functions allow you to manipulate strings. Though you cannot supply strings to the text command directly, you can use the Command function with string variables to enter text, as in the following:

```
(Setq note "This is a test.")
(command "text" point "2.0" "0" note )
```

In this example, *note* is first assigned a string value. Then the command function is used to issue the TEXT command and place the text in the drawing.

Substr

The Substr function returns a portion of a string, called a *substring*, beginning at a specified location. This expression

> (substr "string" 3 4)

returns *ring*. The first argument is the string containing the substring to be extracted. The second argument, 3, tells Substr where to begin the new string; this value must be an integer. The third argument, 4, is optional and tells Substr how long the new string should be. Length must also be an integer.

Strcat

The Strcat function combines several strings, and the result is a string. This expression

> (strcat string1 string2 etc....)

returns *string1 string2 etc....* In this example, the

> etc....

indicates you can have as many string values as you want.

DATA-TYPE CONVERSIONS

▼ TIP

The Angtos and Rtos functions are especially useful for converting radians to any of the standard angle formats available in AutoCAD. For example, using Angtos you can convert 0.785398 radians to 45.0, 45d0'0", or N 45d0'0" E. Using Rtos you can convert the distance value of 42 to 42.00 or 3'–6".

While using AutoLISP, you will often have to convert values from one data type to another. For example, since most angles in AutoLISP must be represented in radians, you must convert them to degrees before you can use them in commands. This can be accomplished by using the Angtos function. Angtos will convert a real number representing an angle in radians, into a string in the degree format you desire. The following example converts an angle of 1.57 radians into surveyor's units with a precision of four decimal places:

> (angtos 1.57 4 4)

V

Customization—Taking
AutoCAD to the Limit

This expression returns *N 0d2'44" E*. The first argument is the angle in radians; the second argument is a code that tells AutoLISP which format to convert the angle to; and the third argument tells AutoLISP the degree of precision desired. (The third argument is optional.) The conversion codes for Angtos are as follows:

0 = degrees

1 = degrees/minutes/seconds

2 = grads

3 = radians

4 = surveyor's units

Now that you've seen an example of what the Angtos data-type conversion can do, let's briefly look at other similar functions.

Atof and Atoi

Atof converts a string to a real number. The expression

        (atof "33.334")

returns 33.334.

Atoi converts a string to an integer. The expression

        (atoi "33.334")

returns 33.

Itoa and Rtos

Itoa converts an integer into a string. The argument must be an integer. The expression

        (itoa 24)

returns 24.

Rtos converts a real number to a string. As with Angtos, a format code and precision value is specified. The expression

(rtos 32.3 4 2)

returns 2′–8 ¼″. The first argument is the value to be converted; the second argument is the conversion code; and the third argument is the precision value. The codes are as follows:

1 = scientific

2 = decimal

3 = engineering

4 = architectural

5 = fractional

Fix and Float

Fix converts a real number into an integer. The expression

(fix 3.3334)

returns 3.

Float converts an integer into a real number. The expression

(float 3)

returns 3.0.

STORING YOUR PROGRAMS AS FILES

▼ WARNING

If you haven't saved the Rectangle program as file, you will have to enter it the Box program from the keyboard as you did in the earlier exercise.

When you exit AutoCAD, the Rectangle program will vanish. But just as you were able to save the keyboard shortcuts in *Chapter 19*, you can create an ASCII file on a disk containing the Rectangle program, or add it to your Acad.LSP file. That way you will have ready access to it at all times.

V

Customization—Taking AutoCAD to the Limit

To save your programs, open a text editor and enter them through the keyboard just as you entered the Rectangle program, including the first line that contains the Defun function. Be sure you save the file with the .LSP file name extension. Then you can recall your program using Tools ➤ Applications which opens the Load AutoLISP, ADS, and ARX Files dialog box.

If you prefer, you can use the manual method for loading AutoLISP programs. This involves the Load AutoLISP function. Just as with all other functions, it is enclosed by parentheses. In *Chapter 19*, you loaded the Chroma.LSP file using the Load AutoLISP, ADS, and ARX Files dialog box. To use the Load function, instead, to load Chroma.LSP, you would enter the following:

    (Load "Chroma")

Load is perhaps one of the simpler AutoLISP functions, since it requires only one argument: the name of the AutoLISP file you want to load. Notice that you do not have to include the .LSP extension.

If the AutoLISP file resides in a directory that isn't in the current path, you need to include the path in the file name, as in the following:

    (Load "c:/acadr13/common/sample/chroma")

Notice that the / is used to indicate directories instead of the usual DOS \. The forward slash is used because the backslash has special meaning to AutoLISP in a string value. It tells AutoLISP that a special character follows. If you attempted to use \ in the above example, you would get an error message.

As you might guess, the Load function can be a part of an AutoLISP program. It can also be included as part of a menu to load specific programs whenever you select a menu item. You'll learn more about customizing the menu in the next chapter.

WHERE TO GO FROM HERE

I hope that you will be enticed into trying some programming on your own and learning more about AutoLISP. For a more detailed look at AutoLISP, review your AutoCAD documentation. Although AutoLISP is somewhat different from other forms of LISP, you may consider studying LISP for background. Versions are available for the PC, and there are a few good introductory books on the subject. *LISP: A Gentle Introduction to Symbolic Computation*, by David S. Touretzky (Harper & Row, 1984), and *Common LISPcraft*, by Robert Wilensky (W. W. Norton & Company, 1987), are good beginning books that cover the theory behind LISP.

In the next and final chapter of this book, you will learn how to make AutoCAD fit into your work environment. You will learn how to set up menus for your specific applications and how to add new hatch patterns and line types. I'll also discuss issues that users face when working in groups and over networks.

V

Customization—Taking AutoCAD to the Limit

21

INTEGRATING AUTOCAD INTO YOUR PROJECTS AND ORGANIZATION

Customizing the Palettes

Customizing Buttons and Icons

Adding Custom Pull-Down Menus

Creating Custom Line Types

Creating Custom Hatch Patterns

Working in an Office Environment

Setting Up Office Standards

FAST TRACK

▽

■▢

972 ▶ **To turn a flyout button menu into a floating tool palette**

Right click on a tool pallet button. At the Toolbars dialog box, locate the name of the flyout you want to open, highlight it, then click on Properties…. At the Toolbar Properties dialog box, un-check the Hide check box. Close the dialog boxes.

■▢

974 ▶ **To create a new tool palette**

Right click on a tool palette button. Click on New from the Toolbars dialog box. Enter a name for the new palette in the Name input box of the New Toolbar dialog box. Click OK then exit the Toolbar dialog box.

■▢

975 ▶ **To add a button to a tool palette**

Right click on a tool palette button to open the Toolbars dialog box. Click on Customize, then from the Customize Toolbar dialog box, click on a tool category from the pop-up list. Click and drag a button from the Customize Toolbar dialog box to your palette.

■▢

978 ▶ **To create a custom tool palette button**

Right click on a tool palette button to open the Toolbars dialog box. Click on Customize, then from the Customize Toolbar dialog box, click on Custom from the pull-down list. Click and drag a blank button from the Customize Toolbar dialog box to your palette, then right click on the new blank button. Add a name, help comment, and macro to the Button Properties dialog box. Select an icon from the icon scroll box or click Edit to create a new icon.

990 ▶ **To pause for input in a menu option**

Enter the backslash (\) where you want AutoCAD to pause in the command keystroke sequence of your menu item.

991 ▶ To include long lines in the menu file

Use a plus sign at the end of a command keystroke line to indicate that the line continues to the next line.

991 ▶ To create a cascading menu

Start the bracketed label with –>, as in [–>line]. The following lines of the menu group will be part of the cascading menu until AutoCAD encounters <– in a menu label, as in [<– Sketch].

992 ▶ To place dividing lines in a pull-down menu

Insert a label containing double hyphens, or a tilde and two hyphens, as in [––] or [~––].

998 ▶ To create a custom line type

Enter **Linetype** ↵ at the command prompt, then **C** ↵, and then the name for your new line type. Select the Acad.LIN file at the dialog box, or enter a name for a new line-type file. Then enter a description for your new line type. Finally, enter the length of each line segment of your new line type, including blank lengths, separated by commas. For example, if you enter **1.5,-1.5**, you will have a line-type pattern of a line for 1.5 units, and then 1.5 blank units before the next 1.5-unit line segment, and so on.

1003 ▶ To create a hatch pattern

In DOS, open the Acad.PAT file, and add your hatch pattern description to the end of the file. The description starts with the name of your pattern preceded with an asterisk, as in ***mypattern**. The subsequent lines describe the line pattern groups. Each group starts with the angle of the line pattern, followed by the origin coordinates, offset coordinates, and finally the line pattern description. The line pattern is described in the same way as a line-type pattern.

The reason microcomputers are so popular may well be their adaptability. Some microcomputer programs, including AutoCAD, offer a high degree of flexibility and customization, allowing you to tailor the software's look and feel to your requirements. In this final chapter, you will examine how AutoCAD can be made to fit into your work group and office environment.

The first part of the chapter shows how you can adapt AutoCAD to fit your particular needs. You will learn how to customize AutoCAD by modifying its menus, and how to create custom macros for commands that your work group uses frequently.

Then we'll examine some general issues of using AutoCAD in an office. In this discussion you may find help with some problems you have encountered when using AutoCAD in a work group. We'll also discuss the management of AutoCAD projects.

CUSTOMIZING TOOL PALETTES

The most direct way to adapt AutoCAD to your way of working is to customize the tool palettes. With Release 13 for Windows, AutoCAD offers new users an easy route to customization. You can create new palettes, customize buttons, and even create new icons. In this section, you'll discover how easy it is to add features to AutoCAD.

▼ TIP

For added convenience, you might want to make the Tool Windows palette appear as a standard part of the AutoCAD screen. The Tool Windows is a palette that lets you open all the other main tool palettes at the click of a button. To open the Tool Windows palette, follow the procedures described here to locate and open ACAD.Tool Windows.

TURNING A FLYOUT INTO A TOOL PALETTE

No two people will use AutoCAD in the exact same way, so AutoCAD has a built-in feature that "remembers" the last button selected from a flyout menu. The theory is that you will use one particular button from a flyout repeatedly. However, this theory doesn't always work. You may in fact, find that you frequently use several options from the same flyout. This situation can quickly become bothersome.

The solution is to simply open the flyout as a floating tool palette. Here's how it's done. In the following example, you'll see how to turn the Arc flyout of the Draw palette into a tool palette.

▼ **NOTE**

You can also choose Tools ➤ Customize Toolbars… from the menu bar to open the Toolbars dialog box.

1. Right-click on any button on the Draw palette. The Toolbars dialog box appears.

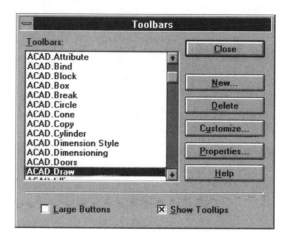

The Toolbars list box shows a listing of all the tool palettes available in AutoCAD. The Draw palette is currently highlighted.

2. Scroll the list box up until you see ACAD.Arc, highlight it, then click on the Properties… button. The Toolbar Properties dialog box appears.

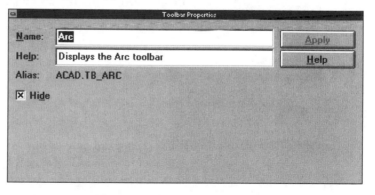

The Name input box controls the title that appears in the palettes title bar. The Help input box controls the help message that appears in the status line.

3. Click on the check box labeled Hide, so that there is no X in the box, then click on Apply. The Arc palette appears in the drawing area.

4. Click on Close from the Toolbars dialog box to close both dialog boxes.

Now you have access to all the different methods for drawing arcs. To close the palette, click on the rectangle in the upper right of the palette.

Before we continue, you may want to know what some of the other options are in the Toolbars dialog box. here's a listing of some of the options with a brief description.

Close closes the dialog box.

New lets you create a new tool palette

Delete deletes a tool palette from the list

Customize... opens the Customize Toolbar dialog box from which you can click and drag pre-defined buttons.

Properties... opens the Toolbar Properties dialog box.

Help displays helpful information about the Toolbars dialog box.

Large Buttons changes all the icon buttons to a larger format.

Show Tooltips lets AutoCAD display the tooltips for the icon buttons.

You'll get to use most of these other options in the following sections.

CREATING YOUR OWN TOOL PALETTE

You may find that instead of using one palette or flyout, you are moving from flyout to flyout from a variety of different tool palettes. If you keep track of the tools you use most frequently, you can create your own custom palette containing your favorite tools. Here's how it's done.

▼ **NOTE**

Typically, AutoCAD stores new palettes and buttons in the Acad.MNS file (see sidebar entitled "The Windows Menu Files"). You can also store them in your custom menu files. Once you've created and loaded your menu file as described in the later section "Adding Your Own Pull-down Menu," choose your menu from the Menu Group pull-down list in the New Toolbar dialog box described here.

▼ **TIP**

Normally AutoCAD stores your custom palettes in the Acad.MNS file (see the sidebar entitled "The Windows Menu Files"). You can also have your palettes stored in your own menu file by selecting its name from the New Toolbar dialog box's Menu Group pull-down list. See "Adding Your Own Pull-Down Menu" later in this chapter.

1. Right-click on an button in any tool palette. The Toolbars dialog box opens.

2. Click on the New button. The New Toolbar dialog box appears.

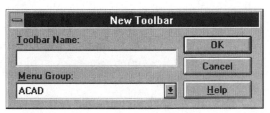

3. Enter **My Palette** in the Toolbar Name input box then click on OK. A blank tool palette appears in the Auto-CAD window.

Notice that ACAD.My Palette now appears in the Toolbars dialog box list. You can now begin to add buttons to your palette.

4. Click on Customize… from the Toolbars dialog box. The Customize Toolbars dialog box appears.

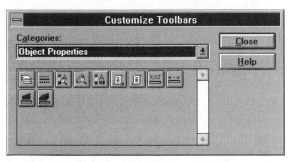

5. Open the Categories pull-down list. Notice that the list contains the main categories of commands.

6. Choose Draw from the list. The list box displays all the Icon buttons available for the Draw category. Notice that the buttons at the top of the list are flyouts. The rest are the individual buttons that issue the commands.

7. Click and drag the Circle flyout button from the Customize Toolbars dialog box into the new tool palette you just created. The button now appears in your palette.

8. Click and drag the Line button to your new palette, then exit the Customize Toolbars dialog box and the Toolbars dialog box.

You now have a custom palette with two buttons. You can add buttons from different categories if you like. You are not restricted to buttons from one category.

AutoCAD will treat your custom palette like any other tool palette. It will appear when you start AutoCAD and will remain until you close it. You can recall it by the same method described in the first exercise.

OPENING PALETTES FROM THE COMMAND LINE

You may want to know how to open tool palettes using the command line. This can be especially helpful if you want to create palette buttons that open frequently used palettes.

1. Type **Toolbar** ↵ at the command prompt.

2. At the Toolbar Name <All> prompt, enter the name of the tool palette you want to open.

3. At the Show/Hide/Left/Right/Top/Bottom/Float: <Show>: prompt, press ↵. The tool palette appears on the screen.

A typical button macro for opening a palette might look like this:

```
^c^cToolbar (space)ACAD.Arc (space)(space)
```

Here, the *[space]* is added for clarity. You would press the spacebar in its place. This example shows a macro that opens the Arc palette (ACAD.Arc).

As the prompt in step 3 indicates, you can specify the location of the tool palette by left, right, top, or bottom. Float lets you specify the location and number of rows for the palette.

▼

The following list shows the palette names available in the standard AutoCAD system. Use these names with the Toolbar command.

ACAD.STANDARD_TOOLBAR	ACAD.TB_TOOL_WINDOWS	ACAD.TB_SELECT_OBJECTS
ACAD.TB_OBJECT_SNAP	ACAD.TB_POINT_FILTERS	ACAD.TB_UCS
ACAD.TB_VIEW	ACAD.TB_REDRAW	ACAD.TB_PAN
ACAD.TB_ZOOM	ACAD.TB_SPACE	ACAD.TB_OBJECT_PROPERTIES
ACAD.TB_INQUIRY	ACAD.TB_DRAW	ACAD.TB_LINE
ACAD.TB_PLINE	ACAD.TB_ARC	ACAD.TB_CIRCLE
ACAD.TB_ELLIPSE	ACAD.TB_POLYGON	ACAD.TB_POINT
ACAD.TB_BLOCK	ACAD.TB_HATCH	ACAD.TB_TEXT
ACAD.TB_MODIFY	ACAD.TB_COPY	ACAD.TB_ROTATE
ACAD.TB_RESIZE	ACAD.TB_TRIM	ACAD.TB_BREAK
ACAD.TB_SPECIAL_EDIT	ACAD.TB_FEATURE	ACAD.TB_EXPLODE
ACAD.TB_DIMENSIONING	ACAD.TB_DIMRADIAL	ACAD.TB_DIMORDINATE
ACAD.TB_DIMTEXT	ACAD.TB_DIMSTYLE	ACAD.TB_SOLIDS
ACAD.TB_BOX	ACAD.TB_CYLINDER	ACAD.TB_CONE
ACAD.TB_WEDGE	ACAD.TB_SURFACES	ACAD.TB_EXTERNAL_REFERENCE
ACAD.TB_BIND	ACAD.TB_ATTRIBUTE	ACAD.TB_RENDER
ACAD.TB_EXTERNAL_DATABASE	ACAD.TB_MISCELLANEOUS	

You may notice that the tool palette names in the Toolbars dialog box do not match those shown in this list. You can find the "true" name of a toolbar by highlighting it in the Toolbars dialog box, then clicking on Properties.... The tool palette's "true" name is displayed under *Alias:*.

V

Customizing —Taking AutoCAD to the Limit

CUSTOMIZING BUTTONS

Now lets move on to some more serious customization. Suppose you want to create an entirely new button with its own functions. For example, you may want to create a set of buttons that will insert your favorite symbols. Or you might want to create a special palette containing a set of buttons that opens some of the existing flyouts as palettes.

Creating a Custom Button

In the following set of exercises, you'll create a button that inserts a door symbol. You'll add your custom button to the palette you just created.

1. Open the Toolbars dialog box again, then click on Customize....

2. Select Custom from the bottom of the pull-down list. The list box now shows two blank buttons, one for a single command and another for flyouts (the one for flyouts has a small triangle in the lower right corner).

3. Click and drag the single command blank button to your new palette.

4. Right click on the blank button in your new palette. The Button Properties dialog box appears.

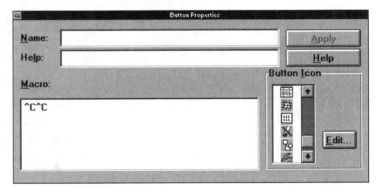

This dialog box lets you define the purpose of your custom button.

Let's pause for a moment to look at this dialog box. The Name input box lets you enter a name for your button. This name will appear as a tool tip. You must enter a name before AutoCAD will create the new button definition.

The Help input box just below the name lets you add a help message. This message will appear in the lower left corner of the AutoCAD window when you point to your button.

The Macro area is the focus of this dialog box. Here, you can enter the keystrokes you want to "play back" when you click on this button.

Finally, to the right, you see a scroll bar that lets you scroll through a set of icons. You'll also see a button labeled Edit. When you highlight an icon in the scroll box, then click on Edit, an Icon editor tool appears allowing you to edit an existing icon, or create a new icon.

Now let's go ahead and add a macro and new icon to this button.

1. In the Name input box, enter Door. This will be your Tool tip for this button.

2. In the Help input box, enter **Inserts a single door**. This will be the help message for this button

3. In the Macro input box, enter the following:

```
^c^cinsert door
```

Note that the two ^c's already appear in the Macro input box. These represent two Cancels being issued. This is the same as pressing the Escape key twice. It ensures that when the macro starts, it cancels any unfinished commands.

You follow the two cancels with the INSERT command as it is issued from the keyboard. If you need help finding the keyboard equivalent of a command, consult *Appendix E*, which contains a listing of all the command names.

After the INSERT command, there is a space, then the name Door appears. This is the same sequence of keystrokes you would enter at the command line to insert the door drawing you created in *Chapters 2* and *3*. You could go on to include an insertion point, scale factor, and rotation angle in this macro, but these options are better left for the time when the door is actually inserted.

▼ TIP

You can put any valid string of keystrokes in the Macro input box, including AutoLISP functions. See Chapters 19 and 20 for more on AutoLISP. You can also include pauses for user input using the backslash (\ ) character. See "Pausing for User Input" later in this chapter.

▼ WARNING

It is important that you enter the exact sequence of keystrokes that follow the command, otherwise your macro may get out of step with the command prompts. This will take a little practice and some going back and forth between testing your button and editing the macro.

V

Customizing —Taking
AutoCAD to the Limit

Creating a Custom Icon

▼ **NOTE**

If you prefer, you can use any of the pre-defined icons in the scroll box. Just click on the icon you want to use, then click on Apply.

You have all the essential parts of the button defined. Now you just need to create a custom icon to go with your door button.

1. In the Icon scroll box, scroll down the list until you see a blank icon.

2. Click on the blank icon, then click on Edit. The Button Editor appears.

The button editor is like a very simple drawing program. Across the top are the tools to draw lines, circles, and points, as well as an eraser. Along the right side, you see a color palette from which you can choose colors for your icon button. In the upper left, you see a preview of your button. The following describes the rest of the options.

Grid turn a grid on and off in the drawing area. This grid can be an aid in drawing your icon.

Clear erases the entire contents of the drawing area.

Open opens a .BMP file to import an icon. The bmp file must be small enough to fit in the 16-by-16 pixel matrix provided for icons (24-by-24 for large format icons).

Save As…   saves your icon as a .BMP file under a name you enter.

Save   saves your icon under a name that AutoCAD provides, usually a series of numbers and letters.

Close   exits the Button Editor.

Help   displays helpful information about the features of the Button Editor.

Now let's continue by creating a new icon.

3. Draw the door icon shown here. Don't worry if its not perfect. you can always go back and fix it.

4. Click on Save, then Close.

5. In the Button Properties dialog box, click on Apply. You'll see the icon appear on the button in your palette.

6. Now click on the Close button of the Toolbars dialog box.

7. Click on the Door button of your new palette. The door appears in your drawing ready to be placed.

▼ WARNING

The Door drawing must be in the default directory, or in the Acad search path before the door button will be inserted.

You can continue to add more buttons to your palette to build a palette of symbols. Of course, you're not limited to a symbols library. You can also incorporate your favorite macros or even AutoLISP routines you accumulate as you work with AutoCAD. The possibilities are endless.

Setting the Properties of Flyouts

Just as you added a new button to your palette, you can also add flyouts. Remember that flyouts are simply another form of a palette. This next example shows how you can add a copy of the Circle palette to your custom palette, then make adjustments to the properties of the flyout.

V

Customizing —Taking AutoCAD to the Limit

▼ TIP

To delete a button from a palette, open the Toolbar dialog
box, then click on Customize.... When the Customize
Toolbar dialog box appears,
click and drag the button you
want to delete out of the palette and into the drawing area.

1. Right click on the door button in the Palette you just finished. The Toolbars dialog box opens with My Palette already highlighted.

2. Click on Customize, then at the Customize Toolbars dialog box,
   open the pull-down list and select Custom at the bottom.

3. Click and drag the flyout button from the list box into the
   My Palette tool palette.

You could have simply clicked and dragged an existing flyout from the
Customize Toolbars dialog box. You now have a blank flyout to which
you can add you own icon. Let's see what options are available for flyout
buttons.

4. Close the Customize Toolbars dialog box, then right-click on
   the new, blank flyout button you just added to your palette.
   The Flyout Properties dialog box appears.

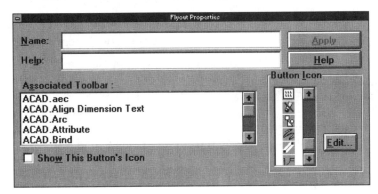

Notice how this dialog box resembles the Button Properties
dialog box you used in the previous exercise. But instead of
the Macro input box, you see a list of button palettes.

5. Scroll down the list of palette names until you find ACAD.Circle. This is a pre-defined palette, though it can be a palette you define yourself.

6. Highlight ACAD.Circle, then enter My Circle Flyout in the Name input box. Enter **My very own flyout** in the Help input box.

7. Locate an icon in the icon scroll box that looks like a simple circle, and click on it.

8. Click on the check box labeled Show This Button's Icon so that an X appears in the box.

9. Click on Apply. The flyout button in the My Palette tool palette shows the icon you selected.

10. Close the Toolbars dialog box, then place the arrow cursor on the flyout to display its tool tip. Notice that your new tool tip and help message appear.

11. Click and drag the circle icon, then select Donut from the flyout Notice that even though you selected donut, the circle icon remains as the icon for the flyout.

Step 11 demonstrates that you can disable the feature that causes the last flyout to appear as the default on the palette. You disabled this feature in step 8 by checking the Show This Button's Icon check box.

Editing Existing Buttons

If you want to edit an existing button or flyout, you can go directly to either the Button Properties or the Flyout Properties dialog box by double-right-clicking on a button. Once one of these dialog boxes is open, you can make changes to any component of the button definition.

The Windows Menu Files

As you create and modify icon buttons and palettes, you see a messages momentarily appear in the status line at the bottom of the AutoCAD window. These messages are telling you that AutoCAD is creating new menu files. The Windows version of AutoCAD creates several menu files it uses in the course of an editing session. Here's a brief rundown of what those different menu files are.

Acad.MNU is the source text file that contains the information required to build the AutoCAD menu. If you are a programmer, you would use this file to do detailed customization of the AutoCAD menu. Here, you can edit the pull-downs, image tiles, buttons, etc. Most users won't have a need to edit this file.

Acad.MNS is a text file containing the source information to create the Acad.MNC file (described next). If you ever customize the Acad.MNU file, you must delete the Acad.MNS file before your changes will take affect.

Acad.MNC is AutoCAD's translation of the Acad.MNS file. AutoCAD translates or "compiles" the Acad.MNU file so that it can read the menu faster.

Acad.MNR is the menu resource file. It is a binary file that contains the bitmap images used for buttons and other graphics.

As you create or edit icon buttons and palettes, AutoCAD first adds your custom items to the Acad.MNS file. It then compiles this file into the Acad.MNC and Acad.MNR files for quicker access to the menus. The Acad.MNS, Acad.MNC, and Acad.MNR files are unique to the Windows version and are not found in the DOS or Unix platforms.

Note that the Acad.MNS file is the file you will want to copy to other computers to transfer your custom buttons and palettes. Also, if you create your own pull-down menu files, as in the Mymenu.MNU example in this chapter, AutoCAD will create the source, compiled, and resource files for your custom menu file. You have the option to store new palettes in your custom menu through the Menu Group pull-down list of the New Toolbar dialog box.

V

Customizing —Taking
AutoCAD to the Limit

ADDING YOUR OWN PULL-DOWN MENU

In addition to adding buttons and tool palettes, AutoCAD lets you add
pull-down menu options. This sections looks at how you might add a
custom pull-down menu.

CREATING YOUR FIRST PULL-DOWN MENU

Let's start by trying the following exercise to create a simple pull-down
menu file called My Menu:

1. Using a text editor, like the Windows Notepad, create a file
   called **Mymenu.MNU,** containing the following lines:

```
***POP1
[My 1st Menu]
[Line]^c^c_line
[--]
[->More]
[Arc-SED]^c^c_arc \_e \_d
[<-Rotate90]^c^c(if (not c:r90)+
(defun c:r90 (/ ss1)(setq ss1 (ssget))+
(command "rotate" ss1 "" pause "90") ) );r90
[Quick Group]^c^c(setq ss2 (ssget))
[Select Quick Group]!ss2
***POP2
[My 2nd Menu]
[door]^c^cInsert door
[Continue Line]^C^CLINE;;
```

2. Save this file, and be sure you place it in your \Acadr13\win
   directory.

Once you've stored the file, you've got your first custom pull-down
menu. You may have noticed some familiar items among the lines
you entered. The menu contains the Line and Arc commands. It also

contains the R90 macro you worked on in *Chapter 19*; this time, that macro is broken into shorter lines.

Now let's see how My Menu works in AutoCAD.

LOADING A MENU

In the following exercise, you will load the menu you have just created and test it out. The procedure described here for loading menus is the same for all menus, regardless of their source.

1. Click on Tools ➤ Customize Menus…. The Menu Customization dialog box appears.

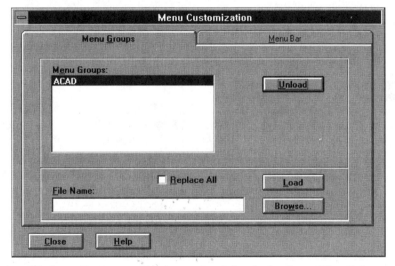

2. Click on Browse at the bottom of the dialog box. The Select Menu file dialog box appears.

3. Locate the Mymenu.MNU file, highlight it, then click on OK. The dialog box closes and you see the name of the file in the File Name input box of the Menu Customization dialog box.

4. Click on Load. The Mymenu.MNU file name appears in the list box.

5. Highlight Mymenu.MNU in the list box then click on the tab at the top of the dialog box labeled Menu Bar. The dialog box changes to show two lists.

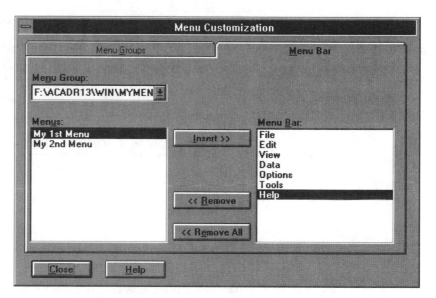

On the left is the name of the menus available in your menu file. The list on the right shows the currently available pull-down menus.

6. Highlight Help in the right hand column. This tells Auto-CAD you want to add your pull-down in front of the help pull-down.

7. Highlight My 1st Menu from the list on the left, then click on the button labeled Insert >>. My 1st Menu moves into the right-hand column and it appears in the AutoCAD menu bar (see Figure 21.1).

8. Highlight My 2nd Menu from the list on the left, then click on Insert >> again. My 2nd Menu is copied to the right-hand column and it too, appears in the menu bar (see Figure 21.1).

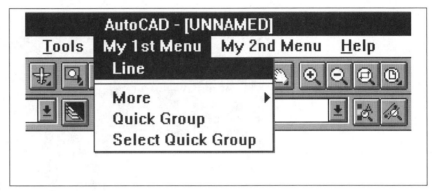

Figure 21.1: The My 1st Menu menu

9. Close the Menu Customization dialog box.

10. Draw some objects on the screen, then try the My 1st Menu ➤ More ➤ Rotate90 option (see Figure 21.2).

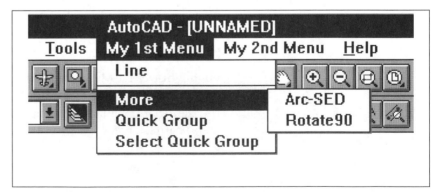

Figure 21.2: The My 1st Menu cascading menu

With just an 11-line menu file, you created a menu that contains virtually every tool used to build menus. Now let's take a more detailed look at how menu files work.

HOW THE PULL-DOWN MENU WORKS

Let's take a closer look at the Mymenu.MNU file. The first item in the file, ***POP1, identifies the beginning of a pull-down menu. The item just below this is the phrase My 1st Menu in square brackets. This is the title of the pull-down menu; it is what appears in the toolbar. Every pull-down menu must have this title element.

Following the title, each item on the list starts with a word enclosed in brackets; these words are the options that actually appear when you open the pull-down menu. If you removed everything else, you would have the menu as it appears on the screen. The text that follows the item in brackets conveys instructions to AutoCAD about the option.

Finally, in the Mymenu sample, you see ***POP2. This is the beginning of a second pull-down menu. Again, you must follow this with a pull-down menu title in square brackets. Below the title, you can add other menu options.

Calling Commands

Now look at the Line option in the Mymenu.MNU listing. The two Ctrl-C (^C) elements that follow the square brackets will cancel any command that is currently operative. The Line command follows, written just as it would be entered through the keyboard. Two Cancels are issued in case you are in a command that has two levels, such as the Edit Vertex option of the PEDIT command (Modify ➤ Edit Polyline ➤ Edit Vertex).

The underline that precedes the LINE command tells AutoCAD that you are using the English-language version of this command. This feature lets you program non-English versions of AutoCAD using the English-language command names.

You may also notice that there is no space between the second ^C and the NEW command. A space in the line would be the same as a ↵. If

V

Customizing —Taking
AutoCAD to the Limit

there were a space between these two elements, a ↵ would be entered between the last Ctrl-C and the New command, causing the command sequence to misstep.

Another way to indicate a ↵ is by using the semicolon, as in the following example:

[Continue Line]^C^CLINE;;

▼ TIP

When you have many ↵s in a menu macro, using semicolons instead of spaces can help make your macro more readable.

In this sample menu option, the LINE command is issued, and then an additional ↵ is added. The effect of choosing this option would be a line that continues from the last line entered into your drawing. The two semicolons following the word LINE tell AutoCAD to start the LINE command, and then issue ↵ twice to begin a line from the endpoint of the last line entered. (AutoCAD automatically issues a single ↵ at the end of a menu line. In this case, however, you want two ↵s, so they must be represented as semicolons.)

Pausing for User Input

Another symbol used in the menu file is the backslash (\ ), used when a pause is required for user input. For example, when you selected the Arc-SED option in My Menu, it started the Arc command and then paused for your input.

▼ NOTE

The underline that precedes the command name and option input tells AutoCAD that you are entering the English-language versions of these commands.

[Arc-SED]^c^c_arc _e _d

The space between ^c^c_arc and the backslash (\ ) represents the pressing of the Spacebar. The backslash indicates a pause to allow you to select the starting endpoint for the arc. Once you have picked a point, the _e represents the selection of the Endpoint option under the Arc command. A second backslash allows another point selection. Finally, the _d represents the selection of the Direction option. Figure 21.3 illustrates this.

If you want the last character in a menu item to be a backslash, you must follow the backslash with a semicolon.

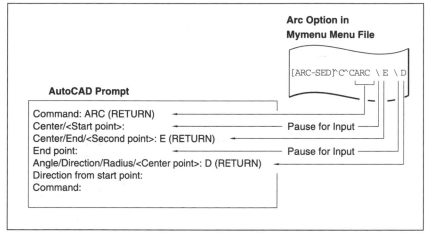

Figure 21.3:   The execution of the Arc menu item

Using the Plus Sign for Long Lines

▼ **TIP**

It's okay to break an AutoLISP program into smaller lines. In fact, it can help you read and understand the program more easily.

As you browse through the Acad.MNU file, you'll notice that many of the lines end with a plus sign (+). The length of each line in the menu file is limited to about 80 characters, but you can break a line into two or more lines by adding a plus sign at the end of the line that continues, like this:

```
[Rotate90]^c^c(if  (not c:r90)+
(defun c:r90 (/ ss1)(setq ss1 (ssget))+
(command "_rotate" ss1 "" pause "90") ) );r90
```

This example shows how you would include the R90 AutoLISP macro in a menu. Everything in this segment is entered just as it would be with the keyboard. The plus is used to indicate the continuation of this long item to the subsequent lines, and the semicolon is used in place of ↵.

Creating a Cascading Menu

Look at the More option in the File pull-down menu group; it starts with these characters: –>. This is the way you indicate a menu item that

V

Customizing —Taking
AutoCAD to the Limit

opens a cascading menu. Everything that follows the [–>More] menu item will appear in the cascading menu. To indicate the end of the cascading menu, you use the characters <–, as in the [<-Rotate90] menu item farther down. Anything beyond this <– item appears in the main part of the menu. If the last item in a cascading menu is also the last item in the menu group, you must use <–<–, as in [<–<–.XZ].

Placing Division Lines and Dimmed Text in Pull-Down Menus

Two symbols are used to place dividing lines in your pull-down menus. One is the *double-hyphen* symbol (—). This is used to divide groups of items in a menu; it will expand to fill the entire width of the pull-down menu with a line of hyphens. The other option is the *tilde* symbol (~). If the tilde precedes a bracketed option name, that option will be dimmed when displayed; when clicked on, it will have no effect. You have probably encountered these dimmed options on various pull-down menus in the programs you use. When you see a dimmed menu item, it usually means that the option is not valid under the current command.

▼ LOADING AUTOLISP ■ MACROS WITH YOUR SUBMENU

As your become a more advanced user, you may find that you want to have many of your own AutoLISP macros load with your menus. This can be accomplished by combining all of your AutoLISP macros into a single file. Give this file the same name as your menu file with the .MNL file name extension. Such a file will be automatically loaded with its menu counterpart. For example, say you have a file called Mymenu.MNL containing the R90 AutoLISP macro. Whenever you load the Mymenu.MNU, Mymenu.MNL will automatically load along with it, giving you access to the R90 Macro. This is a good way to manage and organize any AutoLISP program code you want to include with a menu.

Adding Help Messages to Pull-down Menu Items

Earlier in this chapter, you learned how to include a help message with an Icon button. The help message appears in the status bar of Auto-CAD window when you highlight an option. You can also include a help message with a pull-down menu item. Here's how.

First, you must give your pull-down menu file a menugroup name. This helps AutoCAD isolate your file and its help messages from other menus that might be loaded along with yours. To give your menu file a group name add the following line at the top of the file:

```
***MENUGROUP=MYMENU
```

where *MYMENU* is the name you want for your menugroup name.

Next, you will have to add an ID name to each menu item that requires a help message. The following shows a sample of how this might be done for the My 1st Menu example you used earlier:

```
***MENUGROUP=MYMENU
***POP1
[My 1st Menu]
ID_1line [Line]^c^c_line
[--]
[->More]
ID_1Arc-sed [Arc-SED]^c^c_arc \_e \_d
ID_1Rot90   [<-Rotate90]^c^c(if (not c:r90)+
(defun c:r90 (/ ss1)(setq ss1 (ssget))+
(command "rotate" ss1 "" pause "90") ) );r90
ID_1group   [Quick Group]^c^c(setq ss2 (ssget))
ID_1select  [Select Quick Group]!ss2
```

The ID name starts with the characters **ID** followed by an underline, then the name for the menu item. Several spaces are added so the menu items align for clarity. Each menu item must have a unique ID name.

Finally, you add a section at the end of your file called ***HELP-STRINGS. For this example, it would look like this:

```
***HELPSTRINGS
ID_1line    [Draws a line]
ID_1Arc-sed [Draws an arc with start, end, direction]
```

```
ID_1Rot90    [Rotates an object 90 degrees]
ID_1group    [Groups objects]
ID_1select   [Selects groups]
```

The menu item ID names are duplicated exactly, followed by several spaces, then the actual text you want to appear in the status line, enclosed in brackets. The spaces between the ID and the text are for clarity.

Once you've done this, and then loaded the menu file, you will see these same messages appear in the status bar when these menu options are highlighted. In fact, if you browse your Acad.MNU file, you will see similar ID names. If you prefer, you can use numbers in place of names.

CREATING CUSTOM LINE TYPES AND HATCH PATTERNS

As your drawing needs expand, you may find that the standard line types and hatch patterns are not adequate for your application. Fortunately, you can create your own. This section explains how to go about creating custom line types and patterns.

▼ **NOTE**

AutoCAD stores the line types in a file called Acad.LIN, which is in the ASCII format. When you create a new line type, you are actually adding information to this file. Or, if you create a new file containing your own line-type definitions, it, too, will have the extension .LIN. You can edit line types as described here, or you can edit them directly in these files.

VIEWING AVAILABLE LINE TYPES

Although AutoCAD provides the line types most commonly used in drafting (see Figure 21.4), the dashes and dots may not be spaced the way you would like, or you may want an entirely new line type.

To create a custom line type, you use the LINETYPE command. Let's see how this handy command works by first listing the available line types.

1. Open a new AutoCAD file.

2. Enter **Linetype** ↵ at the command prompt

3. At the ?/Create/Load/Set: prompt, enter **?** ↵.

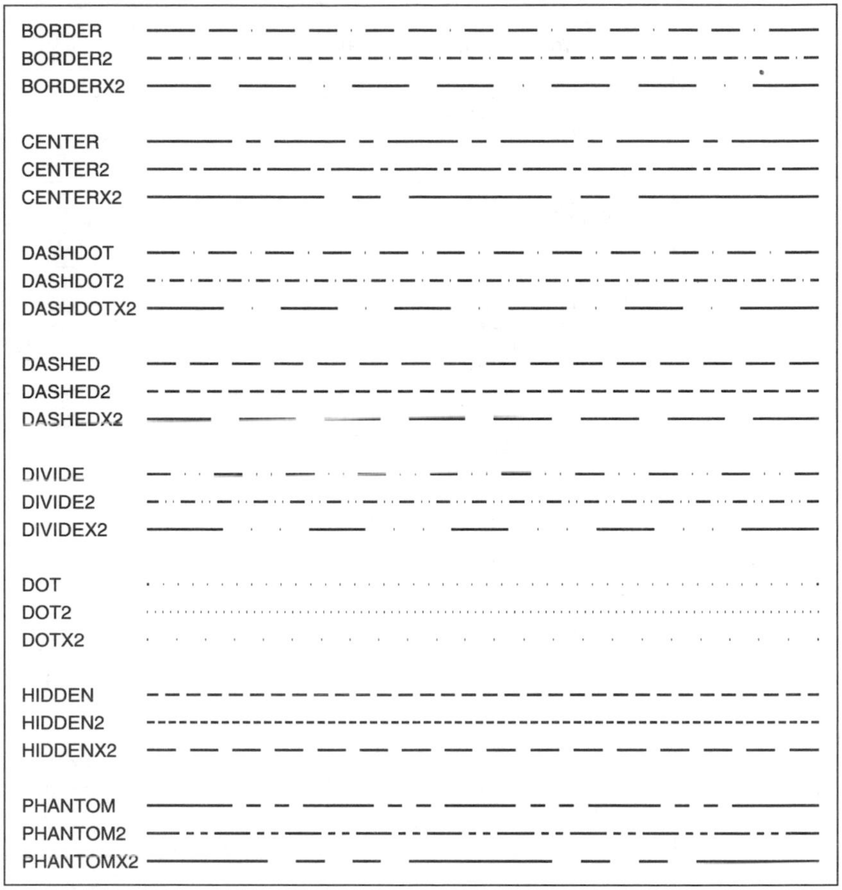

Figure 21.4:   The standard AutoCAD line types

4. In the file dialog box that appears, locate and double-click on ACAD in the listing of available linetype files. You get the listing shown in Figure 21.5, which shows the line types available in the Acad.LIN file, along with a simple description of each line.

Standard AutoCAD Line Types

```
*BORDER,__ __ . __ __ . __ __ . __ __ . __ __ .
A,.5,-.25,.5,-.25,0,-.25
*BORDER2,__.__.__.__.__.__.__.__.__.__.__.__.
A,.25,-.125,.25,-.125,0,-.125
*BORDERX2,____ ____ . ____ ____ . ____ ____ .
A,1.0,-.5,1.0,-.5,0,-.5
*CENTER,____ _ ____ _ ____ _ ____ _ ____ _ ____
A,1.25,-.25,.25,-.25
*CENTER2,___ _ ___ _ ___ _ ___ _ ___ _ ___ _ ___
A,.75,-.125,.125,-.125
*CENTERX2,_____ __ _____ __ _____ __ _____
A,2.5,-.5,.5,-.5
*DASHDOT,__ . __ . __ . __ . __ . __ . __ . __ .
A,.5,-.25,0,-.25
*DASHDOT2,_._._._._._._._._._._._._._._._._._.
A,.25,-.125,0,-.125
*DASHDOTX2,____ . ____ . ____ . ____ . ____ .
A,1.0,-.5,0,-.5
*DASHED,__ __ __ __ __ __ __ __ __ __ __ __ __
A,.5,-.25
*DASHED2,_ _ _ _ _ _ _ _ _ _ _ _ _ _ _ _ _ _ _
A,.25,-.125
*DASHEDX2,____ ____ ____ ____ ____ ____ ____
A,1.0,-.5
*DIVIDE,____ . . ____ . . ____ . . ____ . .
A,.5,-.25,0,-.25,0,-.25
*DIVIDE2,__..__..__..__..__..__..__..__..__..__.
.
A,.25,-.125,0,-.125,0,-.125
*DIVIDEX2,_____ . . _____ . . _____ . .
A,1.0,-.5,0,-.5,0,-.5
*DOT,. . . . . . . . . . . . . . . . . . . . .
A,0,-.25
*DOT2,.....................................
A,0,-.125
*DOTX2,.  .  .  .  .  .  .  .  .  .  .  .  .
A,0,-.5
*HIDDEN,__ __ __ __ __ __ __ __ __ __ __ __ __
A,.25,-.125
*HIDDEN2,_ _ _ _ _ _ _ _ _ _ _ _ _ _ _ _ _ _ _
A,.125,-.0625
*HIDDENX2,____ ____ ____ ____ ____ ____ ____
A,.5,-.25
*PHANTOM,_____ __ __ _____ __ __ _____ __ __
A,1.25,-.25,.25,-.25,.25,-.25
*PHANTOM2,____ _ _ ____ _ _ ____ _ _ ____ _ _ _
__
A,.625,-.125,.125,-.125,.125,-.125
*PHANTOMX2,_____ ____ ____ _____
A,2.5,-.5,.5,-.5,.5,-.5
```

Figure 21.5: A listing of standard line types. The lines in the figure were generated with the underline key and the period, and are only rough representations of the actual lines.

```
Iso Line Types

; dashed line
*ACAD_ISO02W100,__ __ __ __ __ __ __ __ __ __ __ __ __ __
A,12,-3
; dashed space line
*ACAD_ISO03W100,__    __    __    __    __    __    __    __
A,12,-18
; long dashed dotted line
*ACAD_ISO04W100,____ . ____ . ____ . ____ . ____ . ____ .
A,24,-3,.5,-3
; long dashed double dotted line
*ACAD_ISO05W100,____ .. ____ .. ____ .. ____ .. ____ ..
A,24,-3,.5,-3,.5,-3
; long dashed triplicate dotted line
*ACAD_ISO06W100,____ ... ____ ... ____ ... ____ ... ____ ...
A,24,-3,.5,-3,.5,-3,.5,-3
; dotted line
*ACAD_ISO07W100,. . . . . . . . . . . . . . . . . . .
A,.5,-3
; long dashed short dashed line
*ACAD_ISO08W100,____ __ ____ __ ____ __ ____ __ ____ __
A,24,-3,6,-3
; long dashed double-short-dashed line
*ACAD_ISO09W100,____ __ __ ____ __ __ ____ __ __ ____ __
A,24,-3,6,-3,6,-3
; dashed dotted line
*ACAD_ISO10W100,__ . __ . __ . __ . __ . __ . __ .
A,12,-3,.5,-3
; double-dashed dotted line
*ACAD_ISO11W100,__ __ . __ __ . __ __ . __ __ . __ __ .
A,12,-3,12,-3,.5,-3
; dashed double-dotted line
*ACAD_ISO12W100,__ . . __ . . __ . . __ . . __ . .
A,12,-3,.5,-3,.5,-3
; double-dashed double-dotted line
*ACAD_ISO13W100,__ __ . . __ __ . . __ __ . . __ __
A,12,-3,12,-3,.5,-3,.5,-3
; dashed triplicate-dotted line
*ACAD_ISO14W100,__ . . . __ . . . __ . . . __ . . . __
A,12,-3,.5,-3,.5,-3,.5,-3
; double-dashed triplicate-dotted line
*ACAD_ISO15W100,__ __ . . . __ __ . . . __ __ . . . __ __
A,12,-3,12,-3,.5,-3,.5,-3,.5,-3
```

Figure 21.5 (continued): A listing of standard line types. The lines in the figure were generated with the underline key and the period, and are only rough representations of the actual lines.

CREATING A NEW LINE TYPE

Next, try creating a new line type.

1. At the ?/Create/Load/Set: prompt, enter **C** ↵.

2. At the Name of linetype to create: prompt, enter **Custom** ↵ as the name of your new line type.

3. Notice that the file dialog box you see next is named Create or Append Linetype File. You need to enter the name of the line-type file you want to create or add to. If you pick the default line-type file, ACAD, your new line type will be added to the Acad.LIN file. If you choose to create a new line-type file, AutoCAD will open a file containing the line type you create and add .LIN to the file name you supply.

4. Let's assume you want to start a new line type file; enter **Newline** ↵ at the File Name input box.

5. At the Creating new file... Descriptive text: prompt, enter a text description of your line type. You can use any keyboard character as part of your description, but the actual line type can be composed only of a series of lines, points, and blank spaces. For this exercise, enter

    Custom - My own center line _____ _ _____ ↵

    using the underline key to simulate the line appearance.

6. At the Enter pattern (on next line): prompt, enter the following numbers (after the a that appears automatically):

    1.0,-.125,.25,-.125 ↵

7. At the New definition written to file. ?/Create/Load/Set: prompt, press ↵ to exit the LINETYPE command.

Remember, once you've created a line type, you must load it in order to use it, as discussed in the "Assigning Line Types to Layers" section of *Chapter 4.*

▼ NOTE

If you had accepted the default line-type file, ACAD, the prompt in step 5 would say Wait, checking if line-type already de-fined.... This protects you from inadvertently overwriting an existing line type you may want to keep.

▼ WARNING

If you use the Set option of the LINETYPE command to set a new default line type, you will get that line type no matter what layer you are on. Changing this setting is the same as using the Line-type option in the Object Creation dialog box (Data ➤ Object Creation) to set a default line type.

The Line-Type Code

▼ **NOTE**

The values you enter for the line segment lengths are multiplied by the Ltscale factor, so be sure to enter values for the *plotted* lengths.

In step 6 of the previous exercise you entered a series of numbers separated by commas. This is the line-type code, representing the different lengths of the components that make up the line type. The separate elements of the line-type code are explained as follows:

- The 1.0 following the *a* is the length of the first part of the line. (The *a* that begins the line-type definition is a code that is applied to all line types.)

- The first −.125 is the blank or broken part of the line. The minus sign tells AutoCAD that the line is *not* to be drawn for the specified length, which is 0.125 units in this example.

- Next comes the positive value of 0.25. This tells AutoCAD to draw a line segment 0.25 units long after the blank part of the line.

- Finally, the last negative value, −.125, again tells AutoCAD to skip drawing the line for the distance of 0.125 units.

This series of numbers represents the one segment that is repeated to form the line (see Figure 21.6). You could also create a very complex line type that looks like a random broken line, as in Figure 21.7.

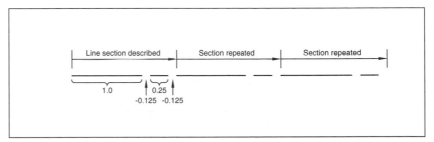

Figure 21.6: Line-type description with plotted line

Customizing —Taking AutoCAD to the Limit

V

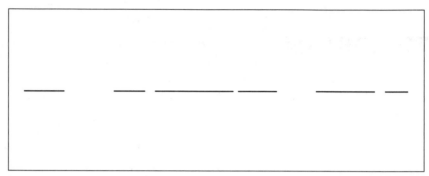

Figure 21.7:   Random broken line

You may be wondering what purpose the *a* serves at the beginning of the line-type code. A line type is composed of a series of line segments and points. The *a*, which is supplied by AutoCAD automatically, is a code that forces the line type to start and end on a line segment rather than a blank space in the series of lines. At times, AutoCAD stretches the last line segment to force this condition, as shown in Figure 21.8.

As mentioned in the beginning of this section, you can also create line types outside AutoCAD by using a word processor or text editor such as Windows Notepad. The standard Acad.LIN file looks like Figure 21.6. This is the same file you saw earlier, with the addition of the code used by AutoCAD to determine the line segment lengths.

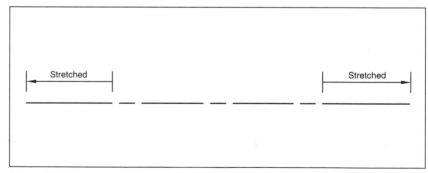

Figure 21.8:   AutoCAD stretches the beginning and end of the line as necessary.

Normally, to use a line type you have created, you have to load it, through either the Layer or the Linetype dialog box (Data ➤ Layers…, or Data ➤ Linetype…). If you use one of your own line types frequently, you may want to create an icon button macro, so it will be available as an option on a menu.

CREATING COMPLEX LINE TYPES

A complex line type is one that incorporates text or special graphics. For example, if you want to show an underground gas line in a site plan, you normally show a line with an intermittent G, as shown in Figure 21.9. Fences are often shown with an intermittent X.

For the graphics needed to compose complex line types, you can use any of the symbols found in the AutoCAD font files shown in *Chapter 8*. Just create a text style using these symbols fonts, and then specify

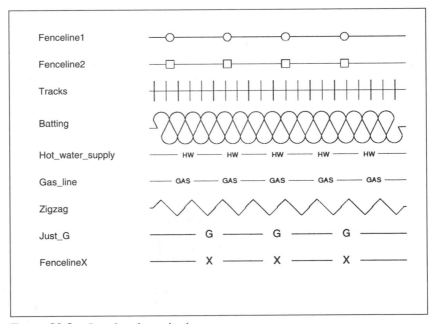

Figure 21.9: Samples of complex line types

the appropriate symbol by using its corresponding letter in the line-type description.

To create a line type that includes text, follow the same procedure for creating a new line type as shown in the previous section, and add the necessary font file information in brackets. For example, say you want to create the line type for the underground gas line mentioned above. You would add the following to your Acad.LIN file:

```
*Gas line ---- G ---- G ----
a,1.0,–0.25, [ "G", standard, S=.2, R=0, X=–.1, Y=–.1], –0.25
```

The information in the square brackets describes the characteristics of the text. The text itself that you want to appear in the line is surrounded by quotes. Next come the text style, scale, rotation angle, x displacement, and y displacement.

You can substitute the rotation angle (the R value) with an A, as in the following example:

```
a,1.0,–0.25, [ "G", standard, S=.2 A=0, X=.1, Y=.1], –0.25
```

This has the effect of keeping the text at the same angle, regardless of the line's direction. Notice that in this sample, the x and y values are a –.1; this will center the Gs on the line. The scale value of .2 will cause the text to be .2 units high, so the –.1 is half the height.

In addition to fonts, you can also specify shapes for line-type definitions. Instead of letters, shapes display symbols. Shapes are stored not as drawings, but as definition files, similar to text-font files. In fact, shape files have the same .SHX extension as text and are defined similarly, as well. Figure 21.10 shows some symbols from shape files supplied with AutoCAD.

To use a shape in a line-type code, you use the same format as shown previously for text; instead of using a letter and style name, however, you use the shape name and the shape file name, as in the following:

```
*Capline, ====
a,1.0,–0.25, [ CAP,ES.SHX,S=.2,R=0,X=–.1,Y=–.1],–0.25
```

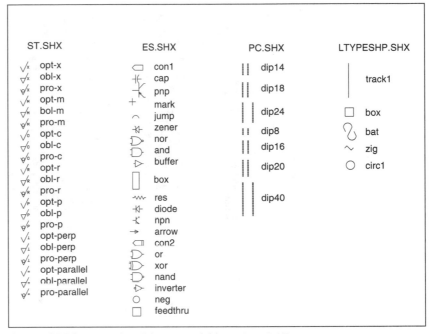

Figure 21.10: Samples of shapes available in AutoCAD

This example uses the Cap symbol from the Es.SHX shape file. The symbol is scaled to .2 units with 0 rotation and an x and y displacement of −.1.

CREATING HATCH PATTERNS

AutoCAD provides several predefined hatch patterns you can choose from (see Figure 21.11), but you can also create your own. This section demonstrates the basic elements of pattern definition.

Unlike line types, hatch patterns cannot be created while you are in an AutoCAD file. The pattern definitions are contained in an external file named Acad.PAT. This file can be opened and edited with a text

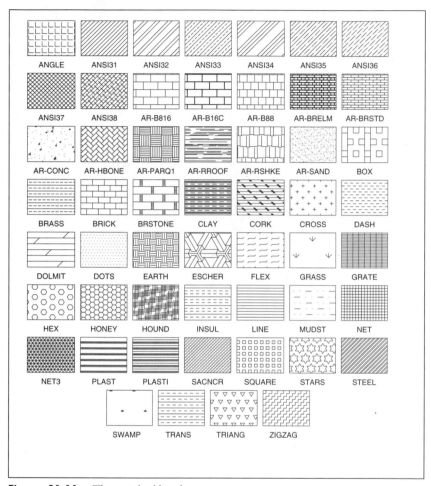

Figure 21.11: The standard hatch patterns

editor that can handle ASCII files, like the Windows Notepad. Here is one hatch pattern definition from that file:

```
*square,Small aligned squares
0, 0,0, 0,.125, .125,–.125
90, 0,0, 0,.125, .125,–.125
```

You can see some similarities between pattern descriptions and line-type descriptions. They both start with a line of descriptive text, and then give numeric values defining the pattern. The numbers in pattern descriptions have a different meaning, however. This example shows two lines of information. Each line represents a line in the pattern. The first line determines the horizontal line component of the pattern, and the second line represents the vertical component. Figure 21.12 shows the hatch pattern defined in the example.

A pattern is made up of *line groups*. A line group is like a line type that is arrayed a specified distance to fill the area to be hatched. A line group is defined by a line of code, much as a line type is defined. In the

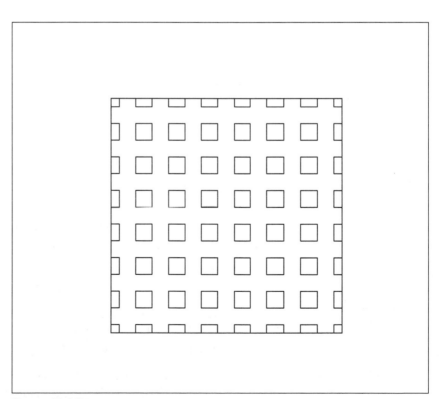

Figure 21.12: Square pattern

square pattern, for instance, two lines—one horizontal and one vertical—are used. Each of these lines is duplicated in a fashion that makes the lines appear as boxes when they are combined. Figure 21.13 illustrates this point.

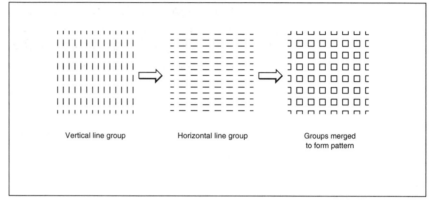

Vertical line group   Horizontal line group   Groups merged to form pattern

Figure 21.13: The individual and combined line groups

Look at the first line in the definition:

0, 0,0, 0,.125, .125,–.125

This example shows a series of numbers separated by commas, and it represents one line group. It actually contains four sets of information, separated by blank spaces:

▼ NOTE

If you have forgotten the numeric values for the various directions, refer back to Figure 2.6 in *Chapter 2*, which shows AutoCAD's system for specifying angles.

■ The first component is the 0 at the beginning. This value indicates the angle of the line group, as determined by the line's orientation. In this case it is 0 for a horizontal line that runs from left to right.

■ The next component is the origin of the line group, 0,0. This does not mean that the line actually begins at the drawing origin (see Figure 21.14). It gives you a reference point to

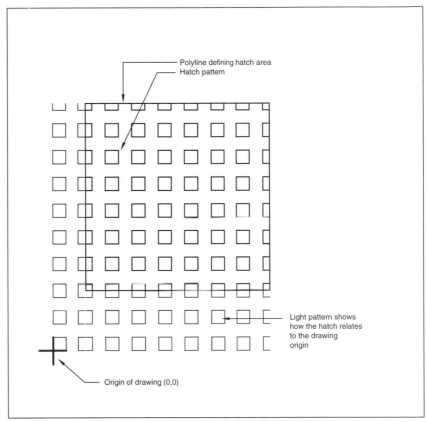

Figure 21.14: The origin of the patterns

determine the location of other line groups involved in generating the pattern.

■ The next component is 0,.125. This determines the distance for arraying the line and in what direction, as illustrated in Figure 21.15. This value is like a relative coordinate indicating x and y distances for a rectangular array. It is not based on the drawing coordinates, but on a coordinate system relative to the orientation of the line. For a line oriented at a 0° angle, the

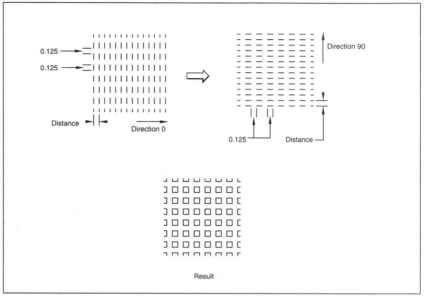

Figure 21.15: The distance and direction of duplication

code 0,.125 indicates a precisely vertical direction. For a line oriented at a 45° angle, the code 0,.125 represents a 135° direction. In this example, the duplication occurs 90° in relation to the line group, because the x value is 0. Figure 21.16 illustrates this point.

■ The last component is the actual description of the line pattern. This value is equivalent to the value given when you create a line type. Positive values are line segments, and negative values are blank segments. This part of the line group definition works exactly as in the line-type definitions you studied in the previous section.

This system of defining hatch patterns may seem somewhat limiting, but you can actually do a lot with it. Autodesk managed to come up with 53 patterns—and that was really only scratching the surface.

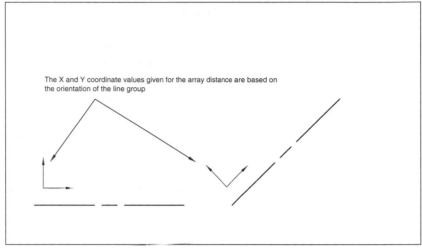

The X and Y coordinate values given for the array distance are based on the orientation of the line group

Figure 21.16: How the direction of the line group copy is determined

SUPPORTING YOUR SYSTEM AND WORKING IN GROUPS

So far in this book you have worked with AutoCAD as an individual learning a program. However, you are usually not alone when you use AutoCAD on a project. Your success with AutoCAD may depend as much on the people you work with as on your knowledge of the program. In the last half of this chapter, we'll look at some of the issues you may face as a member of an interactive group: selecting a system and obtaining support for it; what happens once that system arrives in the office; and some ways you can manage your system.

GETTING OUTSIDE SUPPORT

It helps to have knowledgeable people to consult when questions arise. Most often, the vendor who sells the CAD system is also the source for technical support. Another source is the independent CAD consultant. And don't overlook colleagues who have had some solid experience with AutoCAD. Most likely, you will tap all three of these sources at

▼ **TIP**

It is well worth searching for a knowledgeable vendor. Your vendor can save you several times their sales commission in workhours your office might otherwise spend trying to solve hardware and software problems. The vendor can also help you set up a system of file organization and management—something that can become a nightmare if left unattended.

one point or another as you start to implement an AutoCAD system in your work.

It can be difficult to find a vendor who understands your special needs. This is because the vendor must have specialized knowledge of computers as well as design or production. A good vendor should offer training and phone support, both of which are crucial to productive use of a program with as much complexity as AutoCAD. Some vendors even offer user groups as a means of maintaining an active and open communication with their clients. Here are some further suggestions:

- Find an independent consultant who is familiar with Auto-CAD. Although it may be harder to find a good CAD consultant than to find a good vendor, the consultant's view of your needs is unbiased by the motivation to make a sale. The consultant's main goal is to help you gain productivity from your CAD system, so he or she will be more helpful in these areas than your average vendor.

- Get references before you use anyone's services. Your own colleagues may be the best source of information on vendors, consultants, and even hardware. You can learn from their good fortune or mistakes.

- Don't rely on magazine reviews and product demonstrations at shows. These can often be misleading or offer incomplete information. If you see something you like, test it before you buy it. For some products this may be difficult, but because of the complex nature of computer-aided design and drafting, it is important to know exactly what you are getting.

CHOOSING IN-HOUSE EXPERTS

Perhaps even more important than a good vendor is an individual within your office who knows your CAD system thoroughly. Ideally, everyone closely involved in your drafting and design projects should be a proficient AutoCAD user, but it is impractical to expect everyone to give time to system management. Usually one individual is chosen for this task. It can often be a thankless one, but when the going gets rough, an in-house expert is indispensable.

▼ NOTE

If you find that a task can be automated, a knowledgeable in-house person can create custom macros and commands on the spot, saving your design or production staff hundreds of workhours—especially if several people are performing that task. Your in-house authority can also train new personnel and answer users' questions.

In a smaller office, the in-house authority may need to be an expert on design, production, and computers, all rolled into one. The point is that to really take advantage of AutoCAD or any CAD system, you should provide some in-house expertise. AutoCAD is a powerful tool, but that power is wasted if you don't take advantage of it.

You must be aware, however, that the role of the in-house expert will require significant time spent away from other tasks. Dealing with questions about the program's use can be disruptive to the expert's own work, and writing custom applications is often at least a part-time job in itself. Keep this under consideration when scheduling work or managing costs on a project. It also pays to keep the following in mind:

- The in-house expert should be a professional trained in your firm's field of specialization, rather than someone with a computer background. Every architect or engineer on your staff represents years of training. Learning AutoCAD can take a matter of weeks or months. The expert-to-be, however, should be willing to develop some computer expertise.

- Running a CAD system is not a simple clerical task. It takes not only clear thinking and good organizational skills, but also good communication skills. The in-house authority should have some interest in teaching, and the patience to deal with interruptions and "stupid" questions. He or she may be a manager, and will need access to the same information as any key player on your design team.

- If you have several computers, you may also want to obtain some general technical support. If your company is implementing its first computer environment, many questions will arise that are not directly related to AutoCAD. The technical support person will be able to answer highly technical questions for which a computer background is required more so than familiarity with your professional specialty.

- Consider contracting with an outside consultant to occasionally provide additional support. This will allow development of custom applications without waiting for your staff to develop the necessary skills. A consultant can also help train your staff and even fill in from time to time when production schedules become too tight.

ACCLIMATIZING THE STAFF

Once an AutoCAD system is installed and operational, the next step is to get the staff acquainted with that system. This can be the most difficult task of all. In nearly every office, there is at least one key person who resists the use of computers. This can be a tremendous obstacle, especially if that individual is at management level—though nearly anyone who is resisting the project goals can do damage. The human capacity to undermine the sincerest efforts is astounding, and when coupled with a complex computer system, the results can be disastrous. Unfortunately, there is no easy solution to this problem aside from fostering a positive attitude toward the CAD system's capabilities and its implementation.

AutoCAD has a way of adding force to everything you do, both good and bad. Because it is capable of reproducing work rapidly, it is very easy to unintentionally multiply errors until they are actually out of hand. This also holds true for project management. Poor management tends to be magnified when AutoCAD comes into the picture. You are managing yet another dimension of information—blocks, symbols, layers…. If the users cannot manage and communicate this information, problems are sure to arise.

On the other hand, a smoothly running, well-organized project is reflective of the way AutoCAD enhances your productivity. In fact, good management is essential for realizing productivity gains with Auto-CAD. A project on AutoCAD is only as good as the information you provide and the manner in which the system is administered. Open communication and good record keeping are essential to the development and integrity of a design or a set of drawings. The better managed a project is, the fewer problems arise, and the less time is required to get results.

Discussing CAD management procedures in your project kickoff meetings will help accustom people to the idea of using the system. Exchanging information with your consultants concerning your CAD system standards is also an important step in keeping a job running smoothly from the start, especially if they are also using AutoCAD.

▼ TIP

If any of your staff members are absolutely frightened by computers, you may want to consider using the AutoCAD file viewers mentioned in *Chapter 19*.

LEARNING THE SYSTEM

Learning AutoCAD can be time consuming. If you are the one who is to operate the AutoCAD system, at first you won't be as productive as you were when you were doing everything manually, and don't expect to perform miracles overnight. Once you have a good working knowledge of the program, you still have to integrate it into your day-to-day work. It will take you a month or two, depending on how much time you spend studying AutoCAD, to get to a point where you are entering drawings with any proficiency. It also helps to have a real project you can work on while you are in training. Choose a job that doesn't have a tight schedule, so that if anything goes wrong you have enough time to make corrections.

Remember that it is important to communicate to others what they can expect from you. Otherwise, you may find yourself in an awkward position because you haven't produced the anticipated results.

MAKING AUTOCAD USE EASIER

Not everyone in your organization needs to be an AutoCAD expert, but in order for your firm to obtain maximum productivity from AutoCAD, almost everyone involved in design or production should be able to use the system. Designers especially should be involved, since AutoCAD can produce significant time savings in the design phase of a project.

You may want to consider an add-on software package to aid those who need to use AutoCAD but who are not likely to spend a lot of time learning it. These add-ons automate some of the typical functions of a particular application. They can also provide ready-made office standards for symbols and layers. Add-ons are available for architects, circuit board designers, electrical engineers, civil engineers, and mechanical designers, to name a few.

Add-ons shouldn't be viewed as the only means of using AutoCAD within your office, but rather as aids to casual users, and partners to your own custom applications. No two offices work alike and no two projects are exactly the same, so add-ons cannot be all things to all people. Remember, AutoCAD is really a graphics tool whose commands and interface can be manipulated to suit any project or office. And that is the way it should be.

▼ **TIP**

If you are serious about being productive with AutoCAD, you will want to develop custom applications. See *Chapters 19 and 20* to find out more about customization and third-party software.

V

Customizing —Taking AutoCAD to the Limit

MANAGING AN AUTOCAD PROJECT

If you are managing a project that is to be put on AutoCAD, be sure you understand what it can and can't do. If your expectations are unreasonable, or if you don't communicate your requirements to the design or production team, friction and problems may occur. Open and clear communication is of the utmost importance, especially when using AutoCAD or any CAD program in a workgroup environment. Here are some further points to consider:

- If your office is just beginning to use AutoCAD, be sure you allow time for staff training. Generally, an individual can become independent on the program after 24 to 36 hours of training. ("Independent" means able to produce drawings without having to constantly refer to a manual or call in the trainer.) This book should provide enough guidance to accomplish this level of skill.

- Once at the point of independence, most individuals will take another month or so to reach a work rate comparable to hand drafting. After that, the individual's productivity will depend on his or her creativity and problem-solving ability. These are very rough estimates, but they should give you an idea of what to expect.

- If you are using a software add-on product, the training period may be shorter, but the user won't have the same depth of knowledge as someone who isn't using the enhancements. As mentioned earlier, this kind of education may be fine for casual users, but you will reach an artificial upper limit on productivity if you rely too heavily on add-ons.

As you or your staff members are learning AutoCAD, you will need to learn how to best utilize this new tool in the context of your office's operations. This may mean rethinking how you go about running a project. It may also mean training coworkers to operate differently.

For example, one of the most common production challenges is scheduling work so that check plots can be produced on a timely basis.

Normally, project members are used to looking at drawings at convenient times as they progress, even when there are scheduled review dates. With AutoCAD, you won't have that luxury. You will have to consider plotting time when scheduling drawing review dates. This means the person doing the drawings must get accurate information in time to enter last-minute changes and to plot the drawings.

ESTABLISHING OFFICE STANDARDS

Communication is especially important when you are one of many people working on the same project on separate computers. A well-developed set of standards and procedures helps to minimize problems that might be caused by miscommunication. In this section, you'll find some suggestions on how to set up these standards.

ESTABLISHING LAYERING CONVENTIONS

You have seen how layers can be a useful tool. But they can easily get out of hand when you have free reign over their creation and naming. This can be especially troublesome when more than one person is working on the same set of drawings. The following scenario illustrates this point.

One day the drawing you are working on has twenty layers. Then the next day, you find that someone has added six more, with names that have no meaning to you whatsoever. You don't dare delete those layers or modify the objects on them, for fear of retaliation from the individual who put them there. You ask around, but no one seems to know anything about these new layers. Finally, after spending an hour or two tracking down the culprit, you discover that the layers are not important at all.

With an appropriate layer-naming convention, you can minimize this type of problem (though you may not eliminate it entirely). A too-rigid naming convention can cause as many problems as no convention at all, so it is best to give general guidelines rather than force everyone to stay within narrow limits. As mentioned in *Chapter 6*, you can create layer names in a way that allows you to group them using wildcards.

V

Customizing —Taking
AutoCAD to the Limit

AutoCAD allows up to 31 characters in a layer name, so you can use descriptive names.

Line weights should be standardized in conjunction with colors. If you intend to use a service bureau for plotting, check with them first; they may require that you conform to their color and line-weight standards.

ESTABLISHING DRAWING NAME CONVENTIONS

As with layers, you will also need a system to keep track of your drawing files and blocks. If you are using an MS-DOS computer, this control will be a little more difficult to maintain than keeping track of layers, because DOS limits file names to eight characters. Blocks on AutoCAD can have 31-character names, but because you will want to turn blocks into external files, you should limit block names to eight characters.

Design a file-naming system that allows you to identify your drawing files by job number, drawing type, and revision number. For instance, the job number can be three digits, the drawing type can be an alphabetic code, and the revision can be an alphanumeric code. With this system, a coded file name would look like this: *704B061A.DWG*. Here, the first three numbers are an abbreviation of job number 8704. The next two characters are a symbol for drawing type B on sheet number 6. Finally, the last two characters indicate revision number 1 and series designation A. You may even want to include a code number to designate symbols.

Unfortunately, this type of code is difficult to remember. Most people prefer easily recognizable names, such as *ELM02.DWG* for Elm Street project sheet number 2. Although this recognizable type of name can't convey as much information as a coded name, it is usually better to base your file-naming system on recognizable names—most designers and drafters have enough to think about without having to learn special codes. You may be able to devise a combination of names plus numbers that offers a word or phrase in conjunction with a code.

LABELING HARD COPIES

A problem you will run into once you start to generate files is keeping track of which AutoCAD file goes with which hardcopy drawing. It's a good idea to place an identifying tag on the drawing (and that will plot with the drawing) in some inconspicuous place. As well as the file name, the tag should include such information as the date and time the drawing was last edited, who edited it, and for which submission the plot was done. All these bits of information can prove helpful in the progress of a design or production project (see Figure 21.17).

USING NETWORKS WITH AUTOCAD

▼ NOTE

In simplified terms, a *dedicated file server* is a storage device, often a computer with a large-capacity hard disk, that acts as a repository of data. A server will often have a tape-backup device to facilitate regular system backup.

In an effort to simplify your file maintenance, you may want to consider installing a network to connect your computers electronically. Networks offer a way to share files and peripherals among computers in different locations. They come in a variety of styles—from very simple software and cable connectors, to systems that use what are called *dedicated file servers*, whose special hardware and fiber optics communicate with the computers on the network.

Two basic types of networks can be used with AutoCAD: *server/client systems* and *peer-to-peer systems*. The file server offers you a way to maintain files on a single computer. The computers connected to the server are referred to as *clients* or *nodes*. You can store all of your common symbols, AutoLISP programs, custom menus, and working files on the server, thus reducing the risk of having duplicate files. The client computers are simpler and less powerful. They use the server as their main storage device, accessing the programs and data stored on the server through the network. Networks with servers also have all the peripheral output devices connected to the server. This centralized type of system offers the user an easier way of managing files.

A peer-to-peer network does not use a server. Instead, each computer has equal status and can access files and peripherals on other computers on the network. Generally, this type of network is less expensive, since you don't need to dedicate a computer to the single task of server. Peripherals such as plotters and printers are shared among computers. Even hard disks are shared, though access to directories can be controlled at each computer.

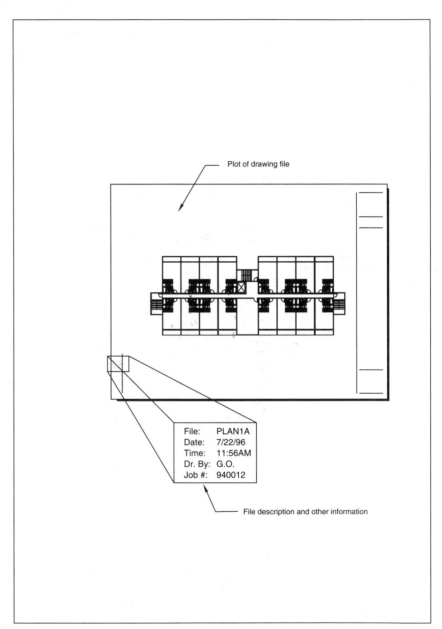

Figure 21.17: You can promote good drawing management by using a small note identifying the file used to generate the drawing.

A third type of network, a *multitasking/multiuser system*, might also be used. This system is similar to a server/client system, with each client computer being nothing more than a monitor and keyboard connected to the "server." Since AutoCAD is so power-hungry, it would be difficult to run more than a few AutoCAD stations on such a system.

Networks can be useful tools in managing your work, but they can also introduce new difficulties. For some network users, file-version control becomes a major concern. Speed of file access can be another problem. No matter what form of network you install, you will need a system manager whose duties include backing up files in the server and making sure the network's output devices are operating as they should. Used properly, a network can save time by easing the flow of information between computer users; it must, however, be managed carefully.

Here are some tips for using AutoCAD on a network:

- If you can afford it, use a star topology for your network, with an active hub and a dedicated server.

- Configure AutoCAD to store temporary files on the client or node computer.

- Use the Acadcfg OS environment setting to force AutoCAD to store configuration settings locally on the client or node computer (see *Appendix A* for more on Acadcfg).

- Configure your network version of AutoCAD for multiple swap files and local code pages, and set the DOS environment to use the client or node computer for swap files (see *Appendix A* for more on these tasks).

KEEPING RECORDS

Computers are said to create "the paperless office." As you work more and more with them, however, you may find that quite the opposite is true. Although you can store more information on magnetic media, you will spend a good deal of time reviewing that information on hardcopy, because it is very difficult to spot errors on a computer monitor. When

▼ NOTE

Release 13 of AutoCAD offers many features for the network user. Features such as file locking and cross-reference files—both discussed in earlier chapters—let you maintain better control of file versions over your network. The network version of AutoCAD can operate with systems such as Novell, 3Com, and NFS (3Com users, however, must pay special attention to AutoCAD's installation and performance guide).

V

Customizing —Taking
AutoCAD to the Limit

you use AutoCAD on large projects, another level of documentation must also exist: a way of keeping track of the many elements that go into the creation of drawings.

▼ TIP

Your companion CD has AutoLISP utilities that will generate log files for you automatically. See *Appendix C* for details.

Because job requirements vary, you may want to provide a layer log to keep track of layers and their intended uses for specific jobs. Also, to manage blocks within files, a log of block names and their insertion values can help. Finally, plan to keep a log of symbols. You will probably have a library of symbols used in your work group, and this library will grow as your projects become more varied. Documenting these symbols will help to keep track of them.

Another activity that you may want to keep records for is plotting—especially if you bill your clients separately for computer time or for analyzing job costs. A plot log might contain such information as the time spent on plotting, the type of plot done, the purpose of the plot, and even a list of plotting errors and problems that arise with each drawing.

Although records may be the last thing on your mind when you are working to meet a deadline, in the long run they can save time and aggravation for you and the people you work with.

UNDERSTANDING WHAT AUTOCAD CAN DO FOR YOU

Many of us have only a vague idea of what AutoCAD can contribute to our work. We think it will make our drafting tasks go faster, but we're not sure exactly how; or we believe it will make us produce better-quality drawings. Some people expect AutoCAD will make them better designers or allow them to produce professional-quality drawings without having much drawing talent. All these things are true to an extent, and AutoCAD can help you in some ways that are less tangible than speed and quality.

SEEING THE HIDDEN ADVANTAGES

We have discussed how AutoCAD can help you meet your drafting and design challenges, by allowing you to visualize your ideas more clearly and by reducing the time it takes to do repetitive tasks. AutoCAD also forces you to organize your drawing process more efficiently. It changes your perception of problems and, though it may introduce new ones, the additional accuracy and information AutoCAD provides will minimize errors.

AutoCAD also provides drawing consistency. A set of drawings done on AutoCAD is more legible and consistent, reducing the possibility of errors caused by illegible handwriting or poor drafting. In our litigious culture, this is a significant feature.

Finally, because AutoCAD systems are becoming more prevalent, it is easier to find people who can use it proficiently. As this group of experts grows, training will become less of a burden to your company.

TAKING A PROJECT OFF AUTOCAD

As helpful as AutoCAD can be, there are times when making revisions on AutoCAD is simply not worth the effort. Last-minute changes that are minor but pervasive throughout a set of drawings are best made by hand on the most up-to-date hardcopy. That way, you don't waste time and drawing media in plotting drawings.

Also, it is a good idea to have a label on every hardcopy of a file so that users know which file to edit when the time comes to make changes.

Only your experience can help you determine the best time to stop using AutoCAD and start making changes by hand. Many factors will influence this decision—the size and complexity of the project, the people available to work on it, and the nature of the revisions, to name just a few.

As you have seen, AutoCAD is a powerful software tool, and like any powerful program, it is difficult to master. I hope this last chapter has given you the incentive to take advantage of AutoCAD's full potential. Remember—even after you've learned how to use AutoCAD, there are many other issues that you must confront while using AutoCAD in an office environment.

▼ TIP

Once the project is done, however, go back and enter the final changes in AutoCAD just to keep your files up-to-date.

V

Customizing —Taking AutoCAD to the limit

Unlike words, drawings have few restrictions. The process of writing requires adherence to the structures of our language. The process of drawing, on the other hand, has no fixed structure. There are a million ways to draw a face or a building, for example. For this reason, your use of AutoCAD is much less restricted, and there are certainly potential uses for it that are yet to be discovered. I encourage you to experiment with AutoCAD and explore the infinite possibilities it offers for solving your design problems and communicating your ideas.

I hope *Mastering AutoCAD 13 for Windows* has been of benefit to you and that you will continue to use it as a reference. If you have comments, criticisms, or ideas about how to improve the next edition of this book, write to me at the address below. And thanks for choosing *Mastering AutoCAD 13 for Windows*.

George Omura
Omura Illustration
P.O. Box 6357
Albany, CA 94706-0357
E-Mail: 76515.1250@compuserve.com

APPENDICES

Finally, this book has five appendices. *Appendix A, Hardware and Software Tips*, should give you a start on selecting hardware appropriate for AutoCAD. It also provides tips on improving AutoCAD's performance and troubleshooting. If AutoCAD is not already installed on your system, read *Appendix B, Installing and Setting Up AutoCAD*, which contains an installation and configuration tutorial that you should follow before starting Chapter 1. You should read *Appendix C, Using the Companion CD Programs*, around the time you read *Chapter 19*. This appendix describes the utilities available on the companion CD you get with this book. This is also where you'll find out how to install the sample files for the exercises in this book. *Appendix D, System and Dimension Variables*, will illuminate the references to the system variables scattered throughout the book. *Appendix D* also discusses the many dimension settings and system features AutoCAD has to offer. Finally, *Appendix E, Standard AutoCAD Commands*, provides a listing of all the AutoCAD commands, with a brief description of their functions and options. This appendix is especially helpful when you get to chapter 21 and start to create your own macros.

HARDWARE AND SOFTWARE TIPS

AutoCAD is a resource-hungry program; it requires a fairly sophisticated hardware system to run efficiently. Since many of the items that make up an AutoCAD system are not found on the typical desktop computer, I have provided this appendix to help you understand some of the less common items you may need. I also discuss ways you can improve AutoCAD's performance through software and hardware.

UNDERSTANDING DEVICE DRIVERS

Sometimes a program calls for input and output devices that are not normally connected to a microcomputer and that the operating system does not know how to manage. AutoCAD for Windows provides its own instructions in the form of applications called *drivers* for managing the devices. These drivers are in the form of computer files and can be recognized by their .DLL extension. They also have specific prefixes depending on whether they are display (ds), rendering (rc), plotter (pl), or digitizer (dg) drivers. In general, you won't have to concern yourself with these files. When you configure AutoCAD during the installation process, AutoCAD provides you with descriptions of the driver options available.

There are many products available in the market that are not listed in the AutoCAD configuration menu. Fortunately, as a way of maintaining compatibility, most products imitate some of the more popular input and output devices. For example, you may have a plotter that emulates the Hewlett-Packard line of plotters through the Hewlett-Packard Graphics Language (HPGL/HPGL2). If you have a plotter that uses HPGL, you can use it by configuring AutoCAD for a Hewlett Packard plotter, regardless of whether yours is listed in the configuration menu. You can also use the Windows *system printer* option, which tells AutoCAD to use the printer used by Windows. The Windows system printer can be selected through the Control Panel application.

In addition to the standard, built-in drivers, AutoCAD allows third-party drivers that use what is called the *Autodesk Device Interface (ADI)*. Autodesk offers the ADI Toolkit for manufacturers who wish to write drivers for their own hardware. This frees Autodesk from having to write drivers for every device on the market. Virtually every CAD related product on the market today supports AutoCAD through standard

interfaces such as HPGL2 or ADI. For the Windows version of Auto-
CAD, the ADI drivers are also .DLL files.

THE GRAPHICS DISPLAY

A high-resolution display card is a device that allows your computer to
display graphic images in greater detail, or *resolution*, than a standard
graphics display. Many of the so-called *SVGA* display cards are inex-
pensive and offer high-quality output. High-resolution display cards
often require a monitor capable of displaying their output. Because of
this, the card and monitor combination is often considered a unit.

To improve AutoCAD's performance, Autodesk and other third-
party products offer *display list* software. The display list gives you nearly
instantaneous pans and zooms, but it comes at the cost of consuming
more of your memory. If you are shopping for a display system, consider
one that utilizes a graphics processor that accelerates Windows graphics. If you are in the market for a complete computer system, you might
consider one that uses the VESA or PCI local bus. A computer
equipped with such a bus, and a local bus display card, can greatly improve overall Windows performance.

POINTING DEVICES

Our most basic means of communicating with computers is the keyboard and pointing device. Most likely, you will use a mouse, but if you
are still in the market for a pointing device, choose an input device that
generates smooth cursor movement. Some of the lesser-quality input
devices cause erratic movement. When looking for an input device
other than a mouse, choose one that provides positive feedback, such
as a definitive button click when you pick an object on the screen.
Many low-cost digitizers have a very poor button feel that can cause errors when you are selecting points or menu options.

In general, use a high-resolution mouse if you do not plan to do any
tracing. You may also consider a trackball if you are tight on desk space.
If you must have the use of a tablet menu, or if you know you are going
to trace drawings, then get a digitizer, but be sure it is of good quality.

Appendices

THE DIGITIZING TABLET

If you need to trace drawings, you should consider a digitizing tablet. It is usually a rectangular object with a penlike *stylus*, or a device called a *puck*, which resembles a mouse. It has a smooth surface on which to draw. The most popular size is 11"×11", but digitizing tablets are available in sizes up to 60"×70". The tablet gives a natural feel to drawing with the computer because the movement of the stylus or puck is directly translated into cursor movement. While many digitizers for Windows come with a stylus, you will want a multi-button puck to work with AutoCAD.

A digitizing tablet's puck often has *function buttons*. These buttons can be programmed through the AutoCAD menu file system to start your most frequently used commands, which is much faster than searching through an on-screen menu. You can also select commands from the tablet's surface if you install the *menu template* supplied with AutoCAD. A menu template is a flat sheet of plastic with the AutoCAD commands printed on it. You can select commands simply by pointing at them on the template. If you have a digitizing tablet, refer to *Appendix B*, which tells you how to install a template.

Most digitizers can be used as pointing devices for Windows. Unfortunately, this precludes their use as a tracing device for AutoCAD. For this reason, you may want to have both a digitizer and a mouse connected to your computer. AutoCAD allows you to switch easily from digitizer to mouse using the Mouse/Digitizer Arbitration option under the Options ➤ Preferences dialog box.

OUTPUT DEVICES

Output options vary greatly in quality and price. Quality and paper size are the major considerations for both printers and plotters. Nearly all printers give accurate drawings, but some produce better line quality than others. Some plotters give merely acceptable results, while others are quite impressive in their speed and accuracy. Color is optional on both printers and plotters. Some printers produce color prints, while all pen plotters allow color.

AutoCAD for Windows can use the Windows *system printer*, so any device that Windows supports is also supported by AutoCAD. AutoCAD also gives you the option of plotting directly to an output device. By plotting directly to the output device, instead of going through Windows, AutoCAD can offer more control over the final output.

PRINTERS

The dot-matrix printer is the least expensive choice for producing a quick-check plot, as long as your drawing isn't larger than 13"×16". It will do a reasonable job of printing your drawing, though it won't produce the best-quality line work, and drawing size is limited to the carriage width of the printer (anywhere from $8^1/2$" to 13"). The printer's chief advantage is speed. A dot-matrix printer can print any drawing in under ten minutes, regardless of complexity. In contrast, a pen plotter can take an hour or more, particularly if your drawing contains a lot of text. Some dot-matrix printers also offer color printing.

As far as AutoCAD is concerned, most laser printers, with the exception of PostScript printers, fall into the category of dot-matrix printers. Laser printers have the same limitations as dot-matrix printers (limted sheet sizes), but they are capable of better line quality and higher speeds. They are usually limited to $8^1/2$×11" paper, though you can get 11"×17" laser printers at a premium.

A third alternative is the ink-jet or bubble-jet printer. These printers offer speed and quality output with the added advantage of low noise. Some ink-jet printers even accept 17"×22" paper and offer PostScript emulation at up to 720 dots per inch. Since ink-jet printers are competitively priced, they can offer the best solution for low-cost check plots. And the 17"×22" paper size is quite acceptable for half-size plots, a format that more architects and engineers are using.

PLOTTERS

A plotter is a mechanical drafting device used to draw a computer image on sheets of paper, vellum, or polyester film. Most plotters use pens, though some offer ink-jet, laser, thermal, or electrostatic technology to get the image on paper.

Appendices

If your drawing is fairly simple, a pen plotter can give you results in minutes. However, many applications require fairly complex drawings, which in turn take much longer to plot. A typical architectural drawing, for example, takes 45 minutes on a good-quality, large-format plotter using wet-ink pens on polyester film. By using pens capable of faster speeds, you can reduce the time it takes to plot a drawing by 40 percent and still get an accurate reproduction. When you want large plots, sharp clear lines, or reproduction quality, the pen plotter is the way to go.

Raster plotters, especially ink-jet plotters, are perhaps the most flexible general-purpose output devices available. These plotters can produce large-format drawings in less than half the time taken by pen plotters. Many ink-jet plotters offer high speed and good quality, at a competitive price. If speed and large-format drawings are top priorities, nothing can match these devices.

If you need large plots but feel you can't afford a large plotter, many blueprint companies offer plotting as a service. This can be a good alternative to purchasing your own plotter. Check with your local blueprinter.

POSTSCRIPT PRINTER OUTPUT

If you want to use a PostScript device to output your drawings, the best method is to use File ➤ Export or the PSOUT command. These options convert your drawing into a true PostScript file. You can then send your file to a PostScript printer or typesetting machine. This can be especially useful for PCB layout where you require photo negatives for output. If you are an architect who needs presentation-quality drawings, you may want to consider using the Encapsulated PS (*.EPS) option in the Export Data dialog box. Often blueprinters who offer a raster plotter service can produce E-size PostScript output from a PostScript file. The uses of this option are really quite open-ended.

FINE-TUNING POSTSCRIPT FILE EXPORT

AutoCAD provides the PostScript user with a great deal of control over the formatting of the PostScript file that is output with the File ➤ Export and the PSOUT command; the options range from font-substitution mapping to custom PostScript Prologue data. Most of this control is offered through a file named Acad.PSF. This is the master support file for the PSIN and PSOUT commands. You can customize the PostScript file created by PSOUT by making changes in the Acad.PSF file. Acad.PSF is divided into sections that affect various parts of the PostScript output. Each section begins with a title preceded by an asterisk. The following briefly describes these sections.

> ***fonts** lets you control font substitution. You can assign a Post-Script font to an AutoCAD font file or PostScript .PFB file used in the drawing.
>
> ***figureprologue** defines the procedures used for embedding figures included with PSIN PostScript images.
>
> ***isofontprologue** defines the procedures used to re-encode fonts in order to be compatible with the ISO 8859 Latin/1 character set.
>
> ***fillprologue** defines the code used in the PSOUT file to describe area fills.
>
> ***fill** is a section where you can include your own custom fill patterns.

Most of these sections, with the exception of the *fonts section, will be of little use to the average user; but if you are a PostScript programmer, you can take advantage of these sections to customize your PostScript output.

You will also want to know about the *Psprolog* system variable. This system variable instructs PSOUT to include your custom prolog statement in its PostScript output. (See *Chapter 14* for details on using PSOUT.) You add your custom prolog to the Acad.PSF file using a text editor. The prolog should begin with a section heading that you devise. The heading can say anything, but it must begin with an asterisk like all the other section headings. Everything following the heading, up to the next heading or the end of the file, and excluding comments, will be included in the PSOUT output file. The following shows a sample prolog that converts color assignments to line widths in a way similar to pen plotters.

Appendices

```
*widthprolog
/ACADLayer { pop } def
/ACADColor { pop pop pop dup 0.5 mul setlinewidth pop } def
/ACADLtype { pop
userdict /Linedict known not { /Linedict 100 dict def } if
1 index cvn Linedict exch known not {
mark 1 index { dup 0 eq { pop 1 72.0 div } if abs } forall
counttomark 2 add −1 roll astore exch pop
1 index cvn exch Linedict begin def end }
{ pop } ifelse
Linedict begin cvx exec 0 setdash end } bind def
/bd{bind def}bind def /m{moveto}bd /1{lineto}bd
/s{stroke}bd
/a{arc}bd /an{arcn}bd /gs{gsave}bd /gr{grestore}bd
/cp{closepath}bd /tr{translate}bd /sc{scale}bd /co{concat}bd
/ff{findfont}bd /sf{setfont}bd /sh{show}bd /np{newpath}bd
/sw{setlinewidth}bd /sj{setlinejoin}bd /sm{setmiterlimit}bd
/cl{clip}bd /fi{fill}bd
%%EndProlog
```

A complete discussion of PSOUT and PSIN's PostScript support is beyond the scope of this book. If you are interested in learning more, consult the PostScript section of the AutoCAD Customization manual. You can also learn a lot by looking at the PostScript files produced by PSOUT, browsing the Acad.PSF file, and consulting the following publications:

Understanding PostScript, David Holzgang, SYBEX Inc.

PostScript Language Program Design, Adobe Systems Incorporated, Addison-Wesley Publishing Company, Inc.

PostScript Language Reference Manual, Adobe Systems Incorporated, Addison-Wesley Publishing Company, Inc.

PostScript Language Tutorial and Cookbook, Adobe Systems Incorporated, Addison-Wesley Publishing Company, Inc.

You can also add a PostScript plotter to the plotter configuration. When you do this, AutoCAD plots the drawing as a series of vectors, just like any other plotter. If you have any filled areas in your drawing and you are plotting to a PostScript file, the vectors that are used to plot those filled areas can greatly increase plot file size and the time it takes to plot your PostScript file.

MEMORY AND AUTOCAD PERFORMANCE

Next to your computer's CPU, memory has the greatest impact on AutoCAD's speed. How much you have, and how you use it, can make a big difference in whether you finish that rush job on schedule or work late nights trying. In this section, I hope to clarify some basic points about memory and how AutoCAD uses it.

AutoCAD Release 13 for Windows is a virtual memory system. This means that when your RAM memory resources reach their limit, part of the data stored in RAM is temporarily moved to your hard disk to make more room in RAM. This temporary storage of RAM to your hard disk is called memory *paging*. Through memory paging, AutoCAD will continue to run, even though your work might exceed the capacity of your RAM.

AutoCAD uses memory in two ways. First, it stores its program code in RAM. The more programs you have open under Windows, the more RAM will be used. Windows controls the use of memory for program code, so if you start to reach the RAM limit, Windows will take care of memory paging. The second way AutoCAD uses memory is for storing drawing data. AutoCAD always attempts to store as much of your drawing in RAM as possible. Again, when the amount of RAM required for a drawing exceeds the actual RAM available, AutoCAD will page parts of the drawing data to the hard disk. The paging of drawing data is controlled strictly by AutoCAD. Since RAM is shared with both program code and drawing data, your drawing size and the number of programs you have open under windows will affect how much RAM you have available. For this reason, if you find your AutoCAD editing session is slowing down, try closing other applications you might have open. This will free up more memory for AutoCAD and the drawing file.

AUTOCAD AND YOUR HARD DISK

You will notice that AutoCAD will slow down when paging occurs. If this happens frequently, the best thing you can do is add more RAM. But you can also improve the performance of AutoCAD under these conditions by ensuring that you have adequate hard-disk space and that any free hard-disk space has been *defragmented* or *optimized*. A defragmented disk will offer faster access, thereby improving paging speed.

You can also set up a permanent swap file under Windows to improve performance. A permanent swap file will improve the speed at which Windows is able to page RAM to your hard disk. To install a permanent swap file, take the following steps:

1. Remove any unnecessary files, then defragment your hard disk.

2. From the Main window of the Windows Program Manager, open the Control Panel program, then double-click on the 386 Enhanced icon. The 386 Enhanced dialog box will appear.

3. Click on the Virtual Memory ... button. The Virtual Memory dialog box appears.

4. Click on the Change button. The dialog box will expand to reveal more options.

5. Select the drive you intend to use for your permanent swap file from the Drive pull-down list, then select Permanent in the Type pull-down list.

6. In the New Size input box, enter the size you want for your permanent swap file.

7. Click on the Use 32-bit Disk Access check box.

8. Close all the dialog boxes by clicking on OK.

Autodesk recommends a swap file that is four times the size of your RAM capacity. This means that if you have 16 megabytes of RAM, you will want a swap file that is 64 megabytes. This gives you a system with up to 64 megabytes of virtual memory.

The permanent swap file will permanently take up space on your hard disk, so when you select a size for the swap file, be sure you leave some room on your drive for other data. If your hard disk is limited in free space, try removing unnecessary files. Autodesk recommends a minimum of 20 Mb of free disk space. If you have a disk optimizer that lets you control which sectors are made free during defragmentation, use the outermost sectors of your hard drive for swap-file space.

WHAT TO DO FOR OUT OF RAM AND OUT OF PAGE SPACE ERRORS

▼ WARNING

If you are in a network environment, check the time and date of any .AC$ files before you remove them. They may belong to another user's current editing session, in which case you should not erase them.

After you have used AutoCAD for some time, you may find some odd-looking files with a .AC$ extension in the directory where your drawings are stored. These files are the temporary files for storing unused portions of a drawing. They often appear if AutoCAD has been terminated abnormally. You can usually erase these files without any adverse effect. (But see my warning in the margin.)

If you've discarded all the old swap files and your disk is still unusually full, there are a few other steps you can take to free up disk space. First, run the Windows 95 ScanDisk utility. This can be found by choosing Programs ➤ Accessories ➤ System Tools ➤ ScanDisk from the Windows 95 Start button. ScanDisk will check your disk for any lost file clusters or defects in the drive. Lost file clusters are pieces of files not actually assigned to a specific file; often they crop up when a program has terminated abnormally. If they go undetected, they will simply use up disk space. ScanDisk lets you locate and delete lost clusters.

▼ NOTE

Users of Windows 3.1 can use the DOS version of ScanDisk. ScanDisk for DOS can be found in the DOS directory in most Windows installations: exit from Windows (this utility should not be used while Windows is running) and type **Help ScanDisk** at the DOS prompt to get information on how to use ScanDisk.

You can also free up disk space by emptying the Recycle Bin (found on the Windows 95 Desktop). Files discarded into the Recycle Bin are not completely deleted from your hard disk until you empty the bin. To do this, right-click on the Recycle Bin, then select Empty Recycle Bin in the pop-up menu.

AUTOCAD MEMORY AND NETWORKS

If you are using a network version of AutoCAD, each computer on the network that uses AutoCAD must have its own configuration file. This

Appendices

means you must set the /C command switch (described in the *Appendix B*) to a local drive and directory. Once this is done, you must run the AutoCAD configuration for each client computer. This will ensure that each node will have its own network node name and default log-in name.

Another point to consider is the location of swap files. When drawing files get large, AutoCAD makes heavy use of your hard disk. Swap files are constantly being written and updated. If you are working with AutoCAD on a network, it is especially important to pay attention to where swap files are being written. If you are using a server-client network system, and the network client or node has its own hard disk, you can improve AutoCAD's performance by forcing the program to place drawing swap files on the local drive, instead of on the server. This reduces network traffic, thereby improving AutoCAD's and the network's performance. The following steps show how this is done.

1. Start AutoCAD from the node, then click on Options ➤ Configure.

2. At the Configuration menu, enter **7** ↵ to select *Operating Parameters*.

3. At the Operating Parameters menu, enter **5** ↵ to select *Placement of temporary files*. You will see the message

   Enter directory name for temporary files, or DRAWING to place them in the same directory as the drawing being edited.
   <DRAWING>:

4. Enter a local drive and directory name where temporary files can be stored.

5. Exit the configuration and make sure you save the configuration at the last prompt.

WHEN THINGS GO WRONG

AutoCAD is a complex program, and at times things don't go exactly right. If you run into problems, chances are the problem is not insurmountable. Here are a few tips on what to do when things don't work.

DIFFICULTY STARTING UP OR OPENING A FILE

If you've recently installed AutoCAD but cannot get it started, you may have a configuration problem. Before you panic, try reconfiguring your system from scratch. To do this, erase the Acad.CFG file found in your Auto-CAD directory, and start AutoCAD. You will be prompted to configure AutoCAD. An Acad.CFG file is created when you first configure Auto-CAD after installation.

Another common problem is having files locked and unavailable. This can happen to drawing files as well as support files—such as line type, hatch pattern, menu, and shape files. If a file is reported as being locked by AutoCAD, and you know no one else is using the system, locate the file in question, then remove its lock file. See *Chapter 14* for a complete listing of files and their lock file equivalents.

If you are on a single-user system, you may want to turn off the file-locking feature altogether. This can save you the frustration of having to unlock files that are accidentally locked as a result of system crashes.

RESTORING CORRUPTED FILES

Perhaps one of the most dreaded sights a computer user can see is the message *Error reading drive C:*. Computer hardware is often taken for granted until something goes wrong with it. Unfortunately, the most vulnerable part of your computer system is the hard disk, with the files it contains. You may even know someone who has lost AutoCAD files to an errant disk drive. One day, while you are trying to open a file, your screen responds *FATAL ERROR* or *INTERNAL ERROR*; then panic sets in.

Fortunately, there is hope for lost files. In most cases, AutoCAD will run through a file-recovery routine automatically when it attempts to load a corrupted file. If you have a file you know is corrupted, you can start the file-recovery utility by clicking on File ➤ Management ➤ Recover. You will get the File dialog box, allowing you to select the file you want to recover. Once you enter the name, AutoCAD goes to work. You get a series of messages, most of which have little meaning to the average user. Then the recovered file is opened. You may lose some data, but a partial file is better than no file at all, especially when the file represents several thousand hours of work.

Appendices

There may be situations when a file is so badly corrupted it cannot be restored. You can only hope and pray this doesn't happen to you. By backing up frequently, the inconvenience of such an occurrence can be minimized. You may also want to invest in a hard disk maintenance program such as SpinRite or Norton Utilities. These programs can spot problem areas on your hard disk before they cause trouble.

CHECKING THE CONNECTION WITH YOUR PLOTTER OR DIGITIZER

The most common problem when connecting devices to your computer's serial port is improper cabling and switch settings. Usually proper cabling is supplied with the device, but sometimes it is not. The wires connecting the various pins on your cable must be arranged a certain way. If your plotter or other serial device does not work, check the cabling on your plotter and be sure it conforms to the cabling diagram shown in your AutoCAD installation guide. Also be sure the switches are properly set on your plotter or other serial device to receive and send data to AutoCAD. Again, these settings can be found in the installation guide.

Some devices require special setting up even after AutoCAD has been configured. These usually come with setup instructions. Check the manual that came with the device to be sure you haven't missed its setup options. When all else fails, call your vendor or manufacturer.

Sometimes when you temporarily switch to another program, you may find that upon returning to AutoCAD your digitizer or plotter won't respond. If this occurs, use the Reinit command. This command re-establishes connections to your peripheral devices. See *Chapter 7* for more details on Reinit.

TROUBLESHOOTING

AutoCAD is a large, complex program, so you are bound to encounter some difficulties from time to time. This section covers a few of the more common problems experienced while using AutoCAD. It is by no means a comprehensive list, but, hopefully, it will cover anything you are likely to encounter.

AutoCAD has stopped
working after the 30-day grace period

AutoCAD now requires an *authorization code*. You are given a grace period of 30 days before you need to enter this code. If for some reason, you let the 30 days lapse before you enter the code, AutoCAD will stop working and you won't have the opportunity to enter the code! If you find yourself in this situation, simply set the date on your computer back to within 30 days of your AutoCAD installation, start AutoCAD, then take the following steps to enter your code:

1. Choose Options Configure or type **Config** ↵ at the command prompt.

2. At the Configuration menu, type **7** ↵ to select the Configure operating parameters option.

3. At the Configure operating parameters menu, type **13** ↵ to select Authorization.

4. Enter your authorization code.

5. Press ↵ at each prompt until you return to the AutoCAD command prompt.

You cannot open a drawing or font file after it has
been opened once before or after a system crash

Usually this problem can be solved by removing the lock file (see *Chapter 14*). This file has the same name as your drawing file but with the .DWK filename extension. Delete this file, and you should be able to open the drawing file once again. Other files, such as menu, font, and configuration files, can also be inadvertently locked—especially after a computer crash. Check to see if you have any of the locked files described in Table 14.1, and if you do, try removing them; this usually takes care of the problem.

In the rare instance that removing the .DWK or other lock file doesn't correct this situation, chances are you are working with a file-safety utility. Such utilities help recover files that are accidentally deleted. Unfortunately, they can also prevent DOS from removing files that are deleted in the normal course of running AutoCAD (such as .BAK files or the temporary .$AC files you will see from time to time).

Appendices

When this happens, AutoCAD will not open files properly. If you are using such a utility and you are experiencing difficulty opening files, try disabling the utility temporarily, and try your AutoCAD file again.

You cannot access objects in a
drawing someone else has worked on   This may be happening because you have a Paper Space view instead of a Model Space view. To make sure you're in Model Space, type **Tilemode** ⏎ and then type **1** ⏎. Or you can turn on the UCS icon (by typing **Ucsicon** ⏎ **On** ⏎, and if you see the triangular UCS icon in the lower-left corner, then you are in Paper Space. You must go to Model Space before you can edit the drawing.

Issuing a REDRAW
does not clear the drawing properly   Check to see if the computer you are working on is using a third-party display list driver. Such drivers require their own special command to perform a redraw.

Grips do not appear when objects are selected
Make sure the Grips feature is set to its default settings (Options ➤ Grips). See *Appendix B* for details.

When you select objects, it doesn't
work the way this book says it should   Check the Selection settings to make sure they are set to their defaults (Options ➤ Selection). See *Chapter 2* for details.

Text appears in the wrong font style, or an
error message says AutoCAD cannot find font files
When you are working on files from another company, it's not uncommon that you will encounter a file that uses special third-party fonts that you do not have. You can usually substitute standard AutoCAD fonts for any fonts you don't have, without adverse effects. AutoCAD automatically presents a dialog box letting you select font files for the substitution. You can either choose a font file or press the Esc key to ignore the message (see *Chapter 8* for more on font files). If you choose

to ignore the error message, you may not see some of the text that would normally appear in the drawing.

If you get this message frequently, you may want to take advantage of AutoCAD's font-substitution capabilities, described in *Chapter 8*. This feature lets you determine in advance which fonts to substitute for missing ones.

DXF files do not import   Various problems can occur during the DXF import, the most common of which is that you are trying to import a DXF file into an existing drawing rather than a new drawing. Under some conditions, you can import a DXF file into an existing drawing, but AutoCAD may not import the entire file.

To ensure that your entire DXF file is safely imported, open a brand-new file using the standard AutoCAD defaults. Choose File ➤ New, and at the dialog box make sure the No Prototype option is checked. Once the new file is opened, proceed with the DXFIN command or use File ➤ Import and select *.DXF from the File Type pull-down list.

A file cannot be saved to disk   Frequently, a hard drive will fill up quickly during an edit session. AutoCAD can generate temporary and swap files many times larger than the file you are editing. This can leave you with no room left to save your file. If this happens, use the Windows File Manager and clear some space on your hard drive, either by moving AutoCAD files to another drive or by deleting old AutoCAD.BAK files you don't need. *Do not delete AutoCAD temporary files.*

At startup, AutoCAD cannot find the Acad.DCL file, or AutoCAD tells you it is not configured, even though you know it is   Chances are your AutoCAD environment is not set up correctly. You will need to use Options ➤ Preferences to open the Preferences dialog box. There you will find the Environment settings. See "Configuring Auto-CAD" in *Appendix B* for details on setting up the environment.

AutoCAD does not display all the Paper Space viewports   AutoCAD uses substantial memory to display Paper Space viewports. For this reason, it limits the

Appendices

number of viewports it will display at one time. Even though viewports don't display, they will still plot. Also, if you zoom in on a blank viewport while in Paper Space, you will be able to see its contents. The viewport regains visibility because you are reducing the number of viewports shown on the screen at one time.

You can increase the number of viewports AutoCAD will display at one time by resetting the *Maxactvp* system variable. (This is usually set to 16.) Be forewarned, however, that increasing the Maxactvp setting will cause AutoCAD to use more memory. If you have limited memory on your system, this will slow down AutoCAD considerably.

AutoCAD becomes impossibly slow when adding more Paper Space viewports
As mentioned for the preceding problem, AutoCAD consumes memory quickly when adding viewports. If your system resources are limited, you can reduce the *Maxactvp* system variable setting so that AutoCAD displays fewer viewports at one time. This will let you work on a file that has numerous viewports without causing a decrease in your computer's performance. Try reducing Maxactvp to 8, and then reduce or increase the setting until you find the optimum value for your situation.

AutoCAD won't open a large file, and displays a "Page file full" message
AutoCAD will open drawing files larger than can fit into your system's RAM. In order to do this, however, AutoCAD attempts to store part of the drawing in a temporary file on your hard drive. If there isn't room on the hard drive, AutoCAD will give up. To remedy this problem, clear off some space on your hard drive.

It is not uncommon for AutoCAD to require as much as 10MB of hard disk space for every 1MB of a drawing file. When you are using a display list driver, AutoCAD needs even more space. If you frequently work on very large files, you may want to set up a dedicated drive just for a Windows permanent swap file. Reserve some space for AutoCAD temporary files. See "AutoCAD and Your Hard Disk" earlier in this appendix.

The keyboard abbreviations for commands are not working
If you are working on an unfamiliar computer, chances are the keyboard abbreviations have

been altered. These usually reside in the Acad.PGP file. See *Chapter 19* for help on adding keyboard abbreviations.

Plots come out blank   Check the scale factor you are using for your plot. Often, a blank plot means your scale factor is making the plot too large to fit on the sheet. Try plotting with the Scale to Fit option. If you get a plot, then you know your scale factor is incorrect. See *Chapter 7* for more on plotting.

**You cannot get your drawing to
be properly oriented on the sheet**   If you want to change the orientation of your drawing on a plotted sheet, and the Plot Configuration orientation options don't seem to work, try rotating the UCS to align with your desired plot view, and then type **Plan** ⏎. Adjust the view to display what you want to have plotted, then use the View command (View ▶ Named Views…) to save this view. When you are ready to plot, use the View option in the Plot Configuration dialog box and plot the saved view, instead of rotating the plot.

INSTALLING AND SETTING UP AUTOCAD

BEFORE YOU DO ANYTHING, BACK UP THE DISKS

Whether you purchased the full disk set or the disk/CD-ROM version, you will want to back up the AutoCAD diskettes. For this, you can use the Copy Disk option on the Disk menu of the File Manager application. You cannot back up the CD-ROM unless you have an optical drive.

▼ **WARNING**

If you have a tablet, do not put disks on top of it, because the tablet uses a small electrical field to operate. This field can destroy data on a disk.

Be sure to label your copies the same way the originals are labeled, including the serial number from Disk 1. Put your originals in a safe place, away from any magnetic sources.

We suggest that you back up the contents of your hard disk so that, in the event you experience problems with the hard disk, you won't have to re-install AutoCAD and other programs and files that reside there.

BEFORE INSTALLING AUTOCAD

Before you begin the installation process, be sure you have a drive with at least 80MB of free disk space. In addition, you should know your dealer's name and phone number.

You will also want to have at least an additional 50MB of free disk space for AutoCAD *temporary files* and *swap files*, plus another 10MB for the tutorial files you will create. (Temporary and swap files are system files AutoCAD creates as AutoCAD works. You don't have to deal with these files directly, but you do have to allow room for them. If you want to know more about these files, see *Appendix A.*)

Finally, have your dealer's name and phone number ready, as you will be asked to enter this information during the installation. You will also want to have your network and single user authorization code ready. These can be obtained by calling the toll-free number listed in your AutoCAD package. Single user systems have a 30-day grace period so you can install and use AutoCAD without having to know your authorization code right away.

INSTALLING WIN32S FOR WINDOWS 3.1

AutoCAD is a 32-bit mode Windows application. If you are planning to run AutoCAD under Windows 3.1, you must install Win32S first. Win32S is a Windows extension that lets it run 32-bit mode applications. It is not required for Windows 95. Here's how to install it:

1. Start Windows and make sure no other applications are running.

2. Insert the Win32S diskette in drive A or B, or, if you have a CD-ROM version of AutoCAD, place the AutoCAD CD-ROM in your CD-ROM drive.

3. Choose File ➤ Run from the Program Manager pull-down menu.

4. Type the following into the Run input box:

   drive:\win32s\disk1\setup.exe

Replace the *drive* in the above example by the drive letter that contains the AutoCAD Win32S diskette or CD-ROM. For example, if your CD-ROM is drive f, you would type **f** in place of the *d* in the example.

Windows will display messages indicating that it is installing Win32S. When installation is done, proceed with the AutoCAD installation.

INSTALLING THE AUTOCAD SOFTWARE

After you've installed Win32S, and you're sure you've got enough disk space, proceed with the following steps to install AutoCAD.

1. To begin your installation, get the backup disk labeled Executables-1, and be sure it is not write-protected. Place the disk in drive A or B. If you are installing from a CD-ROM, be sure the AutoCAD CD is in your CD-ROM drive.

2. From Program Manager or File Manager, choose File ➤ Run.

Appendices

3. At the Run dialog box, enter **A:setup** or **B:setup** into the input box, depending on where the Installation disk is located, then click on OK. You see the opening screen for a moment, and then the next screen informs you that you must first personalize your copy of AutoCAD. Press ↵ to continue.

4. To personalize AutoCAD, you are asked for your name, company, dealer's name, and the dealer's telephone number. This information will be displayed on the opening AutoCAD screen, so don't enter anything you'll regret later.

5. The next group of questions asks which set of files you want to install. Go ahead and install the entire program, including the DOS version.

6. Next, you are asked where to place your AutoCAD files. The tutorial assumes you have AutoCAD on drive C and in a directory called \Acadr13\win—these are the defaults during the installation. Unless you are an experienced computer user, press ↵ to accept these defaults when you see the prompts.

7. You will also be asked where to place *shared support files*. These files, which can be used by both AutoCAD for DOS and AutoCAD for Windows, contain font descriptions, line types, and other features. This tutorial assumes that these files are located in the Common subdirectory of the Acadr13 directory. Since the default location suggested by the Install program is also called \Acadr13\Common, press ↵ to accept the default. Support files that can be used only by AutoCAD for Windows will be put into the Support subdirectory of the Acadr13\win directory.

8. Once you answer all these questions, the actual installation begins and you are prompted for each disk as it is needed. (If you are installing from a CD-ROM disk, you are asked to indicate the CD-ROM drive, and the installation continues uninterrupted.)

9. At the end of the installation, you see a new program group called AutoCAD R 13. It includes on-line documentation, two introductory tutorials, the AutoCAD help file, and several Windows Write files that provide the latest information about AutoCAD.

THE PROGRAM FILES

This book's tutorial assumes you are working from the directory where the program files are stored. However, if you prefer to work from a different directory, be sure you have set a path for the Auto-CAD directory; otherwise, AutoCAD will not start properly. Consult your DOS manual for more information on Path statements.

In the Acadr13\WIN directory, you will see a number of subdirectories. Here are brief descriptions of the contents of each subdirectory:

ADS stands for *AutoCAD Development System.* If you are a C programmer who wants to customize AutoCAD, this directory will be of importance to you. ADS is not discussed in this tutorial, however.

ASE stands for *AutoCAD SQL Extensions.* The files in this directory are for database programmers interested in linking Auto-CAD drawings to SQL servers.

DRV contains the drivers used by AutoCAD to control input and output devices. These drivers include the display drivers for VGA and SVGA.

EDOC contains the online documentation files.

Sample contains sample drawings, menus, and executable files.

Support contains the files that define a variety of AutoCAD's functions that are specifically for the Windows version of AutoCAD.

Tutorial stores sample files used in conjunction with the tutorials that appear in the various AutoCAD manuals.

In the Acadr13\Common directory you will find the subdirectories containing auxiliary files that can be used by both AutoCAD for DOS and AutoCAD for Windows.

ACRX is the new C or C++ program environment that supports the ADS program library, and in the future will support

Appendices

other libraries for developing applications. If you are a C programmer who wants to customize AutoCAD, this directory will be of importance to you. ACRX is not discussed in this tutorial, however.

ADS   stands for *AutoCAD Development System*. The files contained in this directory are programs and sample codes for ADS that can be used in both DOS and Windows.

Fonts   contains the standard AutoCAD font-definition files, as well as some sample TrueType (.TTF) and PostScript (.PFB) files.

Source   contains the uncompiled text shape (.SHP) files.

Sample   has sample drawings and AutoLISP programs; many of the latter are quite useful (see *Chapter 19* for more on AutoLISP).

Support   contains the files that define a variety of AutoCAD's functions common to both DOS and Windows, such as fonts, line types, and patterns. You will take a closer look at all these files in *Chapters 19–21*.

CONFIGURING AUTOCAD

In this section, you will learn how to *configure* AutoCAD. By configure, we mean to set up AutoCAD to work with the particular hardware you have connected to your computer. Programs often rely on their own drivers to operate specialized equipment. By configuring AutoCAD, you tell it exactly what equipment it will be working with. With Release 13, you can configure AutoCAD at any time during an AutoCAD session.

DOING THE BASIC CONFIGURATION

To perform a basic configuration, follow these steps.

1.   Open the AutoCAD program group by double-clicking on its icon, then double-click on the AutoCAD icon. You will get a message that AutoCAD is not yet configured.

2. Press ↵ and you will get the screen shown in Figure B.1. This tells you that AutoCAD needs to be configured.

You are now at the first step in configuring AutoCAD. The following sections will help guide you in selecting configuration options, starting with the display.

Figure B.1: Screen shown when AutoCAD is not configured

Selecting a Display Option

AutoCAD supplies three display drivers for Windows. In most cases, you will want to use the 'WHIP' – HEIDI™ Accelerated Display Driver. This driver offers enhanced speed during AutoCAD display functions. Once selected, you have the option to do a detailed configuration. If you answer Yes to the detailed configuration, you get the following options:

Always   The default setting, Always, causes AutoCAD to store the main graphic display in a buffer in your computer's RAM. The image

Appendices

stored in the buffer is then transferred to your display all at once, resulting in instantaneous redraws and better image quality. The main drawback to this option is that it uses about 1MB of RAM for a typical 1024×768×256 color display; thus, the Always option can actually degrade display performance on systems with limited amounts of RAM.

Never   This setting causes the main graphic display to be sent directly to the video display through the Windows GDI interface. This option should be used in systems with minimal amounts of RAM.

Only When Item Count Exceeds...   This setting causes Auto-CAD to dynamically choose between the Always and Never options, depending on the complexity of the current view of your drawing. You can adjust the value to best suit your system's capacity.

Selecting Input Devices

Once you are done configuring your display, you will get a list of input device options.

1. Check the list for the number of your device and enter that number at the prompt at the bottom of the list. If you have no input device other than the keyboard, choose option 1, *None*. Choosing None causes AutoCAD to use the same pointing device that is used for Windows. The other options listed are various brands of digitizers.

2. Answer any questions regarding your input device. Again, since different input devices offer different options, we cannot provide details on what to select. However, the prompts are usually quite clear, so you shouldn't have any problems.

3. You may also be prompted to select an adapter port for your input device. You will get the prompt

    Connects to Asynchronous Communications
    Adapter port.
    Standard ports are:
    COM1

COM2 Enter port name, or address in hexadecimal <COM1>:

If you have two asynchronous communications ports, or *serial* ports as they are commonly called, you can use this opportunity to tell AutoCAD that you want to connect your input device to a port other than the default, COM1.

4. If you are configuring AutoCAD for a digitizing tablet, see "Configuring Your Digitizing Tablet," later in this appendix. This section also describes how to set up your tablet to use a tablet template.

Be sure you plug your input device into the proper serial port. If you don't know which port is COM2, you may have to experiment by switching ports and seeing which one works.

Selecting Output Devices

Printer and plotter configuration works the same way as display and input device configuration. You are shown a numbered list, at the bottom of which is a prompt asking you to enter the number of the device you wish to connect to.

1. Enter the number corresponding to your printer or plotter.

2. As with the input device, you are prompted for a serial or parallel port assignment. You are also prompted for the printer or plotter default options that are displayed during AutoCAD's PLOT command. *Chapter 7* describes the different options in detail.

3. For now, take the default settings presented to you for the plotter settings. You can always change them later.

You can configure multiple plotters and printers if you so desire. To do this, while in AutoCAD, pull down the Options menu at the far left of

Appendices

the menu bar and click on Configure. At the configuration screen, enter **5**. You are presented with the following list:

Plotter Configuration Menu

0. Exit to configuration menu
1. Add a plotter configuration
2. Delete a plotter configuration
3. Change a plotter configuration
4. Rename a plotter configuration

You have a variety of options to choose from, including the addition of more printers or plotters to the configuration list. You can even have multiple instances of the same plotter or printer if you want.

Answering General Questions about Your System

Once you've finished configuring your peripherals, AutoCAD asks you some general questions about your system configuration. First, you will see the following prompt:

Login Name:
Enter default login name or . for none <*Your name and company.*>:

AutoCAD locks files when they are being edited. This prevents two people on a network from attempting to edit the same file simultaneously. The log-in name is used to identify the computer on the network that is currently using a locked file.

You can press ↵ to accept the default name, which is the same as the one used during the installation. If you enter a period (.) at this prompt, AutoCAD will prompt you for a log-in name every time you open a drawing file. You can always come back and change the log-in name, so press ↵ to accept the default for now.

Next, you will get a different set of options depending on whether you are installing the network version of AutoCAD or the single user version.

Special Options for the Network Version   If you are installing the Network version of AutoCAD, follow these steps:

1. At the next prompt,

   Server authorization:
   AutoCAD serial number is 123-45678900
   Enter the maximum number of users for this package
   <1>:

   enter the number of users your package is authorized for.

2. Once you enter the number, you are prompted for the
   authorization code:

   Enter server authorization code for this package <0>:

3. Once you enter the code, you get the following prompt:

   Do you wish to run the executable from a read-only directory? <N>

   This prompt is significant only if your network requires read-
   only permission on shared executable files, as in 3Com networks. If you answer Y, then you are prompted for a sharable
   directory for server temporary files. You should then enter a
   full path name, including disk-drive designation. Press ⏎ after responding to this prompt.

4. You then see the following prompt:

   Enter a password to restrict unauthorized changes to
   the server authorization or . for none<> :

   Enter a name for a password to protect the server configuration. If you later forget the password, however, you will have
   to reinstall AutoCAD. You are then prompted to reenter the
   password:

   Please retype password to verify:

5. Retype the password. You then get the prompt,

   Do you wish to enable file-locking? <Y>:

Appendices

6. Press ↵ to accept the default, Y.

7. The last prompt asks you to select a spelling dialect for the AutoCAD spell checker dictionary. Make a selection and press ↵.

Options for Single User Systems

If you are installing a single user system, you will not be asked for network related information, as in the previous section. Instead, you will only be asked for your Authorization code. You can choose to skip this option and enter it later at a more convenient date. (See the Troubleshooting section of *Appendix A* for instructions on how to do this.)

You are then asked if you want file locking enabled as in step 5 of the previous instructions. Enter **N** for no file-locking. You are also asked to choose a spelling dialect as in step 7 in the previous section. Do so.

Finishing Up

Once you are done with the configuration, you will get a list of the devices you selected.

1. Press ↵ and you will get the Configuration menu and a prompt asking you to enter a selection.

2. Press ↵ to accept the default, 0. The following message will appear:

   If you answer N to the following question, all configuration changes you have just made will be discarded. Keep configuration changes? <Y>

3. If you wish to save your current configuration, press ↵ to accept the default, Y. AutoCAD will start up. Now you can begin drawing.

SETTING PREFERENCES

Once you've done the basic configuration, you are ready to use AutoCAD. The tutorials in this book assume that you are using the default Preference settings. As you become more familiar with the workings of

AutoCAD, you may want to make adjustments to the way AutoCAD works throughout the Preferences dialog box.

This dialog box can be accessed by clicking on Options ➤ Preferences…. It is further divided into sections shown as tabs across the top of the dialog box. The following describes the settings available in each section according to button groups.

SYSTEM

The System tab options control AutoCAD's appearance and input options as well as the time interval for AutoCAD's automatic save feature.

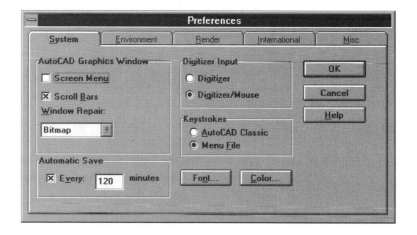

AutoCAD Graphics Window

Here is a listing of the options available under the System tab.

> **Screen Menu**   toggles the screen menu on and off. This is the menu located at the right edge of the drawing area commonly found in earlier versions of AutoCAD.
>
> **Scroll Bars**   toggles the drawing area scroll bars on and off.
>
> **Window Repair**   lets you select the method AutoCAD uses to redraw the graphic window. The options here depend on the display driver you are using. This option is normally set to Bitmap when using the AutoCAD supplied display list driver.

Automatic Save

This group lets you control the time interval between automatic saves. You can also use the Savetime system variable.

Digitizer Input

If you are using a digitizer *and* a mouse, this pair or radio buttons let you control whether the mouse is recognized by AutoCAD.

> **Digitizer/Mouse** let you switch between digitizer and mouse, simply by moving from one pointing device to the other.
>
> **Digitizer** causes AutoCAD to accept input from the digitizer only.

Keystrokes

Many of AutoCAD's drafting tools are controlled by keystroke combinations. These keystrokes can conflict with some of the Windows accelerator keystrokes. This pair lets you control which set of conflicting keystrokes take precedence. If you are a veteran user, you may prefer to choose the AutoCAD Classic button. This option causes AutoCAD to accept the Ctrl key options that toggle drawing modes, like Ctrl-B for the Snap mode, and Ctrl-O for the Ortho mode. The Menu File button forces the accelerator key settings defined in the menu file to take precedence.

Font

The Font button opens a dialog box that lets you select a font for program text display. This has no effect on the text in the AutoCAD drawings.

Color

The Color button opens a dialog box that lets you select colors for the various components of the AutoCAD window. You can, for example, use this button to change the background color of the drawing area.

ENVIRONMENT

The settings under the Environment tab control where AutoCAD looks for files. You can also control memory use here.

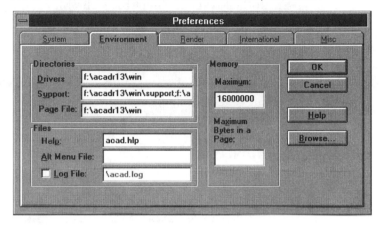

Directories

These settings tell AutoCAD where to look for files it needs during the course of its operation.

> **Drivers** sets the location of device driver files. Under normal circumstances, you don't have to change this.
>
> **Support** sets the location of support files such as fonts, menus, hatch patterns, line types, and drawing libraries. If you add a symbols library, you will want to include the library's path in this input box. Note that each drive and path name is separated by a semicolon.
>
> **Page File** sets the location for temporary swap files. Set this to a drive that has lots of free space for optimum AutoCAD performance.

Files

These settings direct AutoCAD to the Help file (Help) and Alternate tablet menu file (Alt Menu File). The Log file check box and input box allow you to record the data from the command line. When the Check box is checked, the AutoCAD text window is recorded in the file indicated by the Log File input box.

Appendices

Memory

As AutoCAD drawings increase in size, more memory is used. You can limit the amount of memory AutoCAD uses by entering a value in bytes in the Maximum input box. The Maximum Bytes in a Page input box lets you specify a limit for the first page file.

Browse

The Browse button can be used with any of the Directories or Files input boxes to help locate a directory or file.

RENDER

The settings under the Render tab specify where the Render settings are stored.

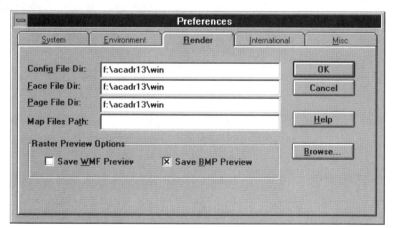

Config File Dir   specifies the directory for the rendering configuration file.

Face File Dir   sets the location for temporary storage of face and mesh data.

Page File Dir   sets the location for the first page file.

Map Files Path   sets the location for map files.

INTERNATIONAL

The options under the International tab let you select the prototype drawing and measurement system. The International Setting's two radio buttons, English and Metric, set the measurement system. By choosing one or the other Automatically selects either the Acad.DWG or Acadiso.DWG prototype drawing. Acad.DWG is set up for English measurement system while Acadiso.DWG is set up for metric. The Drawing Type drop-down list displays the drawing type.

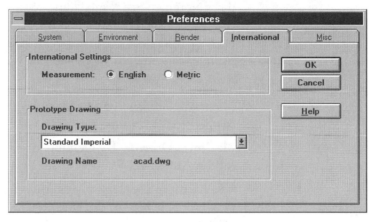

MISC

The options under the Misc tab control text related functions, including the number of lines displayed in the command line window.

Appendices

Options

The options in this group control a variety of text related settings as well as other miscellaneous settings.

Text Editor   specifies the text editor AutoCAD uses when creating Multiline text or when editing Multiline text. The default is Internal, but you can highlight this option, then use the browse button to locate another text editor, such as the Windows Notepad. See "Embedding Codes for Special Text Formatting" in *Chapter 8* for more on this feature.

Font Mapping File   specifies the location of the Font Mapping file. See "Substituting Fonts" in *Chapter 8* for more on this option.

Maximize Application On Startup   causes AutoCAD to fill the desktop (Maximize) at startup.

Maximize Drawing By Default   causes the drawing Window to fill the AutoCAD Window at startup.

Use Menu in Header   causes AutoCAD to attempt to load the menu file specified in the Drawing file's header. Earlier versions of AutoCAD would attempt to load the menu file that was last used with the drawing file. Release 13 removed this requirement, but retained it as an option here.

Text Window

These settings control the text window that displays the command prompt.

History Lines   specifies the number of text lines AutoCAD stores in memory before discarding them. The default setting of 400 means that you will be able to scroll back 400 lines before you reach the top of the command line history.

Docked Visible Lines   specifies the number of lines displayed in the Command line window.

Plot Spooling

This option lets you specify the location and parameters for plot spooling. See "Plot Spooling with ACADPLCMD" in your AutoCAD Installation Guide for Windows for more on this feature.

UNDERSTANDING THE ACAD.INI FILE

If you are comfortable with editing Windows .INI files, you can view and edit the Acad.INI files to set up AutoCAD to your liking. In fact, the Preferences options described here are stored in the Acad.INI file. Here is a listing of the headings in the Acad.INI file and their meaning.

[General] controls many of the environment settings (see Table B.1).

[Prototype Drawing] determines what drawing prototype is used.

[MTE Fonts] controls the fonts used for the AutoCAD Window.

[Application Window] controls the location and size of the AutoCAD window.

[Command Line Windows] controls the appearance of the text window.

[Drawing Window] controls the appearance of the drawing window.

[Toolbars] controls the appearance of toolbars.

[Recent File List] controls the display of recent files at the bottom of the File pull-down menu.

[Browse/Search] controls the options for the Browse/Search option under the Open File dialog box

[Aerial View] Controls the default options for the Aerial View window.

CONFIGURING YOUR DIGITIZING TABLET

If you are using a digitizer with AutoCAD for Windows, you will need to select some additional configuration options. These other options allow you to add flexibility to your digitizer, or to add a menu template. As an alternative, you may choose to configure your tablet as the Windows pointing device; in this case, the options in this section will not apply.

CONFIGURING THE TABLET MENU AREA

If you own a digitizing tablet, and you would like to use it with the AutoCAD tablet menu template, you must configure your tablet menu.

1. The first step is to securely fasten your tablet menu template to the tablet. Be sure the area covered by the template is completely within the tablet's active drawing area.

2. Choose Options ➤ Tablet ➤ Configure. You will get the prompt

   Digitize upper left corner of menu area 1:

   For the next series of prompts, you will be locating the four tablet menu areas, starting with menu area 1 (see Figure B.2).

3. Locate the position indicated in Figure B.2 as the upper-left corner of menu area 1. Place your puck or stylus to pick that point. The prompt will change to

   Digitize lower left corner of menu area 1:

4. Again, locate the position indicated in Figure B.2 as the lower-left corner of menu area 1.

5. Continue this process until you have selected three corners for four menu areas.

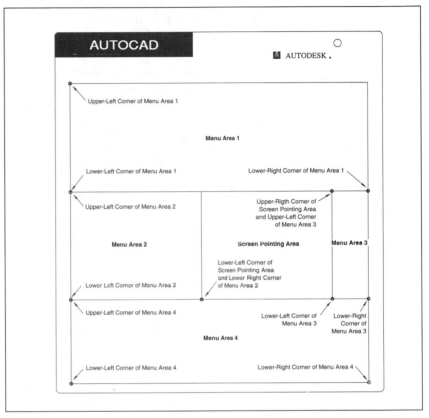

Figure B.2: How to locate the tablet menu areas

6. When you are done selecting the menu areas, you will get the prompt

   Do you want to respecify the Fixed Screen Pointing Area:

   type **Y** ↵ then pick the position indicated in Figure B.2.

7. Finally, you get the prompt

   Digitize upper right corner of screen pointing area:

   Pick the position indicated in Figure B.2.

The 3 prompts that remain refer to a *floating screen pointing area*. This is an area on your tablet that allows you to select menu options and other areas on your screen outside the drawing area. This option is necessary because when you set up a digitizer for tracing, access to areas outside the drawing area are temporarily disabled. The floating screen pointing area lets you access pull-down menus and the status bar during tracing sessions (see *Chapter 11*).

If you never intend to trace drawings with your tablet, then answer **N** to all three prompts. Otherwise do the following:

8. At the following prompt,

Do you want to specify the Floating Screen Pointing Area? <N>:

type **Y** ↵.

9. At the prompt,

Do you want the Floating Screen Pointing Area to be the same size as the Fixed Screen Pointing Area? <Y>:

type **Y** ↵ if you want the Floating Screen Pointing Area to be the same as the Fixed Pointing Screen area, the area you specified in step 6 and 7. Type **N** ↵ if you want to use a separate area on your tablet for the Floating Screen Pointing Area.

10. The last prompt asks you if you want to use the F12 function key to toggle the Floating Screen Area on and off. (This is similar to the F10 key function of earlier releases of Auto-CAD). Enter **Y** ↵ or **N** ↵ depending on whether you want to specify a different function key for the Floating Screen Area or not.

AutoCAD will remember this configuration until you change it again. Quit this file by clicking on File ➤ Exit.

KEEPING MULTIPLE CONFIGURATIONS

There may be times when you want to have AutoCAD configured in more than one way. For example, you may want to have one configuration where the drawing editor's status line, prompt area, and menu area are not shown, so a drawing fills the entire screen. (See *Chapter 1* for the location and appearance of these areas on the display.) This configuration is desirable for presentations. At the same time, you will probably want to use the standard screen configuration when you create and edit drawings.

MAKING A NEW PROGRAM ICON

AutoCAD stores its configuration information in two files. These files are ACAD.CFG and ACAD.INI. When you first install and configure AutoCAD, these two files are created and placed in the \Acadr13\win directory. You can, however, tell AutoCAD to store alternative versions of these files in other directories, then set up an AutoCAD icon to start and run AutoCAD based on these alternate settings. The following guides you through the process of creating a second version of the AutoCAD icon with a different configuration.

1. Double-click on the My Computer icon on your Desktop, then double-click on the icon of the drive that contains your AutoCAD program.

2. Open the \Acadr13\Win directory, then create a new directory called Config2. Copy the files ACAD.CFG and ACAD.INI from the \Acadr13\Win directory into the new Config2 directory.

3. While still in the \Acadr13\Win directory, right-click on the ACAD.EXE file.

Appendices

4. At the pop-up menu, click on Create Shortcut. A new item called Shortcut to ACAD.EXE will appear in the folder.

5. Right-click on the Shortcut to ACAD.EXE icon, then select Properties from the menu. The Properties dialog box appears.

6. Click on the tab labeled Shortcut at the top of the dialog box.

7. In the Target input box, you will see a line similar to this:

   c:\acadr13\win\acad.exe

8. Edit the Target input box so it shows the following:

   c:\acadr13\win\acad.exe /c c:\acadr13\win\config2

9. When you're done, click on OK. Your new configuration is ready to set up.

10. Double-click on the newly created AutoCAD shortcut icon, then run the configuration process described earlier in this appendix. This time, you'll use different settings.

11. Under the Options menu use the Preferences option to set up your preferences for this second configuration.

12. Once you are done, you can add this new AutoCAD shortcut to the Start menu by choosing Settings ➤ Taskbar from the Start menu. Choose the Add button from the Start Menu Programs tab, then choose Browse from the Create Shortcut dialog box.

13. Locate your newly created shortcut, double-click on it, then choose Next.

14. At the Select Program Folder dialog box, locate the Auto-CADr13 folder and double-click on it.

15. Click on Finish. You now have a second option on the Taskbar menu that will start your second configuration of AutoCAD.

In step 8, the Target input box tells Windows where to find the Auto-CAD program. The /C in the example is called a command line switch. The switch is followed by a space, then the file location. This example assumes that AutoCAD is installed in drive C. Be sure to specify the correct drive for installation.

The following describes the switches you can include in the command line:

/C specifies the location for the configuration files Acad.CFG and Acad.INI.

/S specifies the location of support files. For Windows, you need to specify at least \acadr13\win\support and \acadr13\common\support.

/D specifies the path to search for ADI drivers.

/M specifies the maximum amount of memory you want to allocate to AutoCAD.

CHANGING THE AUTOCAD PROGRAM ICON

You can change the icon to a different one by right-clicking on the Program icon; a pop-up menu will appear. Choose Properties and the Properties dialog box will appear. Click on the Shortcut tab, then click on the Change Icon button. This brings up the Change Icon dialog box.

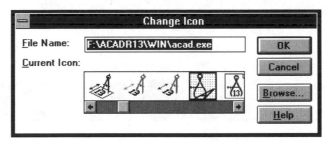

You can select from a set of pre-defined icons that are included with the Acad.EXE file.

The Program Item Properties dialog box also lets you change the title that appears below the icon by editing the Description input box.

Appendices

You can create as many different versions of AutoCAD's startup icon as you like, using these steps. Note that you aren't making copies of the program; you are only making copies of the program items in the Windows program group.

OTHER AUTOCAD SETTINGS

There are a variety of other AutoCAD settings you can control either through command switches or through the *DOS environment*. The DOS environment is a small portion of memory used to store data. When AutoCAD starts up, it looks in that environment for any information that may be specifically set aside for it. You can place data in the environment using the DOS Set command. For example, to direct Auto-CAD to look in \Acadr13\common\Support and \Acadr13\common\font directories for support files, you would enter the following at the DOS prompt:

```
SET ACAD=C:\ACADR13\COMMON\SUP-
PORT;C:\ACADR13\COMMON\FONTS
```

You can include this line in a batch file that starts Windows so the environment is set before you run AutoCAD for Windows. Table B.1 gives a listing of these other environment settings and their uses. It also shows the commands switches that can be used to make some of these settings.

Table B.1: The AutoCAD Windows Environment Variables

Environment Variable	Purpose
ACAD	The directory or directories for support files
ACADCFGW	Location of configuration files for the Windows version
ACADALTMNU	Location of alternate tablet menu files
ACADDRV	Location of protected mode ADI drivers
ACADHELP	Name of AutoCAD help file including path

Table B.1:   The AutoCAD Windows Environment Variables (continued)

Environment Variable	Purpose
ACADMAXMEM	Maximum amount of memory in bytes that AutoCAD requests from the operating system
ACADPAGEDIR	Directory where page files are stored
ACADMAXPAGE	Maximum number of bytes to be sent to the first page file
ACADPLCMD	Shell command AutoCAD is to use for plot spooling
RENDERCFG	Location for storing the AutoCAD Render configuration file, RENDER.CFG
AVEFACEDIR	Location for storing the renderer's temporary files

These variables are entered at the DOS prompt just as described for the ACAD variable in the previous example. You can also control these settings from within AutoCAD. To do this, click on Options ➤ Preferences, then in the Preferences dialog box, click on the Environment tab at the top. The Environment dialog box appears (see "Setting Preferences" earlier in this appendix). You can then enter values for these settings in the appropriate input boxes.

Be aware that there is a hierarchy that AutoCAD follows in the event of conflicting environment settings. Command line settings made in the Windows Program Item Properties dialog box have the highest priority, followed by the Environment settings in the AutoCAD preferences dialog box. The DOS environment settings have the lowest priority.

Appendices

USING THE FILE MANAGER TO OPEN AUTOCAD FILES

You might also want to set up Window's File Manager to automatically start AutoCAD and load a file. Using the File Manager can help you locate and manage your AutoCAD files and keep control over your projects. To set up the File Manager to do this, take the following steps:

1. Open the File Manager.

2. Locate and highlight any AutoCAD drawing file.

3. Pull down the File menu and click on Associate.

4. At the Associate dialog box, click on Browse.

5. At the Browse dialog box, locate Acad.EXE in the \acadr13\win directory and double-click on it.

6. Back at the Associate dialog box, click on OK.

Now you can use the file manager to open AutoCAD files by just clicking on the AutoCAD file drawing name. The directory of the file you double-click on becomes the default working directory.

SETTING UP A WORKING DIRECTORY

The tutorials in this book assume you are working from the directory where the program files are stored. However, if you prefer, you can use another directory to store your files. The following steps describe how you setup a working directory for AutoCAD.

1. Create your working directory either in DOS using the MD command or in the File Manager using File ➤ Create Directory....

2. Highlight the AutoCAD icon in the AutoCAD program group and click on File ➤ Properties from the Program Manager pull-down menu.

3. In the Program Item Properties dialog box, double-click on the Working Directory input box, then enter the name of your working directory. You can use the Browse button to use a file dialog box to locate your directory.

4. Click on OK.

This new working directory will be the default whenever you open the file dialog box in AutoCAD. You can also use these same steps to set a working directory for any other Windows program.

TURNING ON THE NOUN/VERB OPTION

If, for some reason, the Noun/Verb selection method is not available, here are instructions on how to turn it back on.

1. Choose Options ➤ Selection to display the Object Selection Settings dialog box.

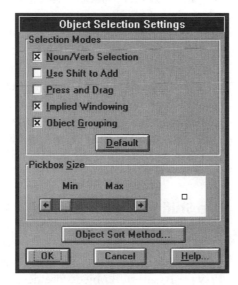

2. In the Selection Modes button group, find the Noun/Verb Selection setting. Click on the check box to turn this option on.

3. Click OK.

If it wasn't there before, you should now see a small square at the intersection of the crosshair cursor. This square is actually a pickbox superimposed on the cursor. It tells you that you can select objects, even while the command prompt appears at the bottom of the screen and no command is currently active. As you saw earlier, the square will momentarily disappear when you are in a command that asks you to select points.

You can also turn on Noun/Verb selection by entering **'Pickfirst** ↵ at the command prompt. When you are asked for New value for PICK-FIRST <0>:, enter **1** ↵ (entering 0 turns the Pickfirst function off). The Pickfirst system variable is stored in the AutoCAD configuration file. See *Appendix D* for more on system variables.

Other Selection Options

The Object Selection Settings dialog box lets you control the degree to which AutoCAD conforms to standard graphical user interface (GUI) methods of operation. It also lets you adjust the size of the object selection pickbox.

In *Chapter 2*, you practiced selecting objects using the Noun/Verb Selection setting—one of several AutoCAD settings that make the program work more like other GUI-environment programs. If you are used to working with other GUIs, you may want to turn on some of the other options in the Selection Settings dialog box. Here are descriptions of them; in brackets are the names of the system variables that control these features.

Use Shift to Add (Pickadd) With this option checked, you can use the standard GUI method of holding down the Shift key to pick multiple objects. When the Shift key is not held down, only the single object picked or the group of objects windowed will be selected. Previously selected objects are deselected, unless the Shift key is held down during selection. To turn this feature on using system variables, set Pickadd to 0.

Click and Drag (Pickdrag)   With this option checked, you can use the standard GUI method for placing windows: You first click and hold down the pick button on the first corner of the window; then, while holding down the pick button, you drag the other corner of the window into position. When the other corner is in place, you let go of the pick button to finish the window. This setting applies to both Verb/Noun and Noun/Verb operations. In the system variables, set Pickadd to 1 for this option.

Implied Window (Pickauto)   When this option is checked, a window or crossing window will automatically start if no object is picked at the Select objects: prompt. This setting has no effect on the Noun/Verb setting (preselection of objects). In the system variables, set Pickadd to 1 for this option.

TURNING ON THE GRIPS FEATURE

If for some reason the grips feature is not available, here are instructions for turning it back on.

1. Choose Options ➤ Grips …. The Grips dialog box appears:

2. At the top of the dialog box are the Select Settings check boxes. Click on the Enable Grips check box

3. Click OK, and you are ready to proceed.

The Grips dialog box also lets you determine whether grips appear on objects that compose a block (see *Chapter 4* for more on blocks), as well as set the grip color and size. These options can also be set using system variables described in *Appendix D*.

You can also turn the Grips feature on and off by entering '**Grips** ↵. At the prompt New value for GRIPS <0>:, enter a **1** to turn Grips on, or **0** to turn Grips off. Grips is a system variable that is stored in the AutoCAD configuration file.

USING DIALOG BOXES

Now that you've seen AutoCAD's workspace layout, you'll want to familiarize yourself with *dialog boxes*. As with pull-down menus, dialog boxes offer an easy way to communicate with the program by offering you command options in an easy-to-understand visual format. If you've used Microsoft Windows or any other graphical user interface, you should feel right at home with AutoCAD Release 13's dialog boxes. If not, here is a brief primer.

THE COMPONENTS

Figure B.3 shows two dialog boxes, each with a set of typical dialog box elements. There are three major components to dialog boxes: the title, the button groups, and the options. At the top of the dialog box is the title, which identifies the dialog box for you. Dialog boxes are divided into groups, enclosed by a rectangle and labeled at the top. We will refer to these groups as *button groups*, even though they don't always contain buttons. Scattered over the dialog boxes are the various buttons, boxes, and so forth (described in the following sections) that you use to specify your choices.

Labeled Buttons

Whenever you see a rectangular button with a *label* on it, you know that clicking on it will immediately execute the action described in the

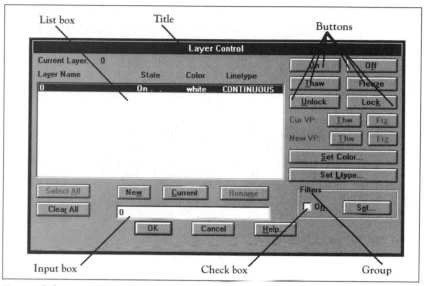

Figure B.3: The parts of a dialog box

label. Buttons whose labels are followed with an ellipsis (…) tell you that a dialog box will be opened when you click. Buttons with a < symbol following the label tell you that the screen will clear, allowing you to perform some activity, such as picking points. When you see a button that is heavily outlined, it means that button is the default choice and will be activated when you press ↵. Dimmed buttons are unavailable in the current use of the dialog box.

Here is a typical set of labeled buttons:

Radio Buttons

When a set of mutually exclusive options are available, they are usually presented as *radio buttons*. These are small square buttons with labels to their right and usually found in groups. You activate a radio button option by clicking on the button itself to fill it in. Here is a set of radio buttons; the Decimal option is turned on:

○ Scientific

◉ Decimal

○ Engineering

○ Architectural

○ Fractional

Check Boxes

Toggled options are presented as *check boxes*. These are squares that are blank when the option is turned off, or have an X in them when the option is turned on. To turn on a check box, you click the square. Here is a set of check boxes; all options except Ortho and Quick Text are turned on:

☐ Ortho

☒ Solid Fill

☐ Quick Text

☒ Blips

☒ Highlight

☒ Groups

List Boxes

You will often be presented with a list of items to choose from. These lists appear in *list boxes*, and you select items from the list by clicking on them. When the list is too long to fit in the list box, a scroll bar appears to the right of the box. You can search for specific items in a list box by typing the first character of the item you are looking for. Edit boxes, explained just below, are often associated with list boxes.

Here is a sample list box; notice the scroll bar on the right:

Layer Name	State	Color	Linetype	
0	. . .	white	CONTINUOUS	▲
ASHADE	On . .	white	CONTINUOUS	
CASEWORK	. . .	blue	CONTINUOUS	
CEILING	On . .	magenta	CONTINUOUS	
DEFPOINTS	. . .	white	CONTINUOUS	
DIM	. . .	white	CONTINUOUS	
DOOR	. . .	red	CONTINUOUS	
DOT	. . .	white	DOT	
F-RAIL	. . .	white	CONTINUOUS	
FIXTURE	. . .	blue	CONTINUOUS	
FLOOR	. . .	cyan	CONTINUOUS	▼

Pull-Down Lists

Sometimes, a *pull-down list* is used instead of a list box. This list first appears as a rectangle with a downward pointing arrow on the right side, and the default item in the rectangle. To pull down the list, you click the arrow, and then you click on the desired option. If the list is long, a scroll bar is provided.

Appendices

Here is a sample pull-down list shown closed and opened with the scroll bar:

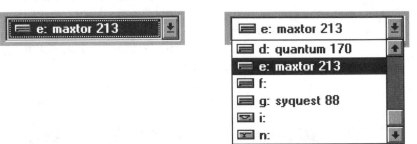

Edit Boxes

If an option requires keyboard input from you, an *edit box* or *input box* is provided. When you click on the edit box, it displays a vertical bar cursor. You can then enter a name, number, or other value for the option next to the box, or you can correct any existing value in the box. Here is a typical group of edit boxes:

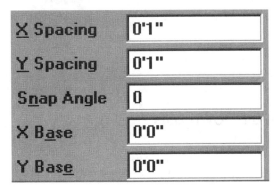

If something already appears in an edit box, you can double-click on the box to highlight the entire text. Then begin to type, and your typing will completely replace the original entry. Clicking once in the text in the box moves the vertical bar cursor to that location, and you can edit or enter from that point. Just as in a word processor, you can toggle between Insert and Overtype modes by pressing the Ins key, and you can use the ← and → keys to move the vertical bar cursor. To highlight a group of characters in the input box, click and drag with the mouse.

KEYBOARD SHORTCUTS

You may have noticed that the labels for the various buttons and boxes have underlined characters in them. Another way to select an option from a dialog box is by holding down the Alt key and pressing the underlined character in the option name. The option label is then highlighted. You can move to any other option in the dialog box by just pressing the underlined character (without Alt), or you can move sequentially from option to option by pressing the Tab key.

Once a button is highlighted, changing the option with the keyboard depends on the type of button it is. To activate radio buttons and check boxes, you use the Spacebar. To open pull-down lists, you press the ↓ key. You can then move up and down in the list using the ↑ and ↓, and use the Esc key to close it. To activate labeled buttons, press ↵ when they are highlighted.

You may want to try using the keyboard shortcuts for a while to see if you like them. They are not for everyone, but since you have one hand free while mousing around, you might as well put it to work.

WHAT'S ON THE COMPANION CD

This appendix describes the software supplied on the companion CD. The CD contains a number of useful utilities that you can load and run at any time. Before you use them, however, it's best to get familiar with AutoCAD. Many of these utilities work within AutoCAD from the command line or as options from pull-down menus, and they offer prompts in a way similar to most other AutoCAD commands. Other utilities are stand-alone applications that run in either DOS or Windows.

THE FILES ON THE CD

The CD contains utilities I've developed, as well as shareware, freeware, and third-party products.

THE MASTERING AUTOCAD BONUS SOFTWARE

To help you get the most from AutoCAD, I've included the following utilities:

AEC.EXE is a self-extracting compressed archive of the set of AEC utilities described later in this appendix. These utilities will enhance your use of AutoCAD regardless of your profession.

AutoPS.EXE is a self-extracting compressed archive of the AutoPS add-on to AutoCAD. AutoPS turns AutoCAD into a high-quality PostScript illustration program.

Blob.EXE is a self-extracting compressed file containing a freeware program called Blob Sculptor. This program is useful for creating complex, organic 3D shapes for use in AutoCAD, such as faces, hands, or other nonlinear shapes. It uses a method, similar to Metaballs, where you form organic shapes by creating and aligning spheres. WinBlob is a Windows port of the program.

Figures.EXE is a self-extracting compressed archive of the drawings used in this book. If you follow the tutorial chapter-by-chapter, you'll create these figures yourself. If you want to do the exercises out of sequence, use these files as needed.

PrintGL and PrintGF are two print utilities from Ravitz Software that enable most dot-matrix and ink-jet printers to produce high-resolution plots. These utilities offer enhanced print and plot capabilities over the standard printer drivers. They also let you view image or plot files before you print them.

WinSpool is a shareware utility that helps simplify your plotting efforts in a network environment. WinSpool monitors a directory on your computer. When a plot file appears in that directory, WinSpool sends it to your printer/plotter. When printing is complete, WinSpool deletes the plot file.

WHIP! contains the Autodesk WHIP! Internet Utilities, which are a set of tools that enable you to publish your AutoCAD drawings on the World Wide Web. The WHIP! Utilities are actually two self-installing tools: an AutoCAD ARX application that lets you convert your drawings into a Web-enabled format, and a plug-in to Netscape Navigator that lets you view, zoom, and pan over a "Web-enabled" AutoCAD drawing.

The Drawings, AEC, and AutoPS

The drawings from the book and my utilities AEC and AutoPS are offered to you free as a part of this book.

You will want to install the drawings in the Samples subdirectory on your hard drive if you plan to do any of the exercises in this book. Whenever you are asked to open a file from the companion disk, you can then look in the Samples subdirectory for the file.

Install the AEC and AutoPS utilities in their own separate subdirectories. You must also edit the AutoCAD Preferences dialog box to include these subdirectories in the Acad path.

Blob Sculptor 2b

Blob Sculptor is a DOS program that lets you create the types of 3D shapes that AutoCAD is so poorly equipped to do—namely, organic, nonlinear shapes. You do this by creating spheres and other primitive 3D shapes. Blob Sculptor "merges" these shapes to form smooth surfaces. (Also included is a Windows port of the product called WinBlob, in the Winblob directory.)

Blob Sculptor is a small program so it will run quite easily in a full-screen DOS window under Windows. It lets you save drawings to a DXF format, which can then be imported into AutoCAD or 3D Studio. The DXF files of version 2b can be read directly by AutoCAD with no modification. I'd like to thank Alfonso Hermida and his associates for taking the time to create version 2b of Blob Sculptor for us. Here is contact information for the Blob Sculptor team:

Pi Square BBS	(301) 725-9080
CompuServe	GO GRAPHDEV
Alfonso Hermida (CIS)	72114,2060
Steve Anger (CIS)	70714,3113(also sanger@hookup.net)
Truman Brown (CIS)	71477,221
Ron Praver (CIS)	70614,400

The PrintGL Utility

Many AutoCAD users elect to plot their drawings to a file, then download the plot file to their plotter or printer. This method lets you keep electronic archives of files you plotted. The drawback to a plot file is that it can be sent only to a specific device, frequently in an HPGL/2 format. The PrintGL utility gives you more flexibility by allowing you to send your HPGL/2 files to virtually any printer or plotter.

To install PrintGL, simply copy the PrintGL folder from the CD-ROM to your computer's hard drive. To run PrintGL, use the Windows File Manager or Explorer to locate Printglw.EXE, then double-click this file.

WinSpool

If you're using AutoCAD on a network, you may want to take a look at WinSpool. It automatically downloads plot files to your plotter from a directory you specify. To install it, open the File Manager or Explorer, locate Winspo.EXE—the WinSpool installation application in the WinSpool directory of the CD—then follow the directions.

This utility can be a real time-saver when you need to plot large documents but don't want to tie up your computer waiting for those plots to finish. WinSpool works with networks and will perform automatic plotting, a process where WinSpool checks a directory from time to time to see if a plot file exists. If one does, the program automatically downloads the plot file to the plotter. You can set up an automatic plot directory, and when you need a plot, simply plot to a file and then move or copy the file to the automatic plot directory. WinSpool will do the rest.

WHIP!

Imagine being able to post your drawings on your Web site so that your consultants or clients can view them at their convenience. The Autodesk WHIP! Internet utilities will enable you to do just that. With the WHIP! Utilities, you can even add URL links to other drawings and Web pages. You can, for example, attach a link to a detail symbol in a floor plan so that when the viewer clicks on the symbol, they will see the associated detail. Or you can decide to link a Web page to the symbol.

To install the WHIP! Utilities, double-click the Whip05.EXE installation file in the WHIP! directory and follow the instructions. You should also read the Readme.TXT file. The WHIP! utilities are 32-bit; they will run only under Windows 95 and Windows NT.

THE AUTOCAD RESOURCE GUIDE

The AutoCAD Resource Guide is an on-line encyclopedia of nearly all the third-party add-on products available for AutoCAD, including hardware and software. Because it's set up as a Windows Help file, you won't have to learn anything new to use it. (The CD-ROM version of the Resource Guide is included with the permission of ICP, Inc., Indianapolis, Indiana.)

The Resource Guide's Table of Contents is the gateway to information on software and hardware solutions, consulting partners, learning resources, training centers, user groups, and new products. You can search for topics using keywords within a topic or you can do a global

Appendices

search. You can search by several different categories, including by application or peripheral. In addition to the Table of Contents and the search engine, there is an alphabetical index available, from which you can jump directly to suppliers or products that interest you.

The AutoCAD Resource Guide also includes demos for a number of products. To go to a demo for an individual product, simply click the Demo icon at the top of the listing. If you need help using the Resource Guide, check out the "How to Use" entry in the main Table of Contents.

AN IMPORTANT WORD ABOUT SHAREWARE

The three utilities—PrintGL, PrintGF, and WinSpool—are distributed as *shareware*, which is a method of making software products available for you to try out before you pay for them. Shareware is not in the public domain and isn't "free," however.

Shareware producers rely on the person receiving the software to pay for and register the program if it is used with any regularity or in a commercial setting. The products included on the Companion CD are quite modest in price, so *please don't hesitate to register your copy if you find it useful to your work.* By doing so, you'll receive a user's manual, and the latest versions of the software as they are released. You will also receive full support from the producer, as well as upgrade information. Most importantly, you'll be supporting the efforts of programmers who offer quality software at an affordable price.

INSTALLING THE COMPANION CD

In the front of this book, you will find the companion CD. The following paragraphs describe how to install and use the files found on the CD.

INSTALLING AND USING THE SAMPLE DRAWING FILES

The archived file named Figures.EXE contains sample drawing files for the exercises in this book. These drawings are provided for you in the event that you decide to skip some of the book's tutorial material. With these files, you can open the book to any chapter and start working, without having to construct the drawings from earlier chapters. An icon in each exercise, like the one shown here in the margin, lets you know when a file is available in the exercise sequence.

Here's how to install the sample files:

▼ NOTE

To copy a file in Windows, remember that you need only click and drag it from one drive to another in the Explorer or File Manager. To make a copy of a file within the same drive, hold down the Ctrl key while clicking and dragging.

1. Use the File Manager to copy the Figures.EXE file from your companion CD into the \Acadr13\win\samples directory.

2. While still in the File Manager, double click on the new copy of Figures.EXE in your \acadr13\win\samples subdirectory. The screen will switch to DOS mode briefly as the sample drawing files are extracted.

Once you've installed the sample files, you have free access to them during the exercises.

INSTALLING THE BONUS ADD-ON PACKAGES

The companion CD also includes two add-on packages called On-Screen AEC and AutoPS. On-Screen AEC is a set of AutoLISP macros and architectural symbols, all integrated with a standard AutoCAD menu. This package offers the basic tools you'll need to start drawing architectural drawings. In addition, it contains many time-saving tools to aid all users, not just architects, in editing your drawings.

AutoPS is a utility that turns AutoCAD into a technical illustration tool. It is designed to help you create high-quality line art for desktop publishing. All the line art in this book was created using AutoPS.

Appendices

Installing On-Screen AEC

Here's how to install On-Screen AEC:

1. Create a subdirectory called AEC under the \Acadr13\win subdirectory.

2. Use the File Manager to copy the AEC.EXE file into the \acadr13\win\aec directory.

3. While still in the File Manager, double click on the AEC.EXE file you just copied into your hard drive. The files will expand into the \acadr13\win\aec directory.

4. Start AutoCAD and choose Options ➤ Preferences....

5. Click on the Environment tab at the top of the dialog box.

6. In the Support input box, add *drive:***Acadr13\WIN\AEC** to the end of the line shown there. The line should be similar to the following:

   C:\Acadr13\COMMON\SUPPORT;
   C:\Acadr13\WIN\SUPPORT;C:\Acadr13\COMMON\
   FONT;C:\Acadr13\WIN;C:\Acadr13\WIN\AEC

   This example shows a typical listing in the Support input box, where AutoCAD is installed on drive C. Replace the C in this example with the drive letter where AutoCAD is installed in your system.

7. Click on OK, then close and re-start AutoCAD.

On-Screen AEC is now installed and ready for use. The next section describes how to load the On-Screen AEC menus.

Loading the On-Screen AEC Menus

Now you are ready to load the On-Screen AEC menus to give you access to the symbols and utilities offered there. You have two menus to choose from. You can replace the standard AutoCAD menu with a full version of the On-Screen AEC menu. This is a copy of the standard AutoCAD menu with the On-Screen AEC functions added. You can also load a partial On-Screen AEC menu to the AutoCAD menu you are now using. This later option gives you more flexibility but will require that you load the AEC menu every time you open a new AutoCAD session. First, we'll describe how to load the full On-Screen AEC menu.

Loading the Full Version   Load the full version of the On-Screen AEC menu when you know you will want access to the AEC tools all the time. Here's how it's done.

1. Once back in AutoCAD, type **Menu** ⏎ at the command prompt. The Select Menu File dialog box appears. This is a typical Windows file dialog box.

2. Locate the file named Acadaec.MNU in the \acadr13\win\aec directory, then double-click on it. You are now ready to use On-Screen AEC.

You can restore the standard version of the AutoCAD menu by following the same steps shown here, but instead of selecting the Acadaec.MNU file, select the Acad.MNU file in the \acadr13\win\support directory.

Loading the Partial Version   Use the partial version of the On-Screen AEC menu when you use the AEC tools infrequently, or with a different third-party menu system. Here's how it's done.

1. Once back in AutoCAD, choose Tools ➤ Customize Menu or type **Menuload** ⏎. The Menu Customization dialog box appears.

Appendices

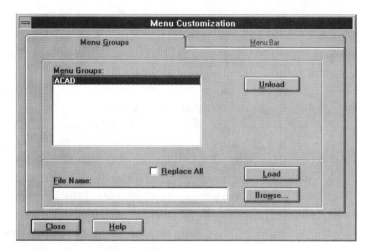

2. Click on the Browse button at the bottom of the dialog box. The Select Menu File dialog box appears

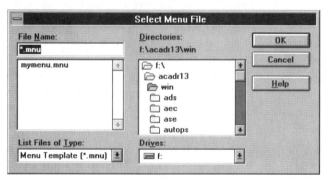

3. Locate the file name OSAEC.MNU, then double click on it. You return to the Menu Customization dialog box and the OSAEC.MNU file name appears in the File Name input box.

4. Click on the Load button just above the Browse button. AutoCAD takes a moment to load the menu. The AEC Tools palette will appear on the screen.

5. In the Menu Group list box in the upper portion of the dialog box, highlight OSAEC, then click the tab labeled Menu Bar at the top of the dialog box. The dialog box changes to reveal the Menu Bar options.

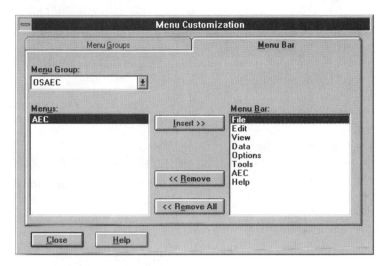

Notice that a menu called AEC appears in the Menus list box to the left. This is a pull-down menu that is contained in the OSAEC.MNU file.

6. In the Menu Bar list box to the right, click on Help to highlight it. This determines where the AEC pull-down menu will appear in the menu bar.

7. Click on the button labeled Insert >>. AEC will appear just above Help in the Menu Bar list box and you will see AEC appear in the AutoCAD menu bar at the top of the AutoCAD Window.

You are now ready to use On-Screen AEC. Follow the instructions presented in the following section.

Installing AutoPS

To install AutoPS and to load the AutoPS menus, perform the same steps as described for installing On-Screen AEC with the following differences:

■ Install AutoPS in a subdirectory called \autops as in \acadr13\win\autops.

Appendices

- Use the Acadaps.MNU file instead of the Acadaec.MNU file for the full menu.

- Use the APS_sub.MNU file instead of the OSAEC.MNU file for the partial menu.

- When inserting a menu bar item during partial menu use, choose AutoPS.

Installing the AutoCAD Resource Guide

To install the AutoCAD Resource Guide take the following steps:

1. Place the companion CD in your CD-ROM drive.

2. Use the File Manager's Run command on the File menu (in Windows 3.1 and NT 3.51), or use the Run command on the Start menu (in Windows 95 and NT 4).

3. At the Run dialog box, enter the following line:

   drive:\argcdrom\setup

   Replace *drive* in the above example with the drive letter of your CD-ROM drive.

4. Click OK, then follow the instructions on your screen.

The Setup program will create a program group and icon that will start the AutoCAD Resource Guide application. You can click and drag the Resource Guide icon to your AutoCAD R13 program group for easier access.

   Note that to use the Resource Guide, you must have the Companion CD in your computer.

USING THE AEC UTILITIES

On-Screen AEC is a basic architectural symbols library package. This package supplies utilities for creating doors, plumbing and electrical fixtures, wall patterns, and wall intersection clean-up. It also includes many timesaving utilities to help you work faster and more efficiently. Even if your application doesn't involve architecture, you may want to install On-Screen AEC just to take advantage of these utilities.

GETTING STARTED WITH ON-SCREEN AEC

Once you've installed the AEC software, you can begin to use On-Screen AEC. You may want to start by clicking on the Setup Drawing option in the AEC menu, to bring up a dialog box you can use to set up your drawing. Once the setup is done, you will have a drawing area equivalent to your sheet size, with a grid representing 1″ intervals on the final plot area.

USING AEC TO ADD WALLS, DOORS, SYMBOLS, AND STAIRS

Let's begin by taking a look at some of the basic architectural features available with AEC.

Adding Walls

To draw walls, you could use the Multiline feature of AutoCAD Release 13, but Multilines are a bit difficult to edit. Another alternative is to use the Walls option on the AEC menu. Here's how it works:

1. Choose AEC ➤ Walls or click on Wall from the AEC palette.

2. At the Enter width prompt, enter a width for your wall in inches.

3. At the Center/Up/Down of line <C>: prompt, enter the desired option. Center (the default) centers the wall along the points you pick. The Up and Down options place one side of the wall on the points you pick.

4. At the Start relative to a position prompt, you can press ↵ to start your wall anywhere, or type **Y** ↵ to place the beginning of the wall relative to another wall.

5. At the Draw Centerline prompt, you can press ↵ to just draw a two-line representation of a wall, or enter **Y** ↵ to add a line along the points you pick.

6. At the Pick beginning of parallel lines: prompt, start picking points for your wall. You will see the Pick next point prompt as you continue to pick points.

7. To stop picking points, press ↵.

8. At the Close last corner prompt, you can enter **Y** ↵ to close your wall, or **N** ↵ to exit the Walls utility without closing the wall.

Adding a Door

The door utility can be used only in the world coordinate system. If you are in another UCS, switch back to the WCS temporarily to insert a door using this utility. Also, you must have drawn walls using the Wall utility to place doors.

1. Choose AEC ➤ Doors then select a door from the cascading menu. (To see what the door styles look like, select the Open Toolbar option at the bottom of the menu to open the Door Palette. You can then select a door type from the palette.)

2. Once you select a door, pick a reference point along the wall (see Figure C.1). This should be a known point, such as an interior corner or the midpoint of a wall. You will later enter a value to determine the distance from this point to the door hinge.

3. Pick a point on the opposite side of the wall, as shown in Figure C.1.

4. Again using Figure C.1 as your guide, pick a point along the wall indicating where the door opening will appear in relation to the last point selected.

5. When the command prompt asks you for a door width, enter a width, or press ↵ to accept the default door width shown in the < > brackets.

6. Enter the distance from the reference point you picked earlier (step 3) that you want to place the door hinge. For

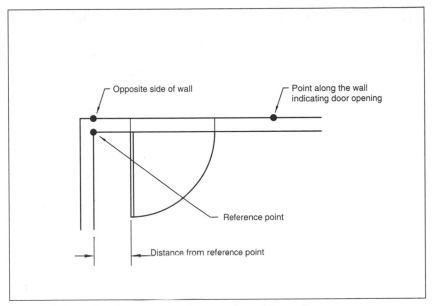

Figure C.1:   Select this sequence of points when adding a door

example, if you picked the inside corner of a room for the reference point and you want the door to be 4″ from that corner, enter 4.

Notice the Settings option near the bottom of the menu; this lets you set the layers on which to place the door, door header, and door jamb. Once these layers are set, AutoCAD will remember them until you change them again. These layer settings affect newly inserted doors only, not previously inserted doors.

Adding a Wall Pattern

Here's how to select and pick points for a wall pattern:

1. Choose AEC ➤ Wall Pattern.

2. From the cascading menu, select the wall pattern you want, or click on Open Toolbar to open the Wall Pattern palette.

Appendices

3. At the Pick wall at beginning of pattern: prompt, use the Osnap modes to select a point along the wall where the pattern is to start. For example, you can pick the intersection of two walls using the Intersect Osnap mode.

4. At the Pick the opposite side of the wall: prompt, pick any point on the opposite side of the wall from the last point you picked.

5. At the Pick end of the wall pattern: prompt, pick a point indicating the end of the wall pattern. This point should be on the same side of the wall as the last point you picked.

The wall pattern appears between the first and last points selected.

Adding Symbols

Here are the steps to add symbols to a drawing. If you would like to modify the AEC-supplied symbols to fit your own work environment, you can find them in the AEC subdirectory.

1. Pull down the AEC menu, and choose one of the three categories of symbols. A cascading menu appears, with a list of symbols.

2. Choose the name of the symbol you want to use, or you can pick Open Toolbar from the menu to have better access to them (see Figure C.2).

3. Answer the Insertion point and rotation angle prompts on the command line. The symbol appears in the location you select.

Adding Stairs

The AEC menu also includes a stair-drawing option, which works as follows:

1. Click on AEC ➤ Draw Stairs.

2. At the Pick first corner of stair: prompt, pick a point locating one corner of the first stair tread nosing (see Figure C.3).

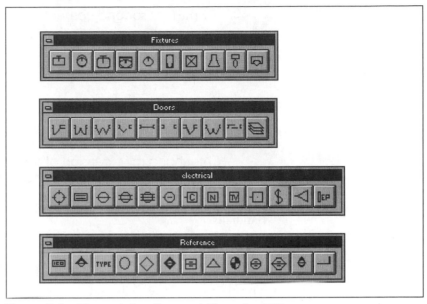

Figure C.2: The symbol toolbars available on the AEC menu.

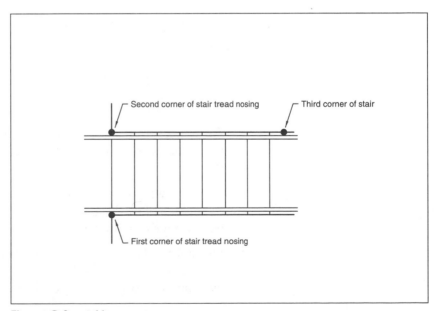

Figure C.3: Adding a stair

3. At the Pick second corner of stair: prompt, pick the other corner of the nosing.

4. At the Pick third corner of stair: prompt, pick the other end of the stair run.

5. Answer the following four prompts:

   Enter minimum run of stair <10.00>:
   Enter maximum rise of stair <7.50>:
   Enter hand rail extension at top of stair <l2.00>:
   Enter hand rail extension at bottom of stair <l2.00>:

The stairs appear within the three points you select complete with handrails.

USING THE WALL CLEANUP UTILITIES

The cleanup utilities will join double lines into tee, corner, and cross formations. The lines joined must be simple lines, not polylines or Multilines. (To join Multilines, you use the MLEDIT command. To join Polylines, use the Join option of the PEDIT command)

Cleaning Up Tee Wall Intersections

To clean up tee wall intersection, do the following:

1. Click on AEC ➤ Wall Cleanup.

2. Select Tee from the cascading menu.

3. At the Pick intersection with window: prompt, use a selection window to enclose the intersection of the walls forming the tee.

4. At the Indicate leg of tee using axis: prompt, pick a point to one side of the leg of the tee. A rubber-banding line appears from the point you select.

5. Pick a second point so that the rubber-banding line crosses over the two lines of the leg of the tee. Take care not to cross over any lines other than those of the tee leg.

The tee intersection joins into a smooth tee intersection as shown in Figure C.4.

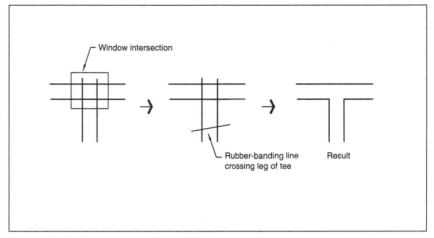

Figure C.4: Joining a tee intersection

Cleaning Up Corner Wall Intersections

To clean up corner wall intersections, do the following:

1. Click on AEC ➤ Wall Cleanup and select Corner.

2. At the Select intersection with window: prompt, window the intersection of the walls forming the corner.

3. At the Pick inside of corner: prompt, a rubber-banding line appears. Pick a point on the inside of the corner. Try to pick this point so that the rubber-banding line divides the angle formed by the two walls exactly in half.

The walls first disappear, then reappear with the corner cleaned up as shown in Figure C.5.

Appendices

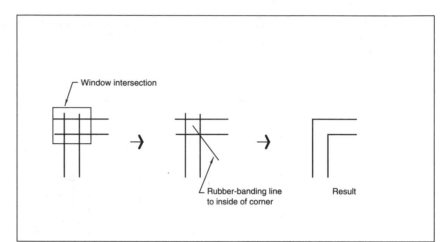

Figure C.5: Joining a corner

Cleaning Up Crossing Wall Intersections

This function only works if all the lines forming the walls are continuous through the intersection. If this is the case, do the following:

1. Click on AEC ➤ Wall Cleanup and choose Intersect.

2. At the Select intersection with window: prompt, window the intersection of the walls.

3. At the Pick narrow bisecting angle of intersection: prompt, pick a point between the intersecting walls, as close to midway between the two walls as possible. If the walls are not perpendicular, pick a point between the narrower angle between the walls.

The walls first disappear, then reappear with the intersection cleaned up as shown in Figure C.6.

Closing the End of a Wall

This function can be used on any two lines that need to be closed.

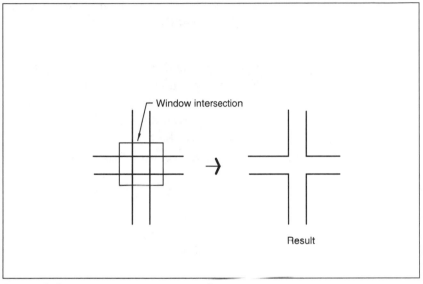

Figure C.6: Joining two intersecting walls

1. Click on AEC ➤ Wall Cleanup and choose Close End.
2. At the Select end of wall with crossing line: prompt, indicate the end of the wall you want to close by picking two points that cross the end of the wall. The end of the wall closes.

USING THE GENERAL UTILITIES

Along with the AEC utilities, On-Screen AEC has several other general-purpose utilities to help you edit your drawings. These utilities are helpful no matter what your field of interest. Take a moment to read through the following descriptions and see if you haven't had a need for at least one or two of these tools.

LAYER UTILITIES

AutoCAD offers many different ways to control layers. Still, there are some shortcuts you can take to setting and controlling layer visibility.

Here are a few tools for improving your productivity that have been useful to me over the years.

Turning Layers Off by Selecting Objects

Sometimes you know that you want the layer of a particular object to be turned off, but you don't know the name of the layer. Normally, you would have to use the LIST command to find the layer of the object, and then use the Layer Control dialog box to turn off that layer. The Layer Off by Obj utility greatly simplifies the operation.

1. Choose AEC ➤ Layers and choose Layer Off by Obj.

2. At the next prompt, select an object whose layer you wish to freeze or turn off. That object's layer name will appear in the command prompt.

3. At the Freeze/<Off>: prompt, enter the appropriate response. A ↵ will turn off the layer of the selected object.

Setting the Current Layer by Objects

This utility may be the oldest and most favorite of all. Match Layer lets you set the current layer by picking an object whose layer you want to work on.

1. Choose AEC ➤ Layers and choose Match Layer.

2. At the Select object whose layer is to be matched: prompt, pick the object whose layer you want to work on.

Recording and Restoring Layer Settings

Layering can often become a nightmare—especially when you want to use several layering settings for the same drawing, or if you want to temporarily turn off layers to work on a drawing and then later turn them back on again. Here is a utility that can help you manage layers.

The AutoLISP file Lrestore.LSP contains two commands, LRECORD and LRESTORE. LRECORD (Record Layer on the AEC ➤ Layers menu) will save your layer settings as a file on disk. LRESTORE (Restore Layers in the AEC ➤ Layers menu) reads that file and resets your layer settings to those found in the file. You can use these utilities as you would an Undo for layer settings; that is, you temporarily change layer settings to view special work layers, and when you are done, restore your layering to its previous condition.

To record layer settings, do the following:

1. Choose AEC ➤ Layers and select Record Layer. The Save Layer Record dialog box appears.

2. Click on OK to accept the default layer record file name, which is the same as the current drawing name with the .LYR extension. Or you can enter a different name.

To restore a previously saved layer setting, do the following:

1. Choose AEC ➤ Layers and select Restore Layers. The Restore Layer Record dialog box appears.

2. Select a layer record file from the files list and click on OK.

3. At the Restore Linetypes? (this can take time) <N>: prompt, you can optionally restore line-type settings. (This is supplied as an option because using it can increase the time it takes to restore layers.) If you haven't made changes to layer line-types, press ↵ at this prompt.

4. AutoCAD works for a moment and then displays A regen may be required to show changes. You may want to issue a REGEN to view the restored layer settings.

TEXT-RELATED UTILITIES

AutoCAD has improved its text-handling capabilities over the years, but you may still want some help in this area. Here are some utilities that will fill many of the voids still remaining in AutoCAD's text-handling functions.

Drawing Text on a Curve

If you work on maps in which text has to follow some geographic feature, this utility will be helpful. The Text on a Path option on the AEC ➤ Text menu draws text on a curved polyline or arc. You must first draw the polyline or arc.

1. Click on AEC ➤ Text and choose Text on a Path.

2. At the Pick path for text prompt, click on the polyline you have created to define the path.

3. At the Enter text prompt, enter the text you want to follow the path, and press ↵.

4. At the Reverse Text? prompt, enter **Y** ↵ if you want the text to appear in a reverse direction. The text will appear momentarily.

Editing Several Lines of Non-Multiline Text

The Edit Dtext Block (Edsp) utility on the AEC ➤ Text menu allows you to use DOS Edit to make changes to a group of single-line text objects created using DTEXT.

1. Click on AEC ➤ Text and choose Edit Dtext Block.

2. At the Save to file/<Edit> ? prompt, enter **S** ↵ to save text in a file for later retrieval. Enter **E** ↵ to edit the text in DOS Edit, and proceed to step 4.

3. If you entered **S** ↵, you are prompted with Enter name of file to be saved <Filename.doc>:. You can enter a different file name, if you want, or press ↵ to accept the default.

4. The next prompt you see is

   Sort text by vertical location (this takes some time) ? <N>:

   Here you have the option to have Edit Dtext Block sort text so it appears in the text file in the same order it appears in the drawing. This only applies to columns of text, so don't use this option unless you plan to select a column of text for editing.

▼ NOTE

At this point, you also have the alternative of exiting AutoCAD entirely and making changes to your text file at a later time. If you choose to do this, be sure you save your file before exiting AutoCAD; otherwise, Edsp won't be able to update your text later. The next time you open the file, load Edsp, enter **Sp_update**, and the text in your drawing will be updated.

5. At the Select text:... Select objects: prompt, select the text you want to edit.

6. Next, you can shell out of AutoCAD and, using a word processor, open the file you just created. Make your changes, and then return to the drawing.

7. Enter **Sp_update** ⏎. The changes you made to your saved file are applied to your drawing.

8. If you chose to enter ⏎ in step 2, AutoCAD loads a text editor and your selected text appears on the screen for you to edit. Once you've made your changes, choose File ➤ Exit; be sure you answer Yes to save your changes. You will return to your drawing, and your text will be updated to reflect the changes you have made.

Quickly Changing Single Lines

You probably often run across the situation where you need to change several lines of text to make them all say the same thing. Instead of changing each line individually, use the Quick Text Edit utility on the AEC ➤ Text menu. It's a very simple utility that lets you select a set of text objects and change them all at once.

1. Click on AEC ➤ Text and choose Quick Text Edit.

2. At the Pick text to be changed-EL Select objects prompt, select the lines of text you want to change.

3. At the Enter new string prompt, enter the text you want to appear in place of the selected lines.

Changing Numeric Sequences

If one of your frequent chores is having to change the sequence of numbers—parking stalls, for example, or sequential numbers in a table—Sequential Numbers (on the AEC ➤ Text ➤ menu) helps you do this quickly and easily. This utility lets you control the unit style of the numbers, as well as the increment of increase for each number in the sequence.

Appendices

1. Click on AEC ➤ Text and choose Sequential Numbers.

2. At the Pick numbers to be changed in order of increment: prompt, select the text objects that are to be converted into a new sequence of numbers. Select the objects in the order the numbers are to appear.

3. At the Enter unit type Scientific/Decimal/Engin/Arch <D>: prompt, enter the unit style you want.

4. At the Enter precision value: prompt, enter the decimal accuracy you want for the numbers.

5. At the Enter increment value: prompt, enter the amount of increase for each number in the sequence.

6. At the Enter new beginning value: prompt, enter the first number of the sequence. AutoCAD then proceeds to change the selected objects into sequential numbers.

Changing the Height of Text Objects

One of the more frequently requested utilities is one that will change text height. The Change Text Style utility on the AEC ➤ Text menu does this—and it also alters nearly any other property of a group of text objects. Unfortunately, it doesn't operate on Multiline text.

1. First, create a text style with the height you want.

2. Click on AEC ➤ Text and choose Change Text Style.

3. At the Select objects prompt, select the text whose height you want to change.

HOUSEKEEPING UTILITIES

When you're working with a group of people, it is often helpful to keep a record of your layers and blocks. Your coworkers can then refer to these records to find out the assigned contents and purpose of existing layers and blocks. The two utilities described in this section create ASCII log files of your work.

Keeping a Log of Your Blocks

The Block Log utility on the AEC ➤ Blocks menu is a simple macro that creates a log file of blocks. You can specify a name for the file or use the default name, which is usually the drawing name with the .BLK extension. The log file will contain the date and a space for remarks. You can edit the file using a text editor to add comments or view and print the file.

Here's how it works:

1. Choose AEC ➤ Blocks ➤ Block Log.

2. At the Enter name of block file <filename>: prompt, enter a block name or press ↵ to accept the default. If no file exists with the name you enter, a new file will be created; otherwise, the current block information will be appended to an existing file.

Keeping a Log of Your Layers

Layer Log does essentially the same thing as the Block Log utility described just above, except it creates an ASCII file log of your layers. This utility creates or appends to a file with the .LAY extension. Here's how to use it:

1. Choose AEC ➤ Layers ➤ Layer Log.

2. At the Enter name of layer file <filename>: prompt, enter a name or press ↵ to accept the default.

GENERAL PRODUCTIVITY TOOLS

The utilities in this section offer general help in drawing and editing.

Changing the Thickness of Lines

The Thicken utility on the AEC ➤ Drawing Aids menu changes the width of a set of lines, polylines, or arcs. This is useful if you like to control line thickness directly in your drawing rather than relying on plotter pen settings.

> **▼ NOTE**
>
> If you want to change the width of circles, you must first turn them into 359° arcs by breaking them with a very small break.

1. Choose AEC ➤ Drawing Aids ➤ Thicken.

2. At the prompt, enter the thickness you want for your lines.

3. At the Select objects prompt, select the lines, arcs, or polylines you want to change, and press ↵.

Drawing Lines a New Way

Drawing lines in AutoCAD can be quite a chore using the standard coordinate notation. With Point Line on the AEC ➤ Drawing Aids menu, there's an easier way. Instead of having to enter **@distance<angle,** Point Line (Nline) lets you indicate the angle using a rubber-banding line, while entering the distance from the keyboard. Here's how it works:

1. Choose AEC ➤ Drawing Aids ➤ Point Line.

2. At the Start point: prompt, pick a point to start your line.

3. At the Enter distance: prompt, indicate the direction of the line using the rubber-banding line and your cursor, then enter the distance you want via the keyboard. As you do this, a temporary line is drawn on the screen.

4. As you enter distances, the prompt reads Enter distance/ Close/eXit:. You can enter **C** ↵ to close a set of lines, or **X** ↵ to exit Nline. Nline then draws a polyline through the path you define.

Joining Broken Lines

> **▼ NOTE**
>
> The Join Lines utility does not work on polylines. You can, however, use grips to first move a polyline endpoint to join the endpoint of the second polyline, and then use the PEDIT command's Join option to connect them.

It is considered bad form to leave disjointed lines in a CAD drawing—"disjointed" meaning lines that appear to be continuous but are actually made up of several line segments. The Join Lines utility on the AEC ➤ Drawing Aids menu will help you clean up such lines, or just close a gap in any broken line except a polyline.

1. Choose AEC ➤ Drawing Aids ➤ Join Lines.

2. At the Select two lines to be joined prompt, pick the lines that are broken.

Attribute Template Files, Simplified

Creating and using attributes can be trying for the beginner and even the intermediate user. Extracting attribute data is even more difficult. The Create Attrib. Templt. option on the AEC ➤ Drawing Aids menu eases these chores by letting you easily create an attribute template file that tells AutoCAD what data to extract.

1. Choose AEC ➤ Drawing Aids ➤ Create Attrib. Templt.

2. At the Name of attribute template file prompt, enter the name you want for your template. Don't bother adding an extension; the utility will do that for you.

3. At the ?/Enter name of attribute tag: prompt, enter the name of the tag you wish to extract. You can also enter **?** ↵ to get a listing of existing tags.

4. At the Is the attribute a Number or Character <C/N>? prompt, enter **C** ↵ or **N** ↵ to specify the attribute as a character or number.

5. At the Enter number of digits or characters: prompt, enter the number of characters or digits you want reserved for the attribute.

6. If you entered **N** ↵ in step 4, you'll see the Enter number of decimal places wanted: prompt next. Enter the number of decimal places you want to reserve for your number.

7. Repeat steps 3 through 5 for each attribute. These prompts will continue until you press ↵ at the ?/Enter name of attribute tag prompt in step 3.

Cookie Cutter for Objects

There may be times when you want to export a portion of a drawing that is enmeshed in a larger set of objects. Cut Out on the AEC ➤ Drawing Aids menu offers a "cookie-cutter" tool for breaking out

Appendices

objects that are bound into a larger system of objects. Here's how to use Cut Out:

1. Choose AEC ➤ Drawing Aids ➤ Cut Out.

2. At the Pick first point of Fence/Select: prompt, pick a point to start a fence. This fence defines that area to be cut out.

3. At the Next point prompt, pick the next point of the fence.

4. At the Next point/Close prompt, continue to pick points defining the area you want to cut out.

5. At the last point of your fence, enter **C** ↵ to close the fence. The program will break each line, polyline, and circle that it encounters.

You can also predefine a fence, by drawing a polyline in the shape of the area you want to cut out. Then, in step 2 you enter **S** ↵. At the prompt Pick line or Pline defining cut location prompt, select an object, and the fence will cut objects along the line or polyline.

There are a few restrictions when using Cut Out:

■ You cannot use polyline arcs or splines for fence paths. If you want to cut an arc path, approximate the arc using a spline curve.

■ The fence cannot cut blocks, text, arcs, or splines and it will not reliably cut fitted polylines.

Counting Blocks

Is there a simple way to count the occurrences of blocks in a drawing? Yes. Perhaps the easiest method is to use the Selection Filters... option on the Assist menu to select the blocks you want, and then choose Assist ➤ Select Objects ➤ Previous to display the number of selected items. This is fine for counting individual block occurrences, but what if you want a quick count of several block definitions? The Count Blocks utility on the AEC ➤ Blocks menu gives you a listing of blocks and the number of times they occur in your drawing. It also saves the list as a file with the same name as your drawing and the .BLK extension.

Here's how it works:

1. Choose AEC ➤ Blocks ➤ Count Blocks.

2. At the Enter name(s) of blocks to count or RETURN for all: prompt, enter the names of the blocks you want to count, separated by commas. Or you can press ↵ to count all the blocks in the drawing.

AutoCAD lists the blocks and their count. When the counting is done, an ASCII file is created to store the information displayed on the screen.

Creating Keyboard Macros

In *Chapter 19*, you learned how you can use AutoLISP to create a keyboard macro. I've included an AutoLISP program utility with On-Screen AEC that will do the work for you. This utility, Macro on the AEC ➤ Drawing Aids menu, allows you to record specific points in your drawing and also lets you insert pauses in your macro where you need them. To create a macro, do the following:

1. Choose AEC ➤ Drawing Aids ➤ Macro.

2. At the Enter keys to define prompt, enter the name of the macro. This is what you will enter at the command prompt to start your macro.

3. At the Will this macro require open ended object selection? prompt, enter **Y** ↵ if you want to be able to select objects without restrictions—this means you can use all the standard selection options whenever you run your macro. If you do enable this option, however, you must use the Previous setting (described at the end of this procedure) in the main part of your macro to indicate where you want the selected objects to be applied.

4. At the Previous/?=Pause/*=Point/# =done/<Keystroke> prompt, enter the keystrokes of your macro or enter one of the options, as described in the following list.

Appendices

Here are descriptions of the options in the Previous/?=Pause/
*=Point/#=done/<Keystroke> prompt:

Previous is used to indicate when the selected objects should
be applied in your macro. Use this option where you anticipate
a Select objects prompt. If you have enabled open-ended object selection (step 3 above), you must include this option.

? places a pause for input in the macro. Use this option when
you want the macro to stop and wait for point or text input.

* lets you pick a point on the screen or enter a coordinate.
This value becomes a fixed value in the macro.

ends the macro keystroke input and stores the macro in
memory (or, optionally, on disk).

A ZOOM Replacement

AutoCAD's ZOOM (View ➤ Zoom) functions are certainly adequate
for most of your work. The Enhanced Zoom utility on the AEC menu
offers some enhancements, however, that may prove useful. Enhanced
Zoom lets you quickly zoom into a maximum zoom level that you set.
You can also zoom in and out incrementally. Other features are real-
time panning and an adjustable overall view setting.

To use Enhanced Zoom, click on AEC ➤ Enhanced Zoom, and select
an option from the cascading menu. The options work as follows:

All displays the entire virtual screen, or a saved view you have
chosen to represent the All option. This view is set using the
Set option, described just below. No regen occurs.

Extents shows the extents of the drawing, without a regen.

In/Out lets you zoom in and out of the current view. You can
change the In/Out zoom factor by using the Set option, described below.

Max zooms in to a maximum magnification, which you designate using the Set option, described below.

Previous shows the previous display.

Real Pan lets you pan your view automatically by moving your cursor in the direction of the pan. By keeping your cursor near the center of the screen, you can pause the panning.

Set is used to set the zoom factors for the Max and In/Out options, as well as the current view that you get with the All option.

Window lets you select a view using a window.

< pan > lets you pan by picking a view center. This is the default that you get by pressing ↵ at the All/Extents/In... prompt. If you enable this option, you will see a rectangular outline moving with the cursor. The outline shows you the area that your pan will take in. If you zoom out using the Extents or All option and then use < pan >, you will zoom in to the point you picked, based on the last zoom factor.

USING AUTOPS

Out of my own frustration with other PostScript drawing programs, which lacked the accuracy offered by AutoCAD, I have created the AutoPS illustration tool. AutoPS gives you the best of both worlds—a decent drawing program with the accuracy and speed of AutoCAD, combined with True PostScript fonts and gray shading.

The illustration shown in Figure C.7 was created with AutoCAD and AutoPS, in about half the time required with the leading PostScript drawing program.

AutoPS works by translating AutoCAD .DXF files into PostScript Vector files. This utility may seem redundant to the AutoCAD PSOUT command, but there are many situations in which AutoPS is useful. First of all, it works either within AutoCAD or as a standalone DOS utility. You can more easily control certain output options, such as corner conditions on wide lines and grayscale screening. Fonts are automatically converted to Helvetica, and you can use aliases to make use of downloadable PostScript fonts. Finally, AutoPS includes a set of AutoLISP utilities that can help you control aspects of your text, such as line spacing and obliqueing.

Appendices

The AutoCAD
PostScript
Editor

AutoPS

Original photograph by Howard Bjornson

Figure C.7:   A sample of what can be done with AutoCAD and AutoPS. The image of the vases is based on an original photograph by Howard Bjornson.

SETTING UP TO USE AUTOPS

Once AutoPS is installed and its menu loaded into AutoCAD, create your drawing. When you are done, take the following steps to create an .EPS (Encapsulated PostScript) file:

1. Choose APS ➤ Psplot. The screen switches to text mode and you are prompted for a PostScript file name. You can enter a name, or accept the default, Psplot.EPS, by pressing ↵.

▼ **NOTE**

Before you can use down-loaded fonts, you must first create a text style named Dlfont1, Dlfont2, or Dlfont3. Text written in these styles can then be assigned to fonts that have been downloaded to your PostScript printer.

▼ **NOTE**

If you need to enter a scale value less than 1, the value must start with a leading zero; for example, if you enter a scale of .5 instead of 0.5, you will get an error message.

2. The current AutoPS settings are displayed. At the bottom is a prompt asking if you want to change these settings. Type **Y** ↵.

3. Next, you are prompted about including downloaded fonts. If you want to use downloaded fonts, type **Y** ↵. You are then asked for font names to be substituted for the Dlfont style in your drawing.

4. Next you are prompted for a drawing scale. If your drawing is to be actual size, enter **1**. If you want the PostScript file to double the drawing size, enter **2**; for half size, enter **0.5**, and so on.

5. The next prompt asks for the standard line weight in points. Enter a value representing the thickness you want for all non-polyline objects.

6. At the next prompt, enter a grayscale value for solid fills. (A value of 100 will leave solid fills solid; a value of 10 will turn solid fills into gray areas with a 10% screen.)

7. At the next prompt you can control the number of dots per inch to be used for screened areas; 60 dpi is the default and offers the best range of grayscales without making the dots too large.

8. At the next prompt you can adjust the dot screen angle, if you intend to create four-color separations.

9. The next prompt lets you control how polyline corners are formed. A Mitered corner is a sharp corner; Rounded will round the corner; Beveled will cut the point off the corner.

10. The last prompt lets you designate landscape or portrait orientation on the final output.

When you are done answering all the prompts, AutoPS will take a few moments to generate the PostScript file.

Appendices

USING AUTOPS AS A STANDALONE PROGRAM

To generate an .EPS file outside of AutoCAD, perform a DXFOUT (File ➤ Export, or type **DXFOUT** ↵) on the drawing you wish to translate. Open a DOS window then go to the \acadr13\win\autops subdirectory. and enter the following:

DXF2EPS (*DXFfilename*.DXF) (*desiredEPSfile_name*)

You can also just enter **DXF2EPS** at the DOS prompt, and you will be prompted for both a source file name and an export file name. You will also be asked for other variables such as typical line thickness, scale, page orientation, and so on. Answer the prompts as needed.

WORKING WITH THE AUTOPS MENU OPTIONS

The AutoPS menu offers some additional tools to help you create your drawings. The first set of tools, Text Tools, are the same as those found in the On-Screen AEC menu and are described in the AEC section earlier under "Text Related Utilities." In addition, you have the following options:

Pline Tools

The Pline tools offer ways to control grayshade screens. They're called Pline Tools because grayscale screens are generated using polylines.

> **Pline Screen** lets you control how a polyline is translated into a screen. You can show polylines as outlines only, outlines with filled screens, and filled screens only. After you choose an option, AutoCAD creates a new layer and assigns the selected polylines to it. The layer is given a name that AutoPS will recognize as a screen type.

> **Move to Front** moves an object so that it appears "on top of" everything else in the drawing. This is important in PostScript work because the topmost object obscures those below it.

Reverse Order reverses the order of objects that are stacked.

Change Thickness changes the thickness of lines, polylines, and arcs.

Set Screen/Layer brings up a dialog box where you can match an existing layer name to a screen type.

Using PostScript Fonts

AutoPS translates text styles into PostScript fonts with the equivalent name. If AutoPS doesn't know the name of a font, it uses Helvetica by default.

Set Current Style on the AutoPS menu offers a simplified way of creating a PostScript style that will be recognized by AutoPS. This option lists all the standard fonts that are normally built into PostScript printers. You are also able to use downloadable fonts by creating an AutoCAD text style called Dlfontl, Dlfont2, or Dlfont3. At plot time, you can then tell AutoPS which fonts to use in place of Dlfonts. The Symb font is included in the menu if you have the Symb Adobe Font. This font is useful for mapping.

SOME CAUTIONS ABOUT AUTOPS

AutoPS was created as an illustration tool for creating original art. It wasn't designed to convert existing AutoCAD drawings to a PostScript format—however, that can be done. If you elect to use AutoPS for converting existing drawings to the PostScript format, here are a few things to watch out for:

■ The AutoPS translator does not recognize Trace objects, nor does it recognize color and line-type assignments other than those of the layer an object is on. For example, if an object is on a layer that has a dashed line type, that object will be dashed in the output file. On the other hand, if objects are assigned the dashed line type individually, using Modify ➤ Properties…, those objects will appear as continuous lines after the translation.

Appendices

■ Associative dimensions do not translate well. If you have associative dimensions, you may want to explode them before you do the translation.

■ Hatch patterns may not translate properly. If you have problems with hatches, explode them just before you translate the drawing. You can always undo an explode command.

■ Avoid nested or large blocks. These can increase file size and translation time.

■ Tapered polylines do not translate as tapered lines. They become wide lines of a constant width.

■ Remember to enter numeric values of less than 1 with a leading zero, as in 0.25.

■ If your drawing won't print, be sure the limits in the original AutoCAD file are set to include all of the drawing. The limits determine the area that gets printed.

SYSTEM AND DIMENSION VARIABLES

This appendix discusses AutoCAD's system variables. It is divided into two sections: *system variables* and *dimension variables*. The general system variables let you fine-tune your AutoCAD environment. Dimension variables govern the specific dimensioning functions of AutoCAD.

System variables are accessible directly from the command prompt, and transparently (while in another command), by entering the variable name preceded by an apostrophe. These variables are also accessible through the AutoLISP interpreter by using the Getvar and Setvar functions.

I've divided this appendix into two main sections, Setting System Variables and Setting Dimension Variables. This division is somewhat artificial, because as far as AutoCAD is concerned, there is no difference between system variables and dimension variables—you use both types of variables the same way. But because the set of dimension variables is quite extensive, they are separated here for clarity.

SETTING SYSTEM VARIABLES

Table D.1 lists the variables, and notes whether they are read-only or adjustable. Most of these variables have counterparts in other commands, as listed in the table. For example, Angdir and Angbase can be adjusted using the UNITS command (Data ➤ Units). Many, such as Highlight and Expert, do not have equivalent commands. These must be adjusted at the command line (or through AutoLISP).

Table D.1: System Variables (continued)

Variable Name	Associated Command	Where Saved	Use
Acadprefix	Preferences	NA	The ACAD environment setting.
Acadver	NA	NA	The AutoCAD version number.
Aflags	UNITS	With drawing	Controls attribute mode settings: 1 = invisible; 2 = constant; 3 = verify; 8 = preset.
Angbase	UNITS	With drawing	Controls direction of 0 angle, relative to the current UCS.
Angdir	UNITS	With drawing	Controls positive direction of angles: 0 = counterclockwise; 1 = clockwise.
Aperture	Aperture	With configuration	Controls the Osnap cursor target height in pixels.
Area (read-only)	Area	NA	Displays last area calculation; use with Setvar or AutoLISP's Getvar function.
Attdia	INSERT/ Attribute	With drawing	Controls the Attribute dialog box: 0 = no dialog box; 1 = dialog box.
Attmode	Attdisp	With drawing	Controls attribute display mode: 0 = off; 1 = normal; 2 = on.
Attreq	Insert	With drawing	Controls the prompt for attributes: 0 = no prompt or dialog box for attributes (attributes use default values); 1 = normal prompt or dialog box upon attribute insertion.
Auditctl	Config	With configuration	Controls whether an audit file is created: 0 = disable; 1 = enable creation of .ADT file.
Aunits	UNITS	With drawing	Controls angular units: 0 = decimal degrees; 1 = degrees-minutes-seconds; 2 = grads; 3 = radians; 4 = surveyor's units.
Auprec	UNITS	With drawing	Controls the precision of angular units determined by decimal place.
Backz (read-only)	DVIEW	With drawing	Displays distance from DVIEW target to back clipping plane.

Appendices

Table D.1: System Variables (continued)

Variable Name	Associated Command	Where Saved	Use
Blipmode	NA	With drawing	Controls appearance of blips: 0 = off; 1 = on.
Cdate (read-only)	TIME	NA	Displays calendar date/time read from DOS: (YYYYMMDD.HHMMSSMSEC).
Cecolor	COLOR	With drawing	Controls current default color assigned to new objects.
Celtscale	NA	With drawing	Controls current linetype scale for individual objects.
Celtype	LINETYPE	With drawing	Controls current default line type assigned to new objects.
Chamfera	CHAMFER	With drawing	Controls first chamfer distance.
Chamferb	CHAMFER	With drawing	Controls second chamfer distance.
Chamferc	CHAMFER	With drawing	Controls chamfer distance for Angle option.
Chamferd	CHAMFER	With drawing	Controls chamfer angle for Angle option.
Chammode	CHAMFER	With drawing	Controls method of chamfer: 0 = use; 2 distances; 1 = use distance and angle.
Circlerad	CIRCLE	NA	Controls the default circle radius: 0 = no default.
Clayer	LAYER	With drawing	Sets the current layer.
Cmdactive (read-only)	NA	NA	Displays whether a command, script, or dialog box is active: 1 = command active; 2 = transparent command active; 4 = script active; 8 = dialog box active (values are cumulative, so 3 = command and transparent command are active).
Cmddia	NA	With configuration	Controls use of dialog boxes for some commands: 0 = don't use dialog box; 1 = use dialog box.
Cmdecho	AutoLISP	NA	With AutoLISP, controls display of prompts from embedded AutoCAD commands: 0 = no display of prompt; 1 = display prompts.

Table D.1: System Variables (continued)

Variable Name	Associated Command	Where Saved	Use
Cmdnames (read-only)	NA	NA	Displays the English name of the currently active command.
Cmljust	MLINE	With configuration	Sets method of justification for Multilines: 0 = top; 1 = middle; 2 = bottom.
Cmlscale	MLINE	With configuration	Sets scale factor for Multiline widths: a 0 value collapses the Multiline to a single line; a negative value reverses the justification.
Cmlstyle (read-only)	MLINE	With configuration	Displays current Multiline style by name.
Coords	F6, Ctrl-D	With drawing	Controls coordinate readout: 0 = coordinates displayed only when points are picked; 1 = absolute coordinates dynamically displayed as cursor moves; 2 = distance and angle displayed during commands that accept relative distance input.
Cvport (read-only)	VPORTS	With drawing	Displays ID number of current viewport.
Date (read-only)	TIME	NA	Displays date and time in Julian format.
Dbmod (read-only)	NA	NA	Displays drawing modification status: 1 = object database modified; 2 = symbol table modified; 4 = database variable modified; 8 = window modified; 16 = view modified.
Dctcust	SPELL	With configuration	Sets default custom spelling dictionary file name, including path.
Dctmain	SPELL	With configuration	Sets default main spelling dictionary file name; requires specific keywords for each language. Use AutoCAD Help for complete list of keywords.
Delobj	NA	With drawing	Controls whether source objects used to create new objects are retained: 0 = delete objects; 1 = retain objects.
Diastat (read-only)	NA	NA	Displays how last dialog box was exited: 0 = Cancel; 1 = OK.

Table D.1: System Variables (continued)

Variable Name	Associated Command	Where Saved	Use
Dispsilh	All curved solids	With drawing	Controls silhouette display of curved 3D solids: 0 = no silhouette; 1 = silhouette curved solids.
Distance (read-only)	DIST	NA	Displays last distance calculated by DIST command.
Donutid	DONUT	NA	Controls default inside diameter of a donut
Donutod	DONUT	NA	Controls default outside diameter of a donut
Dragmode	NA	With drawing	Controls dragging: 0 = no dragging; 1 = if requested; 2 = automatic drag.
Dragp1	NA	With configuration	Controls regeneration-drag input sampling rate.
Dragp2	NA	With configuration	Controls fast-drag input sampling rate.
Dwgcodepage (read-only)	NA	With drawing	Displays code page of drawing (see Syscodepage).
Dwgname (read-only)	OPEN	NA	Displays drawing name and drive/directory, if specified by user.
Dwgprefix (read-only)	NA	NA	Displays drive and directory of current file.
Dwgtitled (read-only)	NA	NA	Displays whether a drawing has been named: 0 = untitled; 1 = named by user.
Dwgwrite (read-only)	NA	NA	Displays read/write status of current drawing: 0 = read-only; 1 = read/write.
Edgemode	TRIM, EXTEND	With configuration	Controls how trim and extend boundaries are determined: 0 = boundaries defined by object only; 1 = boundaries defined by objects and their extension.
Elevation	Elev	With drawing	Controls current 3D elevation relative to current UCS.
Errno (read-only)	NA	NA	Displays error codes from AutoLISP or ADS applications.

Table D.1: System Variables (continued)

Variable Name	Associated Command	Where Saved	Use
Expert	NA	NA	Controls prompts, depending on level of user's expertise: 0 = normal prompts; 1 = suppresses About to regen and Really want to turn the current layer off prompts; 2 = suppresses Block already defined and A drawing with this name already exists prompt for BLOCK command; 3 = suppresses An item with this name already exists prompt for the LINETYPE command; 4 = suppresses An item with this name already exists for the UCS/Save and VPORTS/Save options; 5 = suppresses An item with this name already exists for DIM/Save and DIM/Override commands.
Explmode	EXPLODE	With drawing	Controls whether blocks inserted with different x, y, and z values are exploded: 0 = blocks are not exploded; 1 = blocks are exploded.
Extmax (read-only)	ZOOM	With drawing	Displays upper-right corner coordinate of extents view.
Extmin (read-only)	ZOOM	With drawing	Displays lower-left corner coordinate of extents view.
Facetres	SHADE, HIDE	With drawing	Controls appearance of smooth curved 3D surfaces when shaded or hidden. Value can be between 0.01 and 10. The higher the number, the more faceted (and smoother) the curved surface, and the longer the time needed for shade and hidden-line removal.
Fflimit	Style (fonts)	With configuration	Sets number of PostScript and TrueType fonts that can be stored in memory, from 0 to 100; 0 = no limit.

Appendices

Table D.1: System Variables (continued)

Variable Name	Associated Command	Where Saved	Use
Filedia	Dialog box	With configuration	Sets whether a file dialog box is used by default: 0 = don't use unless requested with a ~; 1 = use whenever possible.
Filletrad	FILLET	With drawing	Controls fillet radius.
Fillmode	FILL	With drawing	Controls fill status: 0 = off; 1 = on.
Fontalt	OPEN, DXFIN, other File ➤ Import options	With configuration	Lets you specify an alternate font when AutoCAD cannot find the font associated with a file. If no font is specified for Fontalt, AutoCAD displays warning message and dialog box where you manually select a font.
Fontmap	Open, Dxfin, other import functions	With configuration	Similar to Fontalt, but lets you designate a set of font substitutions through a font mapping file. Example line from mapping file: romans:c:\Acadr13\fonts\times.ttf. This substitutes Romans font with Times TrueType font. Font mapping file can be any name, with extension .FMP.
Frontz (read-only)	DVIEW	With drawing	Controls front clipping plane for current viewport; use with Viewmode system variable.
Gridmode	GRID	With drawing	Controls grid: 0 = off; 1 = on.
Gridunit	GRID	With drawing	Controls grid spacing.
Gripblock	Grips	With configuration	Controls display of grips in blocks: 0 = show insertion point grip only; 1 = show grips of all objects in block.
Gripcolor	Grips	With configuration	Controls color of unselected grips. Choices are integers from 1 to 255; default is 5.
Griphot	Grips	With configuration	Controls color of hot grips. Choices are integers from 1 to 255; default is 1.
Grips	Grips	With configuration	Controls use of grips: 0 = grips disabled; 1 = grips enabled (default).
Gripsize	Grips	With configuration	Controls grip size (in pixels), from 1 to 255 (default is 3).

Table D.1: System Variables (continued)

Variable Name	Associated Command	Where Saved	Use
Handles (read-only)	NA	With drawing	Displays status of object handles: 0 = off; 1 = on.
Highlight	SELECT	NA	Controls whether objects are highlighted when selected: 0 = none; 1 = highlighting.
Hpang	HATCH	NA	Sets default hatch pattern angle.
Hpbound	HATCH	With drawing	Controls type of object created by HATCH and Boundary commands: 0 = region; 1 = Polyline.
Hpdouble	HATCH	NA	Sets default hatch doubling for user-defined hatch pattern: 0 = no doubling; 1 = doubling at 90°.
Hpname	HATCH	NA	Sets default hatch pattern name; use a period (.) to set to no default.
Hpscale	HATCH	NA	Sets default hatch pattern scale factor.
Hpspace	HATCH	NA	Sets default line spacing for user-defined hatch pattern; cannot be 0.
Insbase	BASE	With drawing	Controls insertion base point of current drawing.
Insname	INSERT	NA	Sets default block or file name for INSERT command; enter a period (.) to set to no default.
Isolines	Curved solids	With drawing	Specifies the number of lines on a Solid's surface to help visualize its shape.
Lastangle (read-only)	ARC	NA	Displays ending angle for last arc drawn.
Lastpoint	NA	NA	Sets or displays coordinate normally referenced by the @.
Lenslength (read-only)	DVIEW	With drawing	Displays focal length of lens used for perspective display.
Limcheck	Limits	With drawing	Controls limit checking: 0 = no checking; 1 = checking.

Table D.1: System Variables (continued)

Variable Name	Associated Command	Where Saved	Use
Limmax	Limits	With drawing	Controls coordinate of drawing's upper-right limit.
Limmin	Limits	With drawing	Controls coordinate of drawing's lower-left limit.
Locale (read-only)	NA	NA	Displays ISO language code used by your version of AutoCAD.
Loginname (read-only)	CONFIG/ Startup	With configuration	Displays user's login name.
Ltscale	LTSCALE	With drawing	Controls the global line-type scale factor.
Lunits	UNITS	With drawing	Controls unit styles: 1 = scientific; 2 = decimal; 3 = engineering, 4 = architectural, 5 = fractional.
Luprec	UNITS	With drawing	Controls unit accuracy by decimal place or size of denominator.
Macrotrace	DIESEL	NA	Controls debugging tool for DIESEL expressions: 0 = disable; 1 = enable.
Maxactvp	VIEWPORTS/ VPORTS	NA	Controls maximum number of viewports to regenerate at one time.
Maxsort	NA	With configuration	Controls maximum number of items to be sorted when a command displays a list.
Menuctl	NA	With configuration	Controls whether side menu changes in response to a command name entered from the keyboard: 0 = no response; 1 = menu response.
Menuecho	NA	NA	Controls messages and command prompt display from commands embedded in menu: 0 = display all messages; 1 = suppress menu item name; 2 = supress command prompts; 4 = Disable ^P toggle of menu echo; 8 = debugging aid for DEISEL expressions.
Menuname (read-only)	Menu	With drawing	Displays name of current menu file.

Table D.1: System Variables (continued)

Variable Name	Associated Command	Where Saved	Use
Mirrtext	MIRROR	With drawing	Controls mirroring of text: 0 = disabled; 1 = enabled.
Modemacro	NA	NA	Controls display of user-defined text in status line.
Mtexted	MTEXT	With configuration	Controls name of program used for editing MTEXT objects.
Offsetdist	Offset	With drawing	Controls default offset distance.
Orthomode	F8, Ctrl-O, ORTHO	With drawing	Controls ortho mode: 0 = off; 1 = on.
Osmode	OSNAP	With drawing	Sets current default Osnap mode: 0 = none; 1 = endpoint; 2 = midpoint; 4 = center; 8 = node; 16 = quadrant; 32 – intersection; 64 = insert; 128 = perpendicular; 256 = nearest; 512 = quick. If more than one mode is required, enter the sum of those modes.
Pdmode	Ddptype	With drawing	Controls type of symbol used as a point during POINT command.
Pdsize	POINT	With drawing	Controls size of symbol set by PDMODE.
Pellipse	ELLIPSE	With drawing	Controls type of object created with ELLIPSE command: 0 = true NURBS ellipse; 1 = polyline representation of ellipse.
Perimeter (read-only)	Area, List	NA	Displays last perimeter value derived from Area and List commands.
Pfacevmax (read-only)	Pface	With drawing	Displays maximum number of vertices per face. (Pfaces are 3D surfaces designed for use by third-party software producers and are not designed for end users.)

Appendices

Table D.1: System Variables (continued)

Variable Name	Associated Command	Where Saved	Use
Pickadd	SELECT	With configuration	Determines how items are added to a selection set: 0 = only most recently selected item(s) become selection set (to accumulate objects in a selection set, hold down Shift while selecting); 1 = selected objects accumulate in a selection set as you select them (hold down Shift while selecting items to remove those items from the selection set).
Pickauto	Select	With configuration	Controls automatic window at Select objects prompt: 0 = window is enabled; 1 = window is disabled.
Pickbox	Select	With configuration	Controls size of object-selection pickbox (in pixels).
Pickdrag	Select	With configuration	Controls how selection windows are used: 0 = click on each corner of the window; 1 = Shift-click and hold on first corner, then drag and release for the second corner.
Pickfirst	Select	With configuration	Controls whether you can pick object(s) before you select a command: 0 = disabled; 1 = enabled.
Pickstyle	Group, HATCH	With drawing	Controls whether groups and/or associative hatches are selectable: 0 = neither are selectable; 1 = groups only; 2 = associative hatches only; 3 = both groups and associative hatches.
Platform (read-only)	NA	NA	Identifies the version of AutoCAD being used.
Plinegen	PLINE/PEDIT	With drawing	Controls how polylines generate line types around vertices: 0 = line-type pattern begins and ends at vertices; 1 = line-type patterns ignore vertices and begin and end at polyline beginning and ending.

Table D.1:   System Variables (continued)

Variable Name	Associated Command	Where Saved	Use
Plinewid	PLINE	With drawing	Controls default polyine width.
Plotid	PLOT	With configuration	Sets default plotter based on its description.
Plotrotmode	PLOT	With drawing	Controls orientation of your plotter output.
Plotter	PLOT	With configuration	Sets default plotter, based on its integer ID.
Polysides	POLYGON	NA	Controls default number of sides for a polygon.
Popups (read-only)	NA	NA	Displays whether the current system supports pull-down menus: 0 = no; 1 = yes.
Projmode	TRIM, EXTEND	With drawing	Controls how TRIM and EXTEND affect objects in 3D: 0 = objects must be coplanar; 1 = trims/extends based on a plane parallel to the current UCS; 2 = trims/extends based on a plane parallel to the current view plane.
Psltscale	PSPACE	With drawing	Controls Paper Space line-type scaling.
Psprolog	PSOUT	With configuration	Controls what portion of the Acad.PSF file is used for the prologue section of a PSOUT output file. Set this to the name of the section you want to use.
Psquality	PSIN	With configuration	Controls how images are generated in AutoCAD with the PSIN command. Value is an integer: 0 = only bounding box is drawn; >0 = number of pixels per AutoCAD drawing unit; <0 = outline with no fills, and absolute value of setting determines pixels per drawing units.
Qtextmode	QTEXT	With drawing	Controls the quick text mode: 0 = off; 1 = on.
Rasterpreview	PSOUT ??	With drawing	Controls whether raster preview inages are saved with the drawing and sets the format type: 0 = BMP only; 1 = BMP and WMF; 2 = WMF only; 3 = No preview image created.

Appendices

Table D.1: System Variables (continued)

Variable Name	Associated Command	Where Saved	Use
Regenmode	REGENAUTO	With drawing	Controls Regenauto mode: 0 = off; 1 = on.
Re-init	REINIT	NA	Reinitializes I/O ports, digitizers, display, plotter, and Acad.PGP: 1 = digitizer port; 2 = Plotter port; 4 = digitizer; 8 = display; 16 = PGP file reload.
Riaspect	TIFFIN, GIFIN	NA	Controls aspect ratio of imported bitmap images. (A setting of 0.8333 is useful for a typical 320x200 8-bit color image.)
Ribackg	TIFFIN, GIFIN, PCXIN	NA	Controls background color of imported bitmap images; use AutoCAD color numbers. To help reduce the size of the imported image, set Ribackg to the color that predominates in the imported image.
Riedge	TIFFIN, GIFIN, PCXIN	NA	Controls how edges are detected in imported image: 0 = complete image is imported; 1 to 255 = outline image is imported (value specifies threshold for edge detection).
Rigamut	TIFFIN, GIFIN, PCXIN	NA	Controls number of colors imported. Value corresponds to Standard AutoCAD color numbers; for instance, 3 results in a black, red, and yellow image (0 = black; 1 = red, and 2 = yellow).
Rigrey	TIFFIN, GIFFIN, PCXIN	NA	Controls whether imported images are converted to gray-shaded images: 0 = disable grayscale conversion; 1 = convert image to grayscale.
Rithresh	TIFFIN, GIFIN, PCXIN	NA	Filters out colors from imported image based on brightness; 0 = off; integer values greater than 0 indicate brightness threshold.
Savefile (read-only)	Autosave	With configuration	Displays file name that is autosaved.
Savename (read-only)	SAVE	NA	Displays user file name under which file is saved.

Table D.1:   System Variables (continued)

Variable Name	Associated Command	Where Saved	Use
Savetime	Autosave	With configuration	Controls time interval between automatic saves, in minutes: 0 = disable automatic save.
Screenboxes (read-only)	Menu	With configuration	Displays number of slots or boxes available in side menu.
Screenmode (read-only)	NA	With configuration	Displays current display mode: 0 = text; 1 = graphics; 2 = dual screen.
Screensize (read-only)	NA	NA	Displays current viewport size in pixels.
Shadedge	SHADE	With drawing	Controls how drawing is shaded: 0 = faces shaded, no edge highlighting; 1 = faces shaded, edge highlighting; 2 = faces not filled, edges in object color; 3 = faces in object color, edges in background color.
Shadedif	SHADE	With drawing	Sets difference between diffuse reflective and ambient light. Value represents percentage of diffuse reflective light.
Shpname	SHAPE	NA	Controls default shape name.
Sketchinc	SKETCH	With drawing	Controls sketch record increment.
Skpoly	SKETCH	With drawing	Controls whether SKETCH uses regular lines or polylines: 0 = line; 1 = polyline.
Snapang	SNAP	With drawing	Controls snap and grid angle.
Snapbase	SNAP	With drawing	Controls snap, grid, and hatch pattern origin.
Snapisopair	SNAP	With drawing	Controls isometric plane: 0 = left; 1 = top; 2 = right.
Snapmode	F9, SNAP	With drawing	Controls snap toggle: 0 = off; 1 = on.
Snapstyl	SNAP	With drawing	Controls snap style: 0 = standard; 1 = isometric.
Snapunit	SNAP	With drawing	Controls snap spacing given in x and y values.

Table D.1: System Variables (continued)

Variable Name	Associated Command	Where Saved	Use
Sortents	NA	With configuration	Controls whether objects are sorted based on their order in database: 0 = disabled; 1 = sort for object selection; 2 = sort for object snap; 4 = sort for redraws; 8 = sort for MSLIDE; 16 = sort for regen; 32 = sort for plot; 64 = sort for PSOUT.
Splframe	PLINE, PEDIT, 3DFace	With drawing	Controls display of spline vertices, defining mesh of a surface-fit mesh, and display of "invisible" edges of 3Dfaces: 0 = no display of spline vertices, display only fit surface of a smoothed 3Dmesh, and no display of "invisible" edges of 3Dface; 1 = spline vertices are displayed, only defining mesh of a smoothed 3Dmesh is displayed, "invisible" edges of 3Dface are displayed.
Splinesegs	PLINE, PEDIT	With drawing	Controls number of line segments used for each spline patch.
Splinetype	PLINE, PEDIT	With drawing	Controls type of spline curve generated by PEDIT spline: 5 = quadratic B-spline; 6 = cubic B-spline.
Surftab1	RULESURF, TABSURF, REVSURF, EDGESURF	With drawing	Controls number of facets in the m direction of meshes.
Surftab2	Revsurf, Edgesurf	With drawing	Controls number of facets in the n direction of meshes.
Surftype	PEDIT	With drawing	Controls type of surface fitting used by PEDIT's Smooth option: 5 = quadratic B-spline surface; 6 = cubic B- spline surface; 8 = Bezier surface.
Surfu	3DMESH	With drawing	Controls surface density in the m direction.
Surfv	3DMESH	With drawing	Controls surface density in the n direction.

Table D.1: System Variables (continued)

Variable Name	Associated Command	Where Saved	Use
Syscodepage (read-only)	NA	With drawing	Displays system code page specified in ACAD.XMF.
Tabmode	TABLET	NA	Controls tablet mode: 0 = off; 1 = on.
Target (read-only)	DVIEW	With drawing	Displays coordinate of perspective target point.
Tdcreate (read-only)	TIME	With drawing	Displays time and date of file creation in Julian format.
Tdindwg (read-only)	TIME	With drawing	Displays total editing time in days and decimal days.
Tdupdate (read-only)	TIME	With drawing	Displays time and date of last file update, in Julian format.
Tdusrtimer (read-only)	TIME	With drawing	Displays user-controlled elapsed time in days and decimal days.
Tempprefix (read-only)	Config (command)	With configuration	Displays location for temporary files.
Texteval	NA	NA	Controls interpretation of text input: 0 = AutoCAD takes all text input literally; 1 = AutoCAD interprets "(" and "!" as part of an AutoLISP expression, unless either the TEXT or DTEXT command is active.
Textfill	TEXT	With drawing	Controls display of Bitstream, TrueType, and PostScript Type 1 fonts: 0 = outlines; 1 = filled.
Textqlty	TEXT	With drawing	Controls resolution of Bitstream, TrueType, and PostScript Type 1 fonts: values from 1.0 to 100.0. The lower the value, the lower the output resolution. Higher resolutions improve font quality but decrease display and plot speeds.
Textsize	TEXT, DTEXT	With drawing	Controls default text height.
Textstyle	TEXT, DTEXT	With drawing	Controls default text style.

Table D.1: System Variables (continued)

Variable Name	Associated Command	Where Saved	Use
Thickness	Elev	With drawing	Controls default 3D thickness of object being drawn.
Tilemode	MSPACE/PSPACE	With drawing	Controls Paper Space and Viewport access: 0 = Paper Space and viewport objects enabled; 1 = strictly Model Space.
Tooltips	Icon tool palettes (Windows only)	With configuration	Controls display of ToolTips: 0 = off; 1 = on.
Tracewid	TRACE	With drawing	Controls trace width.
Treedepth	TREESTAT	With drawing	Controls depth of tree-structured spacial index affecting speed of AutoCAD database search. First two digits are for Model Space nodes; second two digits are for Paper Space nodes. Use positive integers for 3D drawings and negative integers for 2D drawings. Negative values can improve speed of 2D operation.
Treemax	REGEN, TREEDEPTH	With configuration	Limits memory use during regens by limiting maximum number of nodes in spacial index created with TREEDEPTH.
Trimmode	CHAMFER, FILLET	With configuration	Controls whether lines are trimmed during CHAMFER and FILLET commands: 0 = no trim; 1 = trim (as with pre-Release 13 versions of AutoCAD).
Ucsfollow	UCS	With drawing	Controls whether AutoCAD automatically changes to plan view of UCS while in Model Space: 0 = UCS change does not affect view; 1 = UCS change causes view to change with UCS.
Ucsicon	UCSICON	With drawing	Controls UCS icon: 1 = on; 2 = UCS icon appears at origin.
Ucsname (read-only)	UCS	With drawing	Displays name of current UCS.

Table D.1:   System Variables (continued)

Variable Name	Associated Command	Where Saved	Use
UCSORG (read-only)	UCS	With drawing	Displays origin coordinate for current UCS relative to world coordinate system.
UCSXDIR (read-only)	UCS	With drawing	Displays x direction of current UCS relative to world coordinate system.
UCSYDIR (read-only)	UCS	With drawing	Displays y direction of current UCS relative to world coordinate system.
Undoctl (read-only)	Undo	NA	Displays current state of Undo feature: 1 = Undo enabled; 2 = only one command can be undone; 4 = Autogroup mode enabled; 8 = group is currently active.
Undomarks (read-only)	Undo	NA	Displays number of marks placed by Undo command.
Unitmode	UNITS	With drawing	Controls how AutoCAD displays fractional, foot-and-inch, and surveyors angles: 0 = industry standard; 1 = AutoCAD input format.
Useri1–Useri5	AutoLISP, ADS	With drawing	Five user variables capable of storing integer values.
Userr1–Userr5	AutoLISP, ADS	With drawing	Five user variables capable of storing real values.
Users1–Users5	AutoLISP, ADS	With drawing	Five user variables capable of storing string values.
Viewctr (read-only)	NA	With drawing	Displays center of current view in coordinates.
Viewdir (read-only)	DVIEW	With drawing	Displays camera viewing direction in coordinates.
Viewmode (read-only)	DVIEW	With drawing	Displays view-related settings for current viewport: 1 = perspective on; 2 = front clipping on; 4 = back clipping on; 8 = UCS follow on; 16 = front clip not at a point directly in front of the viewer's eye.

Appendices

Table D.1: System Variables (continued)

Variable Name	Associated Command	Where Saved	Use
Viewsize (read-only)	NA	With drawing	Displays height of current view in drawing units.
Viewtwist (read-only)	DVIEW	With drawing	Displays twist angle for current viewport.
Visretain	LAYER	With drawing	Controls whether layer setting for Xrefs is retained: 0 = current layer color; line type and visibility settings retained when drawing is closed; 1 = layer settings of Xref drawing always renewed when file is opened.
Vsmax (read-only)	NA	NA	Displays coordinates of upper-right corner of virtual display.
Vsmin (read-only)	NA	NA	Displays coordinates for lower-left corner of virtual display.
Worlducs (read-only)	UCS	NA	Displays status of WCS: 0 = current UCS is not WCS; 1 = current UCS is WCS.
Worldview	DVIEW, VPOINT	With drawing	Controls whether DVIEW and VIEWPOINT operate relative to UCS or WCS: 0 = current UCS is used; 1 = WCS is used.
Xrefctl	XREF	With configuration	Controls whether Xref log files are written: 0 = no log files; 1 = log files written.

SETTING DIMENSION VARIABLES

In *Chapter 9*, nearly all of the system variables related to dimensioning are shown with their associated options in the Dimension Styles dialog box. Later in this appendix you'll find a complete discussion of all elements of the Dimension Styles dialog box and how to use it.

This section provides further information about the dimension variables. For starters, Table D.2 lists the variables, their default status, and a brief description of what they do. You can get a similar listing by entering **Dimstyle** ↵ at the command prompt, then typing **ST** to select the Status option. Alternatively, you can use the AutoCAD Help system. This section also discusses a few system variables that do not show up in the Dimension Styles dialog box.

Table D.2: The Dimension Variables

General Dimension Controls

Dimension Variable	Default Setting	Description
Dimaso	On	Turns associative dimensions on and off.
Dimsho	Off	Updates dimensions dynamically while dragging.
Dimstyle	*unnamed*	Name of current dimension style.
Dimupt	Off	Controls text positioning control during dimension input: 0 = no text positioning, uses settings; 1 = text positioning allowed during input.

Scale

Dimension Variable	Default Setting	Description
Dimscale	1.0000	Overall scale factor of dimensions.
Dimtxt	3/16″	Text height.
Dimasz	3/16″	Arrow size.
Dimtsz	0″	Tick size.
Dimcen	1/16″	Center mark size.
Dimlfac	1.0000	Linear unit scale factor.

Offsets

Dimension Variable	Default Setting	Description
Dimexo	1/16″	Extension line origin offset.
Dimexe	3/16″	Amount extension line extends beyond dimension line.
Dimdli	3/8″	Dimension line offset for continuation or base.
Dimdle	0″	Amount dimension line extends beyond extension line.

Appendices

Table D.2: The Dimension Variables (continued)

Tolerances

Dimension Variable	Default Setting	Description
Dimalttz	0	Controls zero suppression of tolerance values: 0 = no suppression; 1 = suppression.
Dimdec	4	Sets decimal place for primary tolerance values.
Dimtdec	4	Sets decimal place for tolerance values.
Dimtp	0″	Plus tolerance.
Dimtm	0″	Minus tolerance.
Dimtol	Off	When on, shows dimension tolerances.
Dimtolj	0	Controls vertical location of tolerance values relative to nominal dimension: 0 = bottom; 1 = middle; 2 = top.
Dimtzin	0	Controls supression of 0 dimensions in tolerance values: 0 = no supression; 1 = supression.
Dimlim	Off	When on, shows dimension limits.

Rounding

Dimension Variable	Default Setting	Description
Dimrnd	0″	Rounding value.
Dimzin	0	Controls display of 0 dimensions: 0 = leaves out zero feet and inches; 1 = includes zero feet and inches; 2 = includes zero feet; 3 = includes zero inches.

Dimension Arrow & Text Control

Dimension Variable	Default Setting	Description
Dimaunit	0	Controls angle format for angular dimensions; settings are the same as for Aunits system variable.
Dimblk	Blockname	Alternate arrow block name.
Dimblk1	Blockname	Alternate arrow block name used with Dimsah.
Dimblk2	Blockname	Alternate arrow block name used with Dimsah.

Table D.2:   The Dimension Variables (continued)

Dimension Arrow & Text Control		
Dimension Variable	**Default Setting**	**Description**
Dimfit	3	Controls location of text and arrows for extension lines: 0 = both arrows and text placed outside extensions if space isn't available; 1 = text has priority, so if only enough space for text, arrows are placed outside extension lines; 2 = AutoCAD chooses between text and arrows, based on best fit; 3 = a leader is drawn from dimension line to dimension text when space for text not available (see Dimjust).
Dimgap	1/16″ or 0.09″	Controls distance between dimension text and dimension line.
Dimjust	0	Controls horizontal dimension text position: 0 = centered between extension lines; 1 = next to first extension line; 2 = next to second extension line; 3 = above and centered on first extension line; 4 = above and centered on second extension line.
Dimsah	Off	Allows use of two different arrowheads on a dimension line. See Dimblk1 and Dimblk2.
Dimtfac	1.0″	Controls scale factor for dimension tolerance text.
Dimtih	On	When on, text inside extensions is horizontal.
Dimtoh	On	When on, text outside extensions is horizontal.
Dimtad	Off	When on, slaces text above the dimension line.
Dimtix	Off	Forces text between extensions.
Dimtvp	0	Controls text's vertical position based on numeric value.
Dimtxsty	Standard	Controls text style for dimension text.
Dimunit	2	Controls unit style for all dimension style groups except angular. Settings are same as for Lunit system variable.

Appendices

Table D.2: The Dimension Variables (continued)

Dimension & Extension Line Control

Dimension Variable	Default Setting	Description
Dimsd1	Off	Suppresses the first dimension line.
Dimsd2	Off	Suppresses the second dimension line.
Dimse1	Off	When on, suppresses the first extension line.
Dimse2	Off	When on, suppresses the second extension line.
Dimtofl	Off	Forces a dimension line between extension lines.
Dimsoxd	Off	Suppresses dimension lines outside extension lines.

Alternate Dimension Options

Dimension Variable	Default Setting	Description
Dimalt	Off	When on, alternate units selected are shown.
Dimaltf	25.4000	Alternate unit scale factor.
Dimaltd	2	Alternate unit decimal places.
Dimalttd	2	Alternate unit tolerance decimal places.
Dimaltu	2	Alternate unit style. See Lunits system variable for values.
Dinaltz	0	Suppresses zeroes for alternate dimension values: 0 = no supression; 1 = supression.
Dimpost	*Suffix*	Adds suffix to dimension text.
Dimapost	*Suffix*	Adds suffix to alternate dimension text.

Colors

Dimension Variable	Default Setting	Description
Dimclrd	*byblock*	Controls color of dimension lines and arrows.
Dimclre	*byblock*	Controls color of dimension extension lines.
Dimclrt	*byblock*	Controls color of dimension text.

Finally, for those of you who might want to write macros, scripts, or AutoLISP programs to control dimension styles, we'll talk about using two options of the DIMSTYLE command to set and recall dimension styles from the command line: **Dimstyle**↵ **S** ↵ and **Dimstyle** ↵ **R** ↵.

If you want to change a setting through the command line instead of through the Dimension Styles dialog box, you can enter the system variable name at the command prompt.

CONTROLLING ASSOCIATIVE DIMENSIONING

As discussed in *Chapter 9*, you can turn off AutoCAD's *associative dimensioning* by changing the Dimaso setting. The default for Dimaso is *On*.

The Dimsho setting controls whether the dimension value is dynamically updated while a dimension line is being dragged. The default for this setting is off, because it can slow down the display on less powerful computers.

STORING DIMENSION STYLES THROUGH THE COMMAND LINE

Once you have set the dimension variables as you like, you can save the settings by using the DIMSTYLE command. The Dimstyle/Save command records all of the current dimension variable settings (except Dimaso) with a name you specify.

1. At the command prompt, enter **Dimstyle** ↵

2. At the Save/Restore/STatus/Apply/?: prompt, type **S** ↵

3. When the ?/Name for new dimension style: prompt appears, you can enter a question mark (**?**) to get a listing of any dimension styles currently saved, or you can enter a name under which you want the current settings saved.

Appendices

For example, suppose you change some of your dimension settings through dimension variables instead of through the Dimension Styles dialog box, as shown in the following list:

Dimtsz	0.044
Dimtad	On
Dimtih	Off
Dimtoh	Off

These settings are typical for an architectural style of dimensioning; you might save them under the name Architect, as you did in an exercise *Chapter 9*. Then suppose you change other dimension settings for dimensions in another format—surveyor's dimensions on a site plan, for example. You might save them with the name Survey, again using the Save option of the DIMSTYLE command. When you want to return to the settings you used for your architectural drawing, you use the Restore option of the DIMSTYLE command, described in the next section.

RESTORING A DIMENSION STYLE FROM THE COMMAND LINE

To restore a dimension style saved using the Dimstyle Save option:

1. At the command prompt, enter **Dimstyle** ↵

2. At the Save/Restore/STatus/Apply/?: prompt, type **R** ↵
   The following prompt appears:

   ?/Enter dimension style name or RETURN to select dimension:

   Here you have three options: Enter a question mark (**?**) to get a listing of saved dimension styles; or enter the name of a style, such as Arch, if you know the name of the style you want; or you can use the cursor to select a dimension on the screen whose style you want to match.

NOTES ON METRIC DIMENSIONING

This book assumes you are using feet and inches as units of measure. The AutoCAD user community is worldwide, however, and many of you may be using the metric system in your work. As long as you are not mixing U.S. (feet and inches) and metric measurements, using the English version of AutoCAD is fairly easy. With the UNITS command, set your measurement system to decimal, then draw distances in millimeters or centimeters. At plot time, be sure you specify millimeters at the Size units prompt. Also, be sure you specify a scale that compensates for differences between millimeters (which are the AutoCAD base unit when you are using the metric system) and centimeters.

If your drawings are to be in both foot-and-inch and metric measurements, you will be concerned with several settings, as follows:

Dimlfac sets the scale factor for dimension values. The dimension value will be the measured distance in AutoCAD units times this scale factor. Set Dimlfac to 25.4 if you have drawn in inches but want to dimension in millimeters. The default is 1.00.

Dimalt turns the display of alternate dimensions on or off. Alternate dimensions are dimension text added to your drawing in addition to the standard dimension text.

Dimaltf sets the scale factor for alternate dimensions (i.e., metric). The default is 25.4, which is the millimeter equivalent of 1″.

Dimaltd sets the number of decimal places displayed in the alternate dimensions.

Dimapost adds suffix to alternate dimensions, as in 4.5mm.

If you prefer, you can use the Preferences dialog box to have AutoCAD use a prototype drawing called Acadiso.dwg. This drawing is set up for metric/ISO standard drawings. See *Appendix B* for more on the Preference dialog box.

Appendices

A CLOSER LOOK AT THE DIMENSION STYLES DIALOG BOX

As you saw in *Chapter 9*, you can control the appearance and format of dimensions through dimension styles. To get the Dimension Styles dialog box, you click on the Dimension Styles button on the Dimensioning Palette, or enter **Ddim** ↵ at the command line.

The three buttons in the Dimension Styles dialog box—Geometry, Format, and Annotation—open related dialog boxes that control the variables associated with these three aspects of AutoCAD's dimensioning system.

Within the Dimension Styles dialog box, dimensions are divided into "families" as a way of classifying the different types of dimensions available in AutoCAD. The dimension families are angular, diameter, linear, leader, ordinate, and radial. The Parent family affects all the dimension families globally. You can fine-tune your dimension styles by making settings to each family independently. If you don't set any of the families, their settings default to the Parent settings. To change the settings of a family, click on the family name's radio button before making changes in the Geometry, Format, or Annotation dialog boxes.

The following paragraphs describe the options in the Geometry, Format, and Annotation subdialogs. Each description specifies the dimension variables (in parentheses) that are related to the dialog box option. As you work through this appendix, you may want to refer back to *Chapter 9's* figures that illustrate these subdialogs.

THE GEOMETRY DIALOG BOX

This dialog box lets you control the placement and appearance of dimension lines, arrowheads, extension lines, and center marks. You can also set a scale factor for these dimension components.

The Dimension Line Group   Refer to Figure D.1 for examples of the effects of these options.

> **Suppress (Dimsd1, Dimsd2)** suppresses the dimension line to the left or right of the dimension text.

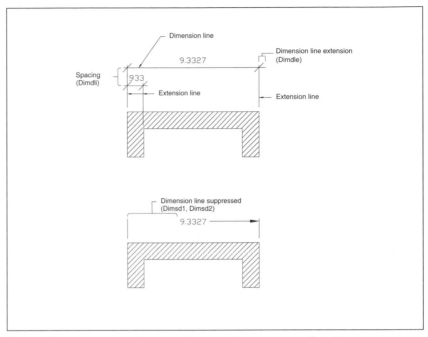

Figure D.1: Examples of how the Dimension Line options affect dimensions

Extension (Dimdle) sets the distance that dimension lines are drawn beyond extension lines, when using the standard Auto-CAD dimension tick for arrows. This option is unavailable (grayed out) when the filled arrow is selected in the Arrowheads group.

Spacing (Dimdli) determines the distance between dimension lines from a common extension line generated by the Baseline Dimension or Continue Dimension options on the Dimensioning palette.

Color (Dimclrd) sets the color of dimension lines. The standard AutoCAD Color dialog box appears, allowing you to visually select a color.

The Extension Line Group Refer to Figure D.2 for examples of the effects of these options.

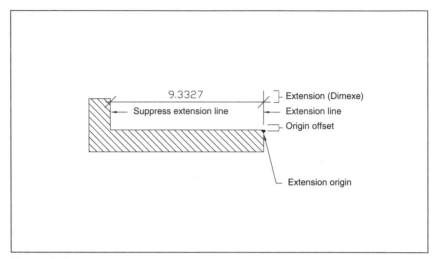

Figure D.2: Examples of how the Extension Line options affect extension lines

Suppress (Dimse1, Dimse2) suppresses the first or second dimension extension line.

Extensions (Dimsexe) sets the distance that extension lines extend beyond the dimension line.

Origin Offset (Dimexo) sets the distance the extension line is offset from its point of origin on the object being dimensioned.

Color (Dimclre) sets the color of extension lines. The standard AutoCAD Color dialog box appears, allowing you to visually select a color.

The Arrowheads Group These options let you control the type of arrowhead AutoCAD applies to dimensions.

1st shows you a pull-down list of choices to set the arrowheads at both ends of the dimension line. When you select an arrowhead, the graphic above the group shows how the arrow will look. You can also click on the graphic to cycle through the selections.

2nd   shows you a pull-down list of choices to set different arrowheads for each side of a dimension. This option works like the 1st option, but sets only one arrowhead.

Size (Dimasz)   sets the size of the arrowhead.

In the 1st and 2nd pull-down lists is a choice called User; this lets you use a block in place of the standard arrows. A dialog box opens, in which you enter the name of the block you wish to use for the arrow. The block must already exist in the drawing before you can add it, and it must follow the guidelines described in the "Using Alternate Dimension Arrows" section of this appendix.

The Center Group

These options let you determine what center mark is drawn when using the DIMCENTER command. Center marks are also drawn when dimension lines are placed outside a circle or arc using the DIAMETER or DIMRADIUS commands. All these settings are controlled by the Dimcen system variable.

Mark   adds a center mark.

Line   creates a center mark and lines.

None   suppresses the creation of center marks and lines.

Size   controls the size of the center marks.

The Scale Group

These options let you control the overall scaling of dimensions.

Overall Scale (Dimscale)   sets the scale factor for the size of dimension components, text and arrow size, and text location. This setting has no effect on actual dimension text or the distances being dimensioned.

Scale to Paper Space   is meaningful only if you dimension objects in a Model Space viewport while you're in Paper Space. When this option is enabled, AutoCAD adjusts the scaling of dimension components to Paper Space.

Appendices

THE FORMAT DIALOG BOX

This subdialog contains the following general settings:

User Defined (Dimupt)   overrides the dimension text location settings and lets you place the text manually when the dimensions are drawn.

Force Line Inside (Dimtofl)   forces a dimension line to be drawn between extension lines under all conditions.

Fit (Dimfit)   lets you determine how dimension text and arrows are placed between extension lines. In the pull-down list, Text and Arrows causes both arrows and text to be placed outside extensions if space isn't available. Text Only gives text priority, so that if space is available for text only, arrows will be placed outside extension lines. With the Best Fit option, AutoCAD determines whether text or arrows fit better, and draws the dimension accordingly. Leader draws a leader line from the dimension line to the dimension text when space for text is not available.

The settings in the Format subdialog control the location of dimension text. The **Text, Horizontal Justification, and Vertical Justification** groups include a graphic that demonstrates the effect of your selected option on the dimension text. You can also click on the graphic to scroll through the options.

The Text Group   These options let you control the text location.

Inside Horizontal (Dimtih)   orients text horizontally when it occurs between extension lines, regardless of the dimension lines' orientations.

Outside Horizontal (Dimtoh)   orients text horizontally when it occurs outside the extension lines, regardless of the dimension lines' orientations.

The Horizontal Justification Group   These settings can also be controlled using the Dimjust system variable.

Centered   centers the dimension text between the extension lines.

1st Extension Line   places the text next to the first extension line.

2nd Extension Line   places the text next to the second extension line.

Over 1st Extension   places the text over the first extension line, aligned with the extension line.

Over 2nd Extension   places the text over the second extension line, aligned with the extension line.

The Vertical Justification Group   These options can also be set using the Dimtad system variable.

Centered   places the dimension text in line with the dimension line.

Above   places the text above the dimension line, as is typical for architectural dimensioning. The distance from the text to the dimension line can be set with the Gap option in the Annotation subdialog.

Outside   places the text outside the dimension line at a point farthest away from the origin point of the first extension line. This effect is similar to the Above option, but is more apparent in circular dimensions.

JIS   places text in conformance with the Japanese Industrial Standards.

THE ANNOTATION DIALOG BOX

This dialog box controls the dimension text. You can determine the style, color, and size of text, as well as the unit style, tolerance, and alternate dimensions.

Appendices

Primary Units and Alternate Units These two groups offer the same options. The Primary Units options affect only the main dimension text, and the Alternate Units options control alternate units when they are enabled. (Alternate units are dimension values that are shown in brackets next to the standard dimension value, and are helpful when two unit systems, such as U.S. —feet and inches—and metric, are used in the same drawing.) The Enable Units check box turns on the alternate units (see Figure D.3).

Prefix lets you include a prefix in dimension text, and **Suffix** lets you include a suffix in dimension text. For the primary dimension text, Prefix and Suffix are controlled by the same Dimpost system variable. For alternate dimension text, Prefix and Suffix share the Dimapost system variable. See Table D.2 for details on Dimpost and Dimapost.

Both the Primary Units and Alternate Units groups have a Units button, which brings up the Primary Units and Alternate Units dialog boxes. Both dialog boxes contain the same options; when enabled, the Primary Units options affect only the main dimension text, and the Alternate

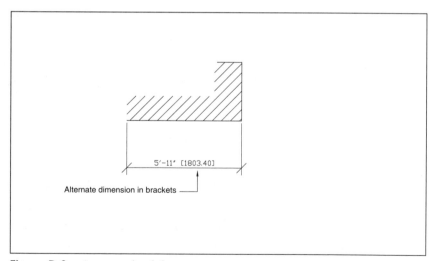

Figure D.3: An example of alternate units

Units options affect only alternate dimension text. Here are descriptions of these options:

Units and **Angles** let you select the unit and angle styles (which are the same styles as for the UNITS command described in *Chapter 3*). For Primary Units, the Units option is controlled by the Dimunit system variable, and the Angles option is controlled by the Dimaunit system variable. For Alternate Units, the Units option is controlled by the Dimaltu.

Dimension Precision and **Tolerance Precision** (Dimdec, Dimtdec, Dimaltd, Dimalttd) set the number of decimal places you want to use for these values. Dimension precision can also be set using the Dimdec system variable, and tolerance precision using Dimtdec. For Alternate Units, dimension precision can be set using Dimaltd, and tolerance precision using Dimalttd.

Dimension Zero Suppression (Dimzin, Dimaltz) controls how AutoCAD handles zeroes in dimensions. The Leading option suppresses leading zeroes in a decimal dimension (for example, 0.3000 becomes .3000). The Trailing option suppresses trailing zeroes (so that 8.8000 becomes 8.8, or 45.0000 becomes 45). The 0 Feet option suppresses zero feet values in an architectural dimension so that 0'–4" becomes 4".

0 Inches suppresses zero inch values in an architectural dimension, so that 12' –0" becomes 12'. The Dimzin system variable controls this option for Primary Units; the Dimaltz system variable controls this option for Alternate Units.

Tolerance Zero Suppression (Dimtzin, Dimalttz) controls how AutoCAD handles zeroes in tolerance dimensions. (See the description for Dimension Zero Suppression, just above.) The Dimtzin system variable controls this option for Primary Units; Dimalttz controls this option for Alternate Units.

Scale lets you specify a scale factor to linear dimensions. This setting affects the dimension text value. For example, say you have drawn an object to one-half its actual size. To have your dimensions reflect the true size of the object, you would set the Linear input box to 2. When you place dimensions in the drawing, AutoCAD multiplies the drawing distances by 2 to derive the dimension text value. By checking the Paper Space Only check box, you tell AutoCAD to apply the scale factor only when dimensioning in Paper Space. These two options in Alternate Units perform the same function for alternate dimension text. In Primary Units, the Scale options are controlled by the Dimlfac system variable. When Paper Space Only is enabled, Dimlfac becomes a negative value. For Alternate Units, the scale options are controlled by the Dimaltf system variable.

The Tolerance Group These options affect both primary and alternate units.

Method sets the type of tolerance displayed in a dimension. Choose among the following: The Symmetrical option adds a single tolerance value with a plus-minus (±) sign; this is the same as Dimtol set to 1 and Dimlim set to 0. The Deviation option adds two stacked values, one a plus value and the other a minus value. The Limits option places two stacked dimension values, showing the allowable range for the dimension instead of the single dimension (this is the same as Dimtol set to 0 and Dimlim set to 1). The Basic option draws a box around the dimension text; the Dimgap system variable set to a negative value produces the same result.

Upper Value sets the maximum tolerance limit. This is stored in the Dimtp system variable.

Lower Value sets the minimum tolerance limit. This is stored in the Dimtm system variable.

Justification sets the vertical location of stacked tolerance values.

Height sets the height for tolerance values. This is stored in the Dimtfac system variable as a ratio of tolerance height to default text height used for dimension text.

The Text Group   These options let you control the appearance of text in a dimension.

Style (Dimtxsty)   sets the text style used for dimension text.

Height (Dimtxt)   sets the current text height for dimension text.

Gap (Dimgap)   sets a margin around the dimension text, within which margin the dimension line is broken.

Color (Dimclrt)   sets the color of the dimension text.

Round Off (Dimrnd)   sets the amount that dimensions are rounded off to the nearest value. This setting works in conjunction with the Dimtol system variable.

IMPORTING DIMENSION STYLES FROM OTHER DRAWINGS

Dimension styles are saved within the current drawing file only. You can, however, import a dimension style from another drawing by using the XBIND command, as described in *Chapter 12*.

To do this, first click on the Attach button on the External References tool palette (**Xref** ↵ **A** ↵). Then click and drag All from the External References palette and choose Dimension Styles (**Xbind** ↵ **D** ↵) to import the dimension style you want. Finally, choose Detach from the External References palette (**Xref** ↵ **D** ↵) to detach the cross-reference file.

DRAWING BLOCKS FOR YOUR OWN DIMENSION ARROWS AND TICK MARKS

If you don't want to use the arrowheads supplied by AutoCAD for your dimension lines, you can create a block of the arrowheads or tick marks you like, to be used in the Arrowheads group of the Dimension Styles/Geometry dialog box.

For example, say you want to have a tick mark that is thicker than the dimension lines and extensions. You can create a block of the tick mark on a layer you assign to a thick pen weight, and then assign that block to the Arrowhead setting. This is done by first opening the Geometry

---

▼ TIP

To get to the Arrowhead options, click on the Dimension Styles button on the Dimensioning palette, or type **Ddim** ↵. At the Dimension Styles dialog box, click on Geometry, and choose User from the pull-down list for the 1st arrowhead.

Appendices

dialog box from the Dimension Styles dialog box (click on the Dimension Styles button on the Dimensioning palette to open the Dimension Styles dialog box). Next, choose User Arrow from the first pull-down list in the Arrowheads group. At the User Arrow dialog box, enter the name of your arrow block.

When you draw the arrow block, make it one unit long. The block's insertion point will be used to determine the point of the arrow that meets the extension line, so make sure you place the insertion point at the tip of the arrow. Because the arrow on the right side of the dimension line will be inserted with a zero rotation value, create the arrow block so that it is pointing to the right (see Figure D.4). The arrow block is rotated 180° for the left side of the dimension line.

To have a different type of arrow at both ends of the dimension line, create a block for each arrow. Then, in the Dimension Styles/Geometry dialog box, choose User in the pull-down list for the 1st arrowhead, and enter the name of one block. Then choose User in the pull-down list for the second arrowhead, and enter the name of the other block.

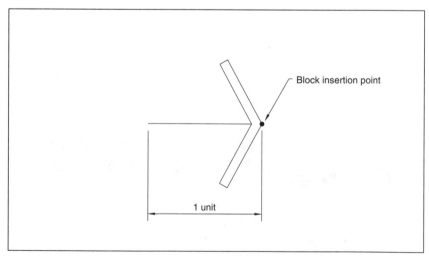

Figure D.4: The orientation and size of a block used in place of the default arrow

E

▼ ▼ ▼ ▼ ▼

STANDARD AUTOCAD COMMANDS

This appendix provides a comprehensive list of all the standard Auto-CAD keyboard commands. If it isn't here, chances are it is an AutoLISP or ADS macro.

If many of these commands look foreign to you, it is probably because they were not discussed directly in the main part of this book. The tutorials and instructions in this book put emphasis on the toolbar and palette buttons. However, the command names are given next to the related toolbar button wherever possible in the main part of this book. For example, in a typical tutorial step, you might see:

1. Click on Hatch from the Draw palette, or type **Bhatch** ↵ at the command prompt.

In this example, the command name, Bhatch, is provided as an alternate.

Command names are also indicated in other parts of the text by enclosing the name in parentheses as in the following example from *Chapter 16*:

"The Revolved Surface option (REVSURF) on the Surfaces palette lets you extrude an object in a linear or circular fashion in any direction in space."

Here, you're given the name of the button, Revolved Surface, and the related command in parentheses (REVSURF).

Be aware that many of the toolbar and palette icon buttons related to these commands automatically provide input for command options. For example, while there is only one ARC keyboard command, you will find eleven buttons in the Draw palette that issue the ARC command. Each of these buttons supply a different set of responses to the ARC commands options. The net result is a set of buttons, each providing a different way to draw an arc. As shown in *Chapter 2*, you can manually enter the ARC command and supply those options yourself. This is how many veteran AutoCAD users work with AutoCAD. For a clearer understanding of how palette and toolbar buttons relate to the keyboard commands, see *Chapter 21*.

Table E.1 briefly describes each command, and provides (where applicable) a listing of options and comments on its operation.

Table E.1: AutoCAD Commands

Command Name	Description	Options/Operations
About	Displays your serial number and a scrolling list box with the contents of the Acad.MSG file	NA
ACISIN	Imports an ACIS (solid model) ASCII file into an AutoCAD drawing	Pick file name from dialog box.
ACISOUT	Exports AutoCAD solid objects to an ACIS file	Enter file name after selecting objects.
Align	Moves and rotates objects to align with other objects	After selecting objects, pick up to three sets of source and destination points.
AMEconvert	Converts AutoCAD Advanced Modeling Extension solid models to AutoCAD Release 13 solid objects	Select AME Release 2 or 2.1 region or solids; all other objects are ignored.
Aperture	Controls the size of the Object Snap cursor	Size of aperture is in pixels.
'Appload	Allows easy location and loading of add-on applications	**Files to Load** lists selected applications, **File** opens a file dialog box, **Remove** removes an item from the list, **Load** loads a highlighted item from the list, **Unload** unloads an ADS or ARX application from memory, **Save List** check box saves the name of a selected application in the list box.
Arc	Draws arcs	**A** = included angle, **C** = center point, **D** = starting direction, **E** = endpoint, **L** = length of cord, **R** = radius.
Area	Calculates area and perimeter of area defined by points, polyline, circle, spline curve, region, and solid	**A** = add mode, **S** = subtract mode, **O** = select object to find area.

Appendices

Table E.1: AutoCAD Commands (continued)

Command Name	Description	Options/Operations
Array	Constructs multiple copies in a matrix or circular pattern	**R** = rectangular, **P** = polar.
ASEadmin	Performs administration functions for external database commands	**E** = environment, **C** = catalog, **S** = schema, **T** = table, **L** = link path, **O** = other options.
ASEexport	Creates a text file containing link data of selected objects	**Database Object Filters** group lets you select the level of link information you want to export, **Export Assignment** group lets you select a format and destination for your export file, **Export** starts the export.
ASElinks	Manipulates links between objects and external database data	The object selected determines links displayed.
ASErows	Manipulates external database table data	**S** = settings, **I** = insert, **C** = cursor state, **T** = textual search, **K** = key value.
ASEselect	Creates a selection set from rows linked to textual selection sets and graphic selection sets	Selection set can be a Union, Intersection, or difference between two sets.
ASESQLed	Executes Structured Query Language (SQL) statements	Dialog box interface simplifies creation of statements.
ASEunload	Unloads the ASE application from memory	No options. Useful in systems that have limited RAM.
Attdef	Creates an attribute definition	**I** = visible/invisible, **C** = constant/variable, **V** = controls verify mode, **P** = controls preset, **Tag** = attribute "ID," **Prompt** = attribute prompt, **default** = attribute default value.
'Attdisp	Controls visibility of attributes	**On** = all are made visible; **Off** = all are made invisible; **N** = normal; only attributes set to invisible are not shown.

Table E.1: AutoCAD Commands (continued)

Command Name	Description	Options/Operations
Attedit	Edits attributes	You can edit attributes globally or one at a time. You can also change attribute text size, orientation, and locations.
Attext	Extracts attribute data	**C** = comma-delimited format, **D** = DXF format, **S** = space-delimited format, **O** = extract from specific objects.
Attredef	Redefines attribute definitions in blocks	Adds, removes, or relocates attribute definitions in a block. You must first have created block components, including new and revised attribute definitions.
Audit	Audits drawing integrity	**Y** = fix errors, **N** = don't fix errors but produce report.
'Base	Changes insertion origin for the current drawing	Pick a point.
Bhatch	Fills an enclosed area with an associative hatch pattern	Automatic boundary and island detection. Hatch preview offered. See also Boundary.
'Blipmode	Controls blips	**On** = show blips, **Off** = don't show blips.
Block	Groups objects into a single, named object	**?** = list existing blocks.
Bmpout	Creates a bitmap image (.BMP file) of objects in your drawing.	Allows you to select specific objects for inclusion.
Boundary	Creates a polyline or region from a closed area	Islands can be excluded; the boundary must be contiguous.
Box	Creates a three-dimensional solid box	Pick corner or **C** = Center.
Break	Breaks objects into two parts	Select object, then second point of break; or **F** = pick first and second point.
'Cal	Starts the AutoCAD Geometry Calculator	The geometry calculator lets you find geometry through a combination of picking points and entering calculator expressions. See *Chapter 12*.

Table E.1: AutoCAD Commands (continued)

Command Name	Description	Options/Operations
Chamfer	Joins two lines or surfaces in a chamfer	**D** = set chamfer distances, **P** = chamfer each vertex of a polyline, **A** = specify angle of chamfer, **T** = trim edges to chamfer-line endpoints, **M** = (select) method; either 2 distances or distance and an angle.
Change	Modify an existing object's properties	**P** = change common properties, such as **C** = color, **E** = elevation, **LA** = layer, **LT** = line type, **S** = line-type scaling, **T** = thickness. Also changes text height, style, angle, value, line endpoints, and circle radius.
Chprop	Modifies common properties of objects	**C** = color, **LA** = layer, **LT** = line type, **S** = line-type scaling, **T** = thickness.
Circle	Draws circles	**2P** = based on 2 diametric points on circle, **3P** = based on 3 points on circumference, **D** = enter diameter, **R** = enter radius, **TTR** = tangent to two objects and a radius.
'Color	Sets default color for new objects	*Number* = color number, *name* = color name for standard colors only, **Bylayer** = use layer color, **Byblock** = floating object color.
Compile	Compiles shape or font file	Indicate file name, with .SHP extension.
Cone	Creates a three-dimensional solid cone with a circular or elliptical base	**E** = elliptical, **A** = apex height and orientation.
Config	Reconfigures AutoCAD	See configuration topics in *Appendix B*.
Copy	Copies objects	**M** = multiple copies.
Copyclip	Copies selected objects to the Windows clipboard for inclusion in other drawings and Windows applications	Selected objects are stored in both image and vector formats; if text-only is selected, it is stored in ASCII format.
Copyhist	Copies the text in the command line history to the Windows clipboard	You may then paste the text into a Windows text processor.

Table E.1: AutoCAD Commands (continued)

Command Name	Description	Options/Operations
Copylink	Copies the current view to the Windows clipboard for linking to other Windows OLE applications	Use the PASTESPEC command to paste and link the view into other documents.
Cutclip	Copies selected objects to the Windows clipboard and erases them from the current drawing	Cutclip does not create links for use in OLE applications.
Cylinder	Creates three-dimensional solid cylinder with a circular or elliptical base	**E** = elliptical, **H** = height.
Dblist	Lists database information for every object in drawing	NA
Ddattdef	Dialog box to create attribute definition	See Attdef.
Ddatte	Dialog box to edit attributes	Displays attribute prompt and value. Values are editable through input box.
Ddattext	Dialog box to extract attribute data	See Attext.
Ddchprop	Dialog box to change properties	See Chprop.
Ddcolor	Dialog box to set color for new objects	See Color.
Ddedit	Dialog box to edit text, multiline text, and attribute definitions	Displays text in an input box, allowing you to edit single lines.
'Ddemodes	Dialog box that sets defaults for new objects	Sets layer, line type, line-type scaling, color, elevation, thickness, and text style.
'Ddgrips	Dialog box to set up the Grips feature	Turns grips on or off, and sets grip color and size.
Ddim	Controls dimensioning settings	Presents a series of dialog boxes for setting dimension styles and variables. See *Appendix D*.

Appendices

Table E.1: AutoCAD Commands (continued)

Command Name	Description	Options/Operations
Ddinsert	Dialog box for the INSERT function	Inserts a block or file and lets you define insertion point, scale, and rotation angle.
Ddlmodes	Dialog box for controlling layers	Sets current layer, creates new layer, and controls visibility, color, line type, etc.
Ddltype	Dialog box for loading and setting line types	See Linetype.
Ddmodify	Dialog box for editing object properties	Similar to Ddchprop, with additional options specific to the object selected. Unlike Ddchprop, you can only select one object.
'Ddosnap	Dialog box for Osnap settings	Controls default Osnap settings and size of Osnap cursor. See Osnap.
'Ddptype	Dialog box for the selection of point styles	Lets you select a point style from a graphic. Point objects are then drawn in the style you select.
'Ddrename	Dialog box for renaming items	Renames blocks, line types, layers, text styles, viewports, UCSs, and dimension styles.
'Ddrmodes	Dialog box for setting standard modes	Sets grid, snap, groups, and other drawing modes.
'Ddselect	Dialog box for setting selection modes	Sets Noun/Verb Selection, shift-pick, click-drag, automatic window, and pickbox size. Also sets object sort method.
Dducs	Dialog box for setting and recalling UCSs	Lets you save a UCS under a name or list a UCS's coordinates.
Dducsp	Dialog box for selecting a predefined UCS	Lets you select a UCS from a predefined set of UCSs.
'Ddunits	Dialog box for unit style settings	Controls unit and angle style, as well as degree of precision for each.
Ddview	Dialog box for saving and restoring views	**Views** lists currently available views. **Restore** restores the highlighted view. **New** opens New View dialog box that lets you save a view through standard methods (see View). **Delete** deletes a view from the list. **Description** displays information about the view.

Table E.1: AutoCAD Commands (continued)

Command Name	Description	Options/Operations
Ddvpoint	Dialog box for setting a 3D viewpoint	Two graphic elements let you set altitude and azimuth of your view in relation to your drawing.
'Delay	In scripts, delays execution of next command	Place just after the command you want to pause in a script. Follow Delay with a value in milliseconds.
Dim	Starts the dimension mode	While in dimension mode, you can only enter dimensioning commands.
Dim1	Lets you enter a single dimension command	After the first one, you can enter any number of dimension commands.
Dimaligned	Creates an aligned linear dimension	Select extension line origins, or ↵ to select object.
Dimangular	Creates an angular dimension	Select objects, or ↵ to specify vertex and angle endpoints.
Dimbaseline	Continues a linear, angular, or ordinate dimension from baseline of previous or selected dimension	Baseline is first extension line of previous dimension, or extension line nearest the selection point.
Dimcenter	Creates a center mark, or the center lines of circles and arcs	Controlled by the value of the Dimcen dimensioning variable (see *Appendix D*).
Dimcontinue	Continues a linear, angular, or ordinate dimension from second dimension line of previous or selected dimension	Continuation is from second extension line of previous dimension, or extension line nearest the selection point.
Dimdiameter	Creates diameter dimensions for circles or arcs	Includes center marks and center lines as determined by value of the Dimcen dimensioning variable (see *Appendix D* for more on Dimcen).
Dimedit	Edits dimensions' text and extension lines	**H** = home text location, **N** = new dimension-line text, **R** = rotate text angle, **O** = oblique extension lines.

Table E.1:

Command Name	Description	Options/Operations
Dimlinear	Creates horizontal, vertical or rotated linear dimensions	Select extension-line origins, or ↵ to specify object.
Dimordinate	Creates ordinate point dimensions	Second point determines x or y datum, or you can specify explicitly.
Dimoverride	Overrides dimension system variables for individual dimensions	Does not affect current dimension style.
Dimradius	Creates radial dimensions for circles or arcs	Includes center marks and center lines by value of the Dimcen dimensioning variable.
Dimstyle	Creates and modifies dimension styles at the command line	Same as the dialog boxes with Ddim command.
Dimtedit	Moves and rotates dimension text	**L** = left side, **R** = right side of dimension line, **H** = middle of dimension line, **R** = angle of rotation.
Dimtfac	Controls the height of stacked fractions	Enter a height at the prompt.
'Dist	Finds the distance between points	Pick two points.
Divide	Marks off an object in equal segments	Select an object, then specify number of segments you want. Uses point objects as markers by default, but you can use blocks.
Donut	Draws a circle with thickness	Specify inside diameter and outside diameter of circle. For a solid circle, make inside diameter 0.
'Dragmode	Controls dynamic dragging	**On** = drag when requested by entering **Drag** ↵, **Off** = don't drag at all, **Auto** = drag when applicable.
Dtext	Draws text directly in graphic area	Select start point, style, or justification; then specify height if style height is set to 0, and rotation angle. You can enter several lines of text. Each ↵ drops cursor down one line.

Table E.1: AutoCAD Commands (continued)

Command Name	Description	Options/Operations
Dview	Controls view of 3D perspectives	**CA** = camera location, **CL** = set clip planes, **D** = camera-to-target distance and turns on perspective mode, **H** = hidden-line removal, **Off** = turns perspective off, **PA** = pan view, **PO** = allows selection of target and camera points, **TA** = allows selection of target point by view, **TW** = twist camera view, **U** = undo last option, **X** = eXit Dview, **Z** = zoom in/out or set camera focal length, **T** = toggle between setting angle from X–Y plane and x-axis of X–Y plane
Dxbin	Inserts .DXB files	NA
DXFin	Inserts .DXF files	NA
DXFout	Exports .DXF files	**B** = write binary .DXF, **O** = select specific objects to export, **0–16** = floating point precision.
Edge	Hides 3Dface edges	**Display** displays hidden edges of selected 3Dfaces. **Select edge** lets you select an edge to hide.
Edgesurf	Draws a three-dimensional mesh based on four contiguous objects	Objects must be joined exactly end-to-end, and can be lines, arcs, or polylines.
Elev	Sets the default elevation and thickness for new objects	Can be set from Ddemodes dialog box.
Ellipse	Draws an ellipse or elliptical arc	**A** = arc, **C** = select center point, **R** = specify eccentricity by rotation, **I** = isometric.
End	Exits AutoCAD	If drawing has been changed, you are offered choice of saving file or discarding changes.
Erase	Deletes objects	Standard selection options.
Explode	Reduces compound objects (blocks, polylines, dimensions, meshes, etc.) to basic objects	Nested blocks are not broken down. Spline polylines break down into line segments.

Table E.1: AutoCAD Commands (continued)

Command Name	Description	Options/Operations
Extend	Extends objects to meet other objects	You can select multiple objects to extend by using a Fence selection option. **P** = project based on UCS or view, **E** = to extended edge, **U** = undo last extend.
Extrude	Creates solids primitives by extruding existing AutoCAD two-dimensional objects	**P** = path to extrude along, **H** = height of extrusion, **T** = taper angle.
'Files	Dialog box to access file utilities	You can copy, list, delete, unlock, or rename files.
'Fill	Controls visibility of filled objects	**On** = fill solids, traces, and wide polylines; **Off** = show outlines only.
Fillet	Rounds and fillets edges of objects	**P** = fillet a polyline, **R** = set radius for fillet, **C** = chain, **E** = edge, **T** = trim lets you choose whether or not to trim lines to arc endpoints.
Filter	Allows you to select objects by their properties	You must first select property you want to use for defining your selection, add it to list using Add to List button, and click on Apply. Dialog box closes and you get object-selection prompt. See *Chapter 12* for more on filters.
Gifin	Imports .GIF files	You supply file name, insertion point, and scale factor. Gifin translates pixels in .GIF file into individual solids of appropriate color in AutoCAD.
'Graphscr	Flips from text to graphics mode	Same as F2.
'Grid	Sets grid settings	**On** = turn on grid, **Off** = turn off grid, **S** = match snap spacing, **A** = set grid aspect ratio, *number* = set grid spacing to number specified, *numberx* = set grid spacing to be multiple of snap setting.

Table E.1: AutoCAD Commands (continued)

Command Name	Description	Options/Operations
Group	Creates a named selection set of objects	**?** = list groups, **O** = change numerical order of objects, **E** = delete group definition, **REN** = rename group, **S** = selectable, **C** = create group.
Hatch	Draws nonassociative hatch patterns within existing entities or by picking points	**Name** = predefined pattern, ***name** = predefined pattern exploded, **U** = simple line or crosshatch (user specifies spacing and rotation), **?** = list predefined hatch patterns. See Bhatch.
Hatchedit	Modifies an existing associative hatch block	**D** = disassociate into regular hatch, **I** = new internal calculation point, **P** = properties (name, scale, etc.) of hatch block.
'Help	Provides information on commands and operations	If used while in middle of a command, provides information regarding the current operation.
Hide	Performs hidden-line removal	NA
'ID	Displays coordinates of selected point	Asks you to select point, which becomes "last point" for reference with @.
Insert	Imports file or inserts block	Use **blockname** = **filename** to redefine internal block; * means insert and explode; other options are independent X, Y, and Z scale, as well as rotation angle. See also Ddinsert.
Insertobj	Allows you to open other Windows applications from inside AutoCAD, create objects in the application format and insert them into the current drawing	Size and position the object in AutoCAD using its Windows handles. To edit an inserted object, double-click on it to return to its native application. (See "Adding Sound, Motion, and Photos to Your Drawings" in *Chapter 14*.)
Interfere	Finds interference of two or more solids and creates a composite solid from their common volume	Select solids, determine highlight, create new solids.
Intersect	Uses interference of solids to create a composite solid	Select solids.

Appendices

Table E.1: AutoCAD Commands (continued)

Command Name	Description	Options/Operations
'Isoplane	Selects plane of isometric grid	**L** = left, **R** = right, **T** = top, ⏎ = toggles between planes (see also Ddrmodes).
'Layer	Provides command-line layer control	**C** = set layer color, **F** = freeze a layer, **L** = set layer line type, **LO** = lock a layer, **M** = create a layer and make it current, **N** = create new layer, **On** = turn on layer, **Off** = turn off layer, **S** = set current layer, **T** = thaw layer, **?** = list layers, **U** = unlock layers. For **F, N, On, Off,** and **T,** you can provide multiple layer names by listing them with comma separators; wildcard characters are also allowed.
Leader	Creates a line that connects to an associative annotation	Format can be **ST** = straight lines, **S** = spline curve, **A** = with arrowhead, and **N** = no arrowhead. Annotation can be **T** = geometric tolerances, **M** = multiline text, **C** = copy of existing annotation, **B** = block insert, **N** = no annotation.
Lengthen	Changes the length of objects and included angle or arcs	Change is by **DE** = delta increment, **P** = percentage of current length, or **T** = absolute total length; **DY** = enters dynamic drag mode.
Light	Opens Light dialog box for creating and editing light sources for Tools ➤ Render feature	See *Chapter 17*.
'Limits	Sets the drawing limits	Select two points to define boundaries of limits. **On** = limits checking on, **Off** = limits checking off (limits checking forces objects to be drawn inside limits).
Line	Draws lines	**C** = close series of lines, **U** = undo last line segment, ⏎ = at Start Point prompt, starts line from last line or arc.

Table E.1: AutoCAD Commands (continued)

Command Name	Description	Options/Operations
'Linetype	Controls line-type settings	**?** = List the line types available from linetype file, **C** = create line-type definition, **L** = load line-type definition, **S** = set current default line type for new objects.
List	Shows properties of objects	Uses standard selection options.
Load	Loads shape and text-style definitions	Uses standard file dialog box.
Logfileoff	Closes log file opened by Logfileon	*NA*
Logfileon	Writes text window contents to a file	*NA*
Ltscale	Sets line-type scale	See Ltscale and Celtscale system variables in *Appendix D*.
Makepreview	Creates .BMP file to allow previewing of Release 12 drawing files	*NA*
Massprop	Calculates and displays mass properties of regions or solids	Information can be written to a file.
Matlib	Opens the renderer's Materials dialog box	You select materials for Tools ➤ Render. You can also assign materials to objects. See *Chapter 12* for more on Matlib.
Measure	Marks off specific intervals on objects	**B** = use a block for marking device. Default marking device is a point object.
Menu	Loads a menu file	Menu's settings are stored with drawings. Any AutoLISP programs with the .MNL file name extension and the same name as the menu are loaded with the menu.
Menuload	Loads partial menu files	Specify name of menu file.
Menuunload	Unloads partial menu files	Specify name of menu group.
Minsert	Multiple inserts of blocks in a rectangular array	Options are similar to those for INSERT command.

Table E.1: AutoCAD Commands (continued)

Command Name	Description	Options/Operations
Mirror	Creates a reflected copy	You can specify a copy, or just mirror an object without copying.
Mirror3D	Mirrors objects in 3D space	**Object** lets you choose a planar object to define a mirror plane; **Last** selects the last mirror plane; **Zaxis** defines a mirror plane using your specified z-axis for the plane; **View** uses a view plane parallel to the current view plane; **XY/XZ/ZX** uses one of the standard planes defined by the x-, y-, and z-axes; **3 point** defines a mirror plane based on your selected 3 points.
Mledit	Edits multiple, parallel lines	Cleans up intersections between Multilines at crossings, tees, corners, and cuts.
Mline	Creates multiple, parallel lines as a single object	**J** = justification on top, middle, and bottom of lines; **S** = scale factor based on width in style definition; **ST** = you enter name of Multiline style.
Mlstyle	Defines a style for multiple, parallel lines	Sets current style; creates new styles by defining elements, offsets, color, line types, and caps; loads from a Multiline library file; copies existing style; and renames a style.
Move	Moves objects	Standard selection options.
Mslide	Makes a slide	Specify file name.
Mspace	Switch to Model Space	Can only be used while in Paper Space.
Mtext	Creates paragraph text	Fits within nonprinting text boundary; allows standard text justification, style, height, and rotation selections.
Mtprop	Changes paragraph text properties	Changes style, height, direction, and attachment point.
Multiple	Repeats the next command	Command is repeated until user enters Ctrl-C.

Table E.1: AutoCAD Commands (continued)

Command Name	Description	Options/Operations
Mview	Controls Paper Space viewports	**On/Off** = turns display of viewport on or off, **Hideplot** = causes hidden-line removal of viewport at plot time, **Fit** = fits new viewport in current view, **2/3/4** = creates two, three, or four viewports, **Restore** = restores viewport configurations saved with VPORTS command.
Mvsetup	Automates the drawing setup process	If issued from Model Space and you answer No to first prompt, you receive options for setting up unit style, paper size, and scale of your drawing. AutoCAD then sets up drawing according to your specifications. If issued from Paper Space, you can create, align, and scale viewports, add a title block, or control other options. See *Chapters 12* and *18* for more on Mvsetup.
New	Creates new drawing	Dialog box lets you choose a prototype drawing.
Offset	Creates parallel copies	**T** = select a point through which offset passes, **number** = offset distance.
Olelinks	Updates, changes and deletes existing OLE links	Dialog box allows you to update any links in the current drawing or set them to update automatically.
Oops	Restores last erasure	*NA*
Open	Opens a new file	Dialog box allows you to save or discard current drawing edits.
'Ortho	Forces lines to be vertical or horizontal	Toggle with F8 key or Ctrl-O.
'Osnap	Allows exact selection of object geometry	You can set object snaps to be the default by using Osnap and entering the Osnap mode you want. Use None to turn default Osnaps off.
'Pan	Shifts the current display in a specified direction	*NA*

Appendices

Table E.1: AutoCAD Commands (continued)

Command Name	Description	Options/Operations
Pasteclip	Allows you to paste AutoCAD objects, text and a variety of file formats into the current drawing	You are prompted for an insertion point, and scale. All objects are inserted in the upper left corner of the drawing area. Text objects become Mtext objects.
Pastespec	Allows you to insert data from the Windows clipboard	The Paste Special dialog box allows you to convert the clipboard data format, from the native application format.
Pcxin	Imports PCX files	You are prompted for a file name, insertion point, and scale. Pixels in .PCX file are translated into AutoCAD solids of same color.
Pedit	Edits polylines, 3D polylines, and meshes	**C** = closes a polyline; **D** = decurves a curved polyline; **Edit** = edits polyline vertices; **F** = curves fitted polyline; **Join** = joins a polyline to other polylines, arcs, and lines; **L** = controls noncontinuous line-type generation through vertices; **O** = opens a closed polyline; **S** = spline curve; **U** = undoes last option; **W** = sets overall width; **X** = exits PEDIT.
Pface	Creates a 3Dmesh	*NA*
Plan	Changes to plan view of a UCS	**C** = current, **U** = specified UCS, **W** = world coordinate system.
Pline	Draws a 2D polyline	**H** = sets half-width value, **U** = undoes last option, **W** = sets beginning and end width of current segment, **A** = switches to drawing arcs, **C** = closes a polyline, **L** = continues previous segment. While in the Arc mode, **A** = arc angle, **CE** = center point, **CL** = close polyline with an arc, **D** = arc direction, **L** = switch to line-drawing mode, **S** = second point of a three point arc.
Plot	Plot a drawing	Uses a dialog box to offer plotter settings. Can be disabled using Cmddia system variable (see *Appendix D*).

Table E.1: AutoCAD Commands (continued)

Command Name	Description	Options/Operations
Point	Draws a point object	Point objects can be changed using Pdmode and Pdsize system variables (see *Appendix D*).
Polygon	Draws a polygon	**E** = draw a polygon by specifying one edge segment, **C** = circumscribe polygon around a circumference, **I** = inscribe a polygon around a circumference.
Preferences	Determine units of current drawing	You specify measurement to be in U.S. (feet and inches) or metric units, and name of prototype drawing.
Psdrag	Controls PSIN drag mode	0 = show only bounding box in dragged image, 1 = show whole image as it is being dragged.
Psfill	Fill polyline with PostScript fill pattern	Pattern appears when plotted to a PostScript device. Not intended for viewing or plotting on pen plotters.
Psin	Import Encapsulated PostScript (.EPS) images	Image quality can be controlled with Psquality.
Psout	Exports drawing to Encapsulated PostScript format	If PostScript fonts are used in the drawing, they will be used with the .EPS file.
Pspace	Switch to Paper Space	Only valid in Paper Space when moving from a Model Space viewport.
Purge	Deletes unused named items	Layers, blocks, text styles, line types, and dimension styles will be removed if not being used.
Qsave	Saves drawing	File is saved, without any messages or requests to you from AutoCAD.
Qtext	Displays text as rectangles	**On** = turn on Qtext, **Off** = turn off Qtext. Can also be set using Ddrmodes.
Quit	Exits AutoCAD	Dialog box appears, letting you save or discard changes to current drawing.
Ray	Creates a semi-infinite line	Pick starting point and specify point(s) through which ray(s) will pass for use as a construction line.

Appendices

Table E.1: AutoCAD Commands (continued)

Command Name	Description	Options/Operations
Rconfig	Reconfigures the renderer	Exits drawing editor and lets you configure renderer display and hardcopy output. See *Appendix B* for more on Rconfig.
Recover	Attempts recovery of damaged drawings	When you try to open a damaged file, AutoCAD automatically attempts a recovery.
Rectang	Draws a rectangle	Prompts you to select two points defining two opposite corners of rectangle. Rectang then draws a closed rectangular polyline.
Redefine	Restores an Undefined command	See Undefine.
Redo	Reverses last Undo	Can only be used to Redo one Undo.
'Redraw	Refreshes the display	Only in current viewport or Model Space.
'Redrawall	Refreshes all viewport displays	NA
Regen	Regenerates a drawing	Refreshes display to reflect latest changes in drawing database.
Regenall	Regenerates all viewports	NA
'Regenauto	Controls automatic regens	Some commands force a regen. With REGENAUTO turned off, you are prompted before a regen is about to occur, allowing you to terminate current command and avoid regen.
Region	Creates a region object from a selection set	Uses standard selection methods.
Reinit	Reinitializes I/O devices	Also reinitializes the ACAD.PGP file.
Rename	Renames named items	Layers, blocks, dimension styles, text styles, line types, UCSs, views, and viewport configurations can be renamed.
Render	Produces a shaded image of your 3D solid or surface drawing	You can make a variety of settings, from light intensity and location to surface reflectance, to control how your image will look. See *Chapter 17*.

Table E.1:   AutoCAD Commands (continued)

Command Name	Description	Options/Operations
Render-unload	Unloads the renderer	Whenever the render commands are issued, the renderer is loaded into memory. For systems with limited RAM, unloading the renderer can help improve performance.
Replay	Displays a GIF, GTA, or TIFF file within AutoCAD	A dialog box lets you set location and size of image. See *Chapter 17*.
'Resume	Resumes a terminated script	See 'Script
Revolve	Creates a solid by rotating a 2D object about an axis	Closed objects can be revolved around an existing or picked axis, at a specified angle of rotation.
Revsurf	Creates a surface of revolution	Requires a polyline profile and a line defining the revolution axis.
Rmat	Lets you modify and assign materials to objects for the renderer	Dialog box gives you control over material definitions in your drawing. See *Chapter 17* for more on this command.
Rotate	Rotates objects	**R** = rotate with respect to an angle.
Rotate3D	Rotates an object in 3D space	Works similarly to Mirror3D.
Rpref	Opens the Render Preferences dialog box	Lets you set general options for renderer, such as render palette, type of smoothing during rendering, whether image is sent to screen or printer, etc. See *Chapter 17*.
Rscript	Restarts a script from the beginning	See 'Script.
Rulesurf	Creates a 3D mesh between two curves	Requires the existence of an arc, line, or polyline between which the mesh is drawn.
Save	Saves a drawing	Dialog box lets you determine name of file and where to save it.
Saveas	Saves and renames a drawing	Same as Save, plus renames the current drawing.
Saveasr12	Saves a drawing in Release 12 format	Same as Save.

Appendices

Table E.1: AutoCAD Commands (continued)

Command Name	Description	Options/Operations
Saveimg	Saves a rendered image to a file	Lets you determine file name and format for image file. You can also save a portion of the image through a selection window.
Scale	Changes size of objects	**R** = scale relative to another object.
Scene	Controls scenes for the renderer	Lets you save and restore scenes through a dialog box. A scene defines lights, materials, and camera position used for rendered image.
'Script	Runs a script file	Script files contain the exact keystrokes to perform a series of actions. Virtually no interaction is allowed; best suited for batch operations.
Section	Uses intersection of a plane and solids to create a region	Section plane can be by **O** = object, **Z** = z-axis, **V** = view, points on the **XY, YZ,** or **ZX** planes, or defined by 3 points.
Select	Selects objects	Lets you preselect objects using standard selection options.
'Setvar	Controls and displays system variables	**?** = show status of all or selected system variables.
Sh	Allows access to DOS commands	See Shell.
Shade	Performs Z-buffer shading on 3D models	See Shadedge and Shadedif system variables (*Appendix D*).
Shape	Places a predefined shape in the drawing	**?** = list available shapes in current drawing. Shapes must be loaded using Load command.
Shell	Temporarily exits AutoCAD to run DOS software	Enter a command or program name after entering **Shell** ↵, or press ↵ again to issue multiple DOS commands. Enter **Exit** ↵ at the DOS prompt to return to AutoCAD.

Table E.1: AutoCAD Commands (continued)

Command Name	Description	Options/Operations
Sketch	Allows freehand drawing	**C** = connect with last sketch endpoint, **E** = back up over previously drawn temporary lines, **P** = start and stop temporary line drawing, **Q** = discard temporary lines, **R** = save temporary lines, **X** = save temporary lines and exit the sketch command, **period (.)** = with pen up, draw straight line to current point.
Slice	Slices a set of solids with a plane	Slicing plane can be set by **O** = object, **Z** – z-axis, **V** = view, points on the **XY, YZ,** or **ZX** planes, or defined by 3 points.
'Snap	Controls Snap function	Snap forces cursor to move in exact increments. **Number** = snap increment, **On/Off** = turns snap feature on and off (same as F9 or Ctrl-B), **A** = allows differing X and Y snap increments, **R** = rotates snap grid, **S** = lets you select between standard and isometric snap grids. See also Snapang and Snapbase system variables (*Appendix D*) and the Ddrmodes command.
Solid	Draws a four-sided, 2D filled polygon	See the Fill command.
Spell	Checks spelling in a drawing	Dictionaries can be added to and changed.
Sphere	Creates a three-dimensional solid sphere	You specify radius or diameter.
Spline	Creates a quadratic or cubic spline (NURBS) curve	**C** = close with tangent to starting point, **F** = fit tolerance through points chosen, **O** = convert 2D or 3D spline fit polylines.
Splinedit	Edits a spline object	**F** = fit data, which determines tangency, tolerances, vertex location, etc.; **C** = close an open spline; **O** = open a closed spline; **M** = move vertex; **R** = refine spline definition by adding, elevating, and changing weight of control points; **E** = rEverse direction; **U** = undo last SPLINEDIT operation; **X** = eXit.

Table E.1: AutoCAD Commands (continued)

Command Name	Description	Options/Operations
Stats	Displays current status of renderer	Tells you scene name, last rendering type, rendering time, total faces, and total triangles. You can save the information to disk.
'Status	Displays general information about the drawing	Offers a quick way to view memory use.
Stlout	Stores a solid in an ASCII or binary file	You select a single object and enter a file name.
Stretch	Stretches vertices	Objects and vertices can be selected separately with careful use of selection options. Last window (i.e., window, crossing window, Wpolygon, or Cpolygon) determines which vertices are moved. The Wpolygon and Cpolygon selection options offer greatest flexibility with this command.
'Style	Creates text styles	You can set text height, width, and obliqueing angles, as well as other orientations; you also specify what font file to use.
Subtract	Creates a composite region or solid by subtracting one set of objects from another	Objects must overlap, and regions must be coplanar.
Syswindows	Allows you to arrange multiple AutoCAD windows	Available options are: Cascade, tile horizontally or vertically and Arrange icons.
Tablet	Controls digitizer tablet alignment	**On/Off** = turns tablet calibration on or off once tablet is calibrated; **Cal** = calibrates a tablet to match coordinates in the draw space; **Cfg** = configures the tablet for use with a digitizer template.
Tabsurf	Extrudes 2D shapes into 3D surfaces	You must supply an object to be extruded and a line to indicate extrusion direction. Command creates a 3Dmesh approximating the extrusion, leaving the original 2D object alone.

Table E.1: AutoCAD Commands (continued)

Command Name	Description	Options/Operations
Tbconfig	Allows you to create and customize toolbars.	Dialog box allows you to create new toolbars, edit and combine toolbars and flyouts, and delete toolbars, and to control the display of icon buttons and tooltips.
Text	Creates text	Select a start point, style, and justification; height if style height is set to 0; and rotation angle. Text does not appear in the drawing until you press ↵ at end of text line.
'Textscr	Flips display to text mode	Same as F2.
3D	Creates three-dimensional polygon mesh objects	**B** = box, **C** = cone, **DI** = dish, **DO** = dome, **M** = mesh, **P** = pyramid, **S** = sphere, **T** = torus, **W** = wedge.
3Dface	Draws a four-sided 3D surface	You can make an edge of a 3Dface invisible by entering **I** ↵ before you pick second point of the side.
3Dmesh	Draws a 3D mesh by specifying each point on the mesh	Points are input column by column in a column-and-row matrix.
3Dpoly	Draws a 3D polyline	3D polylines allow 3D point selection; however, 3Dpolylines cannot have width or thickness.
3Dsin	Imports a 3D Studio file	Each object can be placed on its own layer or on a layer with all other objects of same material or color, or all can be placed on a single layer.
3Dsout	Exports a 3D Studio file from selected objects	Objects can be grouped by layer, color, or object type; smoothed; and welded.
Tiffin	Imports TIFF files	You are prompted for a file name, insertion point, and scale. See also the Riaspect, Ribackg, Riedge, Rigamut, Rigrey, and Rithresh system variables (*Appendix D*).
'Time	Displays time values	Shows date the drawing was created, current time in drawing, and offers an elapsed timer.

Appendices

Table E.1:   AutoCAD Commands (continued)

Command Name	Description	Options/Operations
Tolerance	Creates geometric tolerances	You choose feature control frames from dialog box interface.
Toolbar	Allows you to show, hide and position individual (or all) toolbars	You may specify whether the toolbar is to be docked (at Left/Right/Top/Bottom) or floating.
Torus	Creates a donut-shaped solid	You define by entering diameter or radius of torus, and diameter or radius of tube.
Trace	Draws solid wide lines	Draws lines in one segment behind the current point. You may prefer to use Pline instead of Trace.
Treestat	Displays information on spatial index	AutoCAD uses a binary tree structure to improve its drawing database access. See the Treedepth system variable (*Appendix D*).
Trim	Trims objects back to another object	Several objects can be selected, both for both trimming and as objects to trim to. The Fence option offers a quick way to do multiple trims. U = undo last trim, P = project trim boundary based on UCS or view, E = controls whether the cutting edge is extended beyond it's actual length in order to trim objects that do not actually cross the cutting edge object.
U	Undoes one command at a time	See Undo.
UCS	Controls the user coordinate system function	D = delete UCS, E = set extrusion direction, O = move origin, P = restore previous UCS, S = save the current UCS, V = create a UCS aligned with current view, W = set current UCS to WCS, $X/Y/Z$ = rotate UCS about the x-, y-, or z-axis, ZA = define z-axis using 2 points, 3 = define UCS using 3 points, $?$ = list existing UCSs. See also Dducs.
UCSicon	Controls UCS icon	On/Off = turns display of icon on and off, Or = when possible, places icon at UCS origin.

Table E.1: AutoCAD Commands (continued)

Command Name	Description	Options/Operations
Undefine	Undefines a built-in AutoCAD command	Typically, used when you want to replace a built-in command with another command you have created using ADS or AutoLISP. You can still issue an undefined command by preceding the command name with a period.
Undo	Undoes one or a series of commands	*Number* = number of commands to undo, **A** = turns on or off the treatment of menu macros as single groups, **B** = undoes backward to mark placed with M option, **C** = controls the Undo features. Options are All/None/One. All turns on all the features listed here. None turns off the Undo feature. One limits Undo to one Undo, **E** = marks end of undo group, **G** = marks beginning of undo group, **M** = places the mark used bythe Back option.
Union	Creates a composite region or solid	You can join regions or solids that do not share a common area or volume.
'Units	Selects the unit style	See Ddunits.
'Views	Saves and restores views	**D** = delete a view, **R** = restore a view, **S** = Save a view, **W** = save a windowed view, **?** = list saved views.
Viewres	Controls display of arcs, circles, and line types	When on, enables virtual display, which offers greater display speed. Viewres values affect coarseness of arcs and circles in the virtual display.
Vlconv	Converts Visual Link data to an AutoVision format	Visual Link is an AutoCAD add-on that lets you exchange AutoCAD files with 3D Studio. AutoVision is an enhanced rendering add-on for AutoCAD.

Appendices

Table E.1: AutoCAD Commands (continued)

Command Name	Description	Options/Operations
Vplayer	Controls layer visibility in Paper Space viewports	**?** = lists frozen layers in a viewport, **F** = freezes a layer in a viewport, **T** = thaws a layer in a viewport, **R** = resets layer visibility to default settings, **N** = creates a new layer that is frozen in all viewports, **V** = sets default visibility of existing viewports.
Vpoint	Selects a viewpoint for 3D views	**R** = sets rotation angle in the XY plane, **X,Y,Z** = specifies a viewpoint coordinate, **⏎** = uses tripod and compass to determine viewpoint. In all cases, entire drawing is target location.
Vports	Divides the Model Space display into viewports	**D** = delete a saved viewport configuration, **J** = join two viewports, **R** = restore a viewport configuration, **S** = save the current viewport configuration, **SI** = change to a single viewport, **2/3/4** = divides the current viewport into 2, 3, or 4 viewports, **?** = lists current and saved viewport configurations.
Vslide	Displays slide files	***filename*** = preload *filename* for next Vslide.
Wblock	Saves portions of a file to disk	Generally used to write a block to a file; can also be used to save portions of a drawing. At Block name prompt you can enter **name** = write block name to file, **=** = write block to file using same name as the file, ***** = write the entire current file to a file, **⏎** = write selected objects; you then see object-selection prompt. The * option is a quick way to purge a drawing of all named elements at once.
Wedge	Creates a 3D solid with a sloped face tapering along the X-axis	**C** = cube creates a wedge with sides of equal length, **L** = length along the x-axis, **W** = width along y-axis, **H** = height along the z-axis.

Table E.1: AutoCAD Commands (continued)

Command Name	Description	Options/Operations
WMFin	Imports Windows metafiles	At the Import File dialog box, enter a file name or search for the required file.
Wmfopts	Set the import options for metafile objects	In the dialog box, check to specify Wire Frame and/or Wide Line options.
WMFout	Saves selected AutoCAD objects in Windows Metefile format	N/A
Xbind	Imports named elements from an Xref drawing	Block, dimension styles, layers, line types, and text styles can be imported.
Xline	Creates an infinite line commonly used as construction line	After picking a point, these options define line: **H** = horizontal through point, **V** = vertical through point, **A** = at specified angle, **B** = bisect angle determined by 3 points, **O** = offset from existing object.
Xplode	Breaks blocks, polylines, and other compound object down into their components	You can set layer, color, or line type of component objects globally or one at time. You can also have the component objects inherit the properties of the parent compound object.
Xref	Cross references another drawing with the current one	You can scale, rotate, or mirror cross-referenced files. You can also use object snap modes and set their layers (see Visretain system variable). You cannot edit Xrefs, however. **A** = attach an Xref, **B** = bind or import an Xref to become a permanent part of current drawing, **D** = detach an Xref, **O** = overlay, ignoring nested Xrefs, **P** = allows you to view and edit file names that AutoCAD uses for cross-references, **R** = reload an Xref, **?** = displays a list of Xrefs.

Appendices

Table E.1: AutoCAD Commands (continued)

Command Name	Description	Options/Operations
Xrefclip	Inserts an Xref and creates a viewport that clips the Xref to a view you specify	Xrefclip switches your drawing editor to Paper Space if you are not already in it, and then imports your Xref and prompts you to select an area to be displayed in a viewport.
'Zoom	Controls the display	**Number** = zoom factor relative to drawing limits, **numberx** = zoom factor relative to current view, **A** = displays limits of drawing, **C** = displays view based on center point and height, **D** = dynamic pan/zoom feature, **E** = displays drawing extents, **L** = displays a view based on a lower-left corner and view height, **P** = displays a previous view, **V** = displays entire virtual screen, **W** = displays an enlargement of a window.

TOOLBARS IN AUTOCAD 13

AutoCAD's new toolbar interface makes AutoCAD much easier to use without putting a damper on speed. All of the most commonly used commands are carefully and logically grouped into related tasks. The only tricks are knowing how to open the toolbars and learning to recognize the icons on the toolbar buttons.

Opening the toolbars is fairly painless; choose Tools ➤ Toolbars from the pull-down menu. You'll get a listing of the toolbars. This appendix shows you some of the toolbars from that list as well as the meaning of each button.

Learning the icon buttons may take a little more time. Check the tooltips as you work with the toolbars and palettes; you'll soon start to recognize icons. You might also want to photocopy this appendix and put it on your desktop or wall next to your monitor as a ready reference.

▼ NOTE

You can place individual flyout palettes on the screen as if they were stand-alone toolbars. See *Opening Palettes from the Command Line* in Chapter 21 for specific information on how to do this.

WHERE TO FIND INFORMATION ON SPECIFIC TOOLBARS

The list below shows the chapter and section where you can either find the most complete description of the toolbar or where it appears first in the book. Some of the toolbars, such as Draw and Modify, are described in a variety of places throughout the book, so just their first occurrence is listed.

Attribute	Chapter 10; Creating Attributes
Dimensioning	Chapter 9; Drawing Linear Dimensions
Draw	Chapter 2; Getting to Know the Draw Tool Palette
External Database	Chapter 10; Setting up Ase to Locate Database Tables
External References	Chapter 6; Cross-Referencing Drawings

Appendices

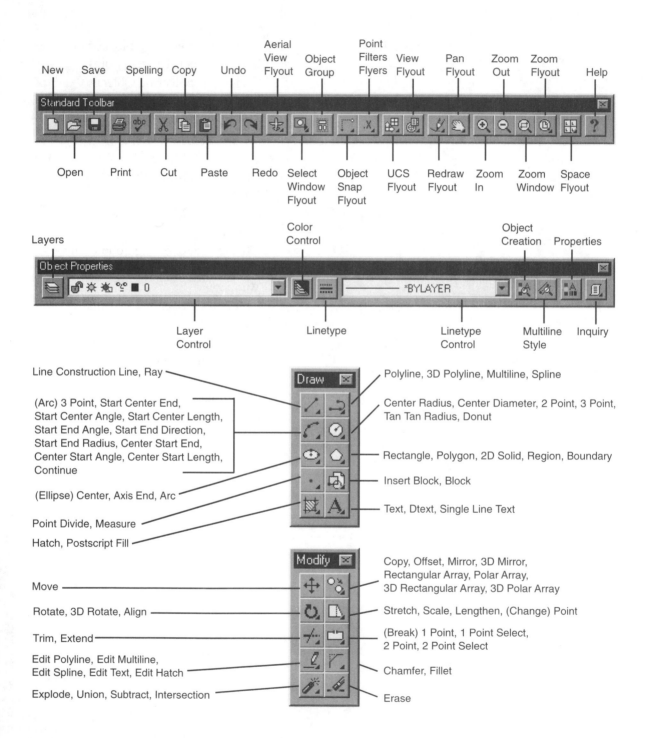

Aerial View Flyout, Object Group, Point Filters Flyers, View Flyout, Pan Flyout, Zoom Out, Zoom Flyout

New, Save, Spelling, Copy, Undo, Help

Standard Toolbar

Open, Print, Cut, Paste, Redo, Select Window Flyout, Object Snap Flyout, UCS Flyout, Redraw Flyout, Zoom In, Zoom Window, Space Flyout

Layers, Color Control, Object Creation, Properties

Object Properties

*BYLAYER

Layer Control, Linetype, Linetype Control, Multiline Style, Inquiry

Line Construction Line, Ray

(Arc) 3 Point, Start Center End, Start Center Angle, Start Center Length, Start End Angle, Start End Direction, Start End Radius, Center Start End, Center Start Angle, Center Start Length, Continue

(Ellipse) Center, Axis End, Arc

Point Divide, Measure

Hatch, Postscript Fill

Draw

Polyline, 3D Polyline, Multiline, Spline

Center Radius, Center Diameter, 2 Point, 3 Point, Tan Tan Radius, Donut

Rectangle, Polygon, 2D Solid, Region, Boundary

Insert Block, Block

Text, Dtext, Single Line Text

Modify

Move

Rotate, 3D Rotate, Align

Trim, Extend

Edit Polyline, Edit Multiline, Edit Spline, Edit Text, Edit Hatch

Explode, Union, Subtract, Intersection

Copy, Offset, Mirror, 3D Mirror, Rectangular Array, Polar Array, 3D Rectangular Array, 3D Polar Array

Stretch, Scale, Lengthen, (Change) Point

(Break) 1 Point, 1 Point Select, 2 Point, 2 Point Select

Chamfer, Fillet

Erase

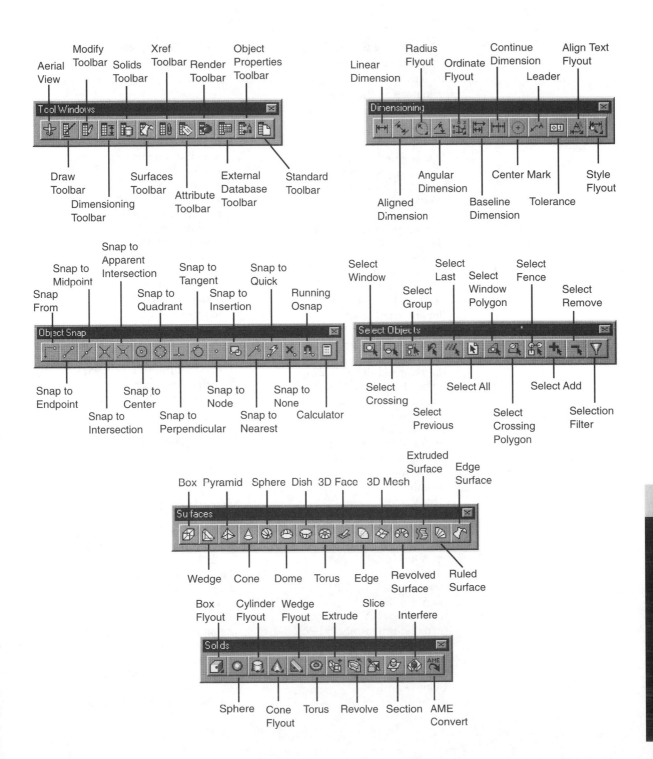

INDEX

Note to the Reader: Throughout this index **boldfaced** page numbers indicate primary discussions of a topic. *Italicized* page numbers indicate illustrations. The letter *n* after a page number indicates that the reference is to a margin note on the page.

Aut
o

D

FOR EVERY COMPUTER QUESTION,
THERE IS A SYBEX BOOK THAT HAS THE ANSWER

Each computer user learns in a different way. Some need thorough, methodical explanations, while others are too busy for details. At Sybex we bring nearly 20 years of experience to developing the book that's right for you. Whatever your needs, we can help you get the most from your software and hardware, at a pace that's comfortable for you.

We start beginners out right. You will learn by seeing and doing with our **Quick & Easy** series: friendly, colorful guidebooks with screen-by-screen illustrations. For hardware novices, the **Your First** series offers valuable purchasing advice and installation support.

Often recognized for excellence in national book reviews, our **Mastering** titles are designed for the intermediate to advanced user, without leaving the beginner behind. A **Mastering** book provides the most detailed reference available. Add our pocket-sized **Instant Reference** titles for a complete guidance system. Programmers will find that the new **Developer's Handbook** series provides a more advanced perspective on developing innovative and original code.

With the breathtaking advances common in computing today comes an ever increasing demand to remain technologically up-to-date. In many of our books, we provide the added value of software, on disks or CDs. Sybex remains your source for information on software development, operating systems, networking, and every kind of desktop application. We even have books for kids. Sybex can help smooth your travels on the **Internet** and provide **Strategies and Secrets** to your favorite computer games.

As you read this book, take note of its quality. Sybex publishes books written by experts—authors chosen for their extensive topical knowledge. In fact, many are professionals working in the computer soft-ware field. In addition, each manuscript is thoroughly reviewed by our technical, editorial, and production personnel for accuracy and ease-of-use before you ever see it—our guarantee that you'll buy a quality Sybex book every time.

To manage your hardware headaches and optimize your software potential, ask for a Sybex book.

FOR MORE INFORMATION, PLEASE CONTACT:

Sybex Inc.
2021 Challenger Drive
Alameda, CA 94501
Tel: (510) 523-8233 • (800) 227-2346
Fax: (510) 523-2373

Let us hear from you.

 alk to SYBEX authors, editors and fellow forum members.

 et tips, hints and advice online.

 ownload magazine articles, book art, and shareware.

Join the SYBEX Forum on CompuServe®

If you're already a CompuServe user, just type GO SYBEX to join the SYBEX Forum. If not, try CompuServe for free by calling 1-800-848-8199 and ask for Representative 560. You'll get one free month of basic service and a $15 credit for CompuServe extended services—a $23.95 value. Your personal ID number and password will be activated when you sign up.

Join us online today. Type GO SYBEX on CompuServe.

If you're not a CompuServe member, call Representative 560 at 1-800-848-8199.

SYBEX

(outside U.S./Canada call 614-457-0802)

TIME-SAVING, QUALITY-ENHANCING SOFTWARE AVAILABLE WITH THIS BOOK

The attached CD is chock-full of useful utilities, as well as all the drawings you'll create while using this book. Together, the book and CD present a unique, performance-based platform for learning, or expanding your mastery of, AutoCAD Release 13 for Windows.

WHAT'S ON THE COMPANION CD-ROM?

These utilities will smooth your way to AutoCAD success:

- On-Screen AEC, a set of AutoLISP macros and architectural symbols developed by the author, all integrated with a standard AutoCAD menu. A $50 value!

- AutoPS, a utility that turns AutoCAD into a technical illustration tool. It is designed to help you create high-quality line art for desktop publishing. A $150 value!

- Alfonso Hermida's Blob Sculptor, a 3D drawing program for creating organic 3D forms (as well as a Windows port of the program, WinBlob).

- PrintGF and PrintGL, shareware utilities that enable most dot-matrix and ink-jet printers to produce high-resolution plots.

- WinSpool, a shareware utility that allows you to download plot files to an HPGL-compatible printer or plotter in a network environment. This utility works in the background so that you can continue to use your computer while you are plotting.

- Autodesk's WHIP! Internet Utilities, a set of tools that allow you to publish and view your AutoCAD drawings on the World Wide Web.

You'll also find:

- All the drawings you'll work on in the course of the book, in various stages of completion, so you can load a drawing without having to start from scratch.

- The most up-to-date version of the AutoCAD Resource Guide, an on-line hypertext encyclopedia with complete information on thousands of third-party products designed for specialized uses of AutoCAD. Many of these come with demos.

For complete information on how to install and use the files included on the CD, refer to Appendix C.